WOBBLIES!

WOBBLIES!

A GRAPHIC HISTORY OF
THE INDUSTRIAL WORKERS OF THE WORLD

EDITED BY **PAUL BUHLE** AND **NICOLE SCHULMAN**

VERSO

London • New York

First published by Verso 2005
© in the collection, Verso 2005
© in the contributions, the individual contributors 2005
All rights reserved

The moral rights of the authors have been asserted

1 3 5 7 9 10 8 6 4 2

Verso
UK: 6 Meard Street, London W1F 0EG
USA: 180 Varick Street, New York, NY 10014–4606
www.versobooks.com

Verso is the imprint of New Left Books

ISBN 1–84467–525–4

British Library Cataloguing in Publication Data
A catalogue record for this book is available from the British Library

Library of Congress Cataloging-in-Publication Data
Wobblies! : a graphic history of the Industrial Workers of the World /
edited by Paul Buhle and Nicole Schulman.
p. cm.
Includes bibliographical references.
ISBN 1-84467-525-4 (pbk.: alk. paper)
1. Industrial Workers of the World – History.
2. Industrial Workers of the World – Pictorial works.
I. Buhle, Paul, 1944– II. Schulman, Nicole, 1975–
HD8055.I4W63 2005
331.88'6'0973–dc22
2005001324

Typeset in Gill Sans Light by Andrea Stimpson
Printed in the USA by R.R. Donnelley & Sons

To the Industrial Workers of the World,
Past, Present and Future—
For another Century of Rebellion!

In 1989 I had the bright idea that a historical/graphic approach to the IWW's 2005 100th anniversary would be a unique way to tell the story. Growing up in a New York City construction-trade household, the idea of industrial unionism came to me with my mother's milk. As the biggest rebel who ever put on a pair of shoes, coming of age in the 1960s, it was inevitable that I would discover the IWW.

Dedicated to my grandfather, Peter Kucewicz, draft resister to the Czar's army, and to my father who taught me that the owning class and the working class have nothing in common.

We never forget!

GEORGE KUCEWICZ

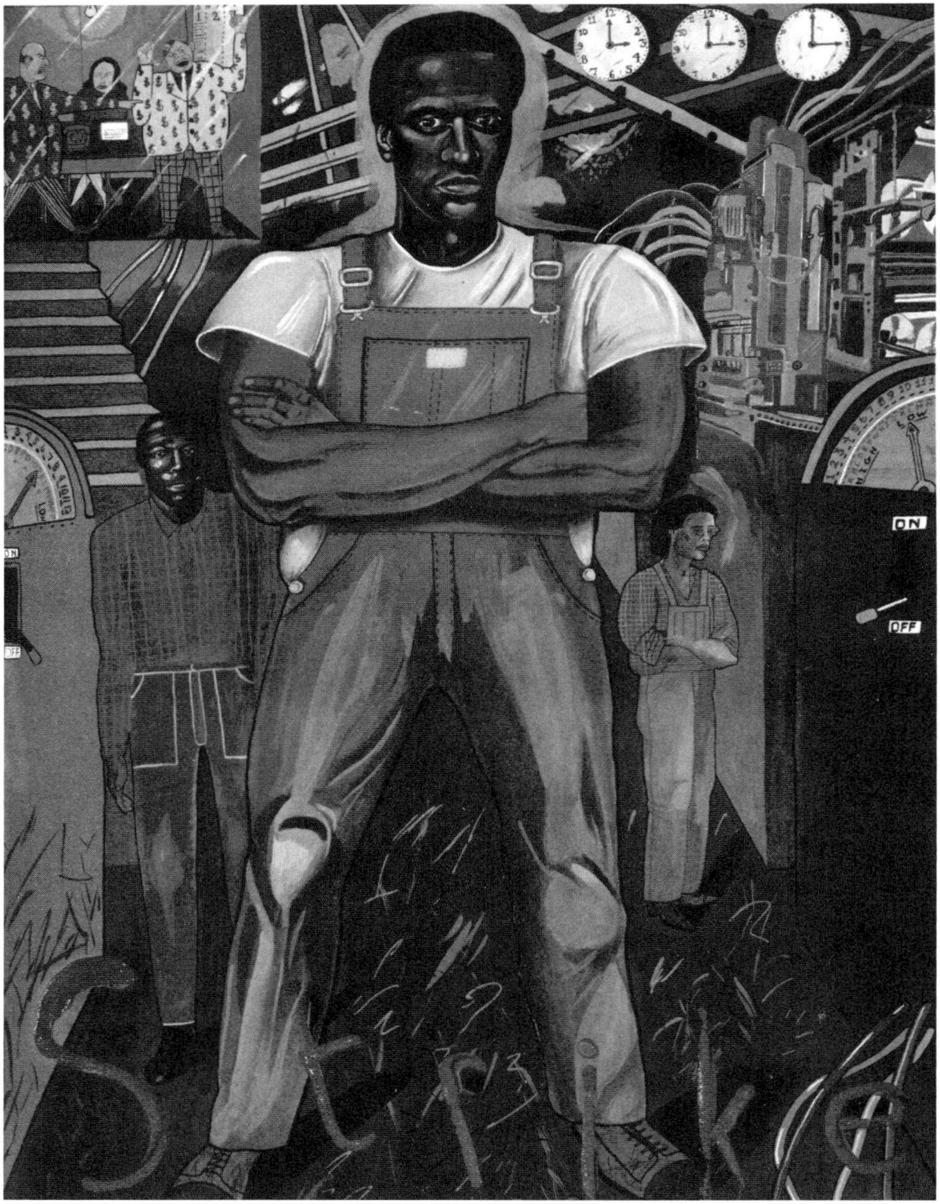
ON
OFF

Sue Coe

CONTENTS

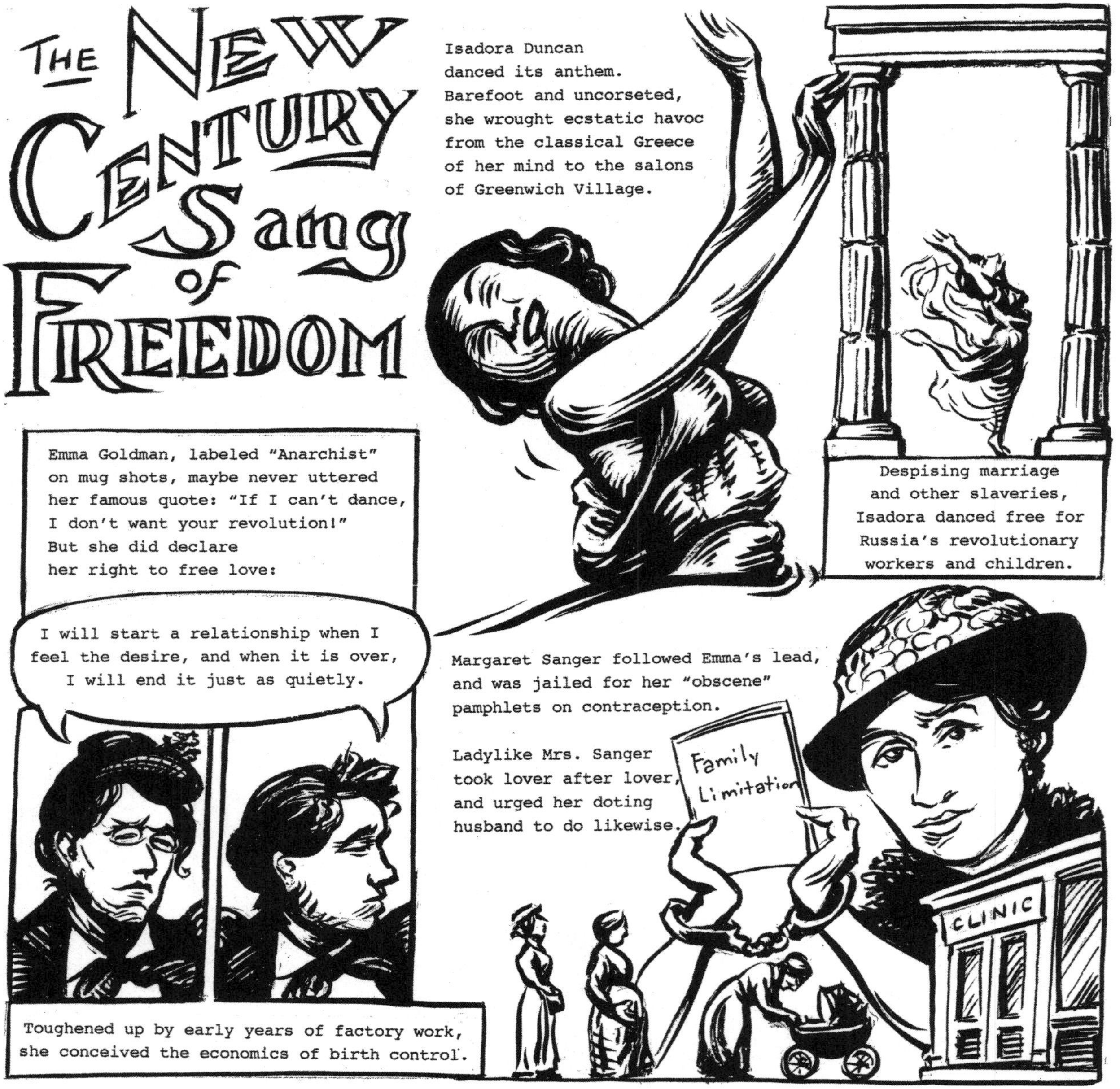
The New Century Sang of Freedom
Isadora Duncan danced its anthem. Barefoot and uncorseted, she wrought ecstatic havoc from the classical Greece of her mind to the salons of Greenwich Village.
Despising marriage and other slaveries, Isadora danced free for Russia's revolutionary workers and children.
Emma Goldman, labeled "Anarchist" on mug shots, maybe never uttered her famous quote: "If I can't dance, I don't want your revolution!" But she did declare her right to free love:
I will start a relationship when I feel the desire, and when it is over, I will end it just as quietly.
Toughened up by early years of factory work, she conceived the economics of birth control.
Margaret Sanger followed Emma's lead, and was jailed for her "obscene" pamphlets on contraception.
Ladylike Mrs. Sanger took lover after lover, and urged her doting husband to do likewise.
Family Limitation
CLINIC

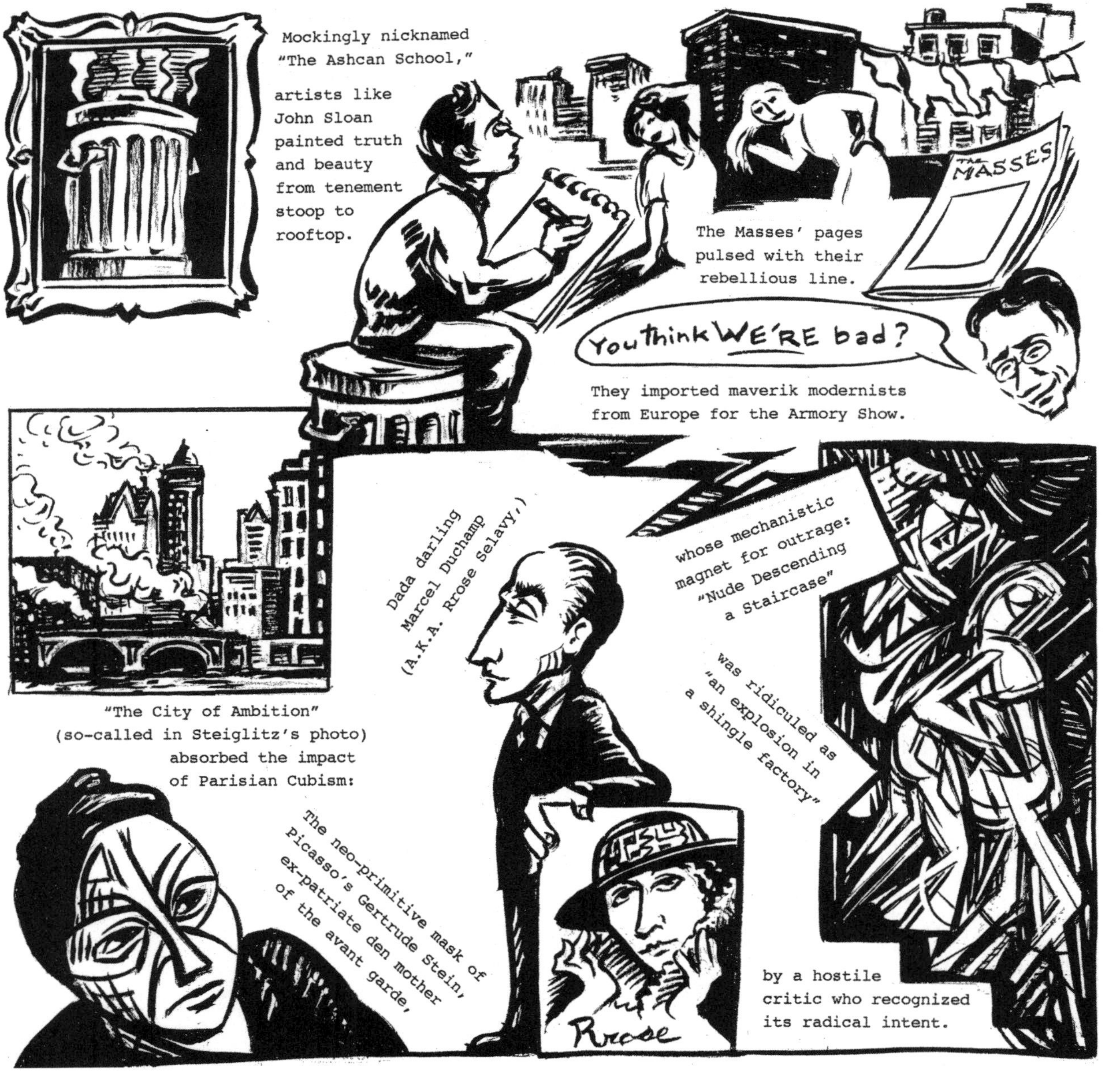
Mockingly nicknamed "The Ashcan School,"
artists like John Sloan painted truth and beauty from tenement stoop to rooftop.
The Masses' pages pulsed with their rebellious line.
THE MASSES
You think WE'RE bad?
They imported maverik modernists from Europe for the Armory Show.
"The City of Ambition" (so-called in Steiglitz's photo) absorbed the impact of Parisian Cubism:
The neo-primitive mask of Picasso's Gertrude Stein, ex-patriate den mother of the avant garde,
Dada darling Marcel Duchamp (A.K.A. Rrose Selavy,)
Rrose
whose mechanistic magnet for outrage: "Nude Descending a Staircase"
was ridiculed as "an explosion in a shingle factory"
by a hostile critic who recognized its radical intent.

ACKNOWLEDGMENTS

To our friends at the Industrial Workers of the World; but also to Richard R. Aarstad and the Montana Historical Society; everyone at Alvarez Fine Art Services; Anthony and Sonya Artis; Alexis Buss; Dustin Chang (for everything!); Christina Di Chiera and her friends in Providence; Esther Cohen and everyone at Bread and Roses; Camillo Viveiros and Mimi; Jonathan Leavitt; Bob Marley House; Barbara and her fellow tenants in Lowell; and the Reagan Babies: Arthur Fonseca; David Grenier (whose suggestion connected the two editors); Julie Herrada; Scott Kramer and Rex Bobbish; Gene Lantz (for his exhaustive research on Frank Little and online bibliography); everyone at Mayday Books and Theater for a New City; Lisa DiPetto and Kate McGreevy (proofreaders extraordinaire); Morgan Miller; Nathaniel Miller; Rebecca Migdal and Kevin Pyle for technical support; Roger Myers; the Rhode Island Labor History Society (and especially Scott Molloy); Franklin and Penelope Rosemont; Ronald and Elaine Schulman; Seth Tobocman (for being there); everyone at Tamiment Library, New York University; everyone at *World War 3 Illustrated*; to our Verso editors, Tariq Ali and Niels Hooper in particular, and Andrea Stimpson and Tim Clark; and to all the artists and writers who made this book possible.

Special thanks to George Kucewicz and the Puffin Foundation.

INTRODUCTION

The Industrial Workers of the World—according to its members and devotees the "Greatest Thing On Earth," but according to employers and labor's conservatives a menace to society—is exactly a century old in 2005. How could a movement that in its best years averaged a hundred thousand members have brought together, for a time, the poorest and most downtrodden working people from every race and group, and written some of the most moving and funniest songs mocking the rich exploiters and their willing slaves? Why would American poets, novelists, and radicals from John Dos Passos and Gary Snyder to Noam Chomsky (whose father was a Wobbly) continue to invoke "the Wobblies" when the memory of most unions is utterly gone from personal or family recollection? These are good questions, all right. The legends of the Wobbly are not so different, in some ways, from the legends of other bigger-than-life characters, like that of Johnny Appleseed (the real-life John

Chapman, who walked the frontier barefoot, preaching peace and planting apple seeds), or John Henry (the folk-mythical African-American who beat the steam engine and died in the process), or Paul Bunyon (the bigger-than-life logger, invented for advertising purposes by a timber company) among others. But the Wobs are very different in other ways.

The Wobbly, male or female, Asian or Occidental, black, brown, red or white, was only an ordinary human being in physique. He or she was different above all because of a "message" that was explained, preached, and sung around the camp fires of "bindle stiffs" (agricultural workers carrying bags or "bindles") and "timber wolves" (lumber workers); at the "mess" or commissary of hard-rock miners and seamen; on the streets of mill villages but also in the social halls of Finnish-American, Hungarian or Russian immigrants; across the borders in Canada and Mexico by men and women who moved from one job to another; and, for a while, even in the parlors of Greenwich Village. Their story was collaborative, collective, not reliant on any one hero or heroine—as heroic (or tragic) as individual Wobblies' lives might be.

The Wobblies were also unique in creating the real-life legend of "hobohemia," a word that does not even exist among today's homeless, rootless, impoverished wanderers. Try to imagine a "hobo university" (in Chicago), or hobo travel etiquette (in order to ride in a boxcar across large regions of the Plains States, you needed to show your IWW red card), or Chicago's "Bughouse Square" with its free-speech zone for anyone willing to stand up on a soapbox and face an audience demanding a lively, convincing presentation. These are images from a lost age; or are they?

This book looks at the Wobblies in many different ways. But perhaps the most important of these is the vision of plain folk running society for their own benefit—without bosses, without politicians, without a coercive State, Army, Navy, Air Force or Marines. But also without hatred and suspicion of "foreigners," or the frequently all-encompassing guilt that because we are rich, someone wants to take our riches away from us. The belief in freedom and internationalism makes the Wobblies just about the most American ideal possible, and got them arrested and sent to prison for long sentences during the First World War—by an acclaimed liberal Democratic administration. Not really because they told anyone to resist that pointless and brutal war, but because their ideas, their very existence, represented a threat to the big men who wanted war.

That way of looking at freedom makes the IWW seem like a lot more than a labor organization, or bigger than all the other labor organizations combined. It looks, for instance, like the grassroots of the ecological/environmental movement. It looks like the Mexicans and Americans who welcomed the Zapatistas taking back the land that had been stolen from their people. It looks like every antiwar movement. It even looks a little like the world John Lennon summed up in the song "Imagine": no distant god, no country, just us humans, all of us, and our world.

It also looks—a lot more than anyone would have suspected, thirty or forty years ago—like the submerged and rapidly submerging America of today. The world of the Wobs was made up of immigrant workers without steady employment, health plans, social security or drug benefits (like the future that Republicans and many a Democrat envision), without any responsibility on the part of the filthy rich for the growing class of poor—so much like the society around us today. The world of the Wobblies was one realized in its best moments by solidarity across race, ethnic, gender and nationality lines. The Wobbly world and promise was wrecked, finally, by the eager collaboration of corporate business and the military, liberals and conservatives, all of them committed firmly to Empire. Will the same thing or something like it happen, as the empire slides into crisis again? Only time will tell. But what the Wobs did was to hold up an alternative, the alternative we need now more than ever.

WHY "WOBBLIES"?

One of the most interesting and never-to-be-resolved questions about the IWW is how they acquired their moniker. We know that it took hold popularly in 1914, with the first line of a song, "I knew he was a Wobbly by the button that he wore." IWW members ever after repeated what little they had heard, or they invented new bits of folklore that might explain how a word that had meant to quiver or tremble became a term for a romantic rebel, male or female.

During the Wheatland, California strike of 6000 impoverished hop pickers in 1913, a strike leader (Herman "Hook Nose" Suhr, soon to be arrested and indicted) sent out a telegram saying "Send all speakers and wobblies possible." In the subsequent trial of Suhr and fellow organizer Richard "Blackie" Ford, a defense attorney asked an IWW publicist what it meant and was told that "Wobbly" was used "generally in the working class to designate IWW." Subsequent publicity prompted the song "Overalls and Snuff," by an anonymous lyricist, identifying the Wobbly as an old-time hop picker with "his blankets on his back." The 1914 edition of the *Little Red Song Book* carried the lyrics. During the next harvest season, in 1915, IWW poet-songster Richard Brazier used the word "Wob" to describe the old-timer, and in 1915, poet Ralph Chaplin announced in "Harvest Song": "The earth is on the button that we wobblies wear/We'll turn the sab cat loose or get our share," effectively combining various symbols.

But where did the word actually come from? Was it that "Eye-Double-You-Double-You," once coined, had a nice ring to it; or could it have derived from the wobbling walk of Wobbly hobos with too much to drink (or just workers on the job with too much to carry on their backs)? Or, more indirectly, from erotic references especially rich in African-American musical slang ("Wobble It a Little, Daddy," by Lillian Glinn, or another phrase, "You wiggle and you wobble, you move it around"), a possibility furthered by the conservatives' description of radical socialists as acting like uncivilized Africans? Or could it possibly have derived from international sources, traveling Australian workers (the IWW was especially popular in Australia) who were called "wallabies," thus translated to "wobbly"? Or is the answer perhaps in the all-time favorite anecdote, the tale of the Chinese cook in a railroad building camp in Oregon around 1912 who had trouble pronouncing "double you" and whose usage was taken up in friendly fashion rather than racist derision?

Whatever its origin, it was forever destined to be a comical word reflecting the IWW outlook on life. Wobblies weren't ashamed of being "wobbly," whether it was used as complaint against them being vulgar (or somehow connected with African-American culture) or unmacho, or anything else. Wobblies most loved, after the *Communist Manifesto*, the booklet by Marx's son-in-law Paul Lafargue: *The Right To Be Lazy*. It notably insisted that the true happiness of pre-civilization had been in leisure, a leisure destined to return when capitalism and class society had vanished once again. There would be plenty of time to wobble then.

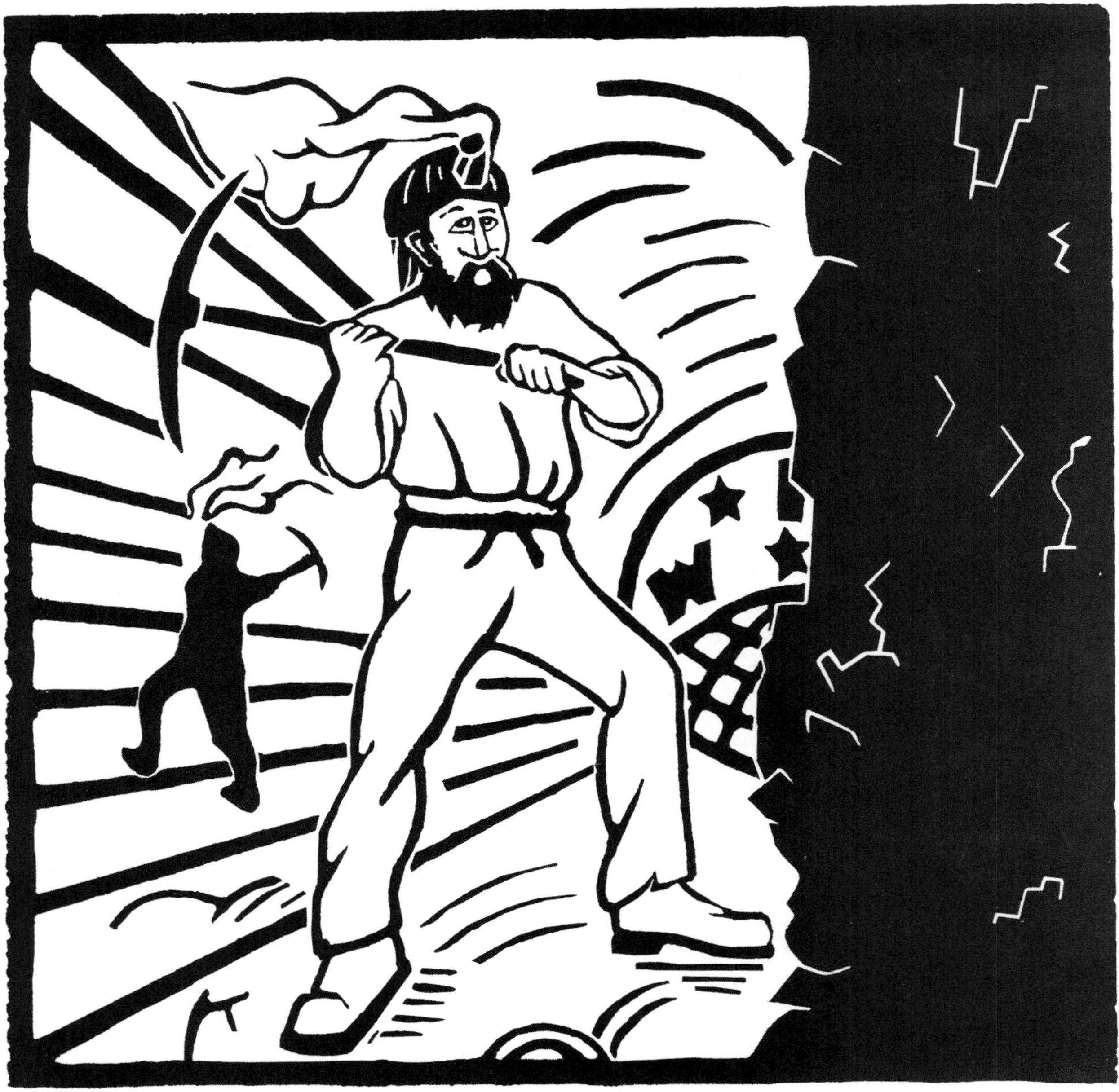

ONE

EARLY DAYS

No one can say exactly where the inspiration for the Industrial Workers of the World came from. The origins are too numerous both in the US and abroad, and over the twenty or forty years prior to 1905 and the consolidation of industrialization (with immigrants making up most of the workers in the new US factories). But the idea of "Solidarity" is so old and so basic that it was known centuries or even millennia earlier. The vision of the romantic rebel or footloose hobo wanderer was a little more recent, dating popularly to the eighteenth or nineteenth century, the response of a free spirit to a society that seemed ever more complex and restrictive.

A considerable number of Wobblies were at least part Indian, and decades after the near-collapse of the IWW, the "old Wobblies" on ships or in lumber camps were often the same men. One of the chief inspirations of socialism's "Founding Fathers," Karl Marx and Friedrich Engels, in their later years, was the American anthropologist

Lewis Henry Morgan. After intensive ethnographic investigations, Morgan claimed to have discovered among Indians the original "communistic" society of extended families and tribes sharing their possessions instead of accumulating private property, and living in nature as harmoniously as they could. The vision of what was called the "Golden Day"—primitive communism before the rise of ruling classes, established churches, armies, and empires—was also widespread among European working classes by time of the rise of modern industrialism. The medieval revolt of European villagers and peasants against Church and Crown created communistic societies of sharing that lasted for weeks or months before being drowned in an ocean of blood by invading soldiers.

These movements left behind memories that fed the dreamers, artists, poets, and philosophers alike, for many generations to come. The mystic Belgian painter Hieronymus Bosch drew murals of a utopian society of (naked) people living in nature with each other and the animals until the armies and priests set upon them. The shoemaker-philosopher Jakob Boehme later described the tree of life that had fed all freely until the merchant had taken over the tree. William Blake, the great British poet-engraver of the 1790s–1810s, pointed to "Satan's Dark Mills" as the plague of modern exploitation, and the return of freedom as the realization of all human (and divine) dreams. In the US, utopians like the Shakers had founded cooperative villages, living without property or harm to nature (also without sex), in hopes of setting an example. New settlements sprung up at the end of the nineteenth century, mostly in response to the utopian novel by newspaperman Edward Bellamy, *Looking Backward* (1888), one of the best-selling books of the century.

But there were other sources less literary and less distant. After the Civil War, massive industry grew up faster than anyone could have imagined, with previously unthinkable wealth accruing to the bankers but with millions of desperately poor working people, employed at low wages or unemployed in the frequent economic recessions. The first nationwide railroad strike took place in 1877, shutting down lines across the whole Eastern United States; troops fired on strikers and rioters who opened freight cars for food. The city of St. Louis was controlled, for a week, by socialists who kept the strike going and who themselves organized deliveries of needed food and public services. It was the first time that virtually a whole US city went on strike and began to reorganize its social relations from the inside.

The earliest mass movement for an eight-hour workday, during 1885–86, highlighted the different roles of two kinds of labor movements. The American Federation of Labor, founded in 1883, sought to organize skilled workers (almost entirely white and male) only, for their self-protection and advancement. It charged high "initiation" fees for new members as a way to limit membership, and frequently invited only the sons or other relatives of existing members to join organized trades. The Knights of Labor, founded in 1869 as a secret society, invited all (except Chinese) to join, enrolled thousands of African-American workers and in some places a majority of women workers of an industry, and promised to roll back the "wage system" in favor of some more cooperative social order.

The radical challenge to society, culminating in strikes across the nation on May Day, 1886, ended in tragedy. In Chicago, following days of police brutality towards strikers, a rally in the city's Haymarket district heard its last speaker and proceeded to disperse when a bomb was thrown at police. Eight well-known anarchists were arrested and put on trial, convicted for "conspiracy"—not because any proof could be offered of their involvement in the bombing but because of their revolutionary ideas. Police swept through the headquarters of socialist groups (mostly German-Americans) across the country, broke up social halls, destroyed the equipment of socialistic newspapers, and initiated the first "Red Scare," more than thirty years before Bolsheviks took power in Russia. The Knights of Labor were destroyed, while the rival AFL survived.

In the years between the railroad strike and the 1886 repression, the Chicago anarchists (they called themselves "Social Revolutionists") were probably the most Wobbly-like of any American labor organization. They held giant parades and picnics with red flags and dance music in the warm weather, and mocked the rich people in giant demonstrations at Thanksgiving. They prepared themselves, in marching societies, to fight the ruling class with weapons if necessary. They also opened revolutionary schools for children, read (and wrote) poetry, created their own theater of radical plays, and published vivid newspapers with lots of illustrations. Some say that after the strike wave was crushed, their hope died and many committed suicide. This last detail cannot be confirmed but has a ring of truth.

The 1890s saw the worst depression in American history. Millions went hungry, and tens of thousands living in miserable tenements, their resistance weakened, were stricken with tuberculosis. Alcoholism soared. With so many workers desperate for jobs, employers drastically reduced wages and sought to wipe out the existing unions. Violent battles broke out, like that involving the highly skilled steelworkers of Homestead, Pennsylvania, who fought a small war with the Carnegie corporation. (Anarchist Alexander Berkman, Emma Goldman's lover, attempted, without success, to assassinate Henry Clay Frick, the Chairman of Carnegie Steel.) But the two most important labor battles of the time made the birth of the IWW both more possible, and more necessary.

The first, and largest, single show of solidarity in American labor to that point was the Pullman Strike. Its champion, and everyone's favorite radical until his death in 1926, was Eugene Victor Debs, a leader of the highly-restricted Brotherhood of Locomotive Firemen, from Terra Haute, Indiana. Named for European radical novelists Eugene Sue and Victor Hugo, young Gene Debs was a Democrat and a promising personality in the AFL. After seeing his union lose strike after strike, he led the formation of a new, all-inclusive body, the American Railway Union. Not long after its founding, it was faced with a dilemma: to support the builders of the ostentatious Pullman Cars, made in a factory town just outside Chicago, or to ignore the plight of these factory workers, and lose the vision of solidarity. Debs chose strike, and railway lines closed again, almost entirely west of the Mississippi. Unlike 1877, this was a peaceful strike, but also unlike 1877, the President declared a national emergency and sent in federal troops. Debs, arrested and sent to the Woodstock, Illinois jail, was said to have read the *Communist Manifesto* in his cell and become a lifelong socialist. He was also a revered working-class leader.

The second event was actually a series of strikes by the hard-rock miners of the West. The Western Federation of Miners, tough men who worked underground, risking their lives daily, learned quickly that their employers intended to have no unions at all. Armed battles broke out in the 1890s, with carbines, dynamite, and plenty of fighting, and with the law almost entirely on the side of the mine owners. The miners also learned that the American Federation of Labor, whose leaders had ridiculed Eugene Debs' railwaymen for abandoning the craft lines of organization, had no interest in defending the miners. What Wobblies would call the "American Separation of Labor" insisted upon what was called "craft autonomy" in which negotiations were entirely separate for each type of job, and workers in one part of a business had no reason to strike with workers in another part of the business. Something better was needed. The "Continental Congress of the Working Class" is how William "Big Bill" Haywood described the meeting in Chicago, June, 1905, with hundreds of delegates and some of the biggest names in American radicalism on hand. It was that, but it might also be described as the something more that was needed. Just prior to the convention, socialist editor Daniel DeLeon had articulated the vision of a stage in human evolution, going beyond the political State to a future global commonwealth of cooperative labor. Drawing upon Lewis Henry Morgan's studies of American Indians, DeLeon declared that collective, cooperative societies had been the basis of civilization; out of their break-up, fostered by the rise in productive possibilities (better tools, trade, and so on) arose the monarchy, the military, and the oppression of ordinary people. After many centuries (and peasant revolts), an industrial working class emerged. In the industrially advanced United States, the working class had been prepared ready to assume control of society and to replace "politics" and the "State" with a government of direct rule. As Marx had pointed out about the Paris Commune (and Lenin would repeat for the Soviets), the existing government apparatus could not be infiltrated and taken over piece-meal; it had to be dissolved and replaced by a truly democratic, modern form of government.

At the convention, held in Brand's Hall in Chicago's north side opening on June 27, 1905, the one-eyed William D. "Big Bill" Haywood called the meeting to order. Within the next few days, ordinary delegates expressed fundamental, practical ideas about the labor movement, emphasizing that labor needed solidarity in practice not in words. The American Federation of Labor's craft unionism was not only out of date (organized for an earlier period of industrial labor) but ineffective, exclusionary and unfair to the masses of industrial workers. As usual, a Wob song (called "The General Strike") explained the logic best:

> "Now we have no fight with the members of the old AF of L
> But we ask you use your reason for the facts we have to tell
> Your craft is but protection for a form of property
> And your skill is the property you're losing, don't you see?
> Improvements on machinery take tools and trade away
> And you'll be among the common slaves some fateful day
> And the things of which we're telling we're mighty sure about
> O, what's the use to strike when you can't win out?"

This was a somewhat oversimplified view, as it turned out: Craft unions persisted, usually because their members became supervisory. They were the "aristocrats of labor" and their exclusionary union structures remained paramount until the rise of the Congress of Industrial Organizations (CIO) in the 1930s, and broadly influential long afterward—most often as a conservative and frequently racist force allied with labor's avid Cold Warriors. (The thuggish George Meany, a plumber and first president of the AFL-CIO, was himself the perfect example of unionism gone rotten.) But the general idea was true in the main, and true even more so as a revolutionary, emancipatory doctrine still unrealized today. Industrial unions were to be the building block for the future cooperative society. By joining an industrial union, workers prepared themselves to take over society directly. Working people who understood their own power had the capacity to act upon their fundamental right to expropriate and share with other workers across the world everything that they collectively produced.

For the IWW, then, the familiar problem of the socialist movement being notoriously small in the US could be solved in a new way. "Educating" workers into becoming socialists, through newspapers, speeches and election campaigns, was too passive and not very successful. Workers needed to educate themselves, in and through their own actions and self-organization. At the founding convention, among seventy delegates nominally representing 50,000 members, two of the delegates, from the Western Federation of Labor and the amorphous American Labor Union, actually represented 40,000 of those members. Contrary to hopes that craft unionists could convert their structures into industrial unions, few craft union locals were represented as such, and many delegates actually represented only themselves. The high points were, then, the statement of principles beginning: "The working class and the employing class have nothing in common," and the memorable soliloquies on the floor of the convention. Thus Lucy Parsons, already renowned for her defense of her husband after the Haymarket Incident in 1886, and a "personality" as an African-American revolutionary in Chicago, famously spoke for the most lowly women driven to prostitution, but also spoke of workers' capacity, arguing: "My conception of the strike of the future is not to strike and go out and starve, but to strike and remain in and take possession of the necessary property of production." In this way, the veteran of nineteenth-century class, race, and gender struggles predicted the sit-down strike of the future, first with the factory and then, in later generations, in the student takeover of classrooms and even presidential offices, to protest the brutal war on Vietnam.

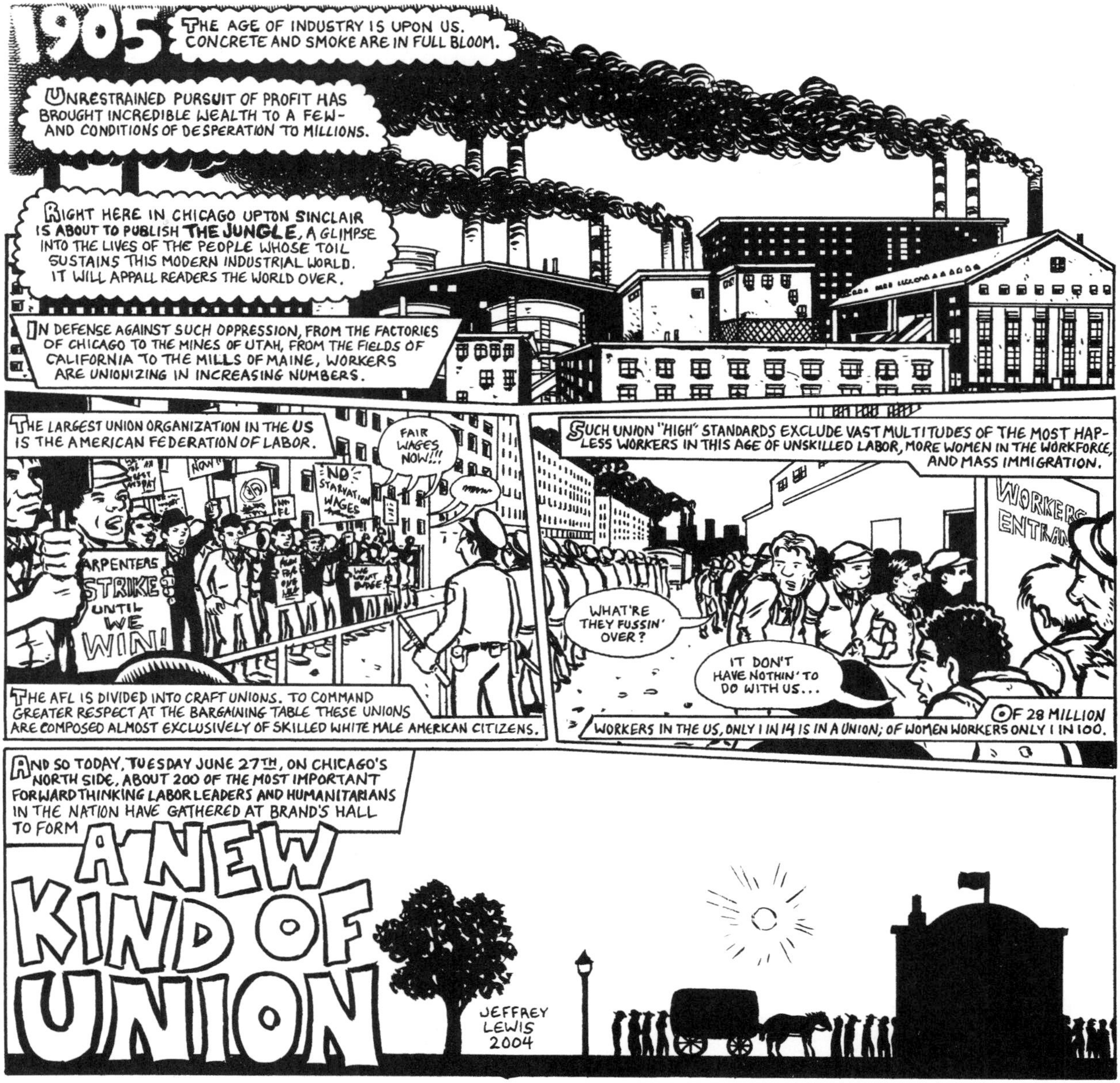
1905
THE AGE OF INDUSTRY IS UPON US. CONCRETE AND SMOKE ARE IN FULL BLOOM.
UNRESTRAINED PURSUIT OF PROFIT HAS BROUGHT INCREDIBLE WEALTH TO A FEW– AND CONDITIONS OF DESPERATION TO MILLIONS.
RIGHT HERE IN CHICAGO UPTON SINCLAIR IS ABOUT TO PUBLISH THE JUNGLE, A GLIMPSE INTO THE LIVES OF THE PEOPLE WHOSE TOIL SUSTAINS THIS MODERN INDUSTRIAL WORLD. IT WILL APPALL READERS THE WORLD OVER.
IN DEFENSE AGAINST SUCH OPPRESSION, FROM THE FACTORIES OF CHICAGO TO THE MINES OF UTAH, FROM THE FIELDS OF CALIFORNIA TO THE MILLS OF MAINE, WORKERS ARE UNIONIZING IN INCREASING NUMBERS.
THE LARGEST UNION ORGANIZATION IN THE US IS THE AMERICAN FEDERATION OF LABOR.
FAIR WAGES NOW!!!
NO STARVATION WAGES
ARPENTERS STRIKE! UNTIL WE WIN!
THE AFL IS DIVIDED INTO CRAFT UNIONS. TO COMMAND GREATER RESPECT AT THE BARGAINING TABLE THESE UNIONS ARE COMPOSED ALMOST EXCLUSIVELY OF SKILLED WHITE MALE AMERICAN CITIZENS.
SUCH UNION "HIGH" STANDARDS EXCLUDE VAST MULTITUDES OF THE MOST HAPLESS WORKERS IN THIS AGE OF UNSKILLED LABOR, MORE WOMEN IN THE WORKFORCE, AND MASS IMMIGRATION.
WHAT'RE THEY FUSSIN' OVER?
IT DON'T HAVE NOTHIN' TO DO WITH US...
OF 28 MILLION WORKERS IN THE US, ONLY 1 IN 14 IS IN A UNION; OF WOMEN WORKERS ONLY 1 IN 100.
AND SO TODAY, TUESDAY JUNE 27TH, ON CHICAGO'S NORTH SIDE, ABOUT 200 OF THE MOST IMPORTANT FORWARD THINKING LABOR LEADERS AND HUMANITARIANS IN THE NATION HAVE GATHERED AT BRAND'S HALL TO FORM
A NEW KIND OF UNION
JEFFREY LEWIS 2004

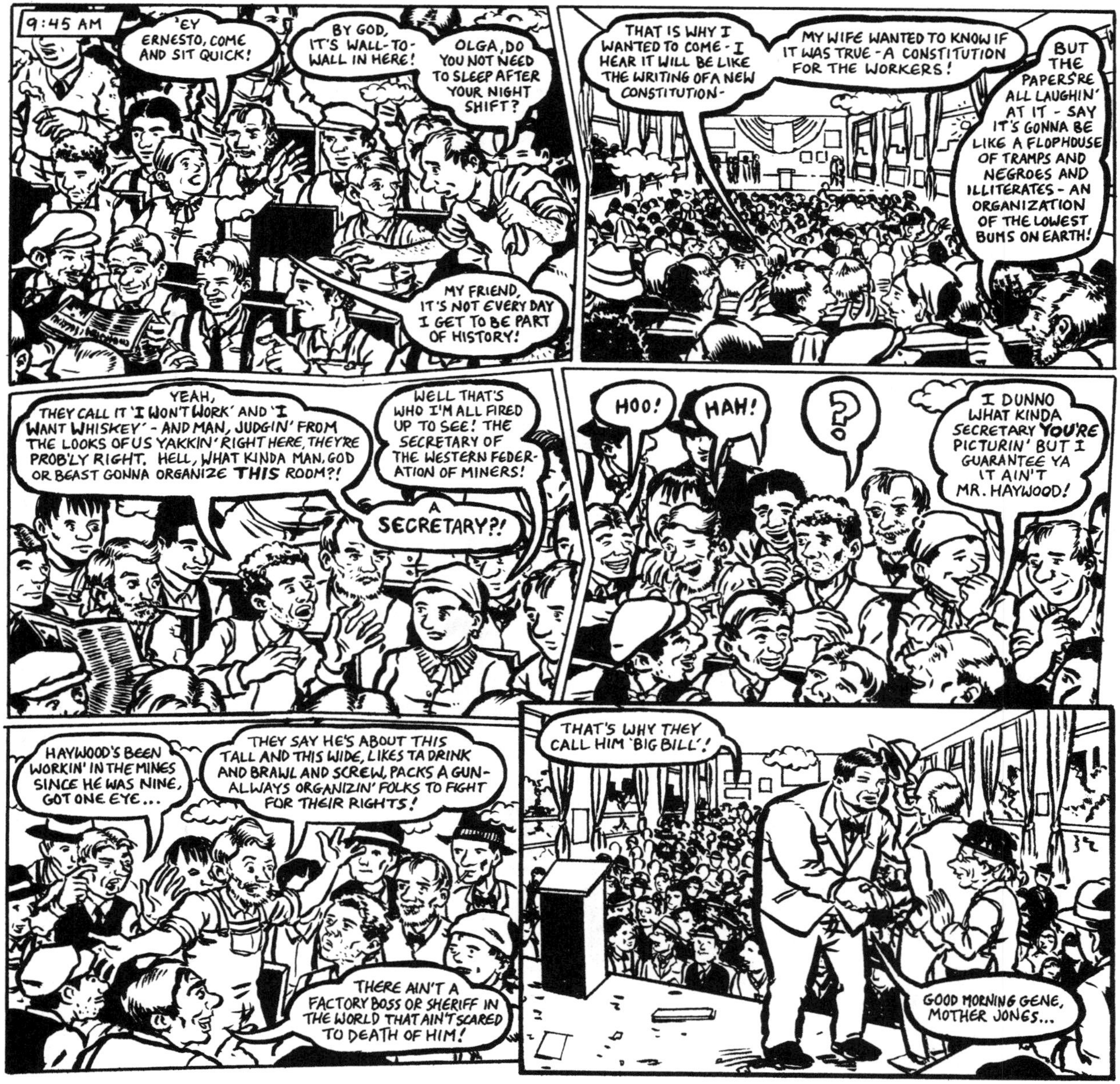
9:45 AM
'EY ERNESTO, COME AND SIT QUICK!
BY GOD, IT'S WALL-TO-WALL IN HERE!
OLGA, DO YOU NOT NEED TO SLEEP AFTER YOUR NIGHT SHIFT?
MY FRIEND, IT'S NOT EVERY DAY I GET TO BE PART OF HISTORY!
THAT IS WHY I WANTED TO COME - I HEAR IT WILL BE LIKE THE WRITING OF A NEW CONSTITUTION-
MY WIFE WANTED TO KNOW IF IT WAS TRUE - A CONSTITUTION FOR THE WORKERS!
BUT THE PAPERS'RE ALL LAUGHIN' AT IT - SAY IT'S GONNA BE LIKE A FLOPHOUSE OF TRAMPS AND NEGROES AND ILLITERATES - AN ORGANIZATION OF THE LOWEST BUMS ON EARTH!
YEAH, THEY CALL IT 'I WON'T WORK' AND 'I WANT WHISKEY' - AND MAN, JUDGIN' FROM THE LOOKS OF US YAKKIN' RIGHT HERE, THEY'RE PROB'LY RIGHT. HELL, WHAT KINDA MAN, GOD OR BEAST GONNA ORGANIZE THIS ROOM?!
WELL THAT'S WHO I'M ALL FIRED UP TO SEE! THE SECRETARY OF THE WESTERN FEDERATION OF MINERS!
A SECRETARY?!
HOO!
HAH!
?
I DUNNO WHAT KINDA SECRETARY YOU'RE PICTURIN' BUT I GUARANTEE YA IT AIN'T MR. HAYWOOD!
HAYWOOD'S BEEN WORKIN' IN THE MINES SINCE HE WAS NINE, GOT ONE EYE...
THEY SAY HE'S ABOUT THIS TALL AND THIS WIDE, LIKES TA DRINK AND BRAWL AND SCREW, PACKS A GUN - ALWAYS ORGANIZIN' FOLKS TO FIGHT FOR THEIR RIGHTS!
THERE AIN'T A FACTORY BOSS OR SHERIFF IN THE WORLD THAT AIN'T SCARED TO DEATH OF HIM!
THAT'S WHY THEY CALL HIM 'BIG BILL'!
GOOD MORNING GENE, MOTHER JONES...

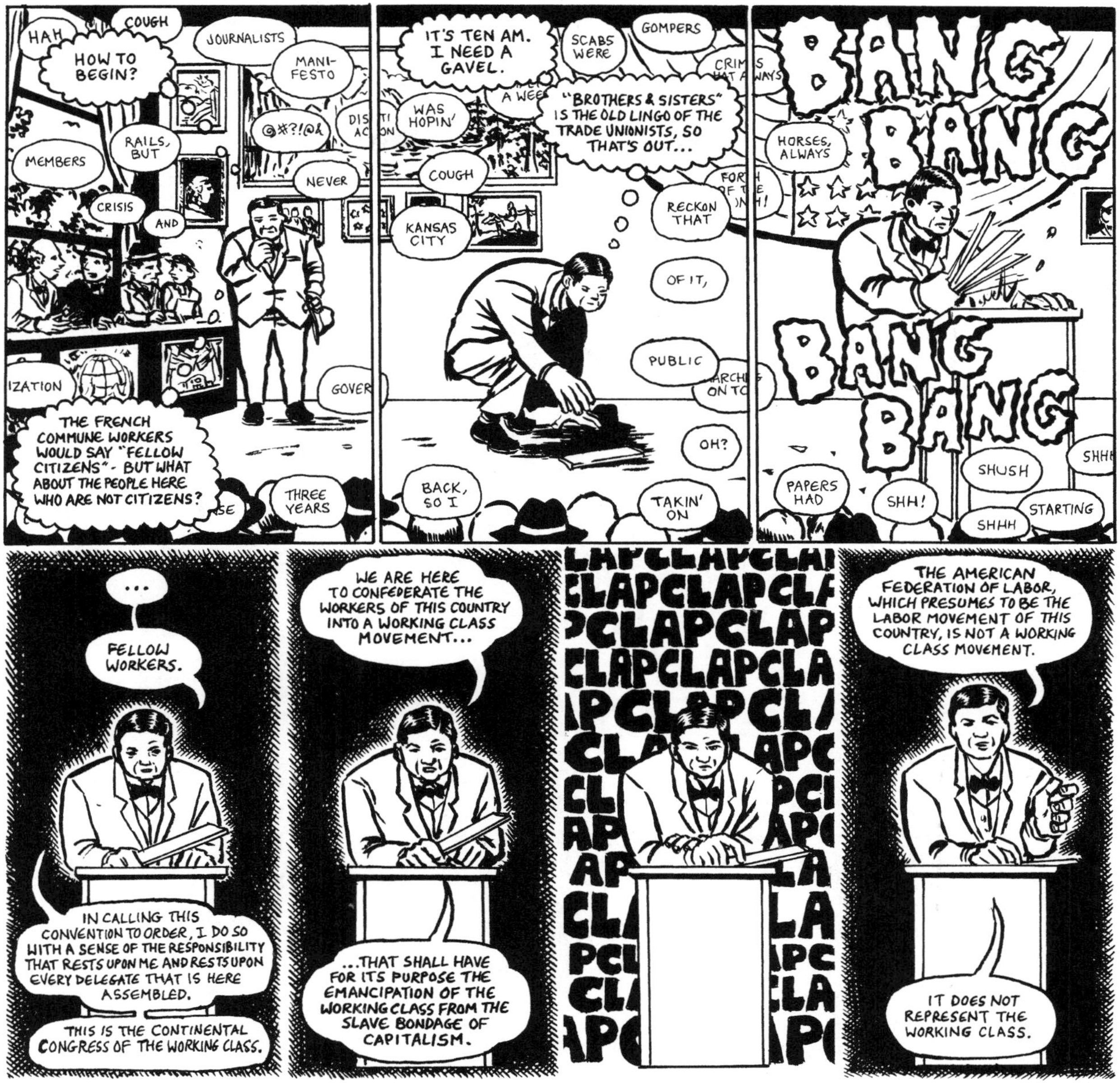
HAH
COUGH
HOW TO BEGIN?
JOURNALISTS
MANI-FESTO
@#?!@&
MEMBERS
RAILS, BUT
NEVER
CRISIS
AND
THE FRENCH COMMUNE WORKERS WOULD SAY "FELLOW CITIZENS" - BUT WHAT ABOUT THE PEOPLE HERE WHO ARE NOT CITIZENS?
THREE YEARS
IT'S TEN AM. I NEED A GAVEL.
SCABS WERE
GOMPERS
WAS HOPIN'
"BROTHERS & SISTERS" IS THE OLD LINGO OF THE TRADE UNIONISTS, SO THAT'S OUT...
COUGH
KANSAS CITY
RECKON THAT
OF IT,
PUBLIC
OH?
BACK, SO I
TAKIN' ON
BANG BANG
HORSES, ALWAYS
BANG BANG
SHUSH
PAPERS HAD
SHH!
SHHH
STARTING
...
FELLOW WORKERS.
IN CALLING THIS CONVENTION TO ORDER, I DO SO WITH A SENSE OF THE RESPONSIBILITY THAT RESTS UPON ME AND RESTS UPON EVERY DELEGATE THAT IS HERE ASSEMBLED.
THIS IS THE CONTINENTAL CONGRESS OF THE WORKING CLASS.
WE ARE HERE TO CONFEDERATE THE WORKERS OF THIS COUNTRY INTO A WORKING CLASS MOVEMENT...
...THAT SHALL HAVE FOR ITS PURPOSE THE EMANCIPATION OF THE WORKING CLASS FROM THE SLAVE BONDAGE OF CAPITALISM.
CLAPCLAPCLAP
THE AMERICAN FEDERATION OF LABOR, WHICH PRESUMES TO BE THE LABOR MOVEMENT OF THIS COUNTRY, IS NOT A WORKING CLASS MOVEMENT.
IT DOES NOT REPRESENT THE WORKING CLASS.

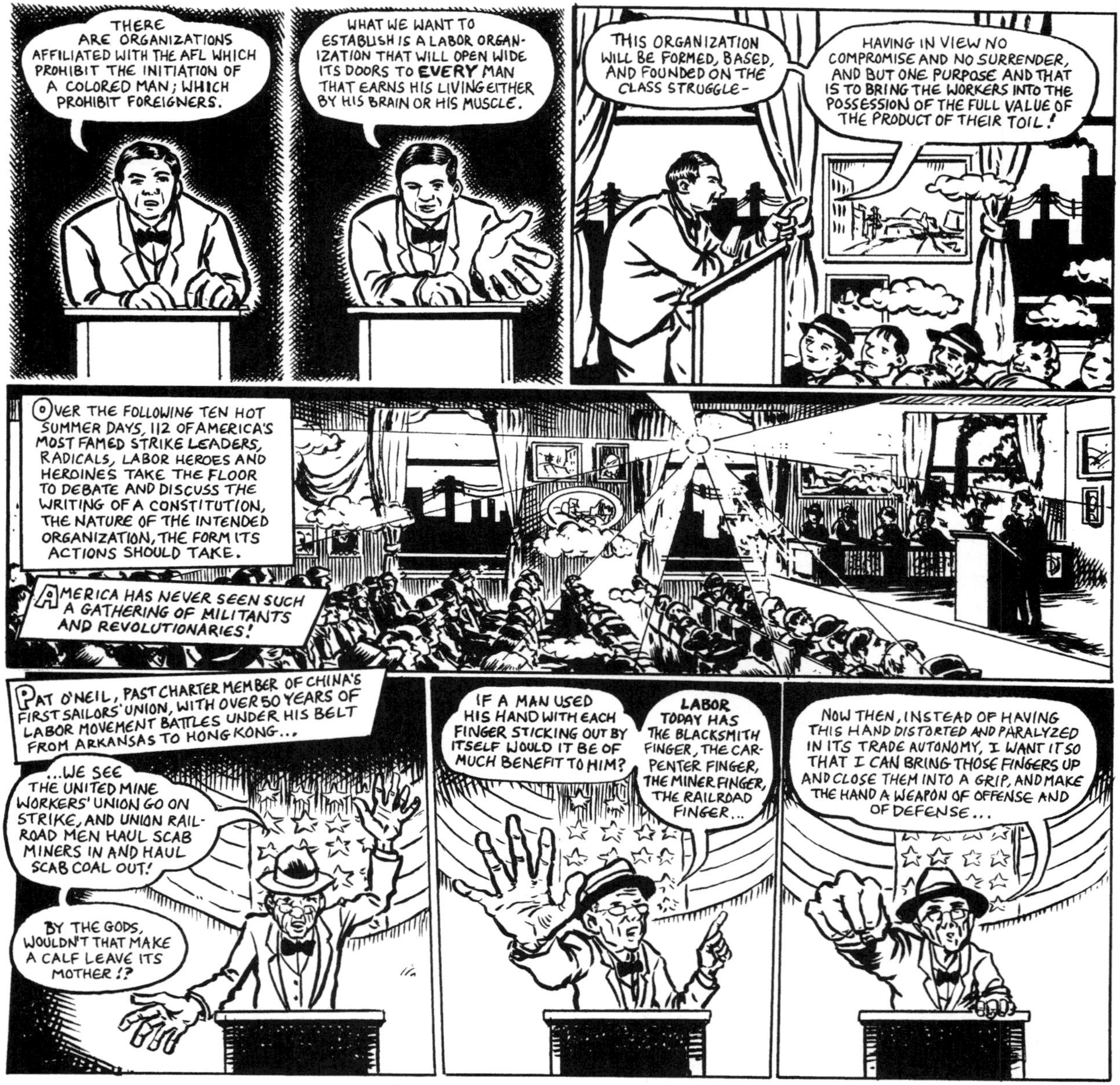
THERE ARE ORGANIZATIONS AFFILIATED WITH THE AFL WHICH PROHIBIT THE INITIATION OF A COLORED MAN; WHICH PROHIBIT FOREIGNERS.
WHAT WE WANT TO ESTABLISH IS A LABOR ORGANIZATION THAT WILL OPEN WIDE ITS DOORS TO EVERY MAN THAT EARNS HIS LIVING EITHER BY HIS BRAIN OR HIS MUSCLE.
THIS ORGANIZATION WILL BE FORMED, BASED, AND FOUNDED ON THE CLASS STRUGGLE-
HAVING IN VIEW NO COMPROMISE AND NO SURRENDER, AND BUT ONE PURPOSE AND THAT IS TO BRING THE WORKERS INTO THE POSSESSION OF THE FULL VALUE OF THE PRODUCT OF THEIR TOIL!
OVER THE FOLLOWING TEN HOT SUMMER DAYS, 112 OF AMERICA'S MOST FAMED STRIKE LEADERS, RADICALS, LABOR HEROES AND HEROINES TAKE THE FLOOR TO DEBATE AND DISCUSS THE WRITING OF A CONSTITUTION, THE NATURE OF THE INTENDED ORGANIZATION, THE FORM ITS ACTIONS SHOULD TAKE.
AMERICA HAS NEVER SEEN SUCH A GATHERING OF MILITANTS AND REVOLUTIONARIES!
PAT O'NEIL, PAST CHARTER MEMBER OF CHINA'S FIRST SAILORS' UNION, WITH OVER 50 YEARS OF LABOR MOVEMENT BATTLES UNDER HIS BELT FROM ARKANSAS TO HONG KONG...
...WE SEE THE UNITED MINE WORKERS' UNION GO ON STRIKE, AND UNION RAILROAD MEN HAUL SCAB MINERS IN AND HAUL SCAB COAL OUT!
BY THE GODS, WOULDN'T THAT MAKE A CALF LEAVE ITS MOTHER!?
IF A MAN USED HIS HAND WITH EACH FINGER STICKING OUT BY ITSELF WOULD IT BE OF MUCH BENEFIT TO HIM?
LABOR TODAY HAS THE BLACKSMITH FINGER, THE CARPENTER FINGER, THE MINER FINGER, THE RAILROAD FINGER...
NOW THEN, INSTEAD OF HAVING THIS HAND DISTORTED AND PARALYZED IN ITS TRADE AUTONOMY, I WANT IT SO THAT I CAN BRING THOSE FINGERS UP AND CLOSE THEM INTO A GRIP, AND MAKE THE HAND A WEAPON OF OFFENSE AND OF DEFENSE...

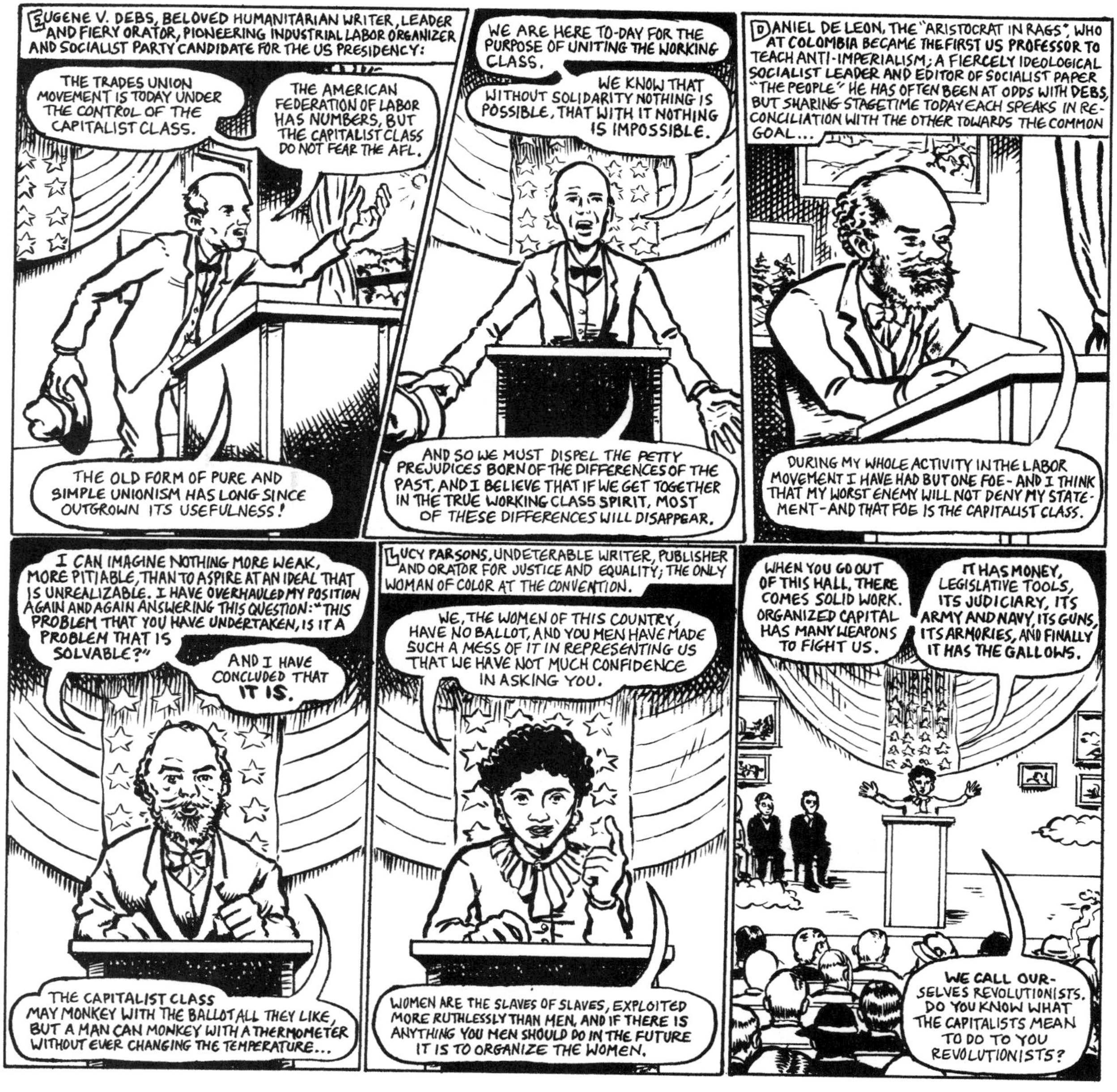
EUGENE V. DEBS, BELOVED HUMANITARIAN WRITER, LEADER AND FIERY ORATOR, PIONEERING INDUSTRIAL LABOR ORGANIZER AND SOCIALIST PARTY CANDIDATE FOR THE US PRESIDENCY:
THE TRADES UNION MOVEMENT IS TODAY UNDER THE CONTROL OF THE CAPITALIST CLASS.
THE AMERICAN FEDERATION OF LABOR HAS NUMBERS, BUT THE CAPITALIST CLASS DO NOT FEAR THE AFL.
THE OLD FORM OF PURE AND SIMPLE UNIONISM HAS LONG SINCE OUTGROWN ITS USEFULNESS!
WE ARE HERE TO-DAY FOR THE PURPOSE OF UNITING THE WORKING CLASS.
WE KNOW THAT WITHOUT SOLIDARITY NOTHING IS POSSIBLE, THAT WITH IT NOTHING IS IMPOSSIBLE.
AND SO WE MUST DISPEL THE PETTY PREJUDICES BORN OF THE DIFFERENCES OF THE PAST, AND I BELIEVE THAT IF WE GET TOGETHER IN THE TRUE WORKING CLASS SPIRIT, MOST OF THESE DIFFERENCES WILL DISAPPEAR.
DANIEL DE LEON, THE "ARISTOCRAT IN RAGS," WHO AT COLOMBIA BECAME THE FIRST US PROFESSOR TO TEACH ANTI-IMPERIALISM; A FIERCELY IDEOLOGICAL SOCIALIST LEADER AND EDITOR OF SOCIALIST PAPER "THE PEOPLE" HE HAS OFTEN BEEN AT ODDS WITH DEBS, BUT SHARING STAGETIME TODAY EACH SPEAKS IN RECONCILIATION WITH THE OTHER TOWARDS THE COMMON GOAL...
DURING MY WHOLE ACTIVITY IN THE LABOR MOVEMENT I HAVE HAD BUT ONE FOE - AND I THINK THAT MY WORST ENEMY WILL NOT DENY MY STATEMENT - AND THAT FOE IS THE CAPITALIST CLASS.
I CAN IMAGINE NOTHING MORE WEAK, MORE PITIABLE, THAN TO ASPIRE AT AN IDEAL THAT IS UNREALIZABLE. I HAVE OVERHAULED MY POSITION AGAIN AND AGAIN ANSWERING THIS QUESTION: "THIS PROBLEM THAT YOU HAVE UNDERTAKEN, IS IT A PROBLEM THAT IS SOLVABLE?"
AND I HAVE CONCLUDED THAT IT IS.
THE CAPITALIST CLASS MAY MONKEY WITH THE BALLOT ALL THEY LIKE, BUT A MAN CAN MONKEY WITH A THERMOMETER WITHOUT EVER CHANGING THE TEMPERATURE...
LUCY PARSONS, UNDETERABLE WRITER, PUBLISHER AND ORATOR FOR JUSTICE AND EQUALITY; THE ONLY WOMAN OF COLOR AT THE CONVENTION.
WE, THE WOMEN OF THIS COUNTRY, HAVE NO BALLOT, AND YOU MEN HAVE MADE SUCH A MESS OF IT IN REPRESENTING US THAT WE HAVE NOT MUCH CONFIDENCE IN ASKING YOU.
WOMEN ARE THE SLAVES OF SLAVES, EXPLOITED MORE RUTHLESSLY THAN MEN, AND IF THERE IS ANYTHING YOU MEN SHOULD DO IN THE FUTURE IT IS TO ORGANIZE THE WOMEN.
WHEN YOU GO OUT OF THIS HALL, THERE COMES SOLID WORK. ORGANIZED CAPITAL HAS MANY WEAPONS TO FIGHT US.
IT HAS MONEY, LEGISLATIVE TOOLS, ITS JUDICIARY, ITS ARMY AND NAVY, ITS GUNS, ITS ARMORIES, AND FINALLY IT HAS THE GALLOWS.
WE CALL OURSELVES REVOLUTIONISTS. DO YOU KNOW WHAT THE CAPITALISTS MEAN TO DO TO YOU REVOLUTIONISTS?

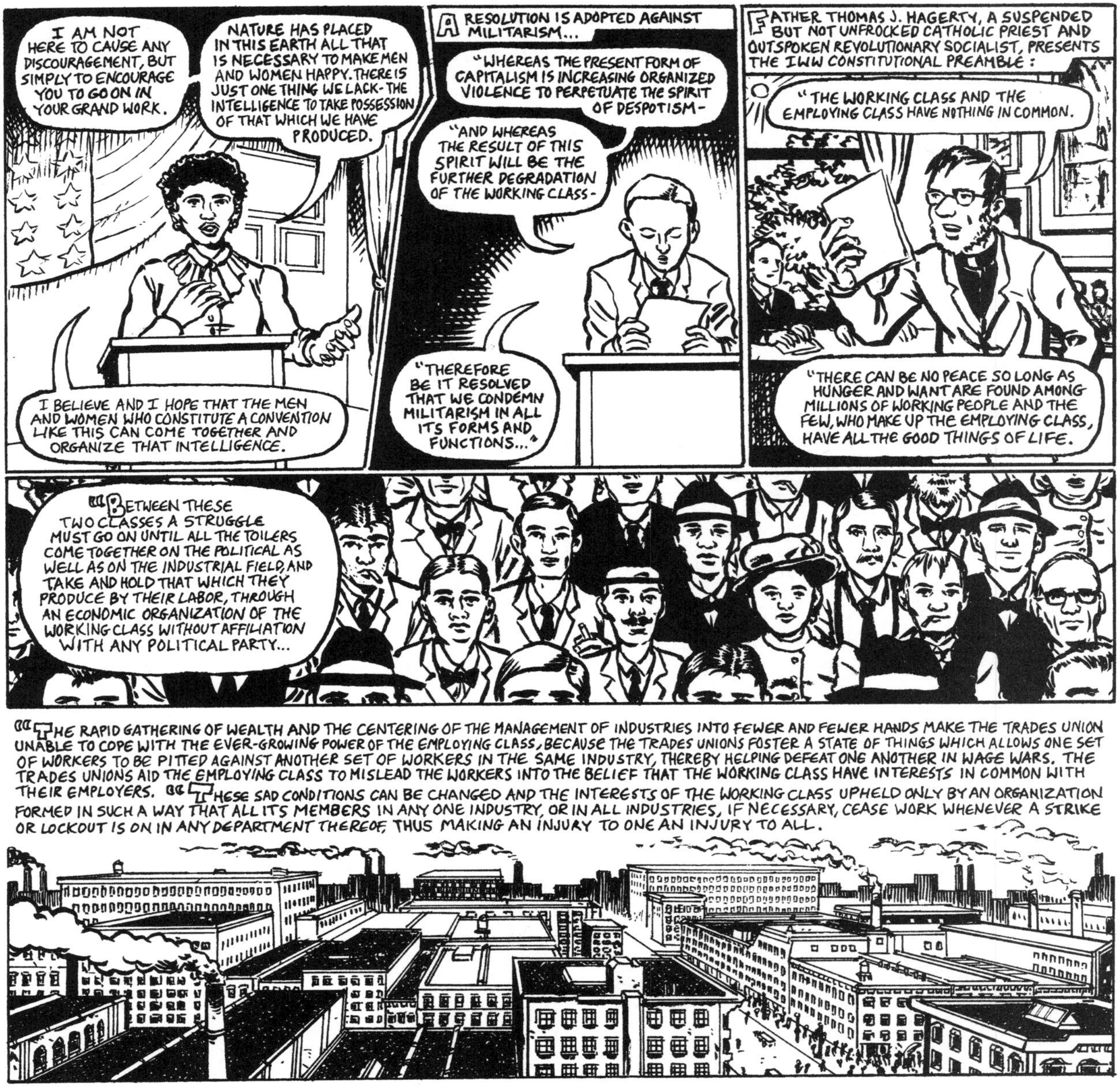
I AM NOT HERE TO CAUSE ANY DISCOURAGEMENT, BUT SIMPLY TO ENCOURAGE YOU TO GO ON IN YOUR GRAND WORK.
NATURE HAS PLACED IN THIS EARTH ALL THAT IS NECESSARY TO MAKE MEN AND WOMEN HAPPY. THERE IS JUST ONE THING WE LACK- THE INTELLIGENCE TO TAKE POSSESSION OF THAT WHICH WE HAVE PRODUCED.
I BELIEVE AND I HOPE THAT THE MEN AND WOMEN WHO CONSTITUTE A CONVENTION LIKE THIS CAN COME TOGETHER AND ORGANIZE THAT INTELLIGENCE.
A RESOLUTION IS ADOPTED AGAINST MILITARISM...
"WHEREAS THE PRESENT FORM OF CAPITALISM IS INCREASING ORGANIZED VIOLENCE TO PERPETUATE THE SPIRIT OF DESPOTISM-
"AND WHEREAS THE RESULT OF THIS SPIRIT WILL BE THE FURTHER DEGRADATION OF THE WORKING CLASS-
"THEREFORE BE IT RESOLVED THAT WE CONDEMN MILITARISM IN ALL ITS FORMS AND FUNCTIONS..."
FATHER THOMAS J. HAGERTY, A SUSPENDED BUT NOT UNFROCKED CATHOLIC PRIEST AND OUTSPOKEN REVOLUTIONARY SOCIALIST, PRESENTS THE IWW CONSTITUTIONAL PREAMBLE:
"THE WORKING CLASS AND THE EMPLOYING CLASS HAVE NOTHING IN COMMON.
"THERE CAN BE NO PEACE SO LONG AS HUNGER AND WANT ARE FOUND AMONG MILLIONS OF WORKING PEOPLE AND THE FEW, WHO MAKE UP THE EMPLOYING CLASS, HAVE ALL THE GOOD THINGS OF LIFE.
"BETWEEN THESE TWO CLASSES A STRUGGLE MUST GO ON UNTIL ALL THE TOILERS COME TOGETHER ON THE POLITICAL AS WELL AS ON THE INDUSTRIAL FIELD, AND TAKE AND HOLD THAT WHICH THEY PRODUCE BY THEIR LABOR, THROUGH AN ECONOMIC ORGANIZATION OF THE WORKING CLASS WITHOUT AFFILIATION WITH ANY POLITICAL PARTY...
"THE RAPID GATHERING OF WEALTH AND THE CENTERING OF THE MANAGEMENT OF INDUSTRIES INTO FEWER AND FEWER HANDS MAKE THE TRADES UNION UNABLE TO COPE WITH THE EVER-GROWING POWER OF THE EMPLOYING CLASS, BECAUSE THE TRADES UNIONS FOSTER A STATE OF THINGS WHICH ALLOWS ONE SET OF WORKERS TO BE PITTED AGAINST ANOTHER SET OF WORKERS IN THE SAME INDUSTRY, THEREBY HELPING DEFEAT ONE ANOTHER IN WAGE WARS. THE TRADES UNIONS AID THE EMPLOYING CLASS TO MISLEAD THE WORKERS INTO THE BELIEF THAT THE WORKING CLASS HAVE INTERESTS IN COMMON WITH THEIR EMPLOYERS. "THESE SAD CONDITIONS CAN BE CHANGED AND THE INTERESTS OF THE WORKING CLASS UPHELD ONLY BY AN ORGANIZATION FORMED IN SUCH A WAY THAT ALL ITS MEMBERS IN ANY ONE INDUSTRY, OR IN ALL INDUSTRIES, IF NECESSARY, CEASE WORK WHENEVER A STRIKE OR LOCKOUT IS ON IN ANY DEPARTMENT THEREOF, THUS MAKING AN INJURY TO ONE AN INJURY TO ALL.

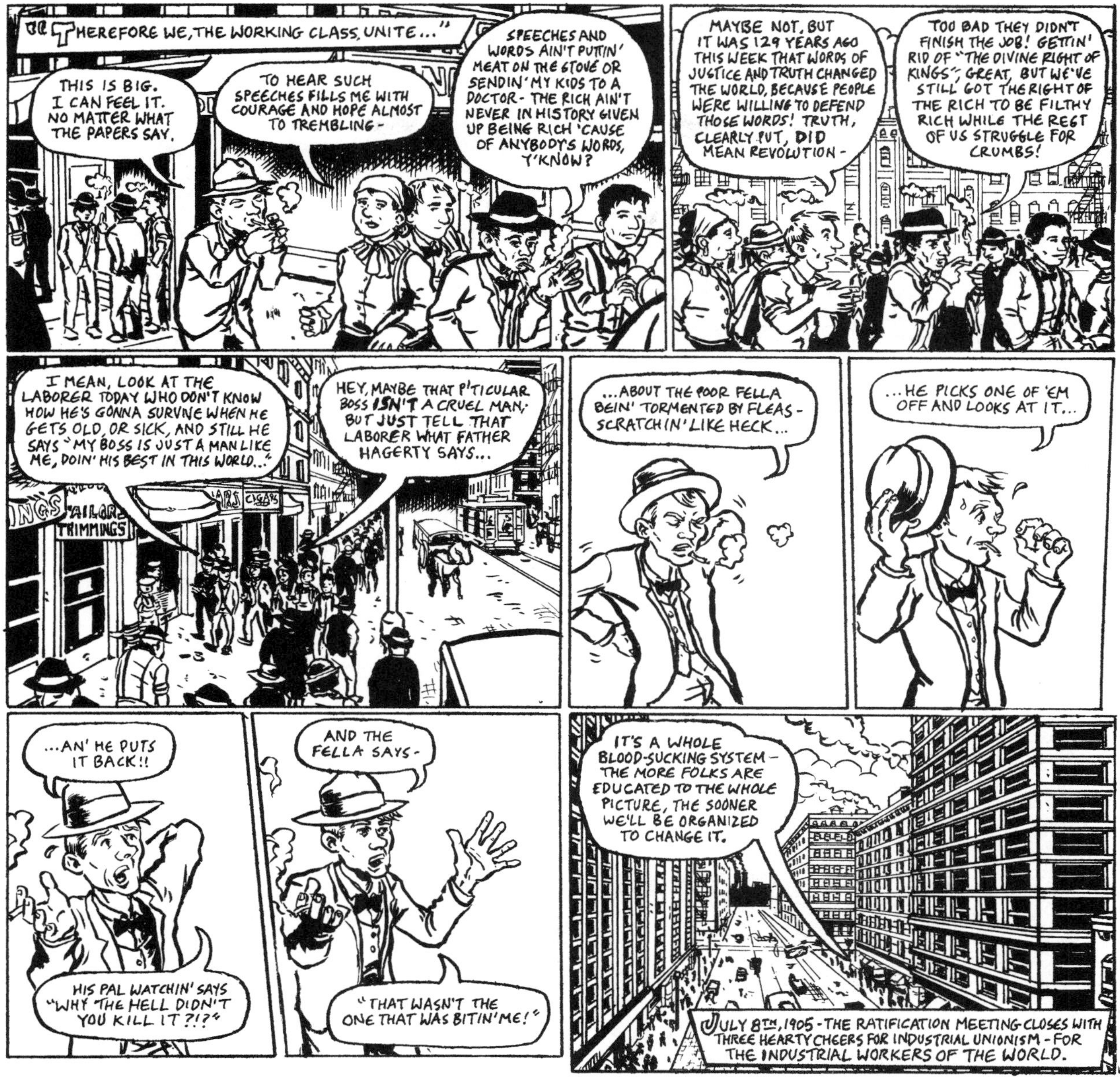
"THEREFORE WE, THE WORKING CLASS, UNITE..."
THIS IS BIG. I CAN FEEL IT. NO MATTER WHAT THE PAPERS SAY.
TO HEAR SUCH SPEECHES FILLS ME WITH COURAGE AND HOPE ALMOST TO TREMBLING-
SPEECHES AND WORDS AIN'T PUTTIN' MEAT ON THE STOVE OR SENDIN' MY KIDS TO A DOCTOR- THE RICH AIN'T NEVER IN HISTORY GIVEN UP BEING RICH 'CAUSE OF ANYBODY'S WORDS, Y'KNOW?
MAYBE NOT, BUT IT WAS 129 YEARS AGO THIS WEEK THAT WORDS OF JUSTICE AND TRUTH CHANGED THE WORLD, BECAUSE PEOPLE WERE WILLING TO DEFEND THOSE WORDS! TRUTH, CLEARLY PUT, DID MEAN REVOLUTION-
TOO BAD THEY DIDN'T FINISH THE JOB! GETTIN' RID OF "THE DIVINE RIGHT OF KINGS", GREAT, BUT WE'VE STILL GOT THE RIGHT OF THE RICH TO BE FILTHY RICH WHILE THE REST OF US STRUGGLE FOR CRUMBS!
I MEAN, LOOK AT THE LABORER TODAY WHO DON'T KNOW HOW HE'S GONNA SURVIVE WHEN HE GETS OLD, OR SICK, AND STILL HE SAYS "MY BOSS IS JUST A MAN LIKE ME, DOIN' HIS BEST IN THIS WORLD..."
HEY, MAYBE THAT P'TICULAR BOSS ISN'T A CRUEL MAN, BUT JUST TELL THAT LABORER WHAT FATHER HAGERTY SAYS...
TAILORS TRIMMINGS
CIGARS
...ABOUT THE POOR FELLA BEIN' TORMENTED BY FLEAS- SCRATCHIN' LIKE HECK...
...HE PICKS ONE OF 'EM OFF AND LOOKS AT IT...
...AN' HE PUTS IT BACK!!
HIS PAL WATCHIN' SAYS "WHY THE HELL DIDN'T YOU KILL IT?!?"
AND THE FELLA SAYS-
"THAT WASN'T THE ONE THAT WAS BITIN' ME!"
IT'S A WHOLE BLOOD-SUCKING SYSTEM- THE MORE FOLKS ARE EDUCATED TO THE WHOLE PICTURE, THE SOONER WE'LL BE ORGANIZED TO CHANGE IT.
JULY 8TH, 1905- THE RATIFICATION MEETING CLOSES WITH THREE HEARTY CHEERS FOR INDUSTRIAL UNIONISM- FOR THE INDUSTRIAL WORKERS OF THE WORLD.

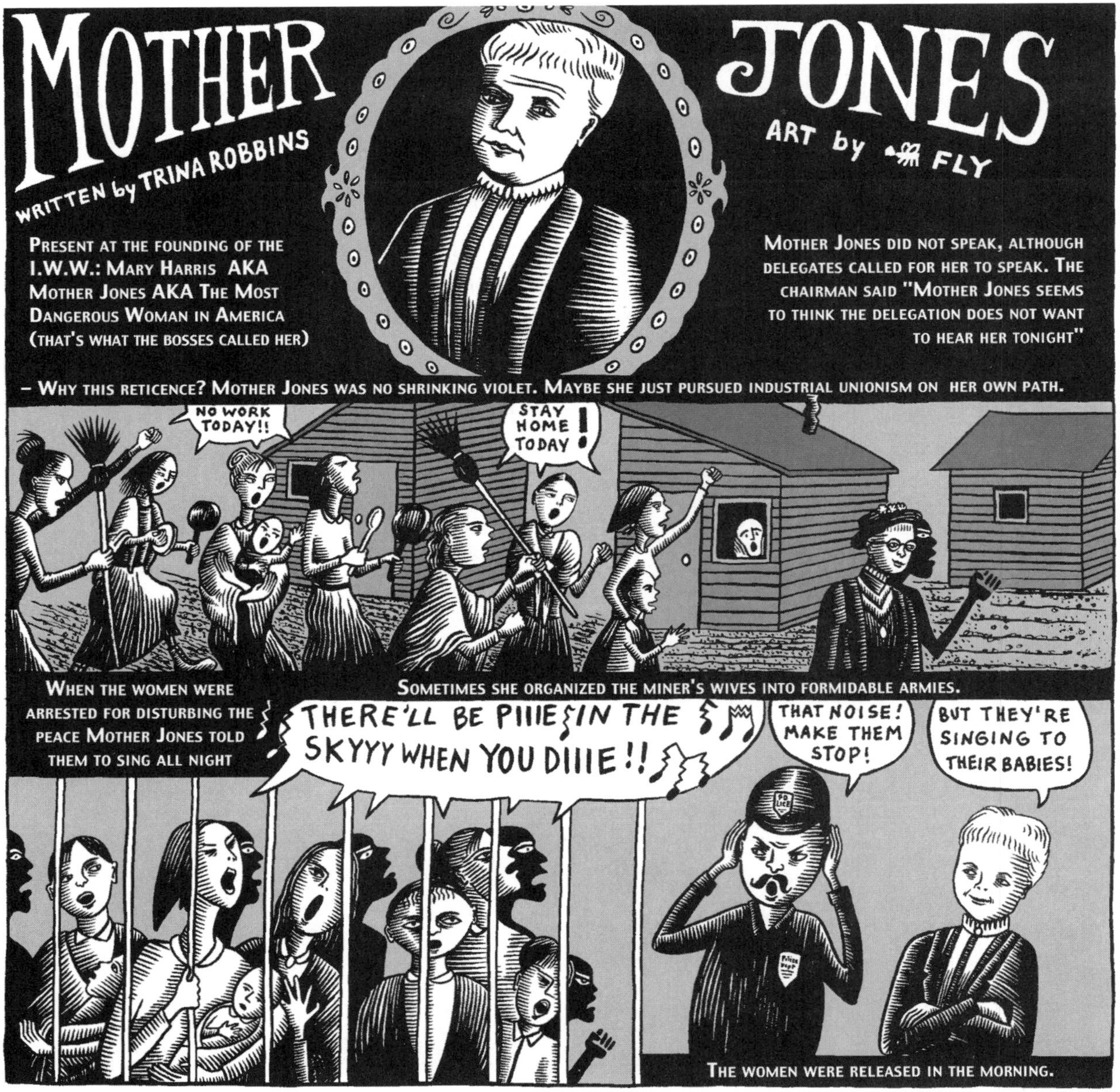
MOTHER JONES
WRITTEN by TRINA ROBBINS
ART by FLY
PRESENT AT THE FOUNDING OF THE I.W.W.: MARY HARRIS AKA MOTHER JONES AKA THE MOST DANGEROUS WOMAN IN AMERICA (THAT'S WHAT THE BOSSES CALLED HER)
MOTHER JONES DID NOT SPEAK, ALTHOUGH DELEGATES CALLED FOR HER TO SPEAK. THE CHAIRMAN SAID "MOTHER JONES SEEMS TO THINK THE DELEGATION DOES NOT WANT TO HEAR HER TONIGHT"
– WHY THIS RETICENCE? MOTHER JONES WAS NO SHRINKING VIOLET. MAYBE SHE JUST PURSUED INDUSTRIAL UNIONISM ON HER OWN PATH.
NO WORK TODAY!!
STAY HOME TODAY!
SOMETIMES SHE ORGANIZED THE MINER'S WIVES INTO FORMIDABLE ARMIES.
WHEN THE WOMEN WERE ARRESTED FOR DISTURBING THE PEACE MOTHER JONES TOLD THEM TO SING ALL NIGHT
THERE'LL BE PIIIE IN THE SKYYY WHEN YOU DIIIE!!
THAT NOISE! MAKE THEM STOP!
BUT THEY'RE SINGING TO THEIR BABIES!
THE WOMEN WERE RELEASED IN THE MORNING.

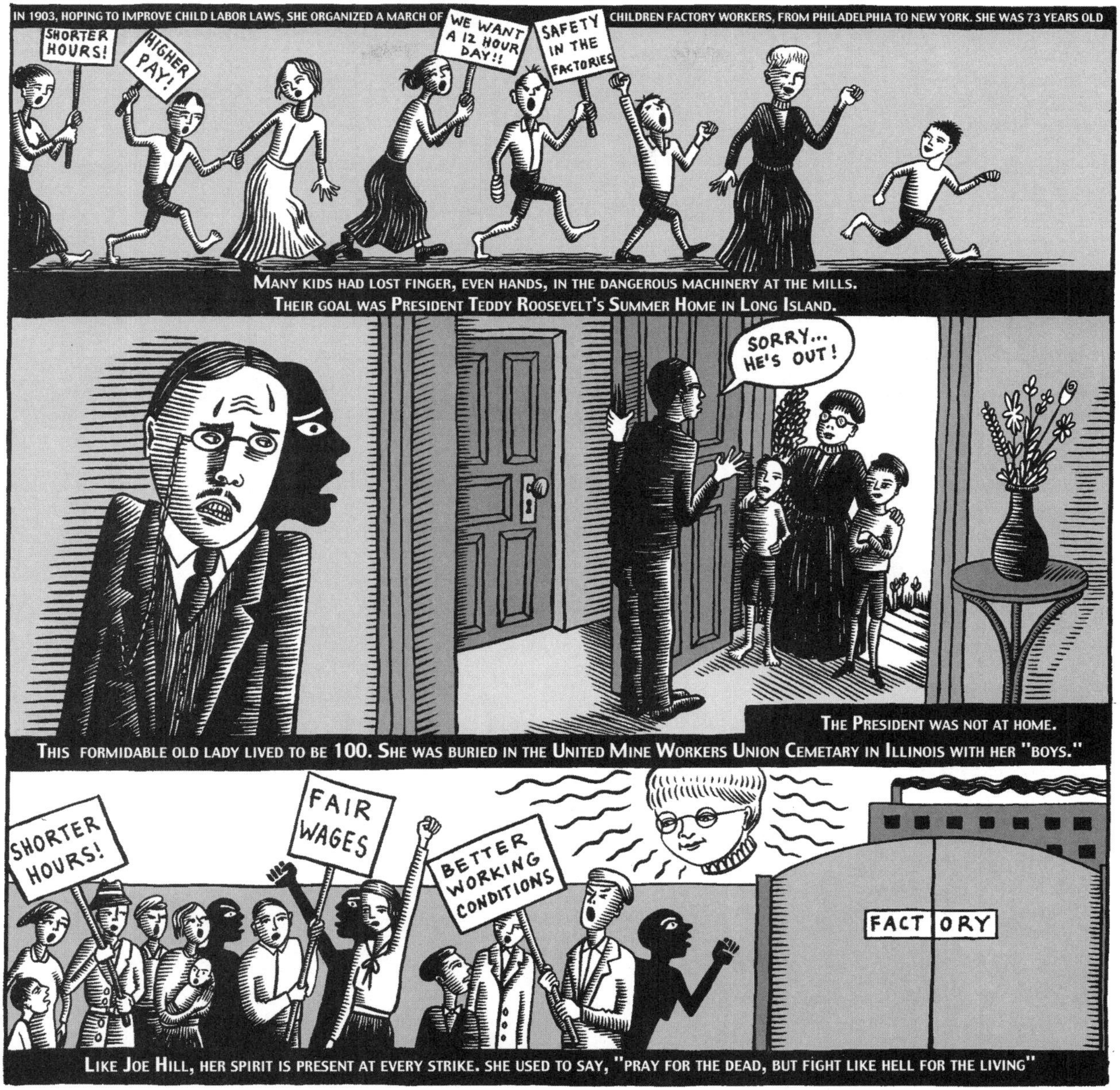
IN 1903, HOPING TO IMPROVE CHILD LABOR LAWS, SHE ORGANIZED A MARCH OF CHILDREN FACTORY WORKERS, FROM PHILADELPHIA TO NEW YORK. SHE WAS 73 YEARS OLD
SHORTER HOURS!
HIGHER PAY!
WE WANT A 12 HOUR DAY!!
SAFETY IN THE FACTORIES
MANY KIDS HAD LOST FINGER, EVEN HANDS, IN THE DANGEROUS MACHINERY AT THE MILLS.
THEIR GOAL WAS PRESIDENT TEDDY ROOSEVELT'S SUMMER HOME IN LONG ISLAND.
SORRY... HE'S OUT!
THE PRESIDENT WAS NOT AT HOME.
THIS FORMIDABLE OLD LADY LIVED TO BE 100. SHE WAS BURIED IN THE UNITED MINE WORKERS UNION CEMETARY IN ILLINOIS WITH HER "BOYS."
SHORTER HOURS!
FAIR WAGES
BETTER WORKING CONDITIONS
FACT ORY
LIKE JOE HILL, HER SPIRIT IS PRESENT AT EVERY STRIKE. SHE USED TO SAY, "PRAY FOR THE DEAD, BUT FIGHT LIKE HELL FOR THE LIVING"

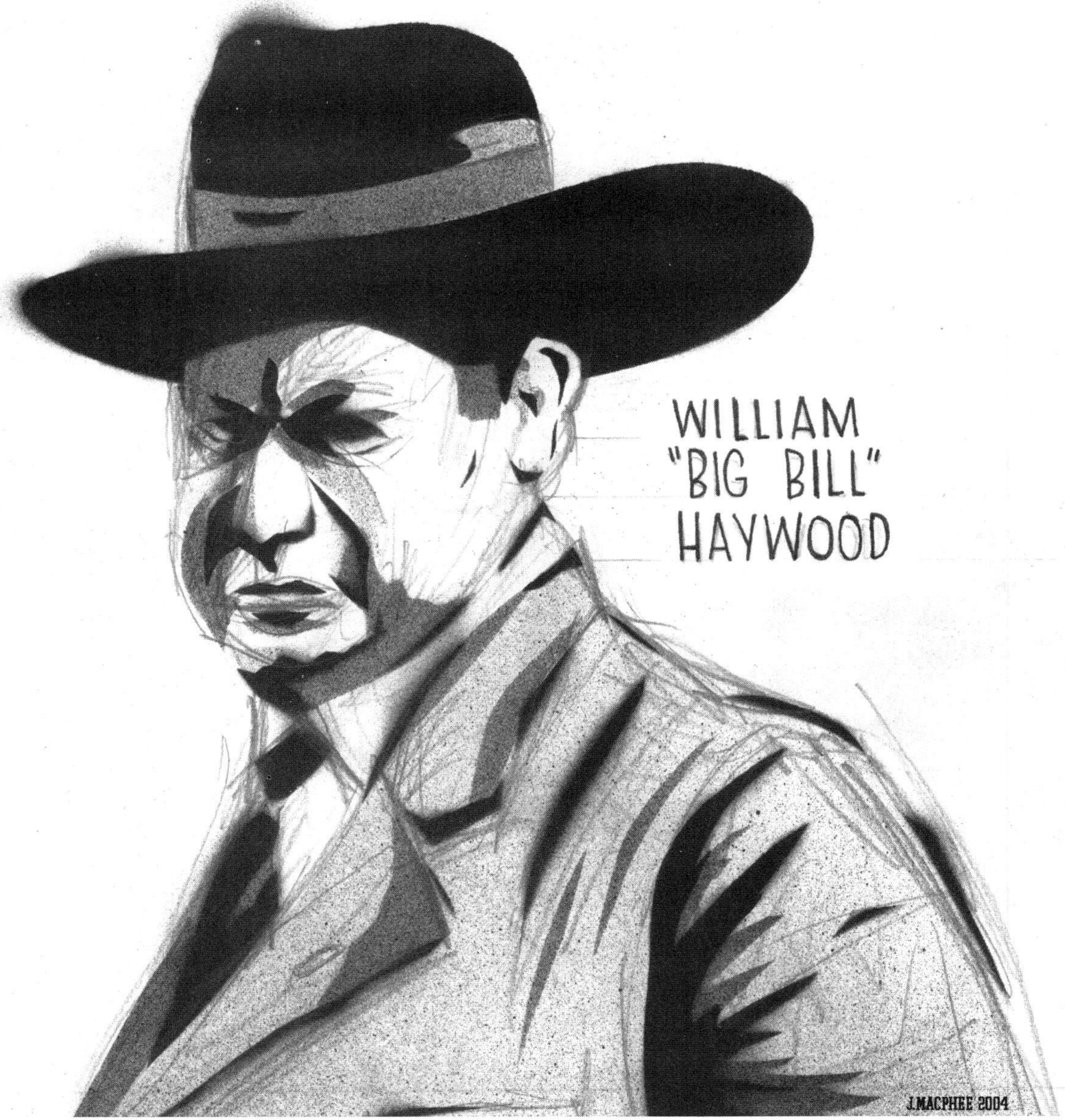
WILLIAM
"BIG BILL"
HAYWOOD
J.MACPHEE 2004

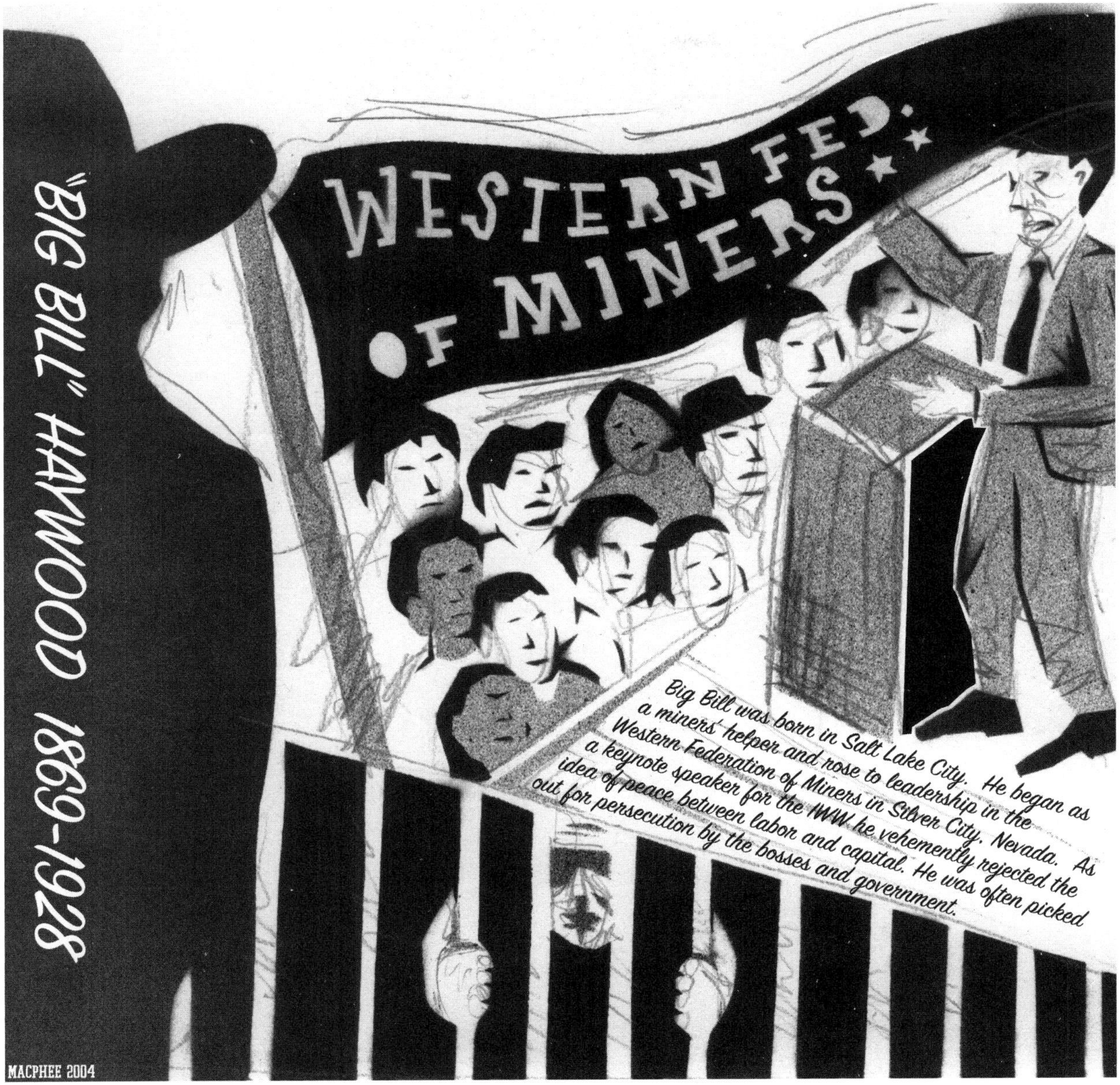
"BIG BILL" HAYWOOD 1869-1928
WESTERN FED. OF MINERS
Big Bill was born in Salt Lake City. He began as a miners' helper and rose to leadership in the Western Federation of Miners in Silver City, Nevada. As a keynote speaker for the IWW he vehemently rejected the idea of peace between labor and capital. He was often picked out for persecution by the bosses and government.
MACPHEE 2004

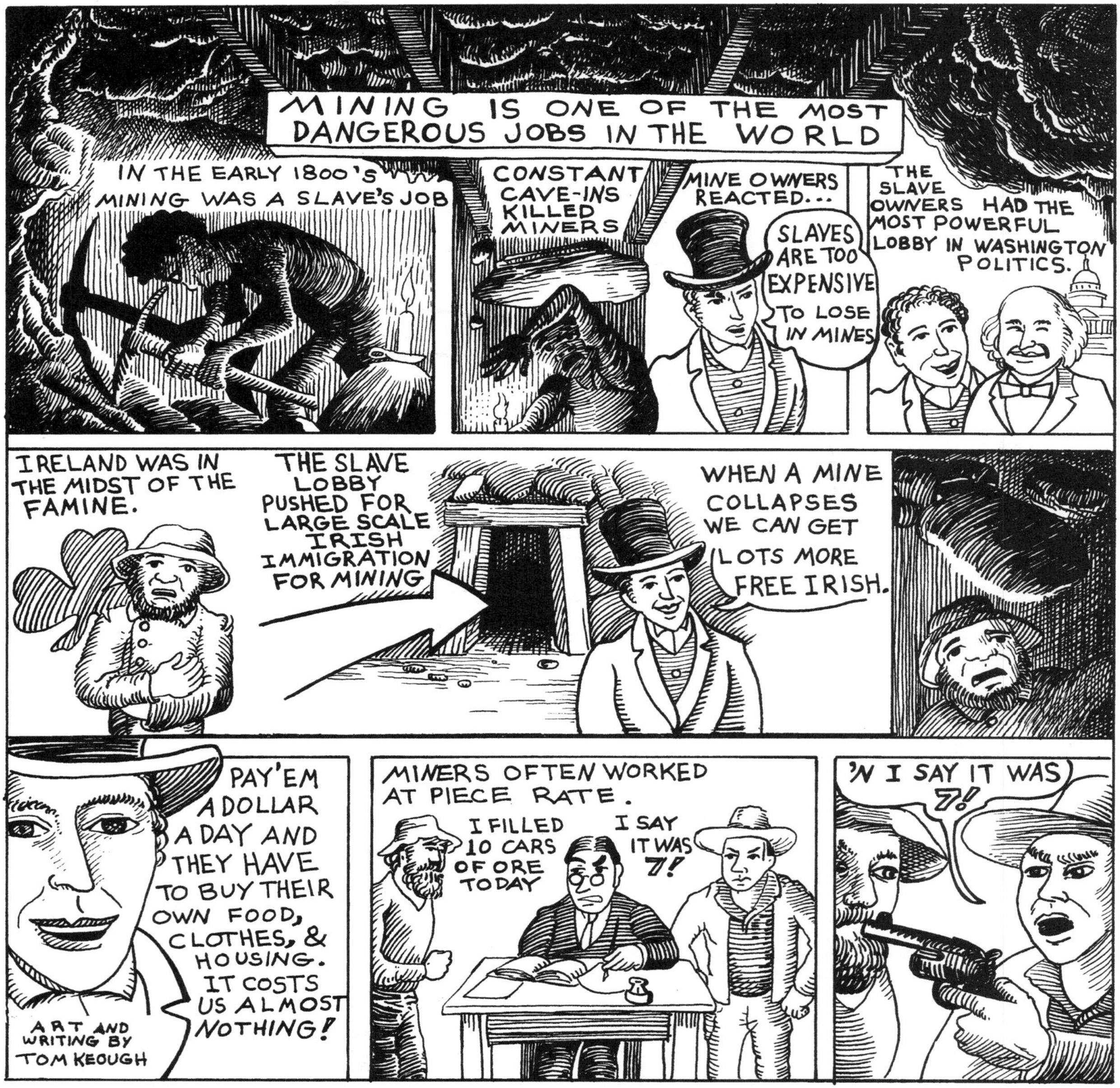
MINING IS ONE OF THE MOST DANGEROUS JOBS IN THE WORLD
IN THE EARLY 1800'S MINING WAS A SLAVE'S JOB
CONSTANT CAVE-INS KILLED MINERS
MINE OWNERS REACTED...
SLAVES ARE TOO EXPENSIVE TO LOSE IN MINES
THE SLAVE OWNERS HAD THE MOST POWERFUL LOBBY IN WASHINGTON POLITICS.
IRELAND WAS IN THE MIDST OF THE FAMINE.
THE SLAVE LOBBY PUSHED FOR LARGE SCALE IRISH IMMIGRATION FOR MINING
WHEN A MINE COLLAPSES WE CAN GET LOTS MORE FREE IRISH.
PAY'EM A DOLLAR A DAY AND THEY HAVE TO BUY THEIR OWN FOOD, CLOTHES, & HOUSING. IT COSTS US ALMOST NOTHING!
ART AND WRITING BY TOM KEOUGH
MINERS OFTEN WORKED AT PIECE RATE.
I FILLED 10 CARS OF ORE TODAY
I SAY IT WAS 7!
'N I SAY IT WAS 7!

MINES ARE LOCATED IN MOUNTAINS, OFTEN FAR FROM THE NEAREST CITIES OR TOWNS.

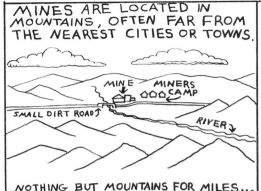

SMALL DIRT ROAD · MINE · MINERS CAMP · RIVER

NOTHING BUT MOUNTAINS FOR MILES...

MINERS NEED TO LIVE NEAR THE MINES. THE ONLY PEOPLE WITH MONEY TO BUILD HOUSES OR STORES NEARBY ARE THE WEALTHY MINE OWNERS.

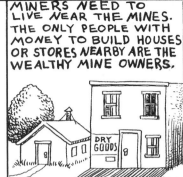

DRY GOODS

FOOD, CLOTHING AND RENT OFTEN COST MORE THAN MINERS GOT PAID. THE MORE THEY WORKED THE DEEPER IN DEBT THEY GOT.

DEBTORS PRISON

IT WAS GENERALLY ONLY THE RICH MINE OWNERS WHO HAD MONEY TO PAY LOCAL JUDGES, SHERIFFS, GUARDS JAILERS, & POLITICIANS

CONSTANT CAVE INS

AIR PRESSURE AND POISON GASES MADE MEN SICK OR DEAD.

I'M NEVER GOING BACK DOWN!

YOU'VE GOT TO!

BY THE LATE 1800'S MINES HAD THOUSANDS OF CHILD LABORERS

"IN KENSINGTON, PA 1903 75,000 COAL MINERS WENT ON STRIKE. OVER 10,000 WERE LESS THAN TWELVE YEARS OLD. EVERYDAY LITTLE CHILDREN CAME TO UNION HEADQUARTERS. SOME WITH THEIR HANDS OFF. SOME WITH THE THUMB MISSING, FINGERS OFF..." MOTHER JONES

MY GRANDMOTHER, HER DAD AND HER 14 BROTHERS AND SISTERS WERE COAL MINERS IN PENNSYLVANIA. HER MOM WAS A MAID FOR THE BOSS.

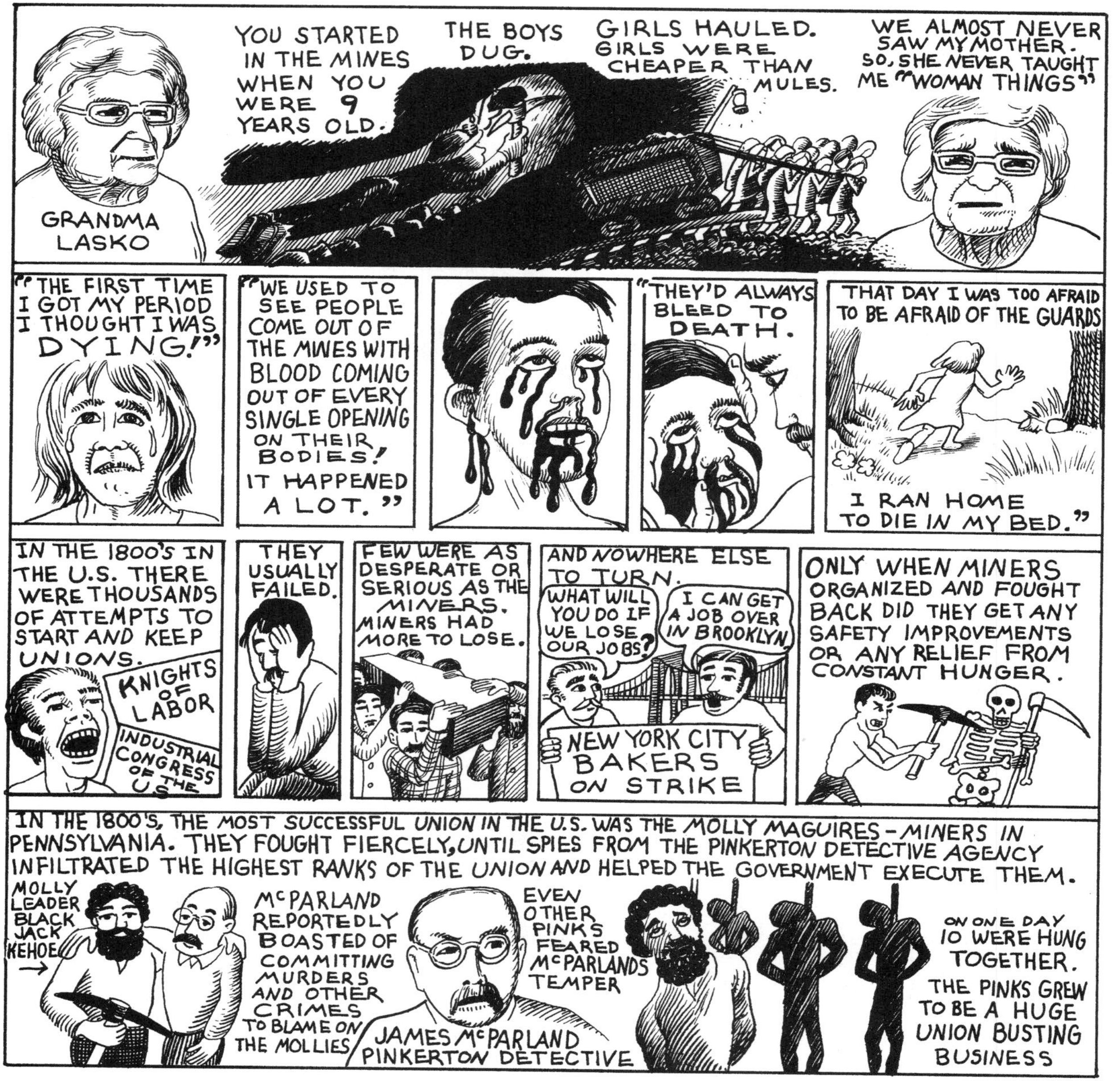
GRANDMA LASKO
YOU STARTED IN THE MINES WHEN YOU WERE 9 YEARS OLD.
THE BOYS DUG.
GIRLS HAULED. GIRLS WERE CHEAPER THAN MULES.
WE ALMOST NEVER SAW MY MOTHER. SO, SHE NEVER TAUGHT ME "WOMAN THINGS"
"THE FIRST TIME I GOT MY PERIOD I THOUGHT I WAS DYING!"
"WE USED TO SEE PEOPLE COME OUT OF THE MINES WITH BLOOD COMING OUT OF EVERY SINGLE OPENING ON THEIR BODIES! IT HAPPENED A LOT."
"THEY'D ALWAYS BLEED TO DEATH.
THAT DAY I WAS TOO AFRAID TO BE AFRAID OF THE GUARDS
I RAN HOME TO DIE IN MY BED."
IN THE 1800'S IN THE U.S. THERE WERE THOUSANDS OF ATTEMPTS TO START AND KEEP UNIONS.
KNIGHTS OF LABOR
INDUSTRIAL CONGRESS OF THE U.S.
THEY USUALLY FAILED.
FEW WERE AS DESPERATE OR SERIOUS AS THE MINERS. MINERS HAD MORE TO LOSE.
AND NOWHERE ELSE TO TURN.
WHAT WILL YOU DO IF WE LOSE OUR JOBS?
I CAN GET A JOB OVER IN BROOKLYN.
NEW YORK CITY BAKERS ON STRIKE
ONLY WHEN MINERS ORGANIZED AND FOUGHT BACK DID THEY GET ANY SAFETY IMPROVEMENTS OR ANY RELIEF FROM CONSTANT HUNGER.
IN THE 1800'S, THE MOST SUCCESSFUL UNION IN THE U.S. WAS THE MOLLY MAGUIRES – MINERS IN PENNSYLVANIA. THEY FOUGHT FIERCELY, UNTIL SPIES FROM THE PINKERTON DETECTIVE AGENCY INFILTRATED THE HIGHEST RANKS OF THE UNION AND HELPED THE GOVERNMENT EXECUTE THEM.
MOLLY LEADER BLACK JACK KEHOE →
McPARLAND REPORTEDLY BOASTED OF COMMITTING MURDERS AND OTHER CRIMES TO BLAME ON THE MOLLIES
JAMES McPARLAND PINKERTON DETECTIVE
EVEN OTHER PINKS FEARED McPARLANDS TEMPER
ON ONE DAY 10 WERE HUNG TOGETHER.
THE PINKS GREW TO BE A HUGE UNION BUSTING BUSINESS

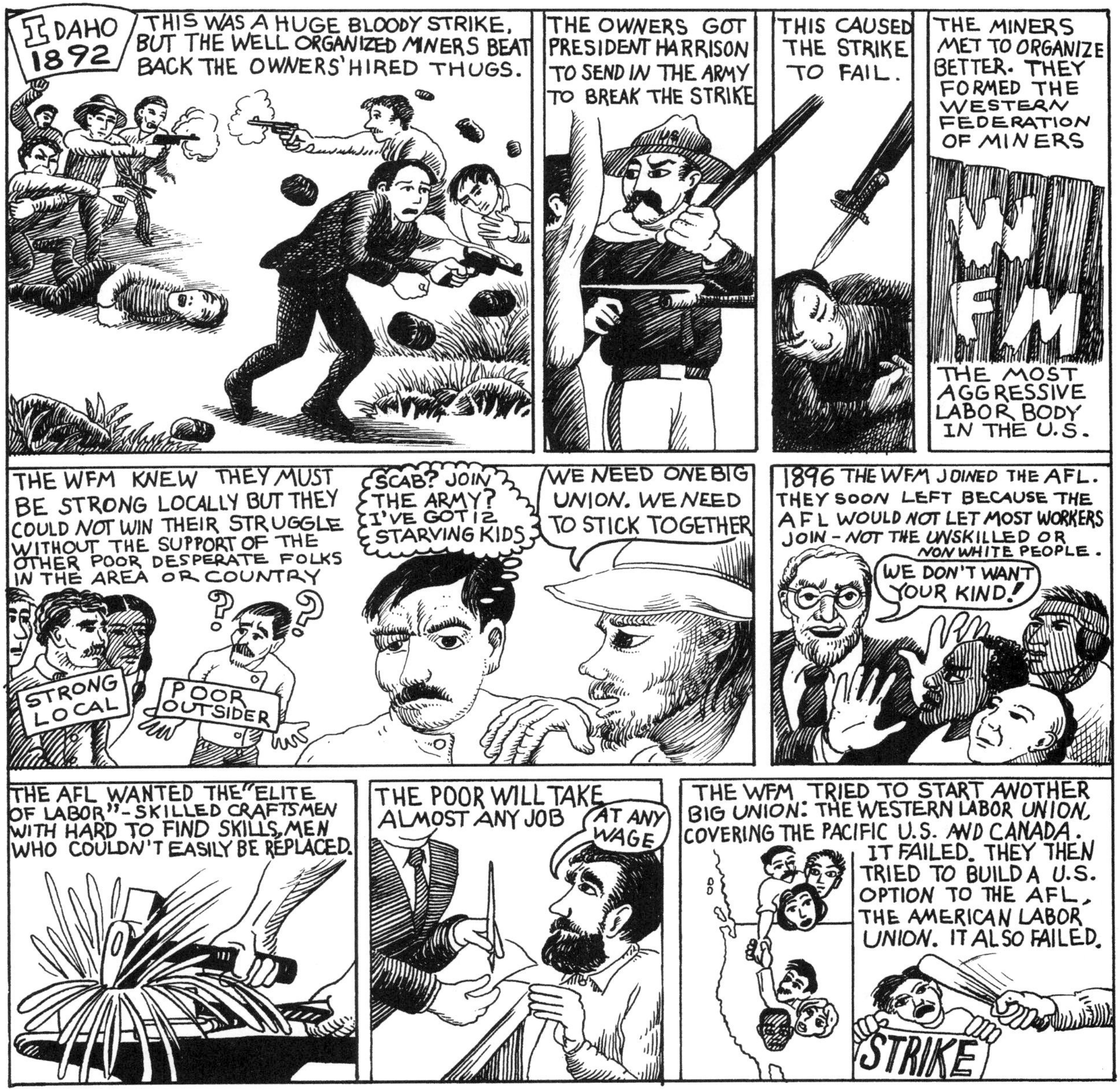
IDAHO 1892
THIS WAS A HUGE BLOODY STRIKE, BUT THE WELL ORGANIZED MINERS BEAT BACK THE OWNERS' HIRED THUGS.
THE OWNERS GOT PRESIDENT HARRISON TO SEND IN THE ARMY TO BREAK THE STRIKE
THIS CAUSED THE STRIKE TO FAIL.
THE MINERS MET TO ORGANIZE BETTER. THEY FORMED THE WESTERN FEDERATION OF MINERS
WFM
THE MOST AGGRESSIVE LABOR BODY IN THE U.S.
THE WFM KNEW THEY MUST BE STRONG LOCALLY BUT THEY COULD NOT WIN THEIR STRUGGLE WITHOUT THE SUPPORT OF THE OTHER POOR DESPERATE FOLKS IN THE AREA OR COUNTRY
STRONG LOCAL
POOR OUTSIDER
SCAB? JOIN THE ARMY? I'VE GOT 12 STARVING KIDS
WE NEED ONE BIG UNION. WE NEED TO STICK TOGETHER
1896 THE WFM JOINED THE AFL. THEY SOON LEFT BECAUSE THE AFL WOULD NOT LET MOST WORKERS JOIN - NOT THE UNSKILLED OR NON WHITE PEOPLE.
WE DON'T WANT YOUR KIND!
THE AFL WANTED THE "ELITE OF LABOR" - SKILLED CRAFTSMEN WITH HARD TO FIND SKILLS, MEN WHO COULDN'T EASILY BE REPLACED.
THE POOR WILL TAKE ALMOST ANY JOB
AT ANY WAGE
THE WFM TRIED TO START ANOTHER BIG UNION: THE WESTERN LABOR UNION, COVERING THE PACIFIC U.S. AND CANADA.
IT FAILED. THEY THEN TRIED TO BUILD A U.S. OPTION TO THE AFL, THE AMERICAN LABOR UNION. IT ALSO FAILED.
STRIKE

1899 A MAJOR WFM STRIKE AT THE BUNKER HILL CO., IDAHO

MINERS HAD ALWAYS BEEN GIVEN DYNAMITE TO BLAST ORE FROM ROCK

THE MINERS WERE ALWAYS HUNGRY, HURT, OPPRESSED.

A $250,000 BUNKER HILL MILL WAS DYNAMITED.

FRANK STEUNENBERG

LABOR'S MAN
A UNION PRINTER

POPULIST PARTY
IDAHO'S GOVERNOR

THE GOVERNOR BEGGED PRES. McKINLEY

TO SEND TROOPS TO BREAK THE STRIKE.

BECAUSE THE WFM OPPOSED BIGOTRY, McKINLEY ORDERED BLACK TROOPS AGAINST THE WFM.

A BLACK MAN SHOULD BE TREATED THE SAME AS A WHITE MAN.

WHITE TROOPS WERE CLOSER. THE BLACK TROOPS WERE BROUGHT AT GREAT EXPENSE.

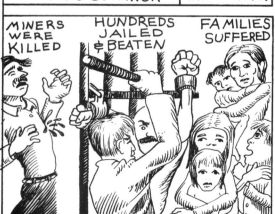

MINERS WERE KILLED

HUNDREDS JAILED & BEATEN

FAMILIES SUFFERED

STEUNENBERG MYSTERIOUSLY GOT VERY WEALTHY. HE RETIRED EARLY AND LIVED ON HIS HUGE SHEEP RANCH...

UNTIL DEC. 30 1905

STEUNENBERG WAS DYNAMITED BY A BOOBY TRAP ON HIS RANCH

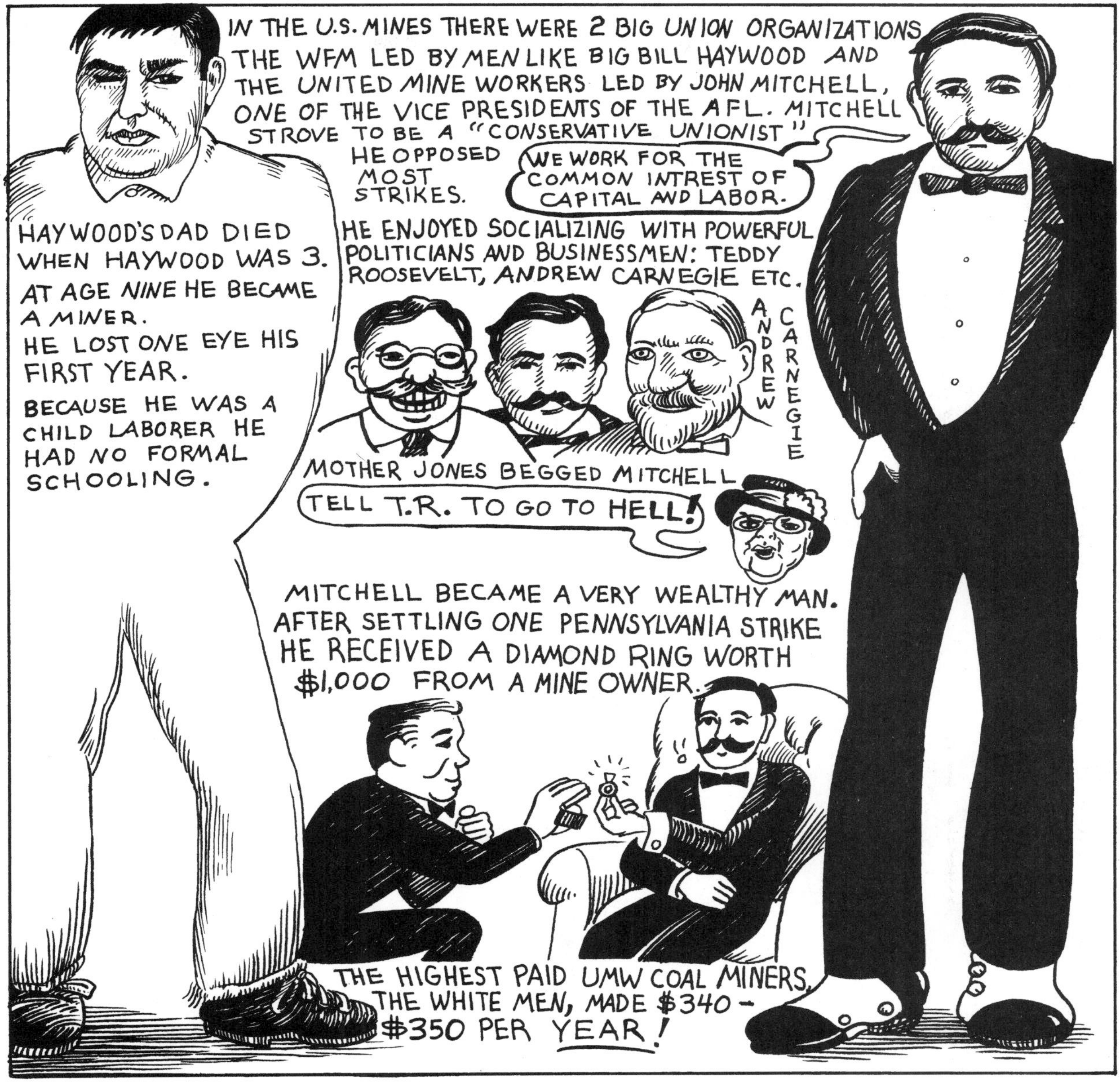

IN THE U.S. MINES THERE WERE 2 BIG UNION ORGANIZATIONS THE WFM LED BY MEN LIKE BIG BILL HAYWOOD AND THE UNITED MINE WORKERS LED BY JOHN MITCHELL, ONE OF THE VICE PRESIDENTS OF THE AFL. MITCHELL STROVE TO BE A "CONSERVATIVE UNIONIST"
HE OPPOSED MOST STRIKES.
WE WORK FOR THE COMMON INTREST OF CAPITAL AND LABOR.
HAYWOOD'S DAD DIED WHEN HAYWOOD WAS 3.
AT AGE NINE HE BECAME A MINER.
HE LOST ONE EYE HIS FIRST YEAR.
BECAUSE HE WAS A CHILD LABORER HE HAD NO FORMAL SCHOOLING.
HE ENJOYED SOCIALIZING WITH POWERFUL POLITICIANS AND BUSINESSMEN: TEDDY ROOSEVELT, ANDREW CARNEGIE ETC.
ANDREW CARNEGIE
MOTHER JONES BEGGED MITCHELL
TELL T.R. TO GO TO HELL!
MITCHELL BECAME A VERY WEALTHY MAN. AFTER SETTLING ONE PENNSYLVANIA STRIKE HE RECEIVED A DIAMOND RING WORTH $1,000 FROM A MINE OWNER.
THE HIGHEST PAID UMW COAL MINERS, THE WHITE MEN, MADE $340 - $350 PER YEAR!

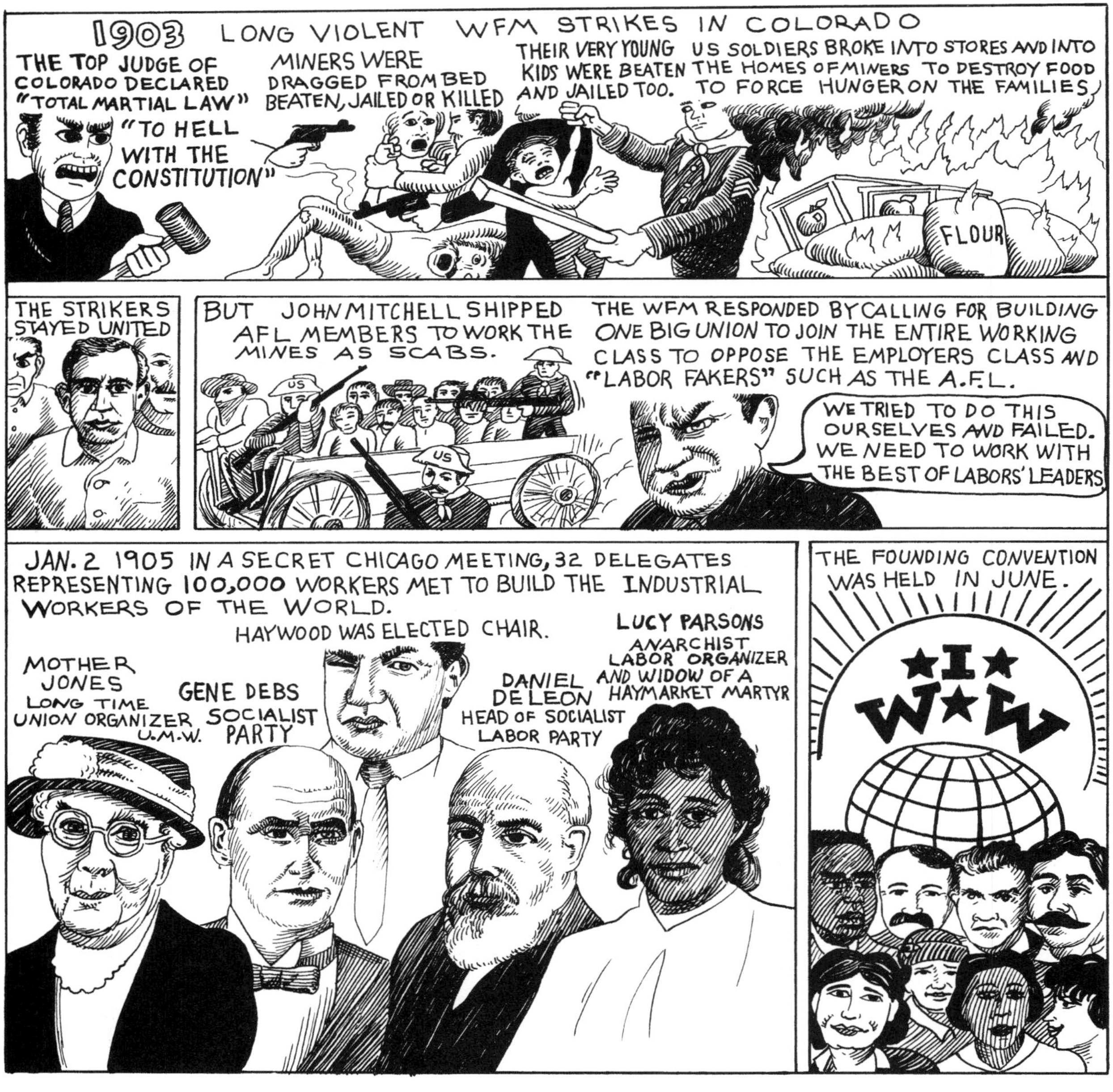
1903 LONG VIOLENT WFM STRIKES IN COLORADO
THE TOP JUDGE OF COLORADO DECLARED "TOTAL MARTIAL LAW"
"TO HELL WITH THE CONSTITUTION"
MINERS WERE DRAGGED FROM BED BEATEN, JAILED OR KILLED
THEIR VERY YOUNG KIDS WERE BEATEN AND JAILED TOO.
US SOLDIERS BROKE INTO STORES AND INTO THE HOMES OF MINERS TO DESTROY FOOD TO FORCE HUNGER ON THE FAMILIES
FLOUR
THE STRIKERS STAYED UNITED
BUT JOHN MITCHELL SHIPPED AFL MEMBERS TO WORK THE MINES AS SCABS.
US
US
THE WFM RESPONDED BY CALLING FOR BUILDING ONE BIG UNION TO JOIN THE ENTIRE WORKING CLASS TO OPPOSE THE EMPLOYERS CLASS AND "LABOR FAKERS" SUCH AS THE A.F.L.
WE TRIED TO DO THIS OURSELVES AND FAILED. WE NEED TO WORK WITH THE BEST OF LABORS' LEADERS
JAN. 2 1905 IN A SECRET CHICAGO MEETING, 32 DELEGATES REPRESENTING 100,000 WORKERS MET TO BUILD THE INDUSTRIAL WORKERS OF THE WORLD.
HAYWOOD WAS ELECTED CHAIR.
LUCY PARSONS ANARCHIST LABOR ORGANIZER AND WIDOW OF A HAYMARKET MARTYR
MOTHER JONES LONG TIME UNION ORGANIZER U.M.W.
GENE DEBS SOCIALIST PARTY
DANIEL DE LEON HEAD OF SOCIALIST LABOR PARTY
THE FOUNDING CONVENTION WAS HELD IN JUNE.
I W W

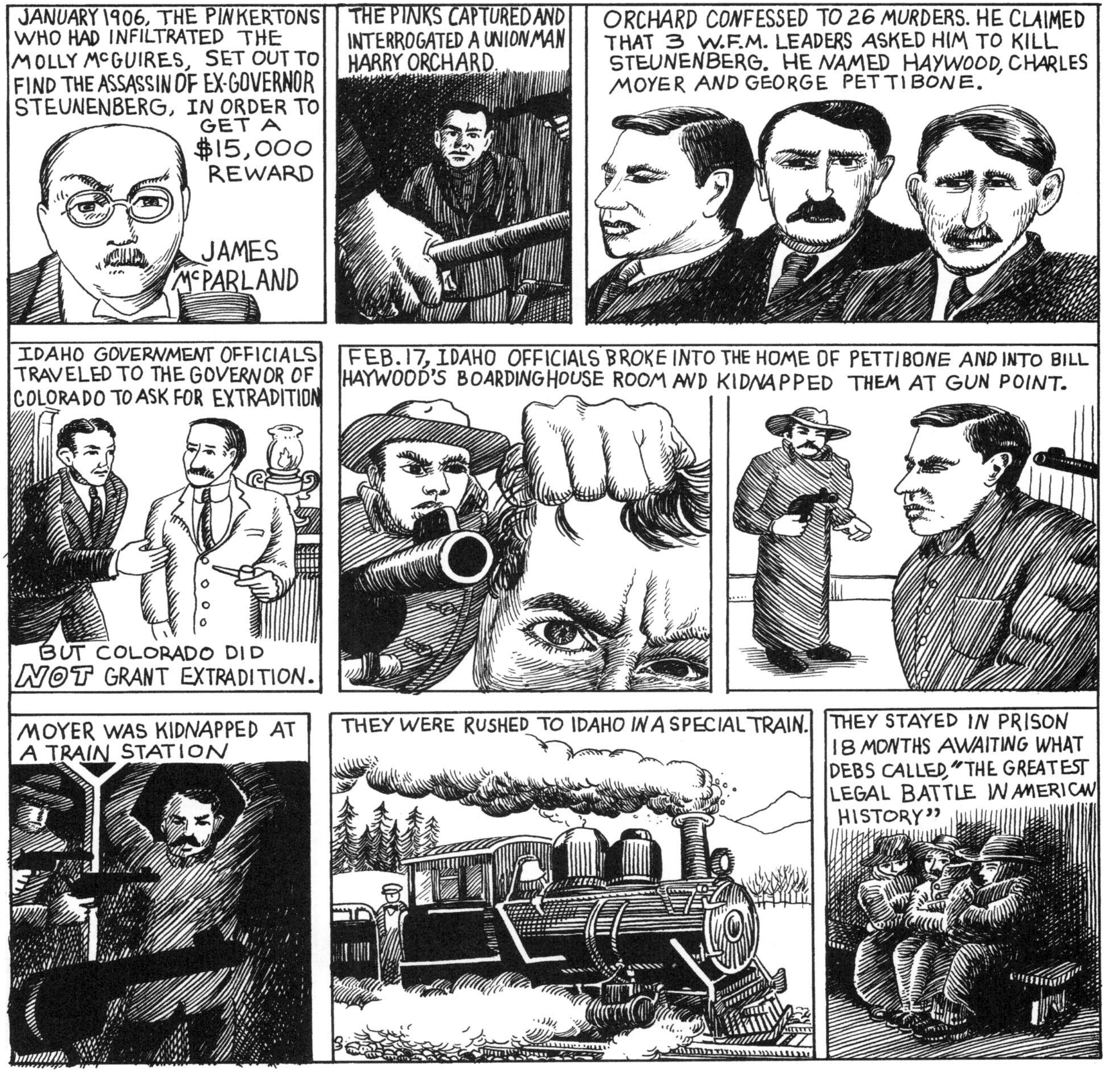
JANUARY 1906, THE PINKERTONS WHO HAD INFILTRATED THE MOLLY McGUIRES, SET OUT TO FIND THE ASSASSIN OF EX-GOVERNOR STEUNENBERG, IN ORDER TO GET A $15,000 REWARD
JAMES McPARLAND
THE PINKS CAPTURED AND INTERROGATED A UNION MAN HARRY ORCHARD
ORCHARD CONFESSED TO 26 MURDERS. HE CLAIMED THAT 3 W.F.M. LEADERS ASKED HIM TO KILL STEUNENBERG. HE NAMED HAYWOOD, CHARLES MOYER AND GEORGE PETTIBONE.
IDAHO GOVERNMENT OFFICIALS TRAVELED TO THE GOVERNOR OF COLORADO TO ASK FOR EXTRADITION
BUT COLORADO DID NOT GRANT EXTRADITION.
FEB. 17, IDAHO OFFICIALS BROKE INTO THE HOME OF PETTIBONE AND INTO BILL HAYWOOD'S BOARDINGHOUSE ROOM AND KIDNAPPED THEM AT GUN POINT.
MOYER WAS KIDNAPPED AT A TRAIN STATION
THEY WERE RUSHED TO IDAHO IN A SPECIAL TRAIN.
THEY STAYED IN PRISON 18 MONTHS AWAITING WHAT DEBS CALLED, "THE GREATEST LEGAL BATTLE IN AMERICAN HISTORY"

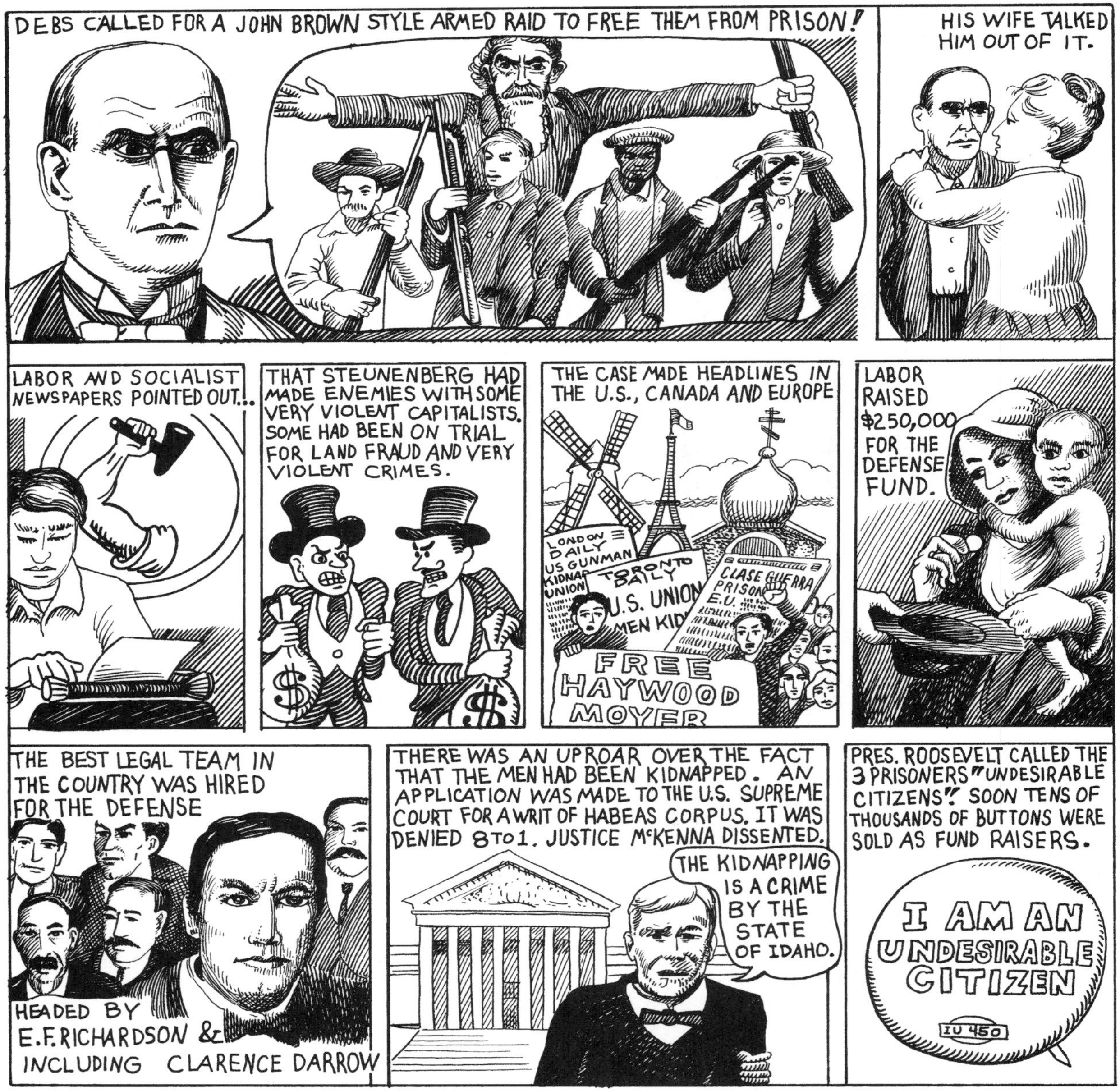
DEBS CALLED FOR A JOHN BROWN STYLE ARMED RAID TO FREE THEM FROM PRISON!
HIS WIFE TALKED HIM OUT OF IT.
LABOR AND SOCIALIST NEWSPAPERS POINTED OUT...
THAT STEUNENBERG HAD MADE ENEMIES WITH SOME VERY VIOLENT CAPITALISTS. SOME HAD BEEN ON TRIAL FOR LAND FRAUD AND VERY VIOLENT CRIMES.
THE CASE MADE HEADLINES IN THE U.S., CANADA AND EUROPE
LONDON DAILY
US GUNMAN
TORONTO DAILY
U.S. UNION
CLASE GUERRA
PRISON
E.U.
FREE HAYWOOD MOYER
LABOR RAISED $250,000 FOR THE DEFENSE FUND.
THE BEST LEGAL TEAM IN THE COUNTRY WAS HIRED FOR THE DEFENSE
HEADED BY E.F. RICHARDSON & INCLUDING CLARENCE DARROW
THERE WAS AN UPROAR OVER THE FACT THAT THE MEN HAD BEEN KIDNAPPED. AN APPLICATION WAS MADE TO THE U.S. SUPREME COURT FOR A WRIT OF HABEAS CORPUS. IT WAS DENIED 8 TO 1. JUSTICE McKENNA DISSENTED.
THE KIDNAPPING IS A CRIME BY THE STATE OF IDAHO.
PRES. ROOSEVELT CALLED THE 3 PRISONERS "UNDESIRABLE CITIZENS". SOON TENS OF THOUSANDS OF BUTTONS WERE SOLD AS FUND RAISERS.
I AM AN UNDESIRABLE CITIZEN
IU 450

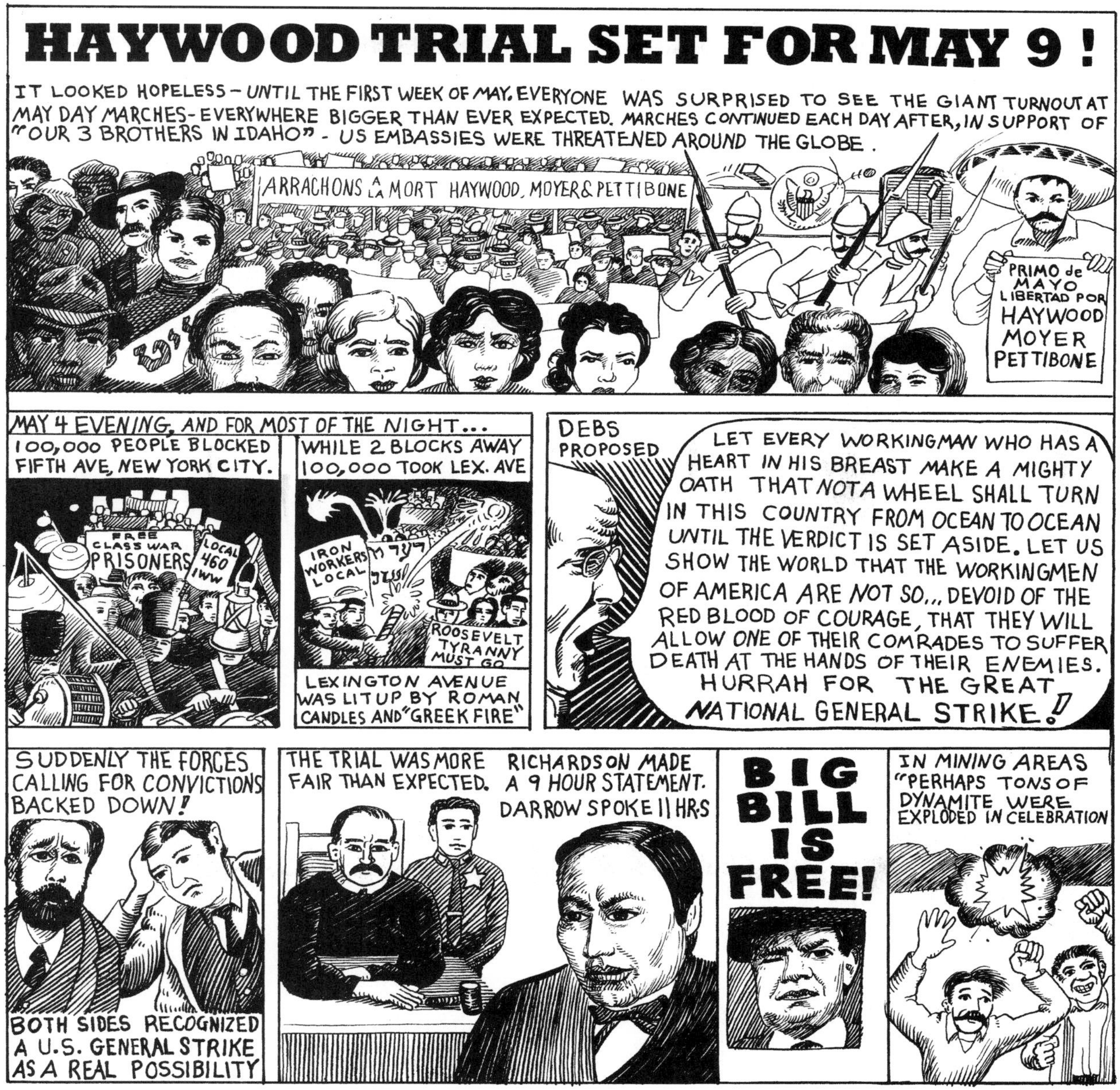
HAYWOOD TRIAL SET FOR MAY 9 !
IT LOOKED HOPELESS – UNTIL THE FIRST WEEK OF MAY. EVERYONE WAS SURPRISED TO SEE THE GIANT TURNOUT AT MAY DAY MARCHES - EVERYWHERE BIGGER THAN EVER EXPECTED. MARCHES CONTINUED EACH DAY AFTER, IN SUPPORT OF "OUR 3 BROTHERS IN IDAHO" - US EMBASSIES WERE THREATENED AROUND THE GLOBE.
ARRACHONS A LA MORT HAYWOOD, MOYER & PETTIBONE
PRIMO de MAYO LIBERTAD POR HAYWOOD MOYER PETTIBONE
MAY 4 EVENING, AND FOR MOST OF THE NIGHT...
100,000 PEOPLE BLOCKED FIFTH AVE, NEW YORK CITY.
FREE CLASS WAR PRISONERS
LOCAL 460 IWW
WHILE 2 BLOCKS AWAY 100,000 TOOK LEX. AVE
IRON WORKERS LOCAL
ROOSEVELT TYRANNY MUST GO
LEXINGTON AVENUE WAS LIT UP BY ROMAN CANDLES AND "GREEK FIRE"
DEBS PROPOSED
LET EVERY WORKINGMAN WHO HAS A HEART IN HIS BREAST MAKE A MIGHTY OATH THAT NOT A WHEEL SHALL TURN IN THIS COUNTRY FROM OCEAN TO OCEAN UNTIL THE VERDICT IS SET ASIDE. LET US SHOW THE WORLD THAT THE WORKINGMEN OF AMERICA ARE NOT SO... DEVOID OF THE RED BLOOD OF COURAGE, THAT THEY WILL ALLOW ONE OF THEIR COMRADES TO SUFFER DEATH AT THE HANDS OF THEIR ENEMIES. HURRAH FOR THE GREAT NATIONAL GENERAL STRIKE!
SUDDENLY THE FORCES CALLING FOR CONVICTIONS BACKED DOWN!
BOTH SIDES RECOGNIZED A U.S. GENERAL STRIKE AS A REAL POSSIBILITY
THE TRIAL WAS MORE FAIR THAN EXPECTED.
RICHARDSON MADE A 9 HOUR STATEMENT. DARROW SPOKE 11 HRS
BIG BILL IS FREE!
IN MINING AREAS "PERHAPS TONS OF DYNAMITE WERE EXPLODED IN CELEBRATION

SOON MOYER AND PETTIBONE WERE FREE!

THE NEWS COVERAGE OF THE CASE HAD EXPOSED THE BRUTALITY OF MINE OWNERS AND SHOWED THAT VIOLENT REACTIONS FROM MINERS WERE UNDERSTANDABLE

THE 3 NEVER DENIED INVOLVEMENT IN THE CRIME OR IN ACTS OF VIOLENCE TO FIGHTBACK.

THROUGHOUT THE TRIAL UNIONS GREW. THE IWW GAINED OVER 10,000 NEW MEMBERS.

SMARTER AND STRONGER IWW ORGANIZING BEGAN

IN GOLDFIELD NEVADA 1907 THE IWW ORGANIZED MINERS AND ALL OCCUPATIONS IN TOWN.

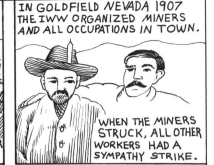

WHEN THE MINERS STRUCK, ALL OTHER WORKERS HAD A SYMPATHY STRIKE.

WOBS WIN STRIKE!

TOWN MINIMUM WAGE LAW $4.50 PER DAY! 8 HOUR DAY! For ALL JOBS IN TOWN

IWW ORGANIZER VINCENT ST. JOHN

THE UNION WON JOB CONTROL. THE IWW SECRETARY POSTED WAGE SCALE AND HOURS, AND IT WAS LAW!

THE EMPLOYERS WERE FORCED TO COME TO SEE THE UNION COMMITTEES NO COMMITTEES WERE EVER SENT TO EMPLOYERS.

IWW WEEKLY LISTING
BILL RY...
JOHN MAR...
MATT...
CAR...
BILL...
JOH...

THE MINE OWNER'S THUGS JUMPED ST. JOHN, LEAVING HIM TO DIE. HE NEVER FULLY RECOVERED.

DEC. 6 1907 361 COAL MINERS KILLED

MONOUGAH WEST VIRGINIA

NOV. 1909 259 MINERS KILLED

CHERRY ILL.

THE IWW GREW IN MINES

IWW? OK

JAN-DEC. 1910 323 KILLED IN COLORADO MINES

SEPT. 1913, LUDLOW COLO. 9,000 MINERS STRIKE AT ROCKEFELLER'S MINES. EVICTED FROM COMPANY TOWNS, THEY LIVED IN TENTS IN A BITTER WINTER. ROCKEFELLER HIRED GUNMEN TO SHOOT AT MINERS CONTINUOUSLY. THEY BOUGHT A GUN THAT SHOT 400 ROUNDS A MIN. APRIL 20 1914 - FAMILY MEMBERS AND MINERS ARE SHOT BOMBED AND BURNED ALIVE.

LUDLOW MASSACRE

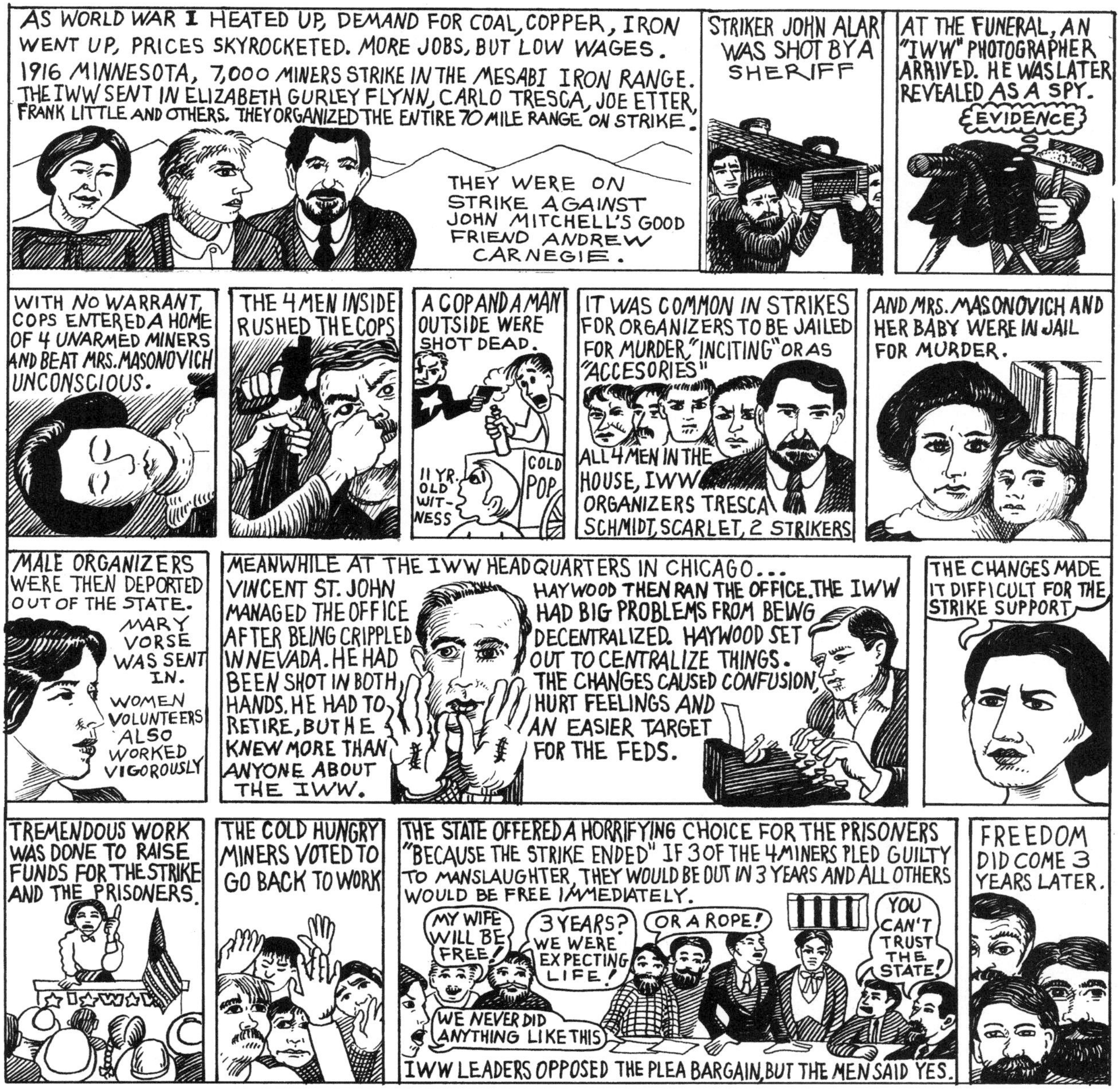
AS WORLD WAR I HEATED UP, DEMAND FOR COAL, COPPER, IRON WENT UP, PRICES SKYROCKETED. MORE JOBS, BUT LOW WAGES.
1916 MINNESOTA, 7,000 MINERS STRIKE IN THE MESABI IRON RANGE.
THE IWW SENT IN ELIZABETH GURLEY FLYNN, CARLO TRESCA, JOE ETTER, FRANK LITTLE AND OTHERS. THEY ORGANIZED THE ENTIRE 70 MILE RANGE ON STRIKE.
THEY WERE ON STRIKE AGAINST JOHN MITCHELL'S GOOD FRIEND ANDREW CARNEGIE.
STRIKER JOHN ALAR WAS SHOT BY A SHERIFF
AT THE FUNERAL, AN "IWW" PHOTOGRAPHER ARRIVED. HE WAS LATER REVEALED AS A SPY.
EVIDENCE
WITH NO WARRANT, COPS ENTERED A HOME OF 4 UNARMED MINERS AND BEAT MRS. MASONOVICH UNCONSCIOUS.
THE 4 MEN INSIDE RUSHED THE COPS
A COP AND A MAN OUTSIDE WERE SHOT DEAD.
11 YR. OLD WIT-NESS
COLD POP
IT WAS COMMON IN STRIKES FOR ORGANIZERS TO BE JAILED FOR MURDER, "INCITING" OR AS "ACCESORIES"
ALL 4 MEN IN THE HOUSE, IWW ORGANIZERS TRESCA SCHMIDT, SCARLET, 2 STRIKERS
AND MRS. MASONOVICH AND HER BABY WERE IN JAIL FOR MURDER.
MALE ORGANIZERS WERE THEN DEPORTED OUT OF THE STATE.
MARY VORSE WAS SENT IN.
WOMEN VOLUNTEERS ALSO WORKED VIGOROUSLY
MEANWHILE AT THE IWW HEADQUARTERS IN CHICAGO...
VINCENT ST. JOHN MANAGED THE OFFICE AFTER BEING CRIPPLED IN NEVADA. HE HAD BEEN SHOT IN BOTH HANDS. HE HAD TO RETIRE, BUT HE KNEW MORE THAN ANYONE ABOUT THE IWW.
HAYWOOD THEN RAN THE OFFICE. THE IWW HAD BIG PROBLEMS FROM BEING DECENTRALIZED. HAYWOOD SET OUT TO CENTRALIZE THINGS. THE CHANGES CAUSED CONFUSION, HURT FEELINGS AND AN EASIER TARGET FOR THE FEDS.
THE CHANGES MADE IT DIFFICULT FOR THE STRIKE SUPPORT
TREMENDOUS WORK WAS DONE TO RAISE FUNDS FOR THE STRIKE AND THE PRISONERS.
IWW
THE COLD HUNGRY MINERS VOTED TO GO BACK TO WORK
THE STATE OFFERED A HORRIFYING CHOICE FOR THE PRISONERS "BECAUSE THE STRIKE ENDED" IF 3 OF THE 4 MINERS PLED GUILTY TO MANSLAUGHTER, THEY WOULD BE OUT IN 3 YEARS AND ALL OTHERS WOULD BE FREE IMMEDIATELY.
MY WIFE WILL BE FREE!
3 YEARS? WE WERE EXPECTING LIFE!
OR A ROPE!
YOU CAN'T TRUST THE STATE!
WE NEVER DID ANYTHING LIKE THIS
IWW LEADERS OPPOSED THE PLEA BARGAIN, BUT THE MEN SAID YES.
FREEDOM DID COME 3 YEARS LATER.

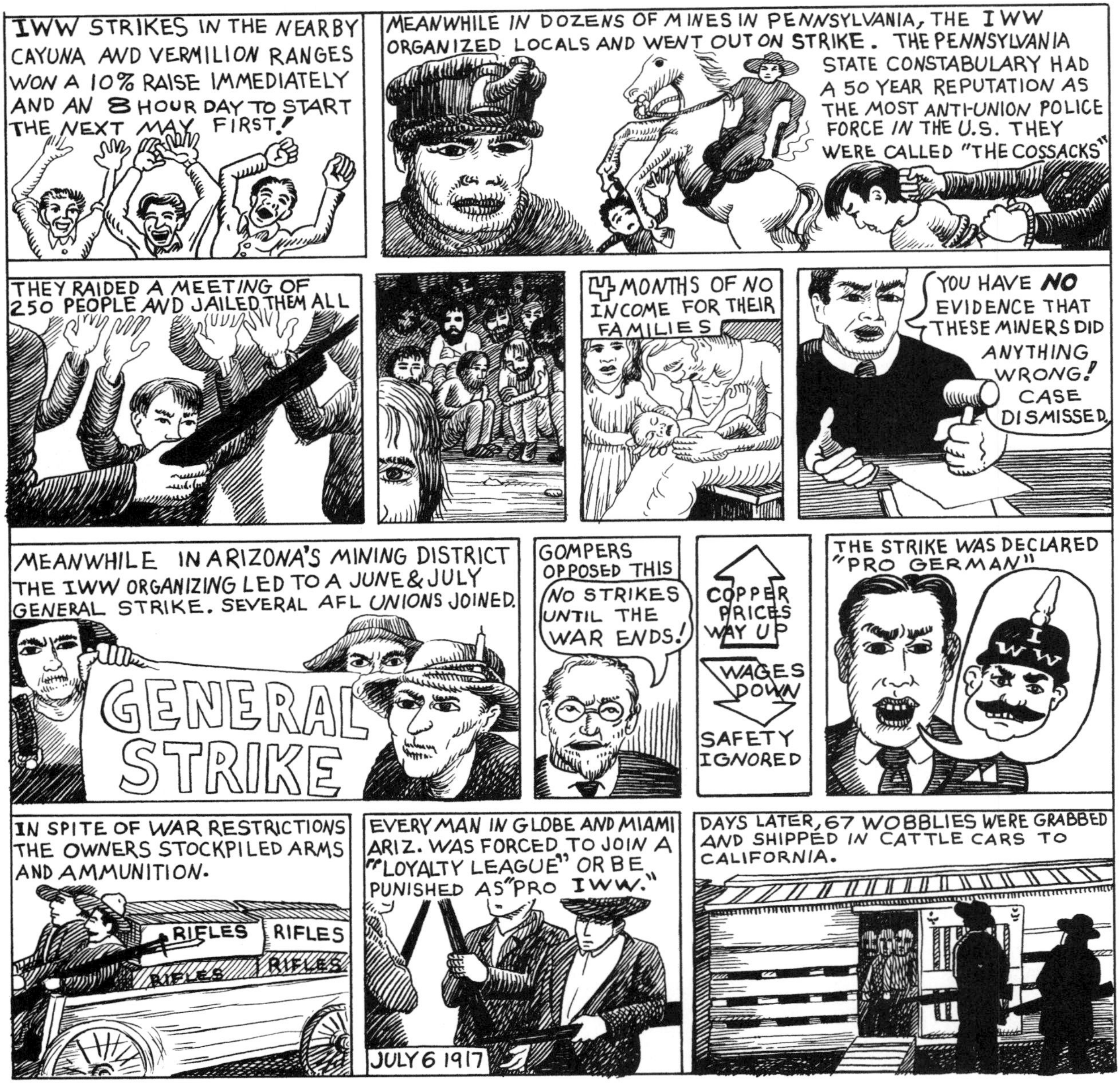
IWW STRIKES IN THE NEARBY CAYUNA AND VERMILION RANGES WON A 10% RAISE IMMEDIATELY AND AN 8 HOUR DAY TO START THE NEXT MAY FIRST!
MEANWHILE IN DOZENS OF MINES IN PENNSYLVANIA, THE IWW ORGANIZED LOCALS AND WENT OUT ON STRIKE. THE PENNSYLVANIA STATE CONSTABULARY HAD A 50 YEAR REPUTATION AS THE MOST ANTI-UNION POLICE FORCE IN THE U.S. THEY WERE CALLED "THE COSSACKS"
THEY RAIDED A MEETING OF 250 PEOPLE AND JAILED THEM ALL
4 MONTHS OF NO INCOME FOR THEIR FAMILIES
YOU HAVE NO EVIDENCE THAT THESE MINERS DID ANYTHING WRONG! CASE DISMISSED.
MEANWHILE IN ARIZONA'S MINING DISTRICT THE IWW ORGANIZING LED TO A JUNE & JULY GENERAL STRIKE. SEVERAL AFL UNIONS JOINED.
GENERAL STRIKE
GOMPERS OPPOSED THIS
NO STRIKES UNTIL THE WAR ENDS!
COPPER PRICES WAY UP
WAGES DOWN
SAFETY IGNORED
THE STRIKE WAS DECLARED "PRO GERMAN"
IWW
IN SPITE OF WAR RESTRICTIONS THE OWNERS STOCKPILED ARMS AND AMMUNITION.
RIFLES
RIFLES
RIFLES
RIFLES
EVERY MAN IN GLOBE AND MIAMI ARIZ. WAS FORCED TO JOIN A "LOYALTY LEAGUE" OR BE PUNISHED AS "PRO IWW."
JULY 6 1917
DAYS LATER, 67 WOBBLIES WERE GRABBED AND SHIPPED IN CATTLE CARS TO CALIFORNIA.

JULY 11, 1917 BISBEE, ARIZONA

WITHOUT ANY TELEGRAPH NO NEWS WILL GET OUT.

THE BISBEE LIBERTY LEAGUE CAPTURED 1,186 MINERS JULY 11–12.

THEY WERE BROUGHT TO A BALL PARK AND TOLD TO RETURN TO WORK OR FACE DEPORTATION.

THEY WERE PUT INTO 27 CATTLE CARS AND SENT TO HERMANAS, NEW MEXICO

IN THE INTENSE HEAT THEY WERE WITHOUT FOOD FOR OVER 2 DAYS.

THEY WERE MET BY FEDERAL AUTHORITIES AND MARCHED TO COLUMBUS, NEW MEXICO.

THEY WERE CAGED IN AN OUTDOOR PEN UNTIL SEPTEMBER.

MOST RETURNED TO BISBEE, MANY WERE ARRESTED IMMEDIATELY

A PRESIDENTIAL MEDIATION COMMISSION WAS SENT TO SETTLE THE STRIKE AND INVESTIGATE THE DEPORTATIONS.

OF THE 1200 DEPORTEES 381 ARE AFL MEN. 426 ARE IN THE IWW. THE REST BELONG TO NO LABOR ORGANIZATION.

THIS STRIKE WAS NEITHER PRO GERMAN NOR SEDITIOUS, BUT SINCE IWWs ARE DISLOYAL TO THE WAR EFFORT, IWW MEMBERS WILL BE EXCLUDED FROM THE SETTLEMENT.

1918

COPPER MINES ARE "WAR PREMISES". TROOPS WILL BE SENT TO ARREST ANYONE ASSEMBLING NEAR THESE "WAR PREMISES".

IN BISBEE, TROOPS STAYED UNTIL 1920, 2 YEARS AFTER THE WAR. THE MINE OWNERS GAVE THEM HOUSING AND DAILY REPORTS FROM PRIVATE DETECTIVES

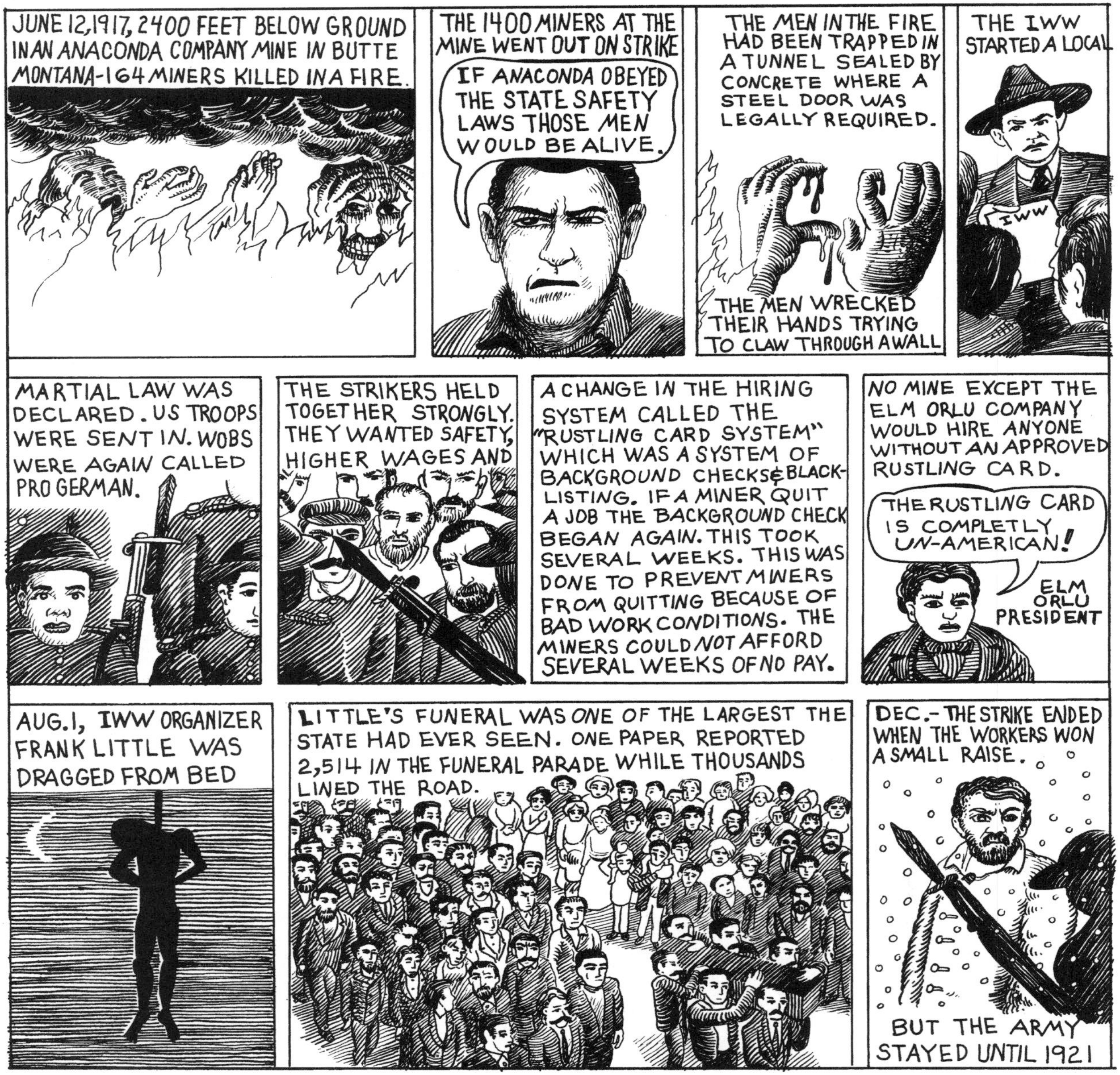
JUNE 12, 1917, 2400 FEET BELOW GROUND IN AN ANACONDA COMPANY MINE IN BUTTE MONTANA-164 MINERS KILLED IN A FIRE.
THE 1400 MINERS AT THE MINE WENT OUT ON STRIKE
IF ANACONDA OBEYED THE STATE SAFETY LAWS THOSE MEN WOULD BE ALIVE.
THE MEN IN THE FIRE HAD BEEN TRAPPED IN A TUNNEL SEALED BY CONCRETE WHERE A STEEL DOOR WAS LEGALLY REQUIRED.
THE MEN WRECKED THEIR HANDS TRYING TO CLAW THROUGH A WALL
THE IWW STARTED A LOCAL
IWW
MARTIAL LAW WAS DECLARED. US TROOPS WERE SENT IN. WOBS WERE AGAIN CALLED PRO GERMAN.
THE STRIKERS HELD TOGETHER STRONGLY. THEY WANTED SAFETY, HIGHER WAGES AND
A CHANGE IN THE HIRING SYSTEM CALLED THE "RUSTLING CARD SYSTEM" WHICH WAS A SYSTEM OF BACKGROUND CHECKS & BLACK-LISTING. IF A MINER QUIT A JOB THE BACKGROUND CHECK BEGAN AGAIN. THIS TOOK SEVERAL WEEKS. THIS WAS DONE TO PREVENT MINERS FROM QUITTING BECAUSE OF BAD WORK CONDITIONS. THE MINERS COULD NOT AFFORD SEVERAL WEEKS OF NO PAY.
NO MINE EXCEPT THE ELM ORLU COMPANY WOULD HIRE ANYONE WITHOUT AN APPROVED RUSTLING CARD.
THE RUSTLING CARD IS COMPLETLY UN-AMERICAN!
ELM ORLU PRESIDENT
AUG. 1, IWW ORGANIZER FRANK LITTLE WAS DRAGGED FROM BED
LITTLE'S FUNERAL WAS ONE OF THE LARGEST THE STATE HAD EVER SEEN. ONE PAPER REPORTED 2,514 IN THE FUNERAL PARADE WHILE THOUSANDS LINED THE ROAD.
DEC.- THE STRIKE ENDED WHEN THE WORKERS WON A SMALL RAISE.
BUT THE ARMY STAYED UNTIL 1921

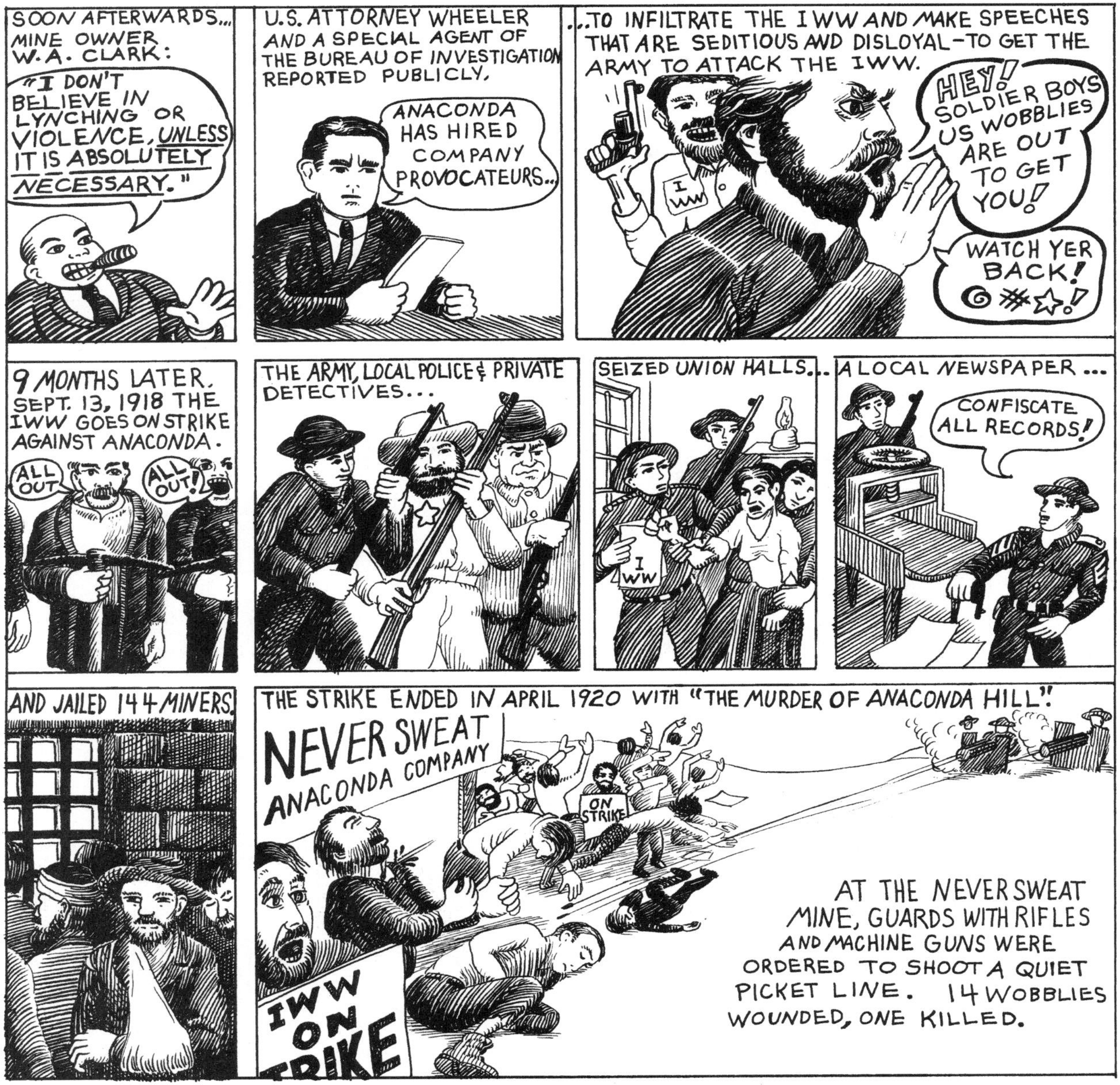
SOON AFTERWARDS... MINE OWNER W.A. CLARK:
"I DON'T BELIEVE IN LYNCHING OR VIOLENCE, UNLESS IT IS ABSOLUTELY NECESSARY."
U.S. ATTORNEY WHEELER AND A SPECIAL AGENT OF THE BUREAU OF INVESTIGATION REPORTED PUBLICLY,
ANACONDA HAS HIRED COMPANY PROVOCATEURS...
...TO INFILTRATE THE IWW AND MAKE SPEECHES THAT ARE SEDITIOUS AND DISLOYAL—TO GET THE ARMY TO ATTACK THE IWW.
I WW
HEY! SOLDIER BOYS US WOBBLIES ARE OUT TO GET YOU!
WATCH YER BACK! @#☆!
9 MONTHS LATER. SEPT. 13, 1918 THE IWW GOES ON STRIKE AGAINST ANACONDA.
ALL OUT
ALL OUT!
THE ARMY, LOCAL POLICE & PRIVATE DETECTIVES...
SEIZED UNION HALLS...
I WW
A LOCAL NEWSPAPER...
CONFISCATE ALL RECORDS!
AND JAILED 144 MINERS.
THE STRIKE ENDED IN APRIL 1920 WITH "THE MURDER OF ANACONDA HILL".
NEVER SWEAT ANACONDA COMPANY
ON STRIKE
IWW ON TRIKE
AT THE NEVER SWEAT MINE, GUARDS WITH RIFLES AND MACHINE GUNS WERE ORDERED TO SHOOT A QUIET PICKET LINE. 14 WOBBLIES WOUNDED, ONE KILLED.

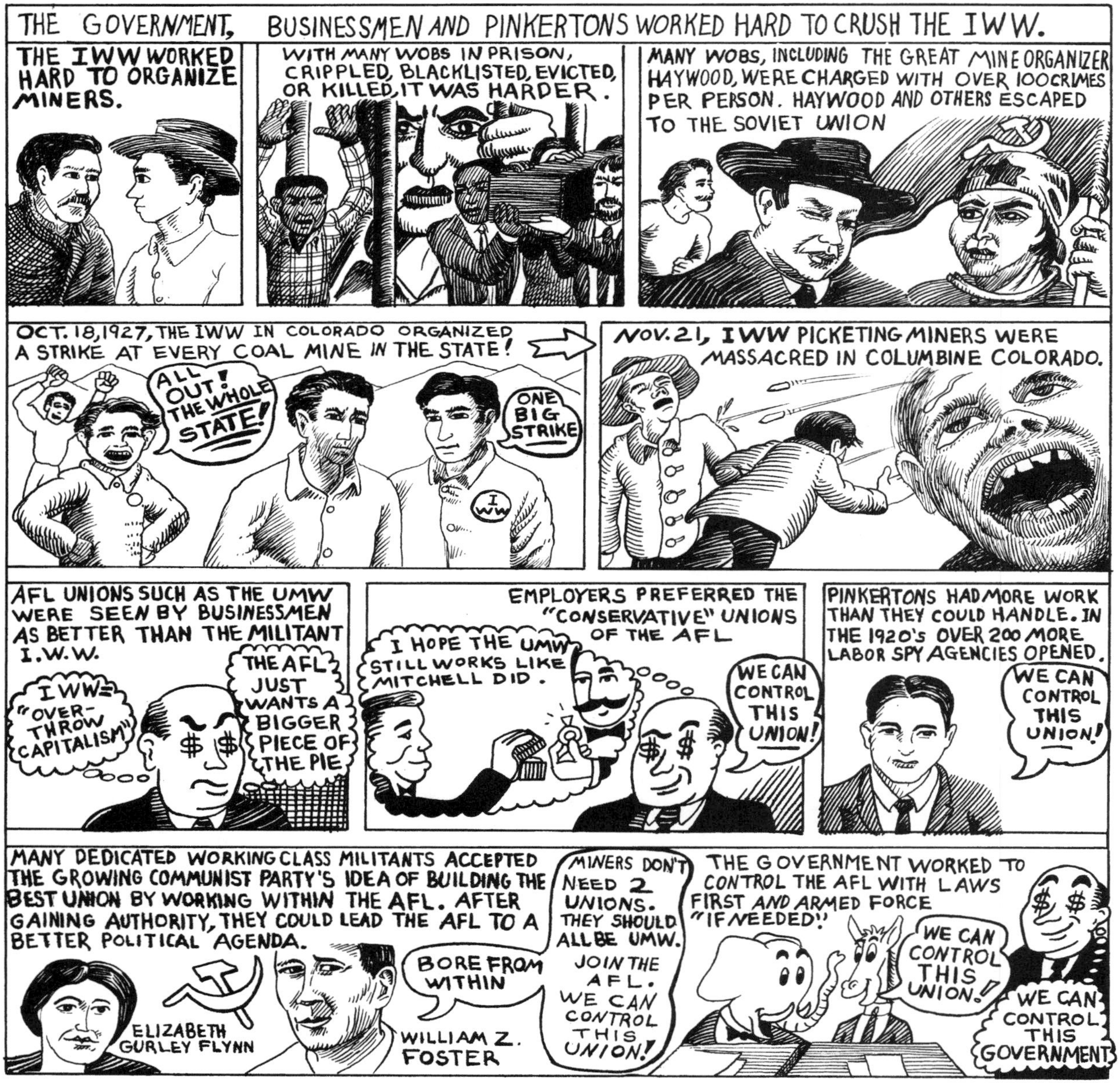
THE GOVERNMENT, BUSINESSMEN AND PINKERTONS WORKED HARD TO CRUSH THE IWW.
THE IWW WORKED HARD TO ORGANIZE MINERS.
WITH MANY WOBS IN PRISON, CRIPPLED, BLACKLISTED, EVICTED, OR KILLED, IT WAS HARDER.
MANY WOBS, INCLUDING THE GREAT MINE ORGANIZER HAYWOOD, WERE CHARGED WITH OVER 100 CRIMES PER PERSON. HAYWOOD AND OTHERS ESCAPED TO THE SOVIET UNION
OCT. 18, 1927, THE IWW IN COLORADO ORGANIZED A STRIKE AT EVERY COAL MINE IN THE STATE!
ALL OUT! THE WHOLE STATE!
ONE BIG STRIKE
I WW
NOV. 21, IWW PICKETING MINERS WERE MASSACRED IN COLUMBINE COLORADO.
AFL UNIONS SUCH AS THE UMW WERE SEEN BY BUSINESSMEN AS BETTER THAN THE MILITANT I.W.W.
IWW= "OVER-THROW CAPITALISM"
THE AFL JUST WANTS A BIGGER PIECE OF THE PIE
EMPLOYERS PREFERRED THE "CONSERVATIVE" UNIONS OF THE AFL
I HOPE THE UMW STILL WORKS LIKE MITCHELL DID.
WE CAN CONTROL THIS UNION!
PINKERTONS HAD MORE WORK THAN THEY COULD HANDLE. IN THE 1920's OVER 200 MORE LABOR SPY AGENCIES OPENED.
WE CAN CONTROL THIS UNION!
MANY DEDICATED WORKING CLASS MILITANTS ACCEPTED THE GROWING COMMUNIST PARTY'S IDEA OF BUILDING THE BEST UNION BY WORKING WITHIN THE AFL. AFTER GAINING AUTHORITY, THEY COULD LEAD THE AFL TO A BETTER POLITICAL AGENDA.
ELIZABETH GURLEY FLYNN
BORE FROM WITHIN
WILLIAM Z. FOSTER
MINERS DON'T NEED 2 UNIONS. THEY SHOULD ALL BE UMW.
JOIN THE AFL. WE CAN CONTROL THIS UNION!
THE GOVERNMENT WORKED TO CONTROL THE AFL WITH LAWS FIRST AND ARMED FORCE "IF NEEDED!"
WE CAN CONTROL THIS UNION!
WE CAN CONTROL THIS GOVERNMENT

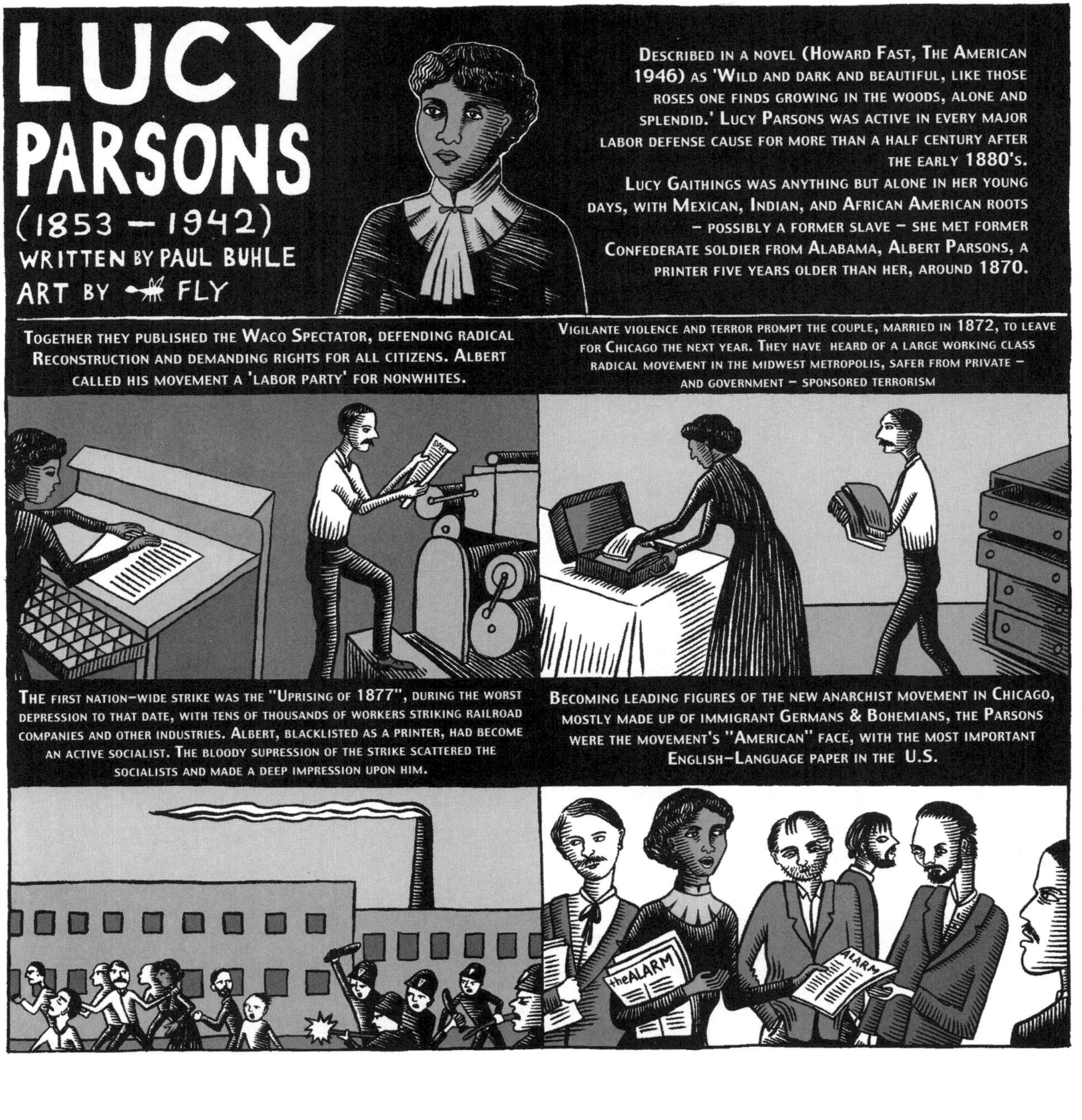
LUCY PARSONS
(1853 – 1942)
WRITTEN BY PAUL BUHLE
ART BY FLY
Described in a novel (Howard Fast, The American 1946) as 'Wild and dark and beautiful, like those roses one finds growing in the woods, alone and splendid.' Lucy Parsons was active in every major labor defense cause for more than a half century after the early 1880's.
Lucy Gaithings was anything but alone in her young days, with Mexican, Indian, and African American roots – possibly a former slave – she met former Confederate soldier from Alabama, Albert Parsons, a printer five years older than her, around 1870.
Together they published the Waco Spectator, defending radical Reconstruction and demanding rights for all citizens. Albert called his movement a 'labor party' for nonwhites.
Vigilante violence and terror prompt the couple, married in 1872, to leave for Chicago the next year. They have heard of a large working class radical movement in the midwest metropolis, safer from private – and government – sponsored terrorism
The first nation-wide strike was the "Uprising of 1877", during the worst depression to that date, with tens of thousands of workers striking railroad companies and other industries. Albert, blacklisted as a printer, had become an active socialist. The bloody supression of the strike scattered the socialists and made a deep impression upon him.
Becoming leading figures of the new anarchist movement in Chicago, mostly made up of immigrant Germans & Bohemians, the Parsons were the movement's "American" face, with the most important English-Language paper in the U.S.
the ALARM
ALARM

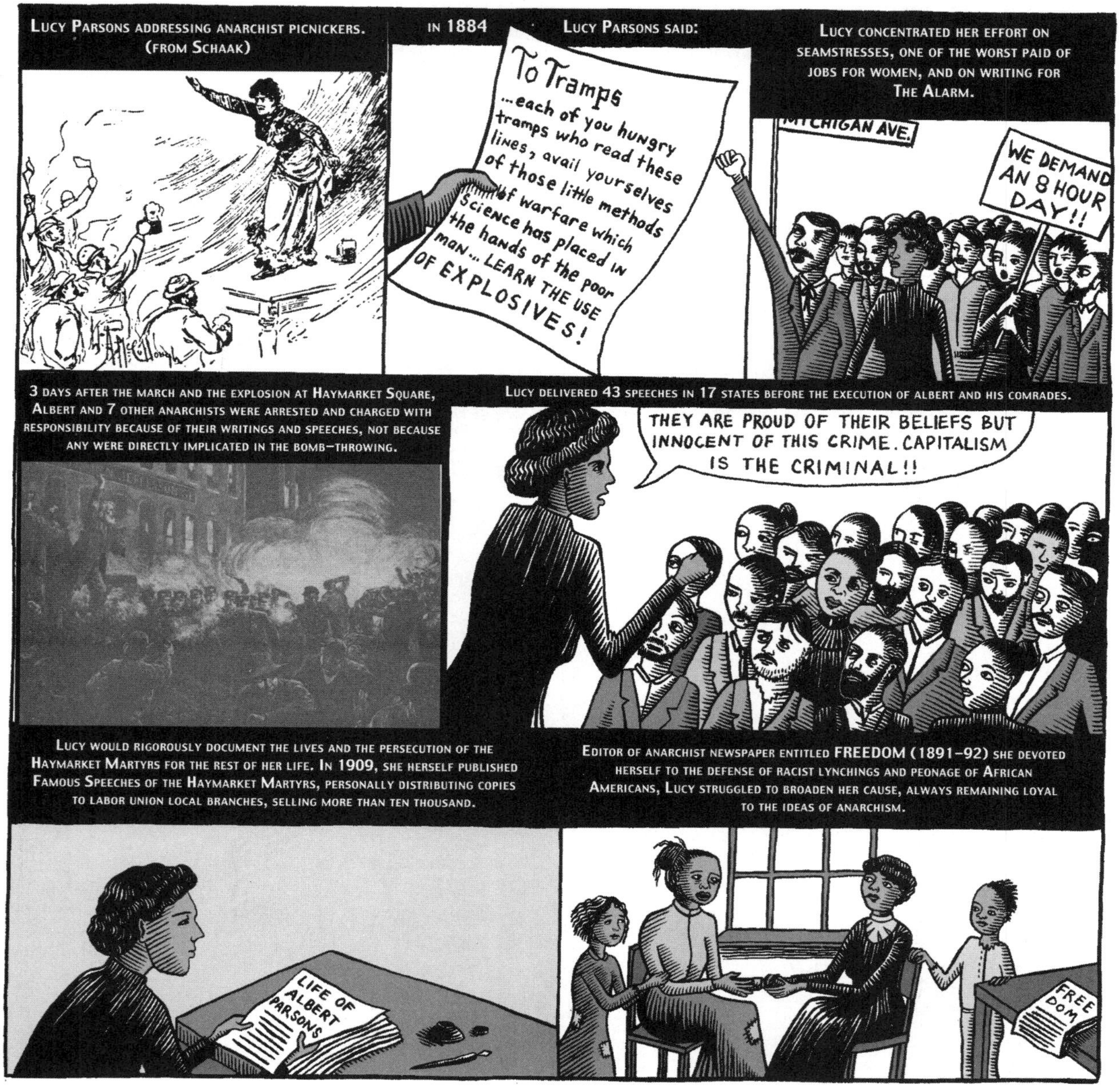
Lucy Parsons addressing anarchist picnickers. (from Schaak)
in 1884 Lucy Parsons said:
To Tramps
...each of you hungry tramps who read these lines, avail yourselves of those little methods of warfare which Science has placed in the hands of the poor man... LEARN THE USE OF EXPLOSIVES!
Lucy concentrated her effort on seamstresses, one of the worst paid of jobs for women, and on writing for The Alarm.
MICHIGAN AVE.
WE DEMAND AN 8 HOUR DAY!!
3 days after the march and the explosion at Haymarket Square, Albert and 7 other anarchists were arrested and charged with responsibility because of their writings and speeches, not because any were directly implicated in the bomb-throwing.
Lucy delivered 43 speeches in 17 states before the execution of albert and his comrades.
THEY ARE PROUD OF THEIR BELIEFS BUT INNOCENT OF THIS CRIME. CAPITALISM IS THE CRIMINAL!!
Lucy would rigorously document the lives and the persecution of the Haymarket Martyrs for the rest of her life. In 1909, she herself published Famous Speeches of the Haymarket Martyrs, personally distributing copies to labor union local branches, selling more than ten thousand.
LIFE OF ALBERT PARSONS
Editor of anarchist newspaper entitled FREEDOM (1891–92) she devoted herself to the defense of racist lynchings and peonage of African Americans, Lucy struggled to broaden her cause, always remaining loyal to the ideas of anarchism.
FREE DOM

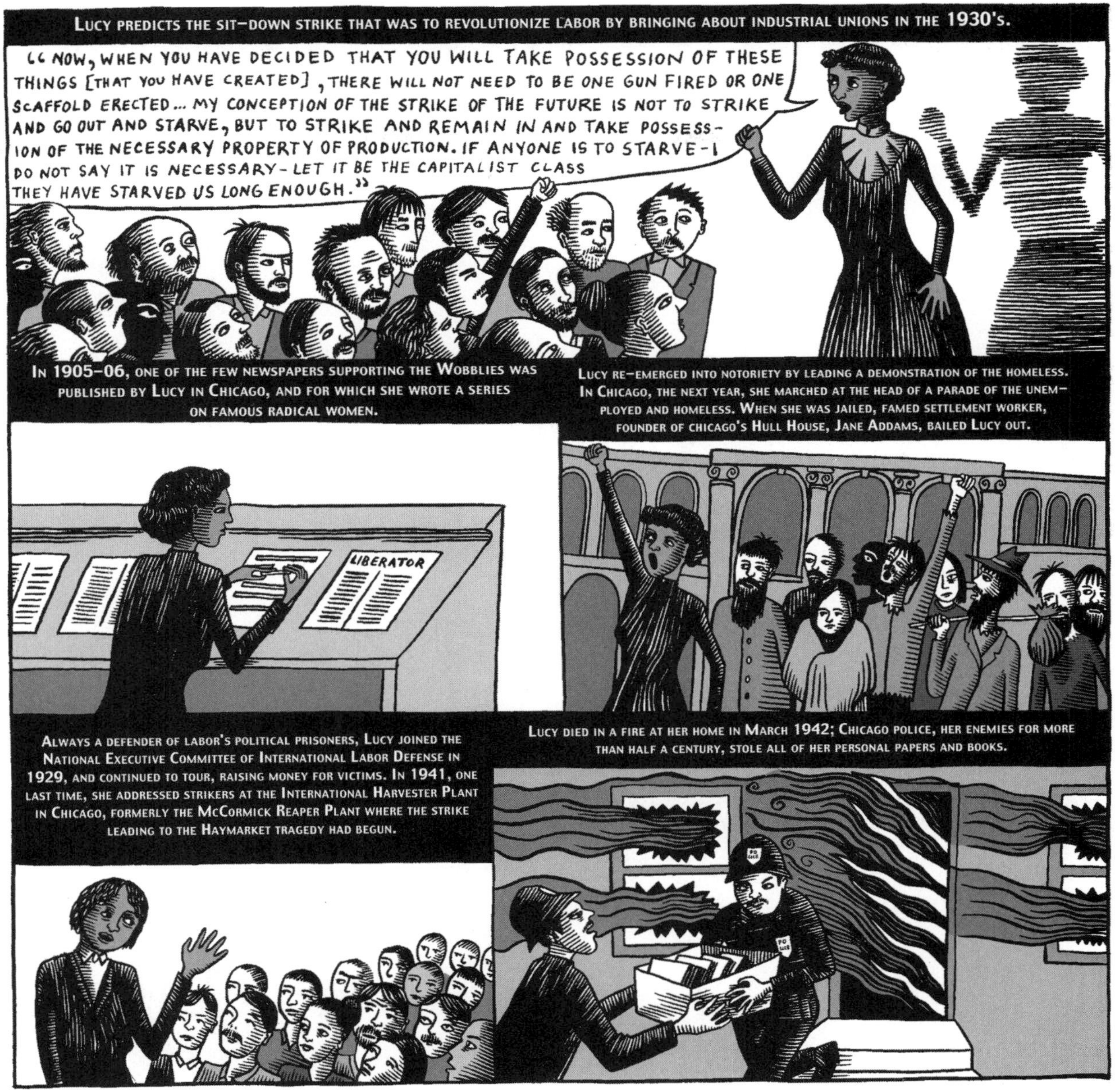
LUCY PREDICTS THE SIT-DOWN STRIKE THAT WAS TO REVOLUTIONIZE LABOR BY BRINGING ABOUT INDUSTRIAL UNIONS IN THE 1930'S.
"NOW, WHEN YOU HAVE DECIDED THAT YOU WILL TAKE POSSESSION OF THESE THINGS [THAT YOU HAVE CREATED], THERE WILL NOT NEED TO BE ONE GUN FIRED OR ONE SCAFFOLD ERECTED... MY CONCEPTION OF THE STRIKE OF THE FUTURE IS NOT TO STRIKE AND GO OUT AND STARVE, BUT TO STRIKE AND REMAIN IN AND TAKE POSSESSION OF THE NECESSARY PROPERTY OF PRODUCTION. IF ANYONE IS TO STARVE - I DO NOT SAY IT IS NECESSARY - LET IT BE THE CAPITALIST CLASS THEY HAVE STARVED US LONG ENOUGH."
IN 1905–06, ONE OF THE FEW NEWSPAPERS SUPPORTING THE WOBBLIES WAS PUBLISHED BY LUCY IN CHICAGO, AND FOR WHICH SHE WROTE A SERIES ON FAMOUS RADICAL WOMEN.
LIBERATOR
LUCY RE-EMERGED INTO NOTORIETY BY LEADING A DEMONSTRATION OF THE HOMELESS. IN CHICAGO, THE NEXT YEAR, SHE MARCHED AT THE HEAD OF A PARADE OF THE UNEMPLOYED AND HOMELESS. WHEN SHE WAS JAILED, FAMED SETTLEMENT WORKER, FOUNDER OF CHICAGO'S HULL HOUSE, JANE ADDAMS, BAILED LUCY OUT.
ALWAYS A DEFENDER OF LABOR'S POLITICAL PRISONERS, LUCY JOINED THE NATIONAL EXECUTIVE COMMITTEE OF INTERNATIONAL LABOR DEFENSE IN 1929, AND CONTINUED TO TOUR, RAISING MONEY FOR VICTIMS. IN 1941, ONE LAST TIME, SHE ADDRESSED STRIKERS AT THE INTERNATIONAL HARVESTER PLANT IN CHICAGO, FORMERLY THE MCCORMICK REAPER PLANT WHERE THE STRIKE LEADING TO THE HAYMARKET TRAGEDY HAD BEGUN.
LUCY DIED IN A FIRE AT HER HOME IN MARCH 1942; CHICAGO POLICE, HER ENEMIES FOR MORE THAN HALF A CENTURY, STOLE ALL OF HER PERSONAL PAPERS AND BOOKS.

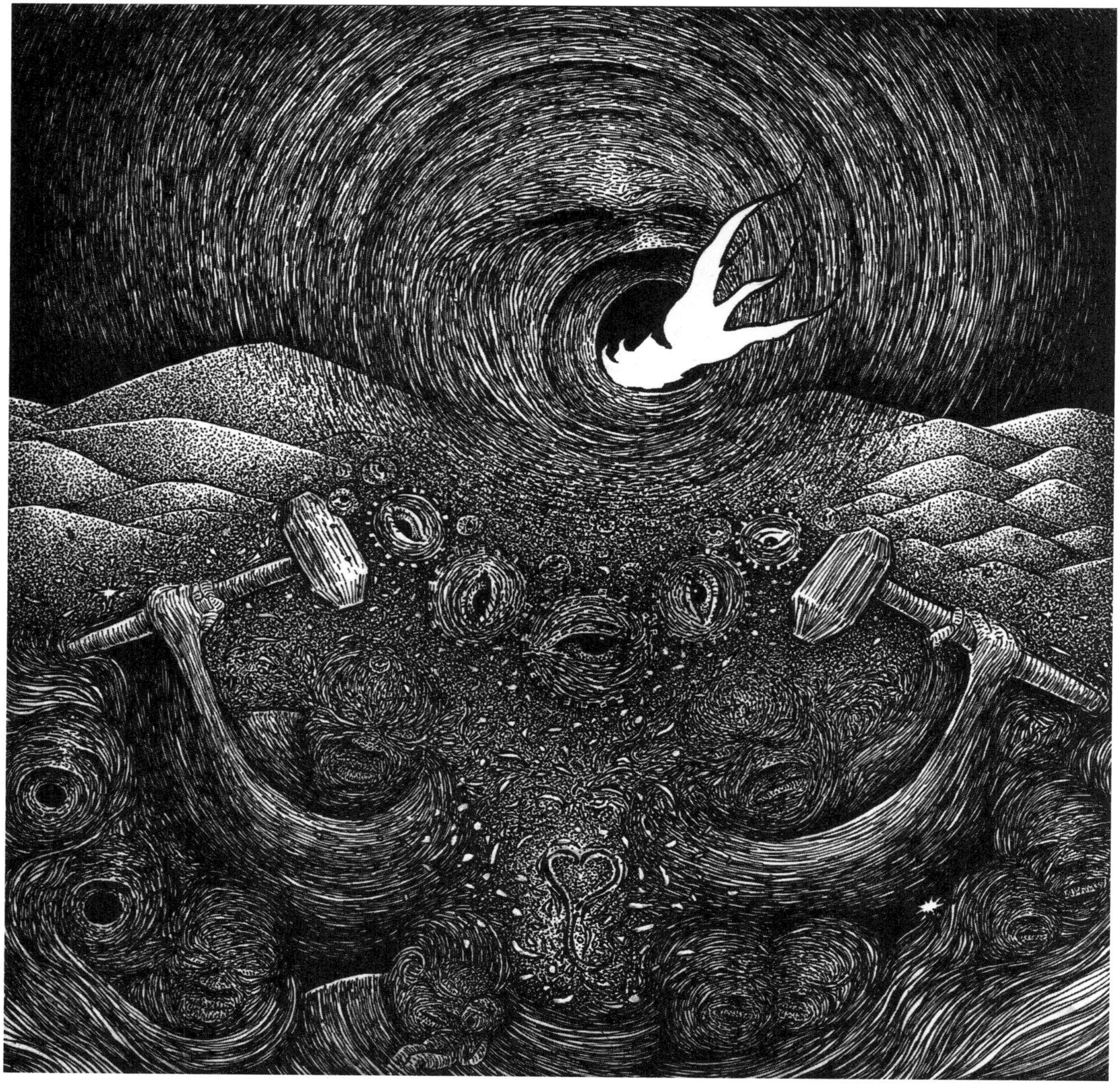

SOLIDARITY FOREVER   Ralph Chaplin

When the union's inspiration through the workers' blood shall run,
There can be no power greater anywhere beneath the sun.
Yet what force on earth is weaker than the feeble strength of one?
But the union makes us strong. (chorus)

Solidarity forever!
Solidarity forever!
Solidarity forever!

Is there aught we hold in common with the greedy parasite
Who would lash us into serfdom and would crush us with his might?
Is there anything left to us but to organize and fight?
For the union makes us strong. (chorus)

It is we who plowed the prairies; built the cities where they trade;
Dug the mines and built the workshops; endless miles of railroad laid.
Now we stand outcast and starving, 'midst the wonders we have made;
But the union makes us strong. (chorus)

All the world that's owned by idle drones is ours and ours alone.
We have laid the wide foundations; built it skyward stone by stone.
It is ours, not to slave in, but to master and to own,
While the union makes us strong. (chorus)

They have taken untold millions that they never toiled to earn,
But without our brain and muscle not a single wheel can turn.
We can break their haughty power; gain our freedom when we learn
That the union makes us strong. (chorus)

In our hands is placed a power greater than their hoarded gold;
Greater than the might of armies, magnified a thousand-fold.
We can bring to birth a new world from the ashes of the old.
For the union makes us strong. (chorus)

"I OBJECT TO ANARCHISM IN THIS BOXCAR"

MR. BLOCK, ERNEST RIEBE, AND THE PROBLEM OF SLAVES WHO THINK IN TERMS OF THEIR MASTERS

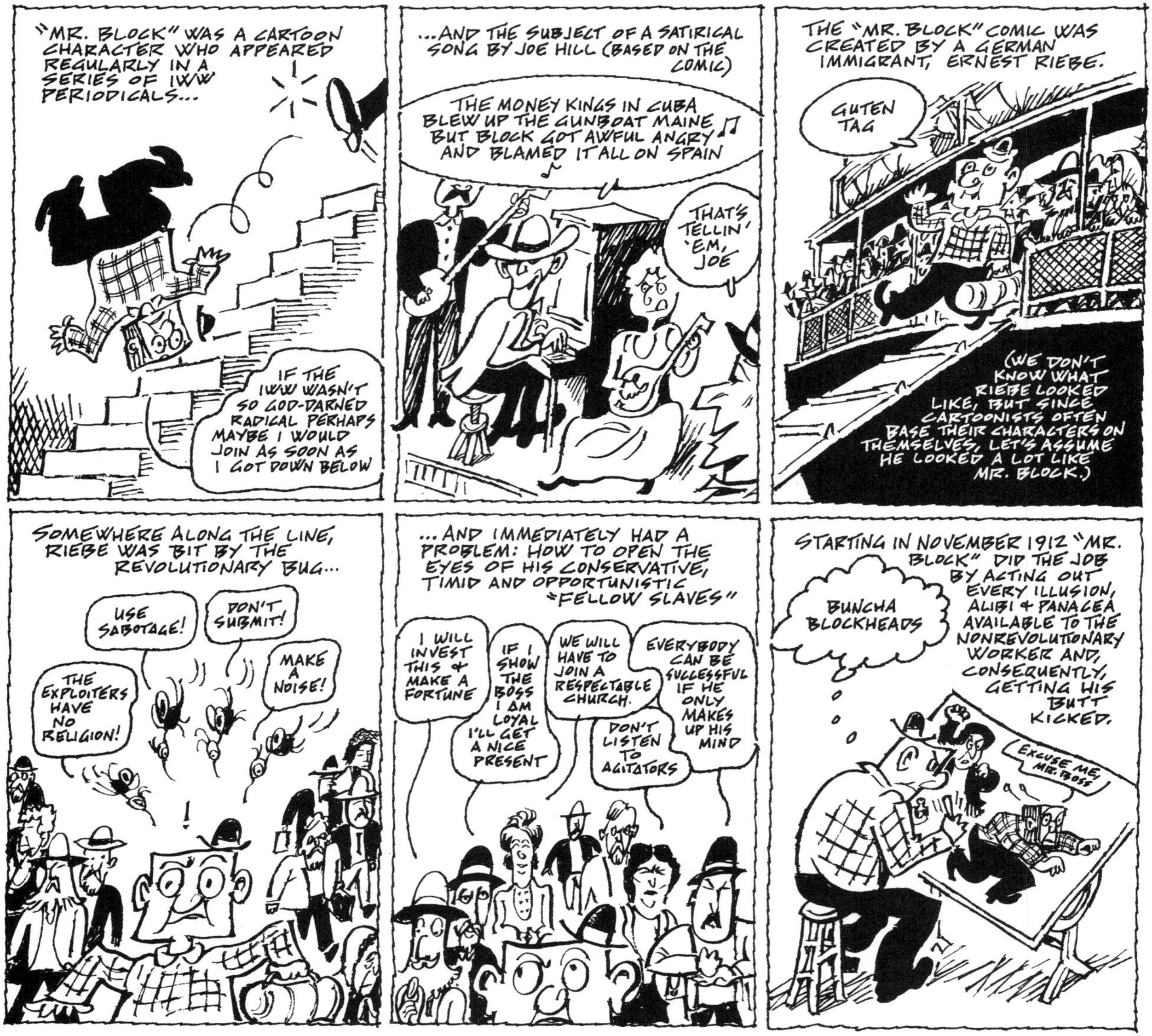
"MR. BLOCK" WAS A CARTOON CHARACTER WHO APPEARED REGULARLY IN A SERIES OF IWW PERIODICALS...
IF THE IWW WASN'T SO GOD-DARNED RADICAL PERHAPS MAYBE I WOULD JOIN AS SOON AS I GOT DOWN BELOW
...AND THE SUBJECT OF A SATIRICAL SONG BY JOE HILL (BASED ON THE COMIC)
THE MONEY KINGS IN CUBA BLEW UP THE GUNBOAT MAINE BUT BLOCK GOT AWFUL ANGRY AND BLAMED IT ALL ON SPAIN
THAT'S TELLIN' 'EM, JOE
THE "MR. BLOCK" COMIC WAS CREATED BY A GERMAN IMMIGRANT, ERNEST RIEBE.
GUTEN TAG
(WE DON'T KNOW WHAT RIEBE LOOKED LIKE, BUT SINCE CARTOONISTS OFTEN BASE THEIR CHARACTERS ON THEMSELVES, LET'S ASSUME HE LOOKED A LOT LIKE MR. BLOCK.)
SOMEWHERE ALONG THE LINE, RIEBE WAS BIT BY THE REVOLUTIONARY BUG...
USE SABOTAGE!
DON'T SUBMIT!
THE EXPLOITERS HAVE NO RELIGION!
MAKE A NOISE!
...AND IMMEDIATELY HAD A PROBLEM: HOW TO OPEN THE EYES OF HIS CONSERVATIVE, TIMID AND OPPORTUNISTIC "FELLOW SLAVES"
I WILL INVEST THIS & MAKE A FORTUNE
IF I SHOW THE BOSS I AM LOYAL I'LL GET A NICE PRESENT
WE WILL HAVE TO JOIN A RESPECTABLE CHURCH.
EVERYBODY CAN BE SUCCESSFUL IF HE ONLY MAKES UP HIS MIND
DON'T LISTEN TO AGITATORS
STARTING IN NOVEMBER 1912 "MR. BLOCK" DID THE JOB BY ACTING OUT EVERY ILLUSION, ALIBI & PANACEA AVAILABLE TO THE NONREVOLUTIONARY WORKER AND, CONSEQUENTLY, GETTING HIS BUTT KICKED.
BUNCHA BLOCKHEADS
EXCUSE ME, MR. BOSS

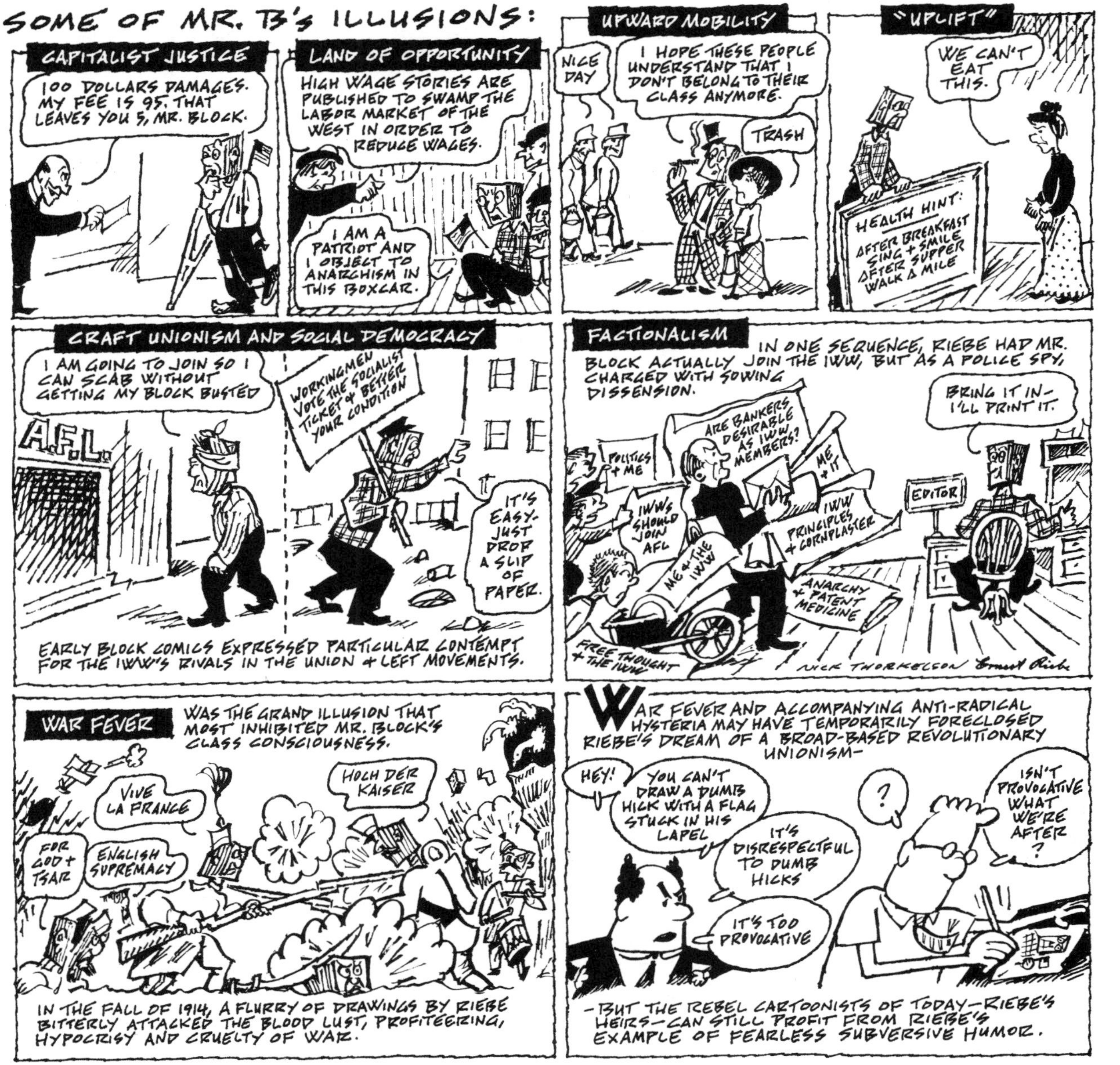
SOME OF MR. B's ILLUSIONS:
CAPITALIST JUSTICE
100 DOLLARS DAMAGES. MY FEE IS 95. THAT LEAVES YOU 5, MR. BLOCK.
LAND OF OPPORTUNITY
HIGH WAGE STORIES ARE PUBLISHED TO SWAMP THE LABOR MARKET OF THE WEST IN ORDER TO REDUCE WAGES.
I AM A PATRIOT AND I OBJECT TO ANARCHISM IN THIS BOXCAR.
UPWARD MOBILITY
NICE DAY
I HOPE THESE PEOPLE UNDERSTAND THAT I DON'T BELONG TO THEIR CLASS ANYMORE.
TRASH
"UPLIFT"
WE CAN'T EAT THIS.
HEALTH HINT: AFTER BREAKFAST SING + SMILE AFTER SUPPER WALK A MILE
CRAFT UNIONISM AND SOCIAL DEMOCRACY
I AM GOING TO JOIN SO I CAN SCAB WITHOUT GETTING MY BLOCK BUSTED
A.F.L.
WORKINGMEN VOTE THE SOCIALIST TICKET & BETTER YOUR CONDITION
IT'S EASY-JUST DROP A SLIP OF PAPER.
EARLY BLOCK COMICS EXPRESSED PARTICULAR CONTEMPT FOR THE IWW'S RIVALS IN THE UNION & LEFT MOVEMENTS.
FACTIONALISM
IN ONE SEQUENCE, RIEBE HAD MR. BLOCK ACTUALLY JOIN THE IWW, BUT AS A POLICE SPY, CHARGED WITH SOWING DISSENSION.
POLITICS + ME
ARE BANKERS DESIRABLE AS IWW MEMBERS?
ME + IT
IWW SHOULD JOIN AFL
ME + THE IWW
IWW PRINCIPLES + CORNPLASTER
ANARCHY + PATENT MEDICINE
FREE THOUGHT + THE IWW
BRING IT IN-I'LL PRINT IT.
EDITOR
NICK THORKELSON
Ernest Riebe
WAR FEVER
WAS THE GRAND ILLUSION THAT MOST INHIBITED MR. BLOCK'S CLASS CONSCIOUSNESS.
VIVE LA FRANCE
HOCH DER KAISER
FOR GOD + TSAR
ENGLISH SUPREMACY
IN THE FALL OF 1914, A FLURRY OF DRAWINGS BY RIEBE BITTERLY ATTACKED THE BLOOD LUST, PROFITEERING, HYPOCRISY AND CRUELTY OF WAR.
WAR FEVER AND ACCOMPANYING ANTI-RADICAL HYSTERIA MAY HAVE TEMPORARILY FORECLOSED RIEBE'S DREAM OF A BROAD-BASED REVOLUTIONARY UNIONISM-
HEY!
YOU CAN'T DRAW A DUMB HICK WITH A FLAG STUCK IN HIS LAPEL
IT'S DISRESPECTFUL TO DUMB HICKS
IT'S TOO PROVOCATIVE
?
ISN'T PROVOCATIVE WHAT WE'RE AFTER?
-BUT THE REBEL CARTOONISTS OF TODAY-RIEBE'S HEIRS-CAN STILL PROFIT FROM RIEBE'S EXAMPLE OF FEARLESS SUBVERSIVE HUMOR.

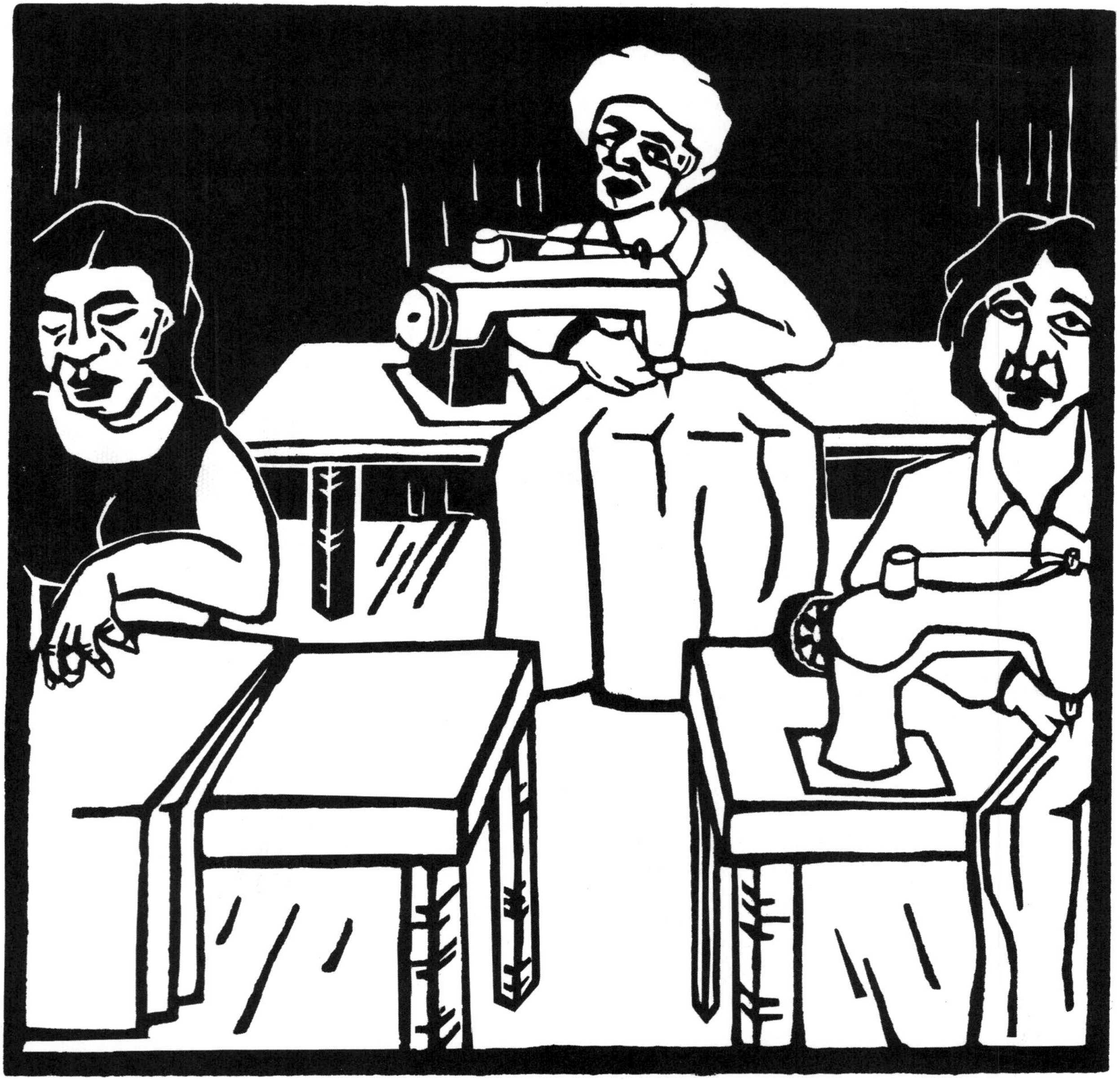

TWO

LAWRENCE AND PATERSON

Even before its famous founding convention, the movement that would become the IWW was attacked as no American labor movement had been attacked at once by the tabloid press, Democratic and Republican politicians, and most especially by the leaders of the American Federation of Labor. The paid propagandists of AFL president Samuel Gompers, some of them former socialists (and some of them still in the Socialist Party), went after the Wobs with a fury. Unionists were informed that no competition would be accepted, strikes would be broken with the help of AFL-led scabs, and employers would be pressured to refuse contracts to Wobblies. A combination of internal disputes and the recession of 1906–7 caused the IWW to lose large sections of its initial membership. The Western Federation of Miners' departure was an especially bitter blow, followed by the expulsion of Daniel DeLeon and his following in the Socialist Labor Party (who formed their own small rival organization, known as the "Detroit IWW" for its home office). Still, the IWW survived, led scattered strikes, conducted a vigorous propaganda campaign for industrial unionism, and invented or reinvented the "sit-down" strike of workers occupying the plant rather than leaving it to the care of the owners. The early Wobblies were above all famous for their Westerners: the part-Indians and the Yankees, sons and daughters of pony-express drivers, and gold prospectors whose families had kept going West but never escaped poverty. But even in these early years many of them were fresh from Europe or were the children of immigrants, radicalized on the other side of the ocean or in their first years of American life. They stayed and stayed in the IWW when native-born "Americans" mostly came and left, published magazines and newspapers that lasted decades, and kept the Wobbly spirit alive for later generations.

The steadiest single group was the Finns. In their homeland, they had been forced in schools to speak Swedish and to turn over half their farm production to the Lutheran church; they staged a massive political strike in 1905 and became the third nation to win the vote for women. Traveling to the US, several hundred thousand concentrated in the "Copper Country" of the northern Midwest, on the coast of Oregon, and a few other places across the country. The non-religious Finnish-Americans, nearly half the population, cultivated their native language and distinctive culture with social halls that put on plays, concerts, political events and economic cooperatives with nearly everyone of all ages taking some part of the fun and the work.

Italian-Americans were not nearly as steady members, but supplied most of the anarchists to the Wobblies. *Il Proletario* (The Worker), the leading weekly paper of the radicals, was the official publication of the Italian Socialist Federation of North America (FSI), loosely affiliated with the IWW, with tens of thousands of readers across the Eastern seaboard and especially among the strikers in Lawrence and

Paterson, along with their supporters. "Free Thought" coffee houses in big cities, especially New York and San Francisco, offered *Il Proletario* to customers. Back in Italy, demonstrations and fund-raising events supported the strikes and strikers in the US. Russians, Hungarians, Croatians, Greeks, Cubans, Mexicans, and other immigrants, like Italians more influenced by anarchism than most American-born Wobblies, also formed their own small Wobbly-friendly propaganda groups and published newspapers and pamphlets.

Strikes by mostly immigrant workers returned the Wobblies from a threatened obscurity during 1906–9 into the center of the picture, not only for the labor movement but for American society at large. At McKees' Rocks, Pennsylvania, in 1909, a Wobbly-led strike brought together mostly Slavic immigrants in ways that thrilled socialists and chilled their enemies. Something was in the air, as the Socialist vote moved toward an apex in 1912 with dozens of communities electing radical working-class candidates to office, and hundreds of local gatherings of immigrants creating their own institutions around the funeral parlor and recreational center, confident that the future would bring a cooperative prospect.

Then came the strikes in Lawrence, Massachusetts, in 1912 and Paterson, New Jersey, in 1913, events with repercussions not only in the US but far beyond. Waves of labor activity among the unskilled (but not only the unskilled) in Britain, the future Irish Republic, Germany, France, and Italy, and even distant Australia, picked up Wobbly slogans and tactics, buoyed by hopes of a global democratic transformation.

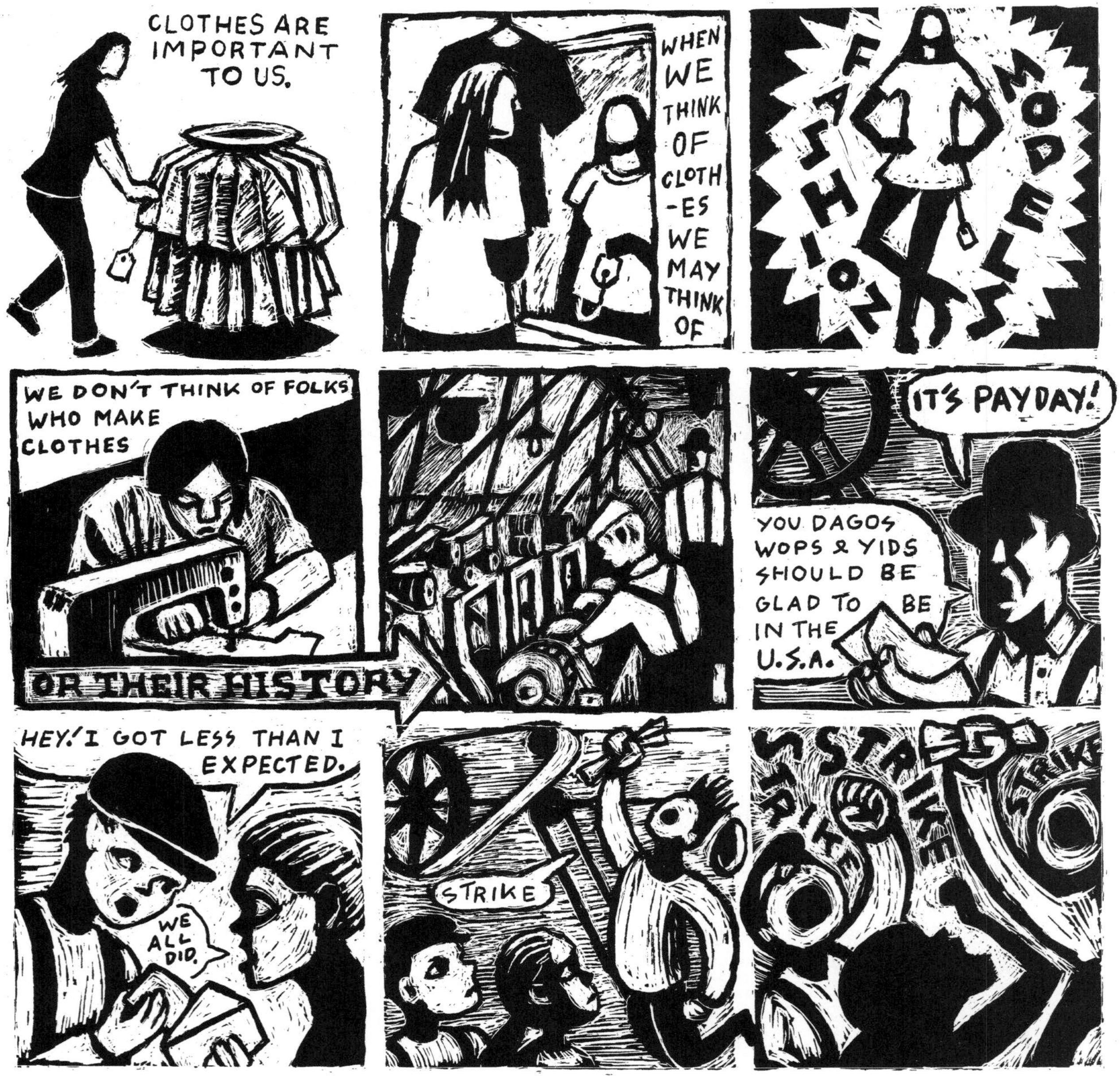
CLOTHES ARE IMPORTANT TO US.
WHEN WE THINK OF CLOTH-ES WE MAY THINK OF
FASHION MODELS
WE DON'T THINK OF FOLKS WHO MAKE CLOTHES
OR THEIR HISTORY
IT'S PAYDAY!
YOU DAGOS WOPS & YIDS SHOULD BE GLAD TO BE IN THE U.S.A.
HEY! I GOT LESS THAN I EXPECTED.
WE ALL DID.
STRIKE
STRIKE
STRIKE

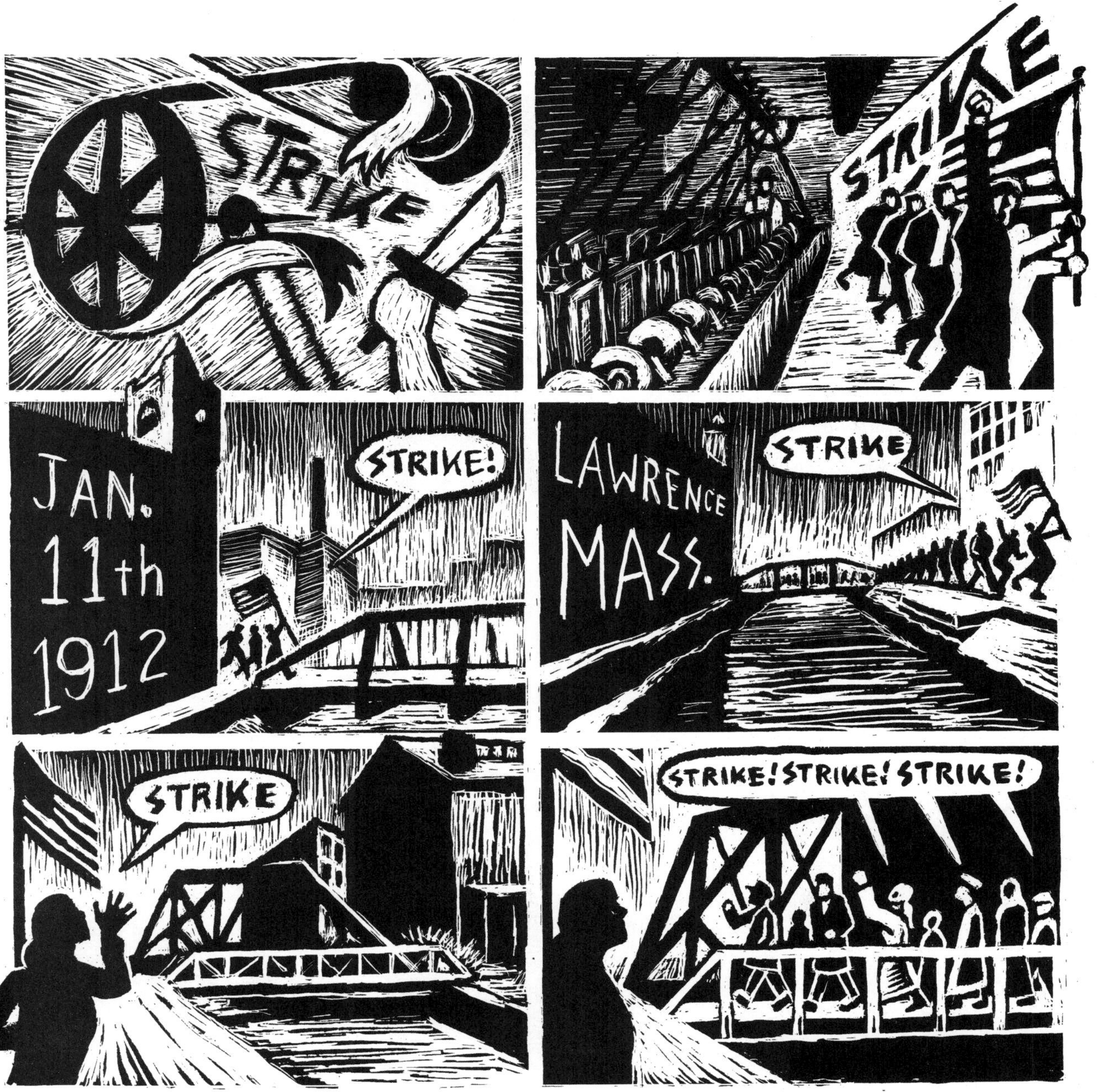
STRIKE
STRIKE
JAN. 11th 1912
STRIKE!
LAWRENCE MASS.
STRIKE
STRIKE
STRIKE! STRIKE! STRIKE!

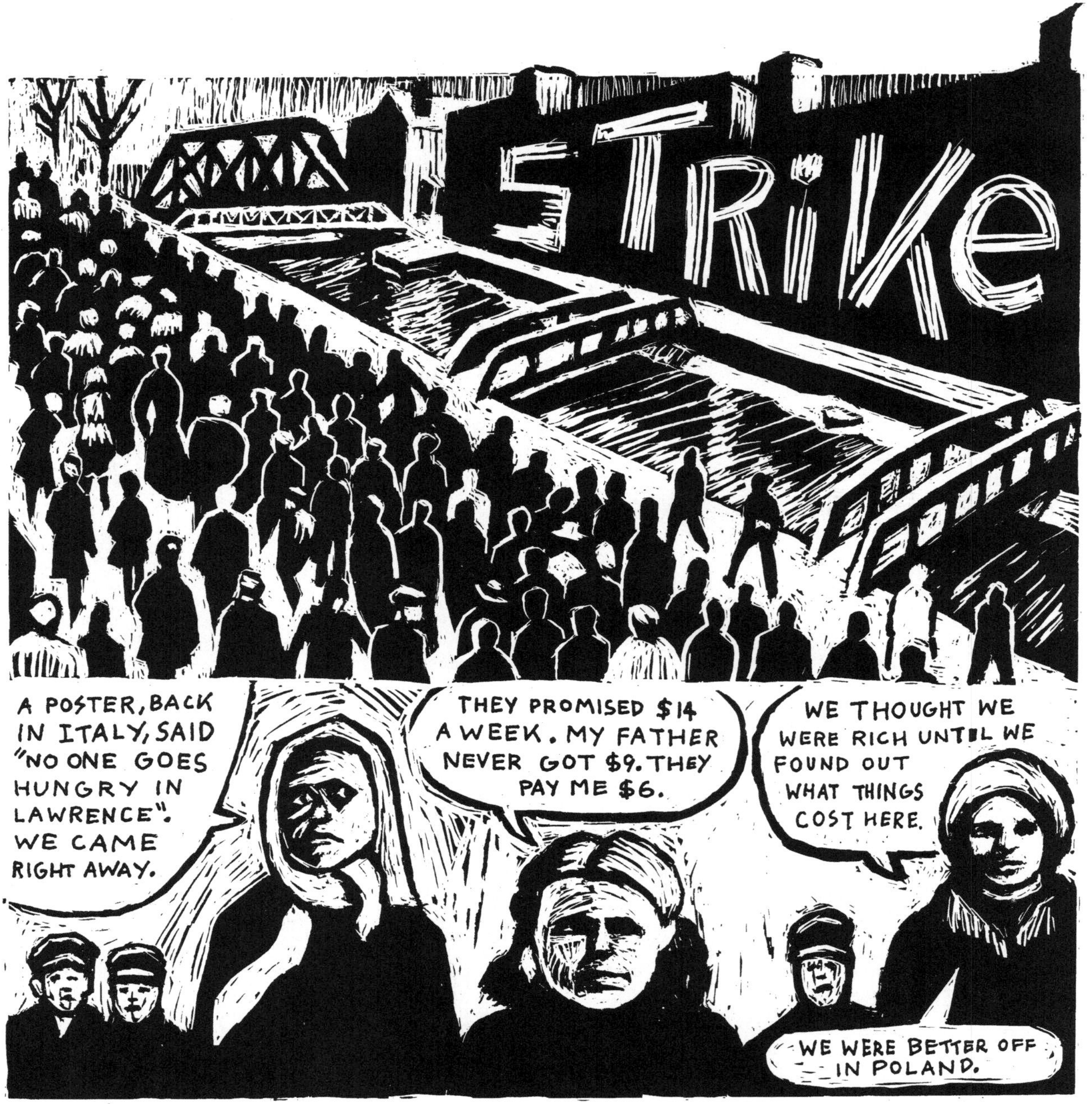
STRIKE
A POSTER, BACK IN ITALY, SAID "NO ONE GOES HUNGRY IN LAWRENCE". WE CAME RIGHT AWAY.
THEY PROMISED $14 A WEEK. MY FATHER NEVER GOT $9. THEY PAY ME $6.
WE THOUGHT WE WERE RICH UNTIL WE FOUND OUT WHAT THINGS COST HERE.
WE WERE BETTER OFF IN POLAND.

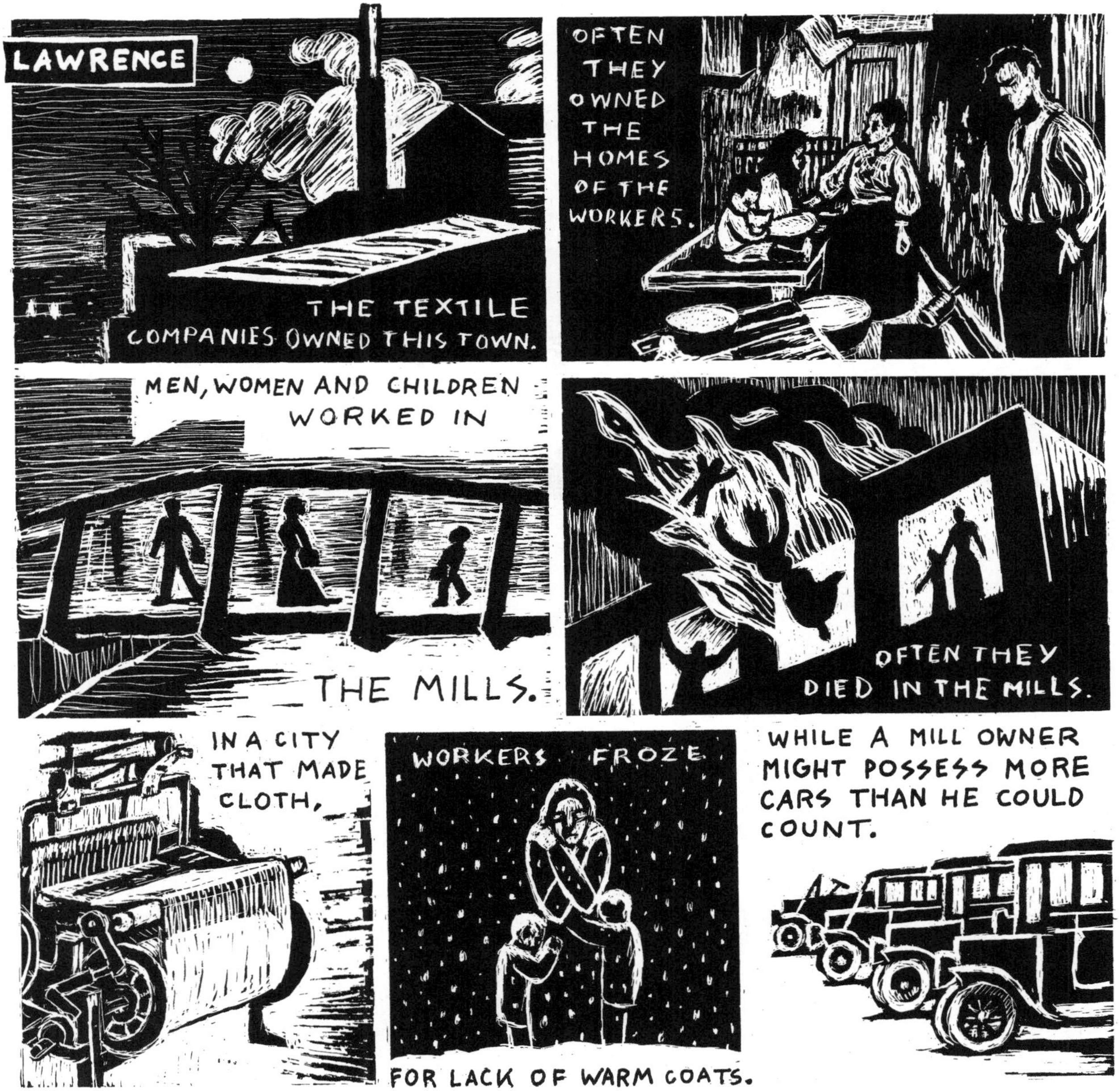
LAWRENCE
THE TEXTILE COMPANIES OWNED THIS TOWN.
OFTEN THEY OWNED THE HOMES OF THE WORKERS.
MEN, WOMEN AND CHILDREN WORKED IN
THE MILLS.
OFTEN THEY DIED IN THE MILLS.
IN A CITY THAT MADE CLOTH,
WORKERS FROZE
FOR LACK OF WARM COATS.
WHILE A MILL OWNER MIGHT POSSESS MORE CARS THAN HE COULD COUNT.

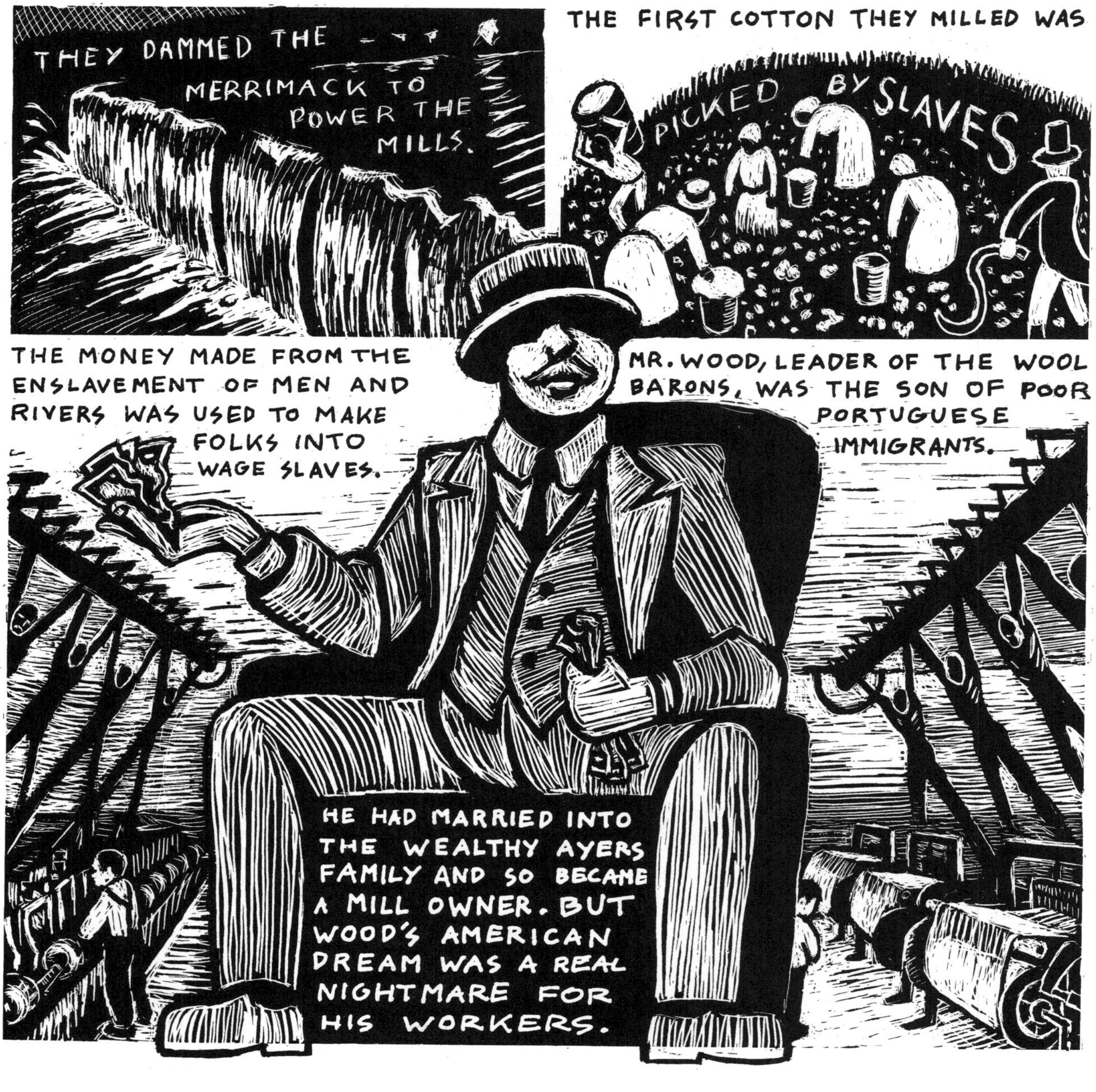
THEY DAMMED THE MERRIMACK TO POWER THE MILLS.
THE FIRST COTTON THEY MILLED WAS
PICKED BY SLAVES
THE MONEY MADE FROM THE ENSLAVEMENT OF MEN AND RIVERS WAS USED TO MAKE FOLKS INTO WAGE SLAVES.
MR. WOOD, LEADER OF THE WOOL BARONS, WAS THE SON OF POOR PORTUGUESE IMMIGRANTS.
HE HAD MARRIED INTO THE WEALTHY AYERS FAMILY AND SO BECAME A MILL OWNER. BUT WOOD'S AMERICAN DREAM WAS A REAL NIGHTMARE FOR HIS WORKERS.

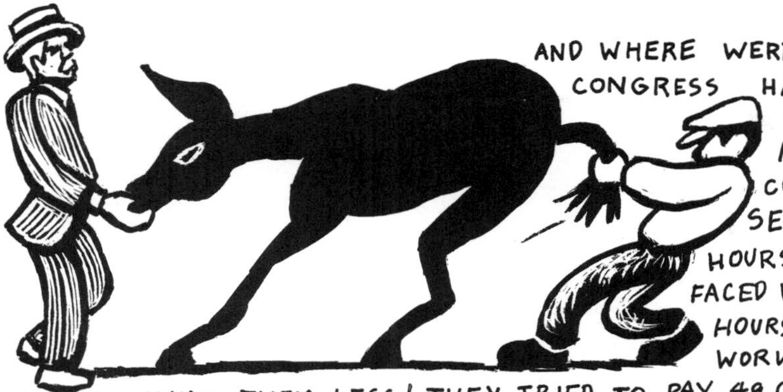

AND WHERE WERE THE DEMOCRATS IN ALL THIS? CONGRESS HAD ENACTED A TARIFF ON FOREIGN FABRICS TO PROTECT MILL OWNERS FROM BRITISH COMPETITION. CONGRESS ALSO SET A LIMIT ON THE NUMBER OF HOURS A PERSON COULD WORK. FACED WITH MANDATORY LIMITS ON HOURS, MILL OWNERS TRIED TO GET WORKERS TO DO MORE WORK IN LESS TIME BY PAYING THEM LESS! THEY TRIED TO PAY 49 CENTS PER CUT INSTEAD OF 79 CENTS, FORCING A MAN TO OPERATE MANY LOOMS AT THE SAME TIME AND WORK FASTER TO BRING HOME LESS PAY. THOSE WHO COULD NOT KEEP UP THE PACE WERE FIRED. IT WAS THIS REDUCTION IN PAY THAT HAD CONVINCED THE WORKERS TO STRIKE.

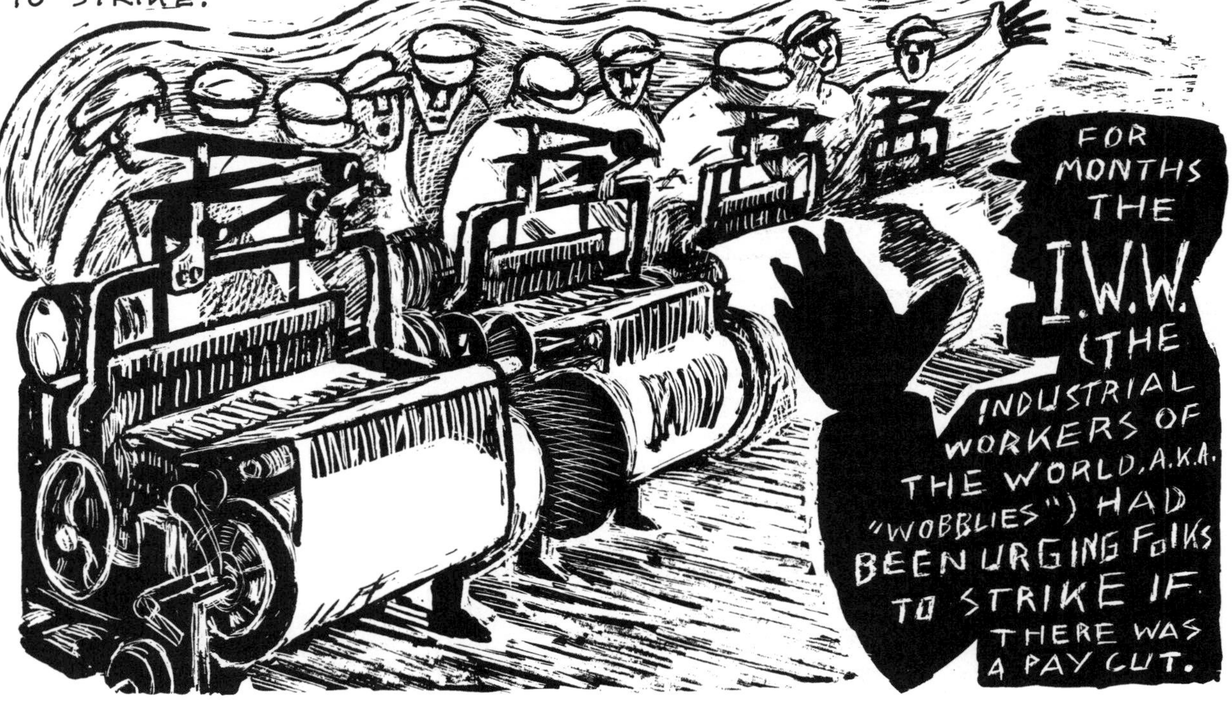
FOR MONTHS THE I.W.W. (THE INDUSTRIAL WORKERS OF THE WORLD, A.K.A. "WOBBLIES") HAD BEEN URGING FOLKS TO STRIKE IF THERE WAS A PAY CUT.

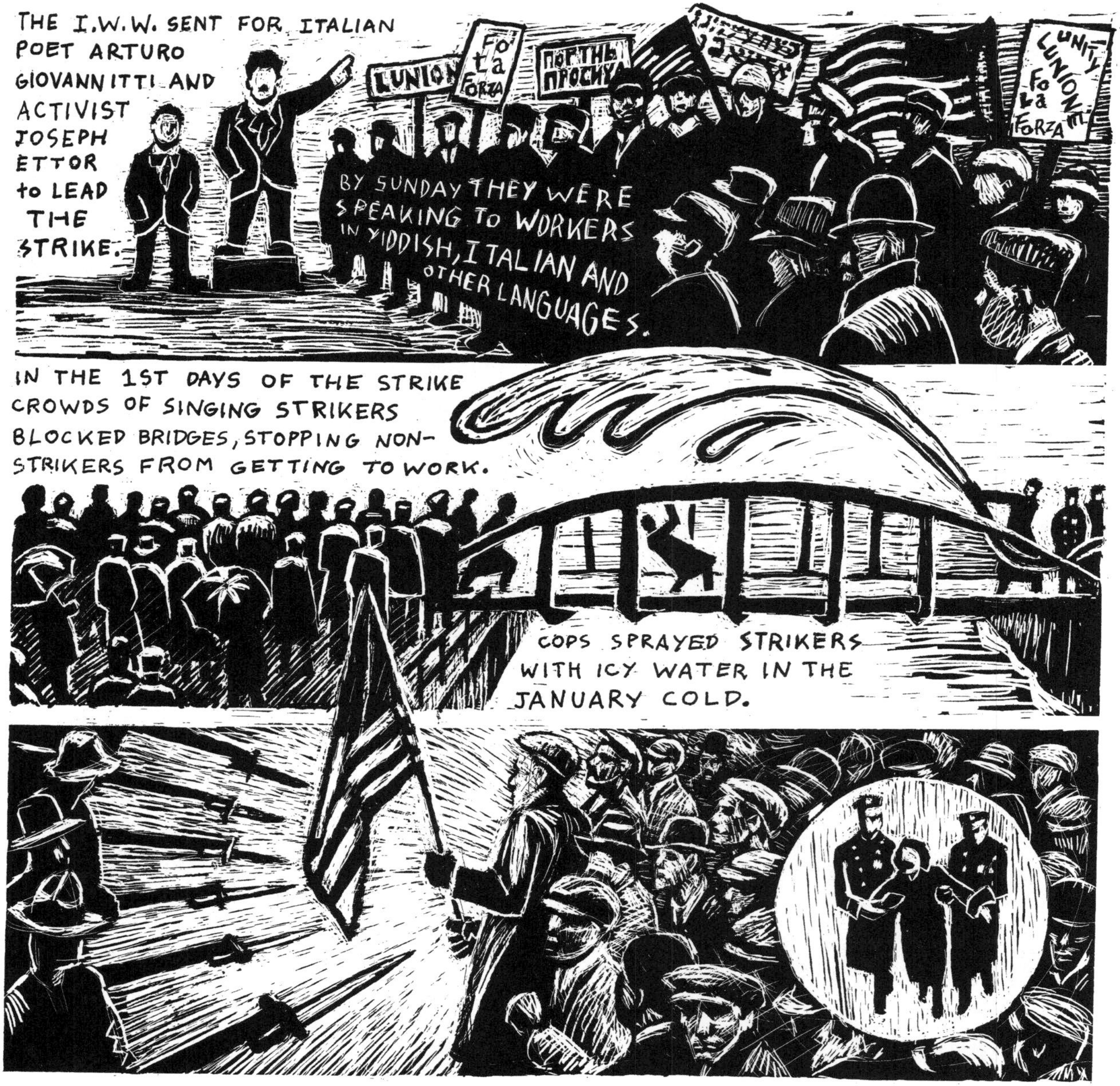
THE I.W.W. SENT FOR ITALIAN POET ARTURO GIOVANNITTI AND ACTIVIST JOSEPH ETTOR to LEAD THE STRIKE.
LUNION
Fo La Forza
BY SUNDAY THEY WERE SPEAKING TO WORKERS IN YIDDISH, ITALIAN AND OTHER LANGUAGES.
UNITY
LUNIONE
Fo La Forza
IN THE 1ST DAYS OF THE STRIKE CROWDS OF SINGING STRIKERS BLOCKED BRIDGES, STOPPING NON-STRIKERS FROM GETTING TO WORK.
COPS SPRAYED STRIKERS WITH ICY WATER IN THE JANUARY COLD.

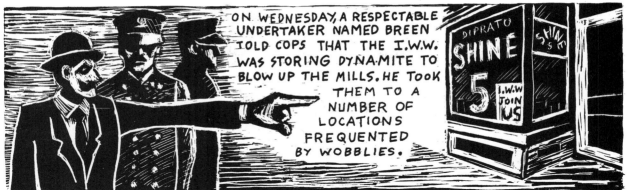

ON WEDNESDAY, A RESPECTABLE UNDERTAKER NAMED BREEN TOLD COPS THAT THE I.W.W. WAS STORING DYNAMITE TO BLOW UP THE MILLS. HE TOOK THEM TO A NUMBER OF LOCATIONS FREQUENTED BY WOBBLIES.
DIPRATO
SHINE
5
I.W.W JOIN US
SHINE 5
DYNAMITE WAS FOUND.
PAPERS RAN WITH IT.
STRIKERS PLOTTING VIOLENCE
'TIL COPS NOTICED THE BOMB WAS WRAPPED IN AN UNDERTAKERS' NEWSLETTER.
BREEN WAS BUST-ED.
ETTOR GAVE WOOD A LIST of the WORKERS' DEMANDS.
WOOD SAID NO.

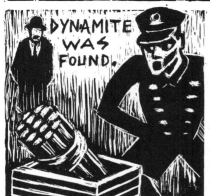

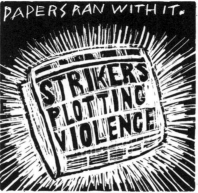

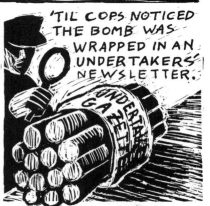

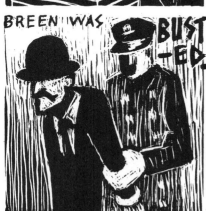

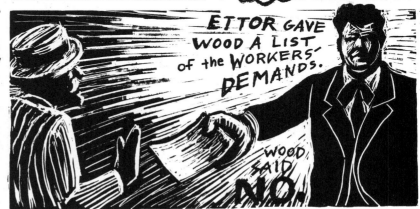

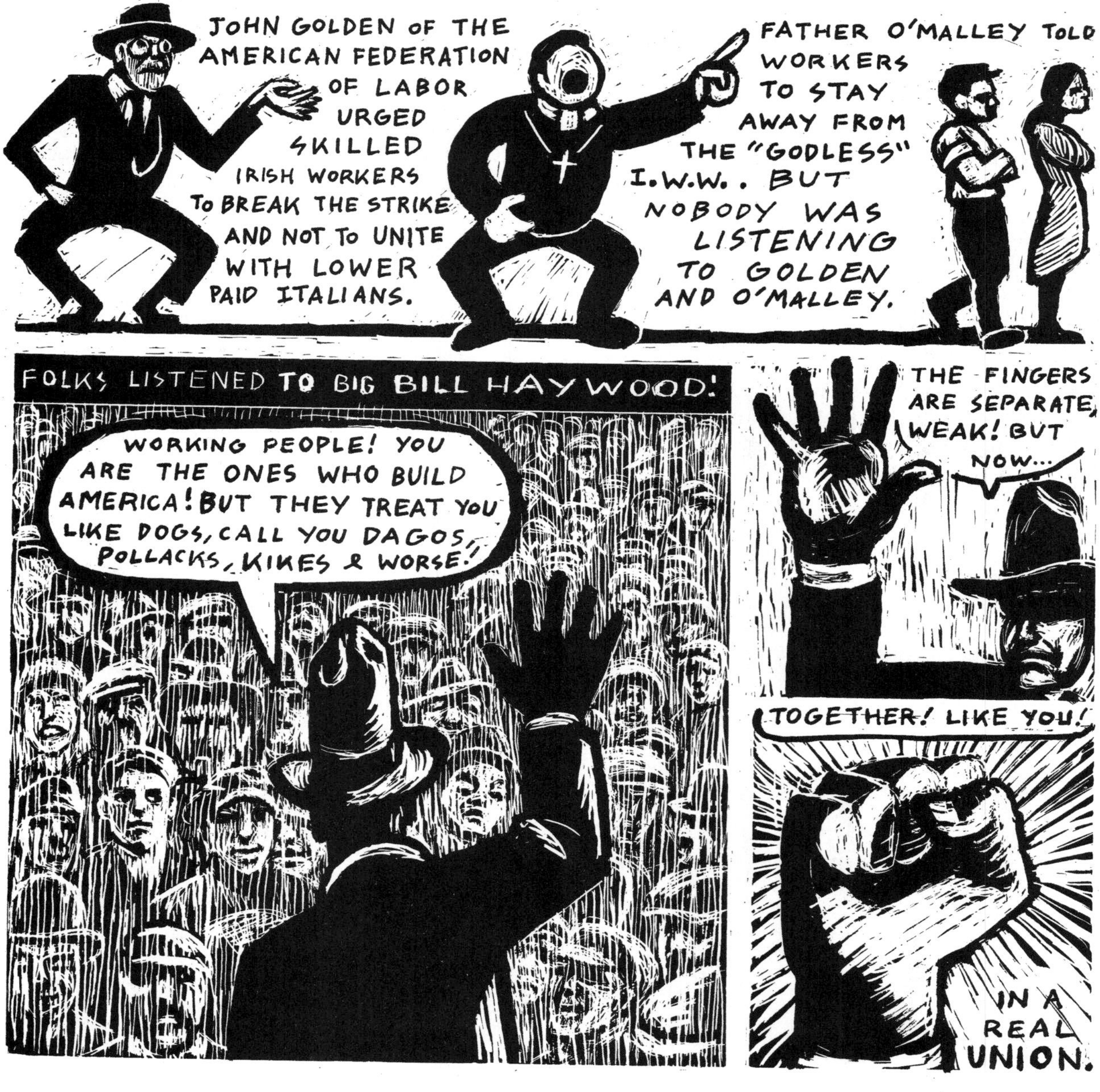
JOHN GOLDEN OF THE AMERICAN FEDERATION OF LABOR URGED SKILLED IRISH WORKERS TO BREAK THE STRIKE AND NOT TO UNITE WITH LOWER PAID ITALIANS.
FATHER O'MALLEY TOLD WORKERS TO STAY AWAY FROM THE "GODLESS" I.W.W.. BUT NOBODY WAS LISTENING TO GOLDEN AND O'MALLEY.
FOLKS LISTENED TO BIG BILL HAYWOOD!
WORKING PEOPLE! YOU ARE THE ONES WHO BUILD AMERICA! BUT THEY TREAT YOU LIKE DOGS, CALL YOU DAGOS, POLLACKS, KIKES & WORSE!
THE FINGERS ARE SEPARATE, WEAK! BUT NOW...
TOGETHER! LIKE YOU!
IN A REAL UNION.

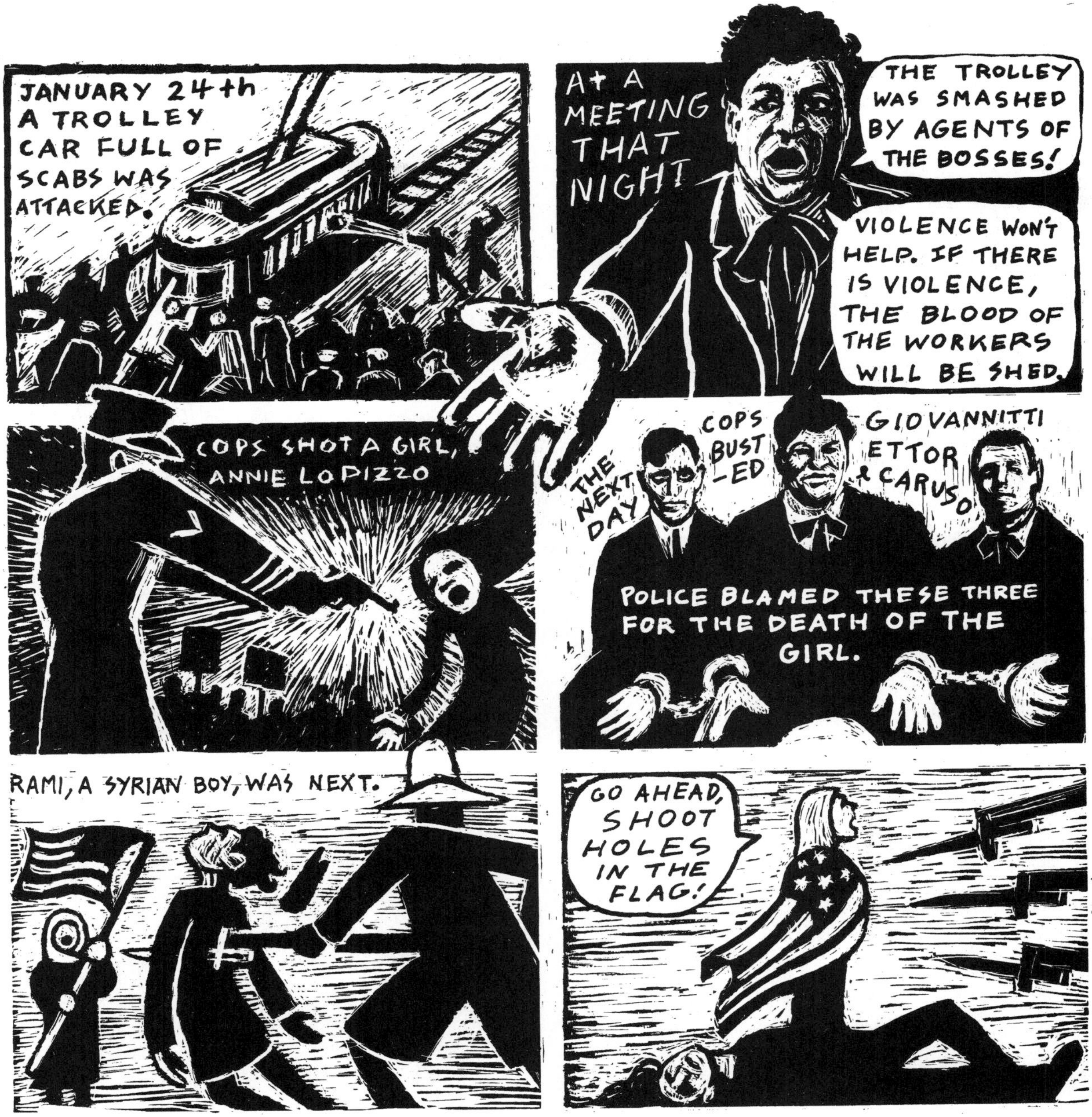
JANUARY 24th A TROLLEY CAR FULL OF SCABS WAS ATTACKED.
AT A MEETING THAT NIGHT
THE TROLLEY WAS SMASHED BY AGENTS OF THE BOSSES!
VIOLENCE WON'T HELP. IF THERE IS VIOLENCE, THE BLOOD OF THE WORKERS WILL BE SHED.
COPS SHOT A GIRL, ANNIE LOPIZZO
THE NEXT DAY
COPS BUST-ED
GIOVANNITTI ETTOR & CARUSO
POLICE BLAMED THESE THREE FOR THE DEATH OF THE GIRL.
RAMI, A SYRIAN BOY, WAS NEXT.
GO AHEAD, SHOOT HOLES IN THE FLAG!

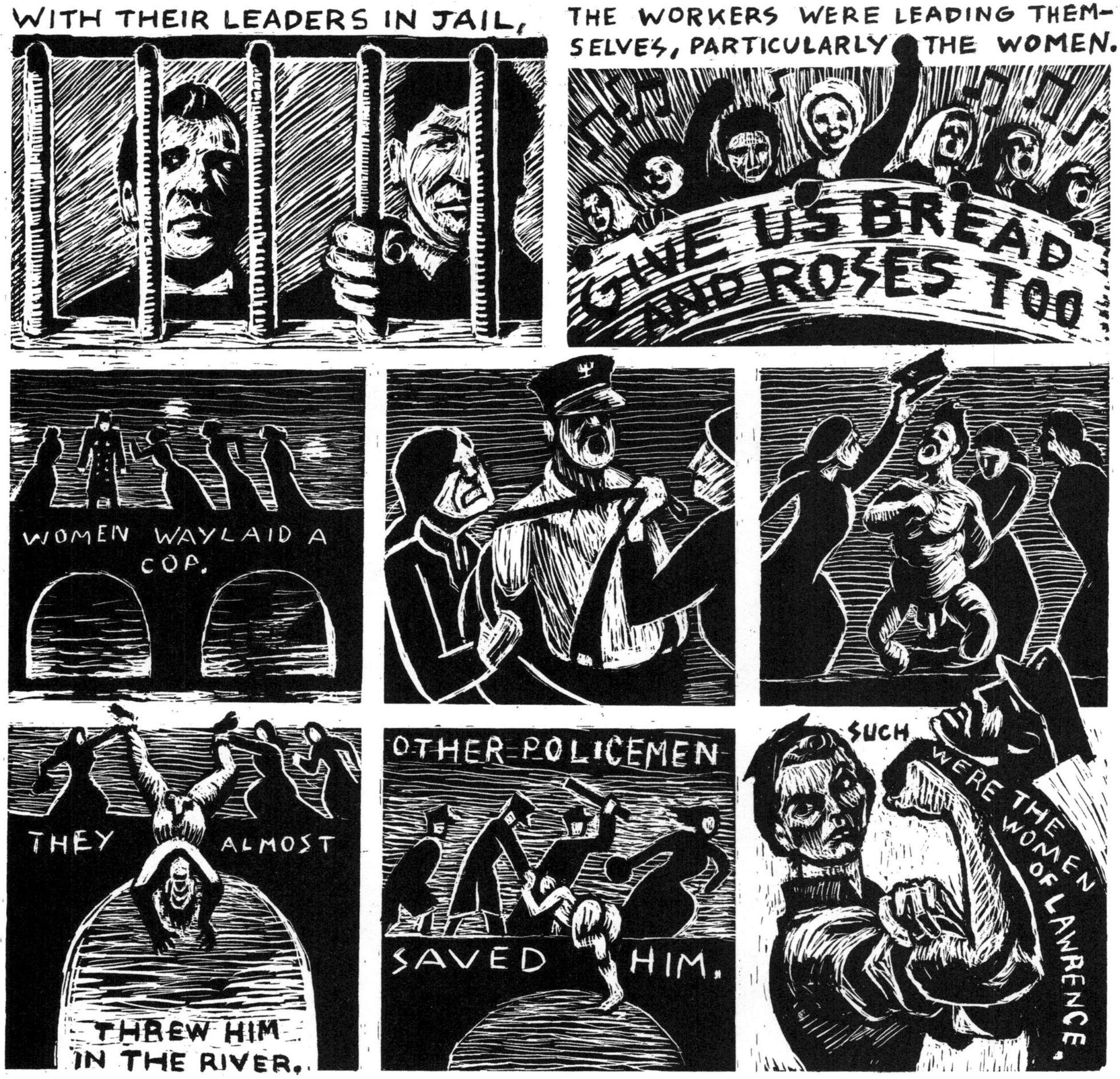

WITH THEIR LEADERS IN JAIL,
THE WORKERS WERE LEADING THEMSELVES, PARTICULARLY THE WOMEN.
GIVE US BREAD AND ROSES TOO
WOMEN WAYLAID A COP.
THEY ALMOST THREW HIM IN THE RIVER.
OTHER POLICEMEN SAVED HIM.
SUCH WERE THE WOMEN OF LAWRENCE.

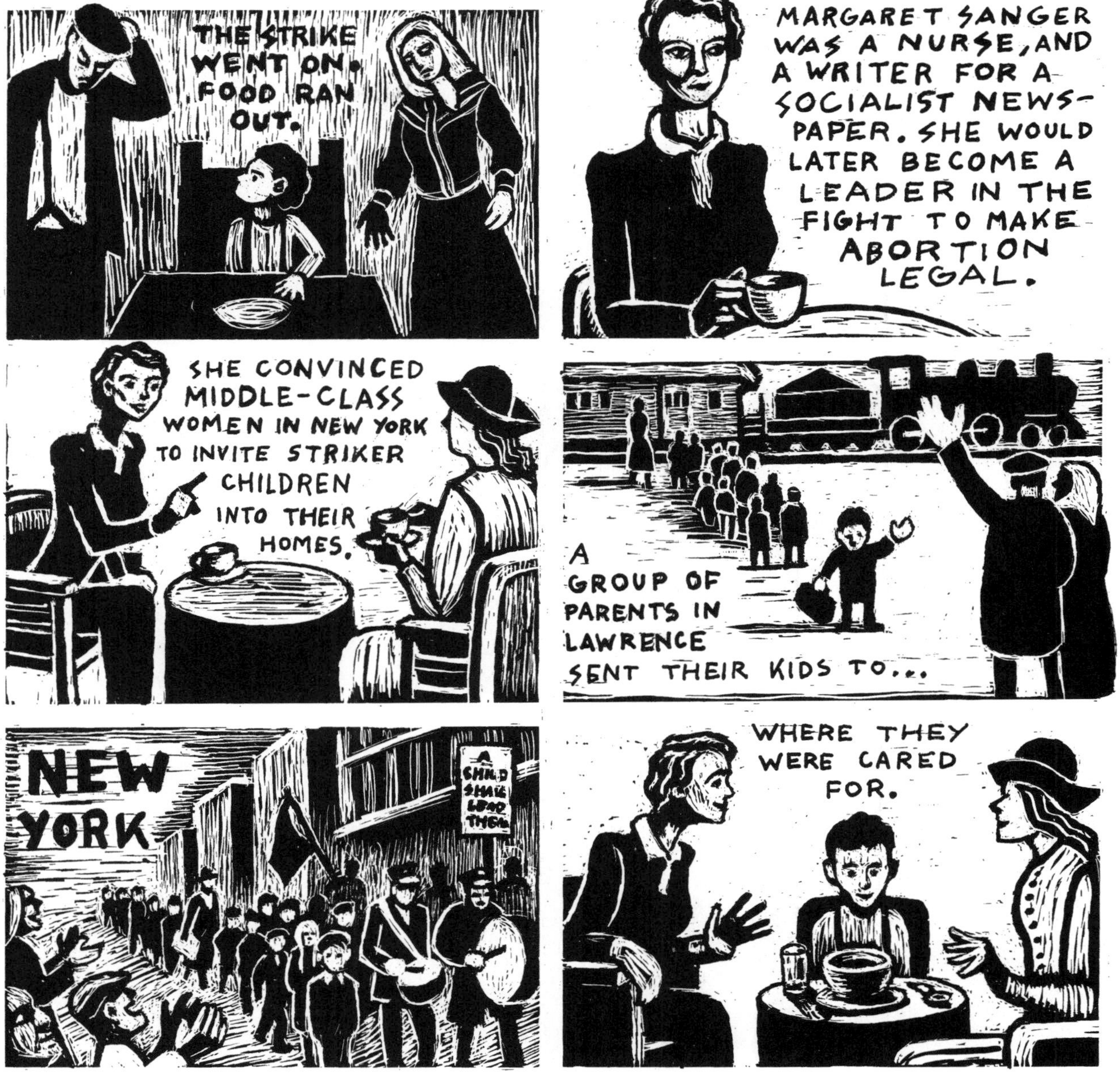
THE STRIKE WENT ON. FOOD RAN OUT.
MARGARET SANGER WAS A NURSE, AND A WRITER FOR A SOCIALIST NEWSPAPER. SHE WOULD LATER BECOME A LEADER IN THE FIGHT TO MAKE ABORTION LEGAL.
SHE CONVINCED MIDDLE-CLASS WOMEN IN NEW YORK TO INVITE STRIKER CHILDREN INTO THEIR HOMES.
A GROUP OF PARENTS IN LAWRENCE SENT THEIR KIDS TO...
NEW YORK
A CHILD
WHERE THEY WERE CARED FOR.

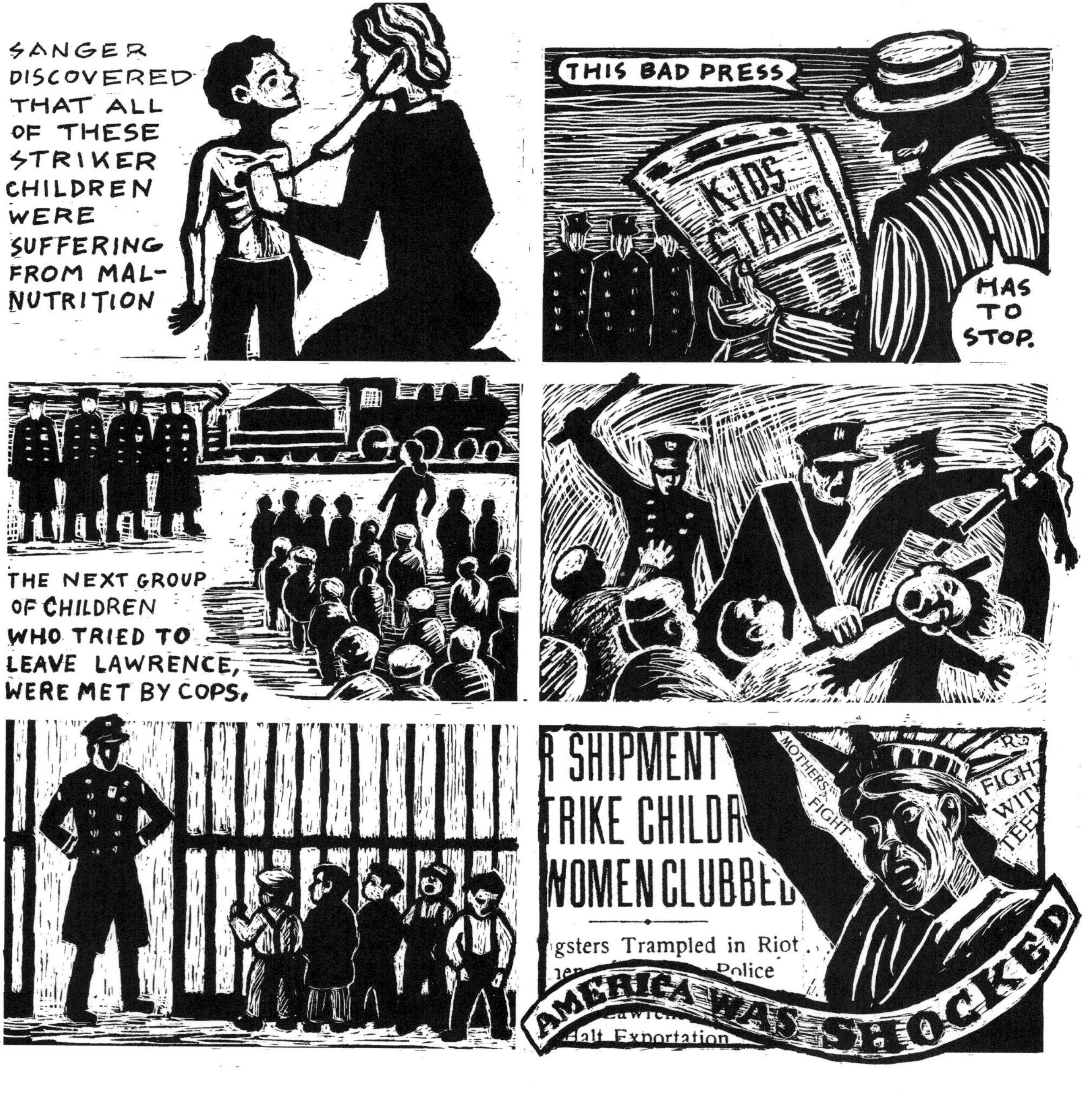
SANGER DISCOVERED THAT ALL OF THESE STRIKER CHILDREN WERE SUFFERING FROM MAL-NUTRITION
THIS BAD PRESS
KIDS STARVE
HAS TO STOP.
THE NEXT GROUP OF CHILDREN WHO TRIED TO LEAVE LAWRENCE, WERE MET BY COPS.
R SHIPMENT
TRIKE CHILDR
WOMEN CLUBBED
gsters Trampled in Riot
Police
Halt Exportation
MOTHERS FIGHT
FIGHT
AMERICA WAS SHOCKED

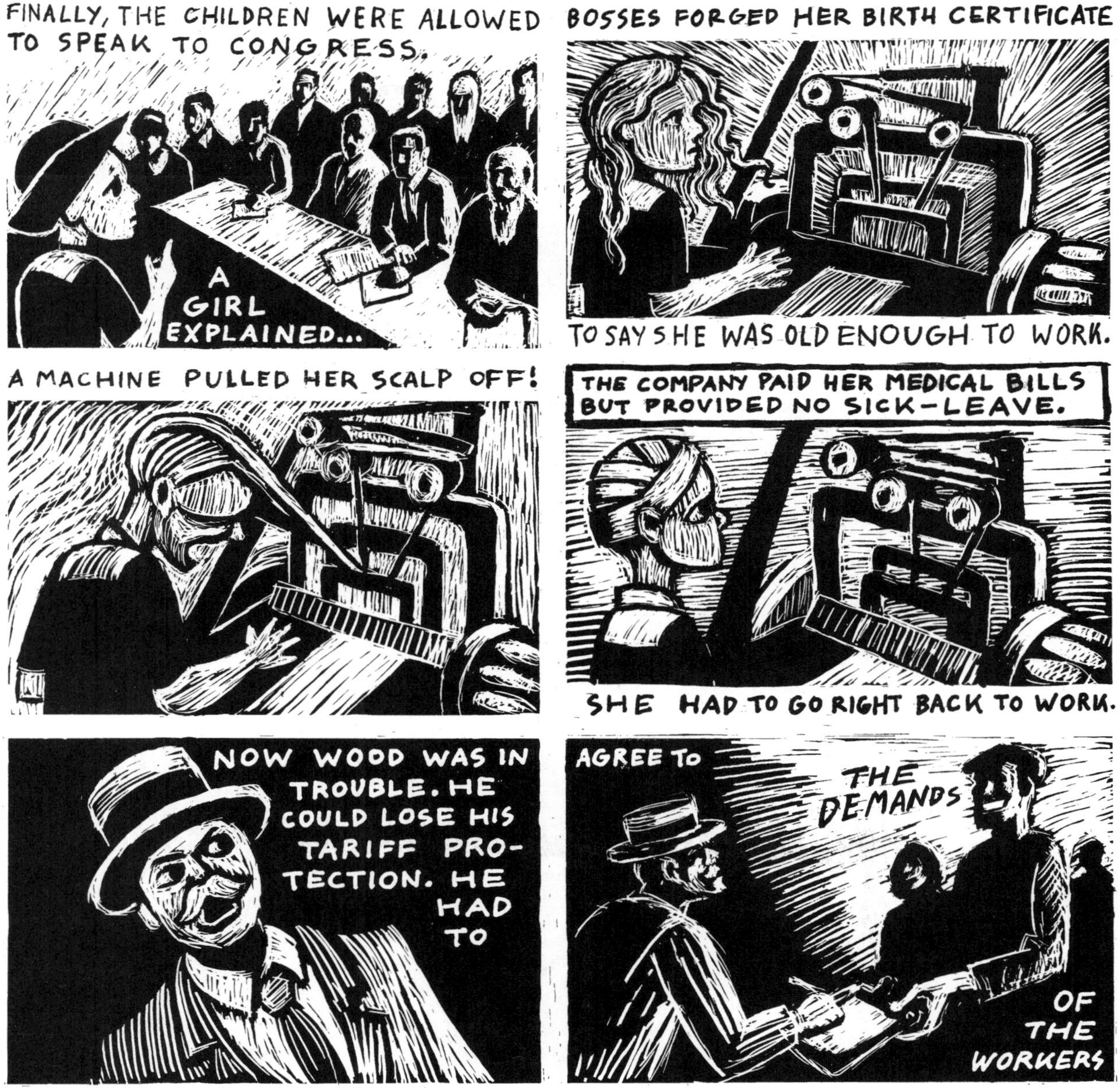
FINALLY, THE CHILDREN WERE ALLOWED TO SPEAK TO CONGRESS.
A GIRL EXPLAINED...
BOSSES FORGED HER BIRTH CERTIFICATE
TO SAY SHE WAS OLD ENOUGH TO WORK.
A MACHINE PULLED HER SCALP OFF!
THE COMPANY PAID HER MEDICAL BILLS BUT PROVIDED NO SICK-LEAVE.
SHE HAD TO GO RIGHT BACK TO WORK.
NOW WOOD WAS IN TROUBLE. HE COULD LOSE HIS TARIFF PROTECTION. HE HAD TO
AGREE TO
THE DEMANDS
OF THE WORKERS

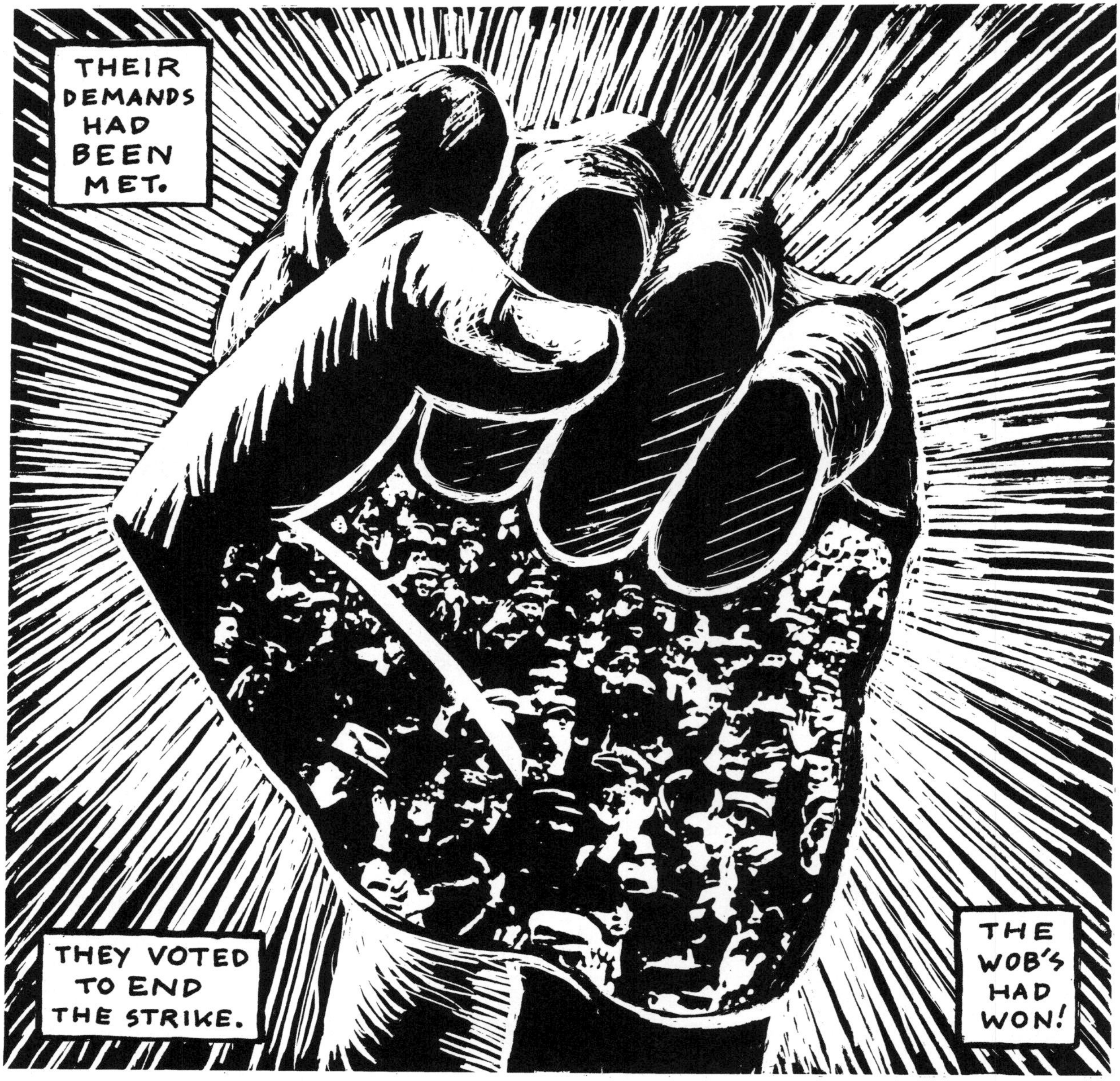
THEIR DEMANDS HAD BEEN MET.
THEY VOTED TO END THE STRIKE.
THE WOB'S HAD WON!

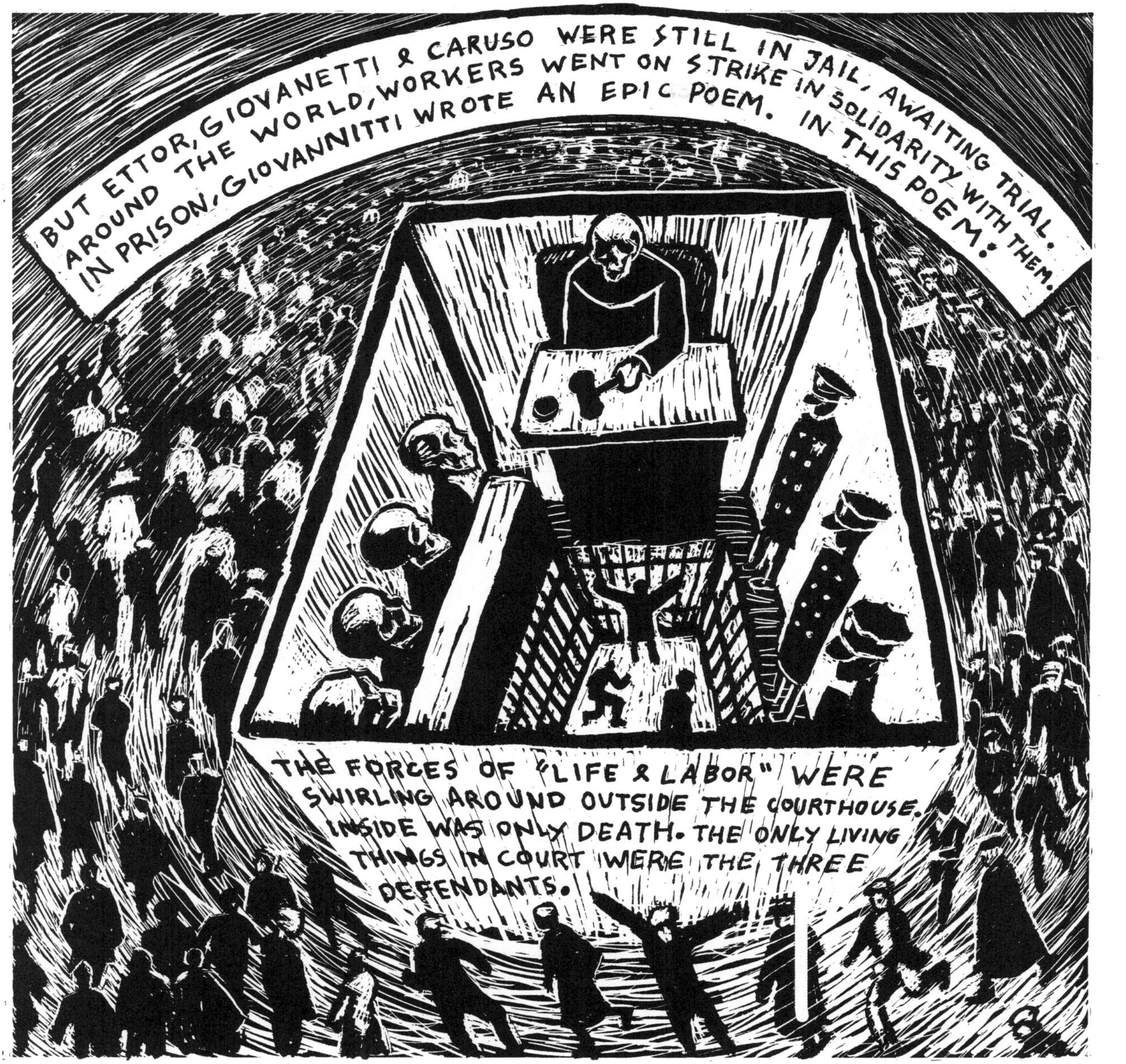
BUT ETTOR, GIOVANETTI & CARUSO WERE STILL IN JAIL, AWAITING TRIAL. AROUND THE WORLD, WORKERS WENT ON STRIKE IN SOLIDARITY WITH THEM. IN PRISON, GIOVANNITTI WROTE AN EPIC POEM. IN THIS POEM:
THE FORCES OF "LIFE & LABOR" WERE SWIRLING AROUND OUTSIDE THE COURTHOUSE. INSIDE WAS ONLY DEATH. THE ONLY LIVING THINGS IN COURT WERE THE THREE DEFENDANTS.

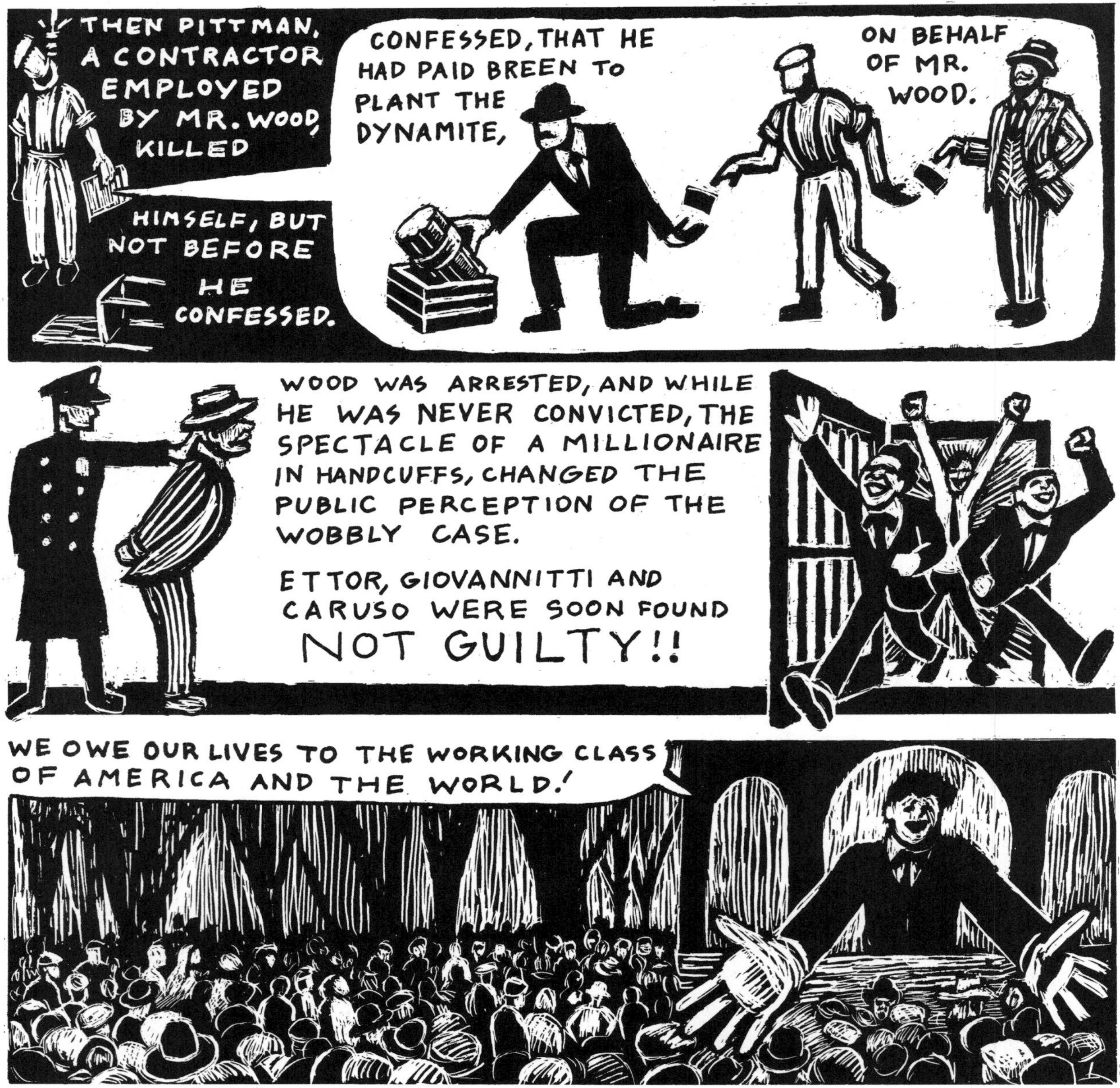
THEN PITTMAN, A CONTRACTOR EMPLOYED BY MR. WOOD, KILLED
HIMSELF, BUT NOT BEFORE HE CONFESSED.
CONFESSED, THAT HE HAD PAID BREEN TO PLANT THE DYNAMITE,
ON BEHALF OF MR. WOOD.
WOOD WAS ARRESTED, AND WHILE HE WAS NEVER CONVICTED, THE SPECTACLE OF A MILLIONAIRE IN HANDCUFFS, CHANGED THE PUBLIC PERCEPTION OF THE WOBBLY CASE.
ETTOR, GIOVANNITTI AND CARUSO WERE SOON FOUND NOT GUILTY!!
WE OWE OUR LIVES TO THE WORKING CLASS OF AMERICA AND THE WORLD!

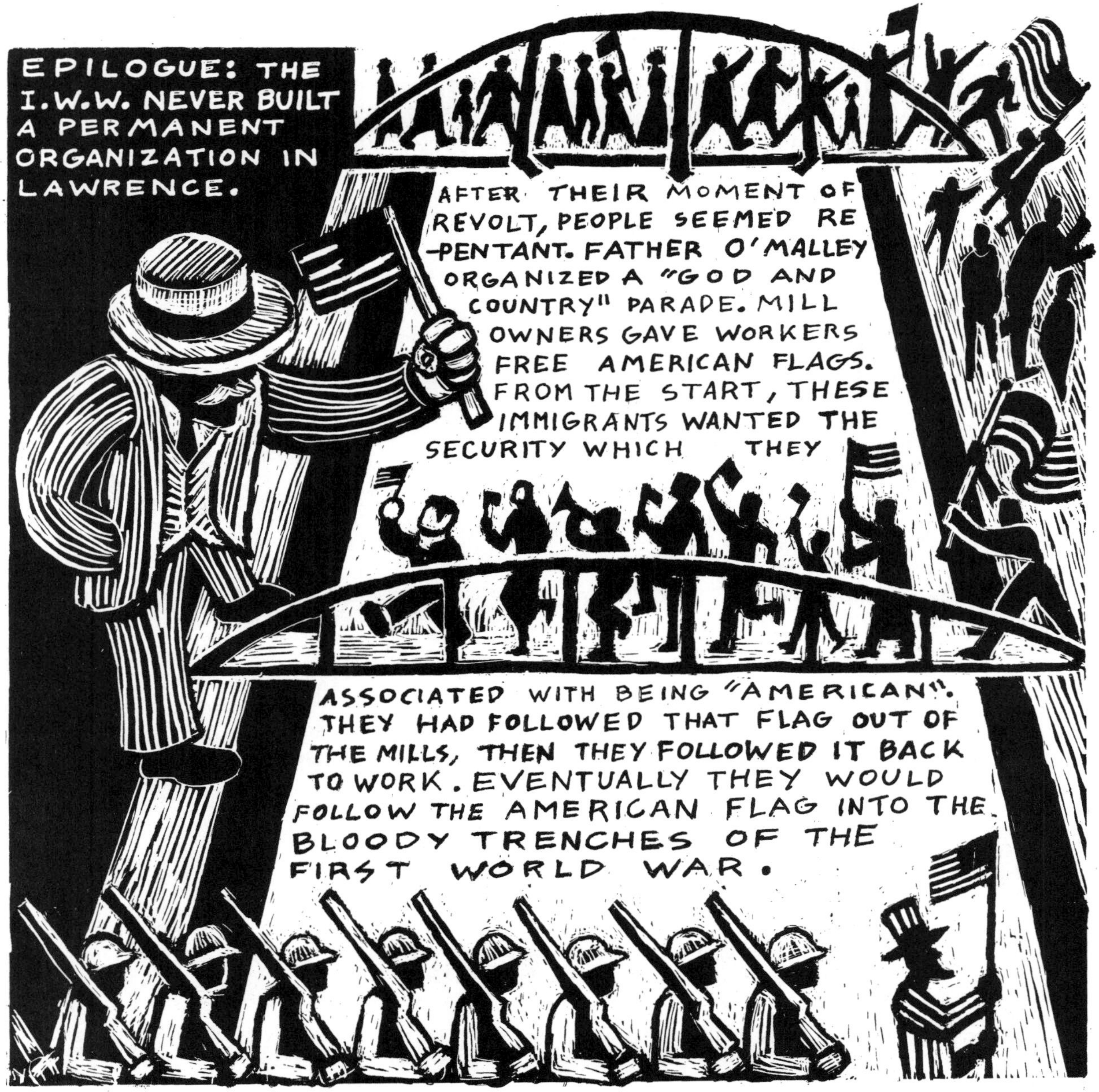
EPILOGUE: THE I.W.W. NEVER BUILT A PERMANENT ORGANIZATION IN LAWRENCE.
AFTER THEIR MOMENT OF REVOLT, PEOPLE SEEMED RE-PENTANT. FATHER O'MALLEY ORGANIZED A "GOD AND COUNTRY" PARADE. MILL OWNERS GAVE WORKERS FREE AMERICAN FLAGS. FROM THE START, THESE IMMIGRANTS WANTED THE SECURITY WHICH THEY
ASSOCIATED WITH BEING "AMERICAN". THEY HAD FOLLOWED THAT FLAG OUT OF THE MILLS, THEN THEY FOLLOWED IT BACK TO WORK. EVENTUALLY THEY WOULD FOLLOW THE AMERICAN FLAG INTO THE BLOODY TRENCHES OF THE FIRST WORLD WAR.

WORKERS JOINED "LESS RADICAL" UNIONS. THESE UNIONS DID NOT OPPOSE THE CAPITALIST SYSTEM, BUT DID FIGHT FOR THE WORKERS. THERE WERE STRIKES IN THE 1930s & 40s, OFTEN LEADING TO "LABOR RIOTS" AND SO THE WORKERS WON SOME IMPROVEMENT IN THEIR CONDITIONS. BUT THIS WAS ONLY TEMPORARY.

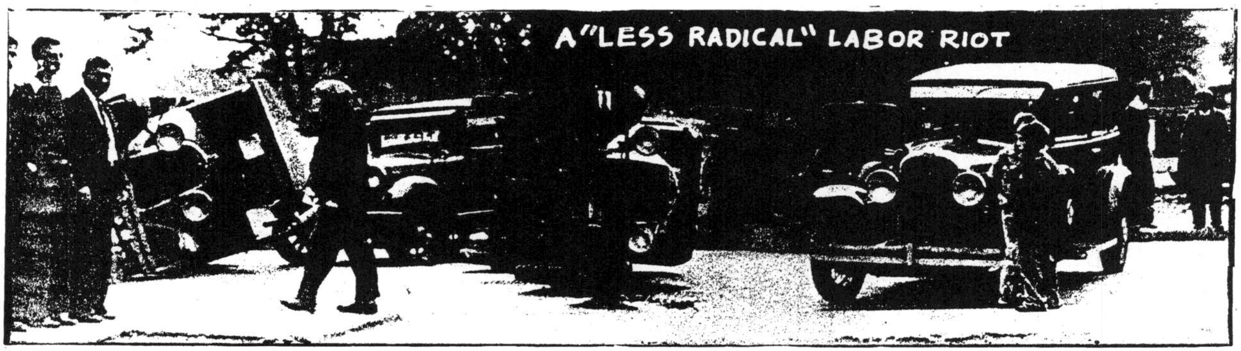
A "LESS RADICAL" LABOR RIOT

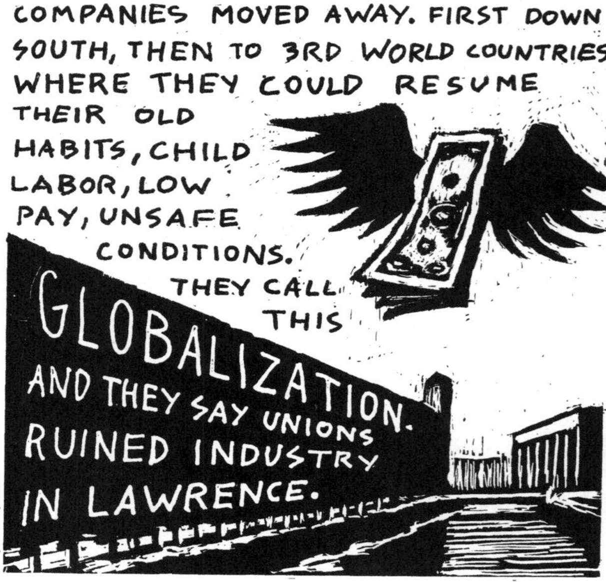
COMPANIES MOVED AWAY. FIRST DOWN SOUTH, THEN TO 3RD WORLD COUNTRIES WHERE THEY COULD RESUME THEIR OLD HABITS, CHILD LABOR, LOW PAY, UNSAFE CONDITIONS.
THEY CALL THIS
GLOBALIZATION.
AND THEY SAY UNIONS RUINED INDUSTRY IN LAWRENCE.

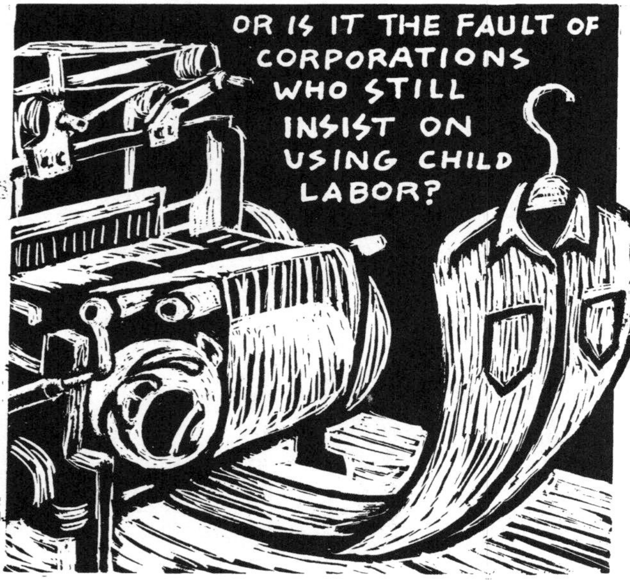
OR IS IT THE FAULT OF CORPORATIONS WHO STILL INSIST ON USING CHILD LABOR?

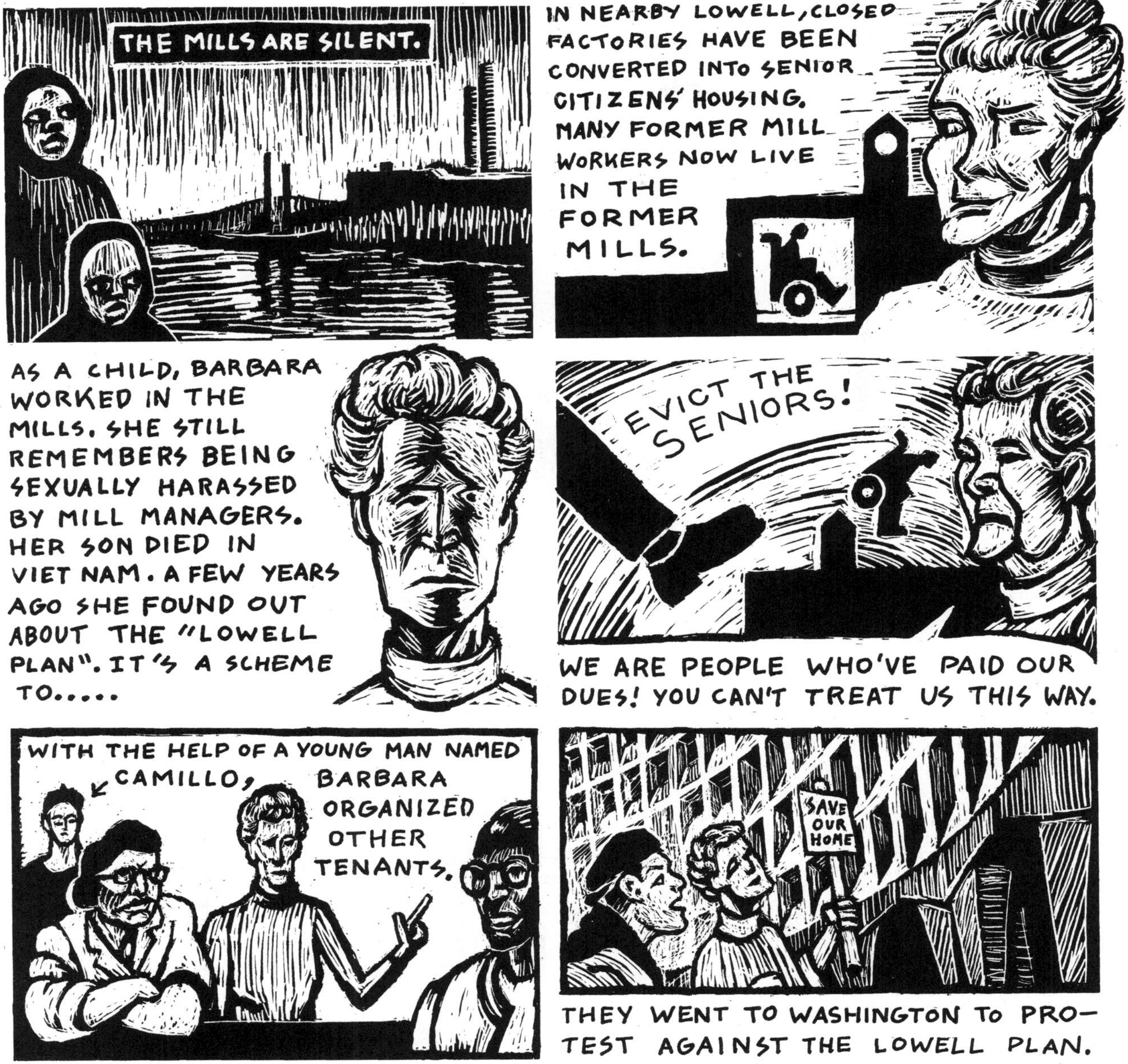
THE MILLS ARE SILENT.
IN NEARBY LOWELL, CLOSED FACTORIES HAVE BEEN CONVERTED INTO SENIOR CITIZENS' HOUSING. MANY FORMER MILL WORKERS NOW LIVE IN THE FORMER MILLS.
AS A CHILD, BARBARA WORKED IN THE MILLS. SHE STILL REMEMBERS BEING SEXUALLY HARASSED BY MILL MANAGERS. HER SON DIED IN VIET NAM. A FEW YEARS AGO SHE FOUND OUT ABOUT THE "LOWELL PLAN". IT'S A SCHEME TO.....
EVICT THE SENIORS!
WE ARE PEOPLE WHO'VE PAID OUR DUES! YOU CAN'T TREAT US THIS WAY.
WITH THE HELP OF A YOUNG MAN NAMED CAMILLO, BARBARA ORGANIZED OTHER TENANTS.
SAVE OUR HOME
THEY WENT TO WASHINGTON TO PROTEST AGAINST THE LOWELL PLAN.

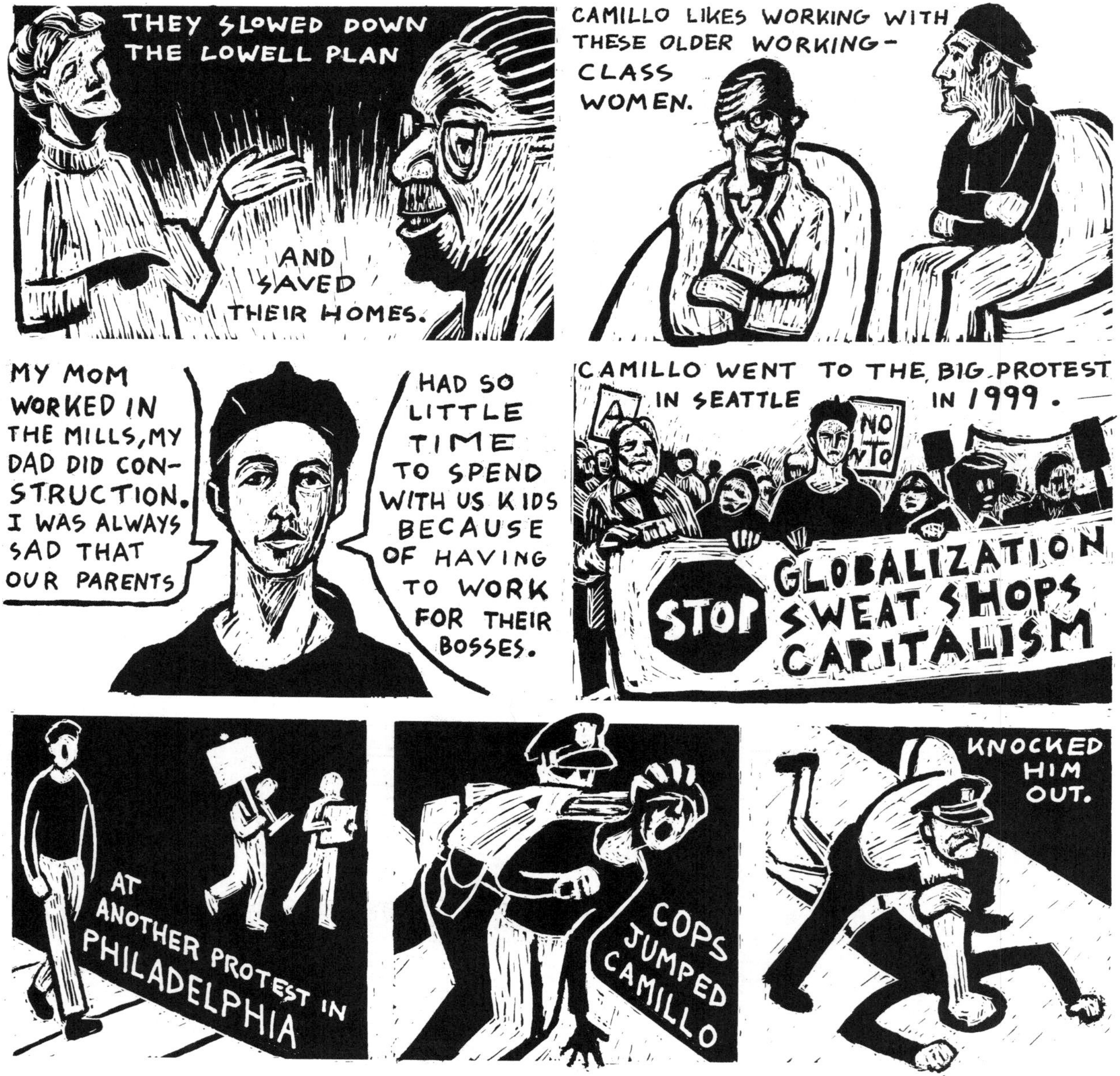
THEY SLOWED DOWN THE LOWELL PLAN
AND SAVED THEIR HOMES.
CAMILLO LIKES WORKING WITH THESE OLDER WORKING-CLASS WOMEN.
MY MOM WORKED IN THE MILLS, MY DAD DID CONSTRUCTION. I WAS ALWAYS SAD THAT OUR PARENTS
HAD SO LITTLE TIME TO SPEND WITH US KIDS BECAUSE OF HAVING TO WORK FOR THEIR BOSSES.
CAMILLO WENT TO THE BIG PROTEST IN SEATTLE IN 1999.
NO WTO
STOP GLOBALIZATION SWEAT SHOPS CAPITALISM
AT ANOTHER PROTEST IN PHILADELPHIA
COPS JUMPED CAMILLO
KNOCKED HIM OUT.

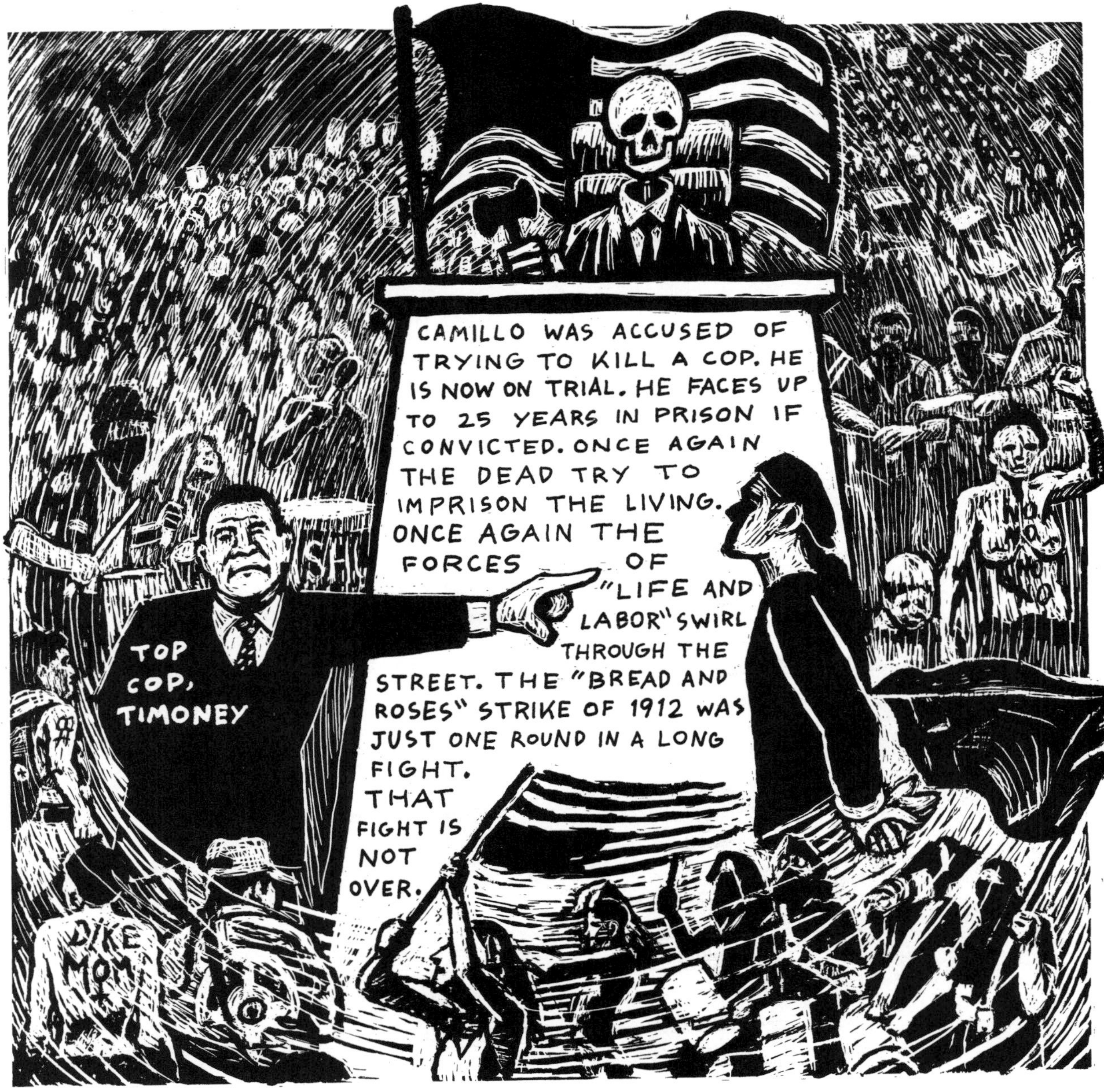
CAMILLO WAS ACCUSED OF TRYING TO KILL A COP. HE IS NOW ON TRIAL. HE FACES UP TO 25 YEARS IN PRISON IF CONVICTED. ONCE AGAIN THE DEAD TRY TO IMPRISON THE LIVING. ONCE AGAIN THE FORCES OF "LIFE AND LABOR" SWIRL THROUGH THE STREET. THE "BREAD AND ROSES" STRIKE OF 1912 WAS JUST ONE ROUND IN A LONG FIGHT.
THAT FIGHT IS NOT OVER.
TOP COP, TIMONEY
DIKE MOM

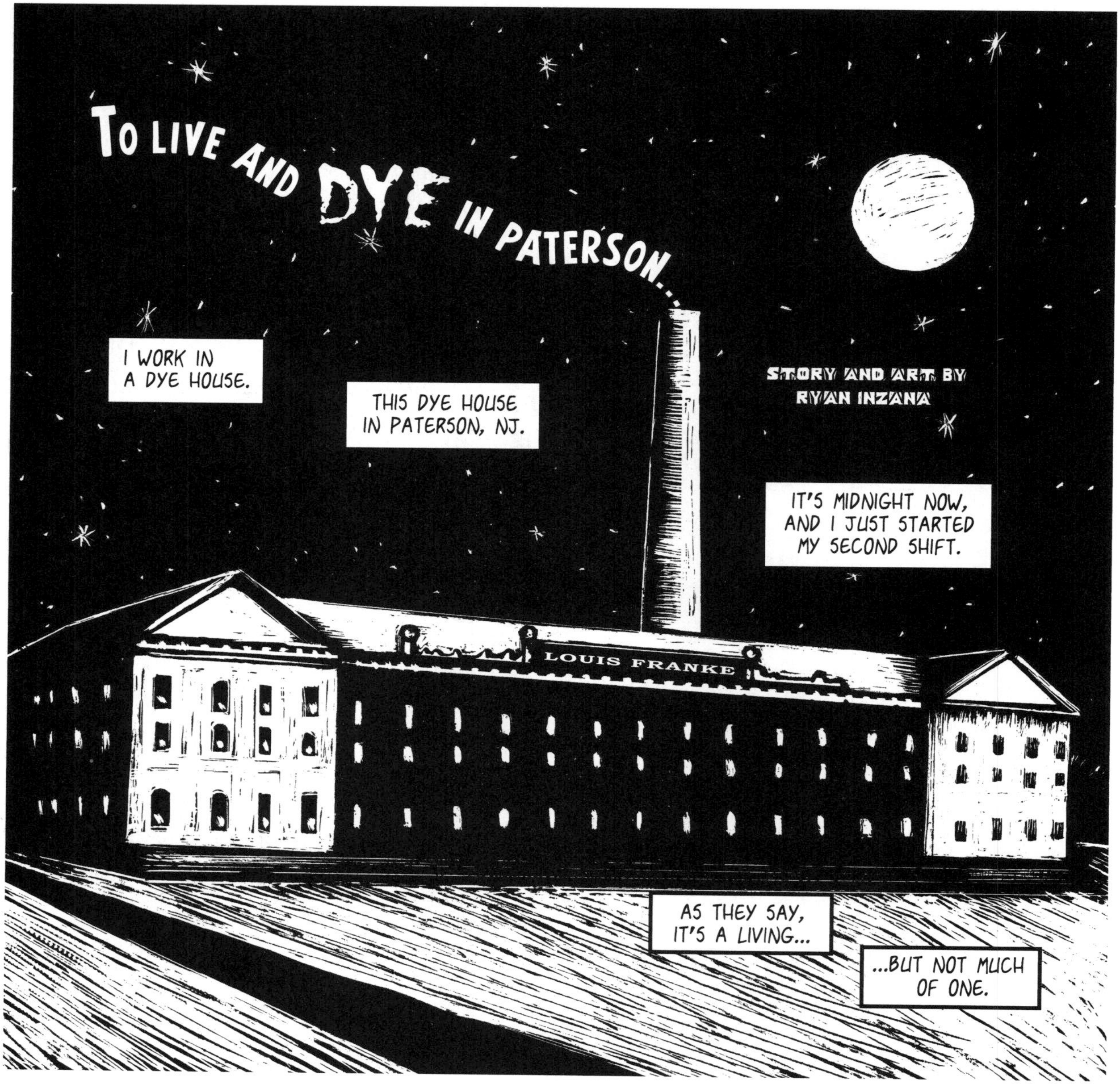
TO LIVE AND DYE IN PATERSON...
I WORK IN A DYE HOUSE.
THIS DYE HOUSE IN PATERSON, NJ.
STORY AND ART BY RYAN INZANA
IT'S MIDNIGHT NOW, AND I JUST STARTED MY SECOND SHIFT.
LOUIS FRANKE
AS THEY SAY, IT'S A LIVING...
...BUT NOT MUCH OF ONE.

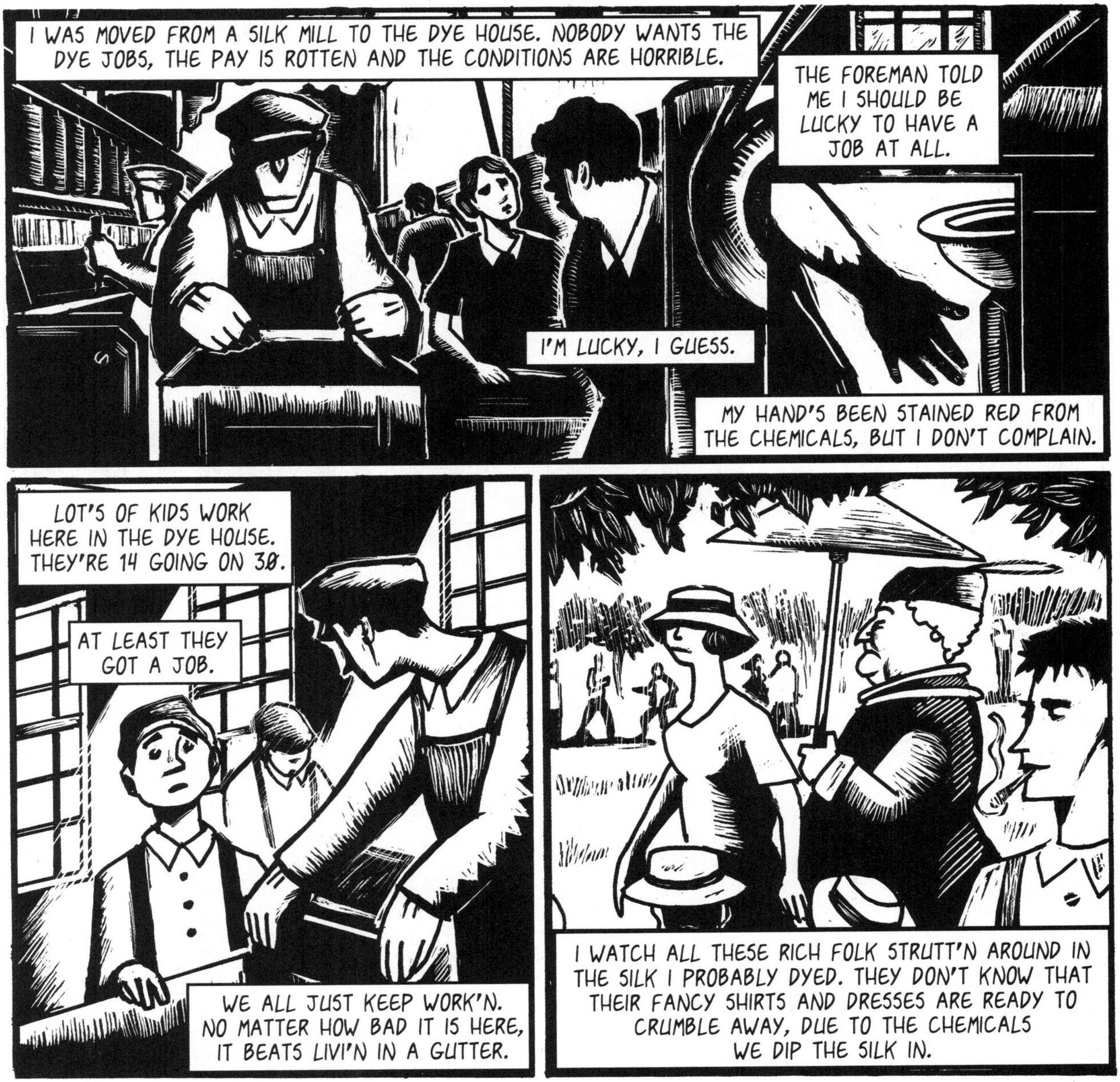
I WAS MOVED FROM A SILK MILL TO THE DYE HOUSE. NOBODY WANTS THE DYE JOBS, THE PAY IS ROTTEN AND THE CONDITIONS ARE HORRIBLE.
I'M LUCKY, I GUESS.
THE FOREMAN TOLD ME I SHOULD BE LUCKY TO HAVE A JOB AT ALL.
MY HAND'S BEEN STAINED RED FROM THE CHEMICALS, BUT I DON'T COMPLAIN.
LOT'S OF KIDS WORK HERE IN THE DYE HOUSE. THEY'RE 14 GOING ON 30.
AT LEAST THEY GOT A JOB.
WE ALL JUST KEEP WORK'N. NO MATTER HOW BAD IT IS HERE, IT BEATS LIVI'N IN A GUTTER.
I WATCH ALL THESE RICH FOLK STRUTT'N AROUND IN THE SILK I PROBABLY DYED. THEY DON'T KNOW THAT THEIR FANCY SHIRTS AND DRESSES ARE READY TO CRUMBLE AWAY, DUE TO THE CHEMICALS WE DIP THE SILK IN.

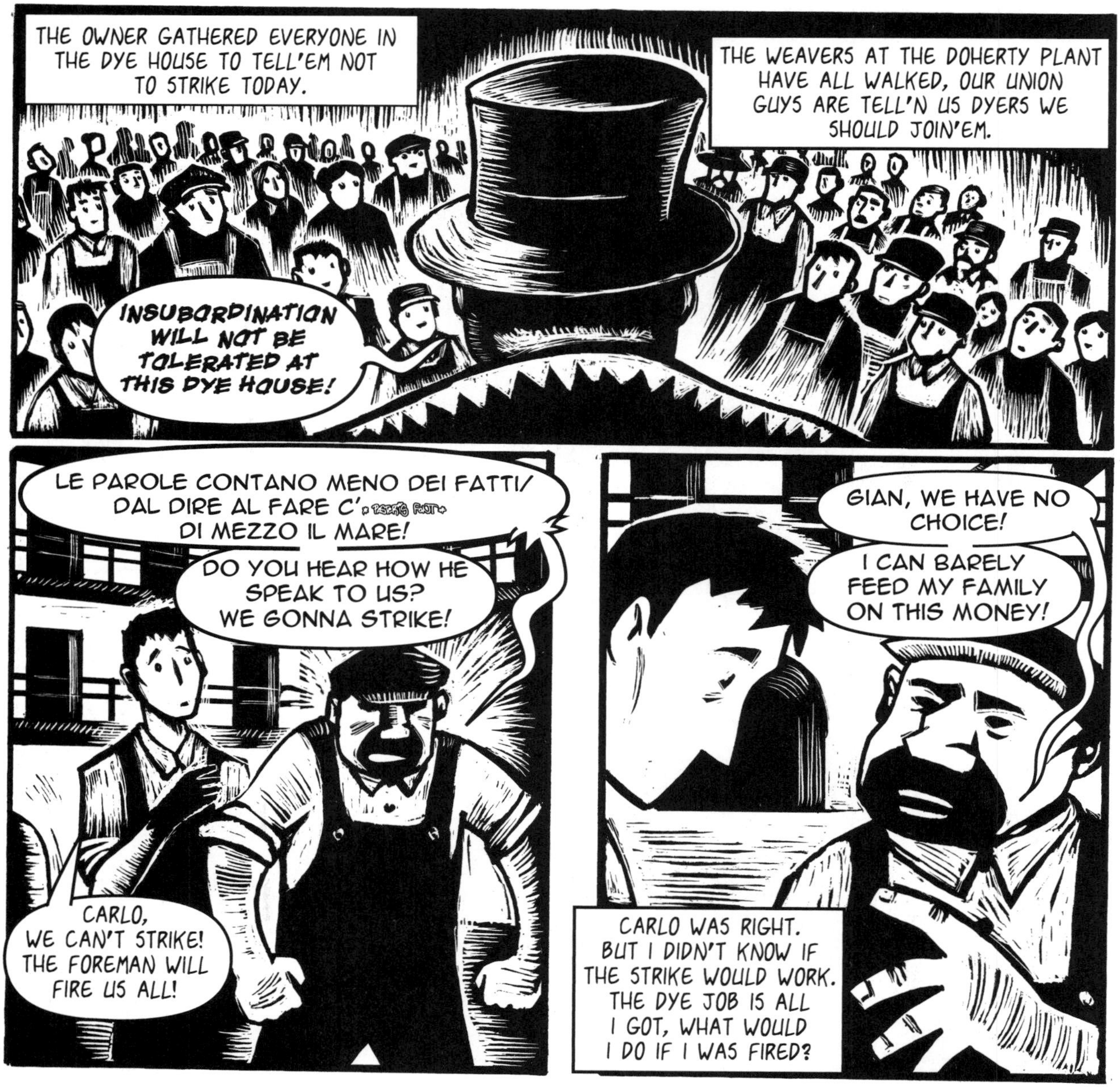
THE OWNER GATHERED EVERYONE IN THE DYE HOUSE TO TELL'EM NOT TO STRIKE TODAY.
THE WEAVERS AT THE DOHERTY PLANT HAVE ALL WALKED, OUR UNION GUYS ARE TELL'N US DYERS WE SHOULD JOIN'EM.
INSUBORDINATION WILL NOT BE TOLERATED AT THIS DYE HOUSE!
LE PAROLE CONTANO MENO DEI FATTI/ DAL DIRE AL FARE C' DI MEZZO IL MARE!
DO YOU HEAR HOW HE SPEAK TO US? WE GONNA STRIKE!
CARLO, WE CAN'T STRIKE! THE FOREMAN WILL FIRE US ALL!
GIAN, WE HAVE NO CHOICE!
I CAN BARELY FEED MY FAMILY ON THIS MONEY!
CARLO WAS RIGHT. BUT I DIDN'T KNOW IF THE STRIKE WOULD WORK. THE DYE JOB IS ALL I GOT, WHAT WOULD I DO IF I WAS FIRED?

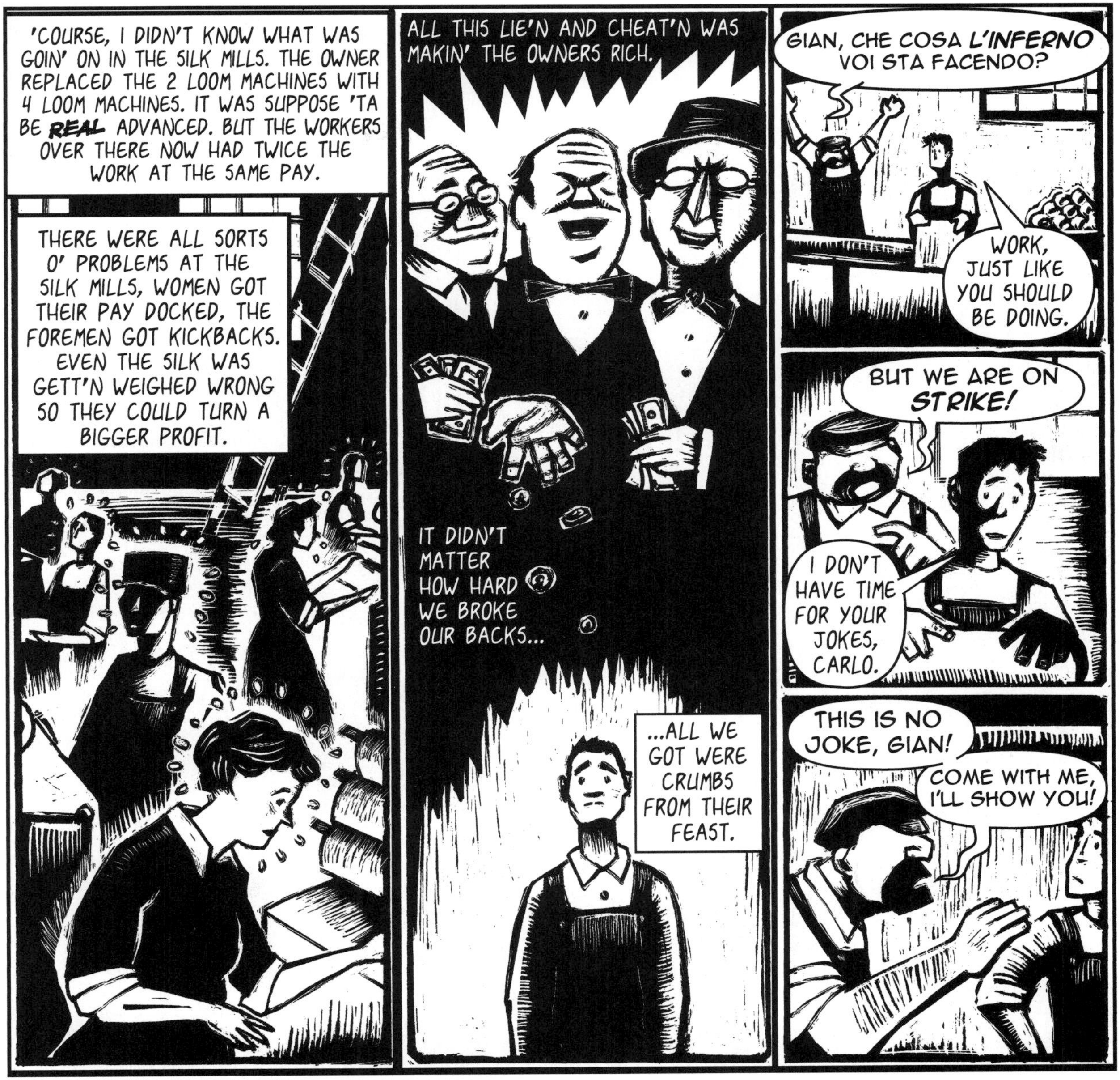
'COURSE, I DIDN'T KNOW WHAT WAS GOIN' ON IN THE SILK MILLS. THE OWNER REPLACED THE 2 LOOM MACHINES WITH 4 LOOM MACHINES. IT WAS SUPPOSE 'TA BE REAL ADVANCED. BUT THE WORKERS OVER THERE NOW HAD TWICE THE WORK AT THE SAME PAY.
THERE WERE ALL SORTS O' PROBLEMS AT THE SILK MILLS, WOMEN GOT THEIR PAY DOCKED, THE FOREMEN GOT KICKBACKS. EVEN THE SILK WAS GETT'N WEIGHED WRONG SO THEY COULD TURN A BIGGER PROFIT.
ALL THIS LIE'N AND CHEAT'N WAS MAKIN' THE OWNERS RICH.
IT DIDN'T MATTER HOW HARD WE BROKE OUR BACKS...
...ALL WE GOT WERE CRUMBS FROM THEIR FEAST.
GIAN, CHE COSA L'INFERNO VOI STA FACENDO?
WORK, JUST LIKE YOU SHOULD BE DOING.
BUT WE ARE ON STRIKE!
I DON'T HAVE TIME FOR YOUR JOKES, CARLO.
THIS IS NO JOKE, GIAN!
COME WITH ME, I'LL SHOW YOU!

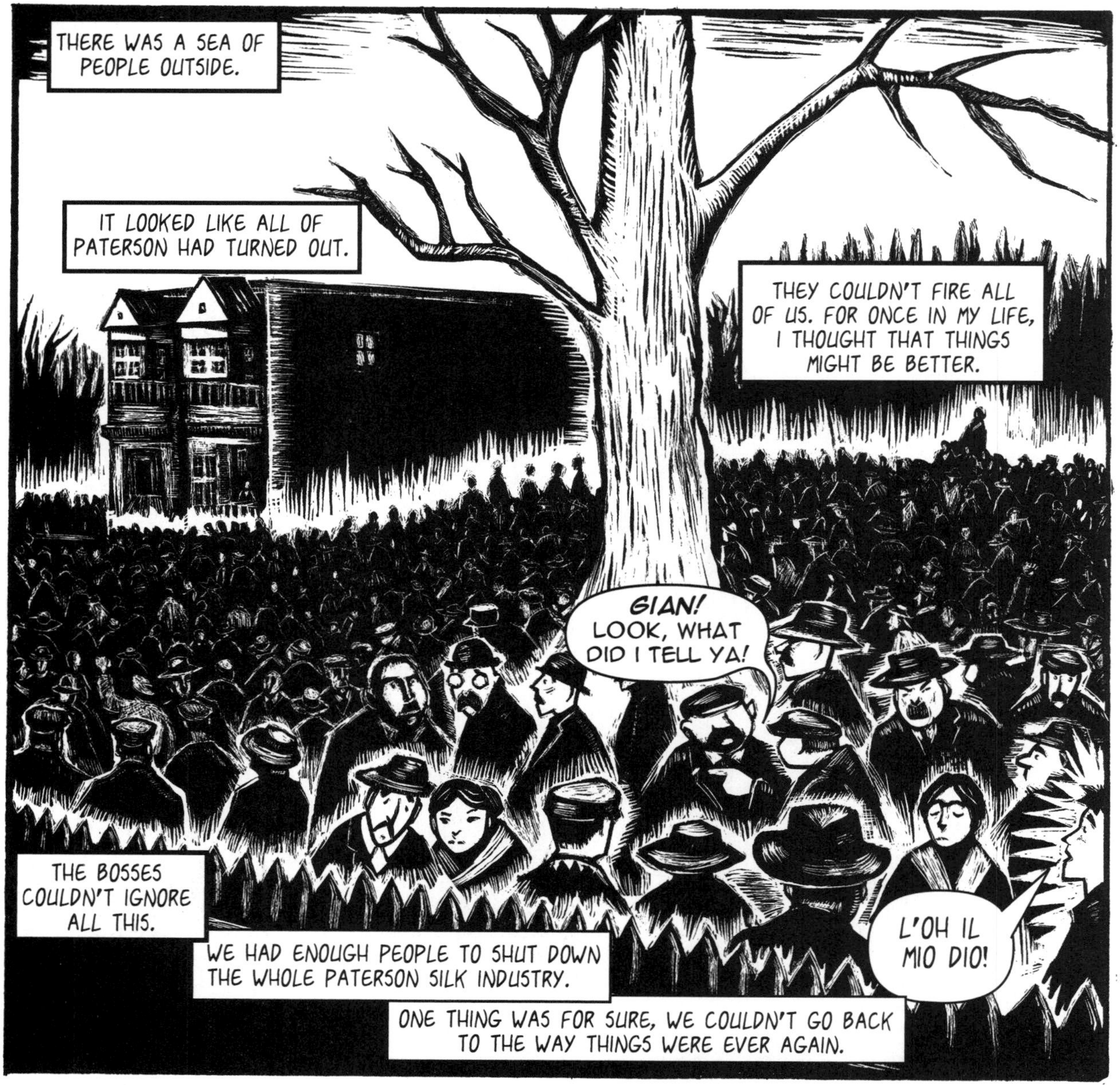
THERE WAS A SEA OF PEOPLE OUTSIDE.
IT LOOKED LIKE ALL OF PATERSON HAD TURNED OUT.
THEY COULDN'T FIRE ALL OF US. FOR ONCE IN MY LIFE, I THOUGHT THAT THINGS MIGHT BE BETTER.
GIAN! LOOK, WHAT DID I TELL YA!
THE BOSSES COULDN'T IGNORE ALL THIS.
WE HAD ENOUGH PEOPLE TO SHUT DOWN THE WHOLE PATERSON SILK INDUSTRY.
L'OH IL MIO DIO!
ONE THING WAS FOR SURE, WE COULDN'T GO BACK TO THE WAY THINGS WERE EVER AGAIN.

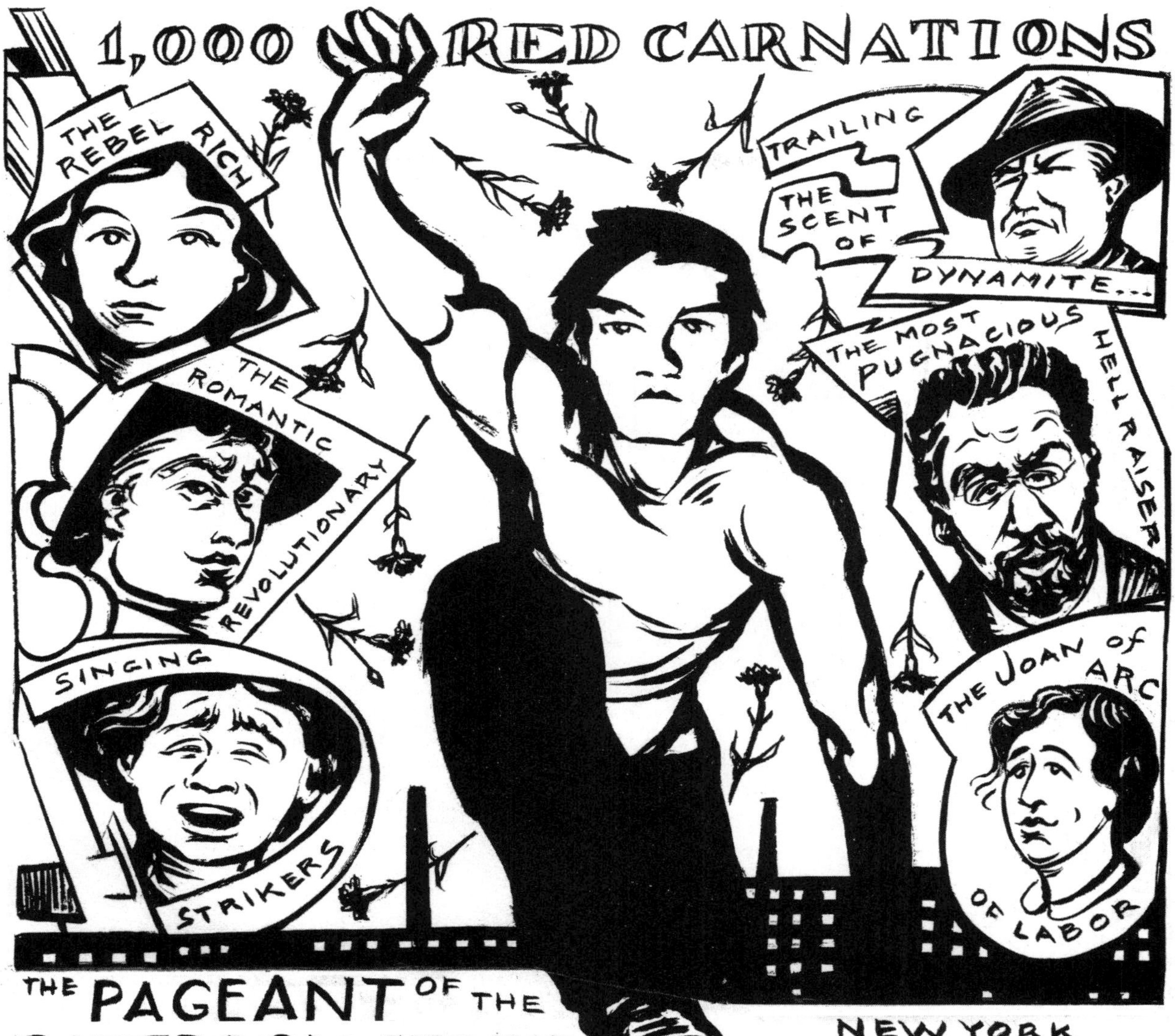
1,000 RED CARNATIONS
THE REBEL RICH
THE ROMANTIC REVOLUTIONARY
SINGING STRIKERS
TRAILING THE SCENT OF DYNAMITE...
THE MOST PUGNACIOUS HELL RAISER
THE JOAN OF ARC OF LABOR
THE PAGEANT OF THE PATERSON STRIKE
NEW YORK 1913
BY SABRINA JONES

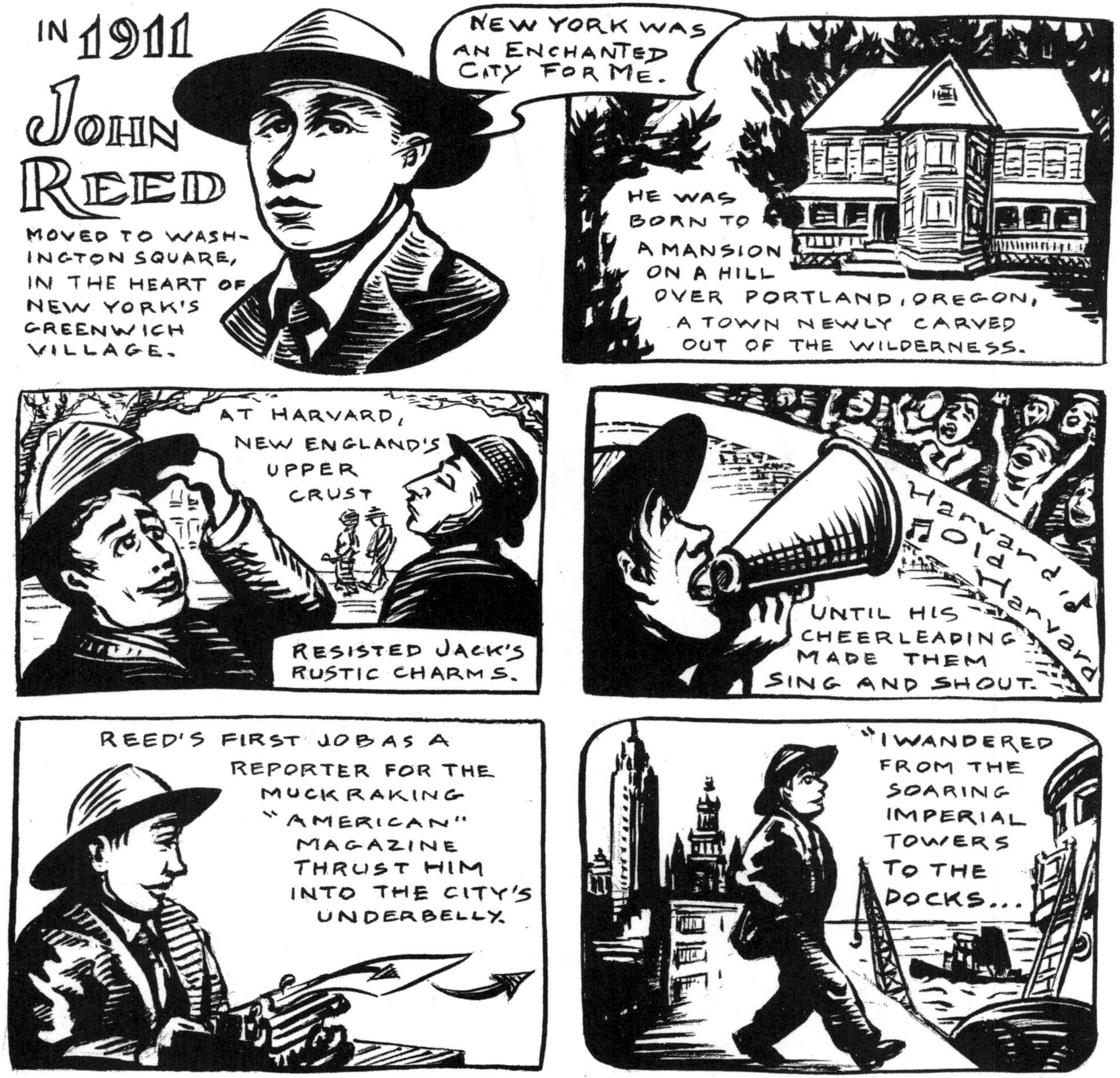
IN 1911
JOHN REED
MOVED TO WASHINGTON SQUARE, IN THE HEART OF NEW YORK'S GREENWICH VILLAGE.
NEW YORK WAS AN ENCHANTED CITY FOR ME.
HE WAS BORN TO A MANSION ON A HILL OVER PORTLAND, OREGON, A TOWN NEWLY CARVED OUT OF THE WILDERNESS.
AT HARVARD, NEW ENGLAND'S UPPER CRUST
RESISTED JACK'S RUSTIC CHARMS.
Harvard, Old Harvard
UNTIL HIS CHEERLEADING MADE THEM SING AND SHOUT.
REED'S FIRST JOB AS A REPORTER FOR THE MUCKRAKING "AMERICAN" MAGAZINE THRUST HIM INTO THE CITY'S UNDERBELLY.
"I WANDERED FROM THE SOARING IMPERIAL TOWERS TO THE DOCKS...

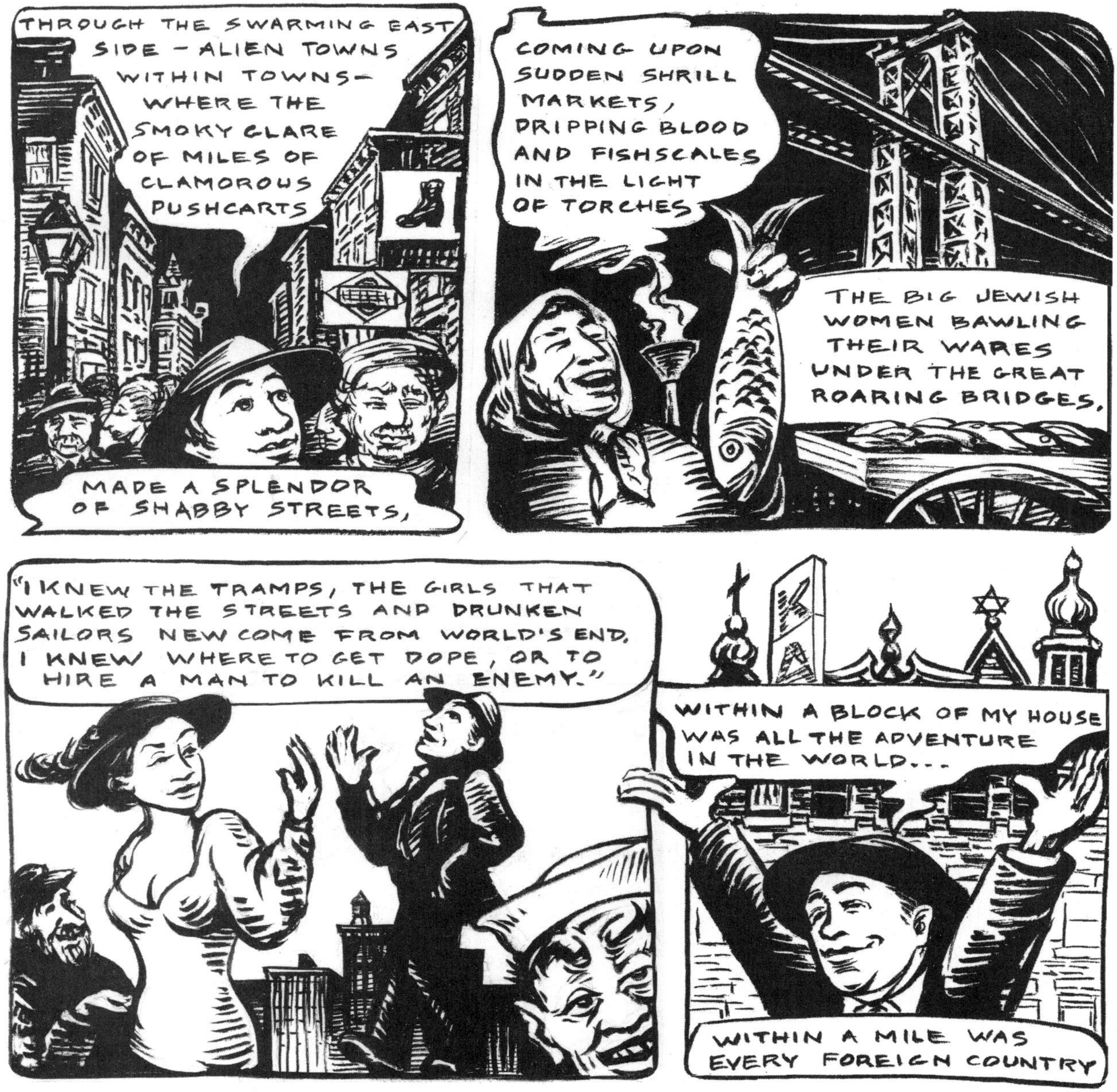
THROUGH THE SWARMING EAST SIDE – ALIEN TOWNS WITHIN TOWNS– WHERE THE SMOKY GLARE OF MILES OF CLAMOROUS PUSHCARTS
MADE A SPLENDOR OF SHABBY STREETS,
COMING UPON SUDDEN SHRILL MARKETS, DRIPPING BLOOD AND FISHSCALES IN THE LIGHT OF TORCHES
THE BIG JEWISH WOMEN BAWLING THEIR WARES UNDER THE GREAT ROARING BRIDGES.
"I KNEW THE TRAMPS, THE GIRLS THAT WALKED THE STREETS AND DRUNKEN SAILORS NEW COME FROM WORLD'S END. I KNEW WHERE TO GET DOPE, OR TO HIRE A MAN TO KILL AN ENEMY."
WITHIN A BLOCK OF MY HOUSE WAS ALL THE ADVENTURE IN THE WORLD...
WITHIN A MILE WAS EVERY FOREIGN COUNTRY

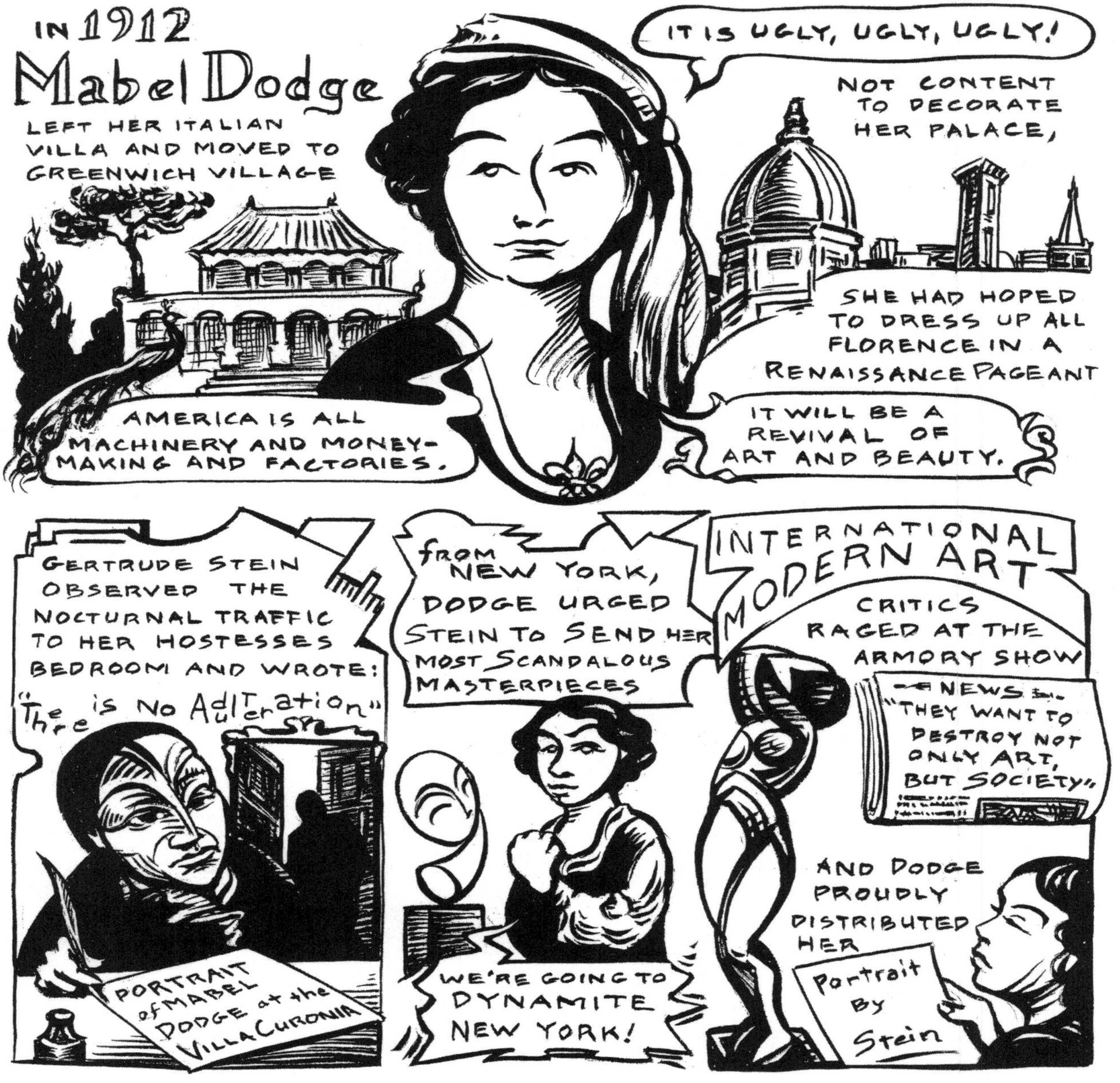

IN 1912
Mabel Dodge
LEFT HER ITALIAN VILLA AND MOVED TO GREENWICH VILLAGE
AMERICA IS ALL MACHINERY AND MONEY-MAKING AND FACTORIES.
IT IS UGLY, UGLY, UGLY!
NOT CONTENT TO DECORATE HER PALACE,
SHE HAD HOPED TO DRESS UP ALL FLORENCE IN A RENAISSANCE PAGEANT
IT WILL BE A REVIVAL OF ART AND BEAUTY.
GERTRUDE STEIN OBSERVED THE NOCTURNAL TRAFFIC TO HER HOSTESSES BEDROOM AND WROTE:
"There is No Adulteration"
PORTRAIT of MABEL DODGE at the VILLA CURONIA
FROM NEW YORK, DODGE URGED STEIN TO SEND HER MOST SCANDALOUS MASTERPIECES
WE'RE GOING TO DYNAMITE NEW YORK!
INTERNATIONAL MODERN ART
CRITICS RAGED AT THE ARMORY SHOW
NEWS
"THEY WANT TO DESTROY NOT ONLY ART, BUT SOCIETY"
AND DODGE PROUDLY DISTRIBUTED HER
Portrait By Stein

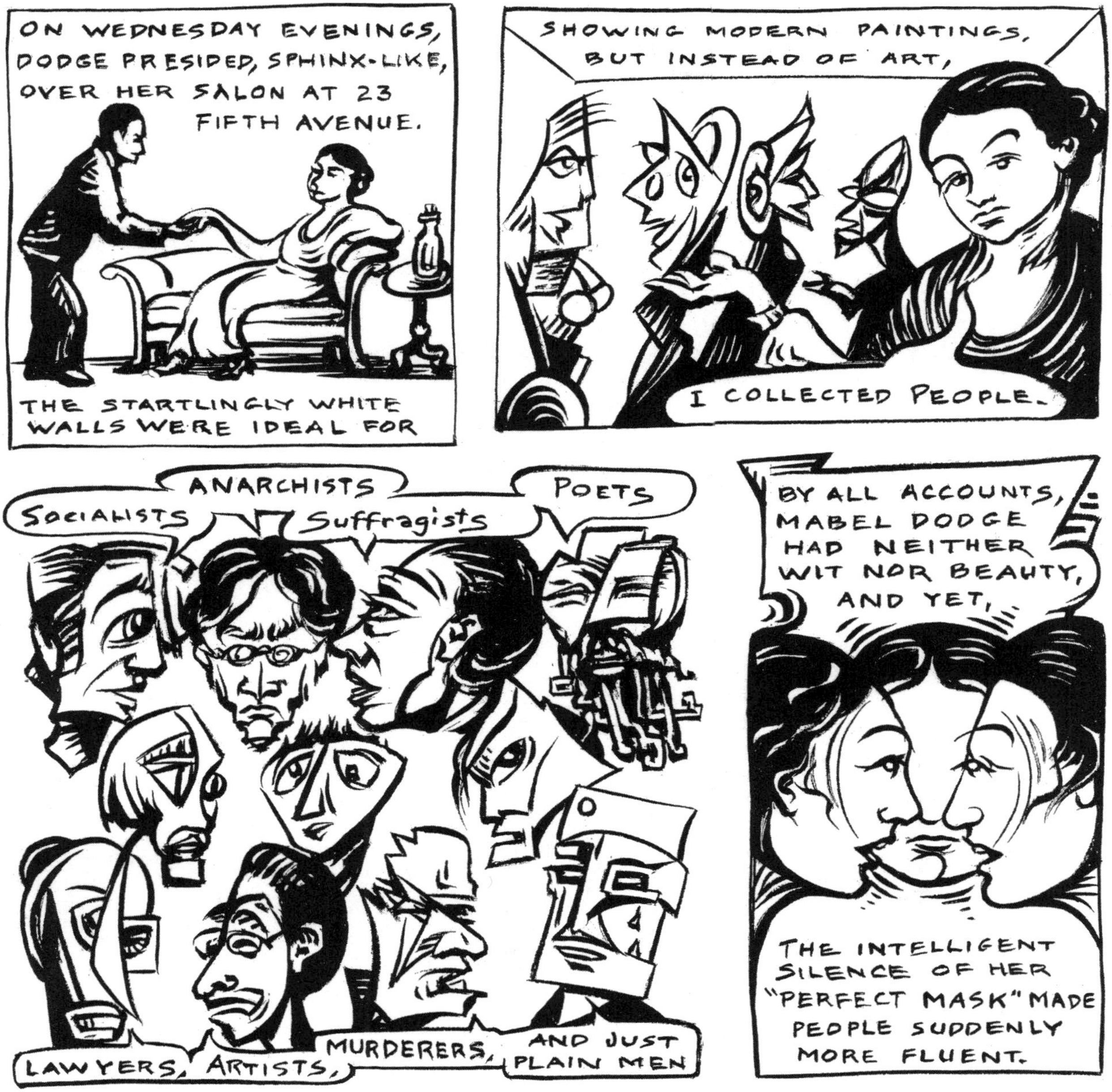
ON WEDNESDAY EVENINGS, DODGE PRESIDED, SPHINX-LIKE, OVER HER SALON AT 23 FIFTH AVENUE.
THE STARTLINGLY WHITE WALLS WERE IDEAL FOR
SHOWING MODERN PAINTINGS, BUT INSTEAD OF ART,
I COLLECTED PEOPLE.
Socialists
ANARCHISTS
Suffragists
POETS
LAWYERS,
ARTISTS,
MURDERERS,
AND JUST PLAIN MEN
BY ALL ACCOUNTS, MABEL DODGE HAD NEITHER WIT NOR BEAUTY, AND YET,
THE INTELLIGENT SILENCE OF HER "PERFECT MASK" MADE PEOPLE SUDDENLY MORE FLUENT.

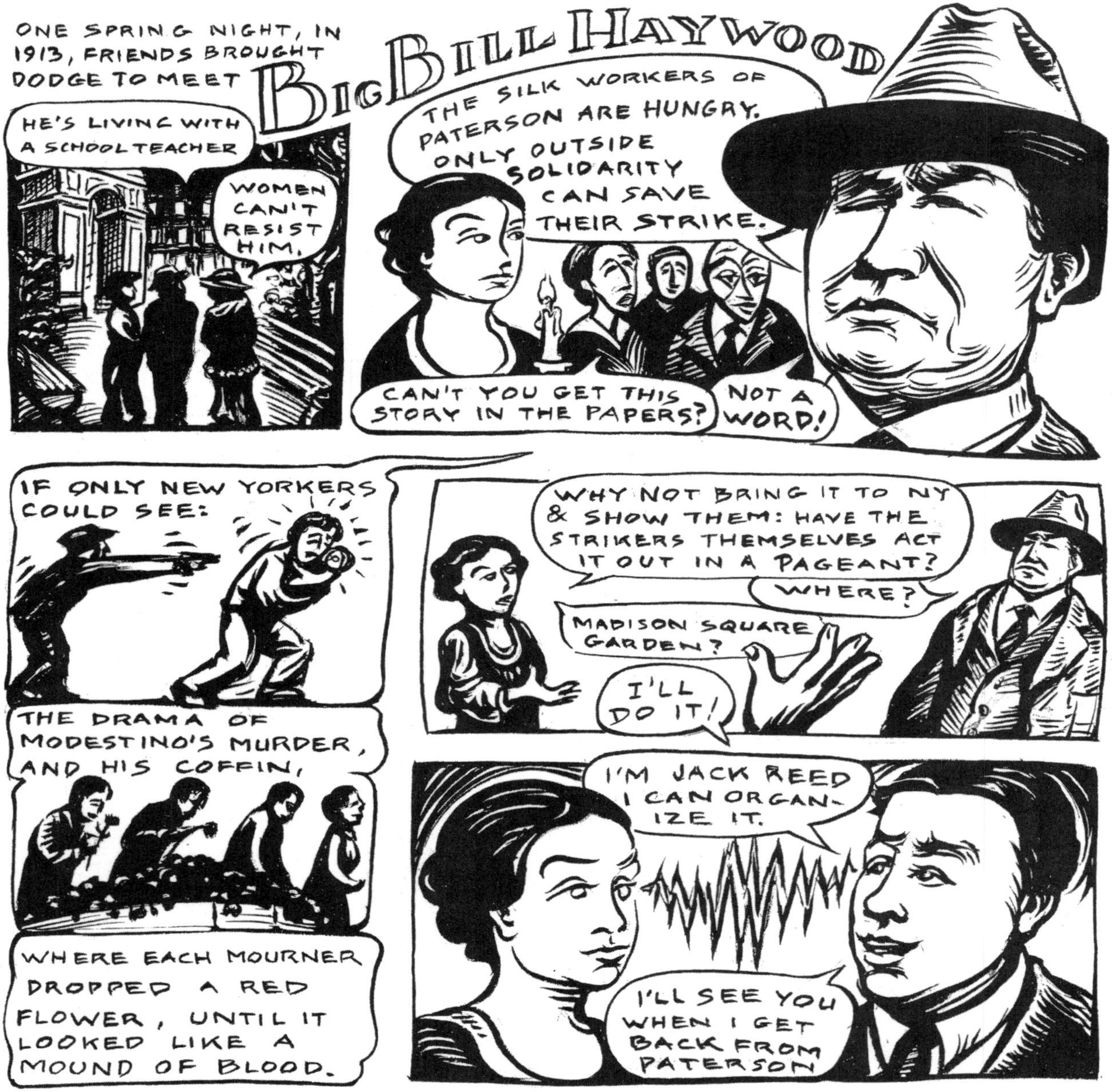

ONE SPRING NIGHT, IN 1913, FRIENDS BROUGHT DODGE TO MEET
BIG BILL HAYWOOD
HE'S LIVING WITH A SCHOOL TEACHER
WOMEN CAN'T RESIST HIM.
THE SILK WORKERS OF PATERSON ARE HUNGRY. ONLY OUTSIDE SOLIDARITY CAN SAVE THEIR STRIKE.
CAN'T YOU GET THIS STORY IN THE PAPERS?
NOT A WORD!
IF ONLY NEW YORKERS COULD SEE:
THE DRAMA OF MODESTINO'S MURDER, AND HIS COFFIN,
WHERE EACH MOURNER DROPPED A RED FLOWER, UNTIL IT LOOKED LIKE A MOUND OF BLOOD.
WHY NOT BRING IT TO NY & SHOW THEM: HAVE THE STRIKERS THEMSELVES ACT IT OUT IN A PAGEANT?
WHERE?
MADISON SQUARE GARDEN?
I'LL DO IT!
I'M JACK REED I CAN ORGANIZE IT.
I'LL SEE YOU WHEN I GET BACK FROM PATERSON

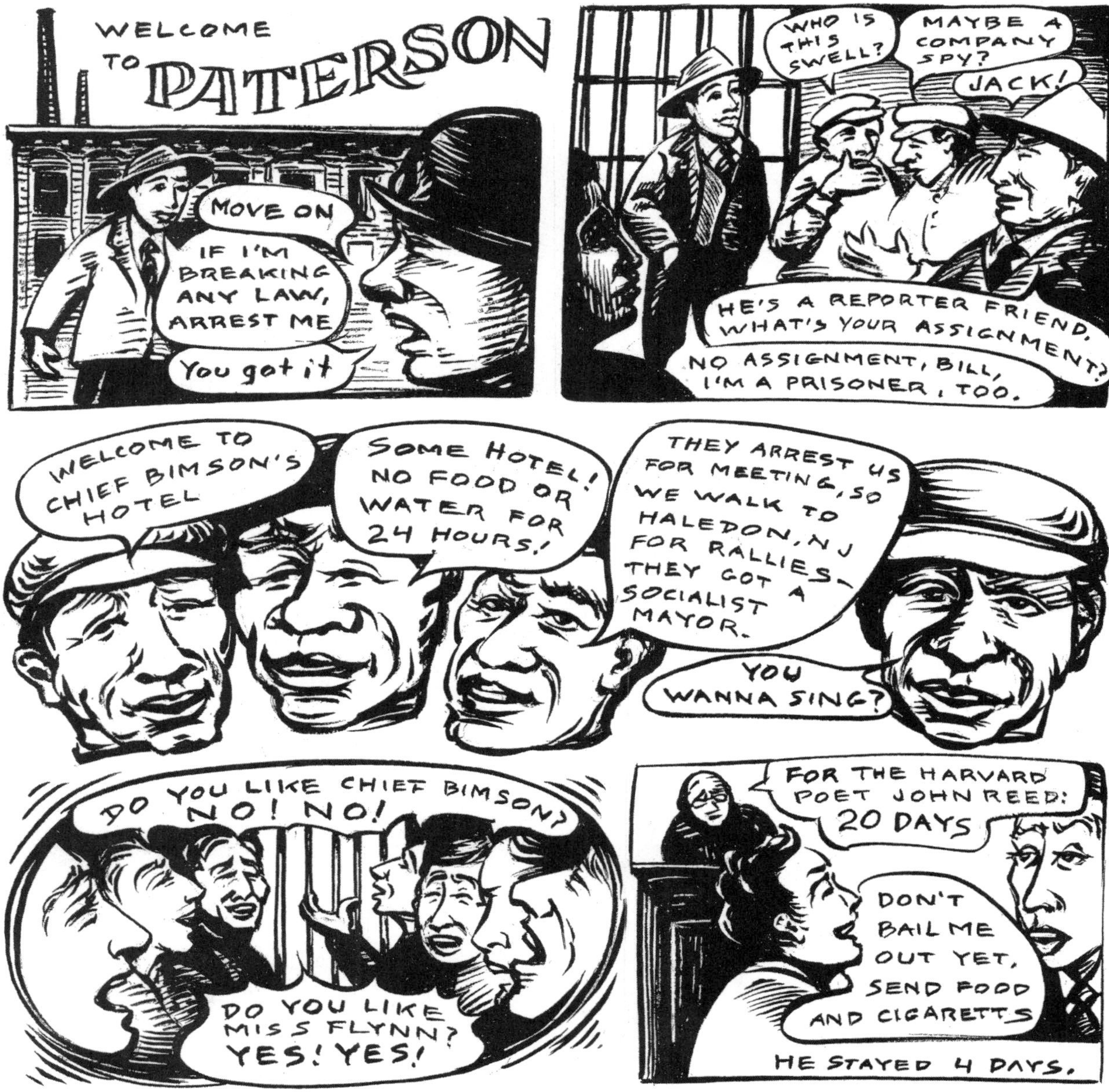
WELCOME TO PATERSON
MOVE ON
IF I'M BREAKING ANY LAW, ARREST ME
You got it
WHO IS THIS SWELL?
MAYBE A COMPANY SPY?
JACK!
HE'S A REPORTER FRIEND. WHAT'S YOUR ASSIGNMENT?
NO ASSIGNMENT, BILL, I'M A PRISONER, TOO.
WELCOME TO CHIEF BIMSON'S HOTEL
SOME HOTEL! NO FOOD OR WATER FOR 24 HOURS!
THEY ARREST US FOR MEETING, SO WE WALK TO HALEDON, NJ FOR RALLIES — THEY GOT A SOCIALIST MAYOR.
YOU WANNA SING?
DO YOU LIKE CHIEF BIMSON?
NO! NO!
DO YOU LIKE MISS FLYNN?
YES! YES!
FOR THE HARVARD POET JOHN REED: 20 DAYS
DON'T BAIL ME OUT YET, SEND FOOD AND CIGARETTS
HE STAYED 4 DAYS.

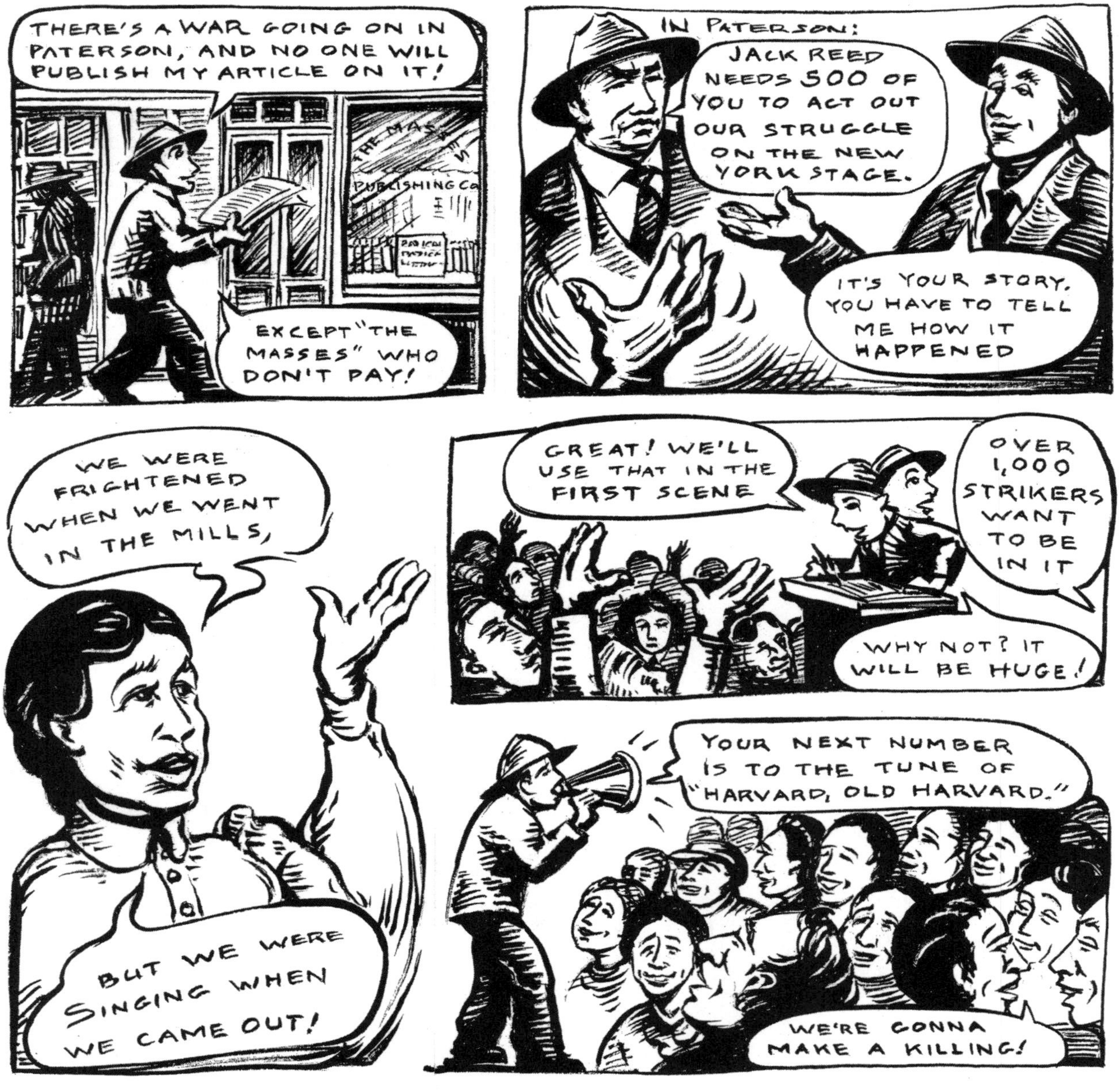
THERE'S A WAR GOING ON IN PATERSON, AND NO ONE WILL PUBLISH MY ARTICLE ON IT!
THE MASSES PUBLISHING CO.
EXCEPT "THE MASSES" WHO DON'T PAY!
IN PATERSON:
JACK REED NEEDS 500 OF YOU TO ACT OUT OUR STRUGGLE ON THE NEW YORK STAGE.
IT'S YOUR STORY. YOU HAVE TO TELL ME HOW IT HAPPENED
WE WERE FRIGHTENED WHEN WE WENT IN THE MILLS,
BUT WE WERE SINGING WHEN WE CAME OUT!
GREAT! WE'LL USE THAT IN THE FIRST SCENE
OVER 1,000 STRIKERS WANT TO BE IN IT
WHY NOT? IT WILL BE HUGE!
YOUR NEXT NUMBER IS TO THE TUNE OF "HARVARD, OLD HARVARD."
WE'RE GONNA MAKE A KILLING!

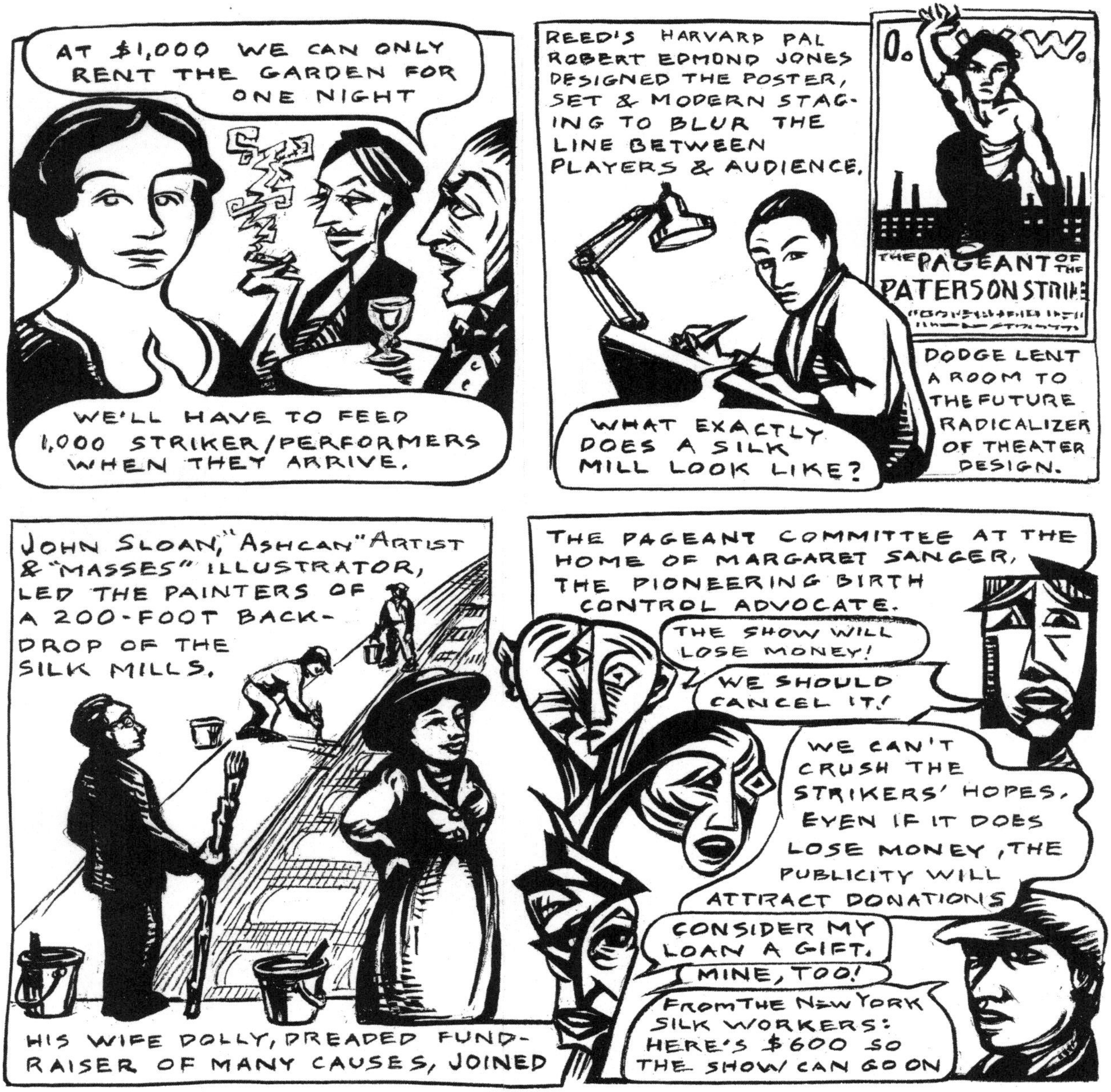

AT $1,000 WE CAN ONLY RENT THE GARDEN FOR ONE NIGHT
WE'LL HAVE TO FEED 1,000 STRIKER/PERFORMERS WHEN THEY ARRIVE.
REED'S HARVARD PAL ROBERT EDMOND JONES DESIGNED THE POSTER, SET & MODERN STAGING TO BLUR THE LINE BETWEEN PLAYERS & AUDIENCE.
THE PAGEANT OF THE PATERSON STRIKE
WHAT EXACTLY DOES A SILK MILL LOOK LIKE?
DODGE LENT A ROOM TO THE FUTURE RADICALIZER OF THEATER DESIGN.
JOHN SLOAN, "ASHCAN" ARTIST & "MASSES" ILLUSTRATOR, LED THE PAINTERS OF A 200-FOOT BACKDROP OF THE SILK MILLS.
HIS WIFE DOLLY, DREADED FUNDRAISER OF MANY CAUSES, JOINED
THE PAGEANT COMMITTEE AT THE HOME OF MARGARET SANGER, THE PIONEERING BIRTH CONTROL ADVOCATE.
THE SHOW WILL LOSE MONEY!
WE SHOULD CANCEL IT!
WE CAN'T CRUSH THE STRIKERS' HOPES. EVEN IF IT DOES LOSE MONEY, THE PUBLICITY WILL ATTRACT DONATIONS
CONSIDER MY LOAN A GIFT.
MINE, TOO!
FROM THE NEW YORK SILK WORKERS: HERE'S $600 SO THE SHOW CAN GO ON

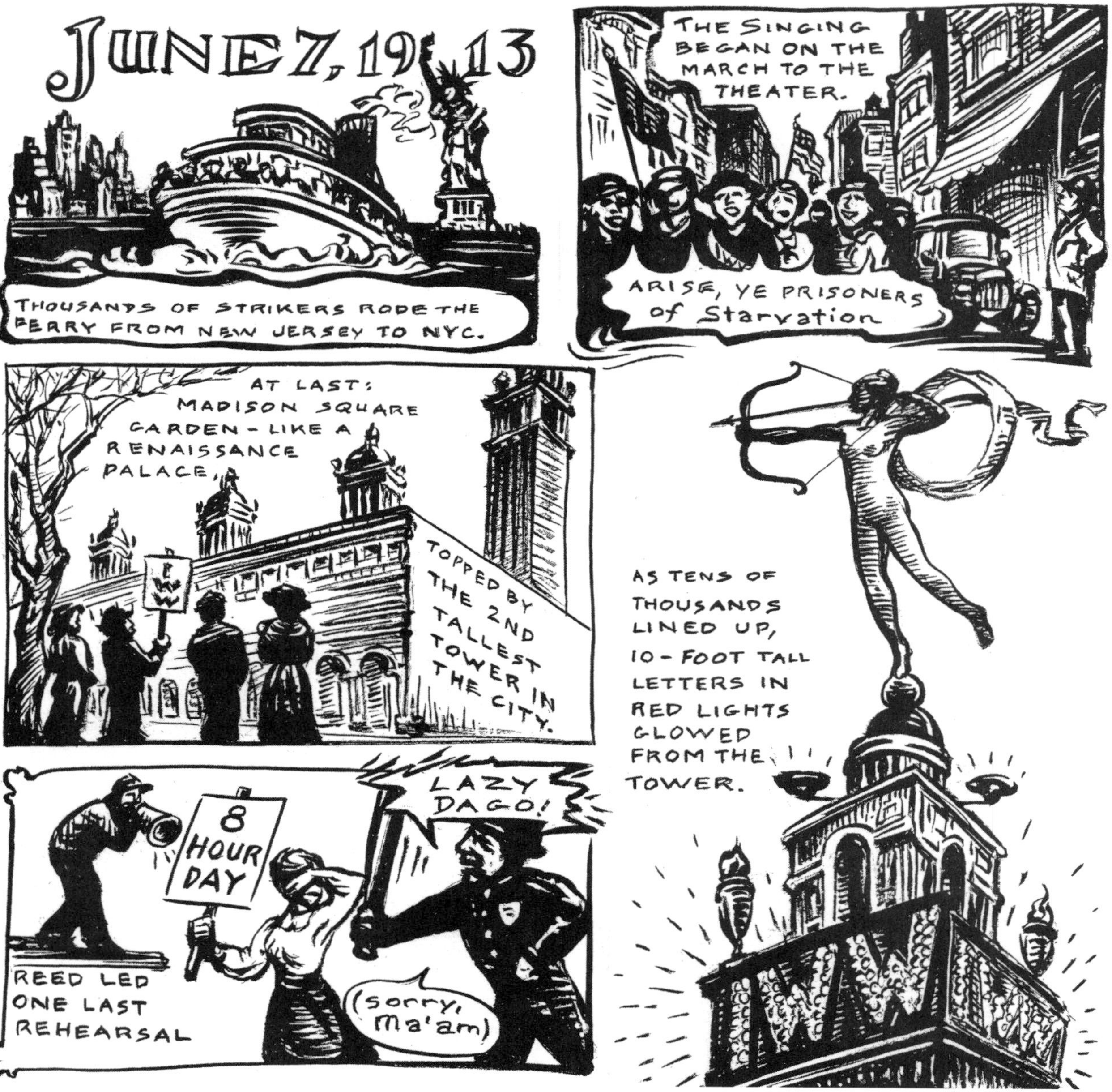
JUNE 7, 1913
THOUSANDS OF STRIKERS RODE THE FERRY FROM NEW JERSEY TO NYC.
THE SINGING BEGAN ON THE MARCH TO THE THEATER.
ARISE, YE PRISONERS of Starvation
AT LAST: MADISON SQUARE GARDEN - LIKE A RENAISSANCE PALACE,
TOPPED BY THE 2ND TALLEST TOWER IN THE CITY.
8 HOUR DAY
LAZY DAGO!
REED LED ONE LAST REHEARSAL
(sorry, Ma'am)
AS TENS OF THOUSANDS LINED UP, 10-FOOT TALL LETTERS IN RED LIGHTS GLOWED FROM THE TOWER.

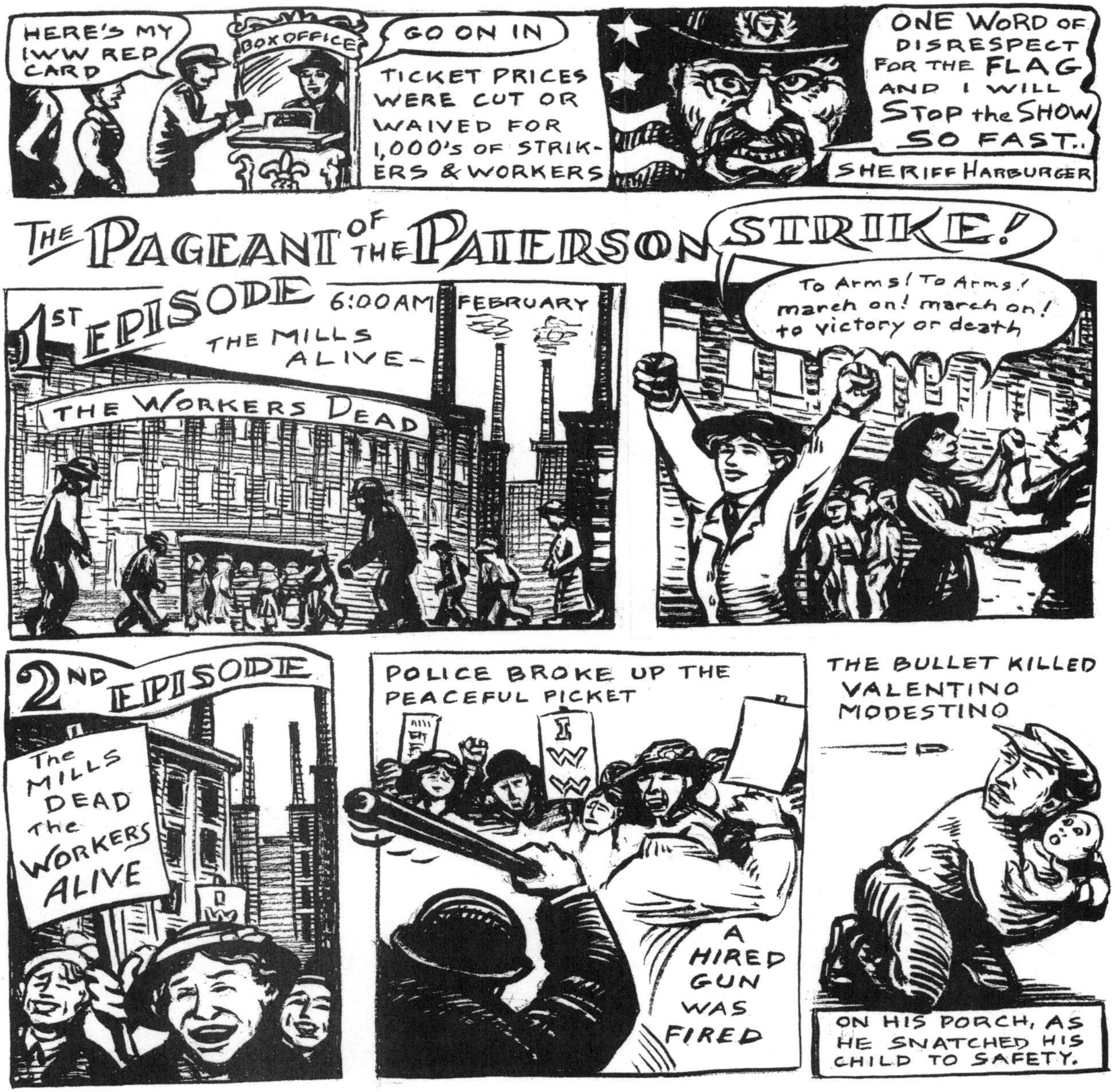
HERE'S MY IWW RED CARD
BOX OFFICE
GO ON IN
TICKET PRICES WERE CUT OR WAIVED FOR 1,000's OF STRIKERS & WORKERS
ONE WORD OF DISRESPECT FOR THE FLAG AND I WILL STOP the SHOW SO FAST.
SHERIFF HARBURGER
THE PAGEANT OF THE PATERSON STRIKE!
1ST EPISODE 6:00AM FEBRUARY
THE MILLS ALIVE-
THE WORKERS DEAD
To Arms! To Arms! march on! march on! to victory or death
2ND EPISODE
The MILLS DEAD the WORKERS ALIVE
I W W
POLICE BROKE UP THE PEACEFUL PICKET
I W W
A HIRED GUN WAS FIRED
THE BULLET KILLED VALENTINO MODESTINO
ON HIS PORCH, AS HE SNATCHED HIS CHILD TO SAFETY.

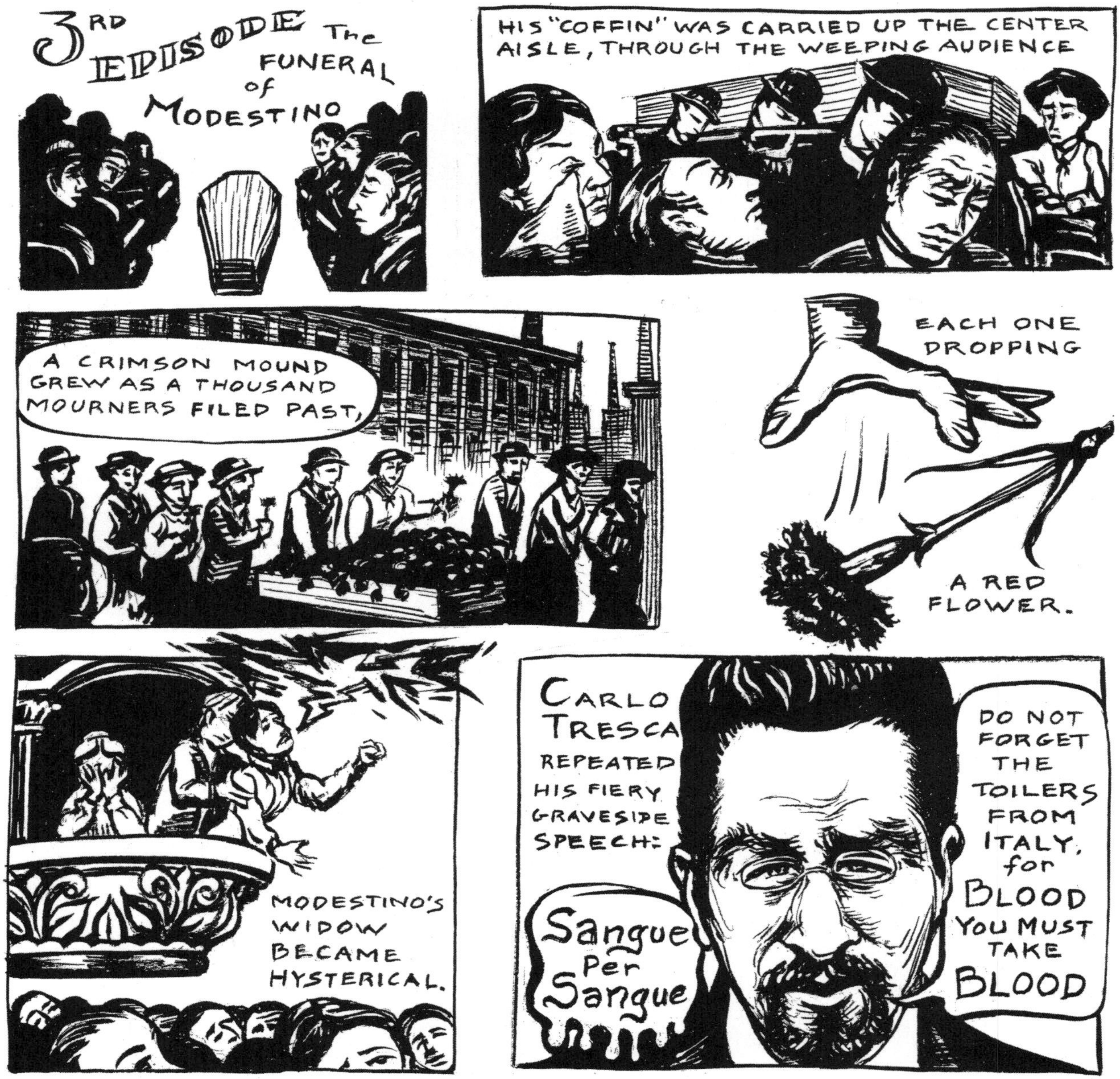
3RD EPISODE The FUNERAL of MODESTINO
HIS "COFFIN" WAS CARRIED UP THE CENTER AISLE, THROUGH THE WEEPING AUDIENCE
A CRIMSON MOUND GREW AS A THOUSAND MOURNERS FILED PAST,
EACH ONE DROPPING
A RED FLOWER.
MODESTINO'S WIDOW BECAME HYSTERICAL.
CARLO TRESCA REPEATED HIS FIERY GRAVESIDE SPEECH:
Sangue Per Sangue
DO NOT FORGET THE TOILERS FROM ITALY, for BLOOD YOU MUST TAKE BLOOD

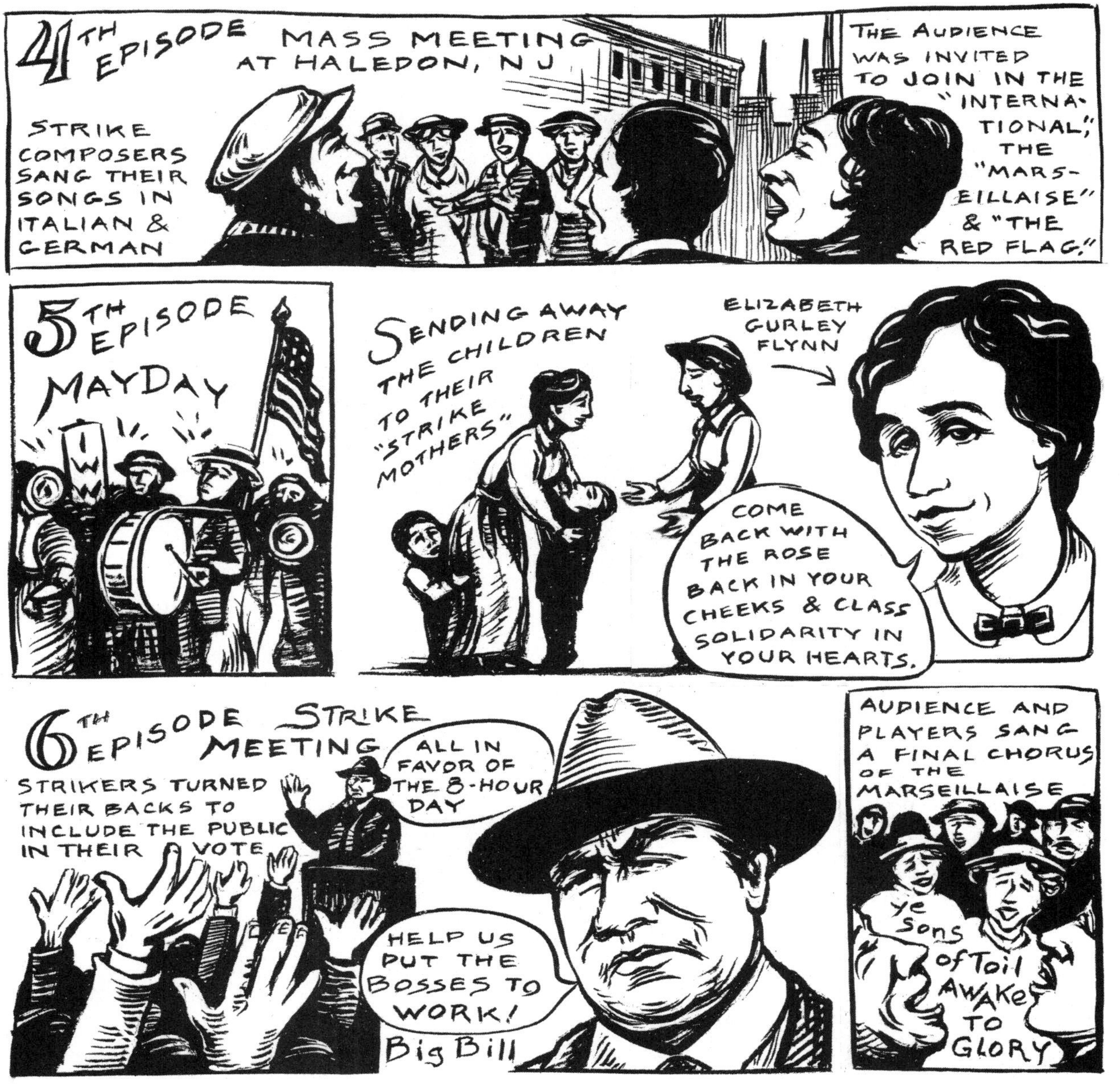
4TH EPISODE
MASS MEETING AT HALEDON, NJ
STRIKE COMPOSERS SANG THEIR SONGS IN ITALIAN & GERMAN
THE AUDIENCE WAS INVITED TO JOIN IN THE "INTERNATIONAL," THE "MARSEILLAISE" & "THE RED FLAG."
5TH EPISODE
MAYDAY
IWW
SENDING AWAY THE CHILDREN TO THEIR "STRIKE MOTHERS"
ELIZABETH GURLEY FLYNN
COME BACK WITH THE ROSE BACK IN YOUR CHEEKS & CLASS SOLIDARITY IN YOUR HEARTS.
6TH EPISODE STRIKE MEETING
STRIKERS TURNED THEIR BACKS TO INCLUDE THE PUBLIC IN THEIR VOTE
ALL IN FAVOR OF THE 8-HOUR DAY
HELP US PUT THE BOSSES TO WORK!
Big Bill
AUDIENCE AND PLAYERS SANG A FINAL CHORUS OF THE MARSEILLAISE
ye sons of Toil AWAKE TO GLORY

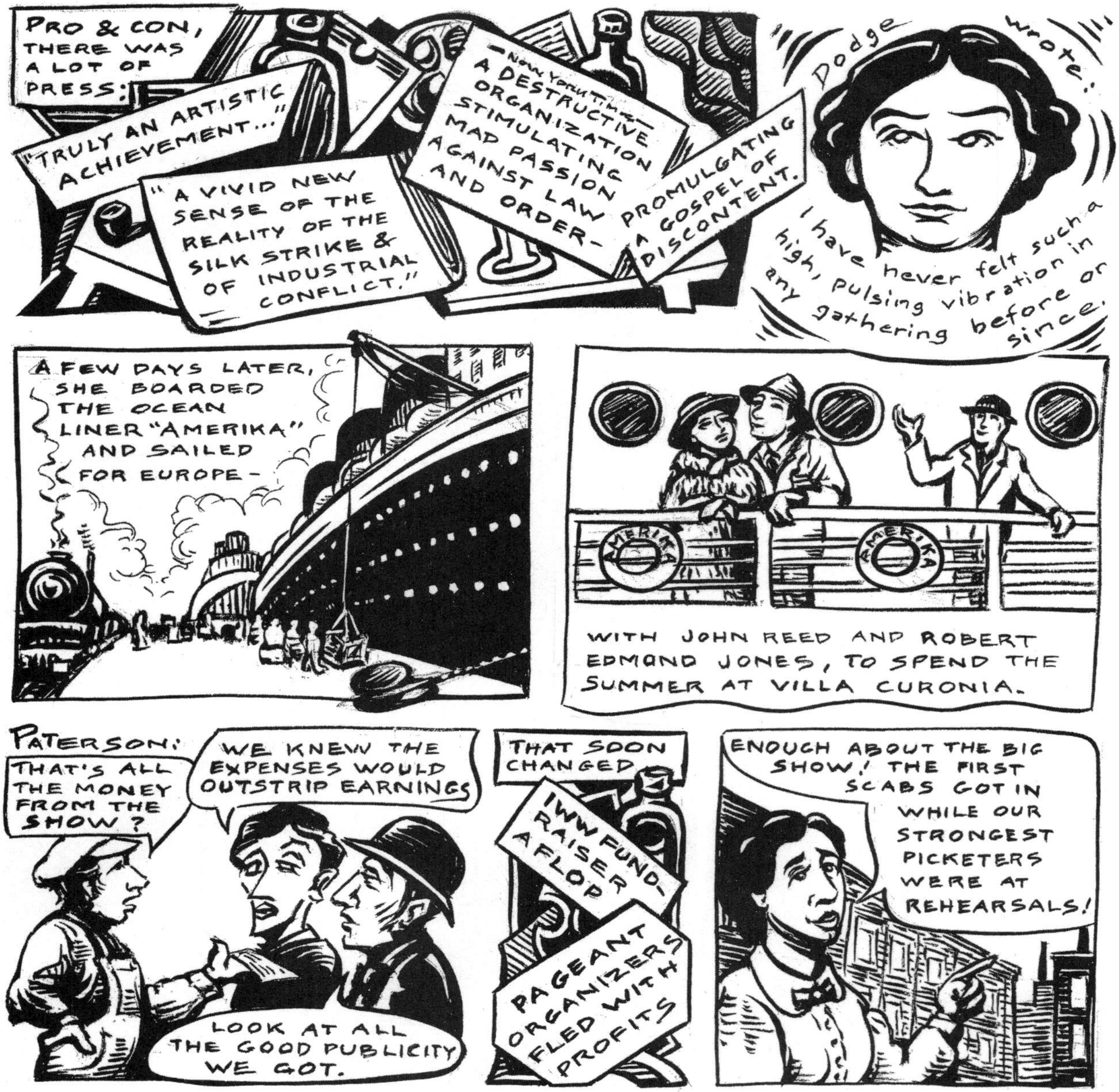
PRO & CON, THERE WAS A LOT OF PRESS:
"TRULY AN ARTISTIC ACHIEVEMENT..."
"A VIVID NEW SENSE OF THE REALITY OF THE SILK STRIKE & OF INDUSTRIAL CONFLICT."
—NEW YORK TIMES—
A DESTRUCTIVE ORGANIZATION STIMULATING MAD PASSION AGAINST LAW AND ORDER—
PROMULGATING A GOSPEL OF DISCONTENT.
Dodge wrote:
I have never felt such a high, pulsing vibration in any gathering before or since.
A FEW DAYS LATER, SHE BOARDED THE OCEAN LINER "AMERIKA" AND SAILED FOR EUROPE—
AMERIKA
AMERIKA
WITH JOHN REED AND ROBERT EDMOND JONES, TO SPEND THE SUMMER AT VILLA CURONIA.
PATERSON:
THAT'S ALL THE MONEY FROM THE SHOW?
WE KNEW THE EXPENSES WOULD OUTSTRIP EARNINGS
LOOK AT ALL THE GOOD PUBLICITY WE GOT.
THAT SOON CHANGED
IWW FUND-RAISER A FLOP
PAGEANT ORGANIZERS FLED WITH PROFITS
ENOUGH ABOUT THE BIG SHOW! THE FIRST SCABS GOT IN WHILE OUR STRONGEST PICKETERS WERE AT REHEARSALS!

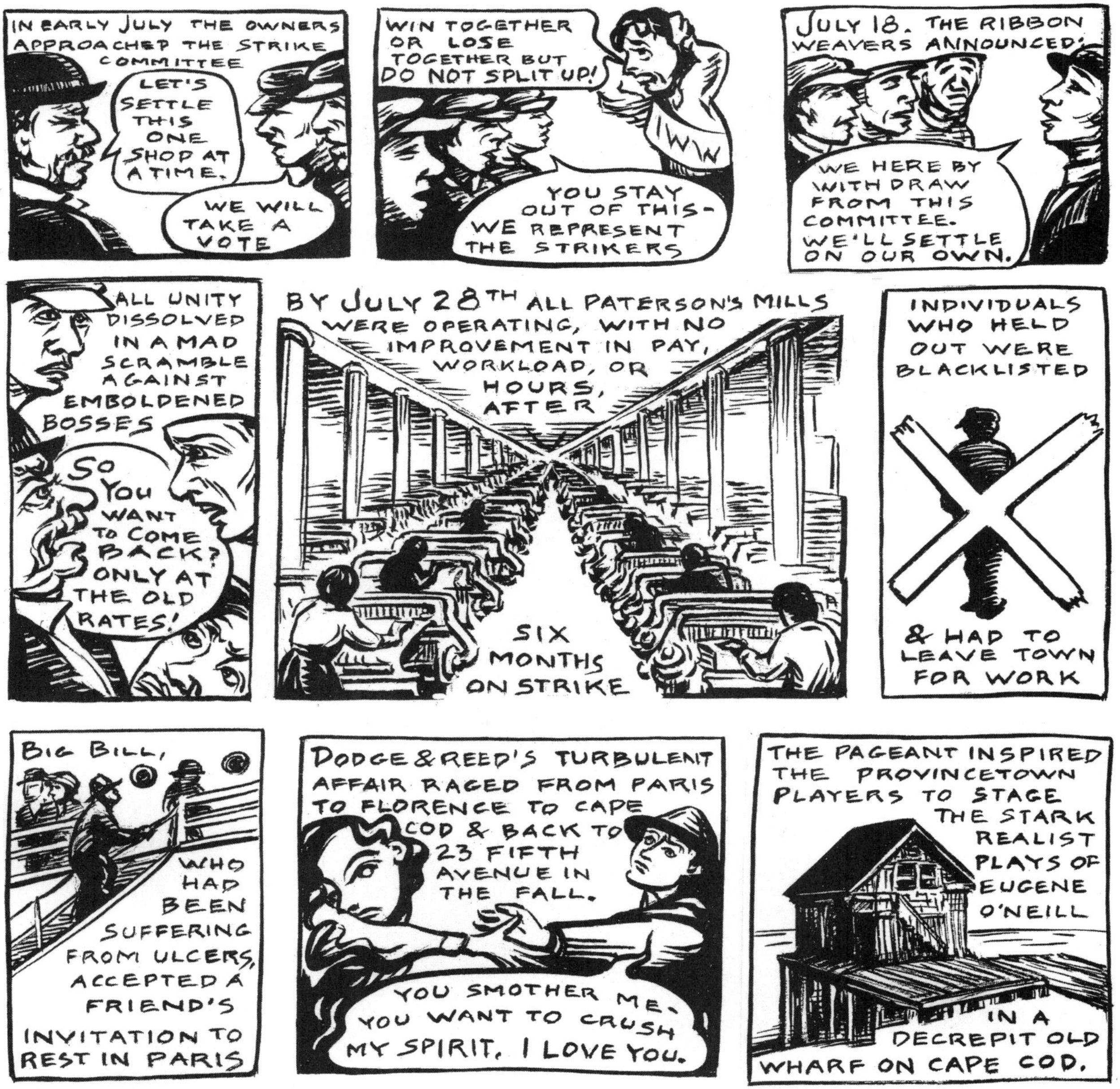
IN EARLY JULY THE OWNERS APPROACHED THE STRIKE COMMITTEE
LET'S SETTLE THIS ONE SHOP AT A TIME.
WE WILL TAKE A VOTE
WIN TOGETHER OR LOSE TOGETHER BUT DO NOT SPLIT UP!
IWW
YOU STAY OUT OF THIS- WE REPRESENT THE STRIKERS
JULY 18. THE RIBBON WEAVERS ANNOUNCED:
WE HERE BY WITH DRAW FROM THIS COMMITTEE. WE'LL SETTLE ON OUR OWN.
ALL UNITY DISSOLVED IN A MAD SCRAMBLE AGAINST EMBOLDENED BOSSES
SO YOU WANT TO COME BACK? ONLY AT THE OLD RATES!
BY JULY 28TH ALL PATERSON'S MILLS WERE OPERATING, WITH NO IMPROVEMENT IN PAY, WORKLOAD, OR HOURS, AFTER
SIX MONTHS ON STRIKE
INDIVIDUALS WHO HELD OUT WERE BLACKLISTED
& HAD TO LEAVE TOWN FOR WORK
BIG BILL,
WHO HAD BEEN SUFFERING FROM ULCERS, ACCEPTED A FRIEND'S INVITATION TO REST IN PARIS
DODGE & REED'S TURBULENT AFFAIR RAGED FROM PARIS TO FLORENCE TO CAPE COD & BACK TO 23 FIFTH AVENUE IN THE FALL.
YOU SMOTHER ME. YOU WANT TO CRUSH MY SPIRIT. I LOVE YOU.
THE PAGEANT INSPIRED THE PROVINCETOWN PLAYERS TO STAGE THE STARK REALIST PLAYS OF EUGENE O'NEILL
IN A DECREPIT OLD WHARF ON CAPE COD.

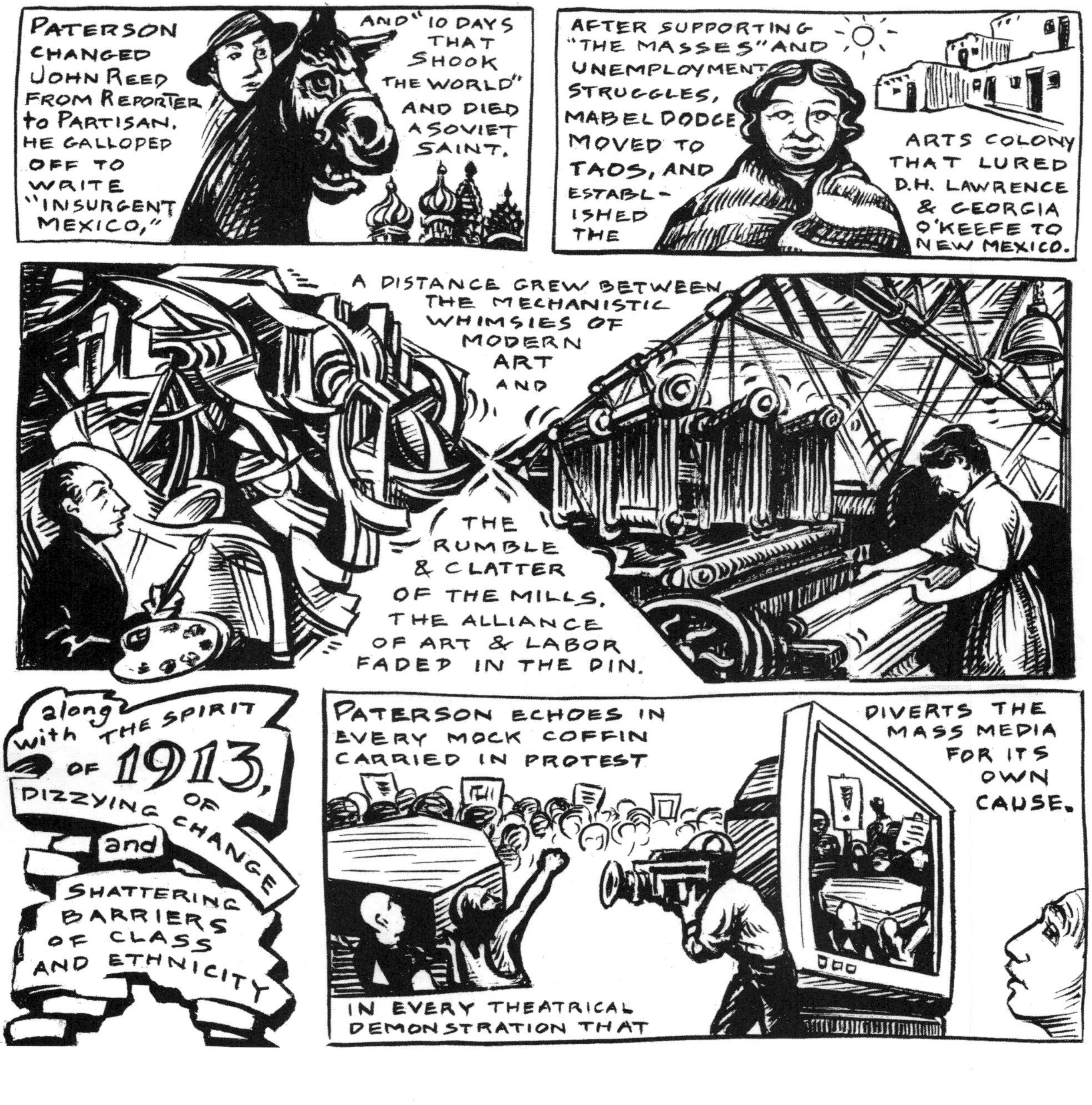

PATERSON CHANGED JOHN REED FROM REPORTER to PARTISAN. HE GALLOPED OFF TO WRITE "INSURGENT MEXICO,"
AND "10 DAYS THAT SHOOK THE WORLD" AND DIED A SOVIET SAINT.
AFTER SUPPORTING "THE MASSES" AND UNEMPLOYMENT STRUGGLES, MABEL DODGE MOVED TO TAOS, AND ESTABL-ISHED THE
ARTS COLONY THAT LURED D.H. LAWRENCE & GEORGIA O'KEEFE TO NEW MEXICO.
A DISTANCE GREW BETWEEN THE MECHANISTIC WHIMSIES OF MODERN ART AND
THE RUMBLE & CLATTER OF THE MILLS. THE ALLIANCE OF ART & LABOR FADED IN THE DIN.
along with THE SPIRIT OF 1913, OF DIZZYING CHANGE
and
SHATTERING BARRIERS OF CLASS AND ETHNICITY
PATERSON ECHOES IN EVERY MOCK COFFIN CARRIED IN PROTEST
IN EVERY THEATRICAL DEMONSTRATION THAT
DIVERTS THE MASS MEDIA FOR ITS OWN CAUSE.

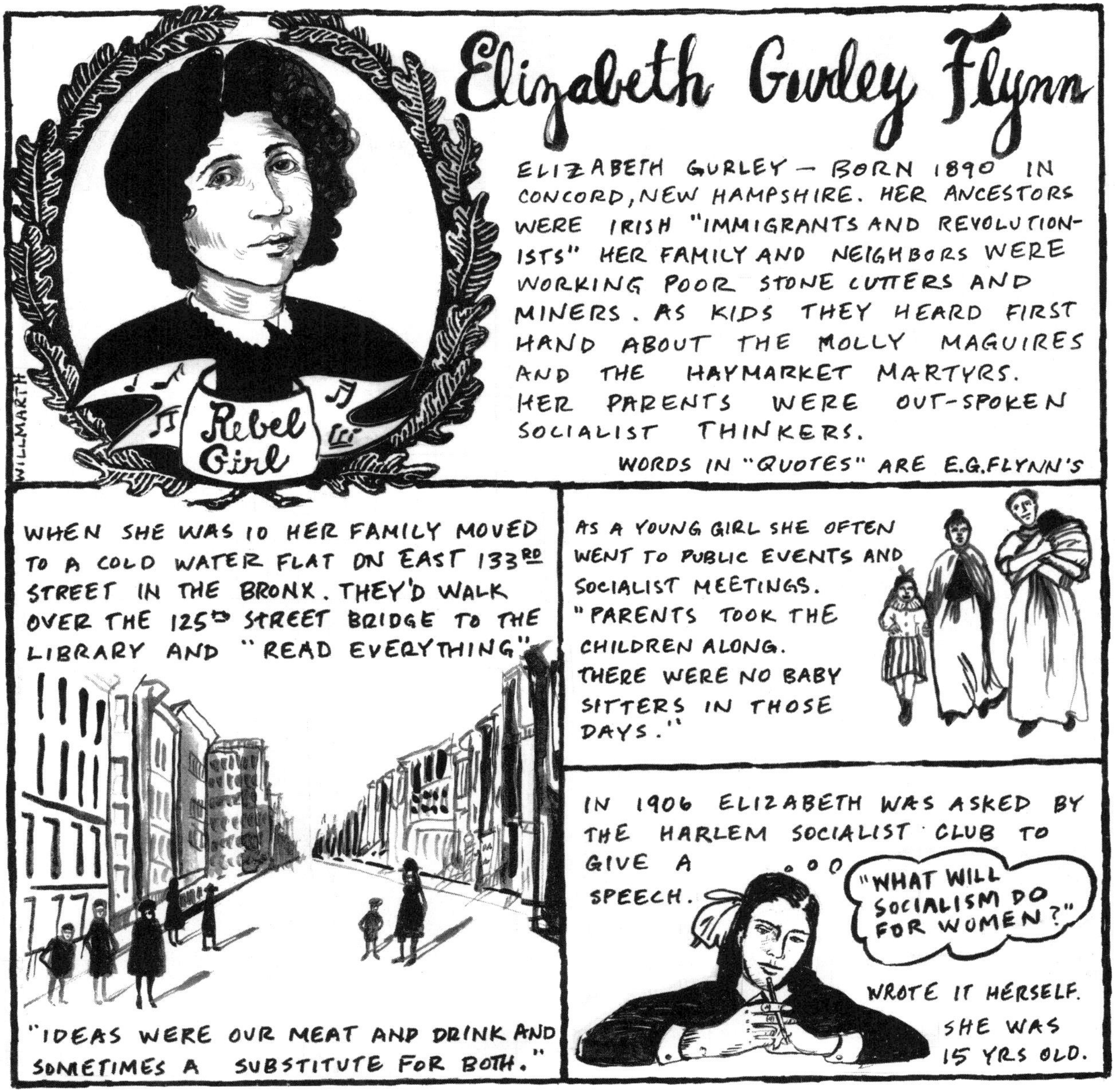

WILLMARTH
Rebel Girl
Elizabeth Gurley Flynn
ELIZABETH GURLEY — BORN 1890 IN CONCORD, NEW HAMPSHIRE. HER ANCESTORS WERE IRISH "IMMIGRANTS AND REVOLUTIONISTS" HER FAMILY AND NEIGHBORS WERE WORKING POOR STONE CUTTERS AND MINERS. AS KIDS THEY HEARD FIRST HAND ABOUT THE MOLLY MAGUIRES AND THE HAYMARKET MARTYRS. HER PARENTS WERE OUT-SPOKEN SOCIALIST THINKERS.
WORDS IN "QUOTES" ARE E.G.FLYNN'S
WHEN SHE WAS 10 HER FAMILY MOVED TO A COLD WATER FLAT ON EAST 133RD STREET IN THE BRONX. THEY'D WALK OVER THE 125TH STREET BRIDGE TO THE LIBRARY AND "READ EVERYTHING".
"IDEAS WERE OUR MEAT AND DRINK AND SOMETIMES A SUBSTITUTE FOR BOTH."
AS A YOUNG GIRL SHE OFTEN WENT TO PUBLIC EVENTS AND SOCIALIST MEETINGS. "PARENTS TOOK THE CHILDREN ALONG. THERE WERE NO BABY SITTERS IN THOSE DAYS."
IN 1906 ELIZABETH WAS ASKED BY THE HARLEM SOCIALIST CLUB TO GIVE A SPEECH.
"WHAT WILL SOCIALISM DO FOR WOMEN?"
WROTE IT HERSELF.
SHE WAS 15 YRS OLD.

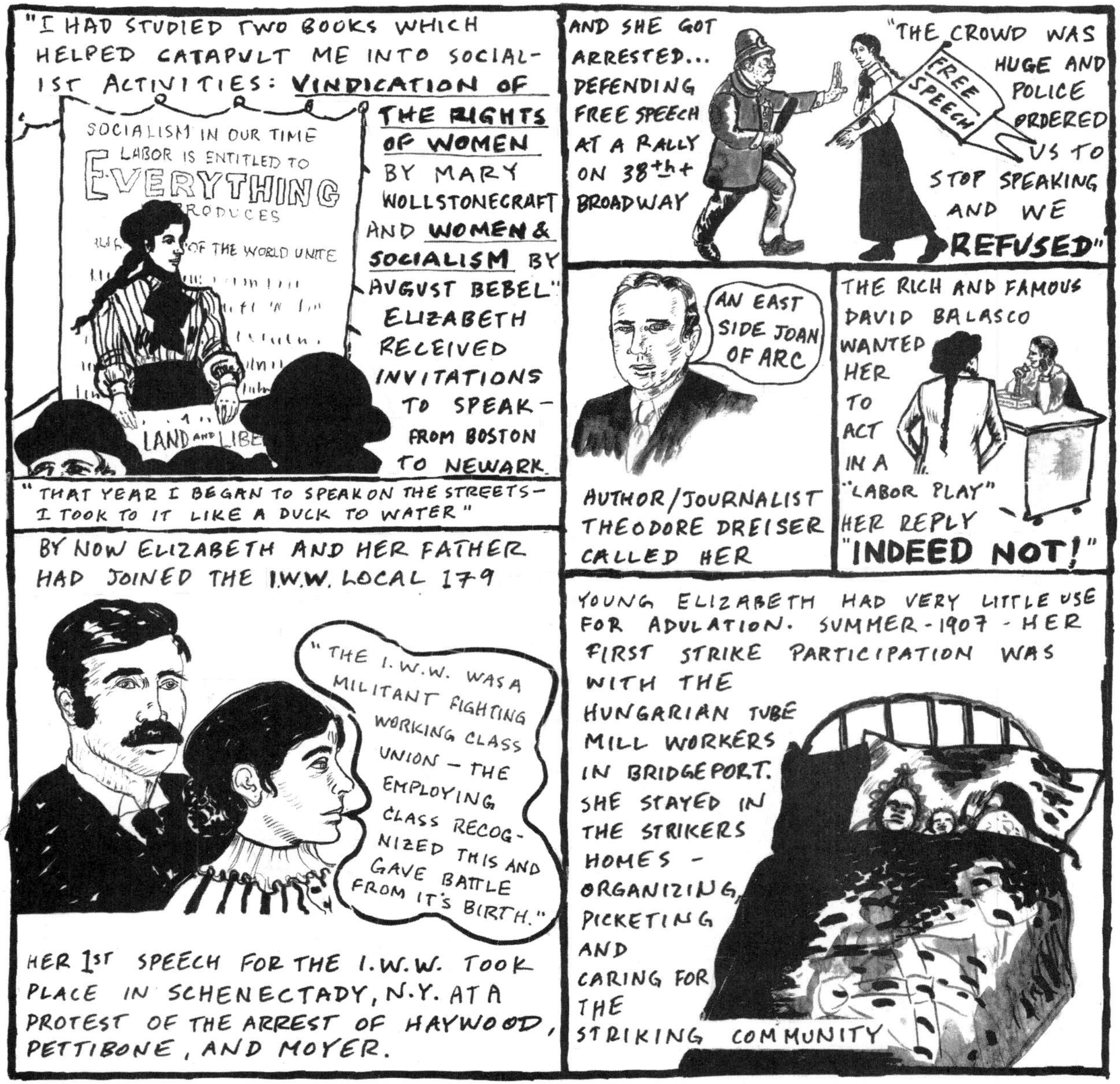
"I HAD STUDIED TWO BOOKS WHICH HELPED CATAPULT ME INTO SOCIALIST ACTIVITIES: VINDICATION OF THE RIGHTS OF WOMEN BY MARY WOLLSTONECRAFT AND WOMEN & SOCIALISM BY AUGUST BEBEL"
SOCIALISM IN OUR TIME
LABOR IS ENTITLED TO EVERYTHING
PRODUCES
OF THE WORLD UNITE
LAND AND LIBE
ELIZABETH RECEIVED INVITATIONS TO SPEAK - FROM BOSTON TO NEWARK
"THAT YEAR I BEGAN TO SPEAK ON THE STREETS - I TOOK TO IT LIKE A DUCK TO WATER"
AND SHE GOT ARRESTED... DEFENDING FREE SPEECH AT A RALLY ON 38th + BROADWAY
FREE SPEECH
"THE CROWD WAS HUGE AND POLICE ORDERED US TO STOP SPEAKING AND WE REFUSED"
AN EAST SIDE JOAN OF ARC
AUTHOR/JOURNALIST THEODORE DREISER CALLED HER
THE RICH AND FAMOUS DAVID BALASCO WANTED HER TO ACT IN A "LABOR PLAY"
HER REPLY "INDEED NOT!"
BY NOW ELIZABETH AND HER FATHER HAD JOINED THE I.W.W. LOCAL 179
"THE I.W.W. WAS A MILITANT FIGHTING WORKING CLASS UNION - THE EMPLOYING CLASS RECOGNIZED THIS AND GAVE BATTLE FROM IT'S BIRTH."
HER 1st SPEECH FOR THE I.W.W. TOOK PLACE IN SCHENECTADY, N.Y. AT A PROTEST OF THE ARREST OF HAYWOOD, PETTIBONE, AND MOYER.
YOUNG ELIZABETH HAD VERY LITTLE USE FOR ADULATION. SUMMER - 1907 - HER FIRST STRIKE PARTICIPATION WAS WITH THE HUNGARIAN TUBE MILL WORKERS IN BRIDGEPORT. SHE STAYED IN THE STRIKERS HOMES - ORGANIZING, PICKETING AND CARING FOR THE STRIKING COMMUNITY

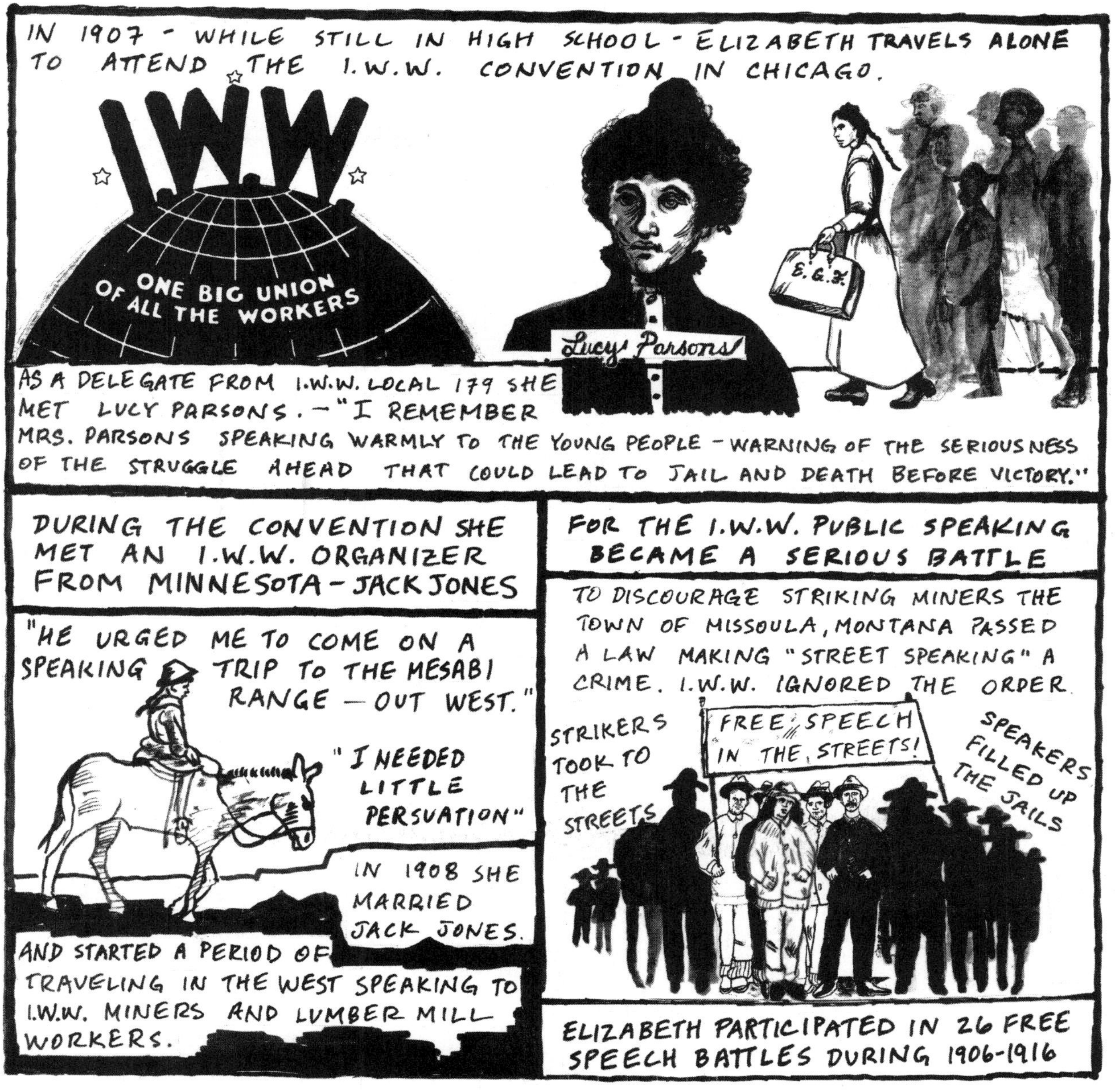
IN 1907 - WHILE STILL IN HIGH SCHOOL - ELIZABETH TRAVELS ALONE TO ATTEND THE I.W.W. CONVENTION IN CHICAGO.
IWW
ONE BIG UNION OF ALL THE WORKERS
Lucy Parsons
E.G.F.
AS A DELEGATE FROM I.W.W. LOCAL 179 SHE MET LUCY PARSONS. — "I REMEMBER MRS. PARSONS SPEAKING WARMLY TO THE YOUNG PEOPLE — WARNING OF THE SERIOUSNESS OF THE STRUGGLE AHEAD THAT COULD LEAD TO JAIL AND DEATH BEFORE VICTORY."
DURING THE CONVENTION SHE MET AN I.W.W. ORGANIZER FROM MINNESOTA - JACK JONES
"HE URGED ME TO COME ON A SPEAKING TRIP TO THE MESABI RANGE — OUT WEST."
"I NEEDED LITTLE PERSUATION"
IN 1908 SHE MARRIED JACK JONES.
AND STARTED A PERIOD OF TRAVELING IN THE WEST SPEAKING TO I.W.W. MINERS AND LUMBER MILL WORKERS.
FOR THE I.W.W. PUBLIC SPEAKING BECAME A SERIOUS BATTLE
TO DISCOURAGE STRIKING MINERS THE TOWN OF MISSOULA, MONTANA PASSED A LAW MAKING "STREET SPEAKING" A CRIME. I.W.W. IGNORED THE ORDER
STRIKERS TOOK TO THE STREETS
FREE SPEECH IN THE STREETS!
SPEAKERS FILLED UP THE JAILS
ELIZABETH PARTICIPATED IN 26 FREE SPEECH BATTLES DURING 1906-1916

1910 - BY NOW ELIZABETH WAS A REGULAR I.W.W. "JAWSMITH" SPEAKING OUT, ORGANIZING AND GETTING ARRESTED.

SHE HAD A BABY - A SON NAMED FRED - HER HUSBAND, JACK, WANTED AN END TO HER TRAVELING - WANTED HER TO SETTLE DOWN IN BUTTE, MONTANA

"HIS ATTITUDE WAS UNDOUBTABLY A NORMAL ONE, BUT I WOULD HAVE NONE OF IT"

FRED STAYED WITH ELIZABETH'S MOTHER.

JACK LEFT.

"I HAVE HAD HEART-ACHES AND EMOTIONAL CONFLICTS ALONG THE WAY. IT WAS NOT EASY IN 1910."

TEN THOUSAND TEXTILE WORKERS ON STRIKE!

1912 LAWRENCE STRIKE

WHEN I.W.W. LEADERS ETTOR AND GIOVANNITTI WERE ARRESTED BILL HAYWOOD AND ELIZABETH FLYNN STEPPED IN TO HELP ORGANIZE THE STRIKE

EMMA GOLDMAN:

"ELIZABETH'S YOUTH, CHARM AND ELOQUENCE EASILY WON EVERYONE'S HEART. THE NAMES OF THE TWO AND THEIR REPUTATION GAINED COUNTRY WIDE SUPPORT FOR THE STRIKE."

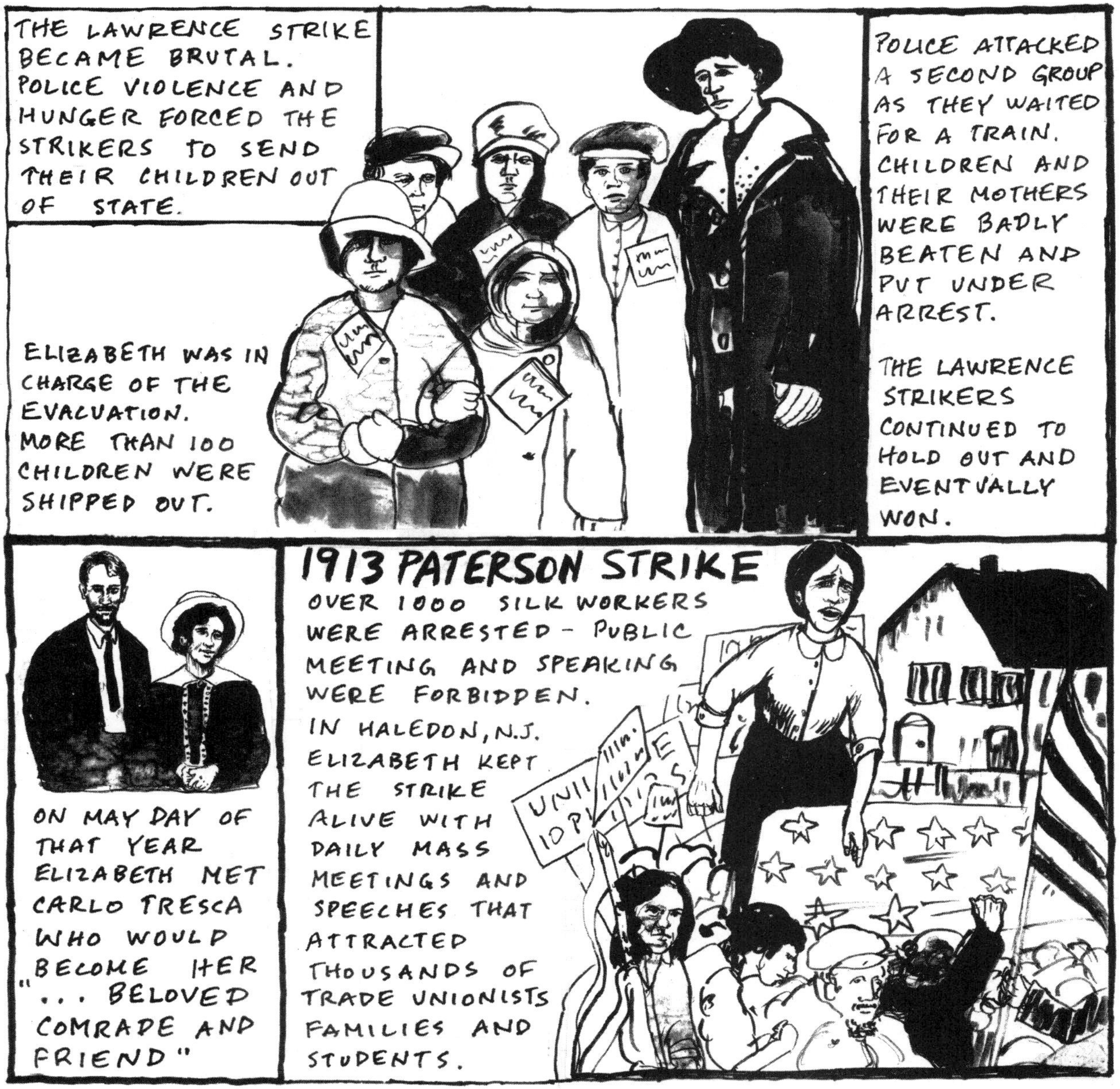

THE LAWRENCE STRIKE BECAME BRUTAL. POLICE VIOLENCE AND HUNGER FORCED THE STRIKERS TO SEND THEIR CHILDREN OUT OF STATE.
ELIZABETH WAS IN CHARGE OF THE EVACUATION. MORE THAN 100 CHILDREN WERE SHIPPED OUT.
POLICE ATTACKED A SECOND GROUP AS THEY WAITED FOR A TRAIN. CHILDREN AND THEIR MOTHERS WERE BADLY BEATEN AND PUT UNDER ARREST.
THE LAWRENCE STRIKERS CONTINUED TO HOLD OUT AND EVENTUALLY WON.
ON MAY DAY OF THAT YEAR ELIZABETH MET CARLO TRESCA WHO WOULD BECOME HER "... BELOVED COMRADE AND FRIEND"
1913 PATERSON STRIKE
OVER 1000 SILK WORKERS WERE ARRESTED - PUBLIC MEETING AND SPEAKING WERE FORBIDDEN.
IN HALEDON, N.J. ELIZABETH KEPT THE STRIKE ALIVE WITH DAILY MASS MEETINGS AND SPEECHES THAT ATTRACTED THOUSANDS OF TRADE UNIONISTS FAMILIES AND STUDENTS.

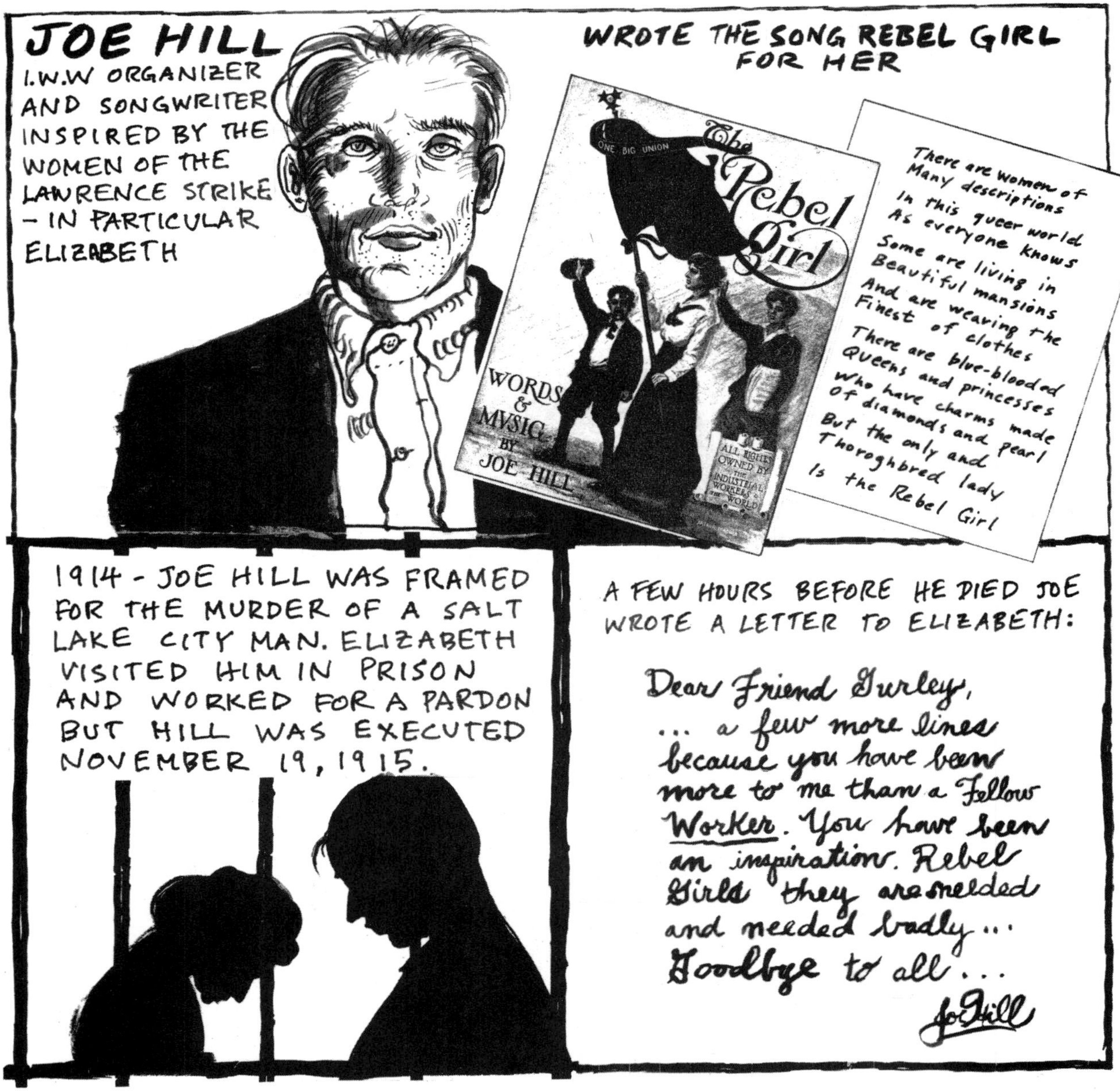
JOE HILL
I.W.W ORGANIZER AND SONGWRITER INSPIRED BY THE WOMEN OF THE LAWRENCE STRIKE – IN PARTICULAR ELIZABETH
WROTE THE SONG REBEL GIRL FOR HER
ONE BIG UNION
The Rebel Girl
WORDS & MUSIC BY JOE HILL
ALL RIGHTS OWNED BY THE INDUSTRIAL WORKERS OF THE WORLD
There are women of Many descriptions In this queer world As everyone knows Some are living in Beautiful mansions And are weaving the Finest of clothes There are blue-blooded Queens and princesses Who have charms made Of diamonds and pearl But the only and Thoroghbred lady Is the Rebel Girl
1914 - JOE HILL WAS FRAMED FOR THE MURDER OF A SALT LAKE CITY MAN. ELIZABETH VISITED HIM IN PRISON AND WORKED FOR A PARDON BUT HILL WAS EXECUTED NOVEMBER 19, 1915.
A FEW HOURS BEFORE HE DIED JOE WROTE A LETTER TO ELIZABETH:
Dear Friend Gurley, ... a few more lines because you have been more to me than a Fellow Worker. You have been an inspiration. Rebel Girls they are needed and needed badly... Goodbye to all...
Joe Hill

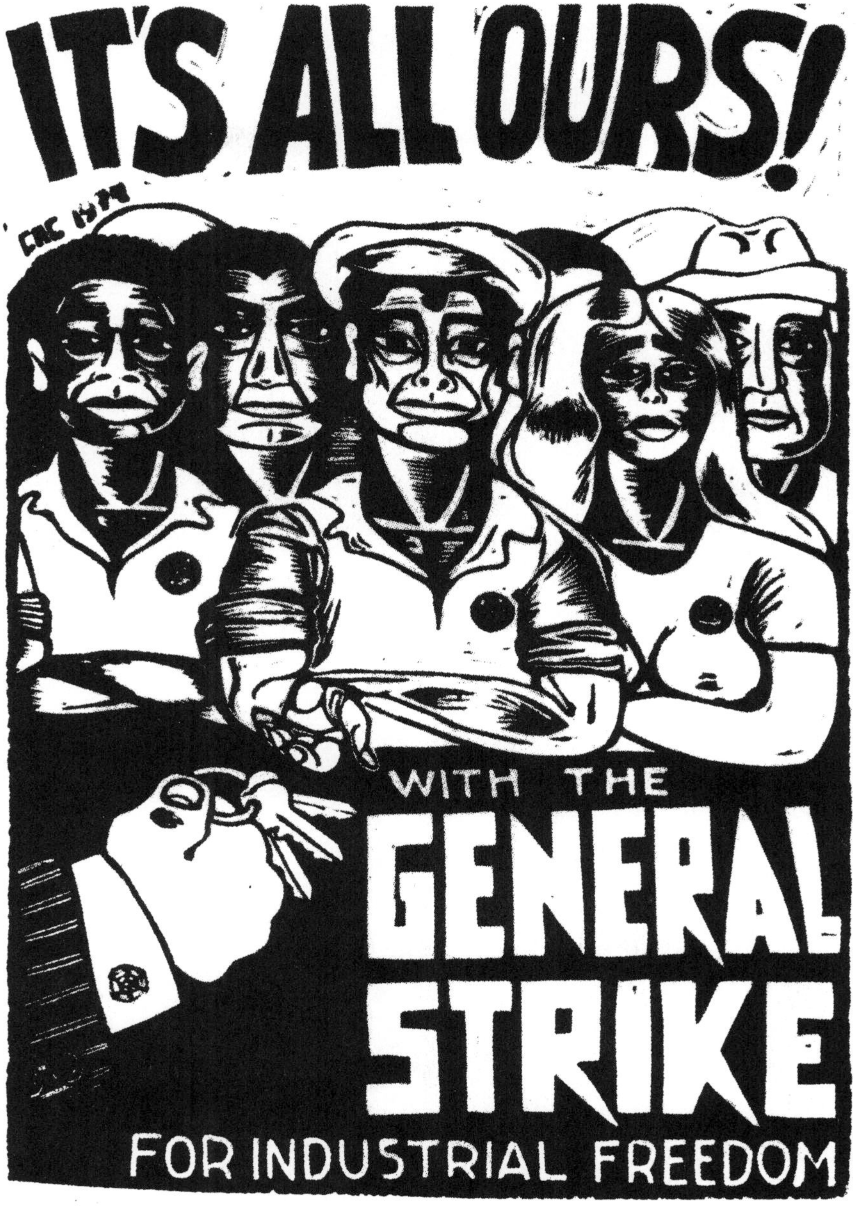
IT'S ALL OURS!
WITH THE
GENERAL
STRIKE
FOR INDUSTRIAL FREEDOM

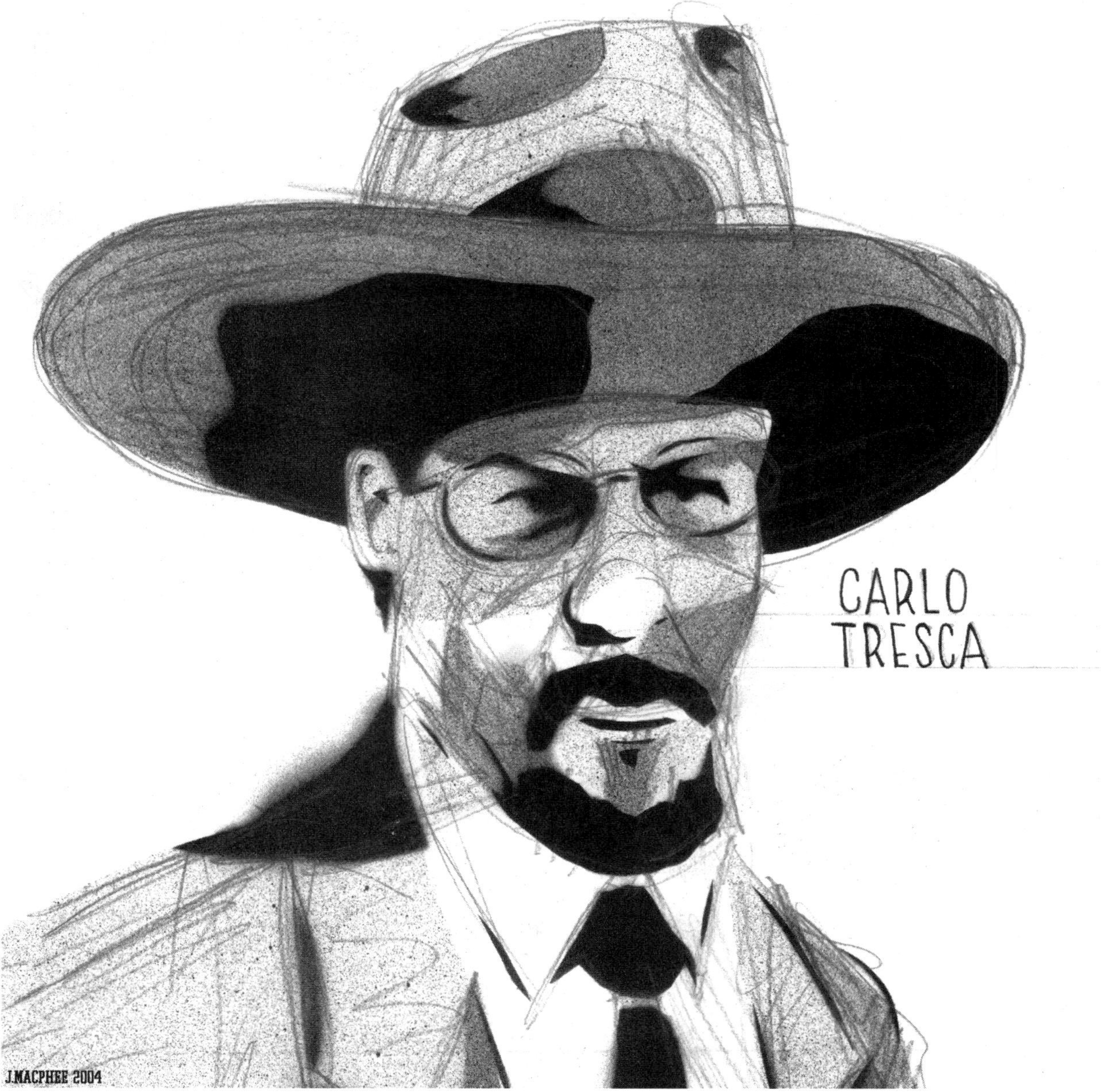
CARLO
TRESCA
J.MACPHEE 2004

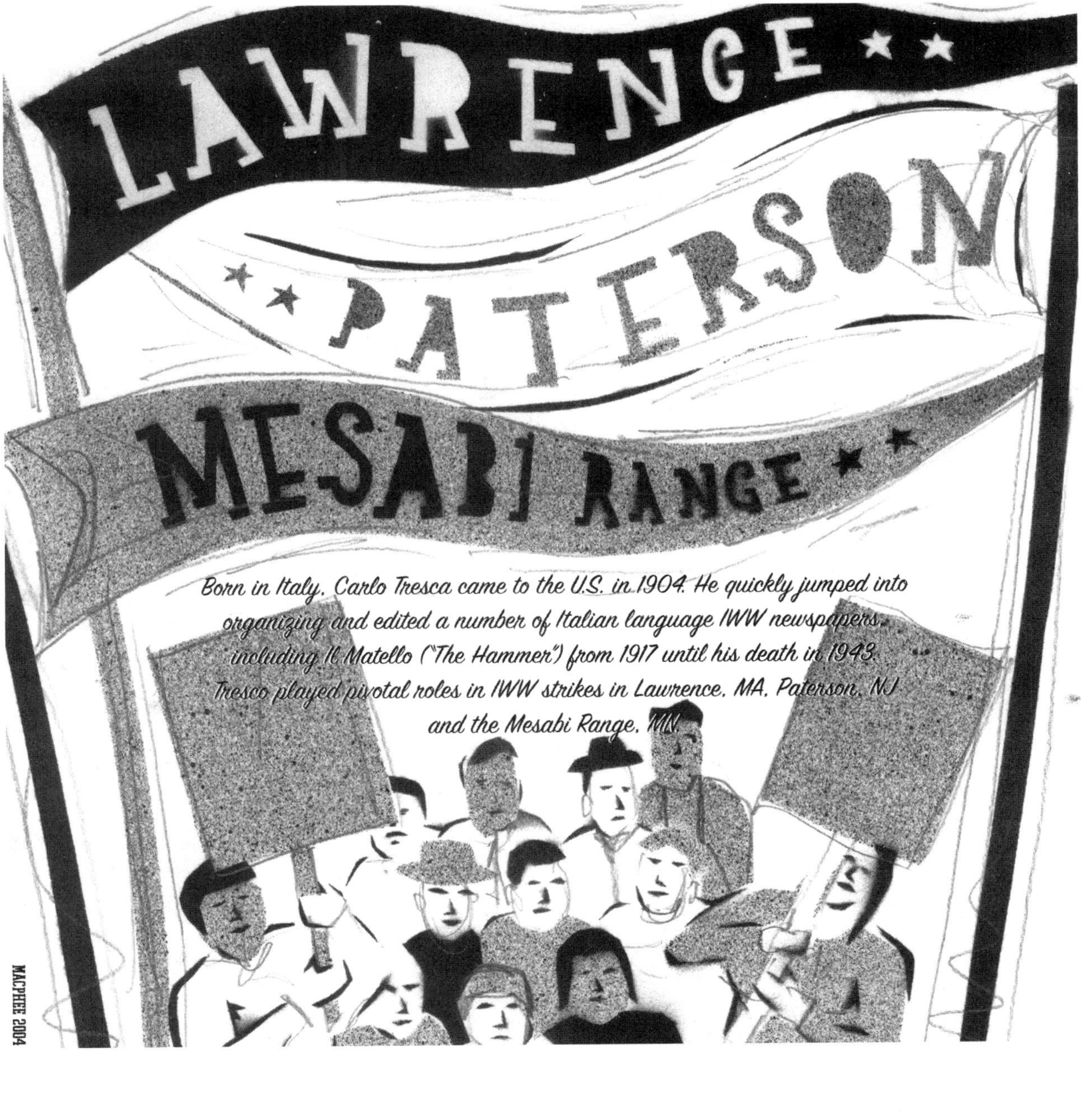
LAWRENCE
PATERSON
MESABI RANGE
Born in Italy, Carlo Tresca came to the U.S. in 1904. He quickly jumped into organizing and edited a number of Italian language IWW newspapers, including Il Matello ("The Hammer") from 1917 until his death in 1943. Tresca played pivotal roles in IWW strikes in Lawrence, MA, Paterson, NJ and the Mesabi Range, MN.
MACPHEE 2004

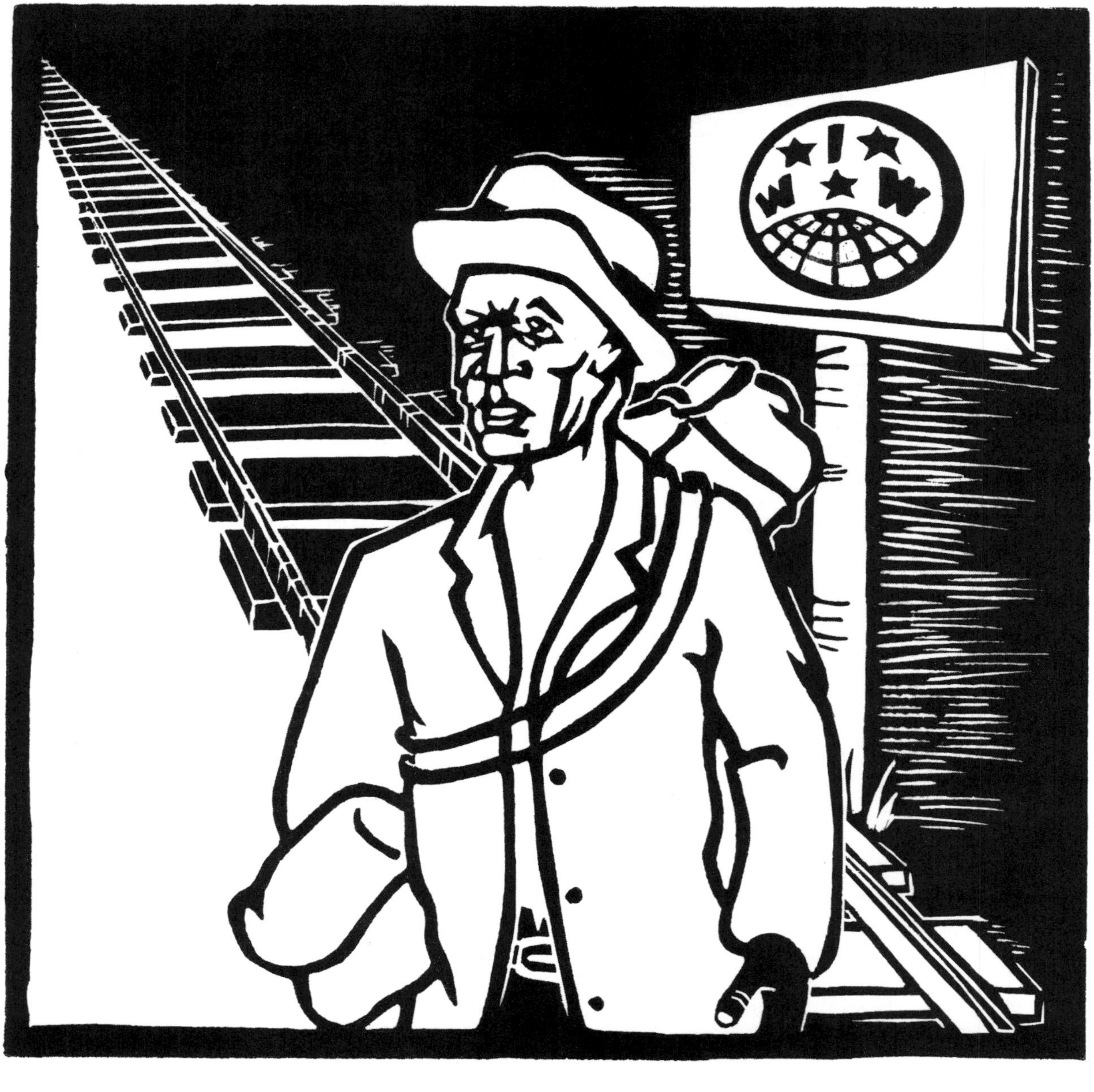
I
W W

THREE

WOBBLIES FAR AND WIDE

After the Paterson disappointment, enemies of the IWW called the organization beaten. It wasn't true, by a long shot. The Wobblies' free-speech fights combined daring with a keen strategic sensibility. But their mobilization of migratory workers offered the best hopes for a large, sustained labor organization. The Agricultural Workers Organization (AWO) planted itself in the work-life culture of the mostly white, male, mobile harvest and threshing workers of the Plains states. Like the Wobs in the mines and timber-mills, they epitomized the Western (and "American") spirit of the organization. Notoriously rebellious and restless, their effective control of box-car riding ("show your red card") was legendary. The Wheatland "riot" and the organizing around it illustrated how effective the Wobs could become under the right circumstances.

The larger AWO also grew strong in the face of repression, peaking in 1918, for a seemingly unlikely reason. Wartime created a labor shortage: it was easier to quit or get fired and move on, because more jobs were available everywhere. Not that AWO organizers succeeded everywhere they tried. Conflicts based on racial differences of many (not all) California farms were difficult to overcome (although they tried); repression during wartime meant suppression of newspapers, arrests of organizers, and threats of vigilante violence. In the longer run, the mechanization of farming would dramatically reduce the numbers of agricultural workers.

Wobblies also learned that organizing in fields was more complicated than in factories. They could not rely on family or ethnic ties, and so had to rely on job actions, slowdowns, and brief strikes in order to attract members. Thus in April, 1915, Frank Little called a conference to organize hobos, creating a "job delegate" system within the IWW, with Wobs setting wage and hour demands beforehand, selecting an individual or a committee to negotiate with a farmer, and then all the Wobs ratifying the agreement. This way, the AWO grew quickly and successfully. Dues were a $2 initiation, then 50 cents per month. By 1915, many had won immediate Wob goals—the ten-hour day, a $3 minimum wage, overtime, good board, clean beds—realizable because war raised the price of wheat. Thus, Wobs would arrive outside town, establish a jungle near a stream, then call a meeting and elect committees to keep the camp clean. A "Spud and Gump Brigade" foraged or begged for food and did the cooking, while some got jobs in town to build up a common fund. This was the IWW world in miniature, a workers' society run by itself, although organizing it and keeping it going sometimes distracted from actual organizing in the fields.

IWW strike leadership would naturally be blamed for causing deaths and injuries handed out by police and private thugs. Huge defense fights exposed terrible conditions, while leaders were handed long sentences. The IWW's reputation spread. Japanese and Chinese workers had their own labor organizations that worked with the IWW, although not usually affiliating directly. The Fresno branch chartered the

Japanese Labor League in 1908 with a thousand members. Mexicans formed their own Wobbly locals (especially San Diego and LA) and published Wobbly pamphlets, leaflets and papers in Spanish. All this activity was unknown and indeed unwanted within the mainstream AFL.

For a historic moment, in 1918, the AWO opened new offices in Minneapolis and Chicago, bought new printing plants, and planned a bright future. Wobblies declared the Russian "Soviets" (literally, "workers' councils") to be mirrors of their own activity. Then came the Red Scares of 1919–21 in the US, followed by the crushing of a vast and powerful Italian working-class uprising and other bitter disappointments.

FREE SPEECH FIGHTS

The IWW conducted some thirty free-speech fights in the decade after 1907, with a great deal of courage but also dramatic flair, and not a little poetry. Even the local repression, driving Wobblies by the hundreds into jail, was often a victory, for very much like the civil rights movement fifty years later, it brought a sense of solidarity marked by singing and good cheer. Only the conspiracies of Woodrow Wilson's federal government bent on war and successful empire-building brought an end, leaving the next generations up to the present to fight for the right to assemble peaceably under constitutional protections.

The prince of the free-speech fight, the very reason for its being, was the soapboxer. Named for the soapboxes that street speakers would stand on in the pre-1920 era, providing a free public entertainment and education to a cash-poor crowd, radical soapboxers often earned their way by selling nickel pamphlets, promoting them (usually including the *Communist Manifesto*) as gateways to wisdom. Wobblies, lacking resources, unable to get their newspapers distributed on (most) newsstands, had no choice. But they liked it, too, because of the direct connection with the workers and the idlers on the streets, from big cities to farming centers, lumber- and mining-towns. The soapbox was their prop, the street their theater, their physical presence, torso in motion, along with the voice, their performance. The voice was especially important, of course. Many of the rousing Wobbly anthems were composed to reach workers through a dose of humor, making fun of the bosses or the preachers, often adopting the language of the Salvation Army in particular to mangle the original intent and put across the logic of the class struggle. The first of the free-speech fights to gain national publicity was held in Missoula, Montana, in 1909. The *Industrial Worker* beseeched its readers in September 1909: "Quit your job. Go to Missoula. Fight with Lumber Jacks for Free Speech!" and taunted gently: "Are you afraid? Do you love the police? Have you been robbed, skinned, grafted on? If so, go to Missoula, and defy the police, the courts and the people who live off the wages of prostitution."

In Spokane, where migratory workers came to winter after a hard season of lumbering or the mines, where flea-bag hotels and bars snapped up their meager savings, the IWW came to town to drive out the "sharks," the agents who charged steep fees for jobs in the woods and mines. Here, in the spring of 1909, the Wobs set up downtown headquarters with a meeting hall, reading room, even a cigar store and hospital plan, and enrolled 1500 new members. The employers struck back, arresting all Wobs who began to speak and locking them up in overcrowded cells with nothing but bread and water. Singing, and holding daily business meetings, they kept up spirits. By the fall, police treatment became considerably more brutal, as authorities closed the Wobbly hall and arrested anyone who peddled a Wobbly paper. Hundreds more came to Spokane in response, the most famous of them the

"Rebel Girl," Elizabeth Gurley Flynn, arriving seven months pregnant and quickly charged with "conspiracy." Soon, the struggle had worn out the authorities' determination and legal budget. City government conceded the right for indoor meetings, sale of literature, and opening the streets to speakers in the near future. The next stop was Fresno, California, near where Wobs were successfully organizing Chicano railroad workers and farmhands. By September, 1910, Wobs flooded the jails, challenging the legal system and prompting a redneck mob to beat the agitators brutally and burn down the makeshift Wobbly tent camp set up outside the city boundaries. Frank Little himself led the fight, which continued with ferocity in city jails. The Wobs had at least gained national publicity with their courage, their humor, their singing and shouting for freedom.

Middle-class San Diego looked like an easier target in some ways because it had a long-standing free-speech zone, and the Wobblies had not been perceived as a threat in organizing the small-scale working class heavily reliant on tourism. Horror awaited.

The Free Speech Fights

Susan Simensky Bietila

NEARER MY JOB TO THEE   BY JOE HILL

NEARER MY JOB TO THEE,
NEARER WITH GLEE,
THREE PLUNKS FOR THE OFFICE FEE,
BUT MY FARE IS FREE.

MY TRAIN IS RUNNING FAST.
I'VE GOT A JOB AT LAST,
NEARER MY JOB TO THEE,
NEARER TO THEE.

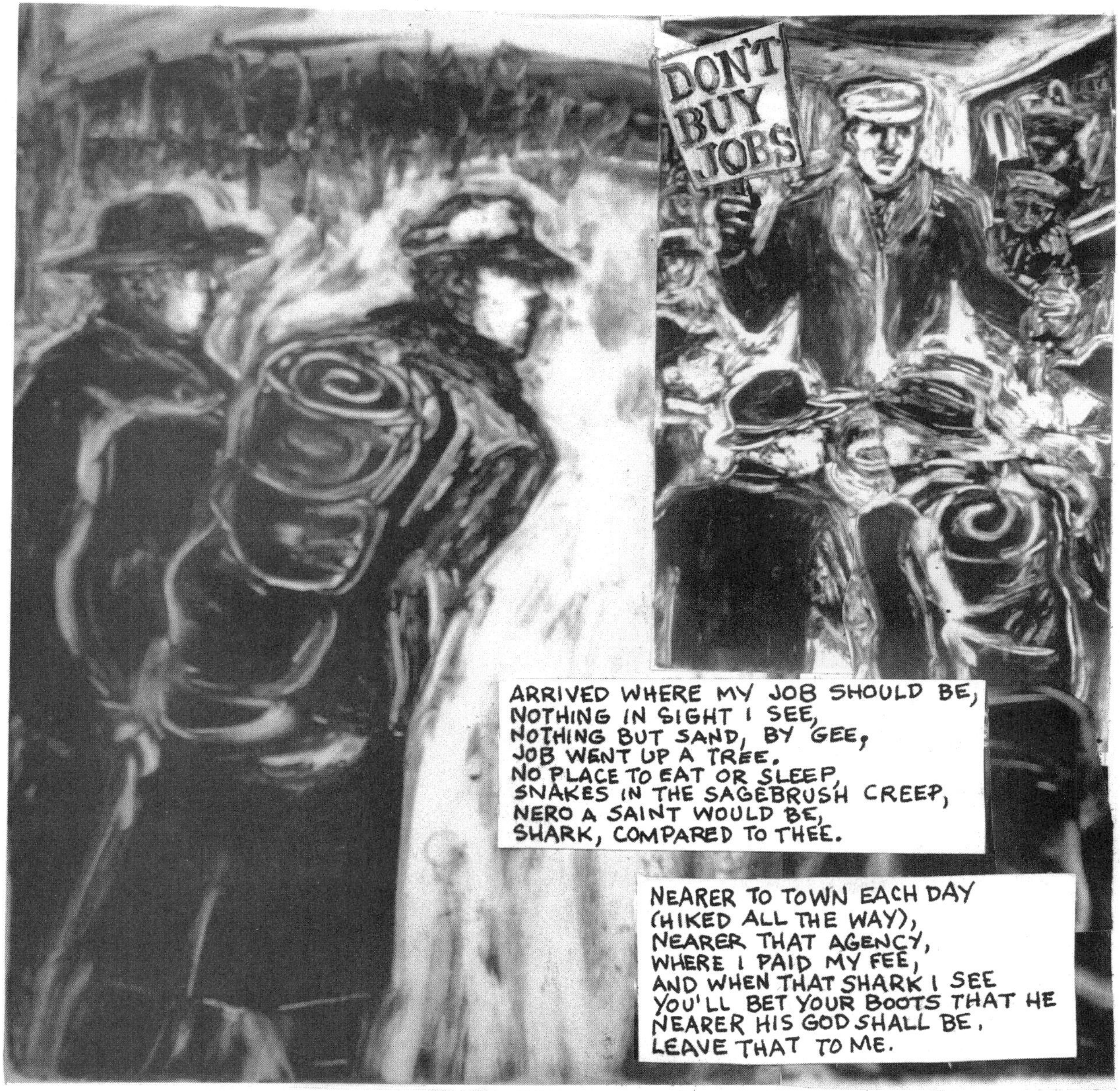
DON'T BUY JOBS
ARRIVED WHERE MY JOB SHOULD BE,
NOTHING IN SIGHT I SEE,
NOTHING BUT SAND, BY GEE,
JOB WENT UP A TREE.
NO PLACE TO EAT OR SLEEP,
SNAKES IN THE SAGEBRUSH CREEP,
NERO A SAINT WOULD BE,
SHARK, COMPARED TO THEE.
NEARER TO TOWN EACH DAY
(HIKED ALL THE WAY),
NEARER THAT AGENCY,
WHERE I PAID MY FEE,
AND WHEN THAT SHARK I SEE
YOU'LL BET YOUR BOOTS THAT HE
NEARER HIS GOD SHALL BE.
LEAVE THAT TO ME.

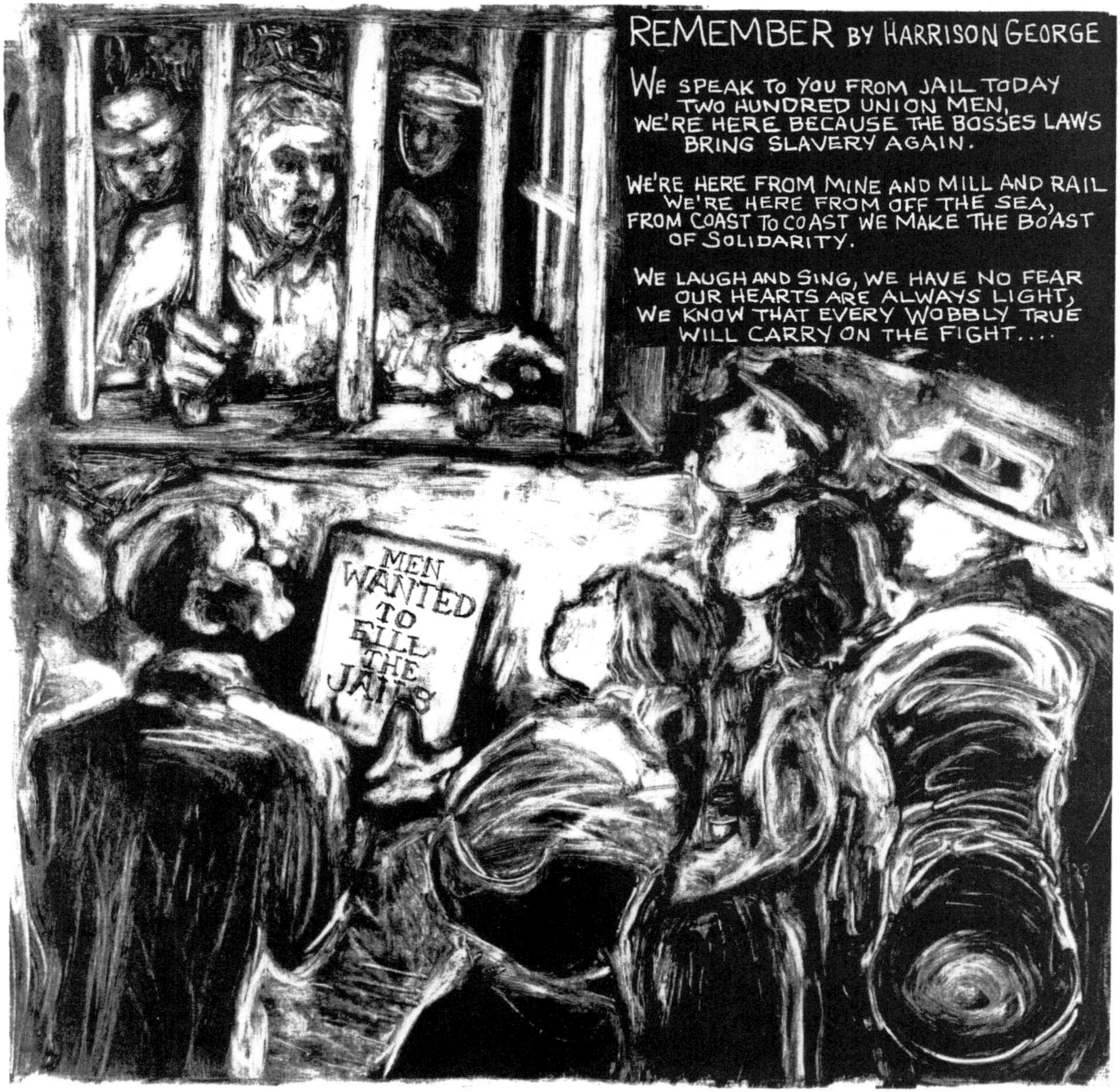
REMEMBER BY HARRISON GEORGE
WE SPEAK TO YOU FROM JAIL TODAY
TWO HUNDRED UNION MEN,
WE'RE HERE BECAUSE THE BOSSES LAWS
BRING SLAVERY AGAIN.
WE'RE HERE FROM MINE AND MILL AND RAIL
WE'RE HERE FROM OFF THE SEA,
FROM COAST TO COAST WE MAKE THE BOAST
OF SOLIDARITY.
WE LAUGH AND SING, WE HAVE NO FEAR
OUR HEARTS ARE ALWAYS LIGHT,
WE KNOW THAT EVERY WOBBLY TRUE
WILL CARRY ON THE FIGHT...
MEN WANTED TO FILL THE JAILS

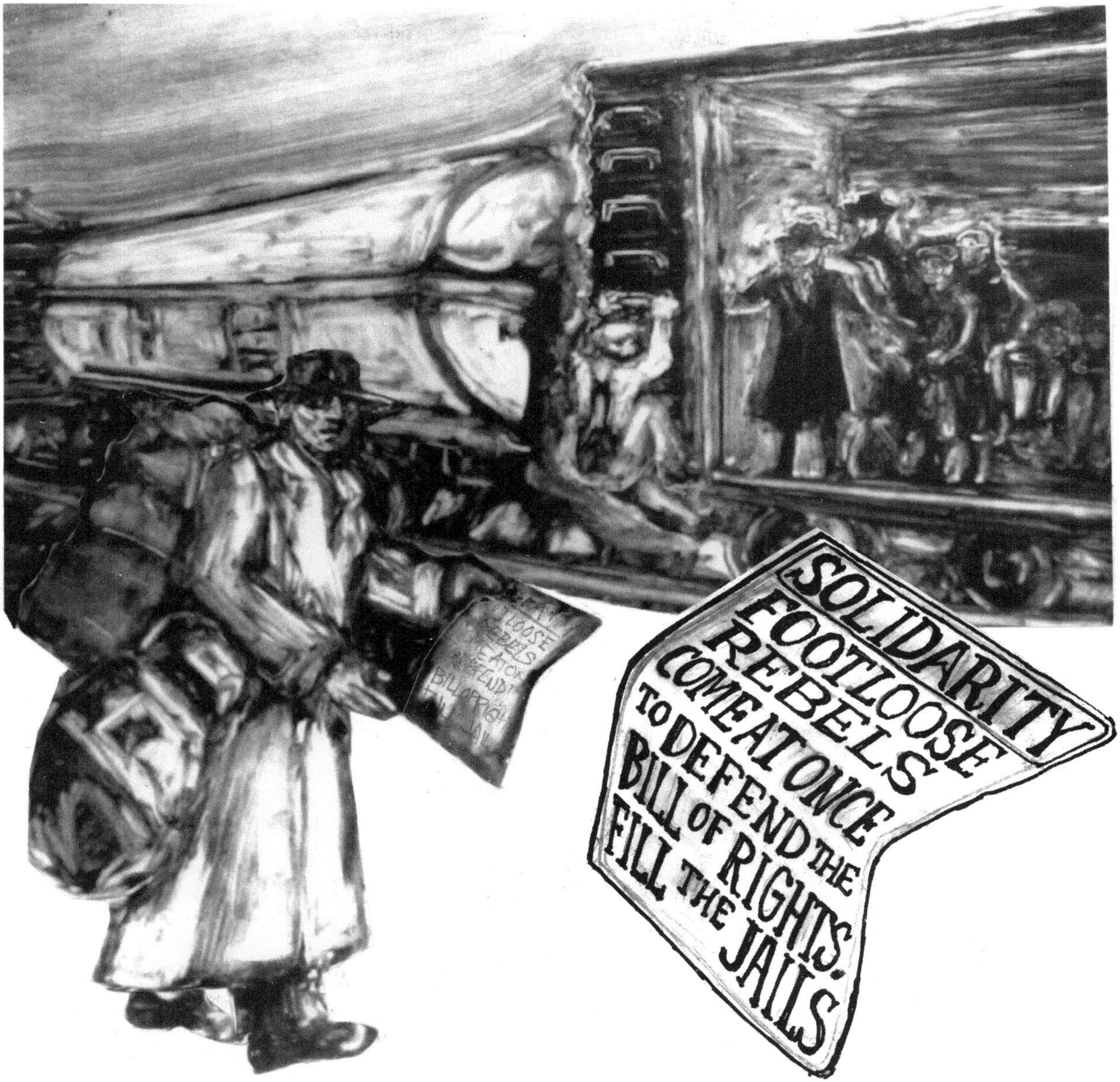
SOLIDARITY
FOOTLOOSE
REBELS
COME AT ONCE
TO DEFEND THE
BILL OF RIGHTS.
FILL THE JAILS

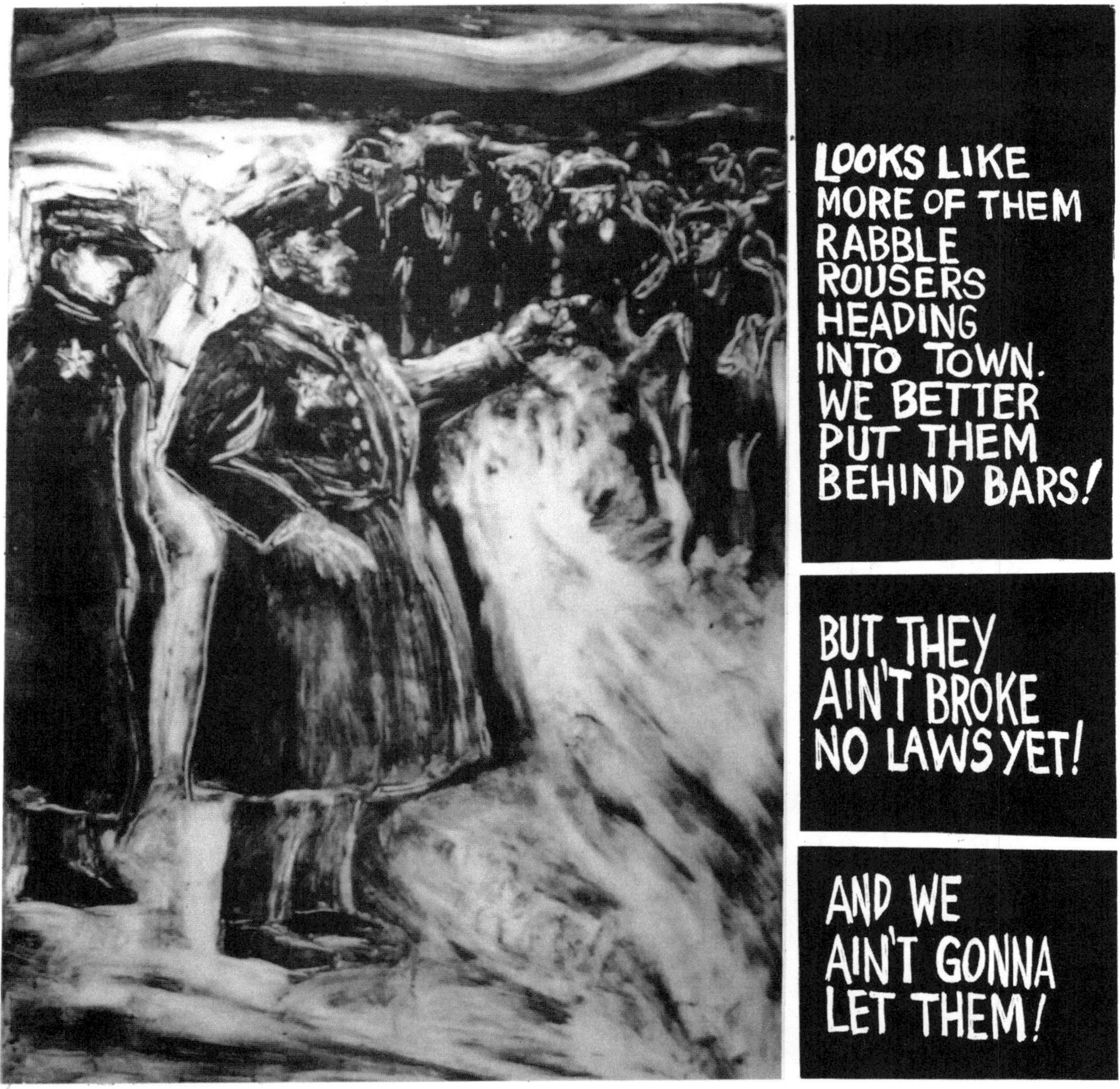
LOOKS LIKE MORE OF THEM RABBLE ROUSERS HEADING INTO TOWN. WE BETTER PUT THEM BEHIND BARS!
BUT THEY AIN'T BROKE NO LAWS YET!
AND WE AIN'T GONNA LET THEM!

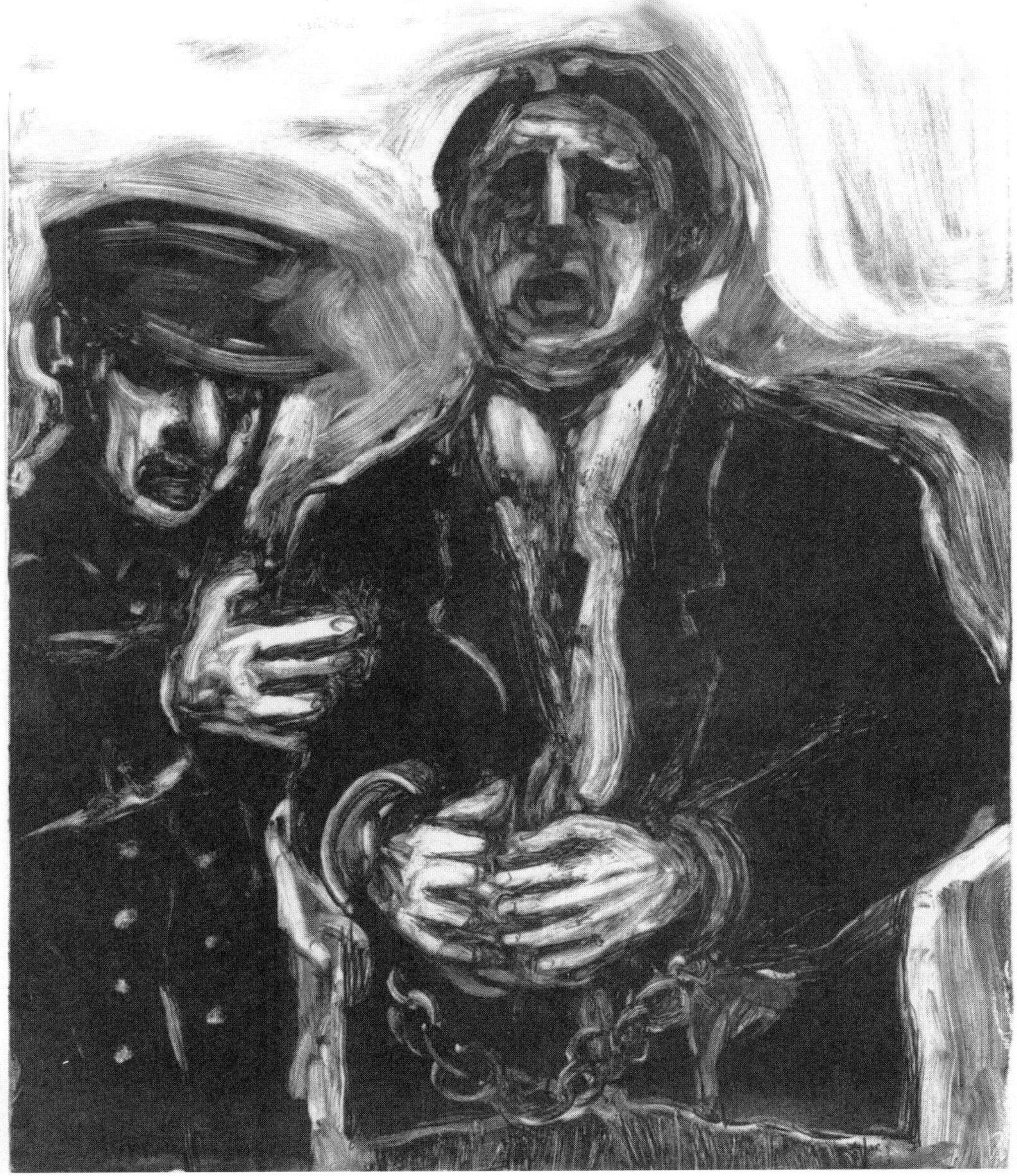

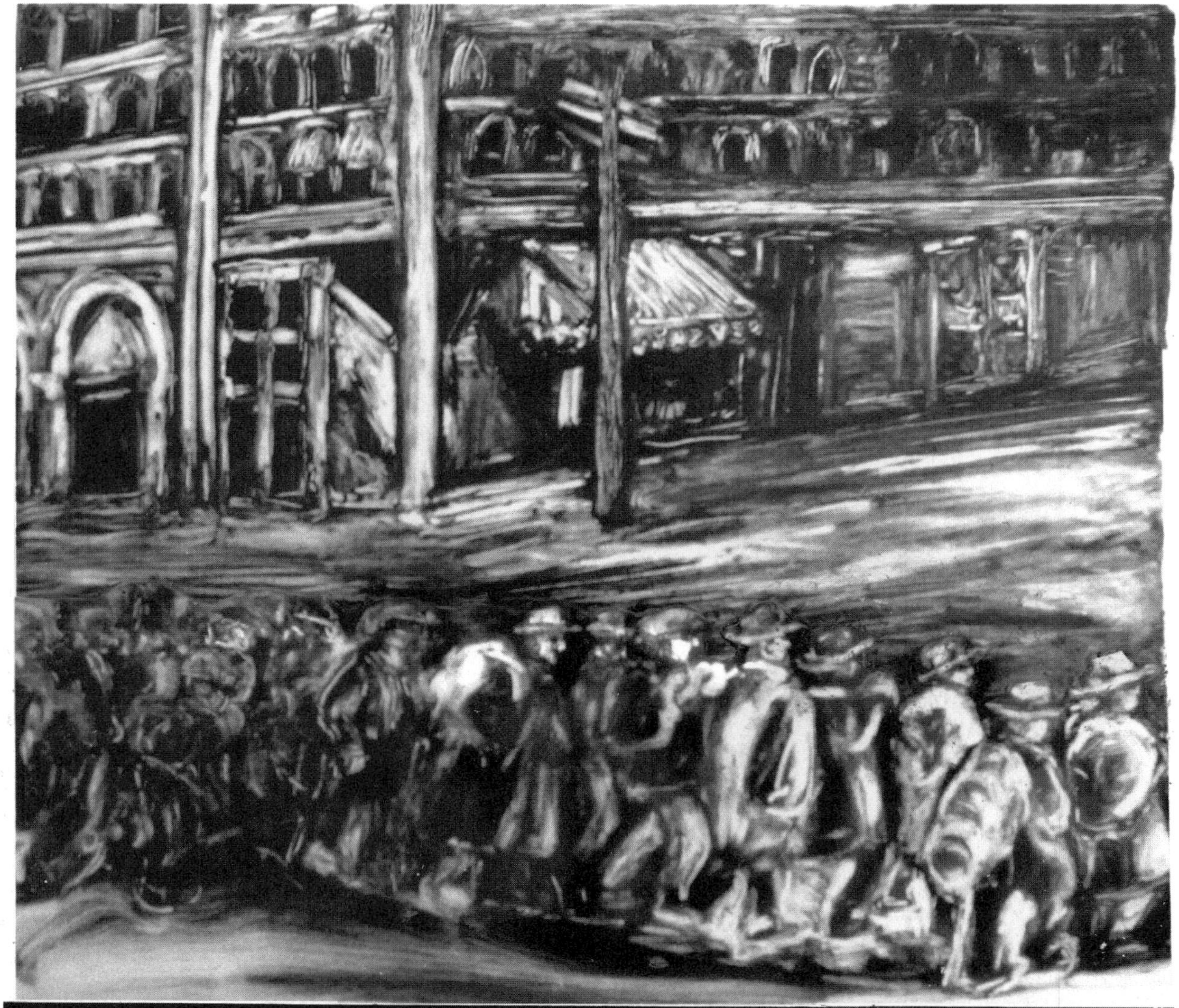

WE'RE BOUND FOR SAN DIEGO

IN THAT TOWN OF SAN DIEGO WHEN THE WORKERS TRY TO TALK, THE COPS WILL SMASH THEM WITH A SAY & TELL 'EM "TAKE A WALK."
THEY THROW THEM IN THE BULL PEN, & THEY FEED THEM ROTTEN BEANS, & THEY CALL THAT "LAW & ORDER" IN THAT CITY, SO IT SEEMS.

THEY'RE CLUBBING FELLOW WORKING MEN WHO DARE THEIR THOUGHTS EXPRESS; & IF OLD OTIS HAS HIS WAY, THERE'S SURE TO BE A MESS,
SO SWELL THIS ARMY, WORKING MEN, & SHOW THEM WHAT WE'LL DO WHEN ALL THE SONS OF TOIL UNITE IN ONE BIG UNION TRUE...

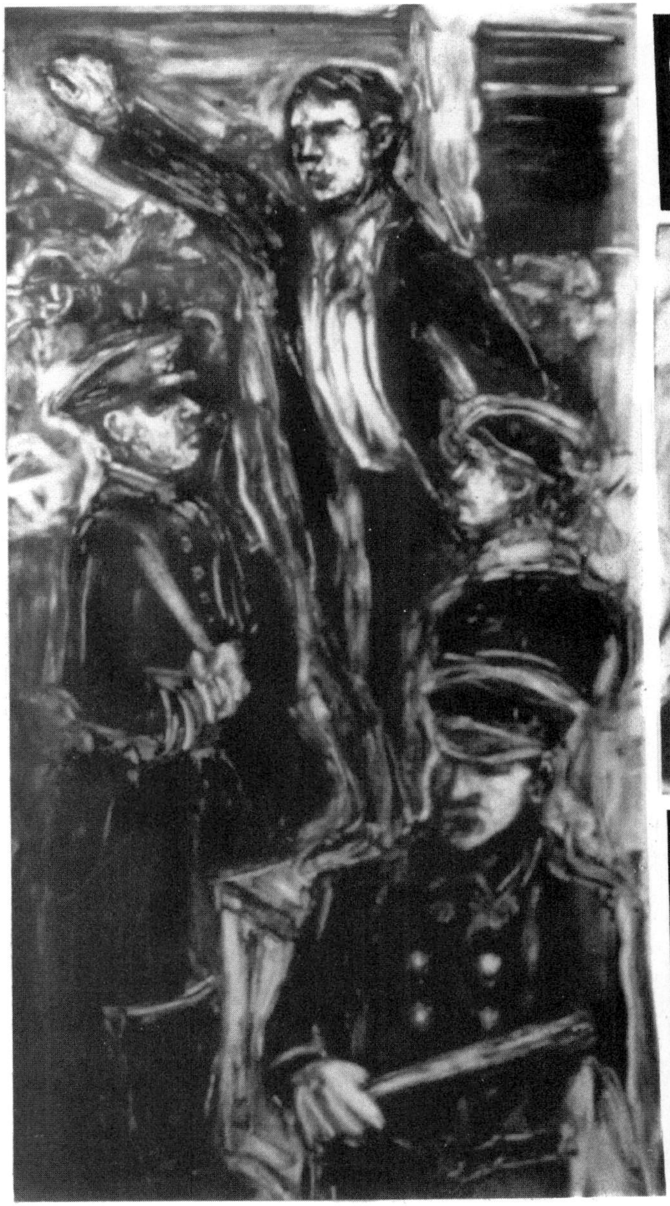

GIVE THEM A "FREE SPEECH ZONE"
OUT NEAR THE RAILROAD YARDS,
BUT GET THEM OUT OF THE
MIDDLE OF THE BUSINESS DISTRICT!

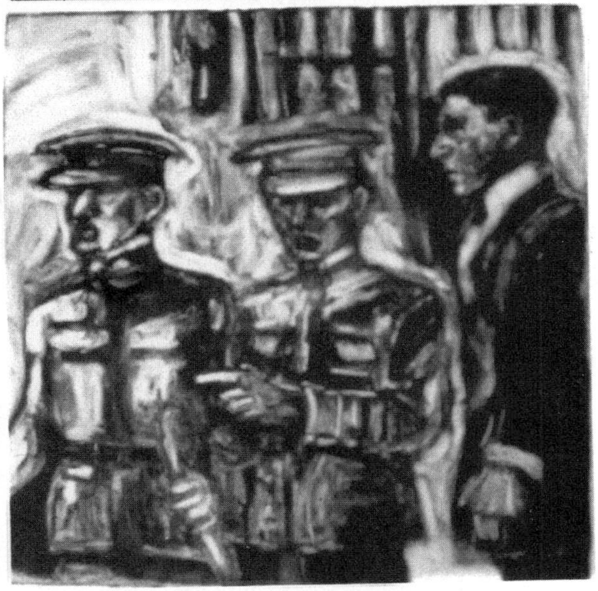

OUT THERE IN SAN DIEGO
WHERE THE WESTERN BREAKERS BEAT
THEY'RE JAILING MEN AND WOMEN
FOR SPEAKING IN THE STREET.

THERE IS ONE THING I CAN TELL YOU
AND IT MAKES THE BOSSES SORE,
AS FAST AS THEY CAN PINCH US
WE CAN ALWAYS GET SOME MORE.

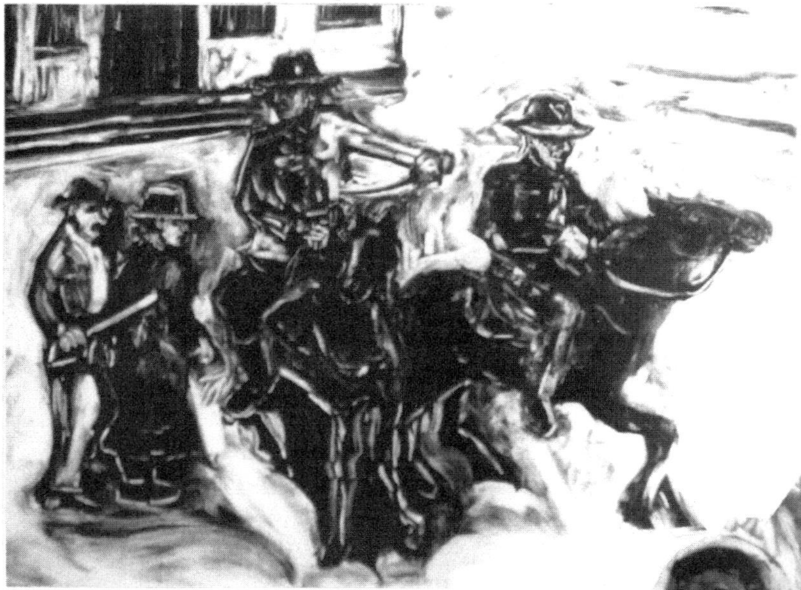

WE'LL END ALL THIS IN AN HOUR! WE'VE GOT THE NOD TO DEAL WITH THESE AGITATORS PRIVATELY. THE POLICE WILL BE GLAD TO LOOK THE OTHER WAY.

THERE'S LIKELY TO BE A PROFITABLE FUTURE IN SUCH HANDIWORK.

PASSER BY: "JUDGE, CAN'T YOU DO SOMETHING TO PREVENT THE BEATING OF INNOCENT MEN?"

JUDGE: "PREVENT? HELL! THERE AIN'T NO USE IN THREATENING THOSE FELLAS WITH KINDNESS. THE ONLY THING TO DO IS TO CLUB THEM DOWN, BEAT THEM UP AND DRIVE THE GODDAMN SONS OF BITCHES INTO THE RIVER AND DROWN THEM ALONG WITH THE SOCIALISTS."

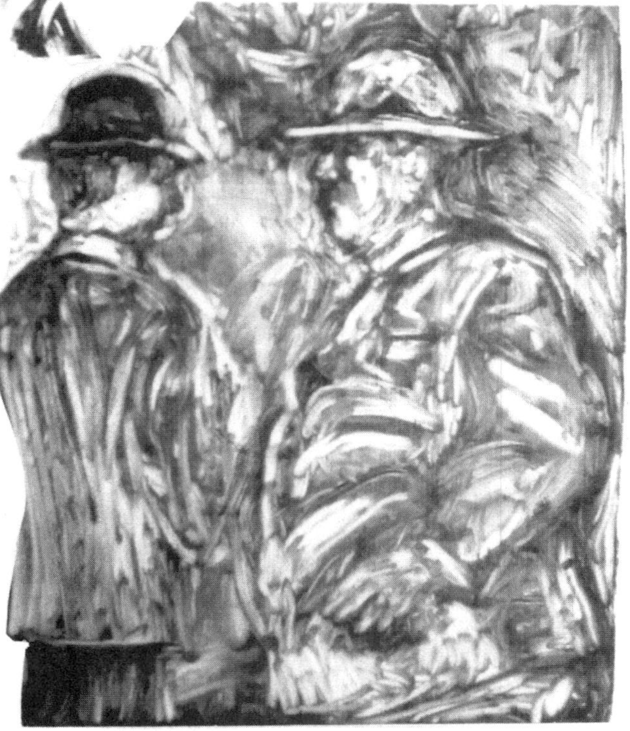

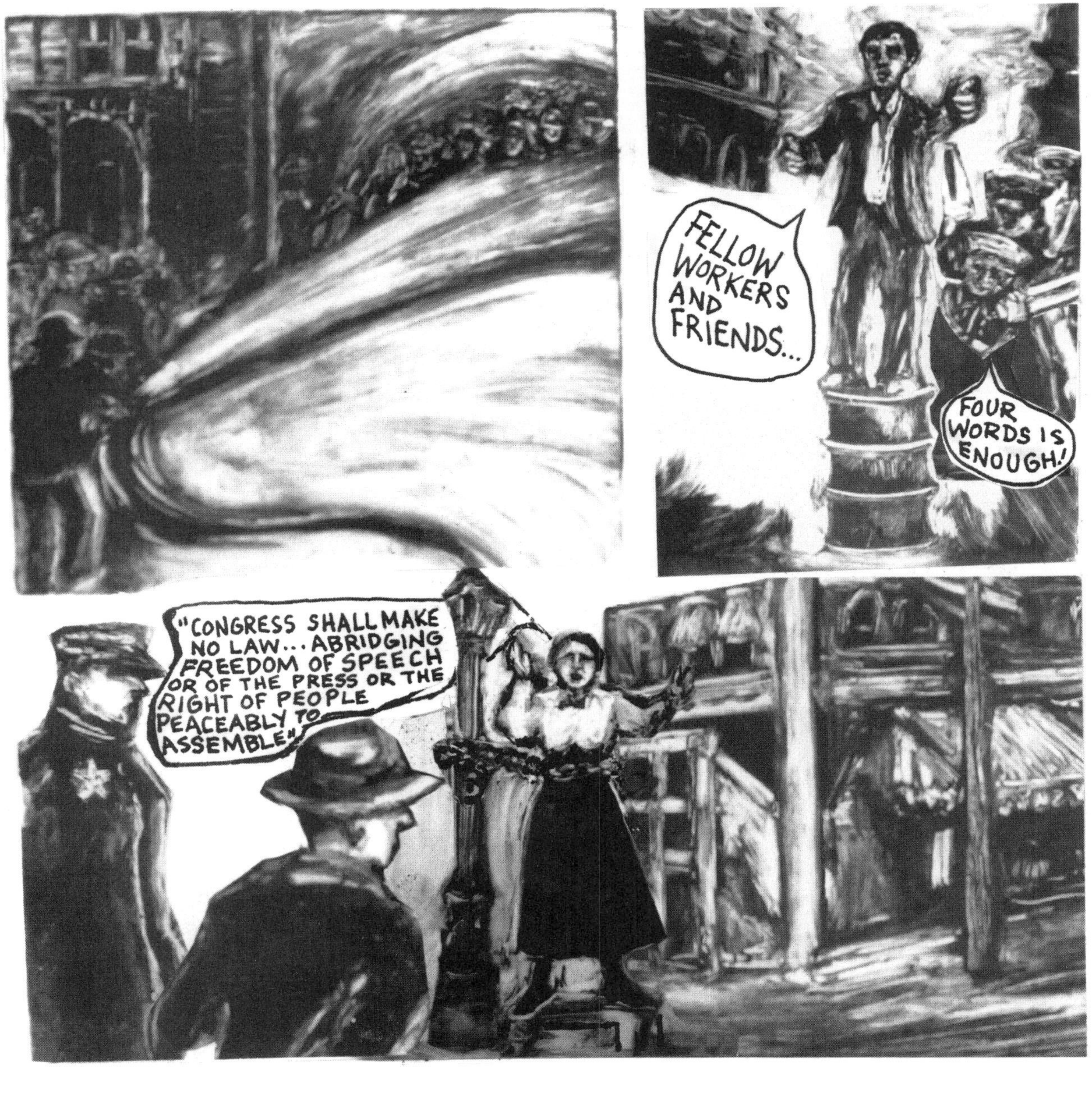
FELLOW WORKERS AND FRIENDS...
FOUR WORDS IS ENOUGH!
"CONGRESS SHALL MAKE NO LAW... ABRIDGING FREEDOM OF SPEECH OR OF THE PRESS OR THE RIGHT OF PEOPLE PEACEABLY TO ASSEMBLE."

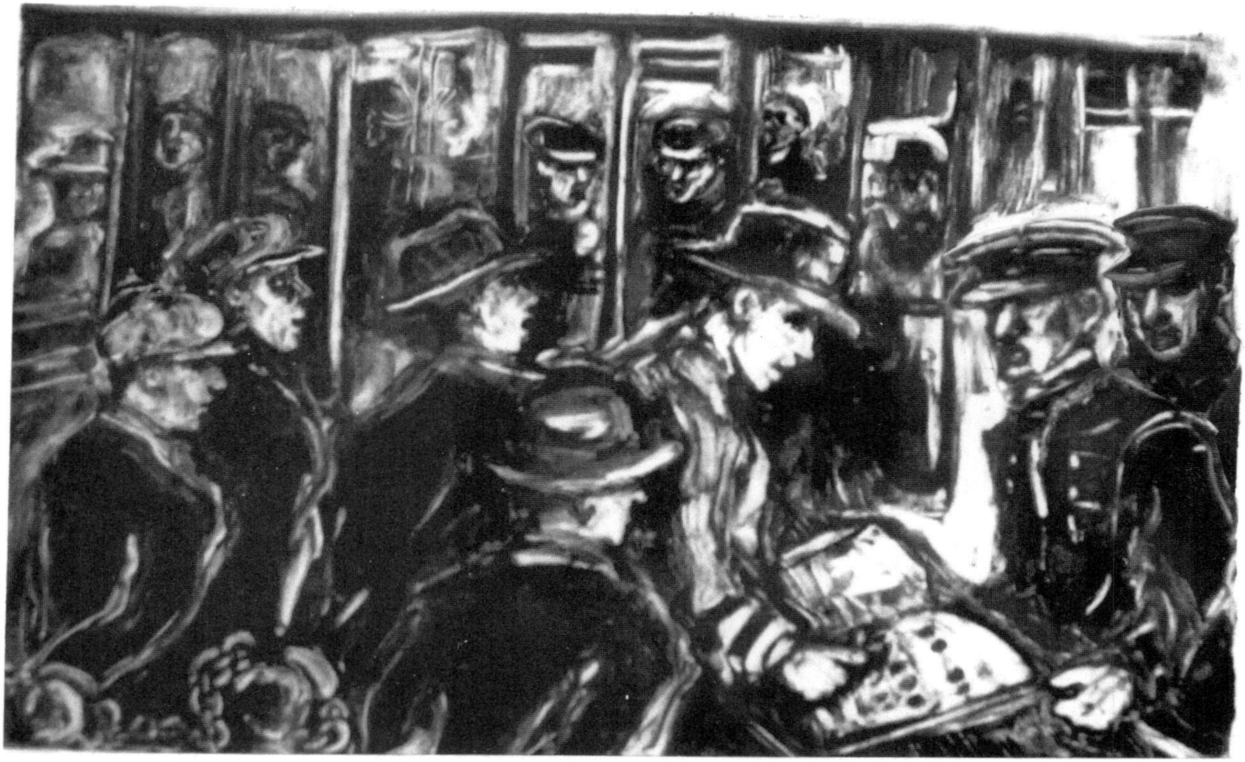

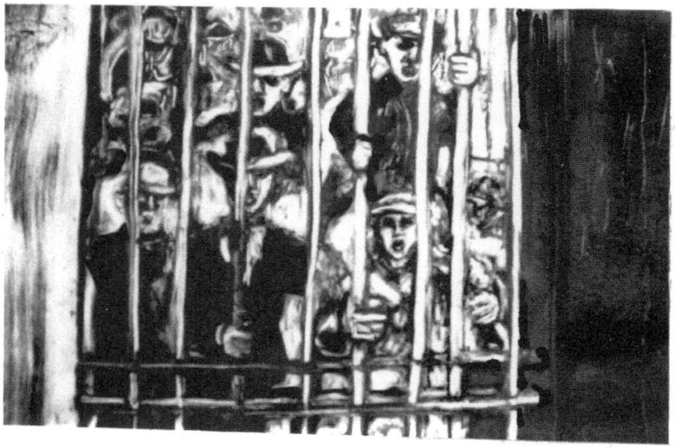

THE JAILS WERE FULL
THE SCHOOLHOUSE TOO
FILTHY ROOMS AND MOLDY FOOD
BUT THE COST JUST GREW AND GREW.

THE CHEER OF ROWDY WOBBLIES
WORE THE JAILORS THIN
SO THE PRISONERS WERE FREED,
LABOR SHARKS CHASED OUT,
AND SOAPBOX SPEAKING RULED IN.

BEWARE HOW HAPPY ENDINGS GO
A VICTORY WAS WON THAT DAY.
BUT THE SAME EXACT INJUSTICES
RING ALL TOO TRUE TODAY.

FROM THE
COMMONWEALTH
OF TOIL
BY RALPH CHAPLIN

THEY HAVE LAID OUR LIVES
OUT FOR US
TO THE UTTER END
OF TIME.
SHALL WE STAGGER ON
BENEATH THEIR HEAVY LOAD?

SHALL WE LET THEM
LIVE FOREVER IN THEIR
GILDED HALLS OF CRIME
WITH OUR CHILDREN
DOOMED TO TOIL
BENEATH THEIR GOAD?

WHEN OUR CAUSE IS
ALL TRIUMPHANT
AND WE CLAIM
OUR MOTHER EARTH,
AND THE NIGHTMARE
OF THE PRESENT
FADES AWAY,

WE SHALL LIVE WITH
LOVE & LAUGHTER,
WE WHO ARE NOW
LITTLE WORTH,
& WE'LL NOT REGRET
THE PRICE WE HAVE
TO PAY.

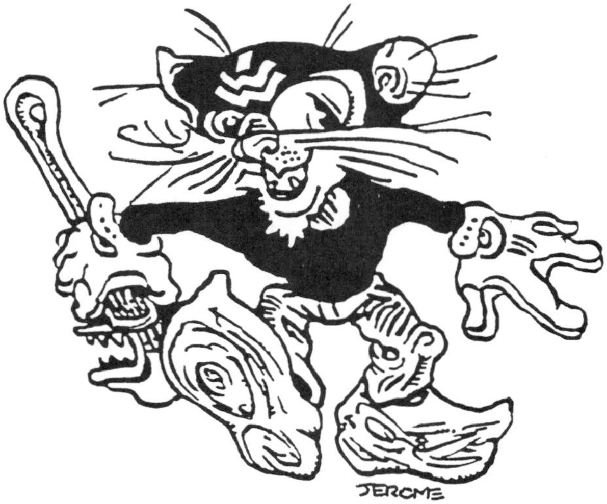
JEROME

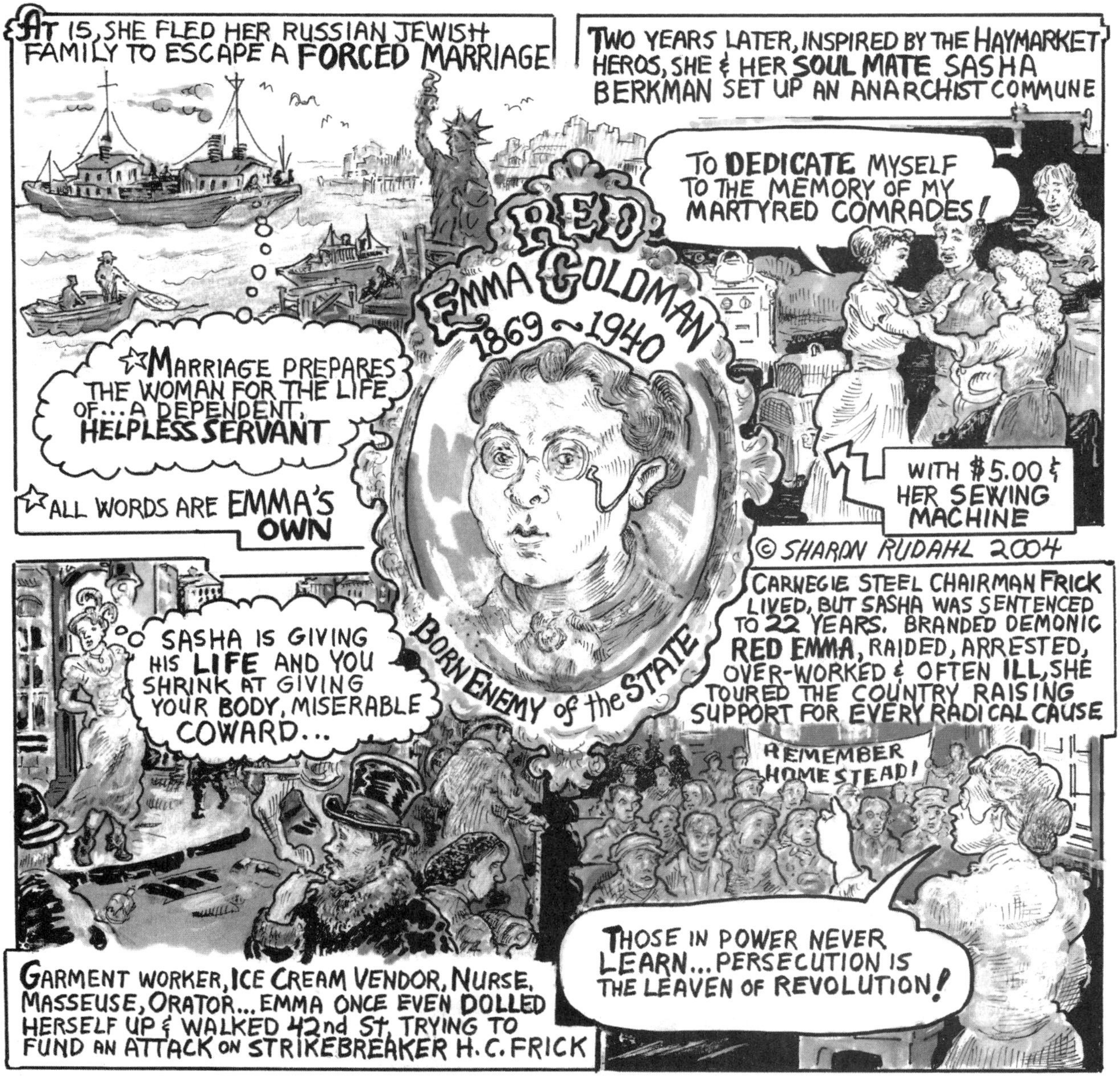
AT 15, SHE FLED HER RUSSIAN JEWISH FAMILY TO ESCAPE A FORCED MARRIAGE
☆MARRIAGE PREPARES THE WOMAN FOR THE LIFE OF... A DEPENDENT, HELPLESS SERVANT
☆ALL WORDS ARE EMMA'S OWN
RED
EMMA GOLDMAN
1869~1940
BORN ENEMY of the STATE
TWO YEARS LATER, INSPIRED BY THE HAYMARKET HEROS, SHE & HER SOUL MATE SASHA BERKMAN SET UP AN ANARCHIST COMMUNE
TO DEDICATE MYSELF TO THE MEMORY OF MY MARTYRED COMRADES!
WITH $5.00 & HER SEWING MACHINE
© SHARON RUDAHL 2004
SASHA IS GIVING HIS LIFE AND YOU SHRINK AT GIVING YOUR BODY, MISERABLE COWARD...
GARMENT WORKER, ICE CREAM VENDOR, NURSE, MASSEUSE, ORATOR... EMMA ONCE EVEN DOLLED HERSELF UP & WALKED 42nd St. TRYING TO FUND AN ATTACK ON STRIKEBREAKER H.C. FRICK
CARNEGIE STEEL CHAIRMAN FRICK LIVED, BUT SASHA WAS SENTENCED TO 22 YEARS. BRANDED DEMONIC RED EMMA, RAIDED, ARRESTED, OVER-WORKED & OFTEN ILL, SHE TOURED THE COUNTRY RAISING SUPPORT FOR EVERY RADICAL CAUSE
REMEMBER HOMESTEAD!
THOSE IN POWER NEVER LEARN... PERSECUTION IS THE LEAVEN OF REVOLUTION!

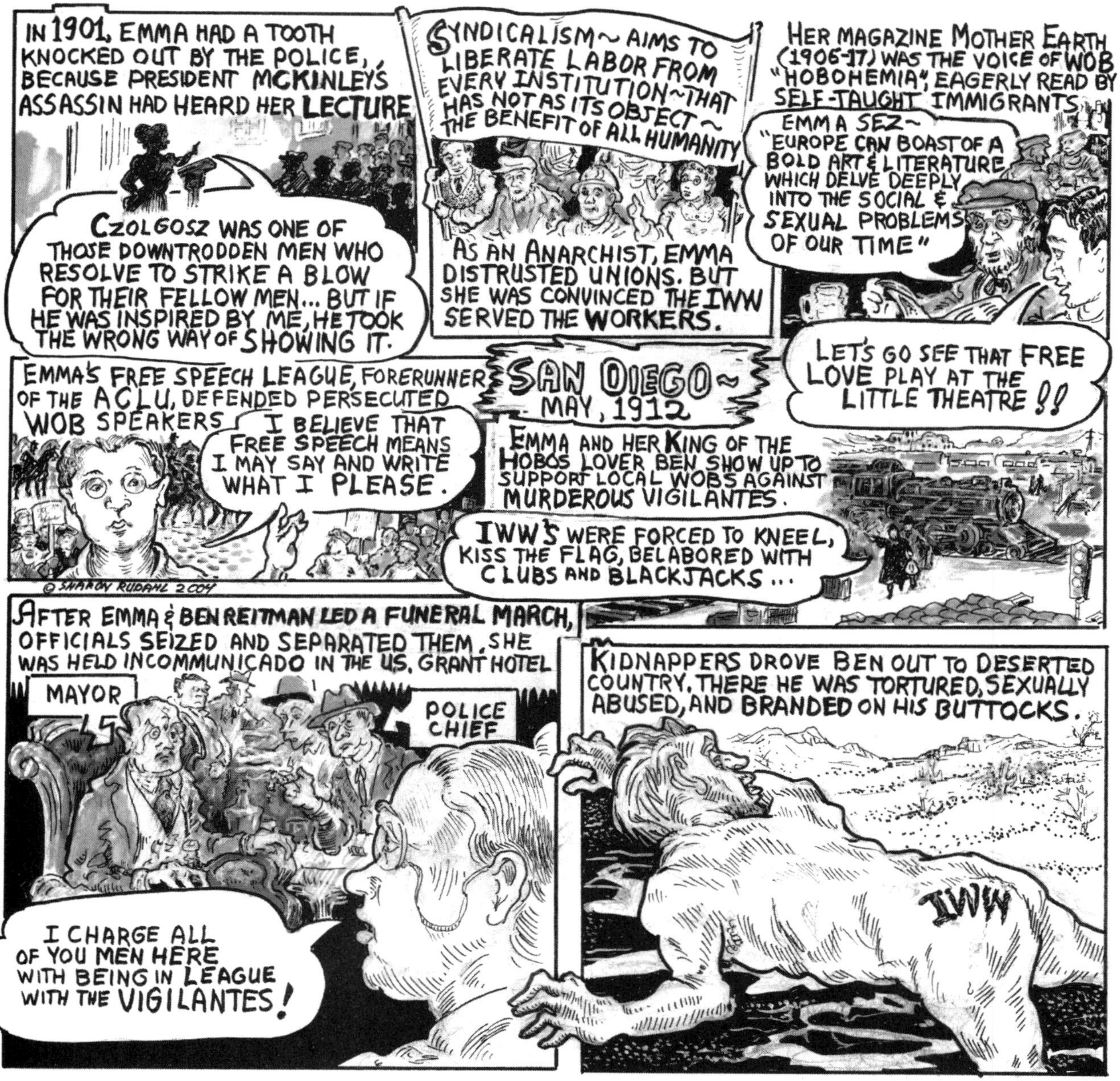

IN 1901, EMMA HAD A TOOTH KNOCKED OUT BY THE POLICE, BECAUSE PRESIDENT MCKINLEY'S ASSASSIN HAD HEARD HER LECTURE
CZOLGOSZ WAS ONE OF THOSE DOWNTRODDEN MEN WHO RESOLVE TO STRIKE A BLOW FOR THEIR FELLOW MEN... BUT IF HE WAS INSPIRED BY ME, HE TOOK THE WRONG WAY OF SHOWING IT.
SYNDICALISM ~ AIMS TO LIBERATE LABOR FROM EVERY INSTITUTION ~ THAT HAS NOT AS ITS OBJECT ~ THE BENEFIT OF ALL HUMANITY
AS AN ANARCHIST, EMMA DISTRUSTED UNIONS. BUT SHE WAS CONVINCED THE IWW SERVED THE WORKERS.
HER MAGAZINE MOTHER EARTH (1906-17) WAS THE VOICE OF WOB "HOBOHEMIA", EAGERLY READ BY SELF-TAUGHT IMMIGRANTS.
EMMA SEZ ~ "EUROPE CAN BOAST OF A BOLD ART & LITERATURE WHICH DELVE DEEPLY INTO THE SOCIAL & SEXUAL PROBLEMS OF OUR TIME"
EMMA'S FREE SPEECH LEAGUE, FORERUNNER OF THE ACLU, DEFENDED PERSECUTED WOB SPEAKERS
I BELIEVE THAT FREE SPEECH MEANS I MAY SAY AND WRITE WHAT I PLEASE.
© SHARON RUDAHL 2004
SAN DIEGO ~ MAY, 1912
LET'S GO SEE THAT FREE LOVE PLAY AT THE LITTLE THEATRE !!
EMMA AND HER KING OF THE HOBOS LOVER BEN SHOW UP TO SUPPORT LOCAL WOBS AGAINST MURDEROUS VIGILANTES.
IWW'S WERE FORCED TO KNEEL, KISS THE FLAG, BELABORED WITH CLUBS AND BLACKJACKS...
AFTER EMMA & BEN REITMAN LED A FUNERAL MARCH, OFFICIALS SEIZED AND SEPARATED THEM. SHE WAS HELD INCOMMUNICADO IN THE U.S. GRANT HOTEL
MAYOR
POLICE CHIEF
I CHARGE ALL OF YOU MEN HERE WITH BEING IN LEAGUE WITH THE VIGILANTES!
KIDNAPPERS DROVE BEN OUT TO DESERTED COUNTRY. THERE HE WAS TORTURED, SEXUALLY ABUSED, AND BRANDED ON HIS BUTTOCKS.
IWW

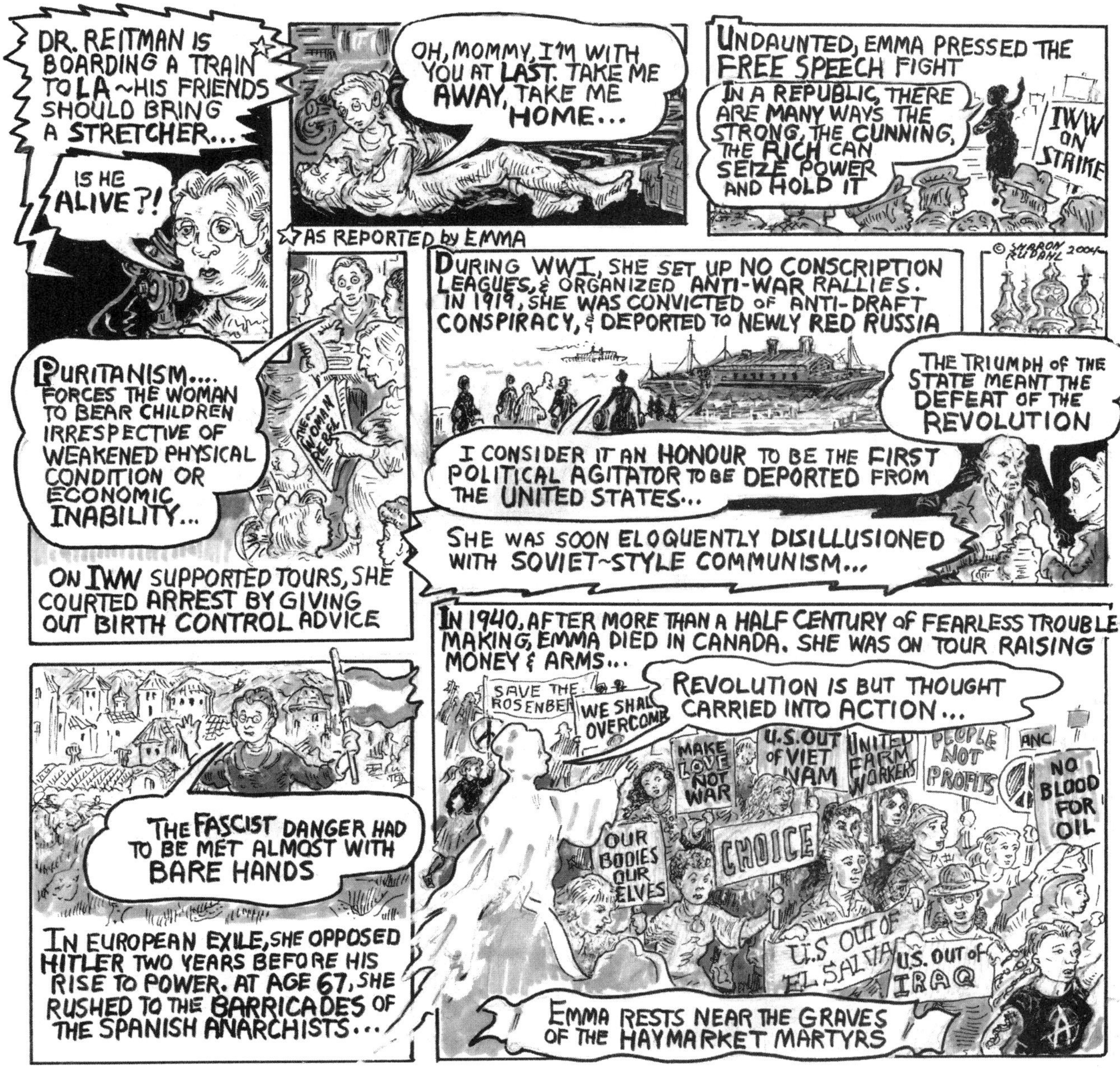
DR. REITMAN IS BOARDING A TRAIN TO LA ~ HIS FRIENDS SHOULD BRING A STRETCHER... ☆
IS HE ALIVE?!
OH, MOMMY, I'M WITH YOU AT LAST. TAKE ME AWAY, TAKE ME HOME...
☆ AS REPORTED BY EMMA
UNDAUNTED, EMMA PRESSED THE FREE SPEECH FIGHT
IN A REPUBLIC, THERE ARE MANY WAYS THE STRONG, THE CUNNING, THE RICH CAN SEIZE POWER AND HOLD IT
IWW ON STRIKE
PURITANISM.... FORCES THE WOMAN TO BEAR CHILDREN IRRESPECTIVE OF WEAKENED PHYSICAL CONDITION OR ECONOMIC INABILITY...
THE WOMAN REBEL
ON IWW SUPPORTED TOURS, SHE COURTED ARREST BY GIVING OUT BIRTH CONTROL ADVICE
DURING WWI, SHE SET UP NO CONSCRIPTION LEAGUES, & ORGANIZED ANTI-WAR RALLIES. IN 1919, SHE WAS CONVICTED OF ANTI-DRAFT CONSPIRACY, & DEPORTED TO NEWLY RED RUSSIA
I CONSIDER IT AN HONOUR TO BE THE FIRST POLITICAL AGITATOR TO BE DEPORTED FROM THE UNITED STATES...
© SHARON RUDAHL 2004
THE TRIUMPH OF THE STATE MEANT THE DEFEAT OF THE REVOLUTION
SHE WAS SOON ELOQUENTLY DISILLUSIONED WITH SOVIET~STYLE COMMUNISM...
THE FASCIST DANGER HAD TO BE MET ALMOST WITH BARE HANDS
IN EUROPEAN EXILE, SHE OPPOSED HITLER TWO YEARS BEFORE HIS RISE TO POWER. AT AGE 67, SHE RUSHED TO THE BARRICADES OF THE SPANISH ANARCHISTS...
IN 1940, AFTER MORE THAN A HALF CENTURY OF FEARLESS TROUBLE-MAKING, EMMA DIED IN CANADA. SHE WAS ON TOUR RAISING MONEY & ARMS...
REVOLUTION IS BUT THOUGHT CARRIED INTO ACTION...
SAVE THE ROSENBER
WE SHAL OVERCOME
MAKE LOVE NOT WAR
U.S. OUT OF VIET NAM
UNITED FARM WORKERS
PEOPLE NOT PROFITS
ANC
NO BLOOD FOR OIL
OUR BODIES OUR ELVES
CHOICE
U.S OUT OF EL SALVA
U.S. OUT OF IRAQ
EMMA RESTS NEAR THE GRAVES OF THE HAYMARKET MARTYRS

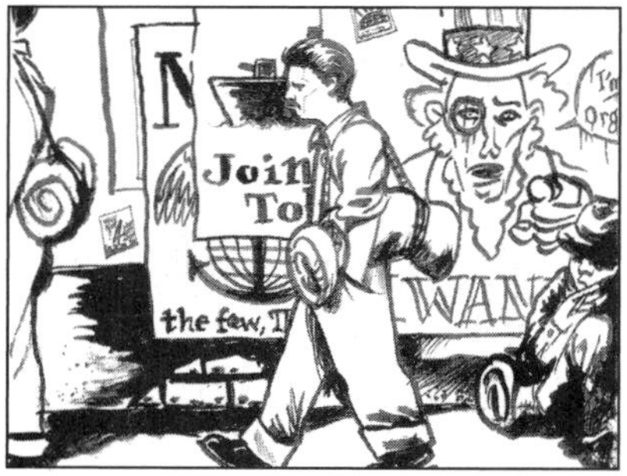

Bindle Stiffs got their name because they carried all their worldly goods rolled up in a blanket and slung by a cord around their shoulders from job to job.

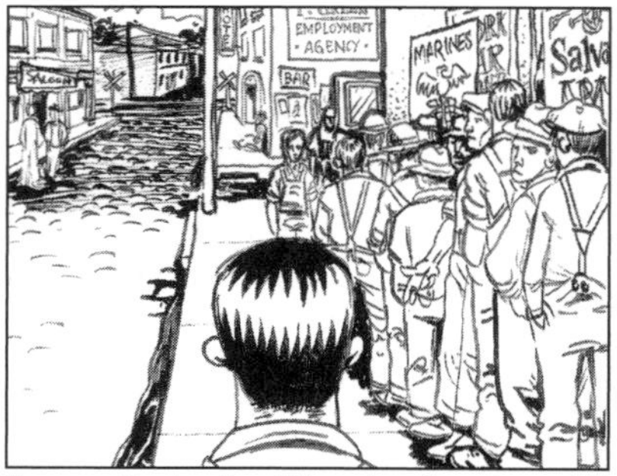
EMPLOYMENT AGENCY
MARINES
BAR

Every city in the West developed a stiff town, a number of streets or blocks that were used as recruiting centers for temporary labor.

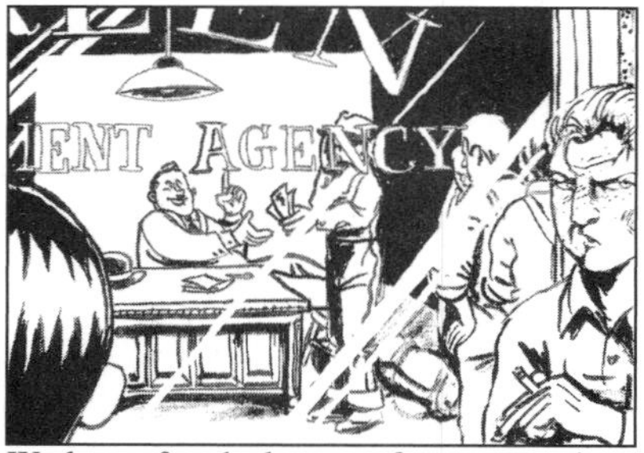
ENT AGENCY

Workers often had to pay fees to rapacious employment agencies, ranging from one to three dollars for a job. The wholesale firing of men by foremen, the arduous nature of the work, and the temporary nature of the employment kept the bindle stiff in constant motion around these job sharks.

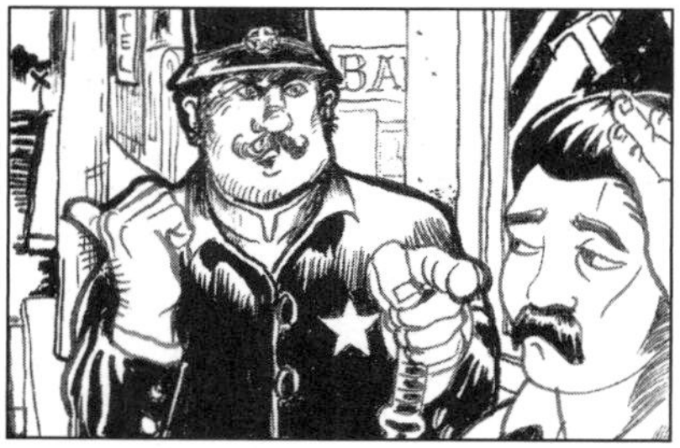

There were cheap hotels, bars and dumps on the drag in this part of town, plenty of places to blow your stake, or what little money you had. But hanging around too long got the attention of the bull and he would give you the horns.

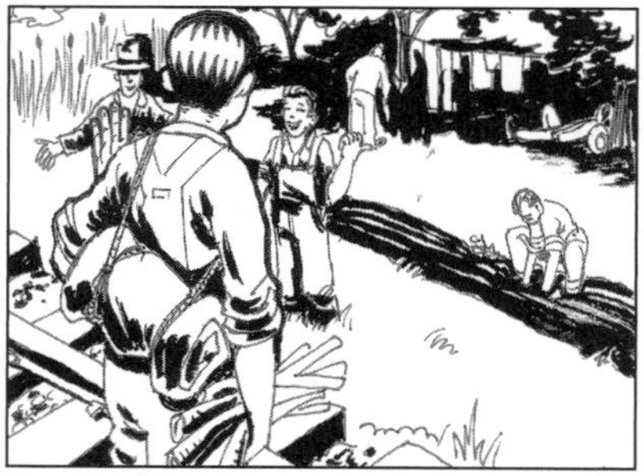

The jungle was a meeting place, usually near a railroad division point, occupied by hoboes and stiffs for preparing food and sleeping. Itinerant workers found acceptance here.

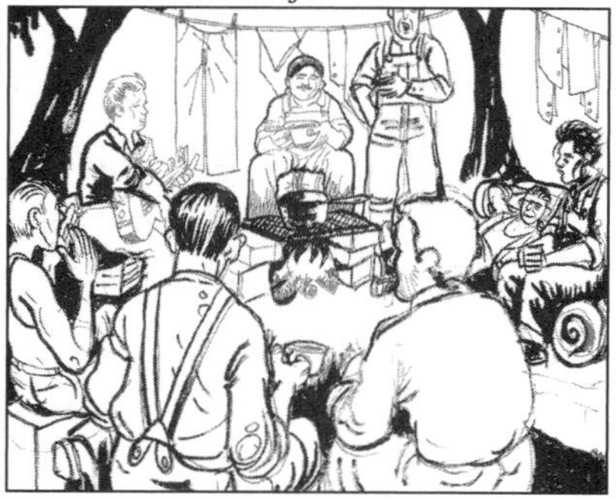

An enlightened Wobbly would often strike up a song from the Little Red Songbook to help get your spirits up and keep you going.

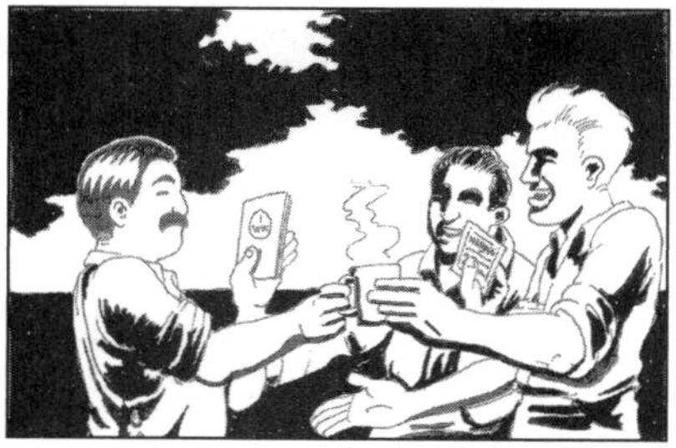

Jungles were a great place to get news. Many of the stiffs were Wobblies or had been in the past. The IWW was the only organization that lifted the lives of these workers to a significant position in society.

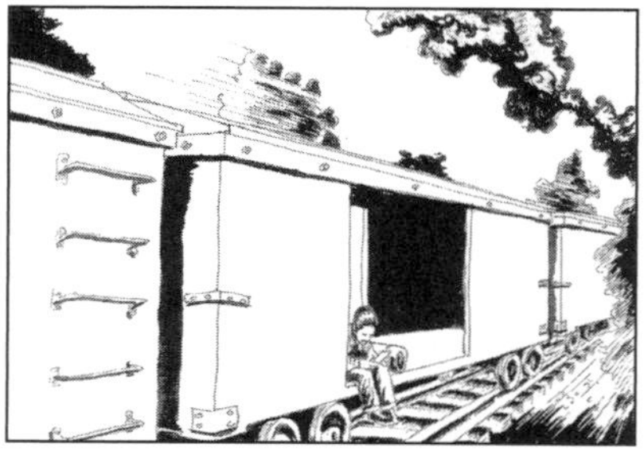

Migratory workers hopped trains to follow the harvest and get from job to job. Your red IWW membership card was your ticket to the rails at times.

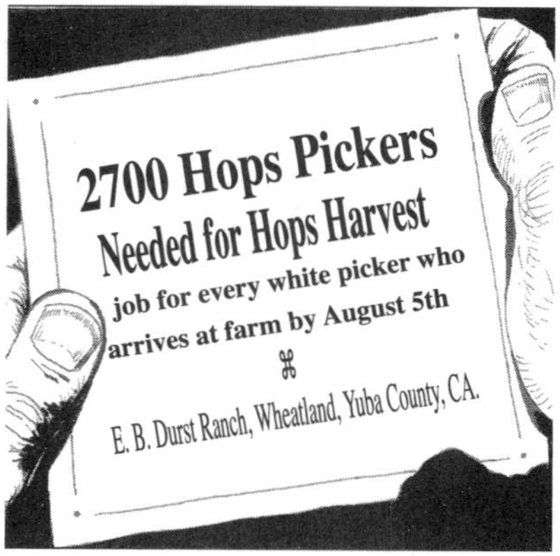
2700 Hops Pickers
Needed for Hops Harvest
job for every white picker who
arrives at farm by August 5th
E. B. Durst Ranch, Wheatland, Yuba County, CA.

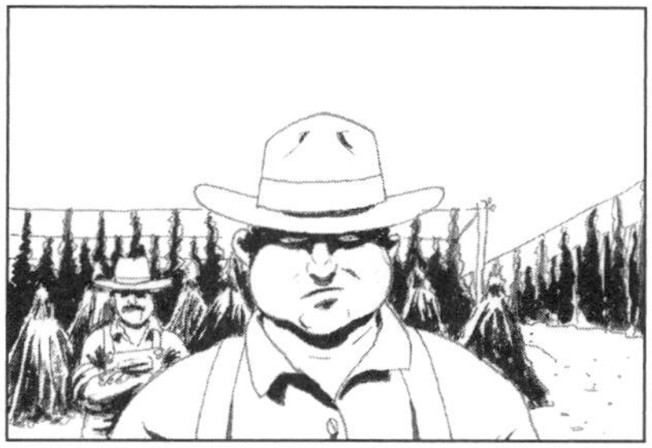
E.B. Durst Ranch was the largest single employer of migratory labor in the state of California. Ralph Durst's ranch was in Wheatland, a short distance south from Marysville.

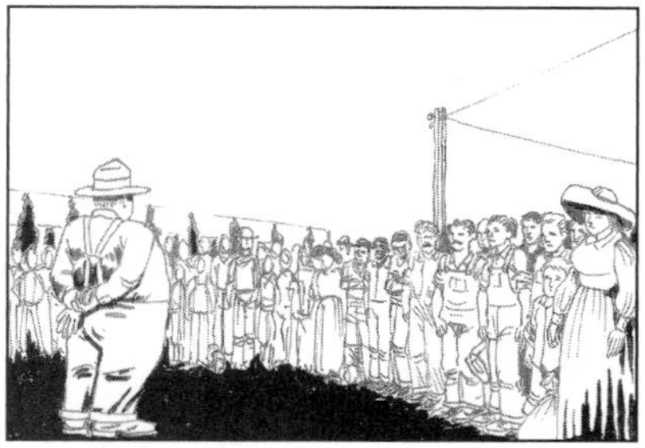
2,800 multiracial workers arrived to find only 1,500 job openings. Durst had deliberately advertised for twice the number of workers he needed. Living conditions were inadequate for even half their number.

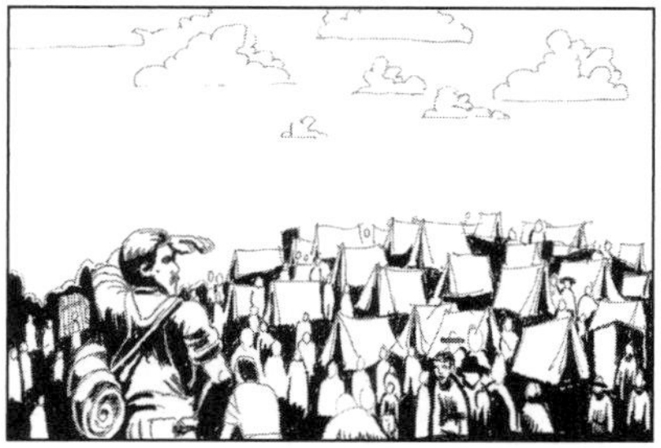
When the workers arrived they discovered a tent and campsite space rented for seventy-five cents a week, but there were too few tents even at that high price.

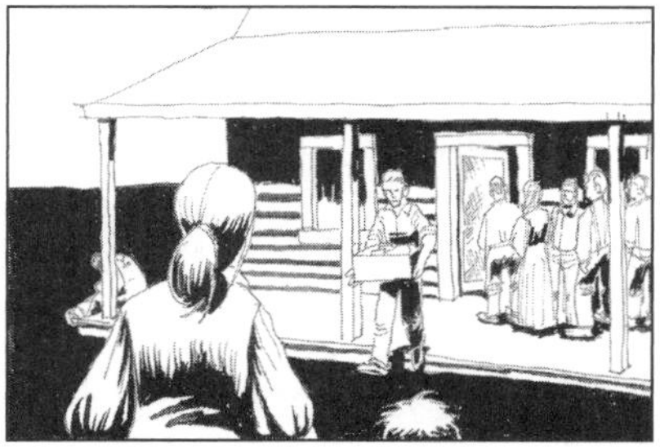
Durst sold food to workers at a grocery store on his property and refused to allow anyone else to deliver groceries to the ranch. A long walk to town was the only way to buy food for less.

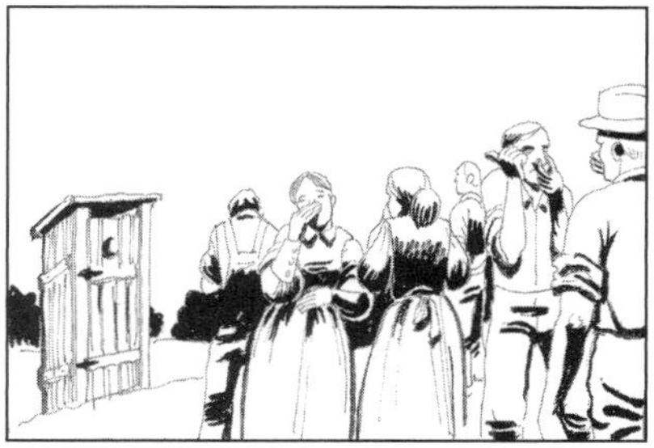
Durst provided only nine crudely built toilets for all the workers. Since the toilets were also the only public trash receptacles, they soon swarmed with maggots and blue flies.

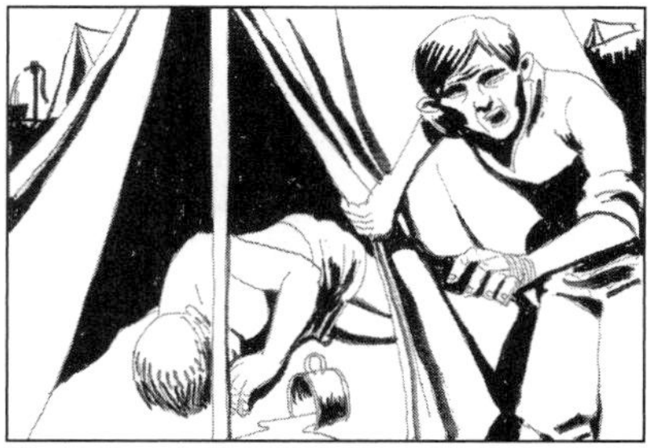
The campsite drinking water was inadequate and dangerous. Wells on the property were dry, full of stagnant water or too close to garbage and toilets areas. Diseases spread among the workers, including typhoid, dysentery, and malaria.

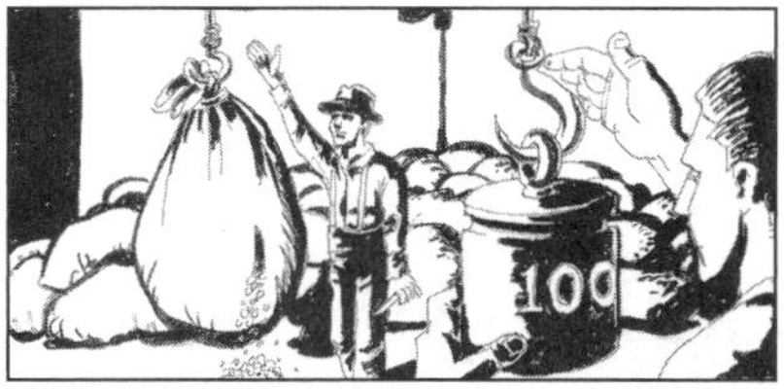
100
Durst offered the going rate at the time of $1 for a hundred weight bag of picked hops. The hops were excessively cleaned before inspection and weighed with no workers present at the time of weighing. Durst withheld 10 cents per hundred pounds until the end of the harvest as a way to coerce workers to stay until the end.

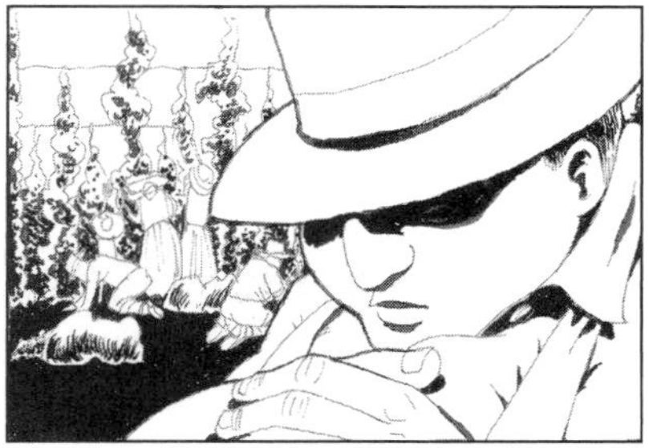
Workers, on average, ended up with less than $1.50 for a twelve-hour day. Twelve-hour workdays were standard at most hop ranches, but a standard day's pay at other ranches was $3 dollars.

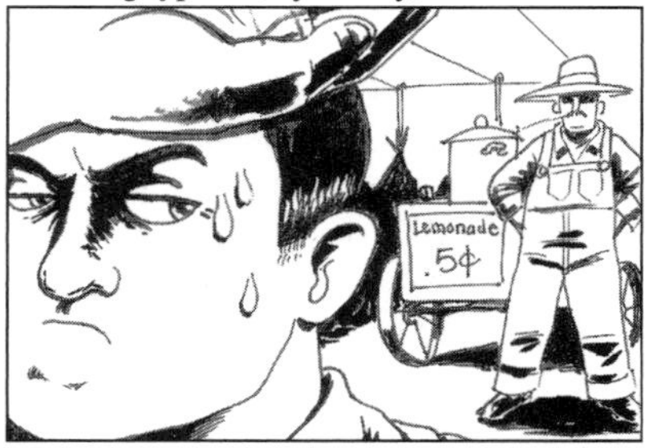
Lemonade
.5¢
Workers that wanted water would have to walk a good distance away from the field, because Durst did not cart water to the field. He did offer lemonade at 5 cents a glass to those workers worried about losing work time and money in the field where temperatures reached 110 degrees on some days.

At most hops ranches men with high poles brought down the tall vines so that women and children could gather the flowers. In Durst's fields there were no high pole men.

The high pole man traditionally helped throw the sacks of hops into the wagons. Without them women and children lifted 80-100 lb hopsacks into the wagons.

By three days into the harvest the conditions were unbearable. The workers began to voice their discontent. Out of the 2,800 workers only about one hundred were current or past IWW members. About thirty of them formed an IWW local, to protest the living and working conditions on the ranch.

In a mass meeting on July 29th the workers chose a committee to voice their demands. They elected Richard "Blackie" Ford as chief spokesman and Herman Suhr as the committee secretary.

Durst caught wind of these events through informants he had in the camp. He invited the workers, on the afternoon of August 3rd to step forward and discuss their complaints. The workers demanded that Durst give them a flat rate of $1.25 per hundred pounds of picked hops, drinking water brought to the fields, inspection of the picked hops by the workers themselves, high-pole men, separate toilets for women, improvements of camp toilets, and lemonade made from real lemons and not powdered citric acid.

Durst agreed only to improve toilets, provide water in the fields, and add one worker to the inspection team.

The committee warned Durst that they would go on strike if their conditions were not fully met. Durst broke off negotiations by slapping Ford with his glove and fired him and all the workers on the committee. He told them to pick up their pay and get off his property

Ford and the committee refused to leave. They had already paid for their accommodations for the week. Durst asked the deputy sheriff Daken to arrest Ford. Workers intervened on Ford's behalf when Daken did not produce a warrant.

Later that day another mass meeting was held on the hill, at the worker's camp. The Wobblies urged their fellow workers to go on strike to force Durst to address their grievances.

During his speech Ford lifted a sick child above the crowd. "It is not so much for ourselves we are fighting as that this little baby may never see the conditions which now exist on this ranch!"

When asked if they would strike, a majority raised their hands. Ford handed the child back to it's mother when he saw two cars approaching the gathering.

Ford begins to lead the workers in the singing of Joe Hill's song; "Mr. Block."

Eleven men arrived in the two cars to arrest Ford and break up the gathering. They were the District Attorney of Yuba county Edward Manwell, who was also Durst's lawyer, Marysville Sheriff Voss, Deputy Sheriffs Daken, Anderson, and Reardon as well as six other deputies. A number of them had been drinking according to some witnesses.

"Please give me your attention, I'll introduce to you. A man that is a credit to "Our Red, White and Blue;" His head is made of lumber, and as solid as a rock;He is a common worker and his name is Mr. Block. And Block thinks he may be President some day."

Oh, Mr. Block you were born by mistake,
  You take the cake,
  You make me ache.
Tie a rock on your block and then jump in the lake, Kindly do that for liberty's sake.

Yes, Mr. Block is lucky; He found a job by gee! The shark got seven dollars, for job and fare and fee. They shipped him to the desert and dumped him with his truck,
But when he tried to find his job he sure was out of luck. He shouted, "That's too raw, I'll fix them with the law."

Oh, Mr. Block you were born by mistake,
  You take the cake,
  You make me ache.
Tie a rock on your block and then jump in the lake, Kindly do that for liberty's sake.

Block hiked back to the city, but wasn't doing well. He said, "I'll join the union- the great A.F. of L." He got a job the next morning, got fired that night, He said, "I'll see Sam Gompers and he'll fix that Foreman right." Sam Gompers said, "You see, You've got our sympathy."

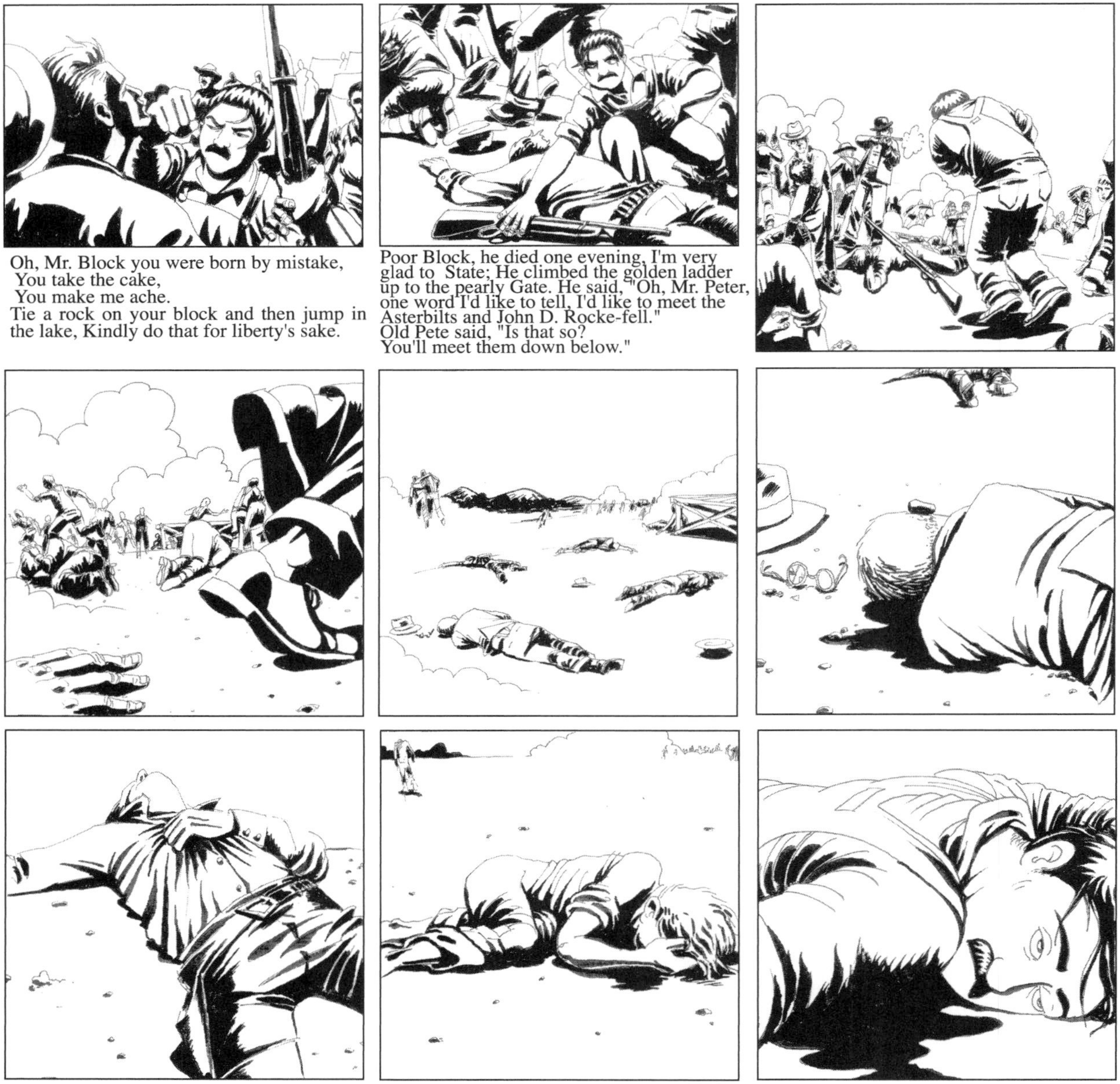
Oh, Mr. Block you were born by mistake,
You take the cake,
You make me ache.
Tie a rock on your block and then jump in the lake, Kindly do that for liberty's sake.
Poor Block, he died one evening, I'm very glad to State; He climbed the golden ladder up to the pearly Gate. He said, "Oh, Mr. Peter, one word I'd like to tell, I'd like to meet the Asterbilts and John D. Rocke-fell."
Old Pete said, "Is that so?
You'll meet them down below."

Fearing more disturbances Governor Hiram Johnson dispatched five companies of the National Guard to Wheatland. Soldiers and law enforcement arrested approximately one hundred workers who remained at camp.

The Marysville coroner's inquest concluded that the IWW strike leadership had caused a riot that led to the death of District Attorney Manwell and Deputy Eugene Reardon.

An extensive manhunt ensued throughout California and the neighboring states to arrest Wobblies involved in the Wheatland affair. Warrants were issued for the arrest of Ford and Suhr for murder.

Burns detectives- a private detective agency known for its antiradical and antilabor tendencies- arrested a number of workers. The law enforcement officers used John Doe warrants, a civil rights abuse that allowed the officers to write in the arrested person's name after the arrest.

In an effort to gain information from the arrested men, Burns men resorted to beating, starving, bribery and kidnapping. Some were kept incommunicado for weeks. One IWW prisoner committed suicide in prison; another went insane from police brutality. Suhr himself was tortured into a confession he recanted later.

Eight months later a trial began. Ford and Suhr were charged with leading a strike that lead to violence. They were convicted of second degree murder. The judge was a lifelong friend of Manwell. Eight of twelve jurors were farmers who knew the deputies. After deliberating one day, they found Ford and Suhr guilty. Both received life sentences.

During the trial, the brutal handling of those under arrest came to light. The trial also revealed the outrageous nature of the hop camp conditions, stirring public condemnation of Durst's behavior, and heightened public interest and concern over the plight of migrant agricultural workers.

The year after the trial IWW membership in California rose to five thousand, with a total of 40 IWW locals. Organizers and soap boxers agitated throughout the state. The IWW blanketed California with stickers and circulars urging a boycott of the hop fields until Ford and Suhr were released, and living and working conditions improved.

Hundreds of thousands of industrial workers left jobless by the 1914 financial depression hopped freight trains in hope of finding work in the harvest fields. American radicalism in the form of the IWW spread rapidly among them. The IWW's Agricultural Worker's Union grew to 70,000 members within three years. It was the first union to organize and negotiate successfully higher wage scales for harvest workers. Farmers learned the meaning of sabotage, strikes for better wages and working conditions. They responded with vigilante mobs, driving agitators and workers from town at gunpoint. Class warfare had broken out in the most "American" sections of rural America. The IWW was determined to build a new world in place of the old, a better one.

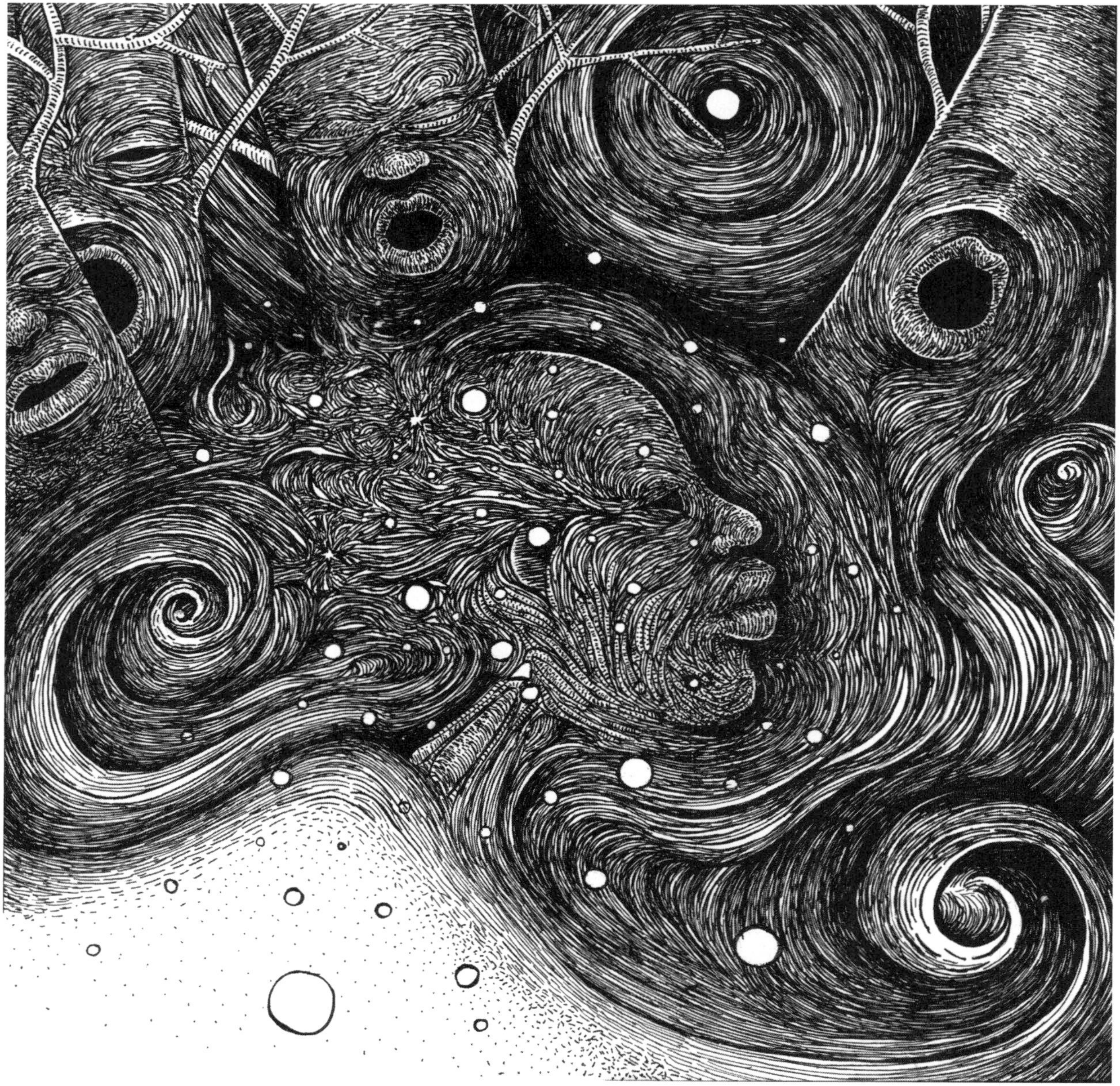

THE TIMBERBEAST'S LAMENT

unsigned IWW poem—source unknown

I'm on the boat for the camp
With a sick and aching head;
I've blowed another winter's stake,
And got the jims instead.

It seems I'll never learn the truth
That's written plain as day,
It's the only time they welcome you
Is when you make it pay.

And it's "blanket-stiff" and "jungle-hound",
And "pitch him out the door",
But it's "Howdy, Jack, old-timer,"
When you've got the price for more.

Oh, tonight the boat is rocky,
And I ain't got a bunk,
Not a rare of cheering likker,
Just a turkey full of junk,

All I call my life's possessions,
Is just what I carry 'round,
For I've blowed the rest on skid-roads,
Of a hundred gyppo towns.

And it's "lumberjack" and "timber-beast",
And "Give these Bums a ride",
But it's "Have one on the house, old boy,"
If you're stepping with the tide.

And the chokers will be heavy,
Just as heavy, just as cold.
When the hooker gives the high-ball,
And we start to dig for gold.

And I'll cuss the siren skid-road,
With its blatant, drunken tune,
But then, of course, I'll up and make
Another trip next June.

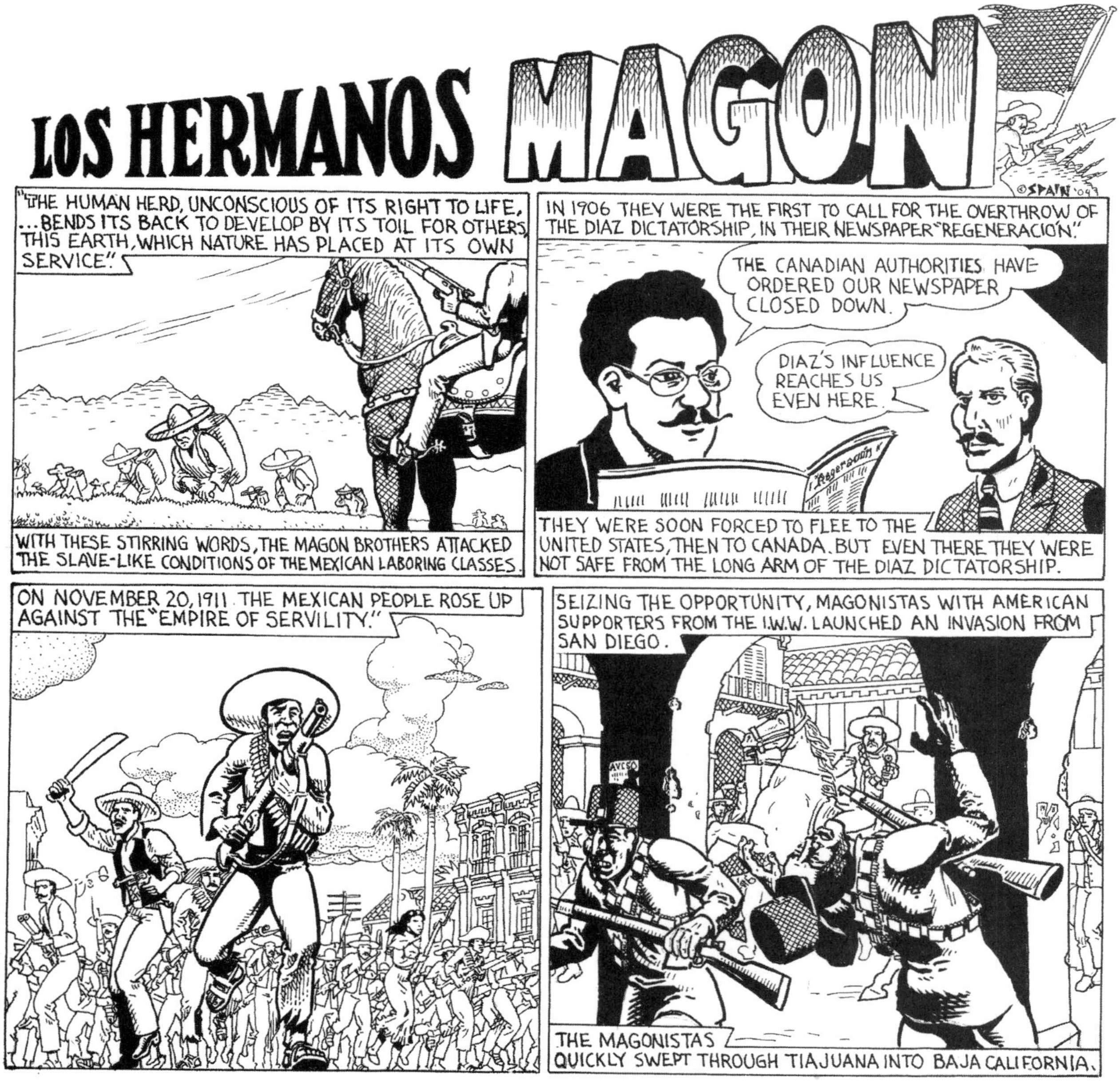
LOS HERMANOS MAGON
©SPAIN '04
"THE HUMAN HERD, UNCONSCIOUS OF ITS RIGHT TO LIFE, ...BENDS ITS BACK TO DEVELOP BY ITS TOIL FOR OTHERS THIS EARTH, WHICH NATURE HAS PLACED AT ITS OWN SERVICE."
WITH THESE STIRRING WORDS, THE MAGON BROTHERS ATTACKED THE SLAVE-LIKE CONDITIONS OF THE MEXICAN LABORING CLASSES.
IN 1906 THEY WERE THE FIRST TO CALL FOR THE OVERTHROW OF THE DIAZ DICTATORSHIP, IN THEIR NEWSPAPER "REGENERACIÓN."
THE CANADIAN AUTHORITIES HAVE ORDERED OUR NEWSPAPER CLOSED DOWN.
DIAZ'S INFLUENCE REACHES US EVEN HERE.
THEY WERE SOON FORCED TO FLEE TO THE UNITED STATES, THEN TO CANADA. BUT EVEN THERE THEY WERE NOT SAFE FROM THE LONG ARM OF THE DIAZ DICTATORSHIP.
ON NOVEMBER 20, 1911 THE MEXICAN PEOPLE ROSE UP AGAINST THE "EMPIRE OF SERVILITY."
SEIZING THE OPPORTUNITY, MAGONISTAS WITH AMERICAN SUPPORTERS FROM THE I.W.W. LAUNCHED AN INVASION FROM SAN DIEGO.
AVISO
THE MAGONISTAS QUICKLY SWEPT THROUGH TIAJUANA INTO BAJA CALIFORNIA.

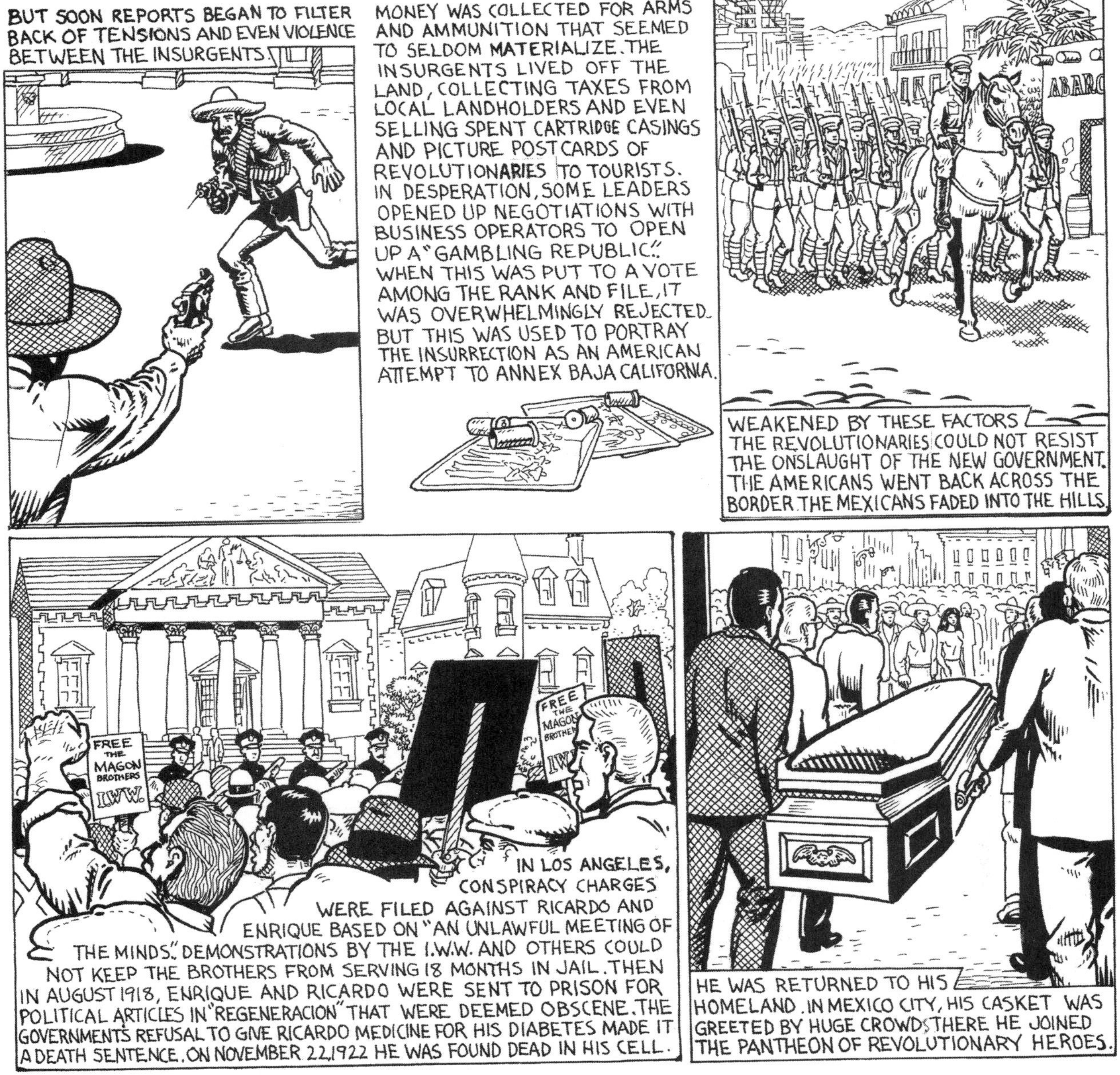
BUT SOON REPORTS BEGAN TO FILTER BACK OF TENSIONS AND EVEN VIOLENCE BETWEEN THE INSURGENTS.
MONEY WAS COLLECTED FOR ARMS AND AMMUNITION THAT SEEMED TO SELDOM MATERIALIZE. THE INSURGENTS LIVED OFF THE LAND, COLLECTING TAXES FROM LOCAL LANDHOLDERS AND EVEN SELLING SPENT CARTRIDGE CASINGS AND PICTURE POSTCARDS OF REVOLUTIONARIES TO TOURISTS. IN DESPERATION, SOME LEADERS OPENED UP NEGOTIATIONS WITH BUSINESS OPERATORS TO OPEN UP A "GAMBLING REPUBLIC." WHEN THIS WAS PUT TO A VOTE AMONG THE RANK AND FILE, IT WAS OVERWHELMINGLY REJECTED. BUT THIS WAS USED TO PORTRAY THE INSURRECTION AS AN AMERICAN ATTEMPT TO ANNEX BAJA CALIFORNIA.
WEAKENED BY THESE FACTORS THE REVOLUTIONARIES COULD NOT RESIST THE ONSLAUGHT OF THE NEW GOVERNMENT. THE AMERICANS WENT BACK ACROSS THE BORDER. THE MEXICANS FADED INTO THE HILLS.
FREE THE MAGON BROTHERS I.W.W.
FREE THE MAGON BROTHERS IWW
IN LOS ANGELES, CONSPIRACY CHARGES WERE FILED AGAINST RICARDO AND ENRIQUE BASED ON "AN UNLAWFUL MEETING OF THE MINDS." DEMONSTRATIONS BY THE I.W.W. AND OTHERS COULD NOT KEEP THE BROTHERS FROM SERVING 18 MONTHS IN JAIL. THEN IN AUGUST 1918, ENRIQUE AND RICARDO WERE SENT TO PRISON FOR POLITICAL ARTICLES IN "REGENERACION" THAT WERE DEEMED OBSCENE. THE GOVERNMENT'S REFUSAL TO GIVE RICARDO MEDICINE FOR HIS DIABETES MADE IT A DEATH SENTENCE. ON NOVEMBER 22, 1922 HE WAS FOUND DEAD IN HIS CELL.
HE WAS RETURNED TO HIS HOMELAND. IN MEXICO CITY, HIS CASKET WAS GREETED BY HUGE CROWDS; THERE HE JOINED THE PANTHEON OF REVOLUTIONARY HEROES.

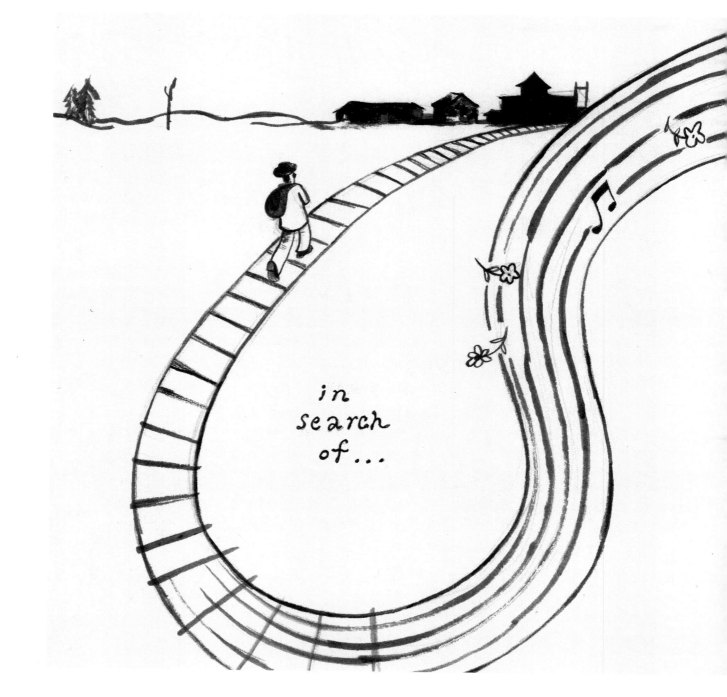

in
search
of...

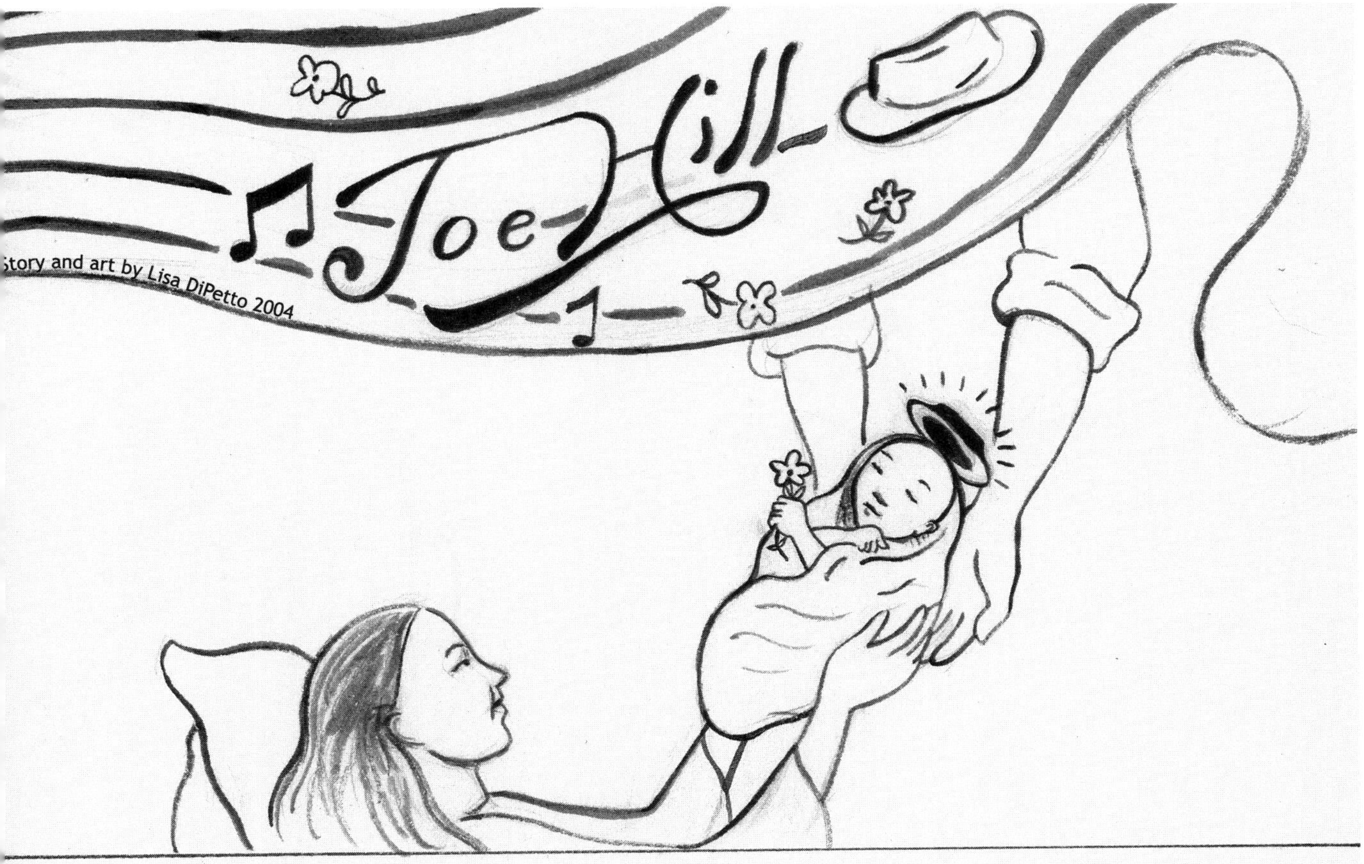
Joe Hill
Story and art by Lisa DiPetto 2004

There are few verifiable facts about the life of Joe Hill other than his birth, death, and the voice his songs gave to the IWW and the labor movement for generations to come. He survives as folk tales and legends do - in stories, recollections, and in his songs.

Joel Emmanuel Haggelund was born on October 7, 1879 in Gavle, Sweden. He was one of 8 children - only 6 would survive childhood.

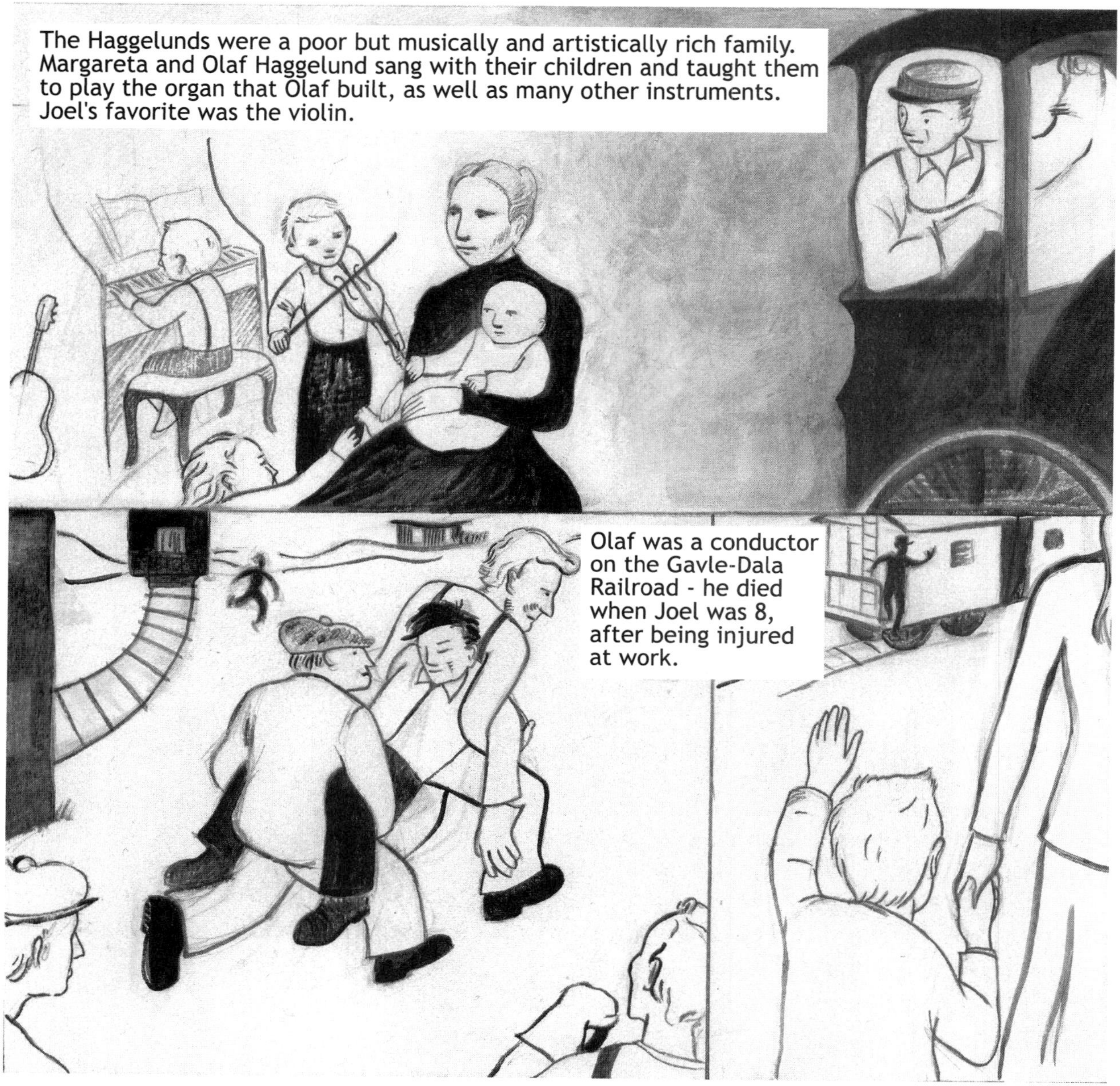
The Haggelunds were a poor but musically and artistically rich family. Margareta and Olaf Haggelund sang with their children and taught them to play the organ that Olaf built, as well as many other instruments. Joel's favorite was the violin.
Olaf was a conductor on the Gavle-Dala Railroad - he died when Joel was 8, after being injured at work.

After the death of their father, the children went to work to support the family. Joel first worked in a rope factory, and when he was older as a fireman on a steam crane.

A fireman kept the engine's fire alive!

In his teens he was diagnosed with skin and joint tuberculosis. The treatment of massive doses of x - rays and many skin grafts left him with scars on his face and neck.

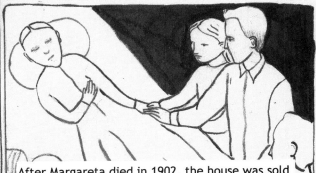

After Margareta died in 1902, the house was sold and the children went their separate ways...

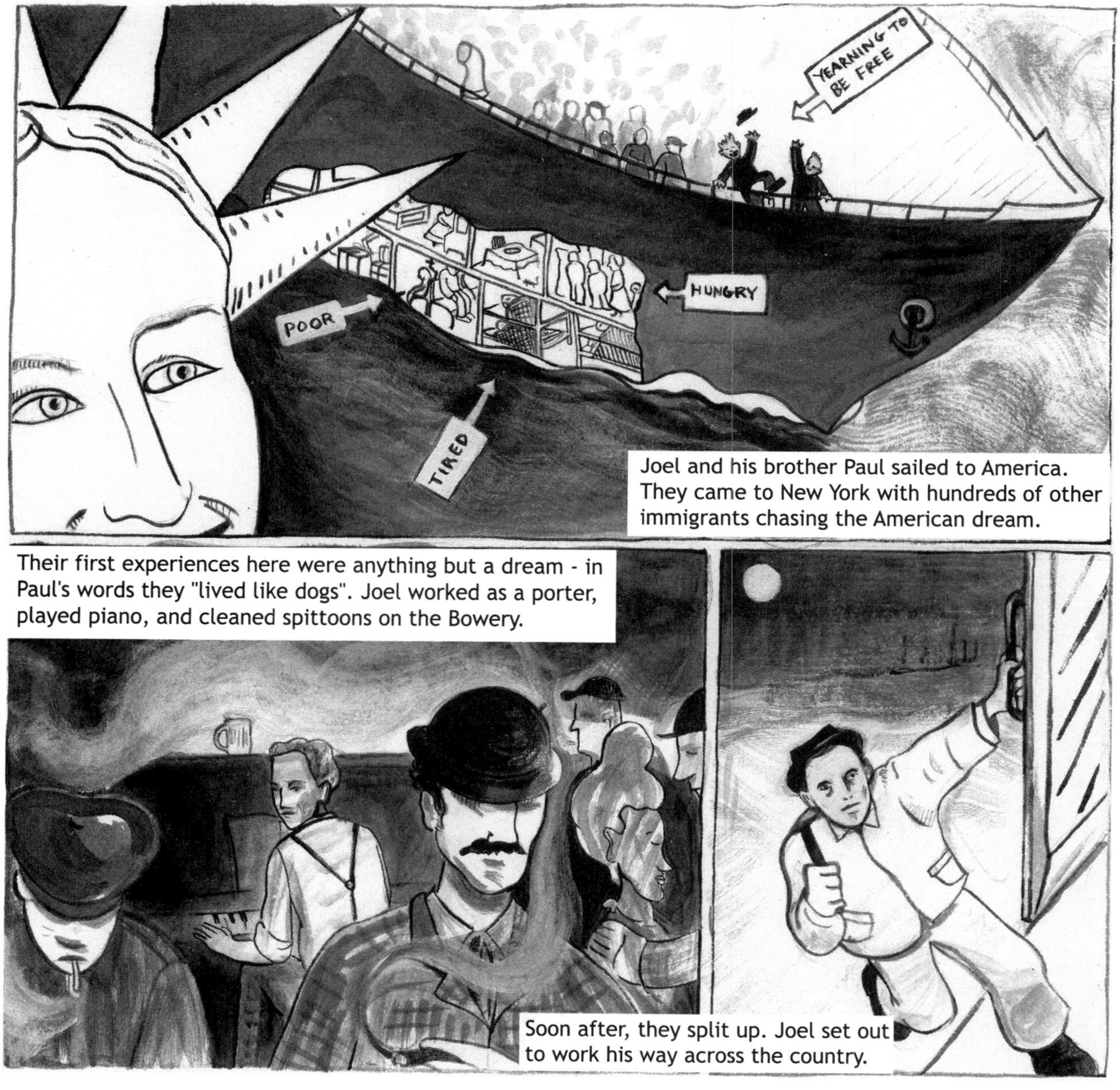
YEARNING TO BE FREE
HUNGRY
POOR
TIRED
Joel and his brother Paul sailed to America. They came to New York with hundreds of other immigrants chasing the American dream.
Their first experiences here were anything but a dream - in Paul's words they "lived like dogs". Joel worked as a porter, played piano, and cleaned spittoons on the Bowery.
Soon after, they split up. Joel set out to work his way across the country.

He traveled across America doing all kinds of jobs: mechanic, longshoreman, machinist, logger - he mastered as many trades as musical instruments. He also stayed up late writing what he called "scribbles" - poems, songs, and cartoons

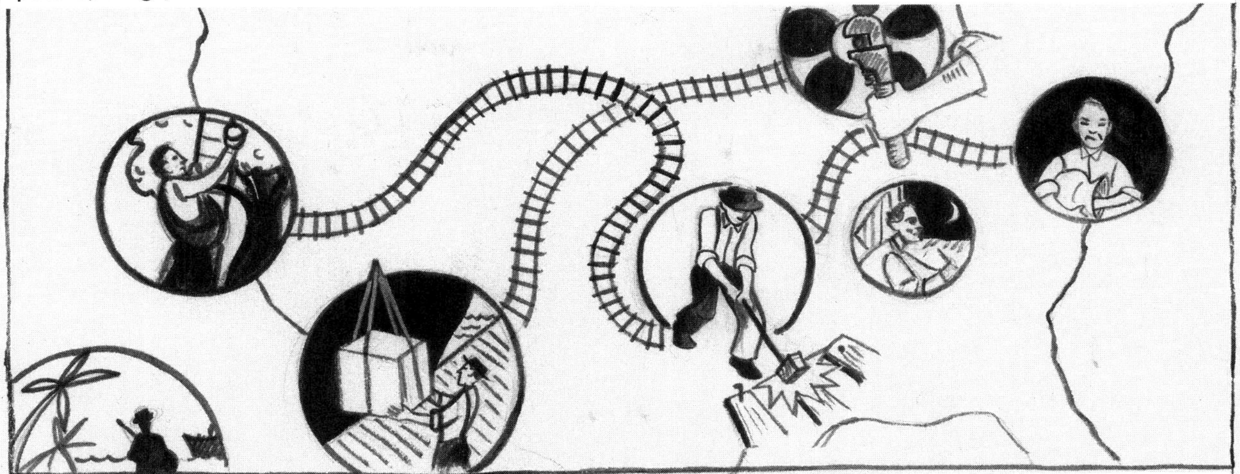

He saw the country from an open boxcar - Joel was a gifted trainhopper, which was a potentially deadly way to travel. He was a gentleman hobo who caught trains in a blue serge suit, white shirt, tie, and his famous hat. He was known to all as a kind and generous man, and a little shy.

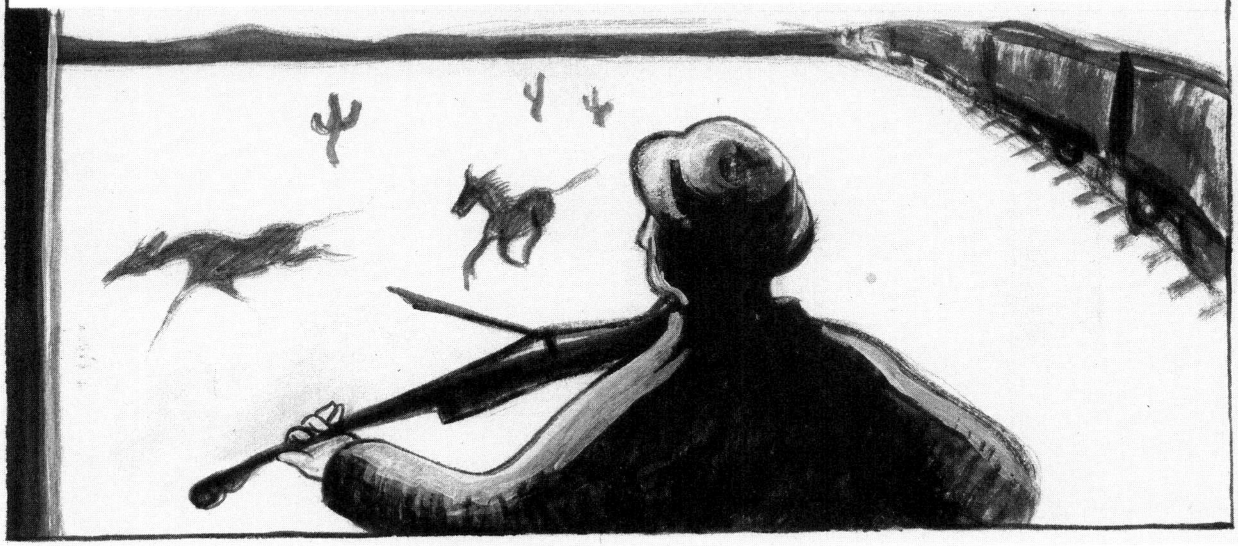

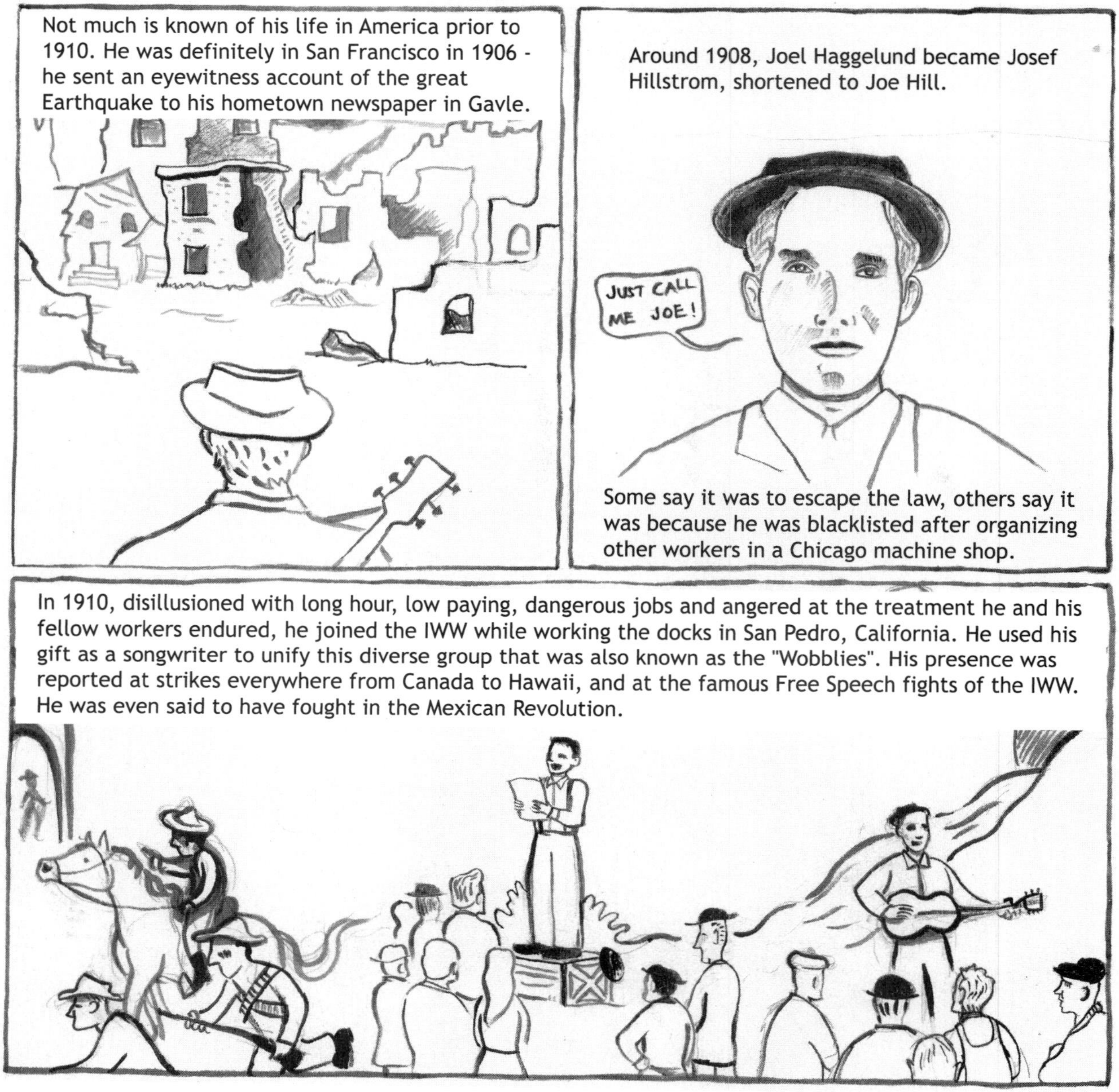
Not much is known of his life in America prior to 1910. He was definitely in San Francisco in 1906 - he sent an eyewitness account of the great Earthquake to his hometown newspaper in Gavle.
Around 1908, Joel Haggelund became Josef Hillstrom, shortened to Joe Hill.
JUST CALL ME JOE!
Some say it was to escape the law, others say it was because he was blacklisted after organizing other workers in a Chicago machine shop.
In 1910, disillusioned with long hour, low paying, dangerous jobs and angered at the treatment he and his fellow workers endured, he joined the IWW while working the docks in San Pedro, California. He used his gift as a songwriter to unify this diverse group that was also known as the "Wobblies". His presence was reported at strikes everywhere from Canada to Hawaii, and at the famous Free Speech fights of the IWW. He was even said to have fought in the Mexican Revolution.

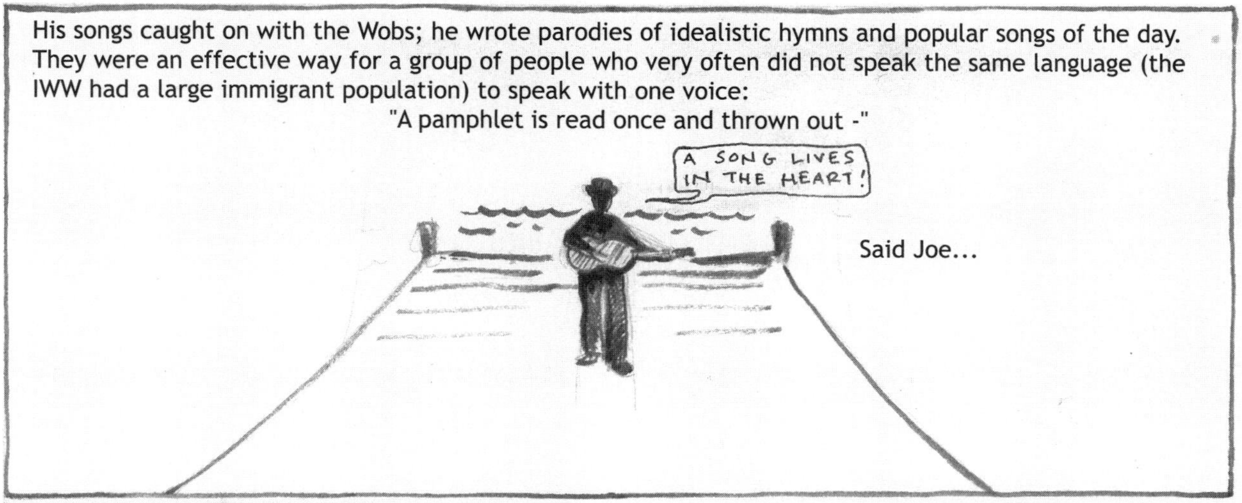
His songs caught on with the Wobs; he wrote parodies of idealistic hymns and popular songs of the day. They were an effective way for a group of people who very often did not speak the same language (the IWW had a large immigrant population) to speak with one voice:
"A pamphlet is read once and thrown out -"
A SONG LIVES IN THE HEART!
Said Joe...

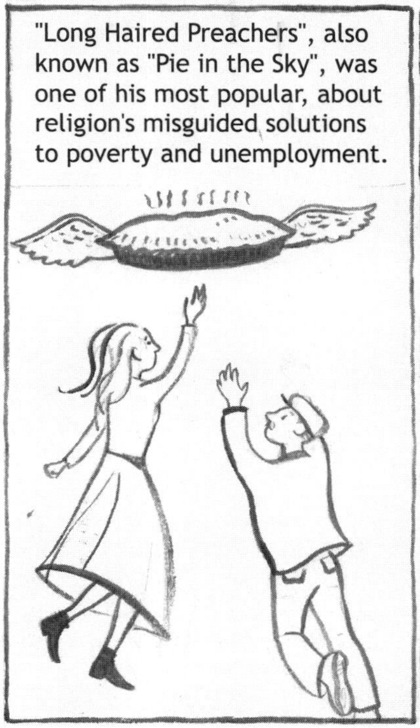
"Long Haired Preachers", also known as "Pie in the Sky", was one of his most popular, about religion's misguided solutions to poverty and unemployment.

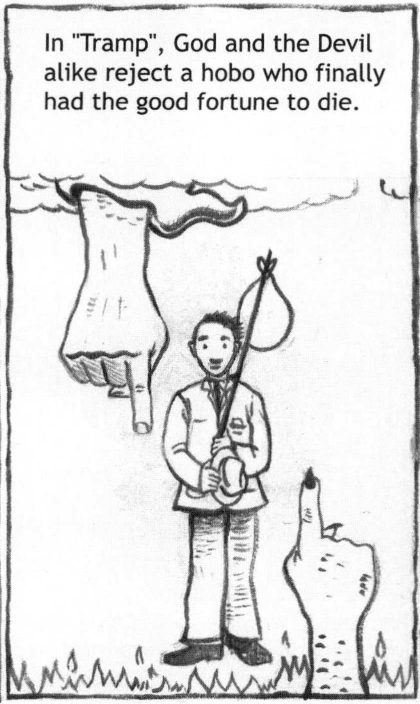
In "Tramp", God and the Devil alike reject a hobo who finally had the good fortune to die.

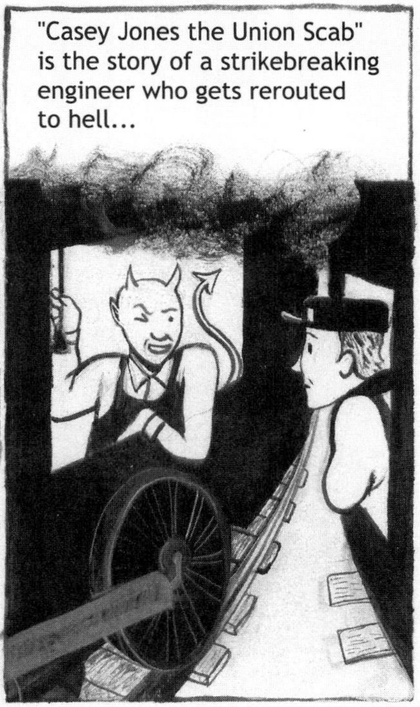
"Casey Jones the Union Scab" is the story of a strikebreaking engineer who gets rerouted to hell...

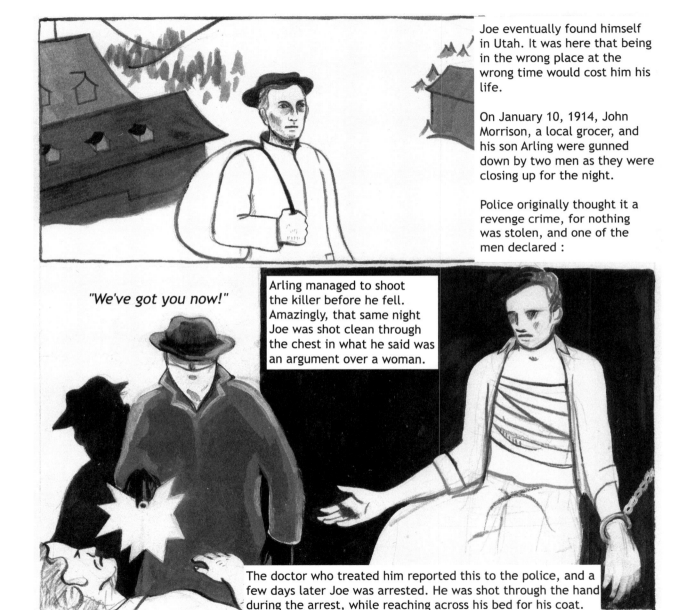

Joe eventually found himself in Utah. It was here that being in the wrong place at the wrong time would cost him his life.

On January 10, 1914, John Morrison, a local grocer, and his son Arling were gunned down by two men as they were closing up for the night.

Police originally thought it a revenge crime, for nothing was stolen, and one of the men declared :

"We've got you now!"

Arling managed to shoot the killer before he fell. Amazingly, that same night Joe was shot clean through the chest in what he said was an argument over a woman.

The doctor who treated him reported this to the police, and a few days later Joe was arrested. He was shot through the hand during the arrest, while reaching across his bed for his coat.

There were other suspects - John Morrison was once a policeman, and had recently said to his wife that he feared retribution from two men he sent to prison some years earlier. These men were never found. There was also another man that Morrison jailed - recently released and seen in the area the night of the murder. The police first thought Joe was this man when they arrested him.

The prosecuting attorney said that he would rely on circumstantial evidence. Indeed, there was no motive, no murder weapon, and the best any witness could say was that Joe resembled the killer in height and build, or in general appearance. No one positively identified him.

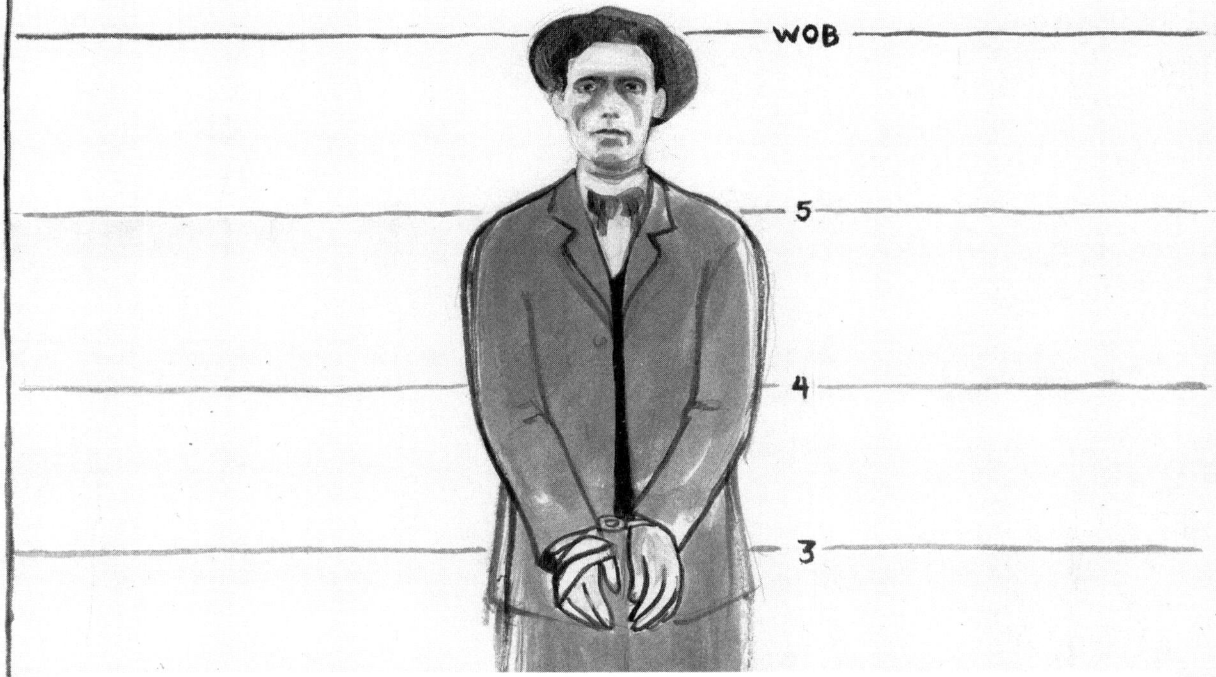
WOB
5
4
3

The climate in Salt Lake City, Utah for a man like Joe Hill - an immigrant, hobo, transient worker, and especially a Wobbly - was not friendly. He was considered an enemy of the companies whose wealth was created by the mining industry that thrived in Utah. He was described in court as a parasite and an undesirable, and presented to the jury as a hardened criminal, when in reality he had only been arrested once for vagrancy. But the biggest obstacle for the defense was his refusal to provide the details of his alibi. He did not want the reputation of the woman to suffer, and remained silent. He was found guilty of murder and sentenced to death.

There was international protest of his sentence. Wobbly Elizabeth Gurley -Flynn corresponded with Joe constantly, and was a fierce advocate for his freedom. Over ten thousand letters from across the country poured into Utah Governor William Spry's office. President Wilson, Helen Keller, and Swedish Minister Ekengren all pleaded for Joe's life, but were rejected.

Joe wrote out his last will in his prison cell:

My Last Will

My Will is easy to decide
For there is nothing to divide
My Kin don't need to fuss and moan
"Moss does not clinge to rolling stone
My body? - Oh! — If I could choose
I would to ashes it reduce
And let the merry breezes blow
My dust to where some flowers grow

Perhaps some fading flower then
Would come to life and bloom again

This is my Last and Final Will. —
Good Luck to All of you

Joe Hill

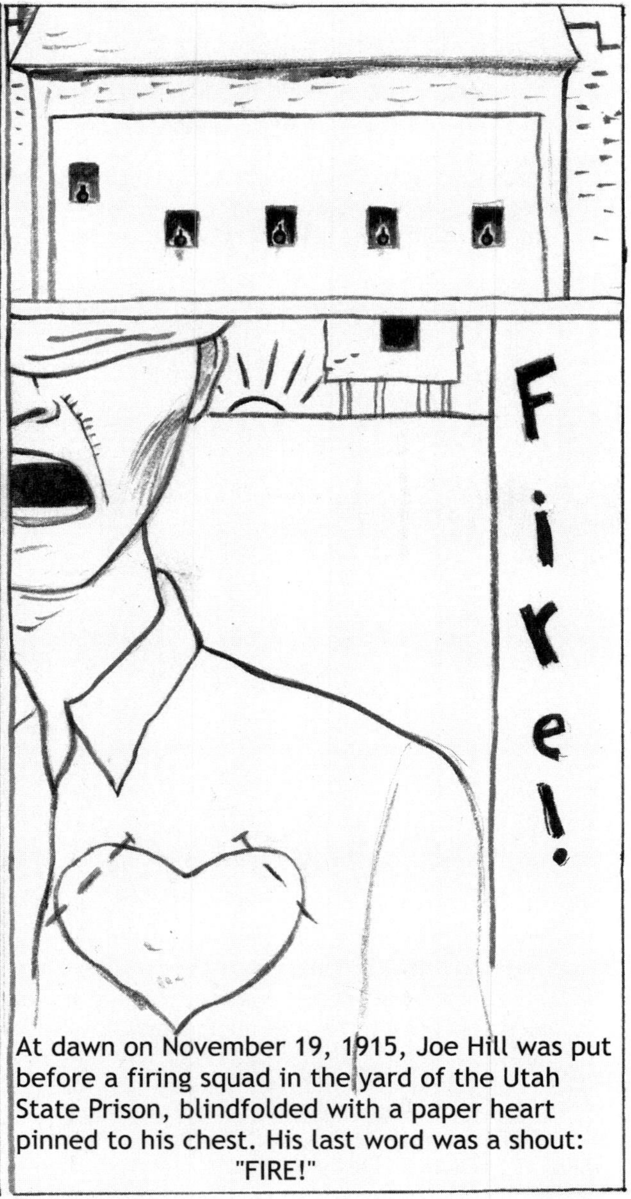
Fire!
At dawn on November 19, 1915, Joe Hill was put before a firing squad in the yard of the Utah State Prison, blindfolded with a paper heart pinned to his chest. His last word was a shout: "FIRE!"

Joe took care to ask Wobbly leader Big Bill Haywood to take him out of Utah to be cremated: "I don't want to be caught dead in Utah." he wrote to Haywood...30,000 people attended his funeral in Chicago. The streets and rooftops were crowded with mourners. Eulogies for this "Citizen of the World" were read in nine languages, and his songs were sung until dark.

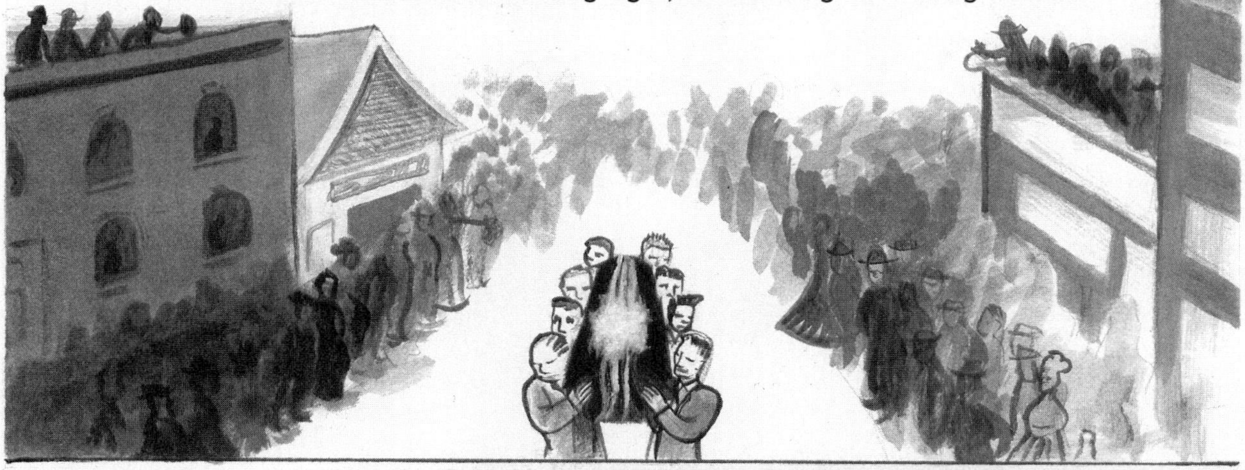

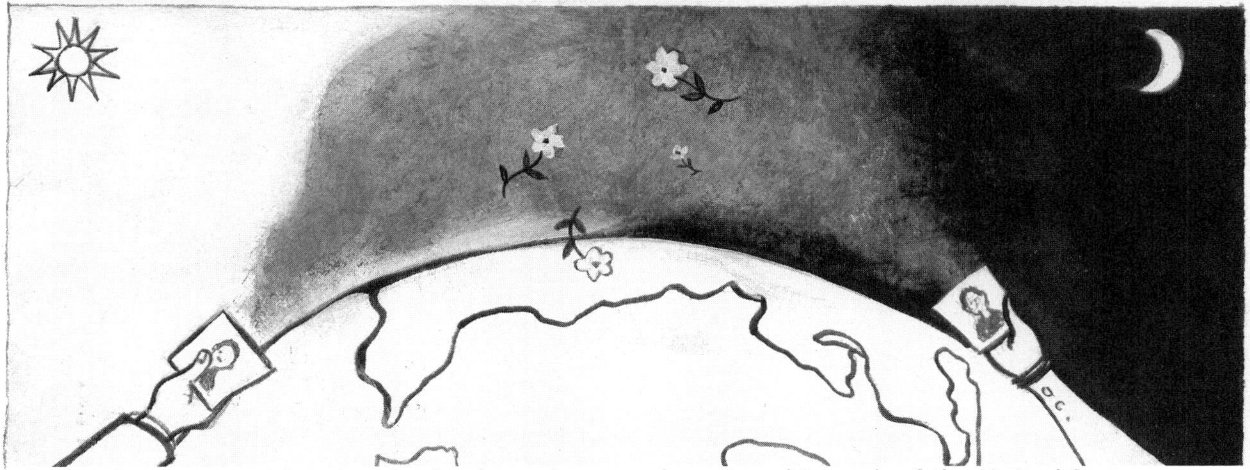

Joe's ashes were put into hundreds of envelopes and scattered in each of the United States (except Utah) and in countries all over the world, except for one envelope. It was confiscated by a postmaster and kept in the national archives of the Post Office. It was found in 1988 - the ashes were returned to the IWW, but the Post Office kept the envelope.

Joe Hill's childhood home in Sweden is now a museum - The Joe Hill House. There is also a garden, and a monument to Joe not far from the house. Despite 2 bombings by local fascists and having it's windows smashed out, it's still standing. After 100 years, Joe Hill is still pissing off the right (wing) people!

Today Salt Lake City is home to the Joe Hill House of Hospitality. The State of Utah now says that under their present law, Joe Hill would never have been executed on the evidence presented at his trial.

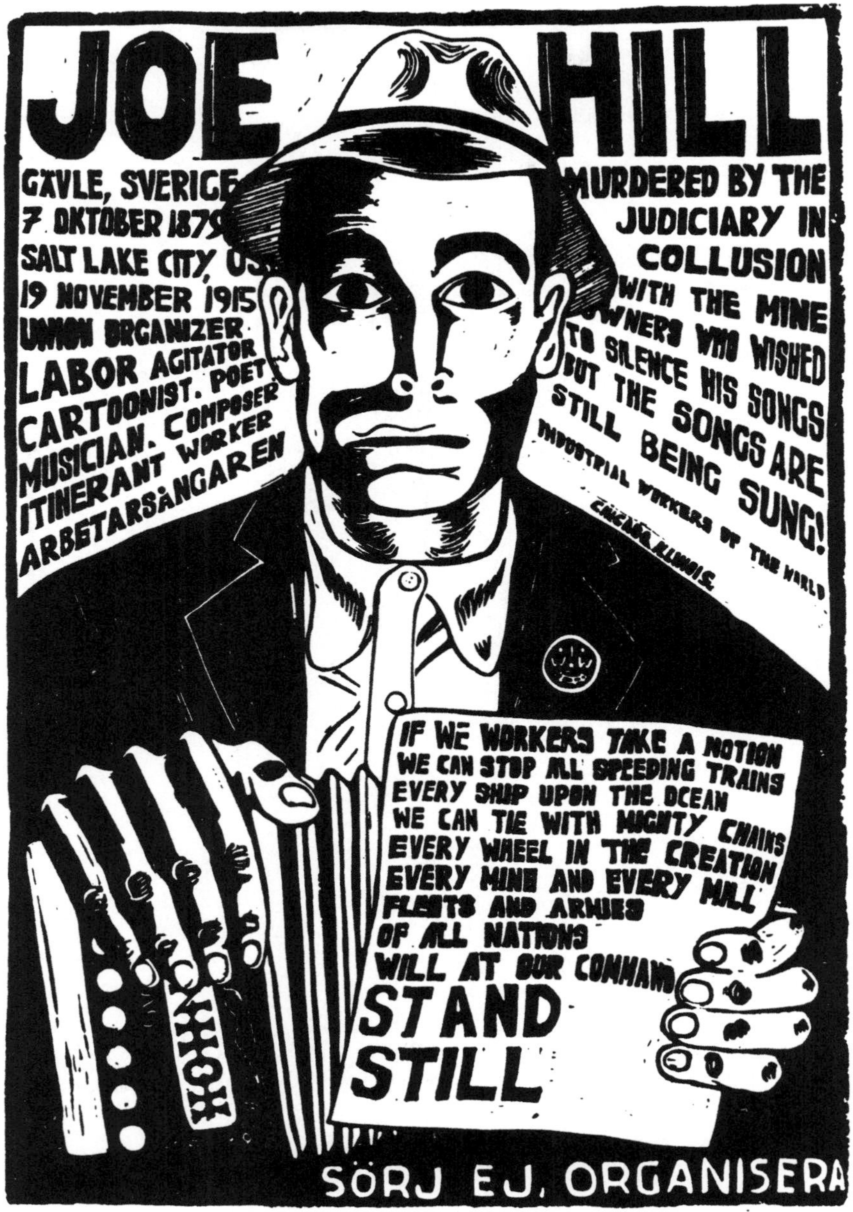
JOE HILL
GÄVLE, SVERIGE
7 OKTOBER 1879
SALT LAKE CITY, US
19 NOVEMBER 1915
UNION ORGANIZER
LABOR AGITATOR
CARTOONIST. POET
MUSICIAN. COMPOSER
ITINERANT WORKER
ARBETARSÅNGAREN
MURDERED BY THE JUDICIARY IN COLLUSION WITH THE MINE OWNERS WHO WISHED TO SILENCE HIS SONGS BUT THE SONGS ARE STILL BEING SUNG!
INDUSTRIAL WORKERS OF THE WORLD
CHICAGO, ILLINOIS.
IF WE WORKERS TAKE A NOTION
WE CAN STOP ALL SPEEDING TRAINS
EVERY SHIP UPON THE OCEAN
WE CAN TIE WITH MIGHTY CHAINS
EVERY WHEEL IN THE CREATION
EVERY MINE AND EVERY MILL
FLEETS AND ARMIES
OF ALL NATIONS
WILL AT OUR COMMAND
STAND
STILL
SÖRJ EJ, ORGANISERA

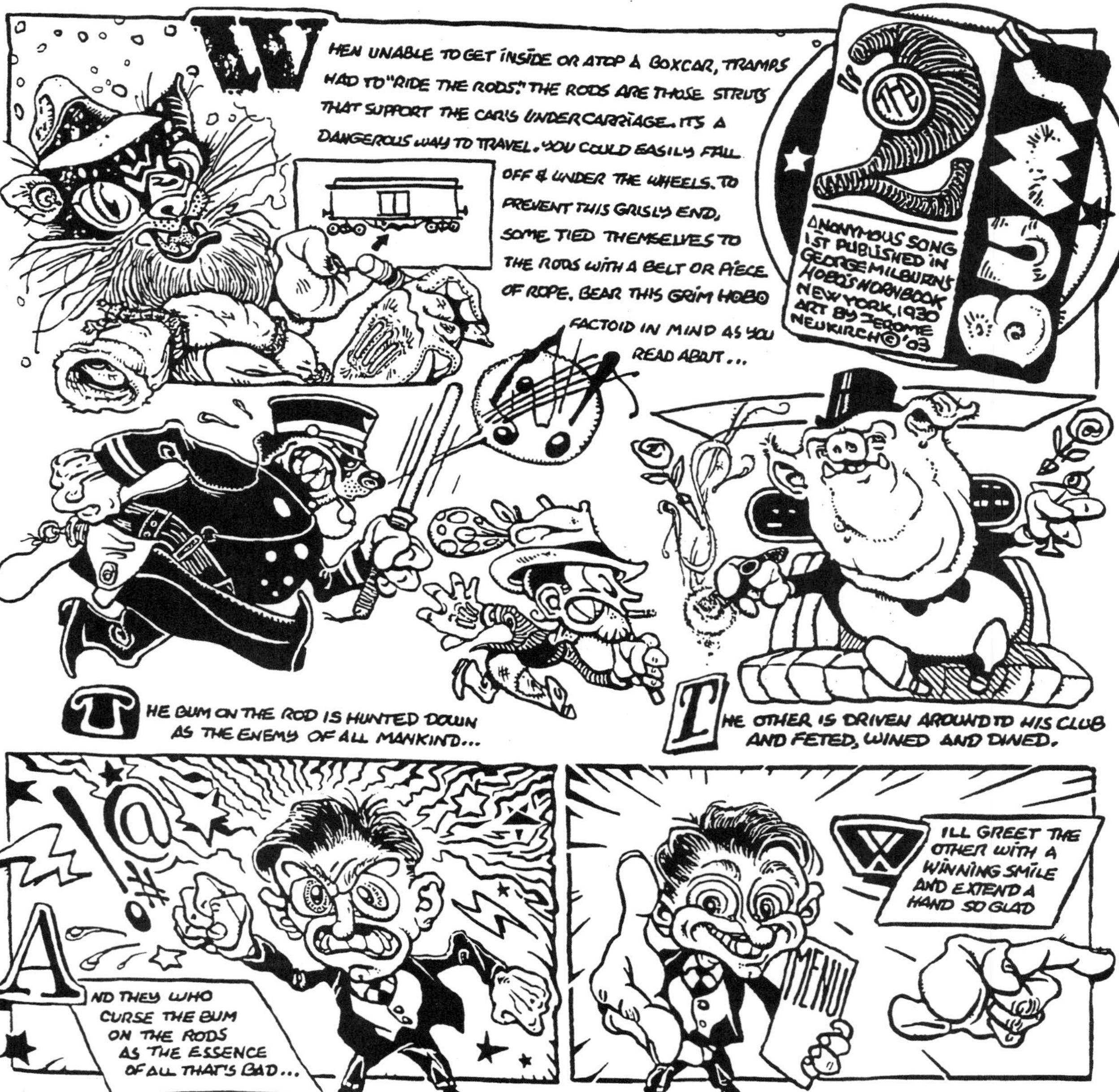
WHEN UNABLE TO GET INSIDE OR ATOP A BOXCAR, TRAMPS HAD TO "RIDE THE RODS." THE RODS ARE THOSE STRUTS THAT SUPPORT THE CAR'S UNDERCARRIAGE. IT'S A DANGEROUS WAY TO TRAVEL. YOU COULD EASILY FALL OFF & UNDER THE WHEELS. TO PREVENT THIS GRISLY END, SOME TIED THEMSELVES TO THE RODS WITH A BELT OR PIECE OF ROPE. BEAR THIS GRIM HOBO FACTOID IN MIND AS YOU READ ABOUT...
THE
ANONYMOUS SONG 1ST PUBLISHED IN GEORGE MILBURN'S HOBO'S HORNBOOK NEW YORK, 1930 ART BY JEROME NEUKIRCH © '03
THE BUM ON THE ROD IS HUNTED DOWN AS THE ENEMY OF ALL MANKIND...
THE OTHER IS DRIVEN AROUND TO HIS CLUB AND FETED, WINED AND DINED.
AND THEY WHO CURSE THE BUM ON THE RODS AS THE ESSENCE OF ALL THAT'S BAD...
WILL GREET THE OTHER WITH A WINNING SMILE AND EXTEND A HAND SO GLAD
MENU

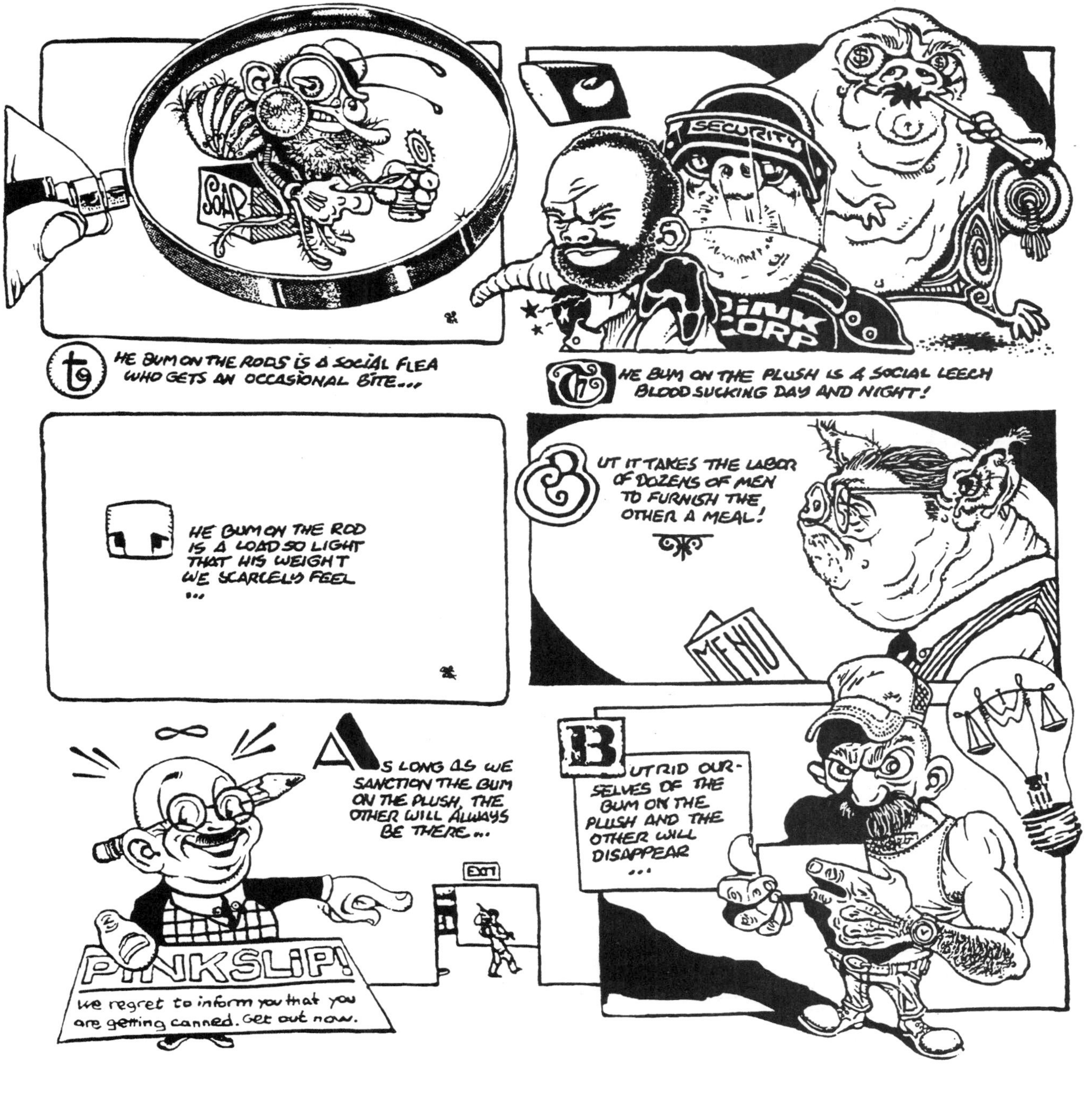
SOAP
THE BUM ON THE RODS IS A SOCIAL FLEA WHO GETS AN OCCASIONAL BITE...
SECURITY
PINK CORP
THE BUM ON THE PLUSH IS A SOCIAL LEECH BLOODSUCKING DAY AND NIGHT!
THE BUM ON THE ROD IS A LOAD SO LIGHT THAT HIS WEIGHT WE SCARCELY FEEL ...
BUT IT TAKES THE LABOR OF DOZENS OF MEN TO FURNISH THE OTHER A MEAL!
MENU
AS LONG AS WE SANCTION THE BUM ON THE PLUSH, THE OTHER WILL ALWAYS BE THERE...
EXIT
PINKSLIP!
we regret to inform you that you are getting canned. Get out now.
BUT RID OURSELVES OF THE BUM ON THE PLUSH AND THE OTHER WILL DISAPPEAR ...

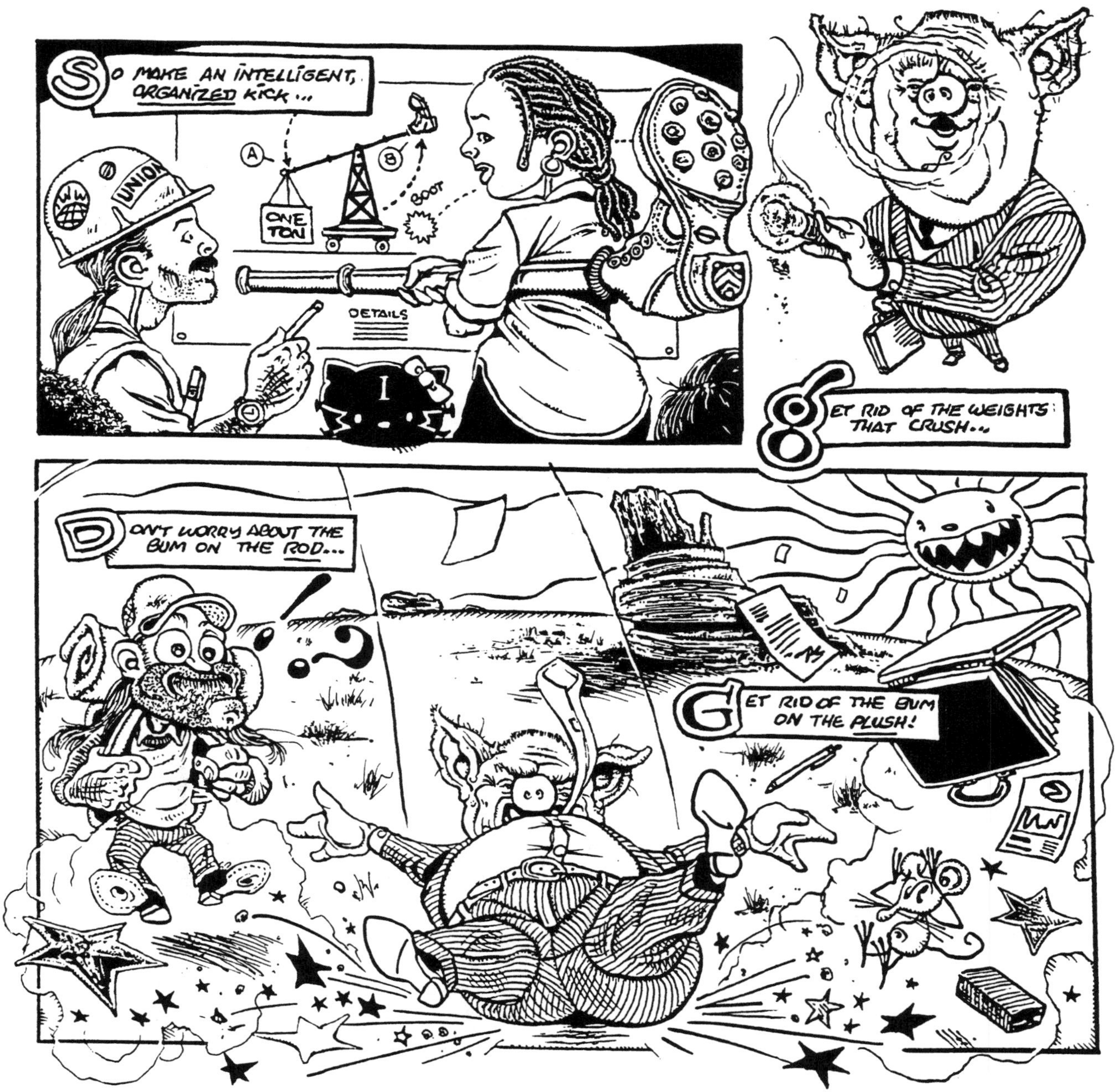

SO MAKE AN INTELLIGENT, ORGANIZED KICK...
UNION
A
B
ONE TON
BOOT
DETAILS
I
GET RID OF THE WEIGHTS THAT CRUSH...
DON'T WORRY ABOUT THE BUM ON THE ROD...
GET RID OF THE BUM ON THE PLUSH!

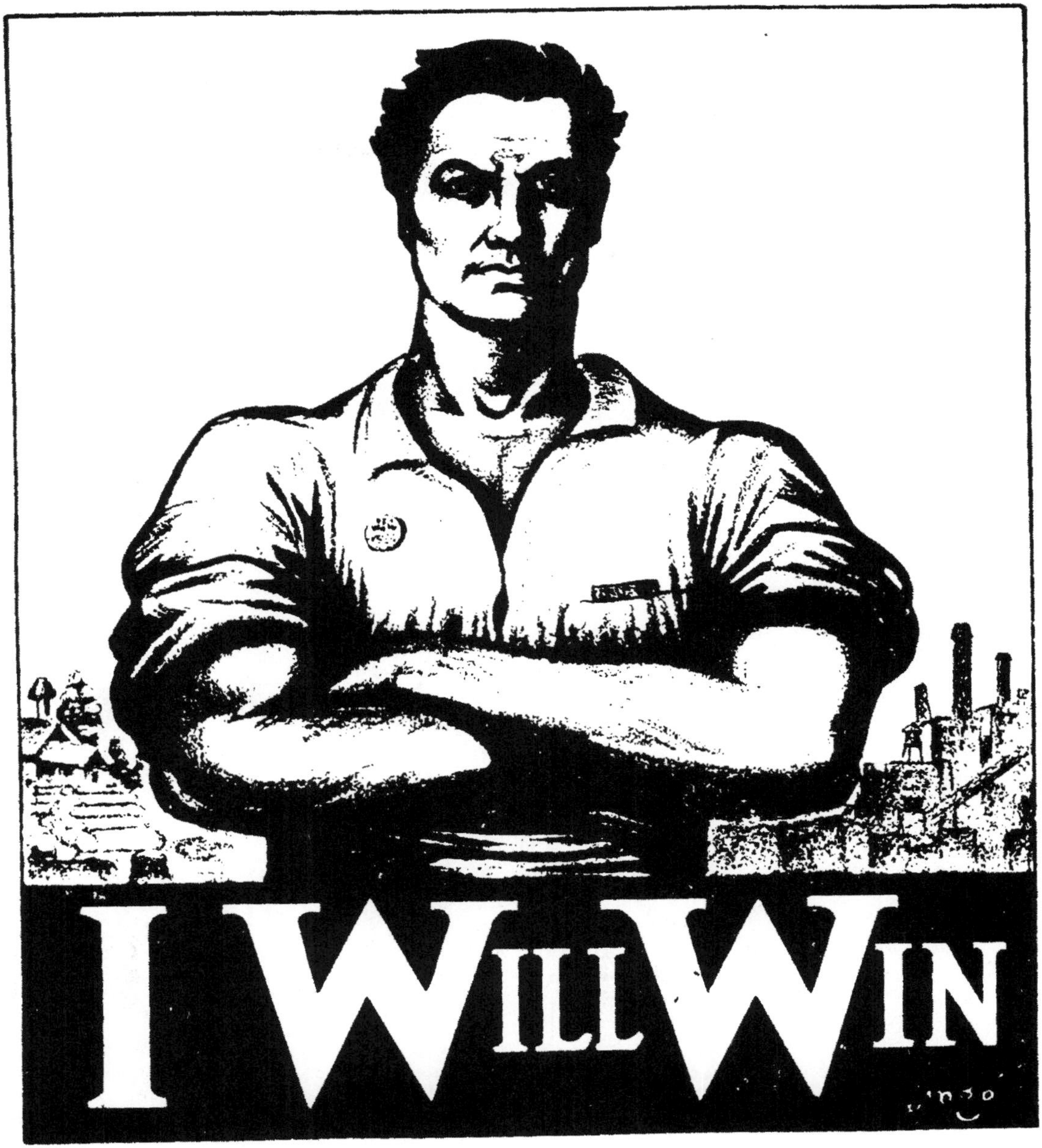
I WILL WIN

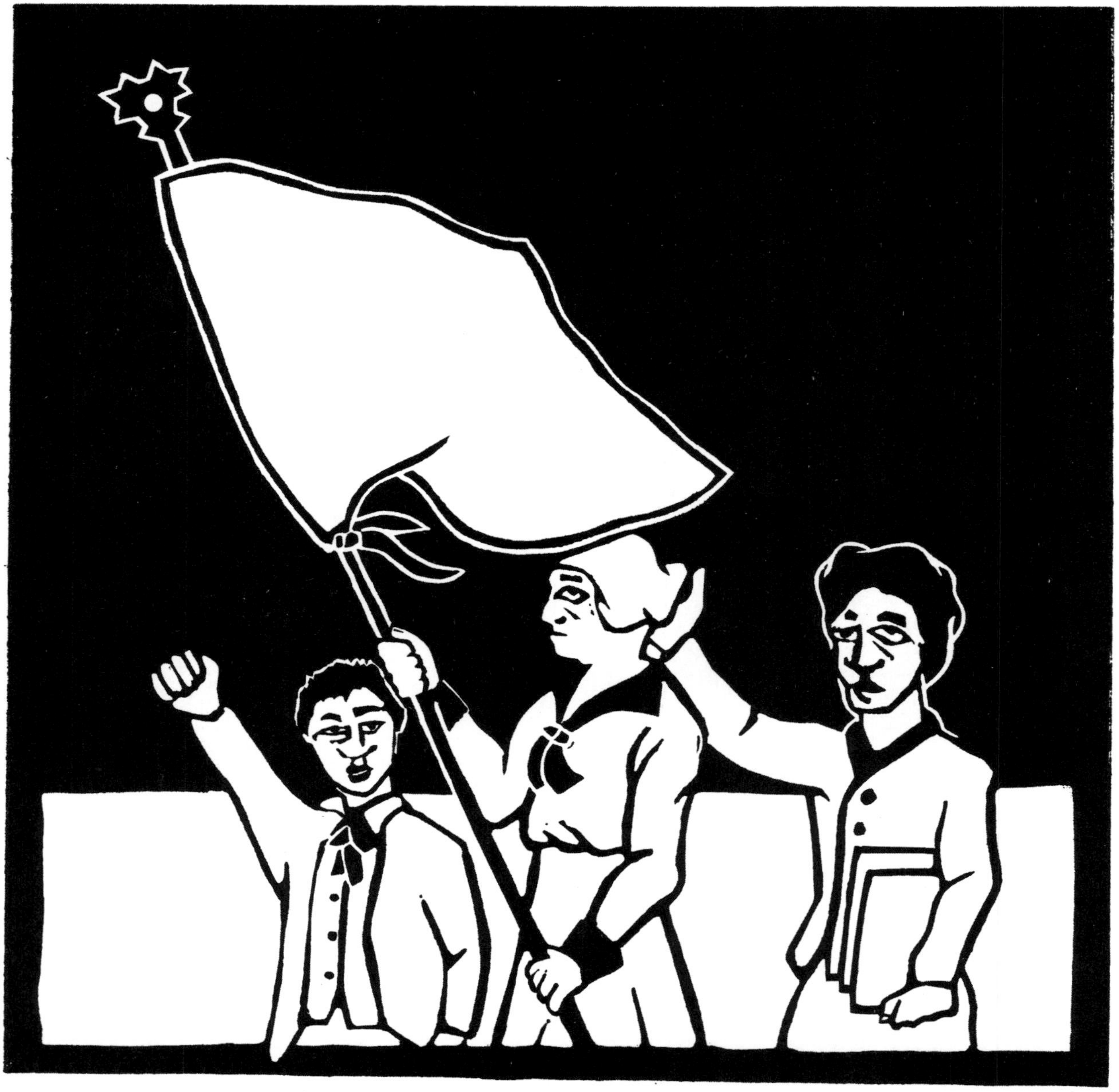

FOUR

REPRESSION, MARTYRDOM, GENERAL STRIKES

The Brotherhood of Timber Workers (BTW) might be taken, as well as any, as the bright promise of the IWW crushed underfoot. It was extraordinary as an interracial union in the South, made up mostly of lumberjacks and sawmill workers in the Louisiana/Texas Piney Woods region being logged out by the big companies. Legendary southern-born poet and agitator-editor Covington Hall quickly transformed the rudimentary and mostly secret BTW into a Wobbly movement. Officially adopting the principles of the IWW, the BTW invited full membership rights to women and nonwhites (including a scattering of Mexicans and Indians), and set out to organize the mill towns one by one. During a series of strikes in 1912–13, it expanded to as many as 20,000 members; then strikebreakers, official and private police rushed in to crush the organization. Violent strikes led to an intensive legal-defense campaign for Wobs framed and put on trial. The BTW struggled on for years but never recovered.

The railroading of Wobbly leaders into federal prisons for long sentences on a variety of charges, the sudden growth of the AFL and independent unions, sometimes recruiting former Wobblies as organizers, combined with the appeal of the new American Communist movement, proved all too daunting. Prosecutorial charges of "criminal syndicalism" mystified later generations of radicals (as well as civil libertarians) and were scarcely understood among most of the defendants. During the McCarthy Era decades later, communists (by their nature wholly opposed to Wobbly or anarchist doctrines) were still being arrested on such creaky statutes. Actress Lucille Ball, facing a House Un-American Activities Committee investigating her past sympathies with communists, was thus quizzed on criminal syndicalism and could honestly respond that she had never heard of it. "Syndicalism," a term popular in France and Italy, and also among some activists in Britain, Germany, and elsewhere, had always been closer to doctrinaire anarchism than the IWW, and sometimes linked to individual acts of violence (rather than a mostly passive sabotage, "accidental" malfunctioning of machines, or just a waitress talking against the food of the restaurant). Those calling themselves syndicalists in the US were mostly competitors to the IWW, urging affiliation of radicals with the mainstream AFL, "boring from within" to achieve their aims by winning over craft-union members. The charge, however, was never intended by prosecutors to be precise in any case. Like the insistence that Wobblies rather than scabs, cops, and assorted thugs had started rough stuff on and around the picket line, "criminal syndicalism" was a convenient label.

The Espionage Acts offered another legalization of outright repression. Enacted in 1917, the Selective Service Act necessarily offered a virtually open definition of what might be deemed to constitute espionage, inasmuch as socialists and Wobblies had no more sympathy for the German Kaiser than the British King or other symbolic nationalisms in the the First World War. The laws governing the naturalization of the foreign-born, altered after the assassination of President McKinley (by a native-born anarchist, son of an immigrant), began to be applied against Wobbly-noncitizens seeking citizenship as early as 1912, soon making it all but impossible for sworn members to naturalize. Meanwhile, Congress and the President (for the moment in a liberal, civil-libertarian mood) debated the merits of further repressive legislation against those who damaged or endangered property. By 1918, federal troops broke up Wobbly picket lines in Arizona by declaring the production of copper to be a "war utility," making those hindering production thus liable to prosecution under the new Sabotage Act. The US State Department and Bureau of Immigration had also set themselves upon yet another distinct rationale of repression. By the time the US had entered the war, immigration officials had been given far more latitude in deciding who to deport and under what conditions. The Immigration Act of 1918 was designed specifically to remove from radical aliens any rights of Constitutional protection. For the first time in US history, guilt of association or belief became a deportable offense. Even before the law was enacted, the Bureau began to plan the deportation of Wobblies by its own standards, in ways eerily familiar to today's civil libertarians: membership, sympathy, financial support or even implied agreement with IWW aims could be used. Faced with initial defeats in the courts, the Bureau secretly devised new standards, and these would be upheld. Any alien known to support the IWW, a perfectly legal organization, could nevertheless be held and deported. The Labor Department, the Attorney General, and the highest circles around the President could join with company officials, sheriff's agents, and paid thugs to attack Wobs most anywhere, but especially in the northwest, where so many loggers swore loyalty to the movement. The foreign-born would not even be allowed legal counsel, setting a further precedent for future methods of illegal repression.

During the uprisings of 1919, amid massive May Day parades, a General Strike in Seattle, and solidarity actions to prevent war goods being shipped to counterrevolutionary forces in embattled Russia, it nevertheless seemed for an extended moment that persecution only deepened the class struggle. Then it was over. Within a year, the young Communist movement had nearly destroyed itself (with considerable help from police agents), along with the Socialist Party, in a round of wild factionalism, seeking the perfect revolutionary formula while real radicals faced immediate problems.

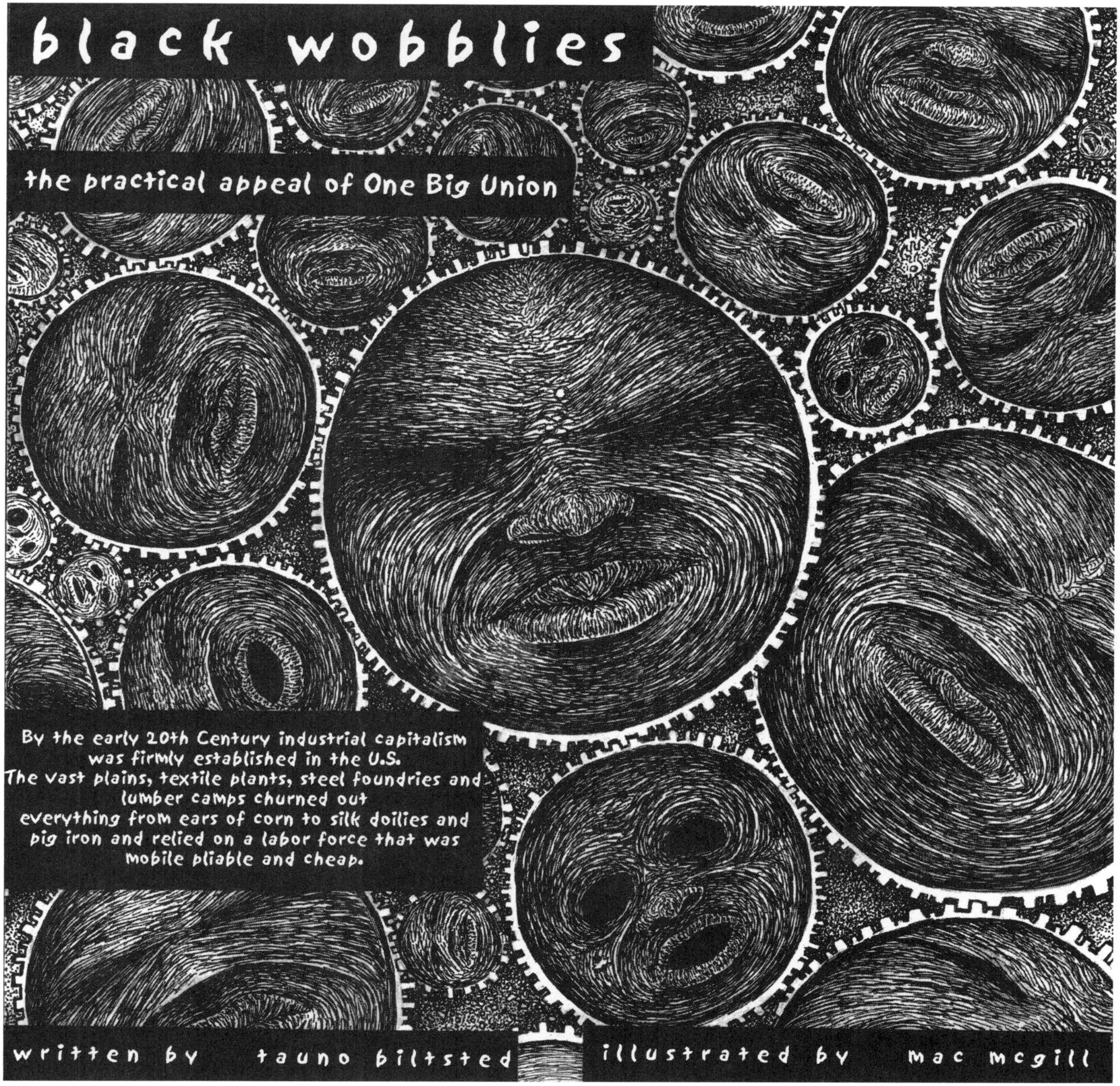
black wobblies
the practical appeal of One Big Union
By the early 20th Century industrial capitalism was firmly established in the U.S. The vast plains, textile plants, steel foundries and lumber camps churned out everything from ears of corn to silk doilies and pig iron and relied on a labor force that was mobile pliable and cheap.
written by tauno biltsted
illustrated by mac mcgill

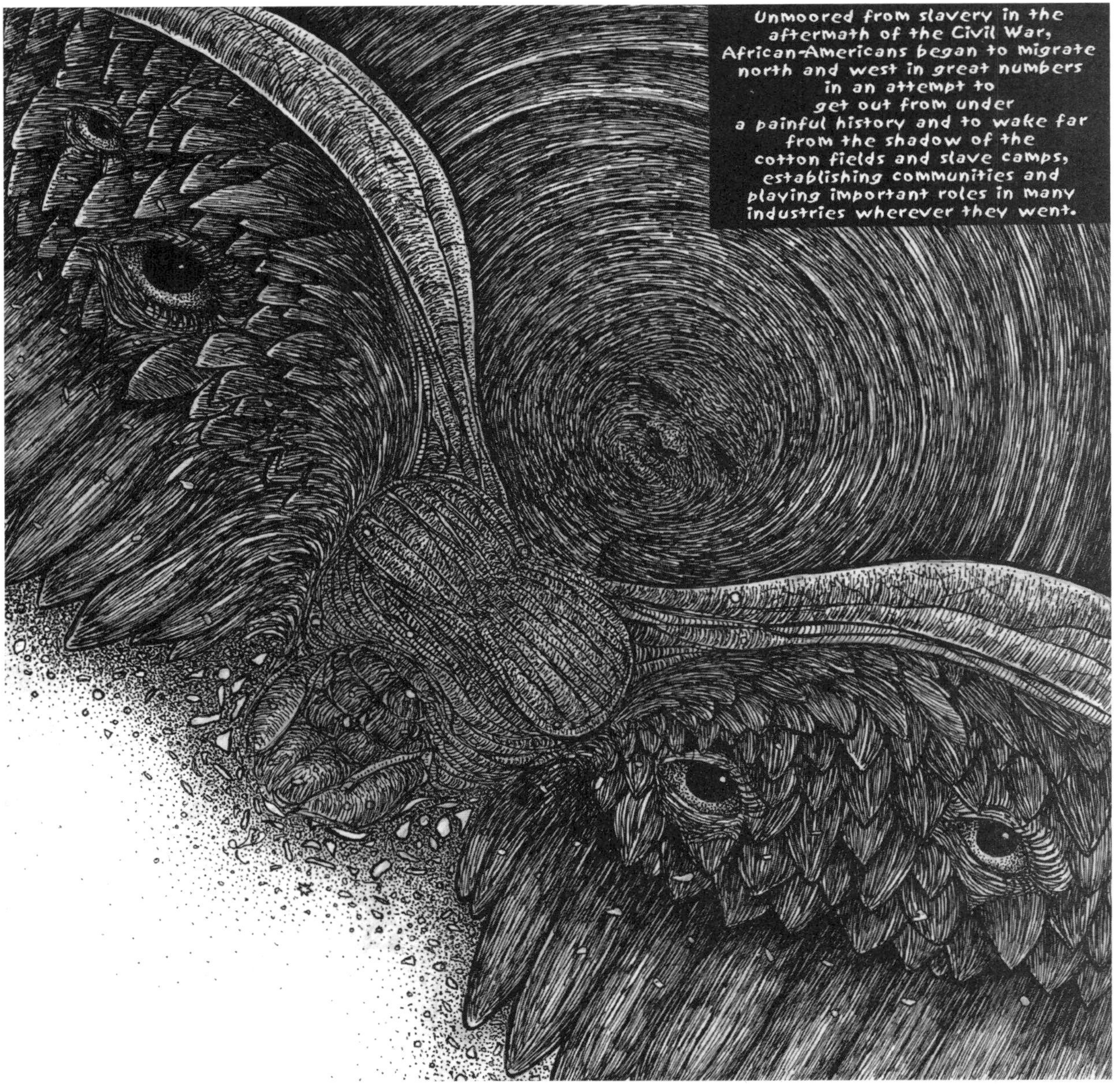
Unmoored from slavery in the aftermath of the Civil War, African-Americans began to migrate north and west in great numbers in an attempt to get out from under a painful history and to wake far from the shadow of the cotton fields and slave camps, establishing communities and playing important roles in many industries wherever they went.

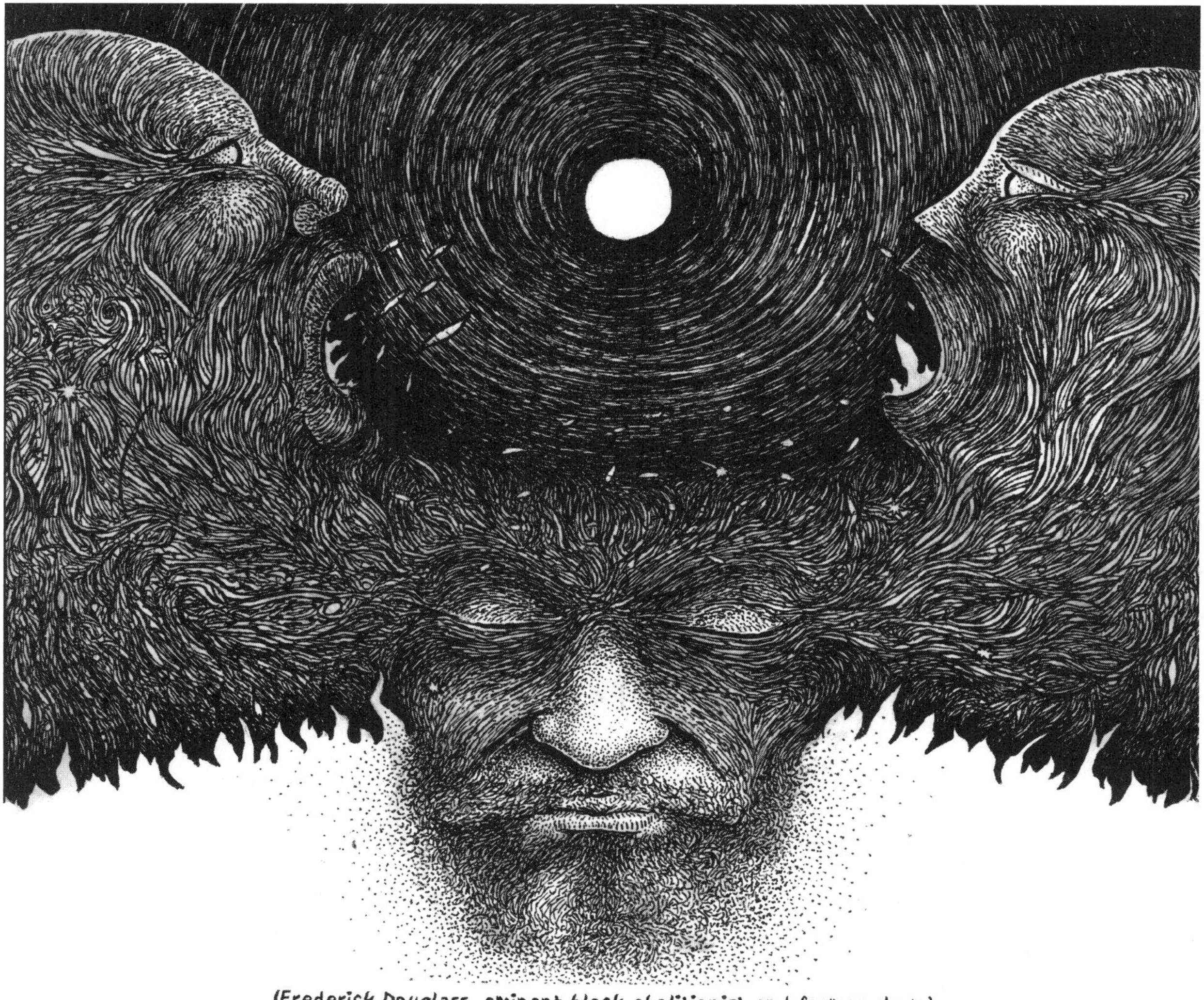

(Frederick Douglass, eminent black abolitionist and former slave)....
"The hostility between the whites and blacks is easily explained. It has its root and sap in the relation of slavery that was incited on both sides by the cunning of the slave masters. Those masters secured their ascendancy over the poor whites and the blacks by putting enmity between them.

They divided both to conquer each..."

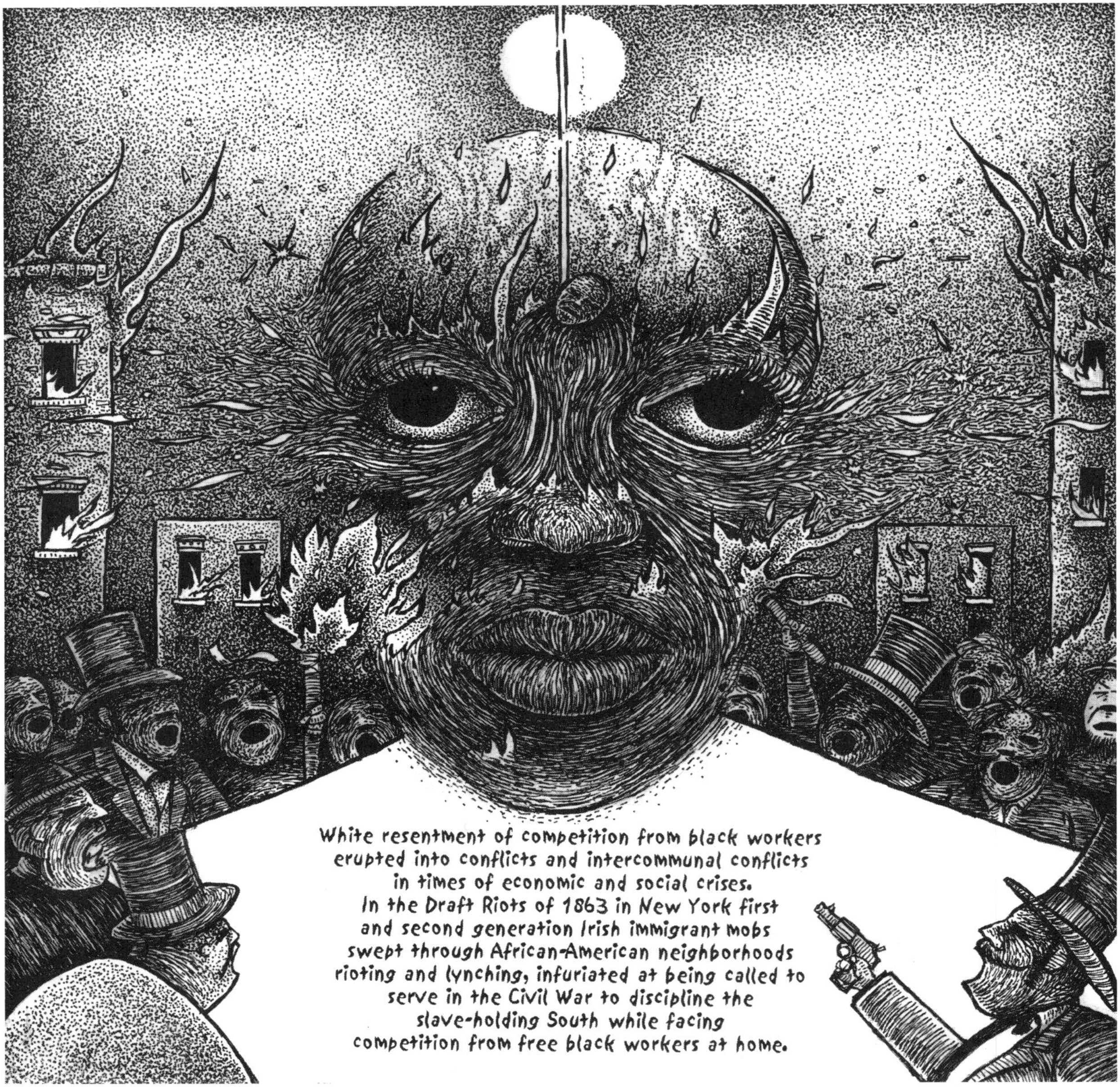
White resentment of competition from black workers erupted into conflicts and intercommunal conflicts in times of economic and social crises. In the Draft Riots of 1863 in New York first and second generation Irish immigrant mobs swept through African-American neighborhoods rioting and lynching, infuriated at being called to serve in the Civil War to discipline the slave-holding South while facing competition from free black workers at home.

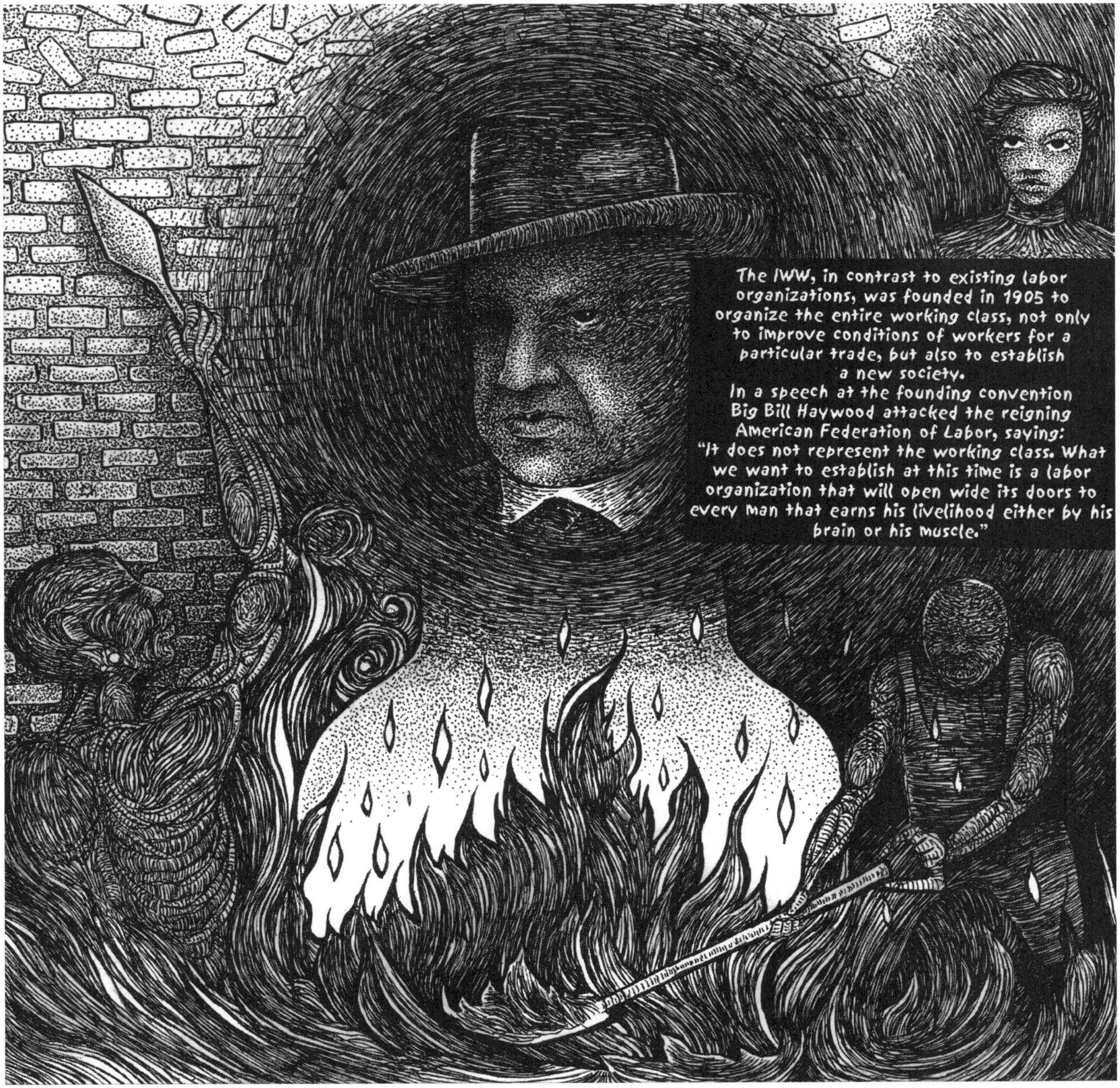
The IWW, in contrast to existing labor organizations, was founded in 1905 to organize the entire working class, not only to improve conditions of workers for a particular trade, but also to establish a new society.
In a speech at the founding convention Big Bill Haywood attacked the reigning American Federation of Labor, saying: "It does not represent the working class. What we want to establish at this time is a labor organization that will open wide its doors to every man that earns his livelihood either by his brain or his muscle."

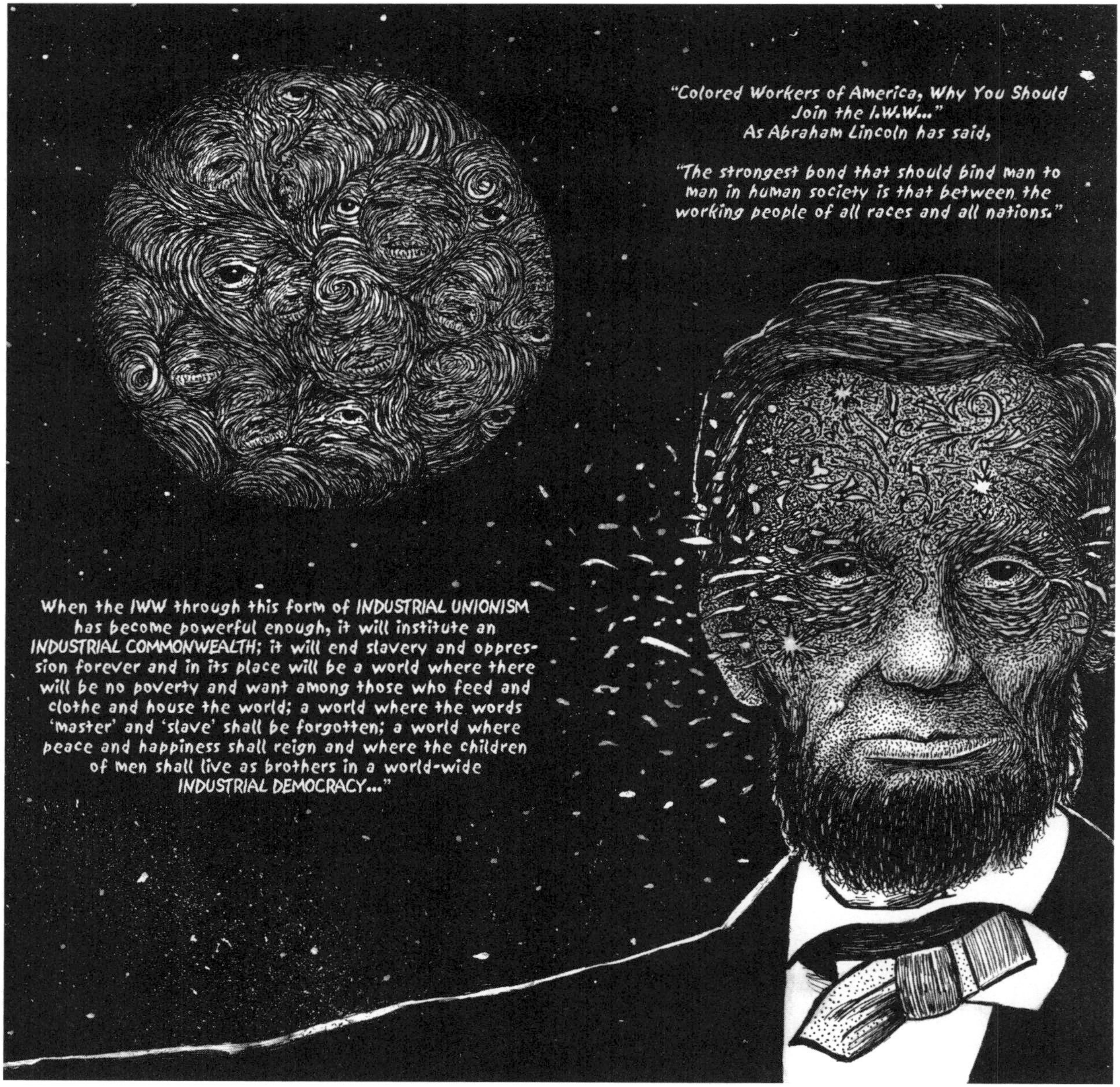
"Colored Workers of America, Why You Should Join the I.W.W..." As Abraham Lincoln has said,
"The strongest bond that should bind man to man in human society is that between the working people of all races and all nations."
When the IWW through this form of INDUSTRIAL UNIONISM has become powerful enough, it will institute an INDUSTRIAL COMMONWEALTH; it will end slavery and oppression forever and in its place will be a world where there will be no poverty and want among those who feed and clothe and house the world; a world where the words 'master' and 'slave' shall be forgotten; a world where peace and happiness shall reign and where the children of men shall live as brothers in a world-wide INDUSTRIAL DEMOCRACY..."

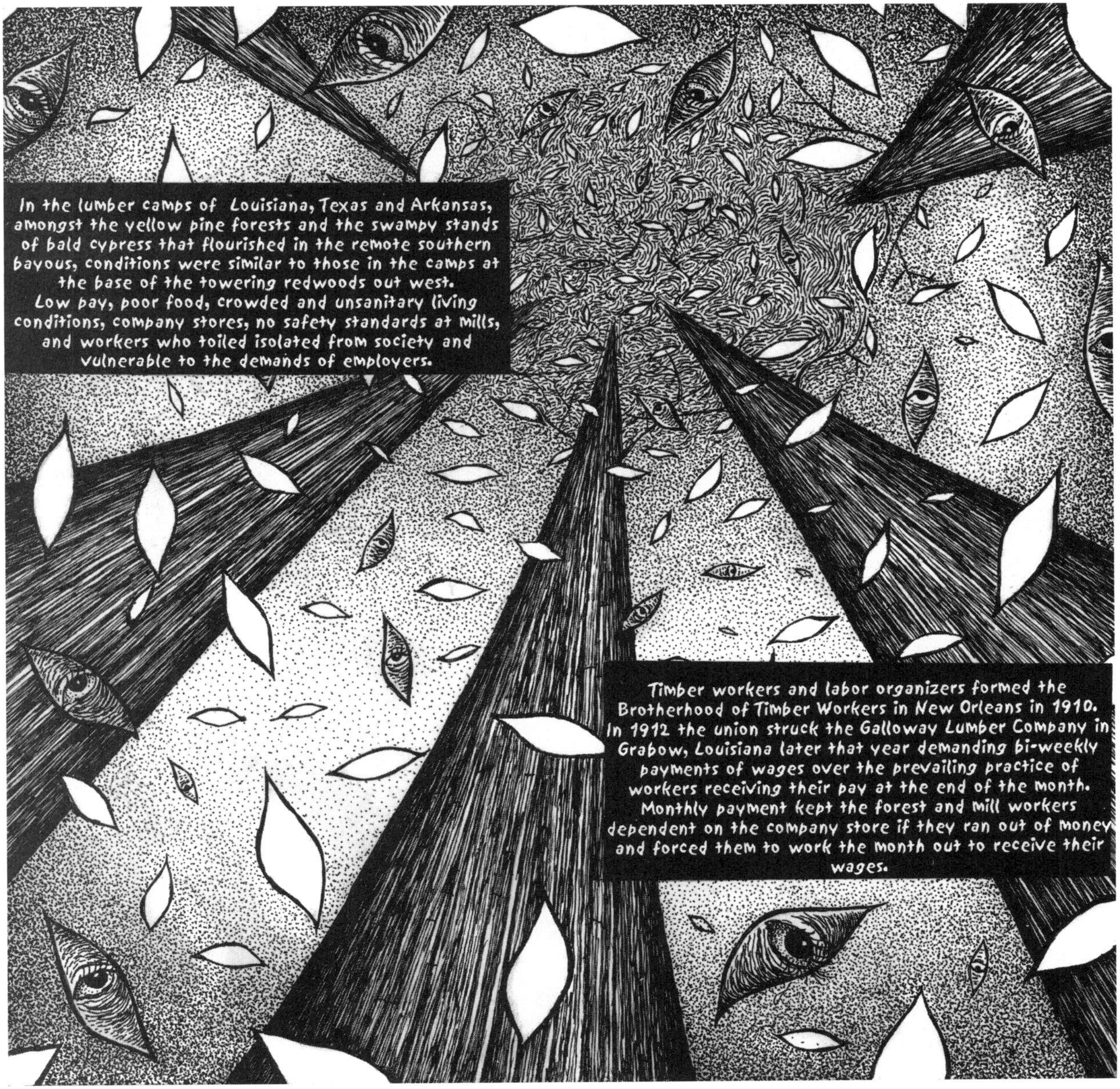
In the lumber camps of Louisiana, Texas and Arkansas, amongst the yellow pine forests and the swampy stands of bald cypress that flourished in the remote southern bayous, conditions were similar to those in the camps at the base of the towering redwoods out west. Low pay, poor food, crowded and unsanitary living conditions, company stores, no safety standards at mills, and workers who toiled isolated from society and vulnerable to the demands of employers.
Timber workers and labor organizers formed the Brotherhood of Timber Workers in New Orleans in 1910. In 1912 the union struck the Galloway Lumber Company in Grabow, Louisiana later that year demanding bi-weekly payments of wages over the prevailing practice of workers receiving their pay at the end of the month. Monthly payment kept the forest and mill workers dependent on the company store if they ran out of money and forced them to work the month out to receive their wages.

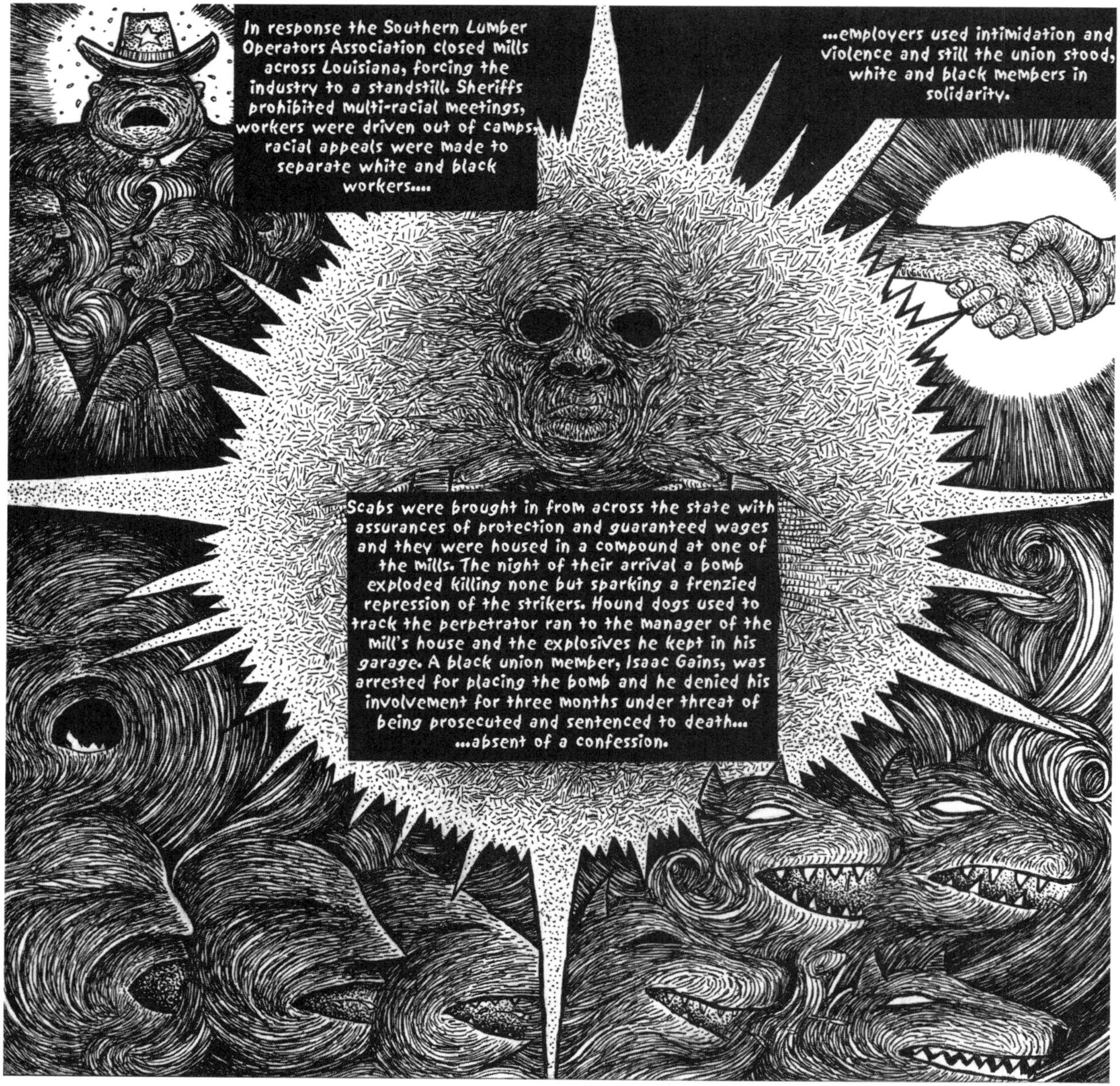
In response the Southern Lumber Operators Association closed mills across Louisiana, forcing the industry to a standstill. Sheriffs prohibited multi-racial meetings, workers were driven out of camps, racial appeals were made to separate white and black workers....
...employers used intimidation and violence and still the union stood, white and black members in solidarity.
Scabs were brought in from across the state with assurances of protection and guaranteed wages and they were housed in a compound at one of the mills. The night of their arrival a bomb exploded killing none but sparking a frenzied repression of the strikers. Hound dogs used to track the perpetrator ran to the manager of the mill's house and the explosives he kept in his garage. A black union member, Isaac Gains, was arrested for placing the bomb and he denied his involvement for three months under threat of being prosecuted and sentenced to death...
...absent of a confession.

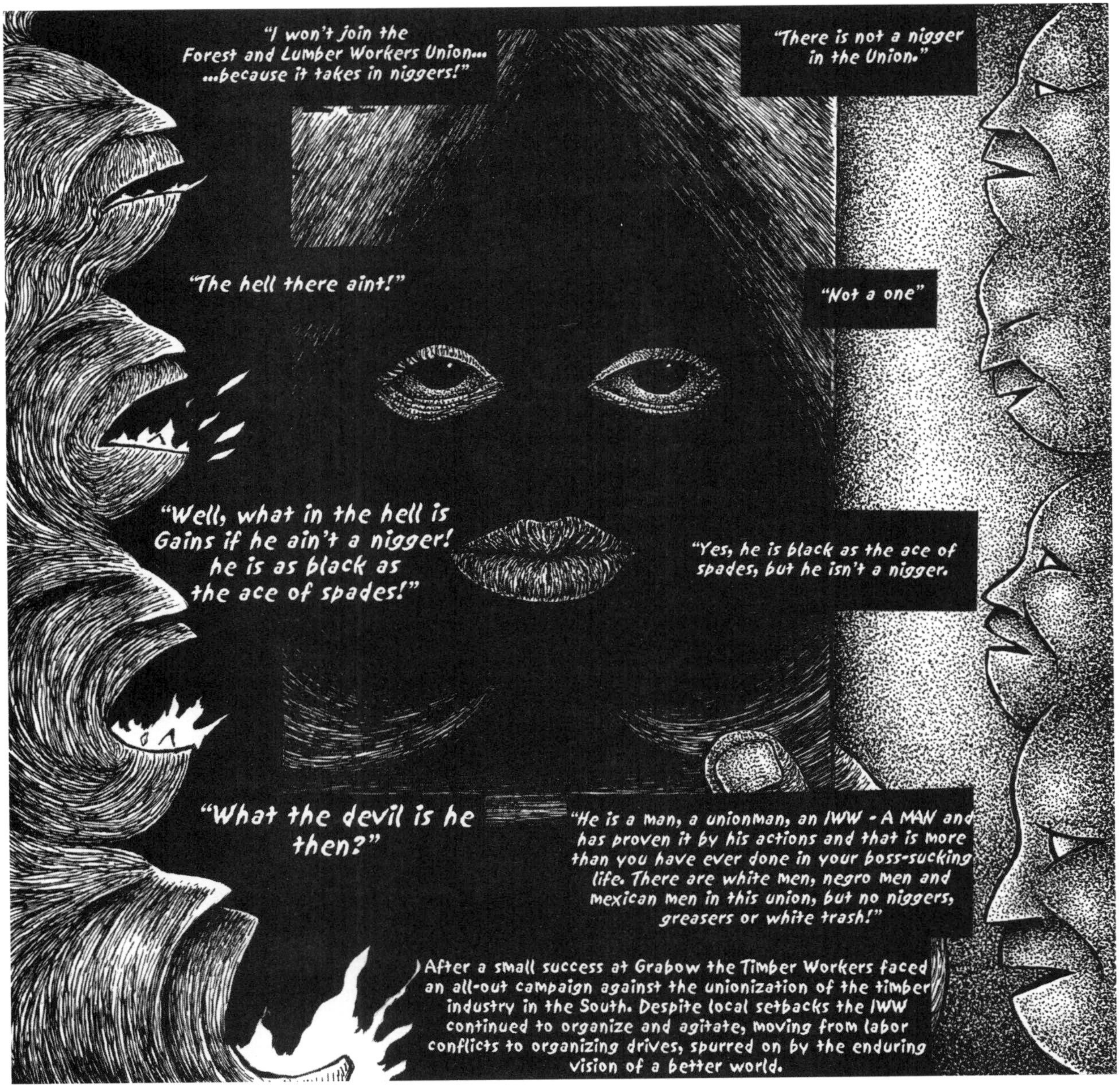
"I won't join the Forest and Lumber Workers Union... ...because it takes in niggers!"
"There is not a nigger in the Union."
"The hell there aint!"
"Not a one"
"Well, what in the hell is Gains if he ain't a nigger! he is as black as the ace of spades!"
"Yes, he is black as the ace of spades, but he isn't a nigger.
"What the devil is he then?"
"He is a man, a unionman, an IWW - A MAN and has proven it by his actions and that is more than you have ever done in your boss-sucking life. There are white men, negro men and mexican men in this union, but no niggers, greasers or white trash!"
After a small success at Grabow the Timber Workers faced an all-out campaign against the unionization of the timber industry in the South. Despite local setbacks the IWW continued to organize and agitate, moving from labor conflicts to organizing drives, spurred on by the enduring vision of a better world.

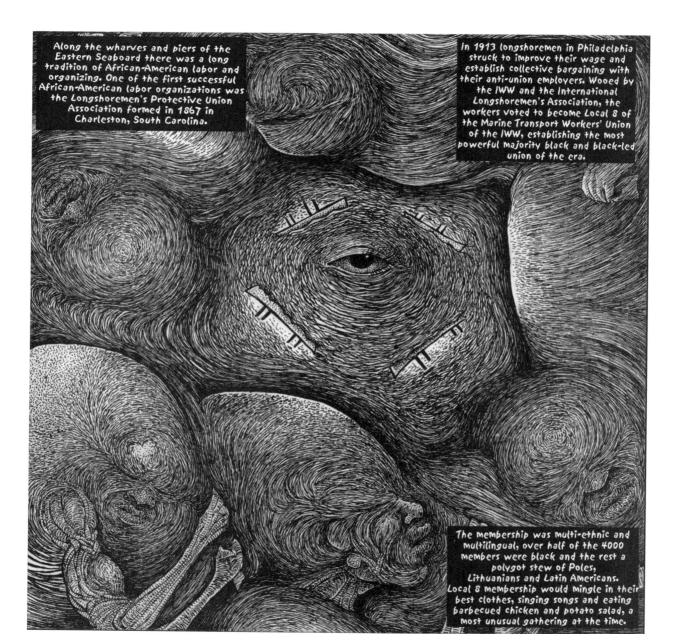

Along the wharves and piers of the Eastern Seaboard there was a long tradition of African-American labor and organizing. One of the first successful African-American labor organizations was the Longshoremen's Protective Union Association formed in 1867 in Charleston, South Carolina.

In 1913 longshoremen in Philadelphia struck to improve their wage and establish collective bargaining with their anti-union employers. Wooed by the IWW and the International Longshoremen's Association, the workers voted to become Local 8 of the Marine Transport Workers' Union of the IWW, establishing the most powerful majority black and black-led union of the era.

The membership was multi-ethnic and multilingual, over half of the 4000 members were black and the rest a polygot stew of Poles, Lithuanians and Latin Americans. Local 8 membership would mingle in their best clothes, singing songs and eating barbecued chicken and potato salad, a most unusual gathering at the time.

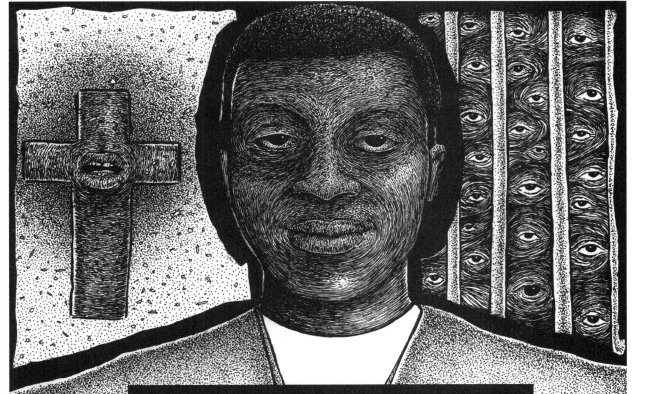

Ben Fletcher was born in Philadelphia in 1890. He had a open and generous face and the few surviving pictures of him invariably show a warm smile. Little is known of his life prior to 1911 when he first became known as a dockworker and local organizer for the IWW. When Local 8 was formed he became part of the leadershp of the union, a prominent African-American who staunchly advocated working-class solidarity over ethnic and racial rivalry.

A local African Methodist minister remarked 'the IWW at least protects the colored man, which is more than I can say for the laws of this country.'

Ben Fletcher's arrest in 1918, as part of a mass arrest of the IWW leadership on charges of encouraging draft resistance, conducting illegal strikes and violating the Espionage Act of 1917, was a blow to the membership of Local 8. He was the only black face amongst the sea of 101 defendants who faced serious charges in the Chicago courts. After a trial that was the biggest mass trial in US history, the judge handed down harsh sentences ranging from 10 to 25 years to life. With a bitter joke Fletcher remarked to his co-defendants...

..."Judge Landis is using poor English today. His sentences are too long."

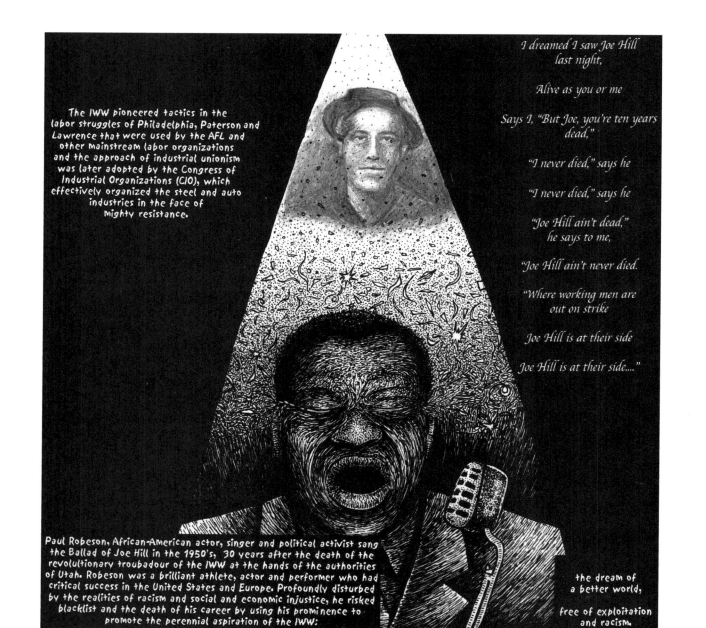

The IWW pioneered tactics in the labor struggles of Philadelphia, Paterson and Lawrence that were used by the AFL and other mainstream labor organizations and the approach of industrial unionism was later adopted by the Congress of Industrial Organizations (CIO), which effectively organized the steel and auto industries in the face of mighty resistance.

I dreamed I saw Joe Hill last night,

Alive as you or me

Says I, "But Joe, you're ten years dead,"

"I never died," says he

"I never died," says he

"Joe Hill ain't dead," he says to me,

"Joe Hill ain't never died.

"Where working men are out on strike

Joe Hill is at their side

Joe Hill is at their side...."

Paul Robeson, African-American actor, singer and political activist sang the Ballad of Joe Hill in the 1950's, 30 years after the death of the revolutionary troubadour of the IWW at the hands of the authorities of Utah. Robeson was a brilliant athlete, actor and performer who had critical success in the United States and Europe. Profoundly disturbed by the realities of racism and social and economic injustice, he risked blacklist and the death of his career by using his prominence to promote the perennial aspiration of the IWW:

the dream of a better world,

free of exploitation and racism.

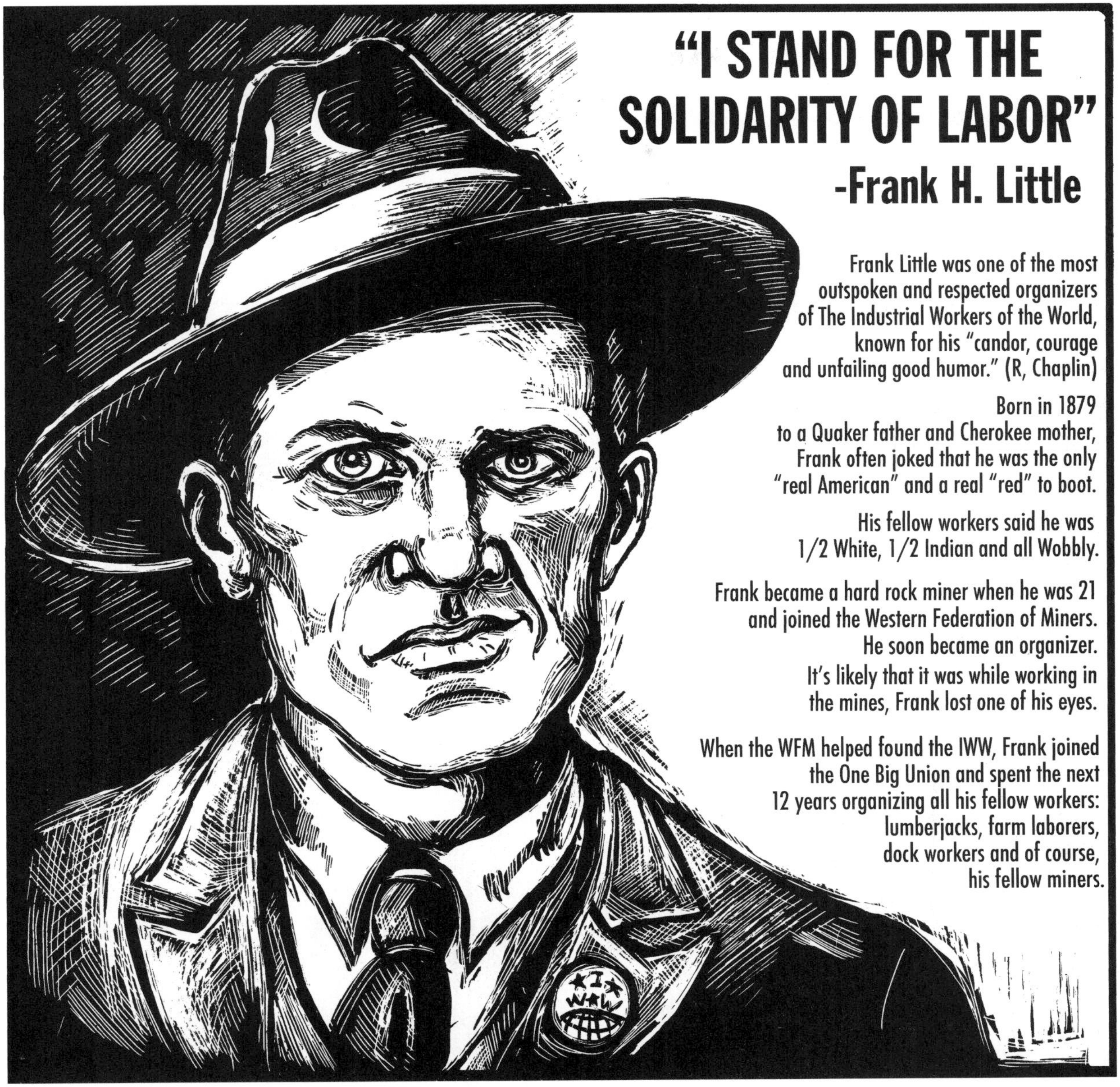
"I STAND FOR THE SOLIDARITY OF LABOR"
-Frank H. Little
Frank Little was one of the most outspoken and respected organizers of The Industrial Workers of the World, known for his "candor, courage and unfailing good humor." (R, Chaplin)
Born in 1879 to a Quaker father and Cherokee mother, Frank often joked that he was the only "real American" and a real "red" to boot.
His fellow workers said he was 1/2 White, 1/2 Indian and all Wobbly.
Frank became a hard rock miner when he was 21 and joined the Western Federation of Miners. He soon became an organizer.
It's likely that it was while working in the mines, Frank lost one of his eyes.
When the WFM helped found the IWW, Frank joined the One Big Union and spent the next 12 years organizing all his fellow workers: lumberjacks, farm laborers, dock workers and of course, his fellow miners.
IWW

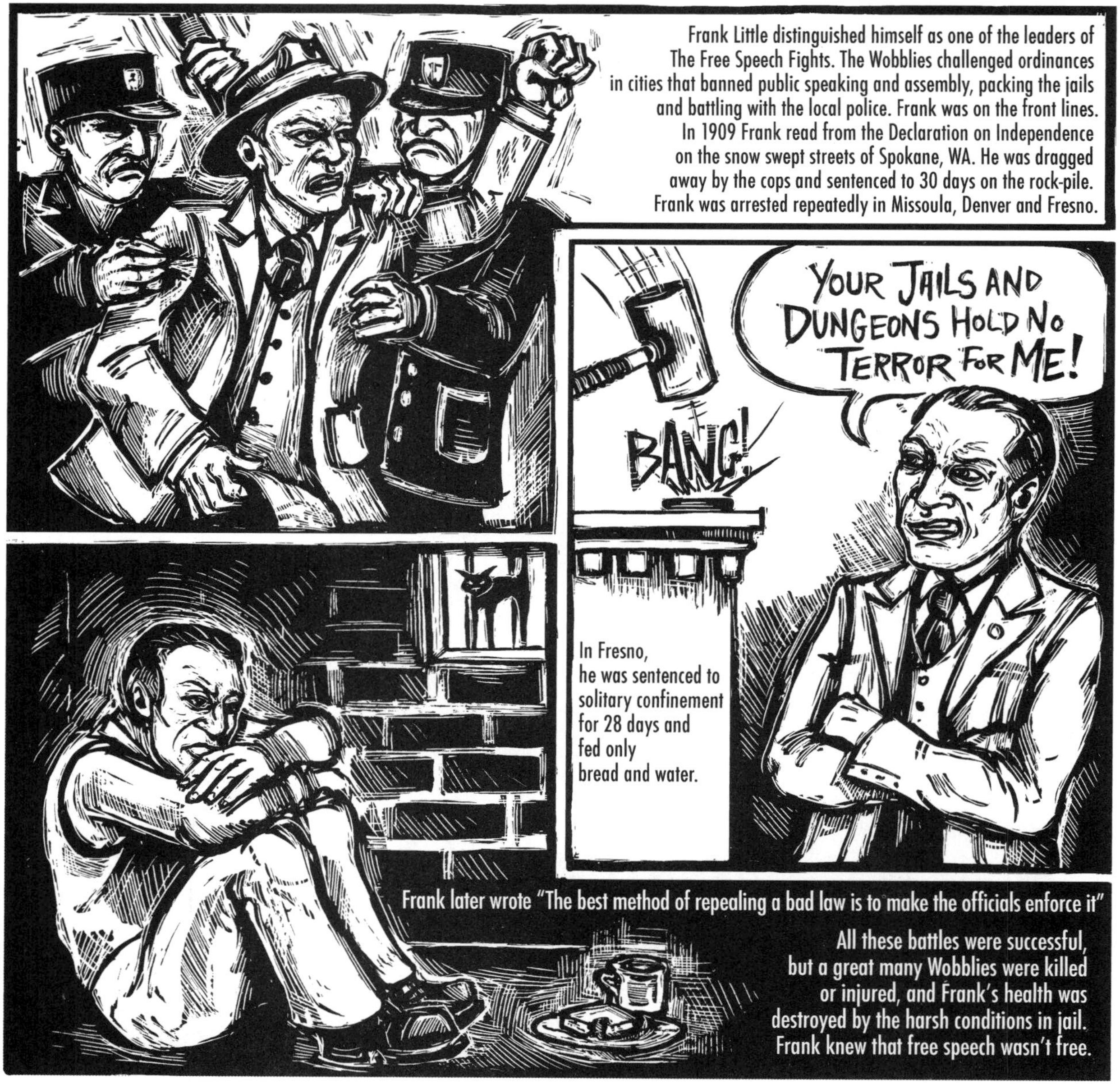
Frank Little distinguished himself as one of the leaders of The Free Speech Fights. The Wobblies challenged ordinances in cities that banned public speaking and assembly, packing the jails and battling with the local police. Frank was on the front lines. In 1909 Frank read from the Declaration on Independence on the snow swept streets of Spokane, WA. He was dragged away by the cops and sentenced to 30 days on the rock-pile. Frank was arrested repeatedly in Missoula, Denver and Fresno.
YOUR JAILS AND DUNGEONS HOLD NO TERROR FOR ME!
BANG!
In Fresno, he was sentenced to solitary confinement for 28 days and fed only bread and water.
Frank later wrote "The best method of repealing a bad law is to make the officials enforce it"
All these battles were successful, but a great many Wobblies were killed or injured, and Frank's health was destroyed by the harsh conditions in jail. Frank knew that free speech wasn't free.

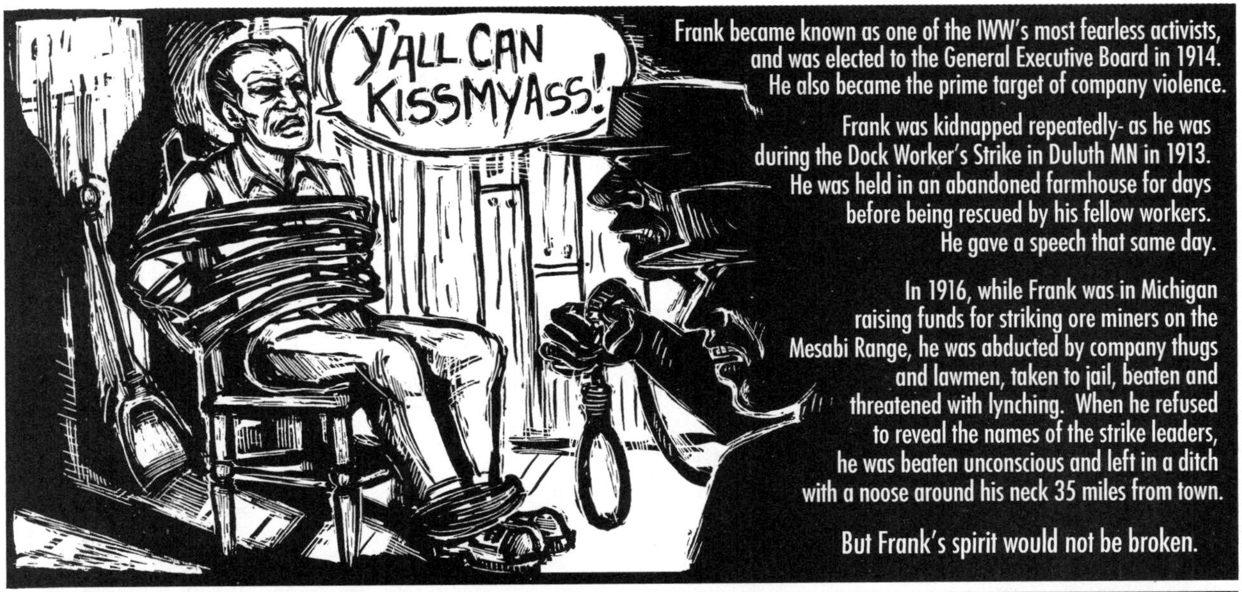
Y'ALL CAN KISSMYASS!
Frank became known as one of the IWW's most fearless activists, and was elected to the General Executive Board in 1914. He also became the prime target of company violence.
Frank was kidnapped repeatedly- as he was during the Dock Worker's Strike in Duluth MN in 1913. He was held in an abandoned farmhouse for days before being rescued by his fellow workers. He gave a speech that same day.
In 1916, while Frank was in Michigan raising funds for striking ore miners on the Mesabi Range, he was abducted by company thugs and lawmen, taken to jail, beaten and threatened with lynching. When he refused to reveal the names of the strike leaders, he was beaten unconscious and left in a ditch with a noose around his neck 35 miles from town.
But Frank's spirit would not be broken.

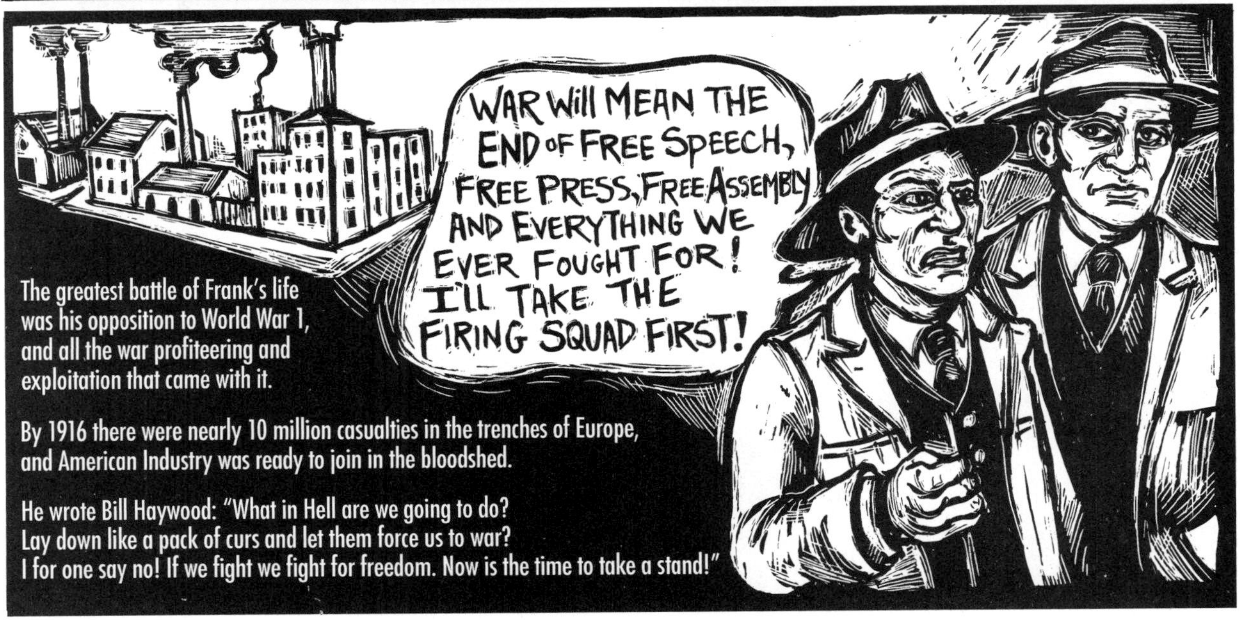
WAR WILL MEAN THE END OF FREE SPEECH, FREE PRESS, FREE ASSEMBLY AND EVERYTHING WE EVER FOUGHT FOR! I'LL TAKE THE FIRING SQUAD FIRST!
The greatest battle of Frank's life was his opposition to World War 1, and all the war profiteering and exploitation that came with it.
By 1916 there were nearly 10 million casualties in the trenches of Europe, and American Industry was ready to join in the bloodshed.
He wrote Bill Haywood: "What in Hell are we going to do? Lay down like a pack of curs and let them force us to war? I for one say no! If we fight we fight for freedom. Now is the time to take a stand!"

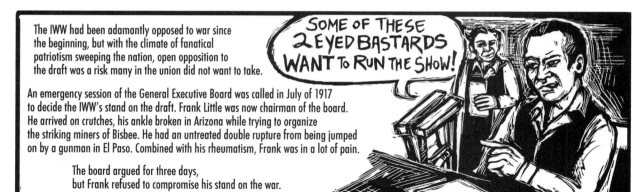

The IWW had been adamantly opposed to war since the beginning, but with the climate of fanatical patriotism sweeping the nation, open opposition to the draft was a risk many in the union did not want to take.

An emergency session of the General Executive Board was called in July of 1917 to decide the IWW's stand on the draft. Frank Little was now chairman of the board. He arrived on crutches, his ankle broken in Arizona while trying to organize the striking miners of Bisbee. He had an untreated double rupture from being jumped on by a gunman in El Paso. Combined with his rheumatism, Frank was in a lot of pain.

The board argued for three days, but Frank refused to compromise his stand on the war.

SOME OF THESE 2 EYED BASTARDS WANT TO RUN THE SHOW!

IF WE OPPOSE THE DRAFT, THEY'LL RUN US OUT OF BUISNESS...

THEY'LL RUN US OUT OF BUISNESS ANYWAY! EITHER WE'RE FOR THIS CAPITALISTIC-SLAUGHTERFEST OR WE'RE AGAINST IT! I'M READY TO FACE THE FIRING SQUAD RATHER THAN COMPROMISE!

No resolution was passed, and Frank volunteered for the most difficult and dangerous assignment of his life.

A FINE SPECIMEN THE IWW IS SENDING TO THAT TOUGH TOWN... ONE LEG, ONE EYE, TWO CRUTCHES-AND NO BRAINS!

DON'T WORRY FELLOW WORKER ALL WE'RE GONNA NEED FROM NOW ON IS GUTS!

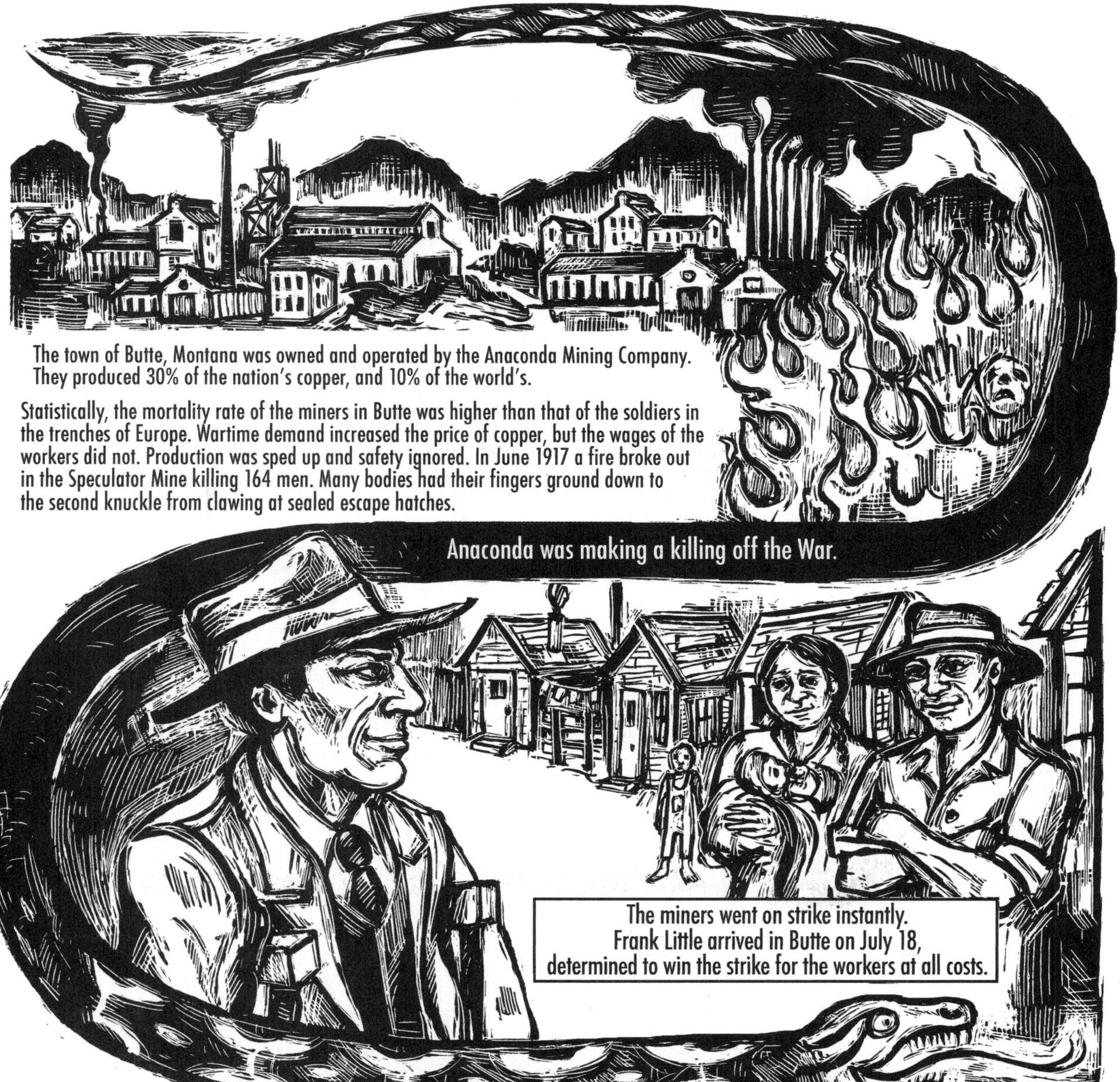

The town of Butte, Montana was owned and operated by the Anaconda Mining Company. They produced 30% of the nation's copper, and 10% of the world's.
Statistically, the mortality rate of the miners in Butte was higher than that of the soldiers in the trenches of Europe. Wartime demand increased the price of copper, but the wages of the workers did not. Production was sped up and safety ignored. In June 1917 a fire broke out in the Speculator Mine killing 164 men. Many bodies had their fingers ground down to the second knuckle from clawing at sealed escape hatches.
Anaconda was making a killing off the War.
The miners went on strike instantly. Frank Little arrived in Butte on July 18, determined to win the strike for the workers at all costs.

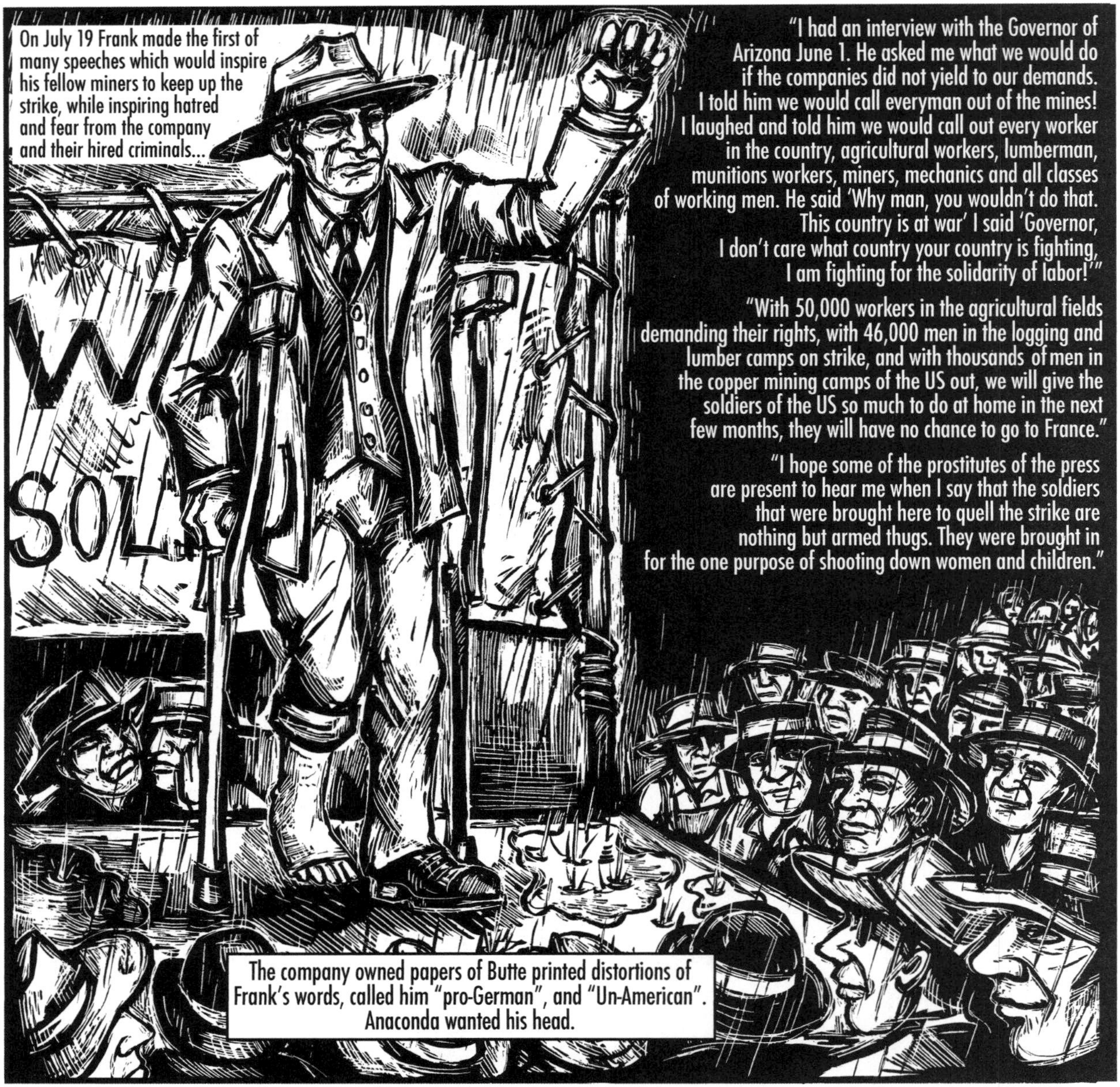
On July 19 Frank made the first of many speeches which would inspire his fellow miners to keep up the strike, while inspiring hatred and fear from the company and their hired criminals...
"I had an interview with the Governor of Arizona June 1. He asked me what we would do if the companies did not yield to our demands. I told him we would call everyman out of the mines! I laughed and told him we would call out every worker in the country, agricultural workers, lumberman, munitions workers, miners, mechanics and all classes of working men. He said 'Why man, you wouldn't do that. This country is at war' I said 'Governor, I don't care what country your country is fighting, I am fighting for the solidarity of labor!'"
"With 50,000 workers in the agricultural fields demanding their rights, with 46,000 men in the logging and lumber camps on strike, and with thousands of men in the copper mining camps of the US out, we will give the soldiers of the US so much to do at home in the next few months, they will have no chance to go to France."
"I hope some of the prostitutes of the press are present to hear me when I say that the soldiers that were brought here to quell the strike are nothing but armed thugs. They were brought in for the one purpose of shooting down women and children."
W
SOL
The company owned papers of Butte printed distortions of Frank's words, called him "pro-German", and "Un-American". Anaconda wanted his head.

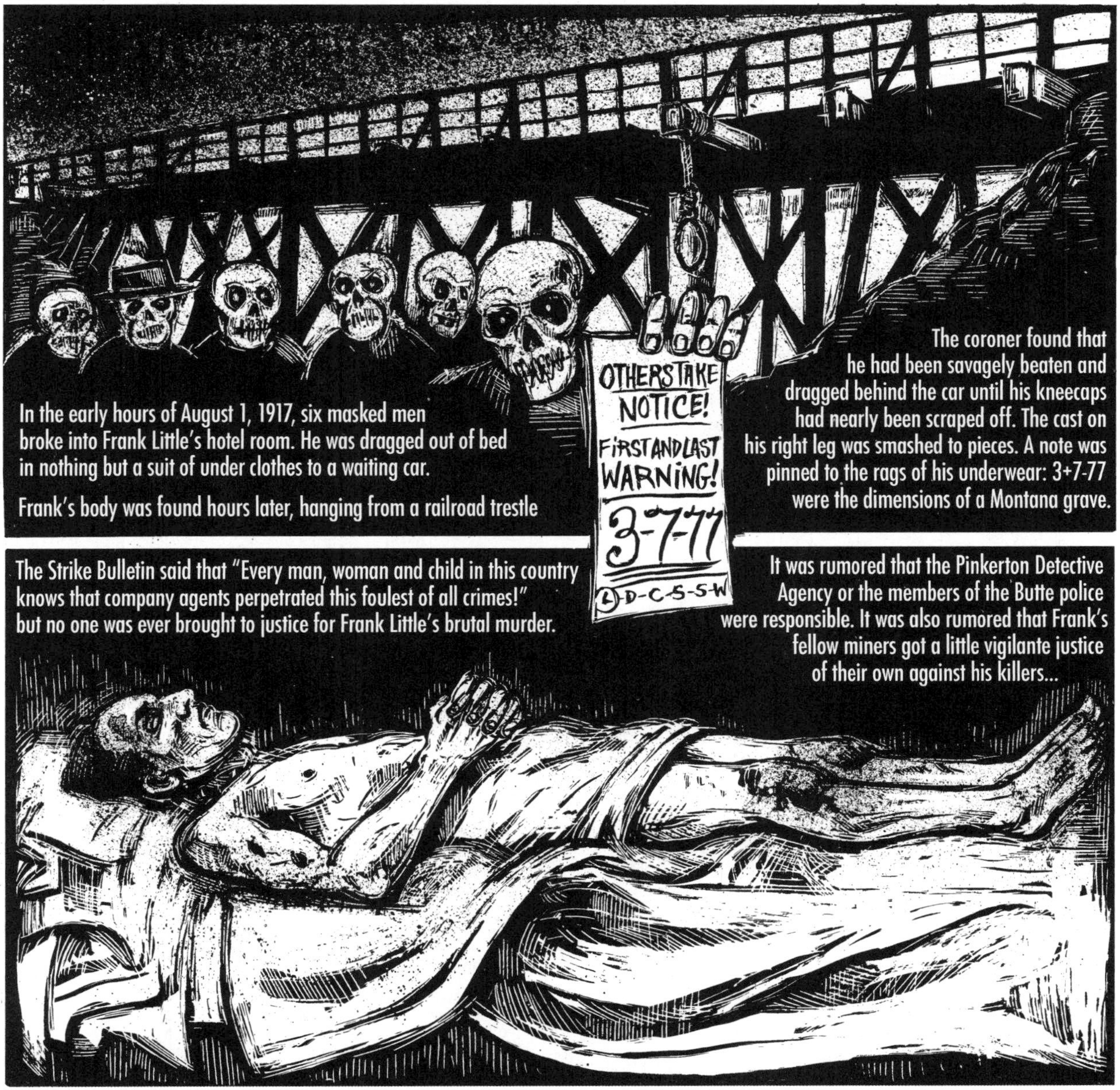
In the early hours of August 1, 1917, six masked men broke into Frank Little's hotel room. He was dragged out of bed in nothing but a suit of under clothes to a waiting car.
Frank's body was found hours later, hanging from a railroad trestle
OTHERS TAKE NOTICE!
FIRST AND LAST WARNING!
3-7-77
L-D-C-S-S-W
The coroner found that he had been savagely beaten and dragged behind the car until his kneecaps had nearly been scraped off. The cast on his right leg was smashed to pieces. A note was pinned to the rags of his underwear: 3+7-77 were the dimensions of a Montana grave.
The Strike Bulletin said that "Every man, woman and child in this country knows that company agents perpetrated this foulest of all crimes!" but no one was ever brought to justice for Frank Little's brutal murder.
It was rumored that the Pinkerton Detective Agency or the members of the Butte police were responsible. It was also rumored that Frank's fellow miners got a little vigilante justice of their own against his killers...

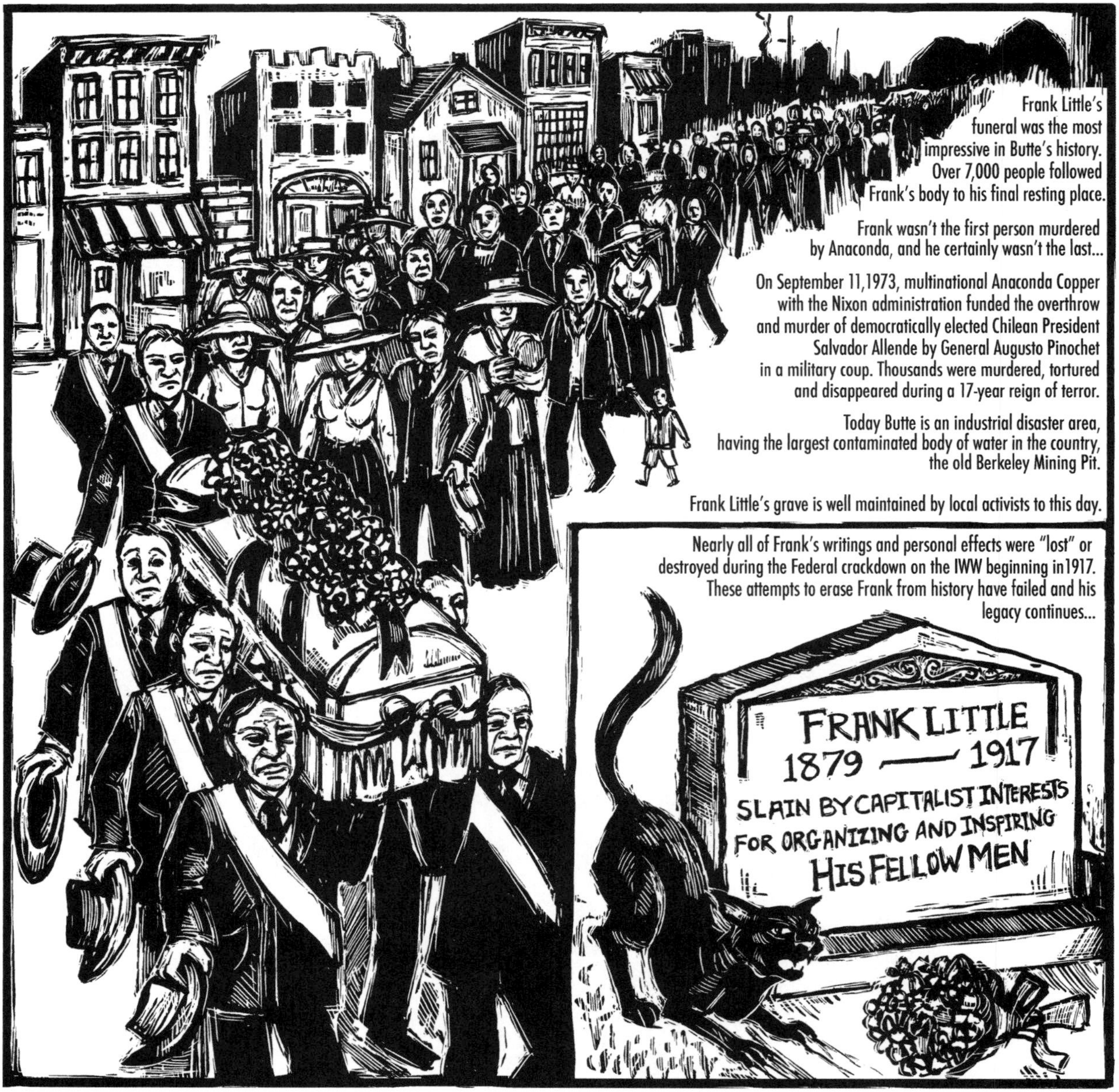
Frank Little's funeral was the most impressive in Butte's history. Over 7,000 people followed Frank's body to his final resting place.
Frank wasn't the first person murdered by Anaconda, and he certainly wasn't the last...
On September 11,1973, multinational Anaconda Copper with the Nixon administration funded the overthrow and murder of democratically elected Chilean President Salvador Allende by General Augusto Pinochet in a military coup. Thousands were murdered, tortured and disappeared during a 17-year reign of terror.
Today Butte is an industrial disaster area, having the largest contaminated body of water in the country, the old Berkeley Mining Pit.
Frank Little's grave is well maintained by local activists to this day.
Nearly all of Frank's writings and personal effects were "lost" or destroyed during the Federal crackdown on the IWW beginning in1917. These attempts to erase Frank from history have failed and his legacy continues...
FRANK LITTLE
1879 — 1917
SLAIN BY CAPITALIST INTERESTS
FOR ORGANIZING AND INSPIRING
HIS FELLOW MEN

1/2 INDIAN
1/2 WHITE
ALL IWW
FRANK H. LITTLE
1879
1917
FREE SPEECH
FIGHTS
FRESNO
MISSOULA
SPOKANE
SLAIN BY CAPITALIST INTERESTS FOR ORGANIZING AND INSPIRING HIS FELLOW WORKERS.
NO WAR BUT CLASS WAR
NS '04

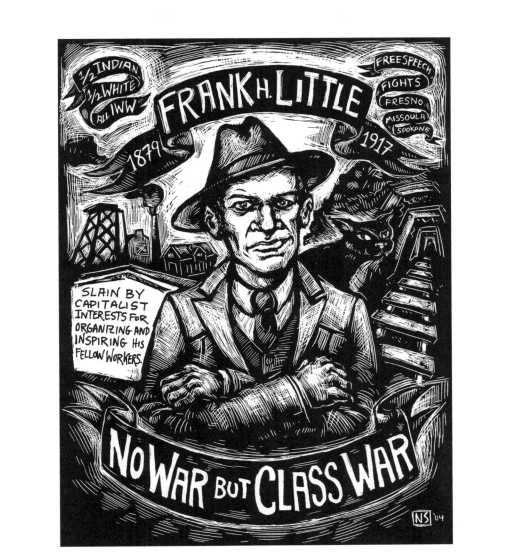

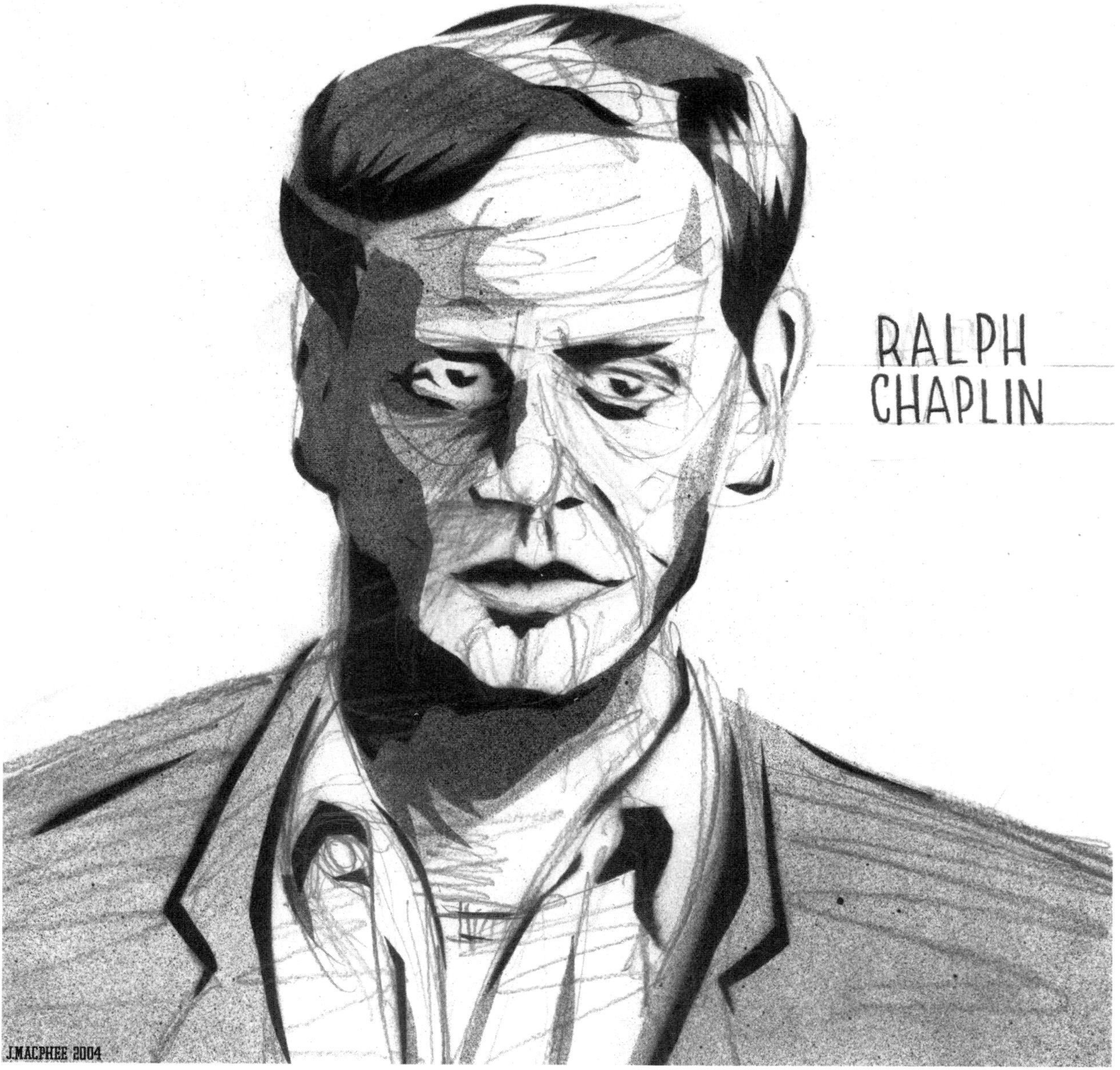
RALPH
CHAPLIN
J.MACPHEE 2004

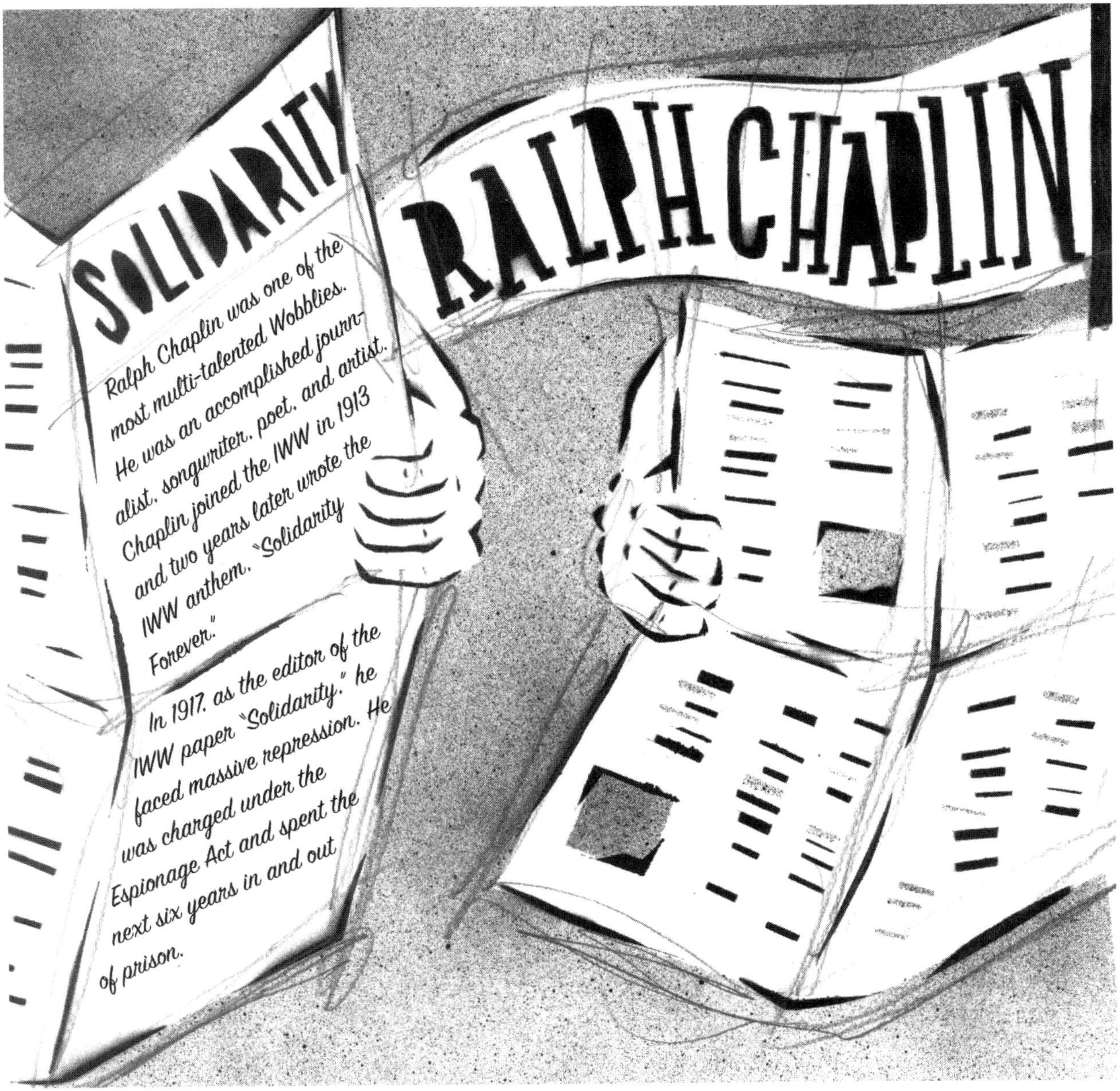

SOLIDARITY
RALPH CHAPLIN
Ralph Chaplin was one of the most multi-talented Wobblies. He was an accomplished journalist, songwriter, poet, and artist. Chaplin joined the IWW in 1913 and two years later wrote the IWW anthem, "Solidarity Forever."
In 1917, as the editor of the IWW paper "Solidarity," he faced massive repression. He was charged under the Espionage Act and spent the next six years in and out of prison.

"The General Executive Board of the I.W.W. in session assembled,
reaffirm with unfaltering determination the un-alterable opposition
of the Industrial Workers of the World and its membership to all wars,
and the participation therein of the membership of the Industrial Workers of the World."

"In this mad chaos of bloodshed and slaughter that has engulfed the world,
all the rights we have fought so long and bitterly to retain and enlarge,
are in danger of being crushed and suppressed by the ruthless powers of Capitalism,
therefore it behooves the membership of the I.W.W. to lock well to their rights, and
to battle for their principles with intensified vigor and courage.
We must not allow the masters of industry, under the cloak of 'military expediency'
or the subtle and hypocritical lie of this being a 'War for Democracy' to destroy every
vestige of our organization, to stifle the voice of the workers, to crush the
working-class press, by abrogating the rights of Free Speech, Free Press
and Free Assemblage, as they are now doing on every hand, these tyrannical acts
and usurpation of power, we cannot and shall not tolerate without protest and
resistance by all methods within our power, we must let these tyrants understand
that they cannot fool us with their 'War for Democracy' lies,
by destroying Democracy here."

"We wish to serve notice on our Capitalist masters, that we are just as bitterly opposed
to their wars of commercialism, today, as we ever were, and our refusal to endorse of
participate in their wars is just as firm to day, as it ever was, and that we will resent with
all power at our command any attempt upon their part, to compel us — the disinherited,
to participate in a war, that can only bring in its wake death and untold misery, privation
and suffering to millions of workers, and only serve to further rivet the
chains of slavery on our necks, and render still more secure the
power of the few to control the destinies of the many."

-Excerpts from the 1916
Statement of the General Executive Board of the I.W.W. on War.

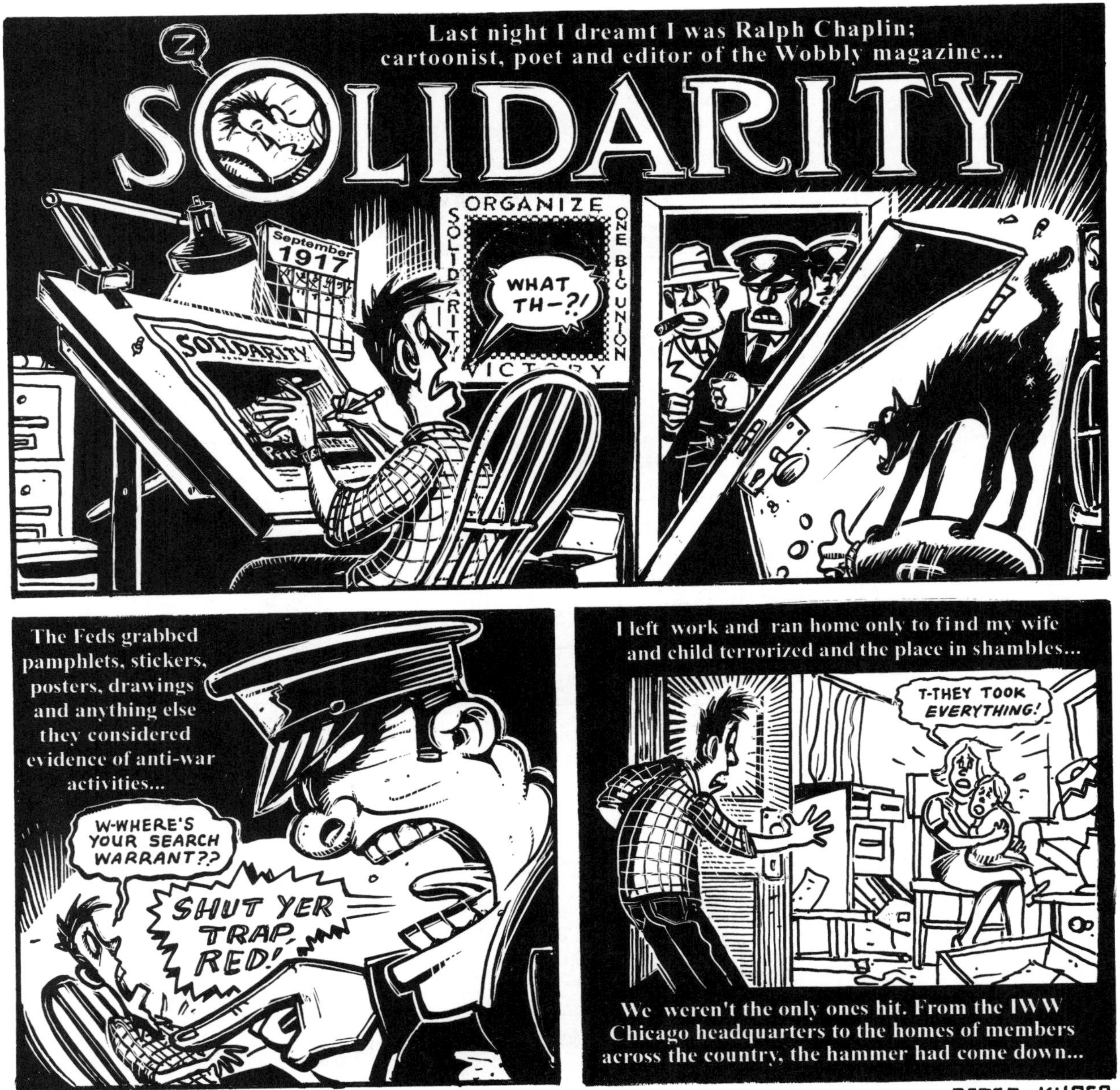
Z
Last night I dreamt I was Ralph Chaplin; cartoonist, poet and editor of the Wobbly magazine...
SOLIDARITY
September 1917
SOLIDARITY
ORGANIZE
SOLIDARITY
ONE BIG UNION
VICTORY
WHAT TH–?!
The Feds grabbed pamphlets, stickers, posters, drawings and anything else they considered evidence of anti-war activities...
W-WHERE'S YOUR SEARCH WARRANT??
SHUT YER TRAP, RED!
I left work and ran home only to find my wife and child terrorized and the place in shambles...
T-THEY TOOK EVERYTHING!
We weren't the only ones hit. From the IWW Chicago headquarters to the homes of members across the country, the hammer had come down...

PETER KUPER

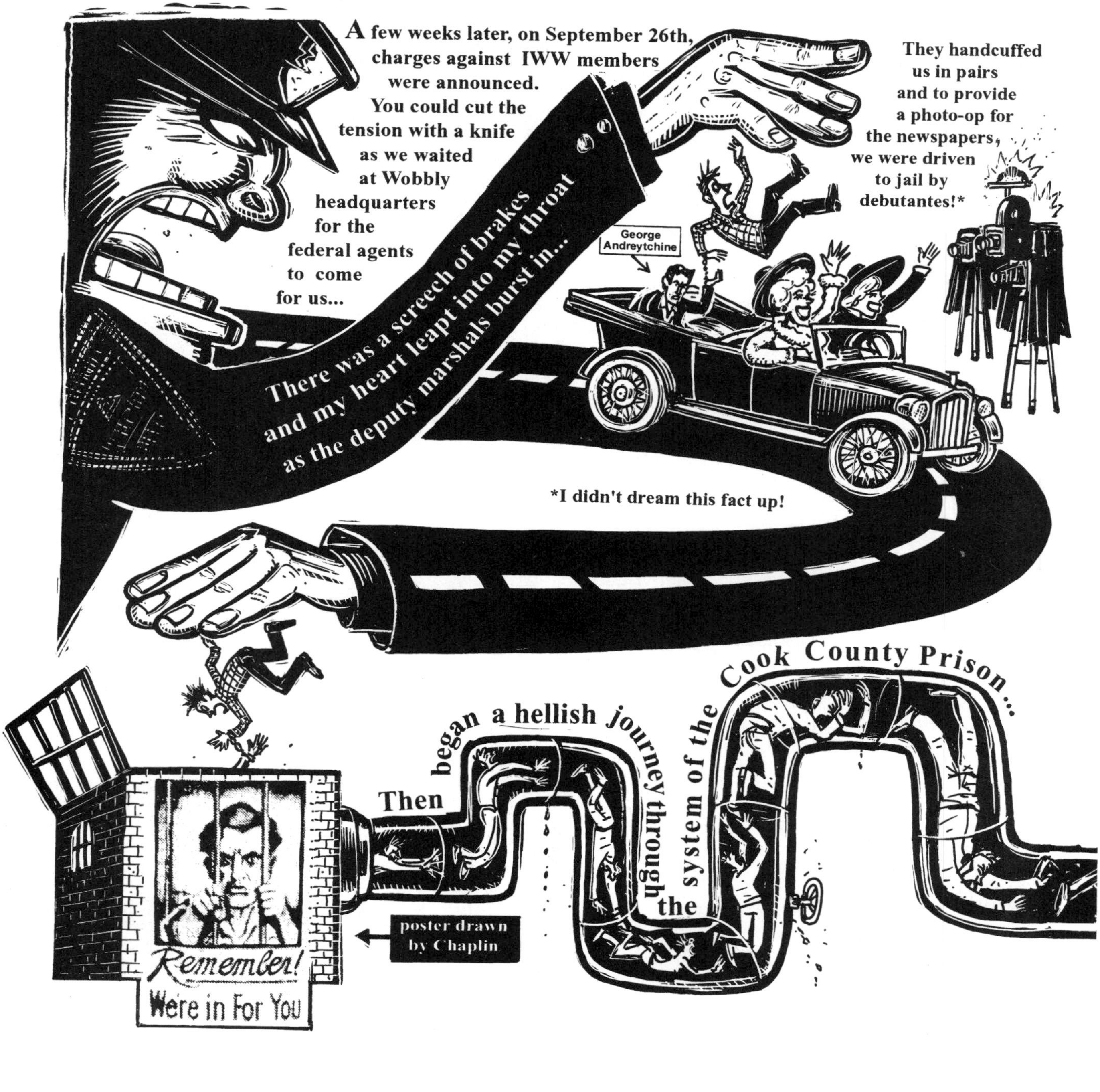

A few weeks later, on September 26th, charges against IWW members were announced. You could cut the tension with a knife as we waited at Wobbly headquarters for the federal agents to come for us...
There was a screech of brakes and my heart leapt into my throat as the deputy marshals burst in...
They handcuffed us in pairs and to provide a photo-op for the newspapers, we were driven to jail by debutantes!*
George Andreytchine
*I didn't dream this fact up!
Then began a hellish journey through the system of the Cook County Prison...
Remember! Were in For You
poster drawn by Chaplin

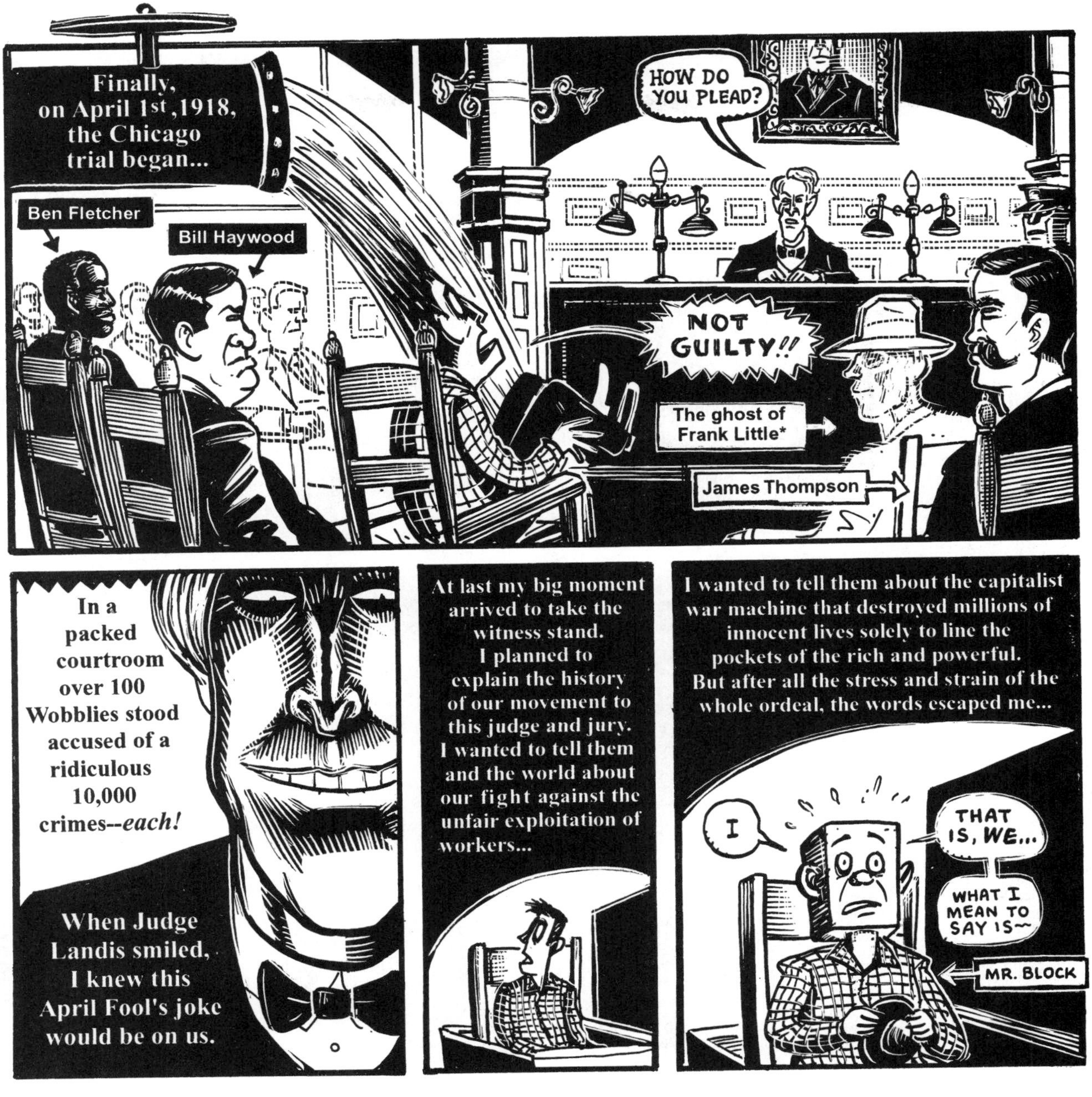

Finally, on April 1st, 1918, the Chicago trial began...
Ben Fletcher
Bill Haywood
HOW DO YOU PLEAD?
NOT GUILTY!!
The ghost of Frank Little*
James Thompson
In a packed courtroom over 100 Wobblies stood accused of a ridiculous 10,000 crimes--*each!*
When Judge Landis smiled, I knew this April Fool's joke would be on us.
At last my big moment arrived to take the witness stand. I planned to explain the history of our movement to this judge and jury. I wanted to tell them and the world about our fight against the unfair exploitation of workers...
I wanted to tell them about the capitalist war machine that destroyed millions of innocent lives solely to line the pockets of the rich and powerful. But after all the stress and strain of the whole ordeal, the words escaped me...
I
THAT IS, WE...
WHAT I MEAN TO SAY IS~
MR. BLOCK

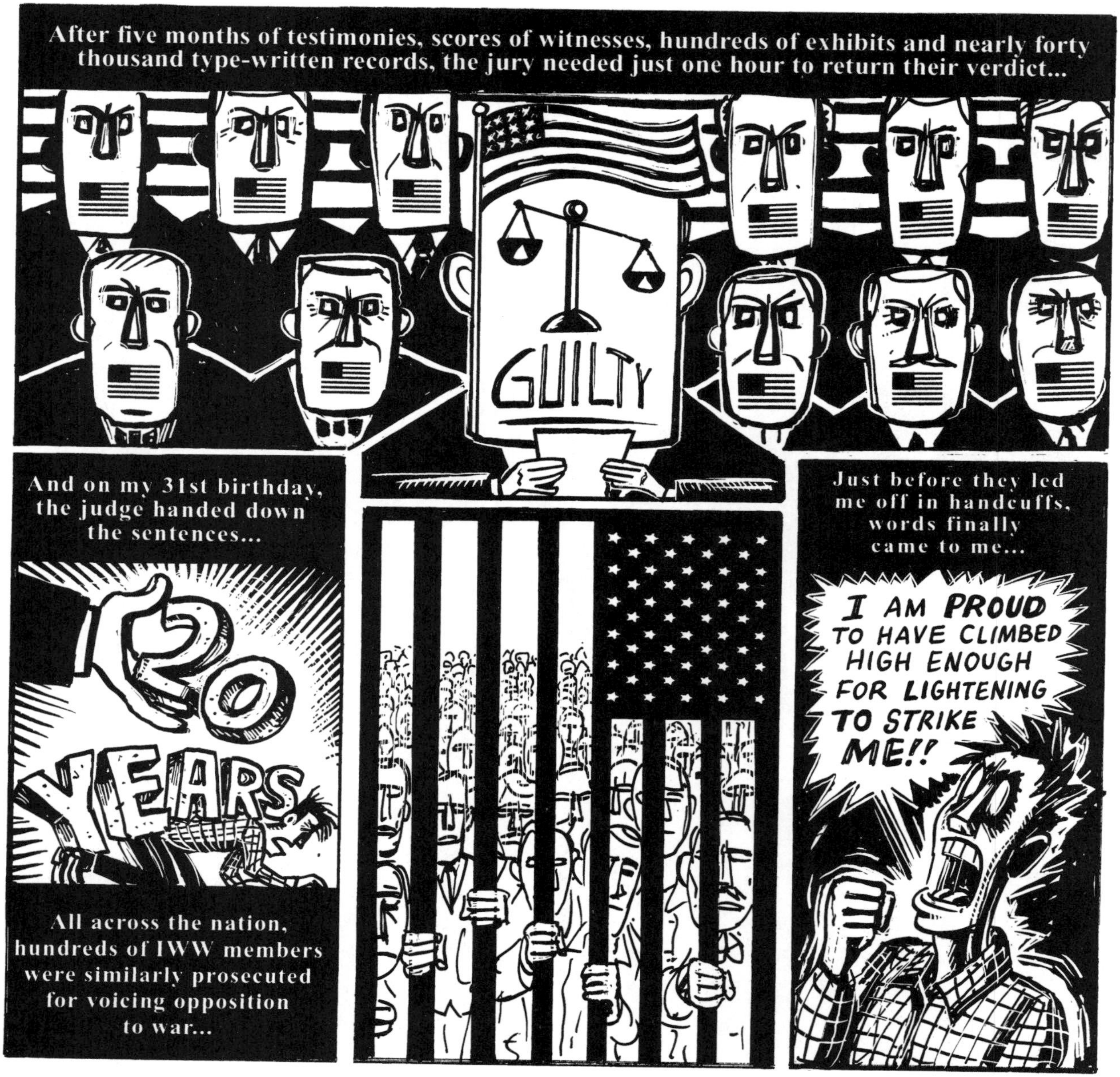
After five months of testimonies, scores of witnesses, hundreds of exhibits and nearly forty thousand type-written records, the jury needed just one hour to return their verdict...
GUILTY
And on my 31st birthday, the judge handed down the sentences...
20 YEARS
All across the nation, hundreds of IWW members were similarly prosecuted for voicing opposition to war...
Just before they led me off in handcuffs, words finally came to me...
I AM PROUD TO HAVE CLIMBED HIGH ENOUGH FOR LIGHTENING TO STRIKE ME!!

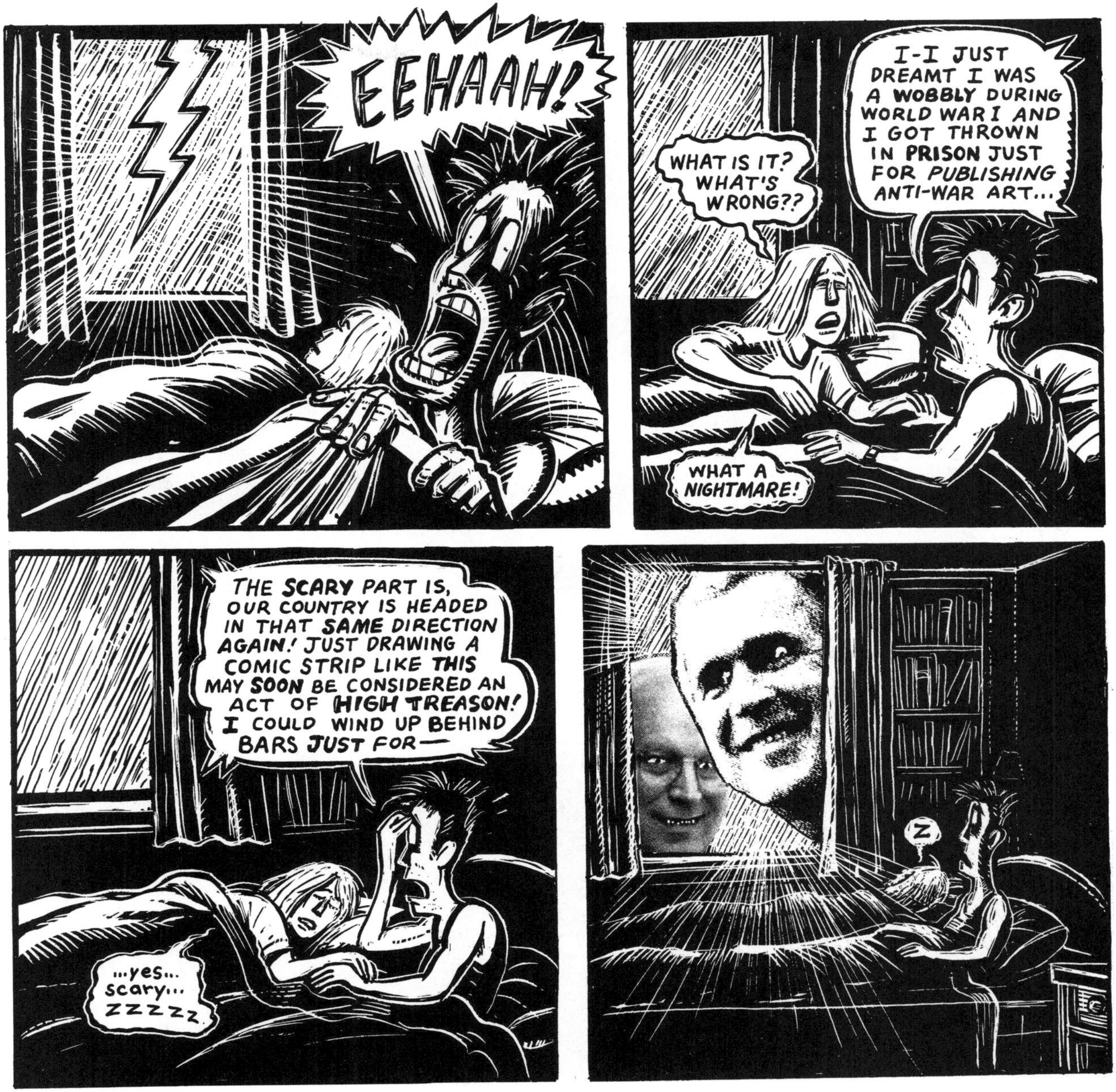
EEHAAH!
WHAT IS IT? WHAT'S WRONG??
I-I JUST DREAMT I WAS A WOBBLY DURING WORLD WAR I AND I GOT THROWN IN PRISON JUST FOR PUBLISHING ANTI-WAR ART...
WHAT A NIGHTMARE!
THE SCARY PART IS, OUR COUNTRY IS HEADED IN THAT SAME DIRECTION AGAIN! JUST DRAWING A COMIC STRIP LIKE THIS MAY SOON BE CONSIDERED AN ACT OF HIGH TREASON! I COULD WIND UP BEHIND BARS JUST FOR—
...yes... scary... zzzzz
Z

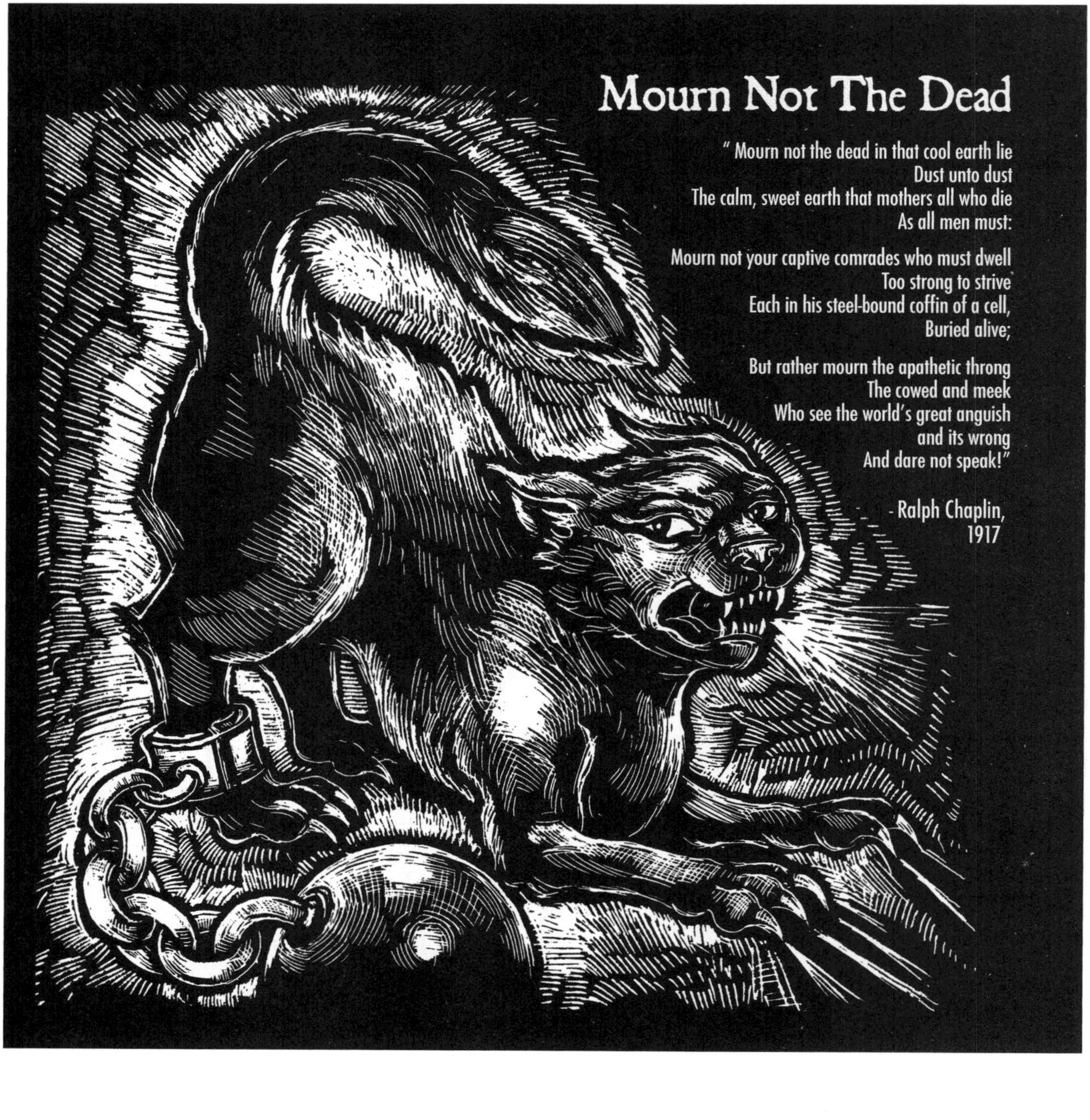
Mourn Not The Dead
" Mourn not the dead in that cool earth lie
Dust unto dust
The calm, sweet earth that mothers all who die
As all men must:
Mourn not your captive comrades who must dwell
Too strong to strive
Each in his steel-bound coffin of a cell,
Buried alive;
But rather mourn the apathetic throng
The cowed and meek
Who see the world's great anguish
and its wrong
And dare not speak!"
- Ralph Chaplin,
1917

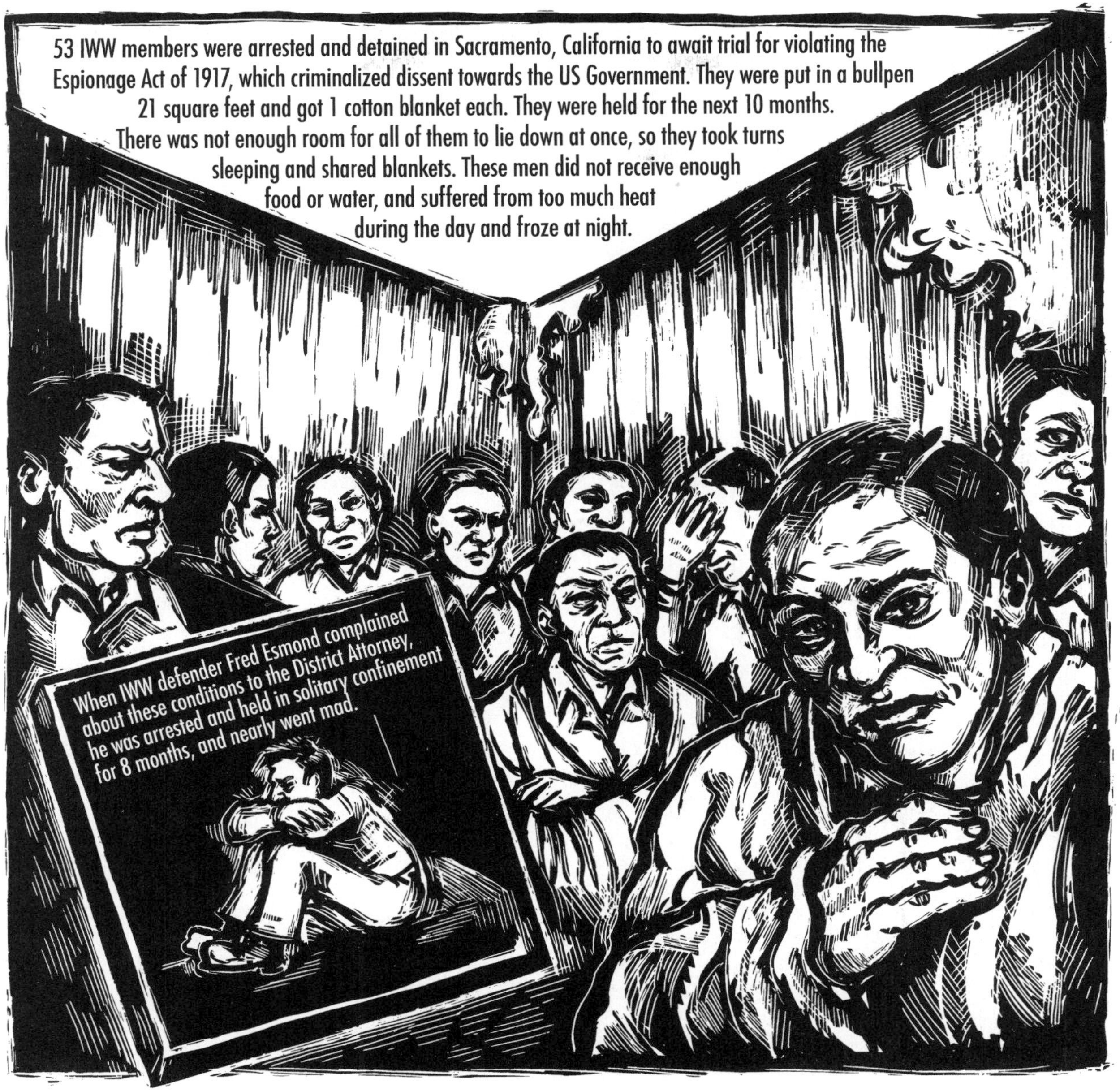
53 IWW members were arrested and detained in Sacramento, California to await trial for violating the Espionage Act of 1917, which criminalized dissent towards the US Government. They were put in a bullpen 21 square feet and got 1 cotton blanket each. They were held for the next 10 months. There was not enough room for all of them to lie down at once, so they took turns sleeping and shared blankets. These men did not receive enough food or water, and suffered from too much heat during the day and froze at night.
When IWW defender Fred Esmond complained about these conditions to the District Attorney, he was arrested and held in solitary confinement for 8 months, and nearly went mad.

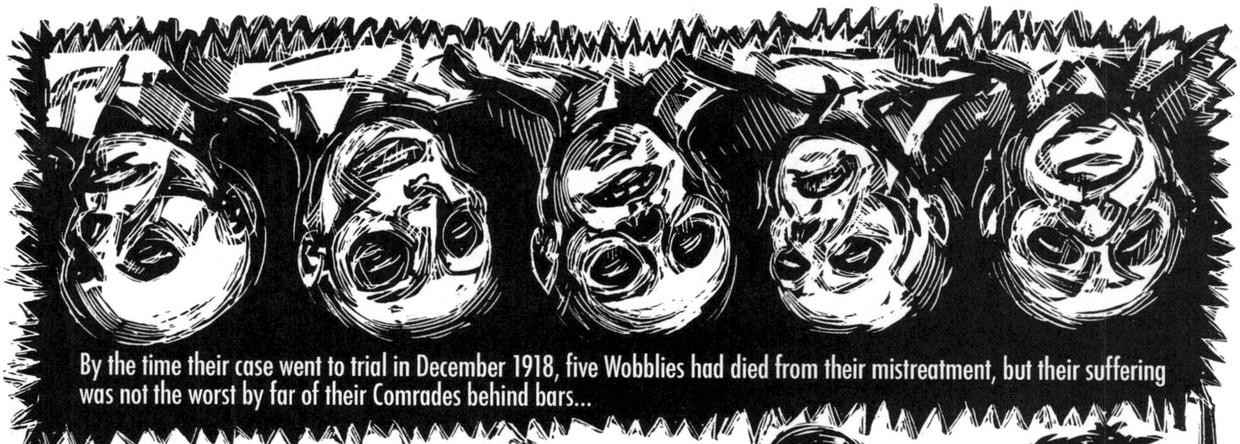
By the time their case went to trial in December 1918, five Wobblies had died from their mistreatment, but their suffering was not the worst by far of their Comrades behind bars...

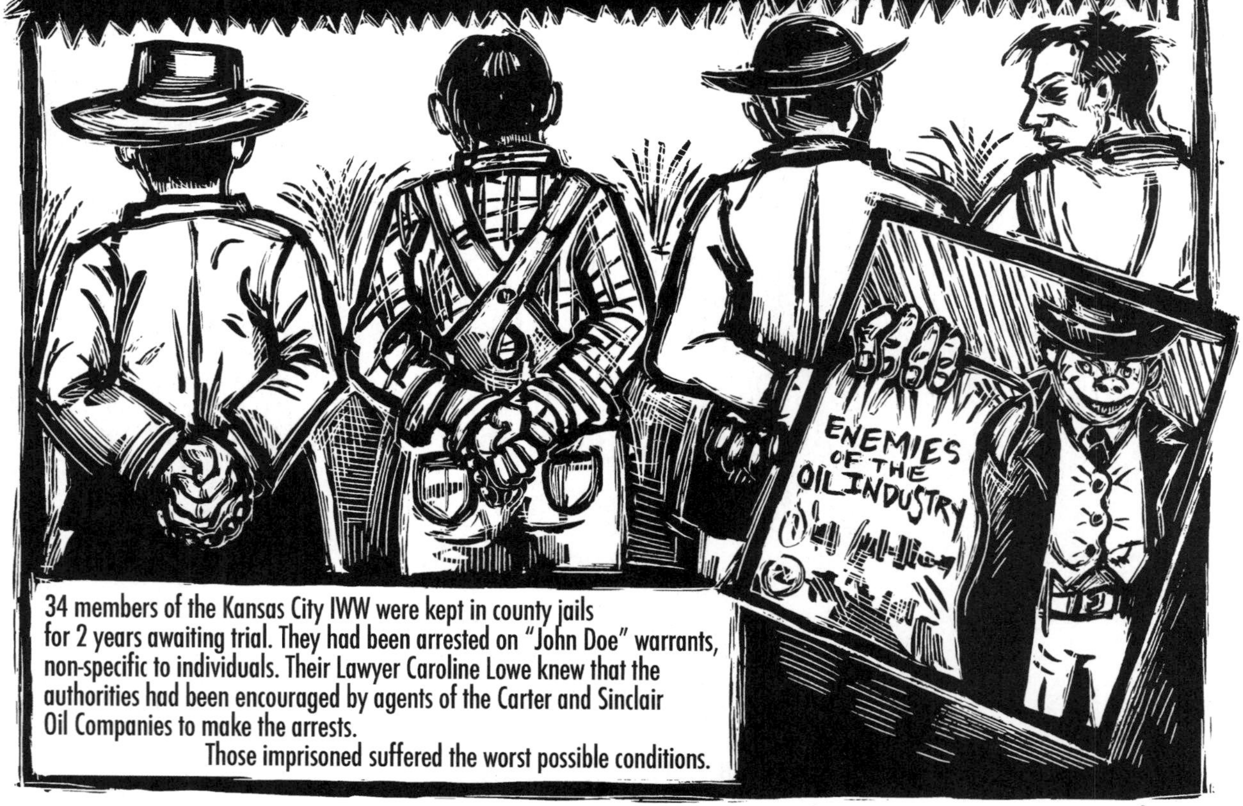
ENEMIES OF THE OIL INDUSTRY
34 members of the Kansas City IWW were kept in county jails for 2 years awaiting trial. They had been arrested on "John Doe" warrants, non-specific to individuals. Their Lawyer Caroline Lowe knew that the authorities had been encouraged by agents of the Carter and Sinclair Oil Companies to make the arrests.
Those imprisoned suffered the worst possible conditions.

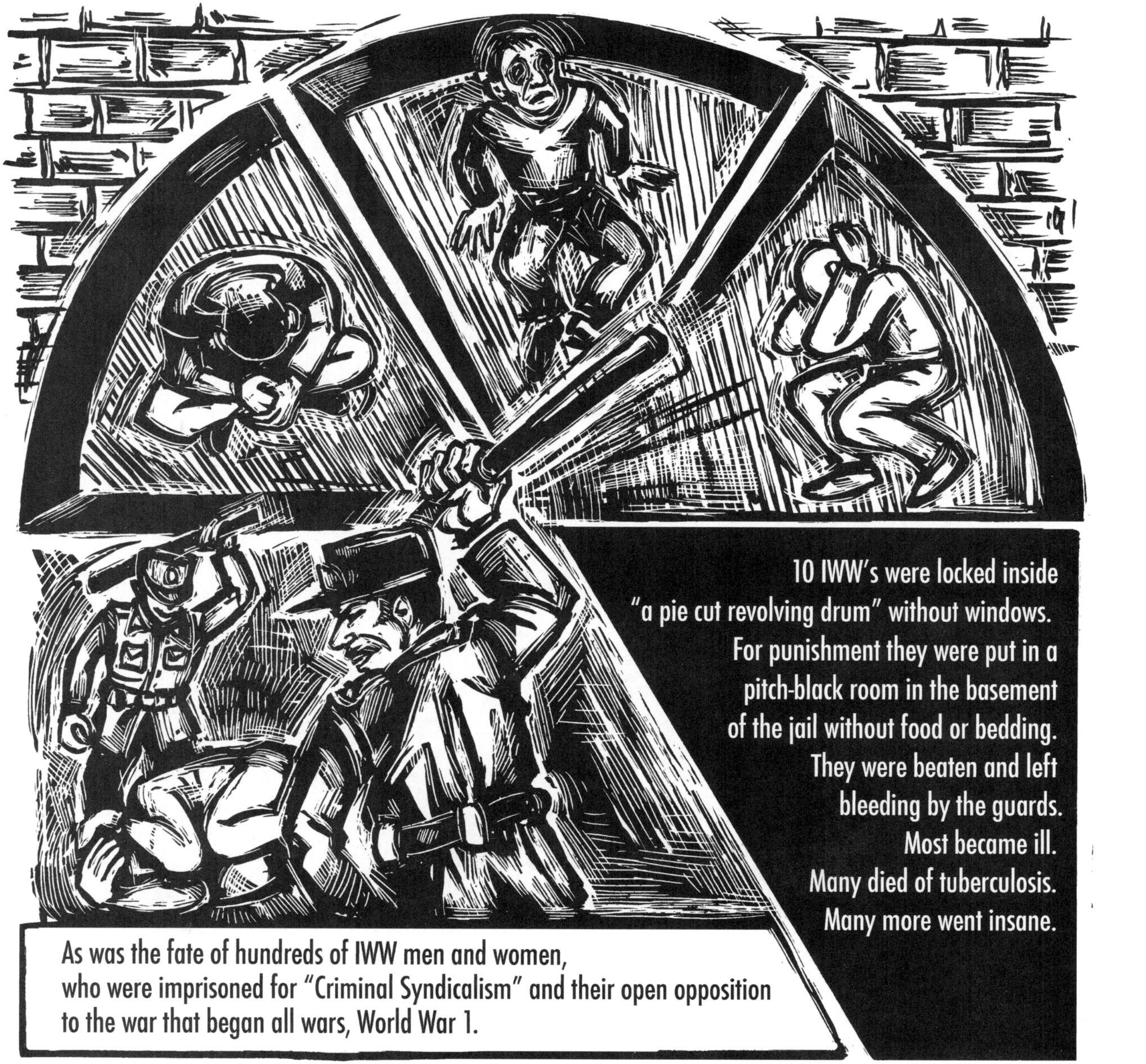
10 IWW's were locked inside "a pie cut revolving drum" without windows. For punishment they were put in a pitch-black room in the basement of the jail without food or bedding. They were beaten and left bleeding by the guards. Most became ill. Many died of tuberculosis. Many more went insane.
As was the fate of hundreds of IWW men and women, who were imprisoned for "Criminal Syndicalism" and their open opposition to the war that began all wars, World War 1.

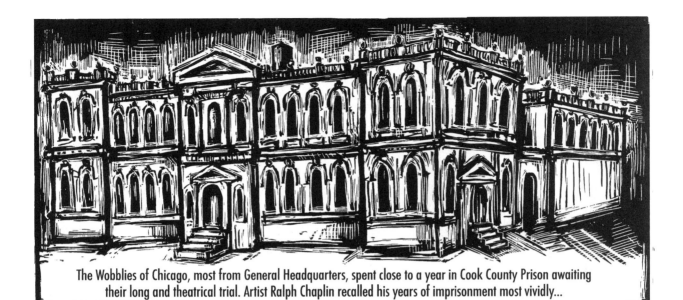

The Wobblies of Chicago, most from General Headquarters, spent close to a year in Cook County Prison awaiting their long and theatrical trial. Artist Ralph Chaplin recalled his years of imprisonment most vividly...

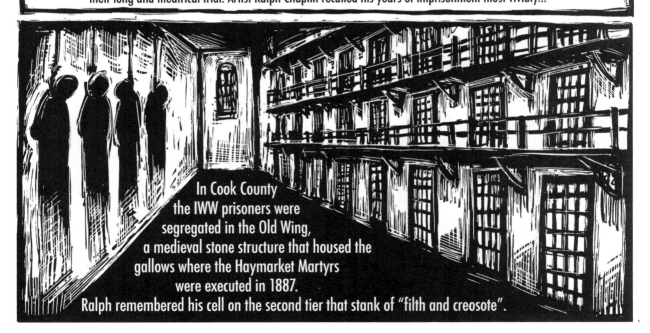

In Cook County the IWW prisoners were segregated in the Old Wing, a medieval stone structure that housed the gallows where the Haymarket Martyrs were executed in 1887. Ralph remembered his cell on the second tier that stank of "filth and creosote".

They could hear faint Jazz music filtering across the Clark Street alley from a cheap dance hall, watching the figures dance in silhouette like "Horrible Marionettes".

AHAAHA AHAHA HAAHA

"Day and night the jailhouse noise and stench were indescribable. From cell to cell, from galley to galley the air was crackling with obscene and blasphemous words. To me it seemed a monstrous cage in which unearthly and monstrous birds were caged."

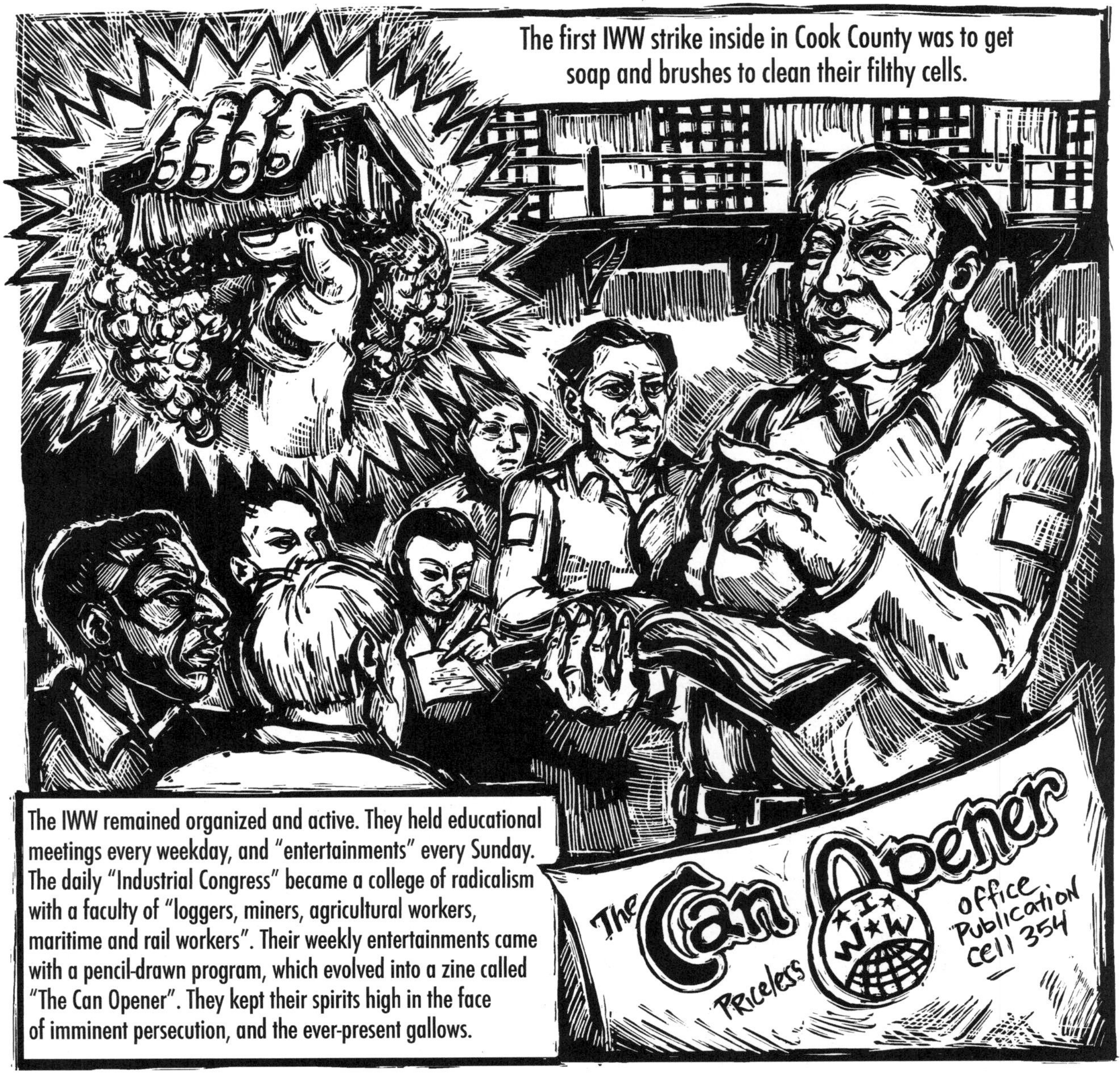

The first IWW strike inside in Cook County was to get soap and brushes to clean their filthy cells.
The IWW remained organized and active. They held educational meetings every weekday, and "entertainments" every Sunday. The daily "Industrial Congress" became a college of radicalism with a faculty of "loggers, miners, agricultural workers, maritime and rail workers". Their weekly entertainments came with a pencil-drawn program, which evolved into a zine called "The Can Opener". They kept their spirits high in the face of imminent persecution, and the ever-present gallows.
The Can Opener
I W W
Priceless
Office Publication Cell 354

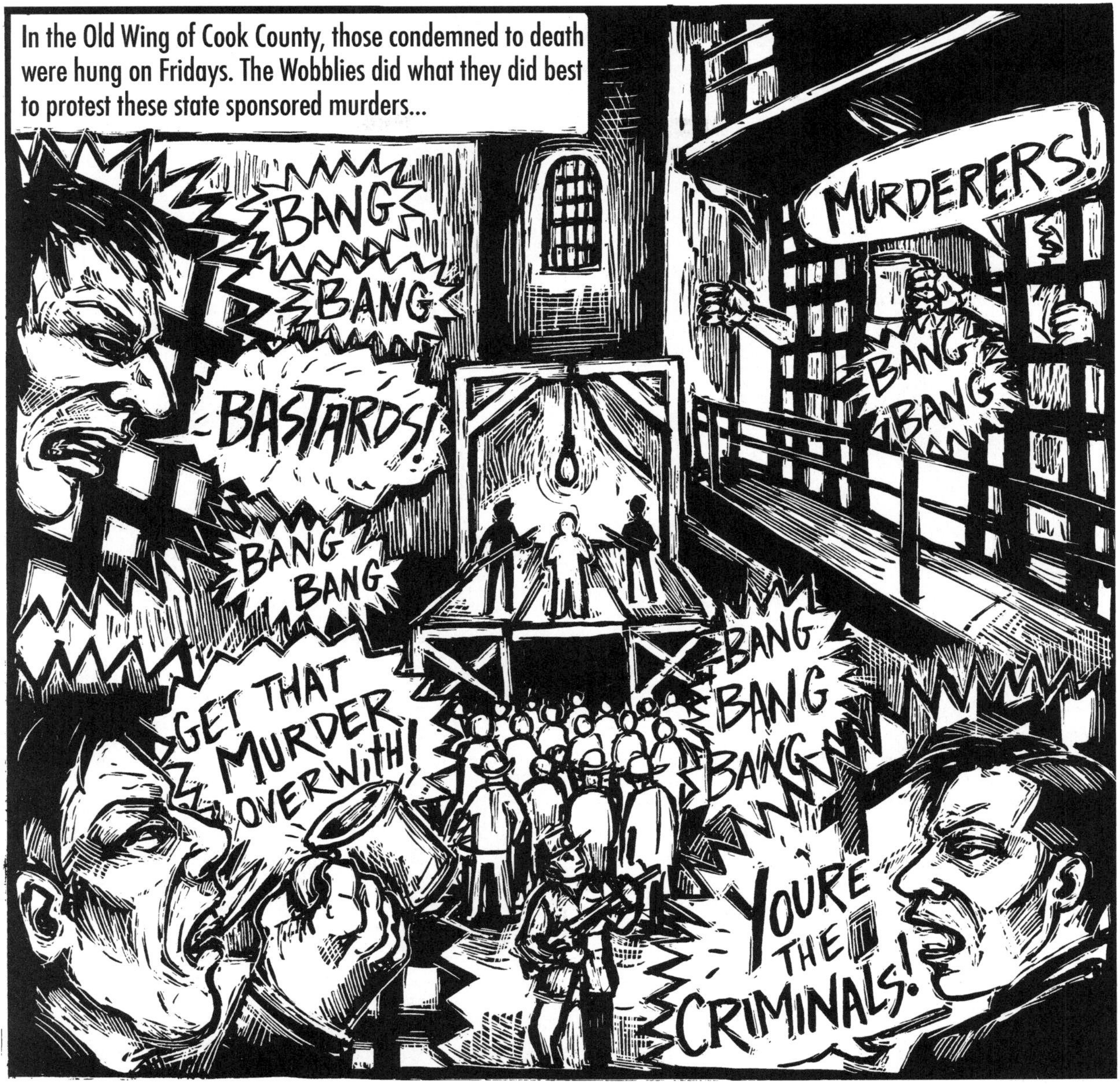
In the Old Wing of Cook County, those condemned to death were hung on Fridays. The Wobblies did what they did best to protest these state sponsored murders...
BANG BANG
BASTARDS!
MURDERERS!
BANG BANG
BANG BANG
GET THAT MURDER OVER WITH!
BANG BANG BANG
YOURE THE CRIMINALS!

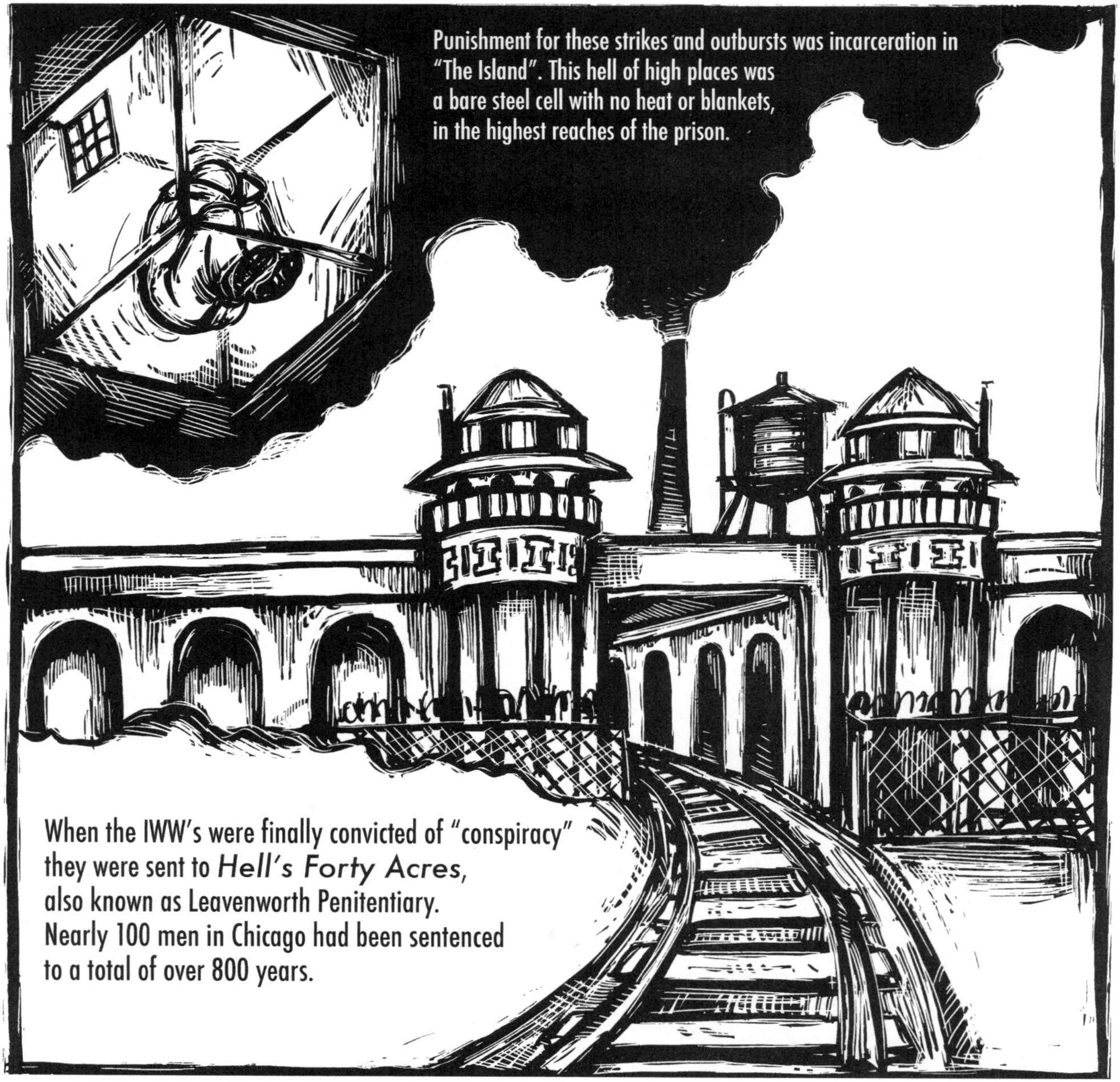
Punishment for these strikes and outbursts was incarceration in "The Island". This hell of high places was a bare steel cell with no heat or blankets, in the highest reaches of the prison.
When the IWW's were finally convicted of "conspiracy" they were sent to *Hell's Forty Acres*, also known as Leavenworth Penitentiary. Nearly 100 men in Chicago had been sentenced to a total of over 800 years.

The Wobblies were mixed in with the general population, though thanks to the war the ranks were swelled with political prisoners, radicals and draft dodgers of all persuasions.

"Prison rules were merciless regarding mutiny" wrote Chaplin. Any prisoners who went on strike were brutally beaten, forced under cold showers and thrown into solitary for days or weeks.

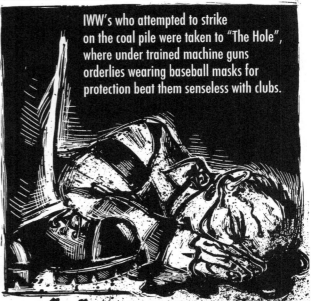

IWW's who attempted to strike on the coal pile were taken to "The Hole", where under trained machine guns orderlies wearing baseball masks for protection beat them senseless with clubs.

Chaplin witnessed the torture of Mennonite conscientious objectors. A dozen of them refused to work because their beards were cut off and were not permitted to remove the buttons from their clothes, as their religious beliefs required. They were handcuffed to the bars of cell block B for more than two weeks.

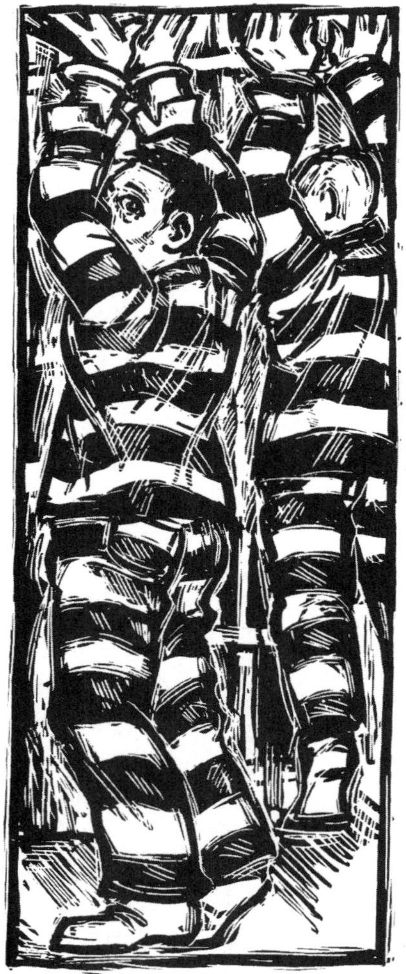

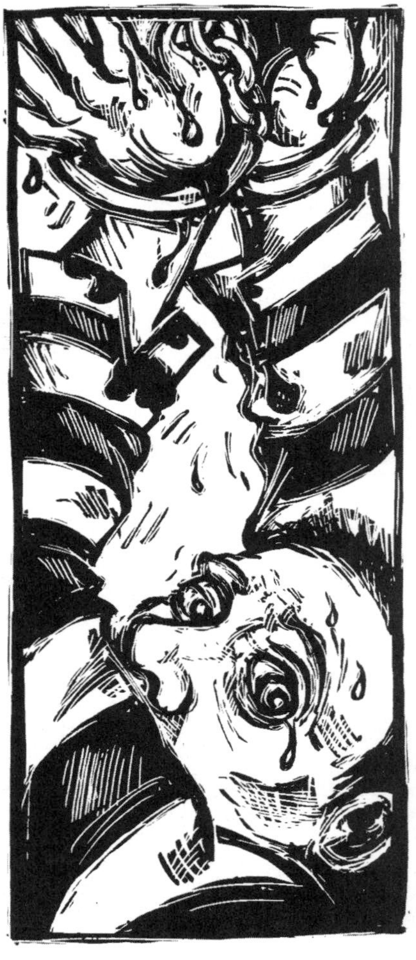

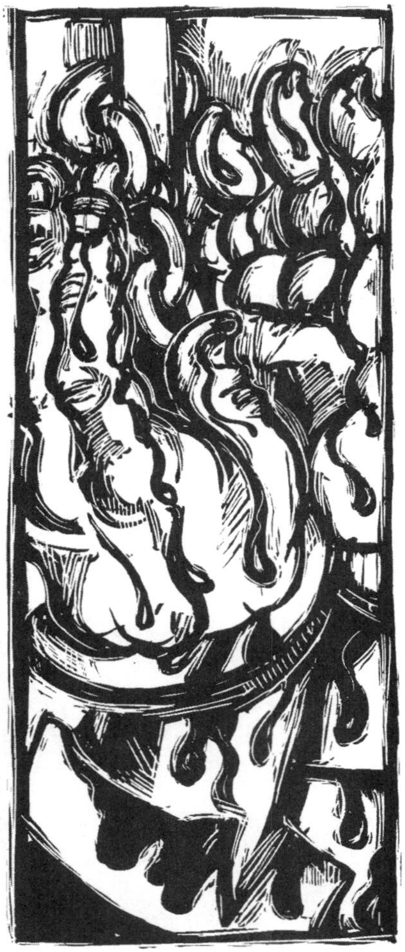

They had to stand on their toes to keep the cuffs from cutting into the flesh of their wrists. When they grew too tired to do this, "their fingers would swell, turn blue and crack open and blood would trickle down the upraised arms". From information leaked by the IWW prisoners and their defense committees, the new organization, the ACLU began to fight for reforms inside US prisons.

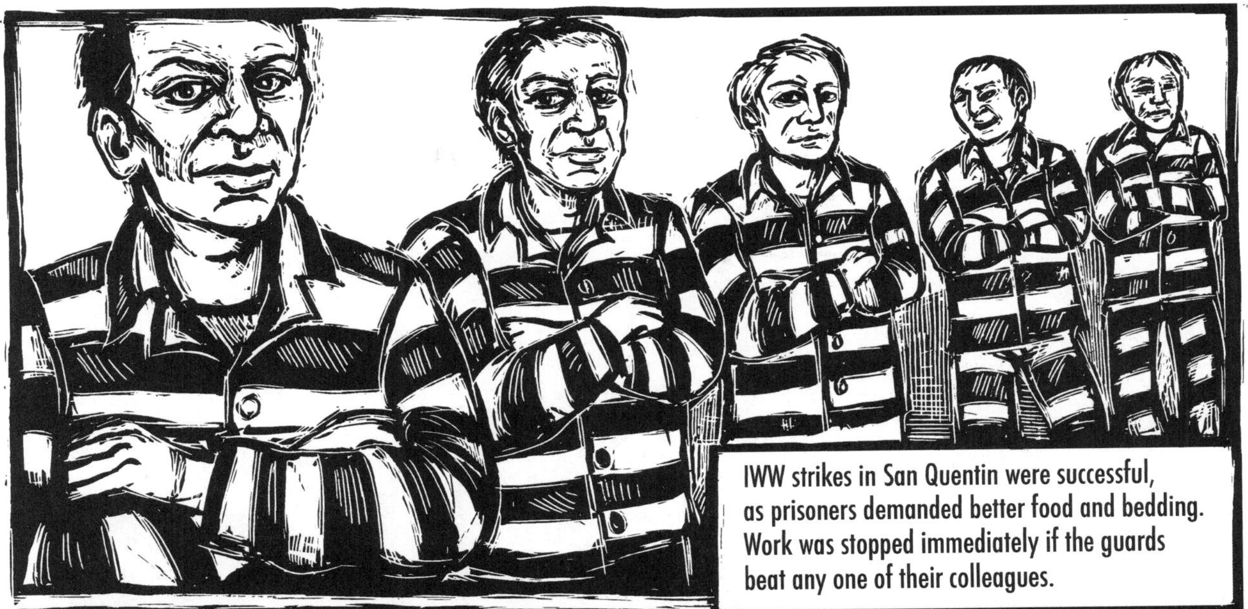
IWW strikes in San Quentin were successful,
as prisoners demanded better food and bedding.
Work was stopped immediately if the guards
beat any one of their colleagues.

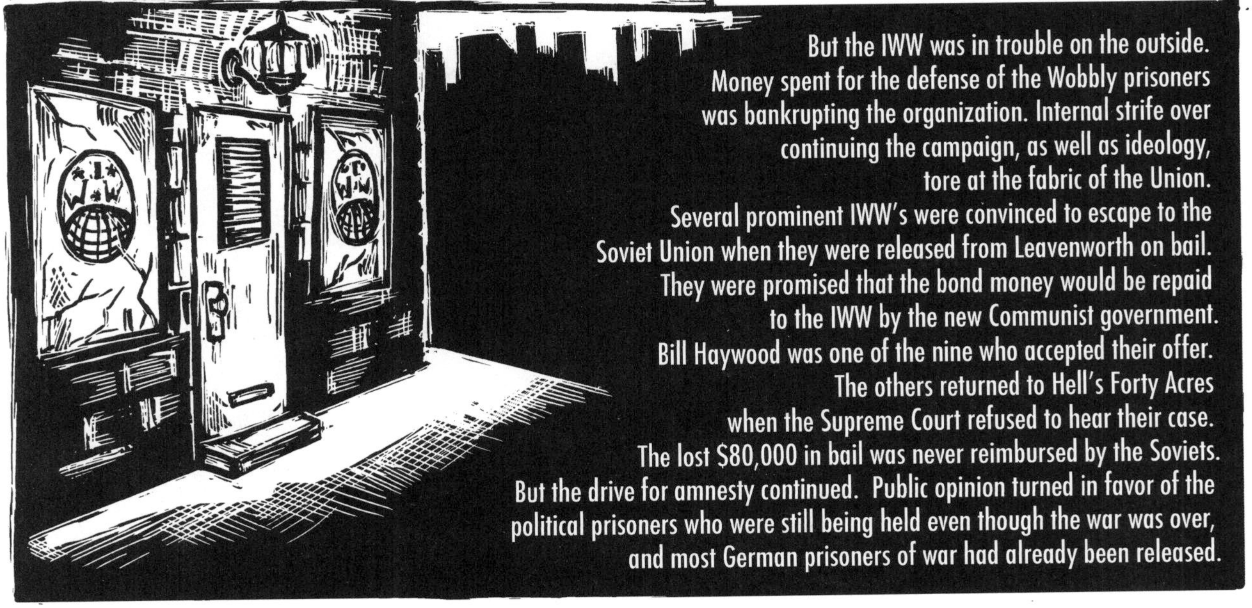
But the IWW was in trouble on the outside.
Money spent for the defense of the Wobbly prisoners
was bankrupting the organization. Internal strife over
continuing the campaign, as well as ideology,
tore at the fabric of the Union.
Several prominent IWW's were convinced to escape to the
Soviet Union when they were released from Leavenworth on bail.
They were promised that the bond money would be repaid
to the IWW by the new Communist government.
Bill Haywood was one of the nine who accepted their offer.
The others returned to Hell's Forty Acres
when the Supreme Court refused to hear their case.
The lost $80,000 in bail was never reimbursed by the Soviets.
But the drive for amnesty continued. Public opinion turned in favor of the
political prisoners who were still being held even though the war was over,
and most German prisoners of war had already been released.

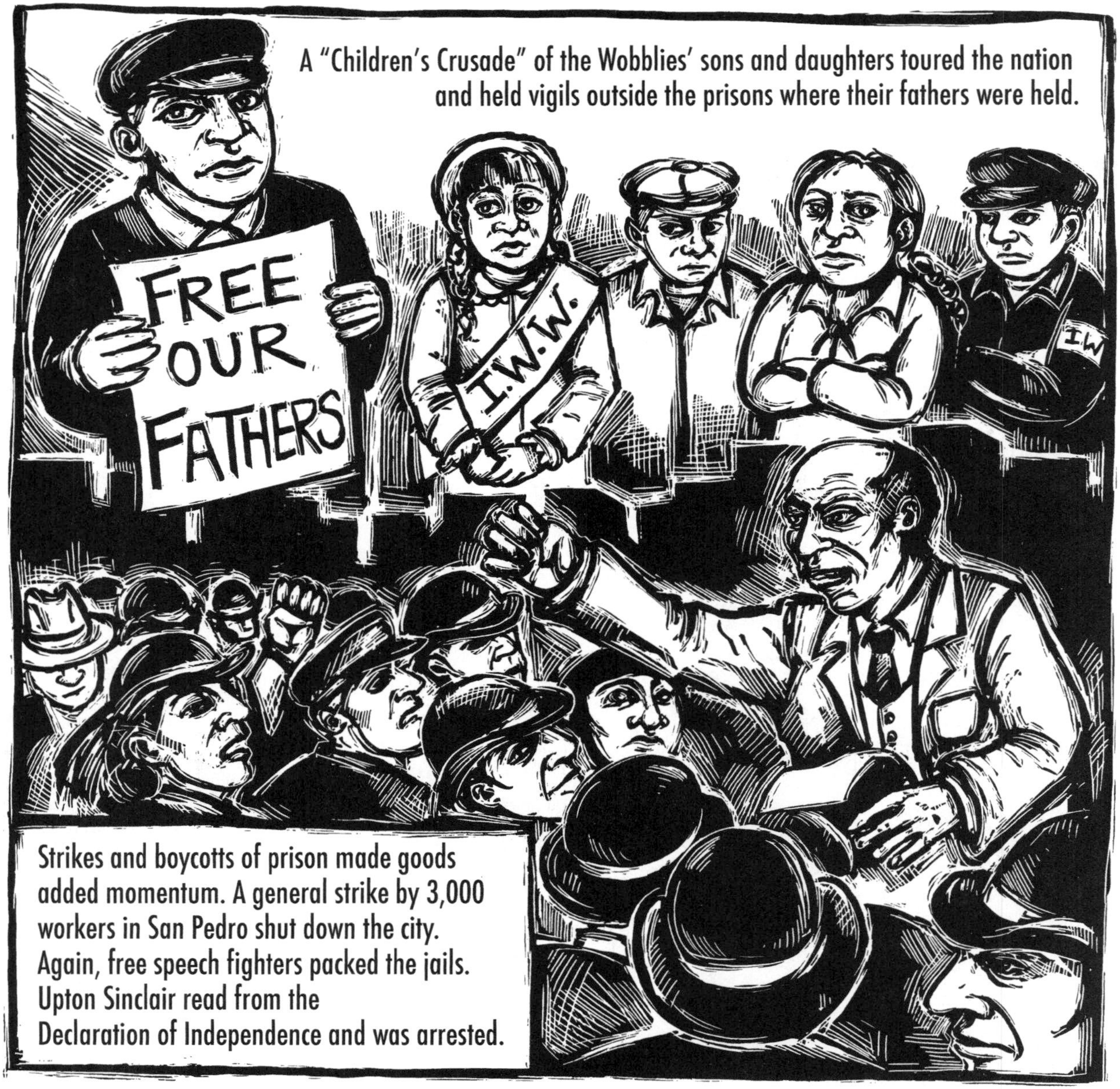
A "Children's Crusade" of the Wobblies' sons and daughters toured the nation and held vigils outside the prisons where their fathers were held.
FREE OUR FATHERS
I.W.W.
I.W
Strikes and boycotts of prison made goods added momentum. A general strike by 3,000 workers in San Pedro shut down the city. Again, free speech fighters packed the jails. Upton Sinclair read from the Declaration of Independence and was arrested.

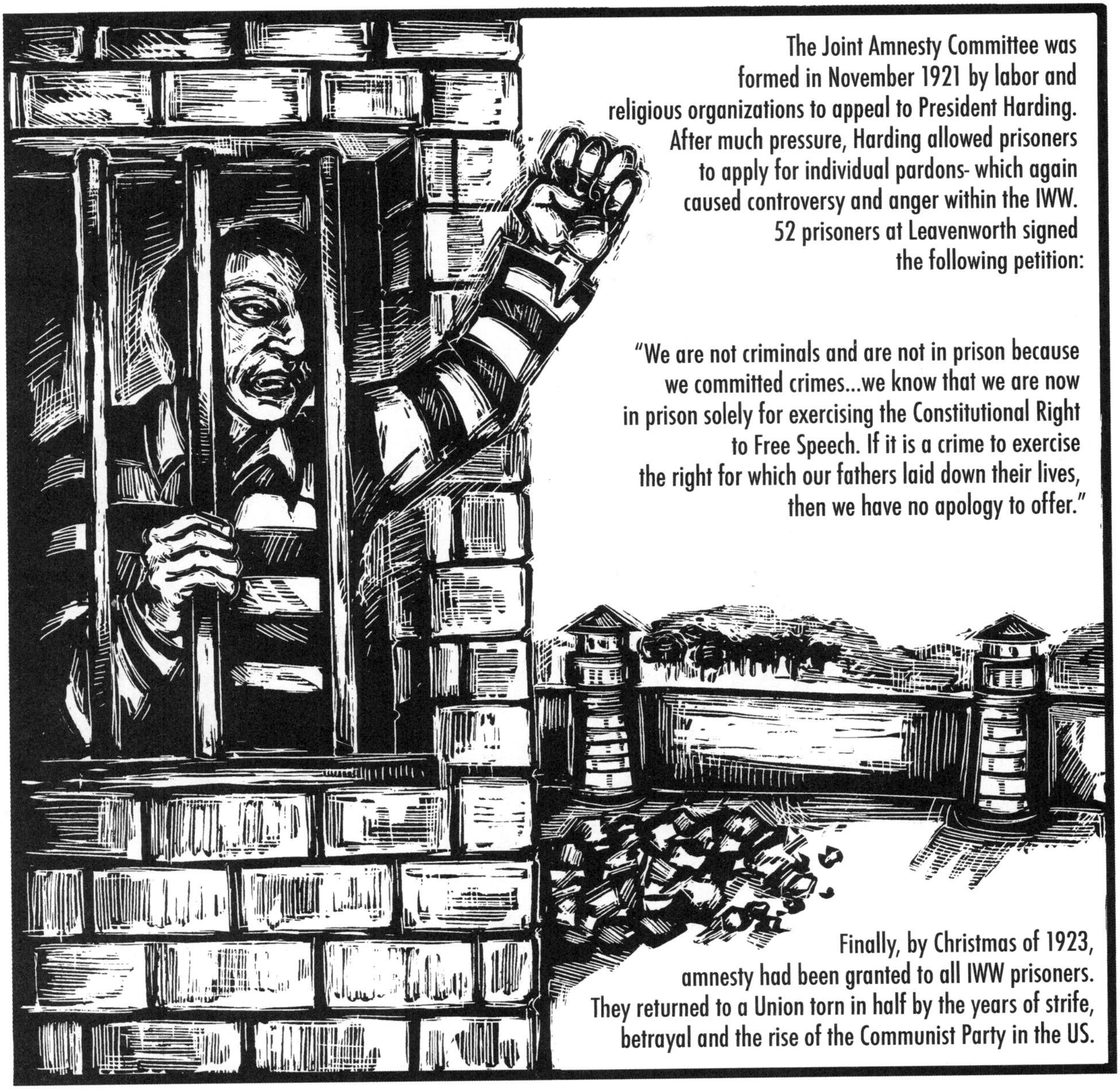
The Joint Amnesty Committee was formed in November 1921 by labor and religious organizations to appeal to President Harding. After much pressure, Harding allowed prisoners to apply for individual pardons- which again caused controversy and anger within the IWW. 52 prisoners at Leavenworth signed the following petition:
"We are not criminals and are not in prison because we committed crimes...we know that we are now in prison solely for exercising the Constitutional Right to Free Speech. If it is a crime to exercise the right for which our fathers laid down their lives, then we have no apology to offer."
Finally, by Christmas of 1923, amnesty had been granted to all IWW prisoners. They returned to a Union torn in half by the years of strife, betrayal and the rise of the Communist Party in the US.

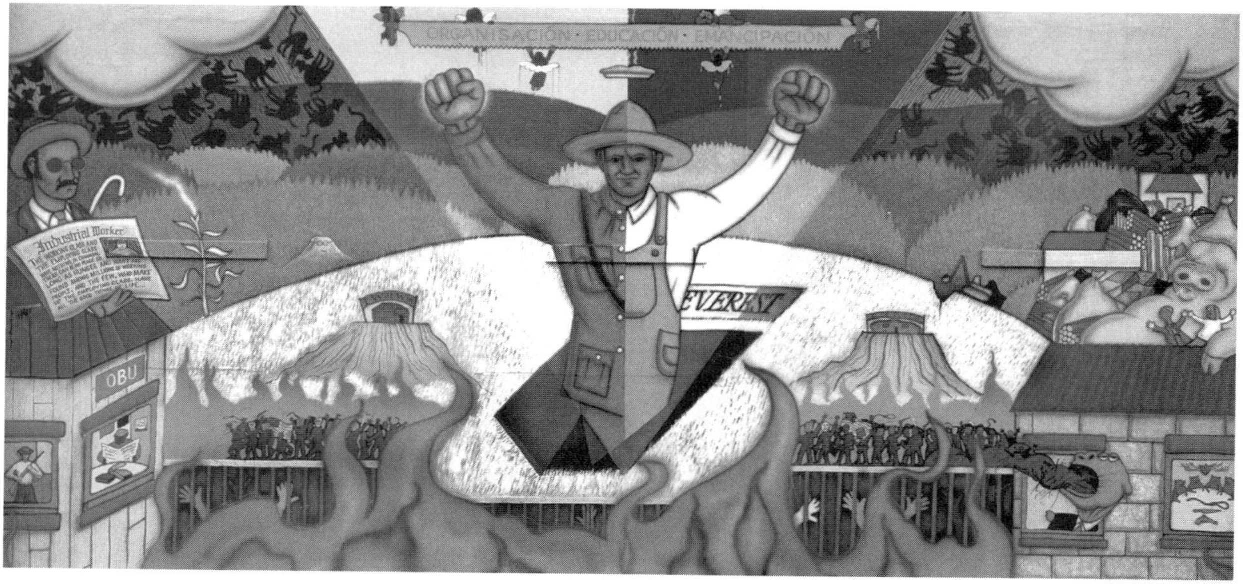
ORGANISACIÓN · EDUCACIÓN · EMANCIPACIÓN
Industrial Worker
OBU
EVEREST

CLASS WAR IN CENTRALIA

I'm Ray Becker, one of the eight Wobblies imprisoned as a consequence of the tragedy that occurred in Centralia, Washington on November 11, 1919. I spent more time in jail than any of my comrades. I was released in 1939, all of the other fellows got out in 1933 or before. I didn't want parole, I wanted a complete pardon. I knew that I was innocent. I didn't kill anybody. I fired my revolver twice towards the gang of vigilantes who had just broken into the IWW hall, but I didn't hit anyone. I had armed myself in the mistaken belief that I could help avert the destruction of the central Wobbly office.

I was born in Chicago in 1893, my dad was a minister and enrolled me in a seminary when I was seventeen. After less than a year, I hopped a freight out to Washington and started in the logging camps. It was not much of a life: the work was brutal and conditions bad, but I joined the IWW early on, and the camaraderie that I found helped me understand the life of hypocrisy I had left behind.

Demand for lumber increased dramatically with the onset of the war in Europe in 1914. The timber trusts were making huge profits by selling to both the Allies and the Germans. Production increased but wages did

not. We organized to better our conditions, but what made bosses hate us was our opposition to war and especially our opposition to conscription. I was drafted in 1917 and refused to register. I went to jail, and managed to escape for nearly a year until the police caught up to me in Spokane. I spent the rest of the war in prison, then went back to work in the timber stands of the Cascade Mountains. I ran into a couple of Wobs in 1919 who had just hopped a freight car from Centralia, and told me about the threat of a raid upon the Wobbly hall during the upcoming Armistice Day parade. I went right on down.

The previous IWW office in Centralia had been raided after a Red Cross Day Parade in 1918, and the Wobs were not going to give up their new hall without a fight. Besides, Wobblies were being arrested and their meeting places broken up across the country: it was a fight for free speech and the right to organize, as the European war ended and the class war bubbled up at home.

There were 300 men in the Centralia post of the American Legion, and the Chief of Police flatly refused to do anything about the threats. We knew that our only chance of defending the hall was by arms. I spent the night in the Wob hall, and met everyone who was going to be arrested or murdered. Wesley Everest had been arrested in Marshfield, near Coos Bay in Oregon, in 1915, dragged out of jail by vigilantes, made to kneel and kiss the flag, beaten and abused. He would never back down while he had a gun in his hand.

The shooting started after the American Legion companies had marched past the Wob hall, leaving only Legionnaires and Wobs on the scene. I fired my pistol twice and was captured without a struggle. Everest ran into a pair of Legionnaires as he fled, and shot them both, then ran to the river, which was too swollen with rain for him to swim, and hid behind a stump on the bank. The nephew of the biggest mill owner in Centralia approached him with an unloaded gun, demanding that he surrender, and Everest dropped him with one shot. Then Everest was captured and kicked, dragged to jail with a belt around his neck.

Everest was kidnapped alone from the cell of the jail; they castrated him, lynched him from a bridge over the Chehalis River and shot his body full of holes. A National Guard unit came in from Tacoma to bring order. A milkman cut Everest's body from the bridge crossbar that his noose had been thrown over and left his bullet-riddled corpse in the mud on the banks of the Chehalis River all day. His body was thrown on the floor between our jail cells and left there through the night of the 12th until the morning of the 13th, when the National Guard escorted us to a vacant lot to bury the body of our comrade in an unmarked grave. Wobs were rounded up by the dozens, anyone holding a Red Card. With Martial Law in the district, the outcome of the trial was inevitable. Myself and seven others were convicted of second-degree murder, and although the jury specifically asked for the most lenient sentence, the judge disregarded the request and sentenced all to 25–40 years.

Lawyer Elmer Smith devoted the rest of his life to the Centralia prisoners, but without success in gaining justice. I refused parole and remained in prison until 1939, when my remaining sentence was commuted, just two days after famed labor martyr Tom Mooney was released in San Francisco. A new war had started in Europe, and the war profiteers had lost interest in the victims of a long past, little understood, and furiously controversial class war in western Washington.

Arthur Fonseca

FELLOW WORKERS:

Remember!

WE ARE IN HERE FOR YOU; YOU ARE OUT THERE FOR US

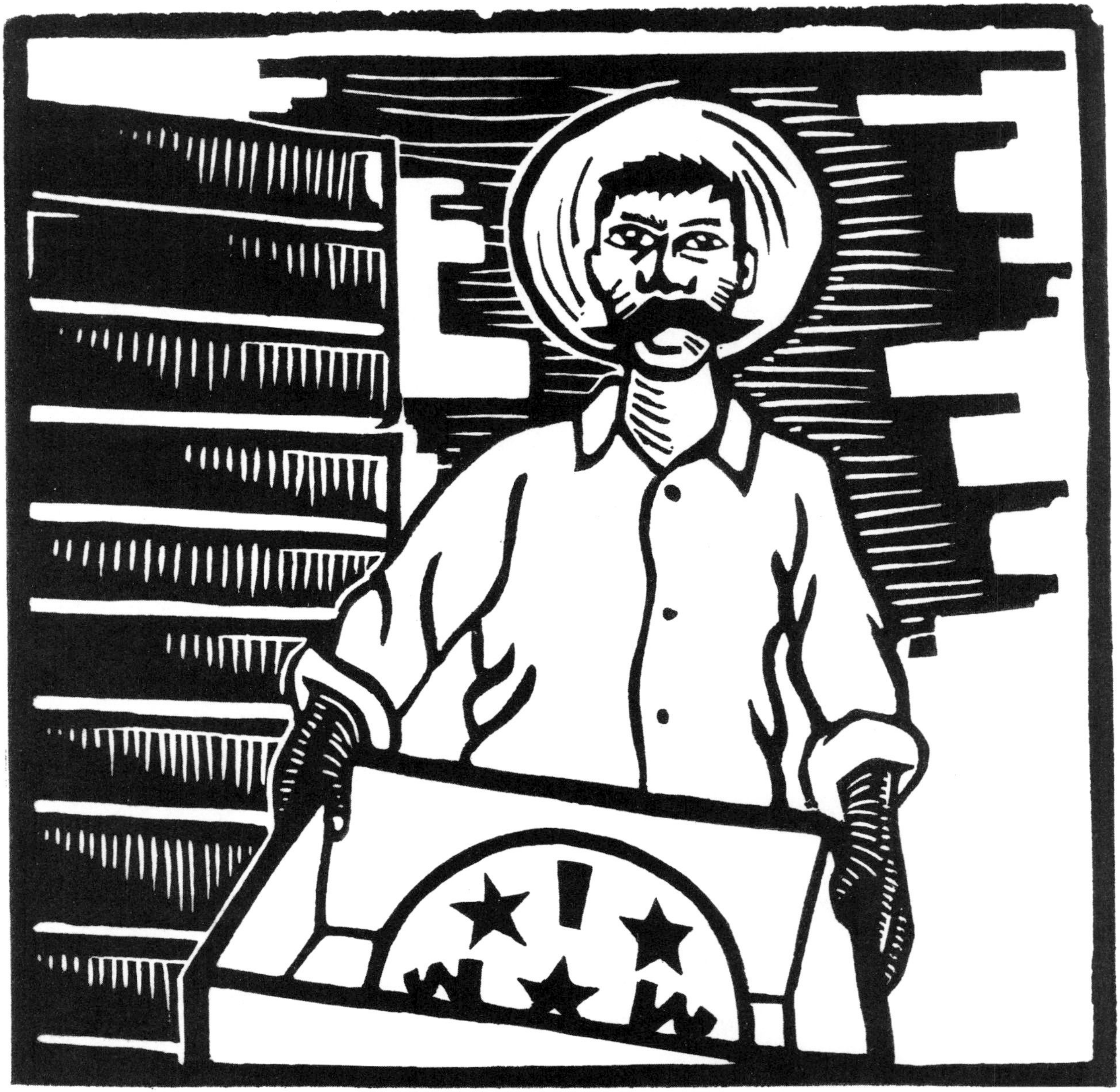

FIVE

BEYOND MARTYRDOM

Official Wobbly historians have been at pains to demonstrate that the IWW did not die from the persecutions and the continuing Red Scare. Indeed, the Wobs' propaganda apparatus took on a new life during the 1920s, nearly a thousand oil workers were added to still more thousands of harvest workers holding steady, miners in the Canadian west drew close to the IWW, and above all the mostly African-American Marine Transport Workers (MTW) sank roots seaward from its Philadelphia base.

But a calamitous split in the IWW developed over a concatenation of internal issues, including centralization of the organizational leadership. Although factions of coal miners in Colorado and Illinois showed sympathy for the IWW later in the decade, and a ghost version of the Wobs continued in Canada (mostly under a different name and sometime rival: the One Big

Union), the movement had definitely retreated into an educational / agitational framework.

In this form it continued, notably in the distant North Country of the Midwest. One group of Finnish-born radicals had left the Socialist Party and joined the Wobblies in 1914, publishing *Industrialistii* (1915–75), with more than 20,000 readers at its height. The same group took over the Finnish-led Work People's College, a labor school that taught radical ideas and skills, and kept it going for more than thirty years. Considerable numbers of these Wobblies actually went over to the Communist Party during the 1920s but many came back to Wobbly ideas after disillusionment with Moscow. Their dues and their loyalty did much to help the IWW keep going through lean times.

Not so far from the North Country was Chicago and what locals called Hobohemia. The Hobo College, the Dil Pickle, the weekly speak-outs in Bughouse Square and other activities showed a kind of radicalism that elsewhere could be found mostly on the fringes of the Communist movement, in mostly constricted form or in groups so obscure to the outside world so as to escape notice (like the Detroit-based Bulgarian Left comic theater). Other playful elements, like the Modikot puppet theater of communist-leaning Yiddishist speakers and the stirrings of folk music around the likes of Woody Guthrie, made a comeback for left-wing popular culture. By the later 1930s and 1940s, there were big audiences for left-wing performers. But the revolutionary temperament had meanwhile damped down: radicals and their friends expected less in a world suffering from the threat of fascism and from the grim collectivism of Stalin.

It might almost be said that the IWW was surviving mainly in memory, as in the memories of older workers influencing the young in the wave of 1934 general strikes, the brief flourishing of assorted independent radical unions, the sit-down strikes of the next few years, and the early, vital era of the Congress of Industrial

Organizations. But that would not be entirely true due to one extraordinary development: the Mexican peasant uprising of Tarascans under Primo Tapia. Such events illustrated the continuing link of peasants and workers mostly ignored by Marxists, at their peril, and also a spirit of anarchism that had not been vanquished and would be seen more vividly again.

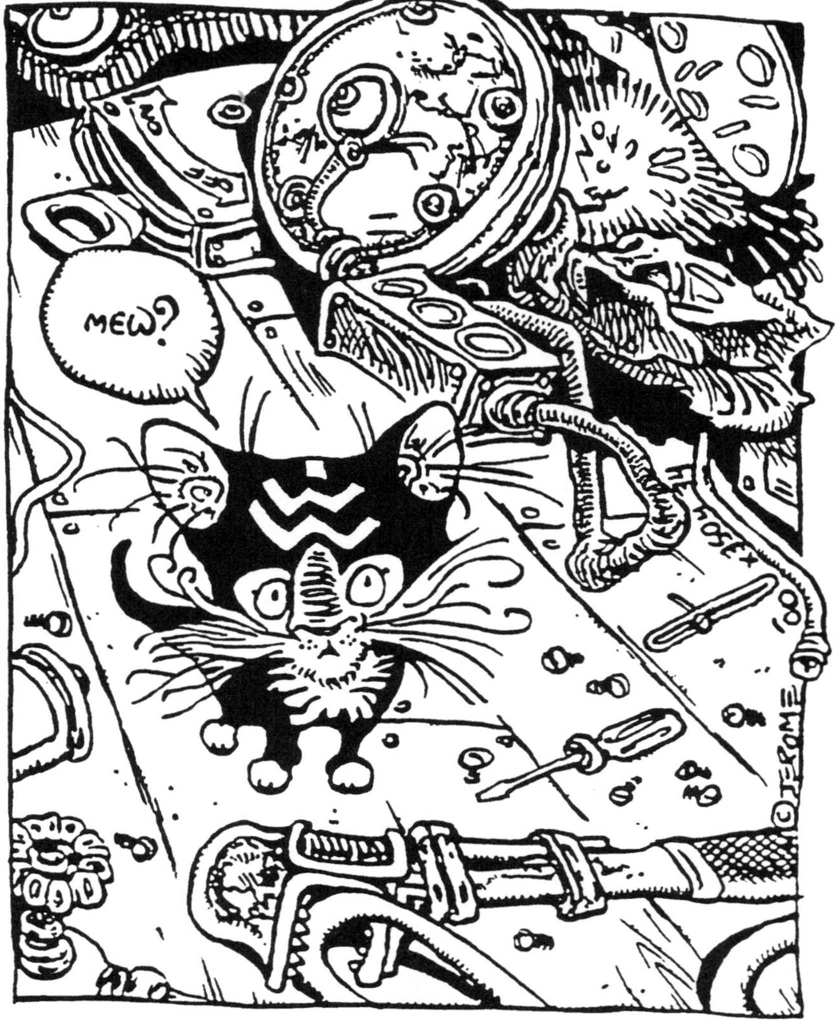
MEW?

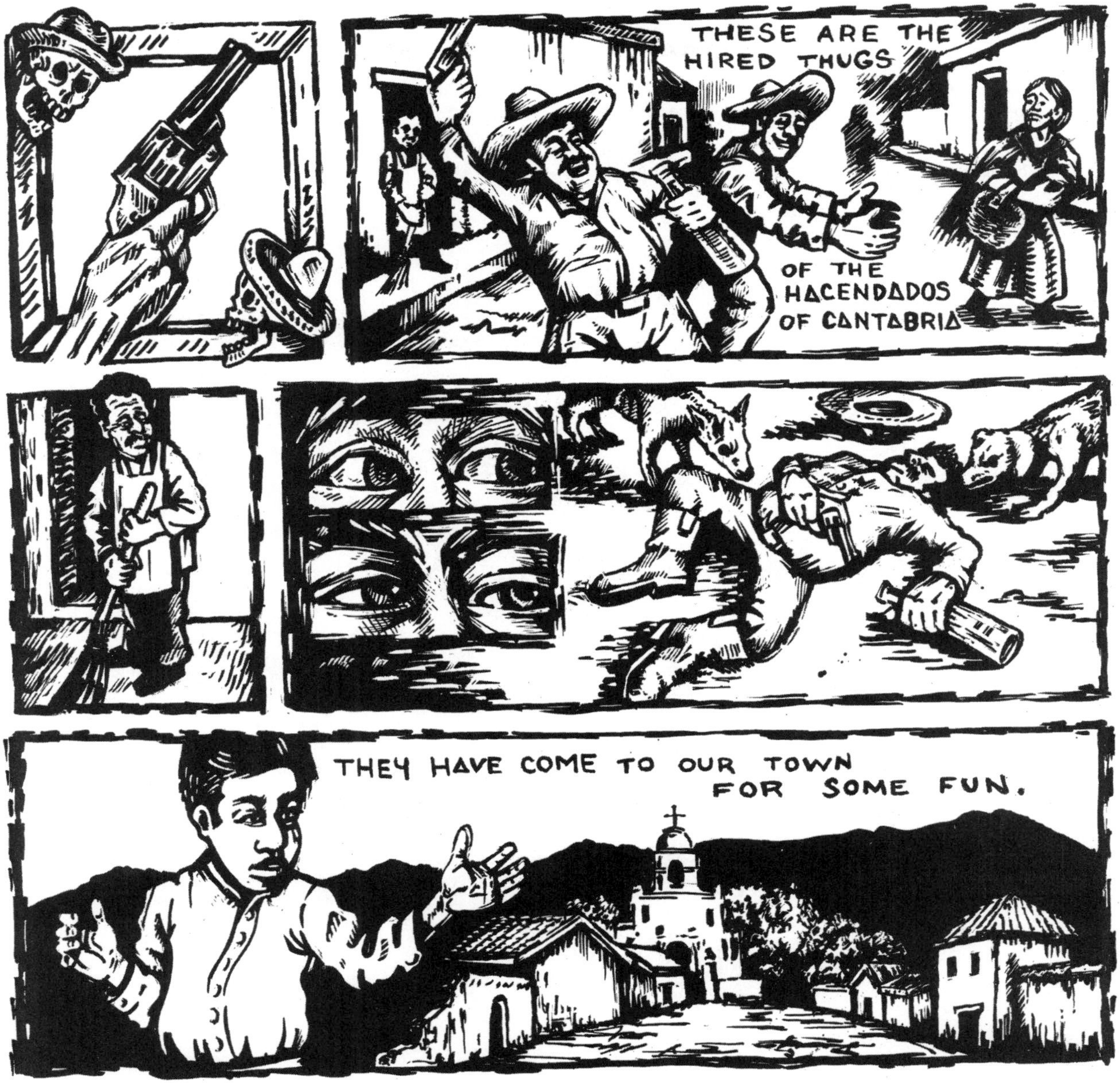
THESE ARE THE HIRED THUGS
OF THE HACENDADOS OF CANTABRIA
THEY HAVE COME TO OUR TOWN FOR SOME FUN.

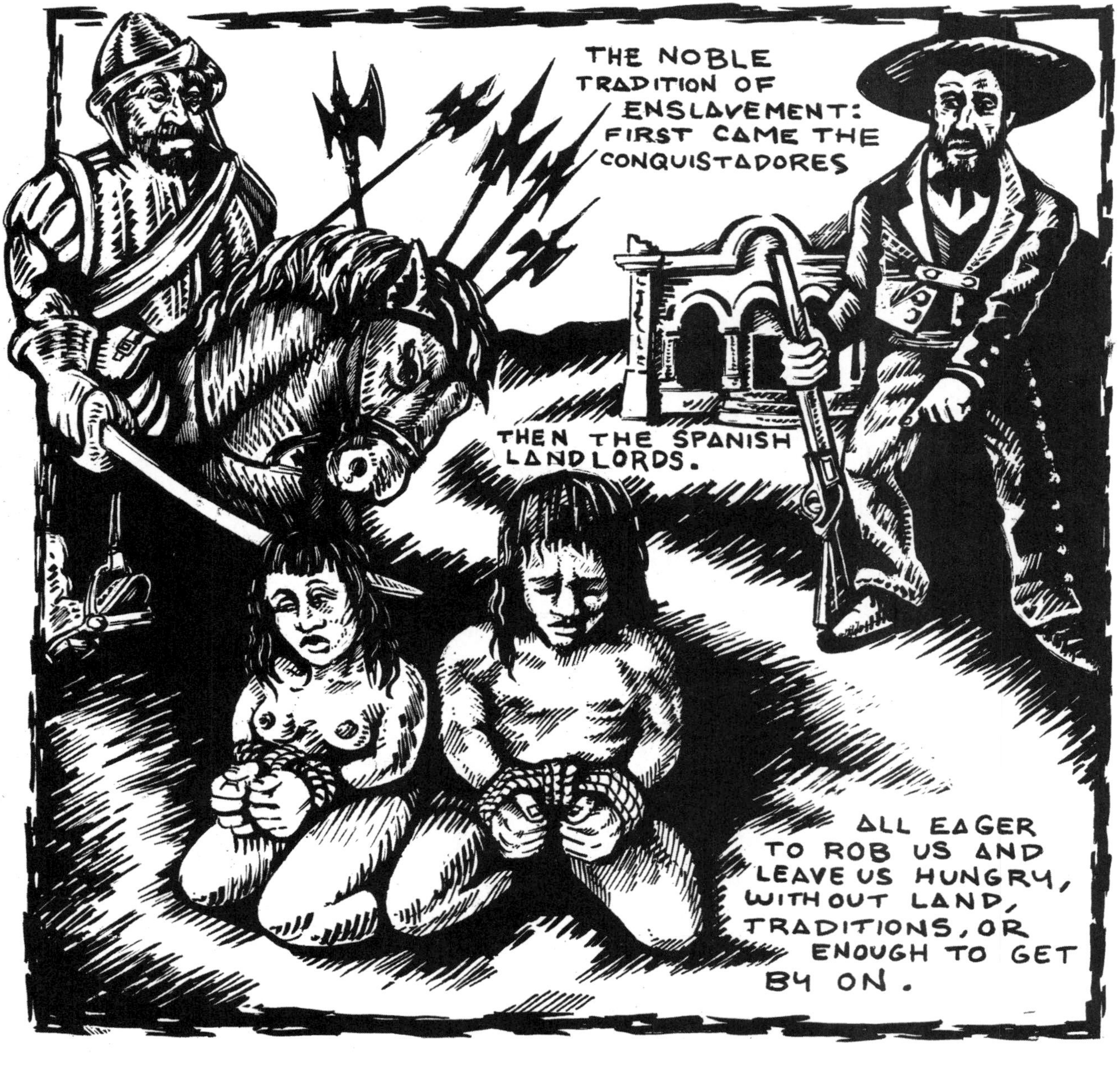
THE NOBLE TRADITION OF ENSLAVEMENT: FIRST CAME THE CONQUISTADORES
THEN THE SPANISH LANDLORDS.
ALL EAGER TO ROB US AND LEAVE US HUNGRY, WITHOUT LAND, TRADITIONS, OR ENOUGH TO GET BY ON.

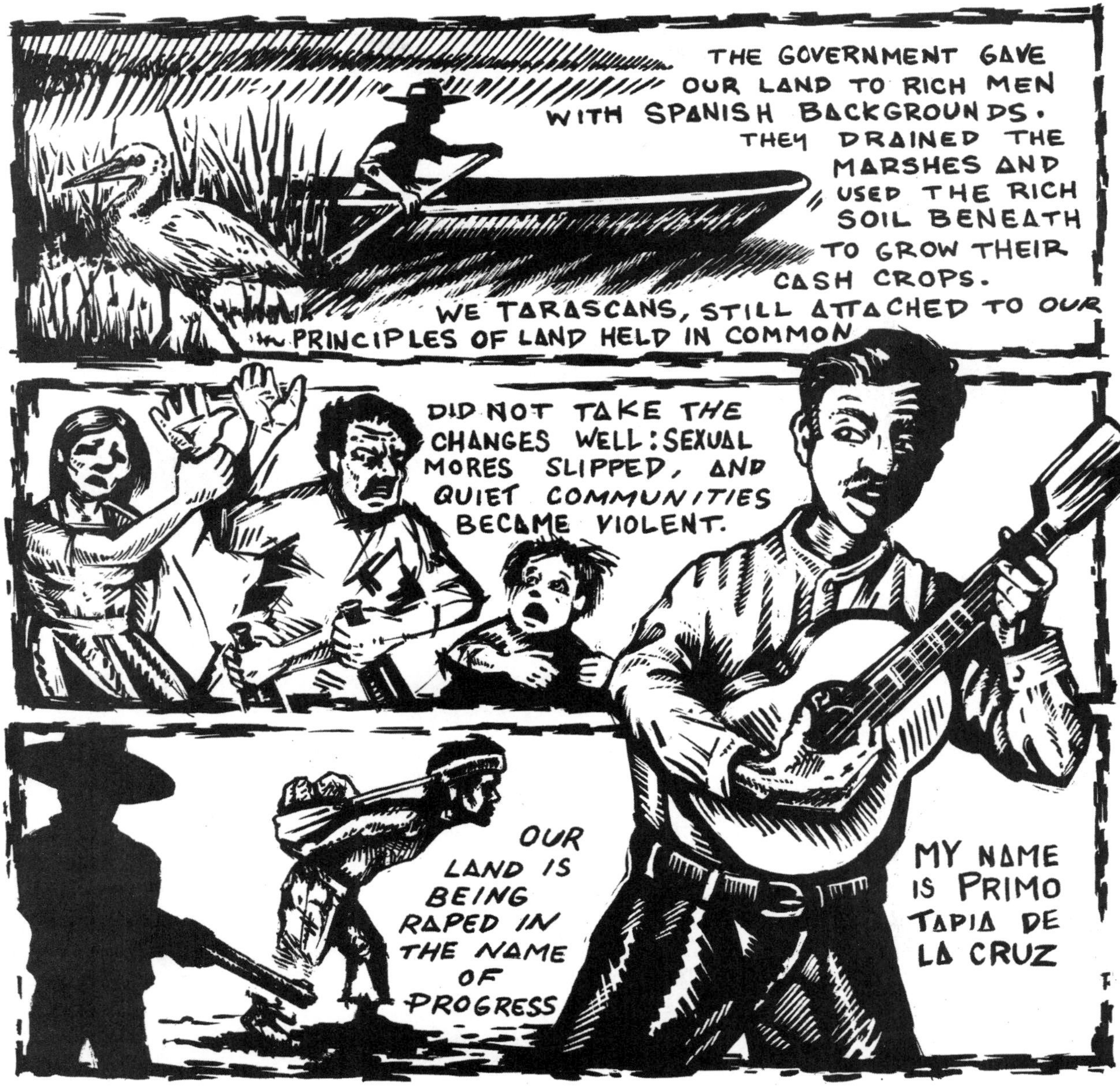
THE GOVERNMENT GAVE OUR LAND TO RICH MEN WITH SPANISH BACKGROUNDS.
THEY DRAINED THE MARSHES AND USED THE RICH SOIL BENEATH TO GROW THEIR CASH CROPS.
WE TARASCANS, STILL ATTACHED TO OUR PRINCIPLES OF LAND HELD IN COMMON
DID NOT TAKE THE CHANGES WELL: SEXUAL MORES SLIPPED, AND QUIET COMMUNITIES BECAME VIOLENT.
OUR LAND IS BEING RAPED IN THE NAME OF PROGRESS
MY NAME IS PRIMO TAPIA DE LA CRUZ

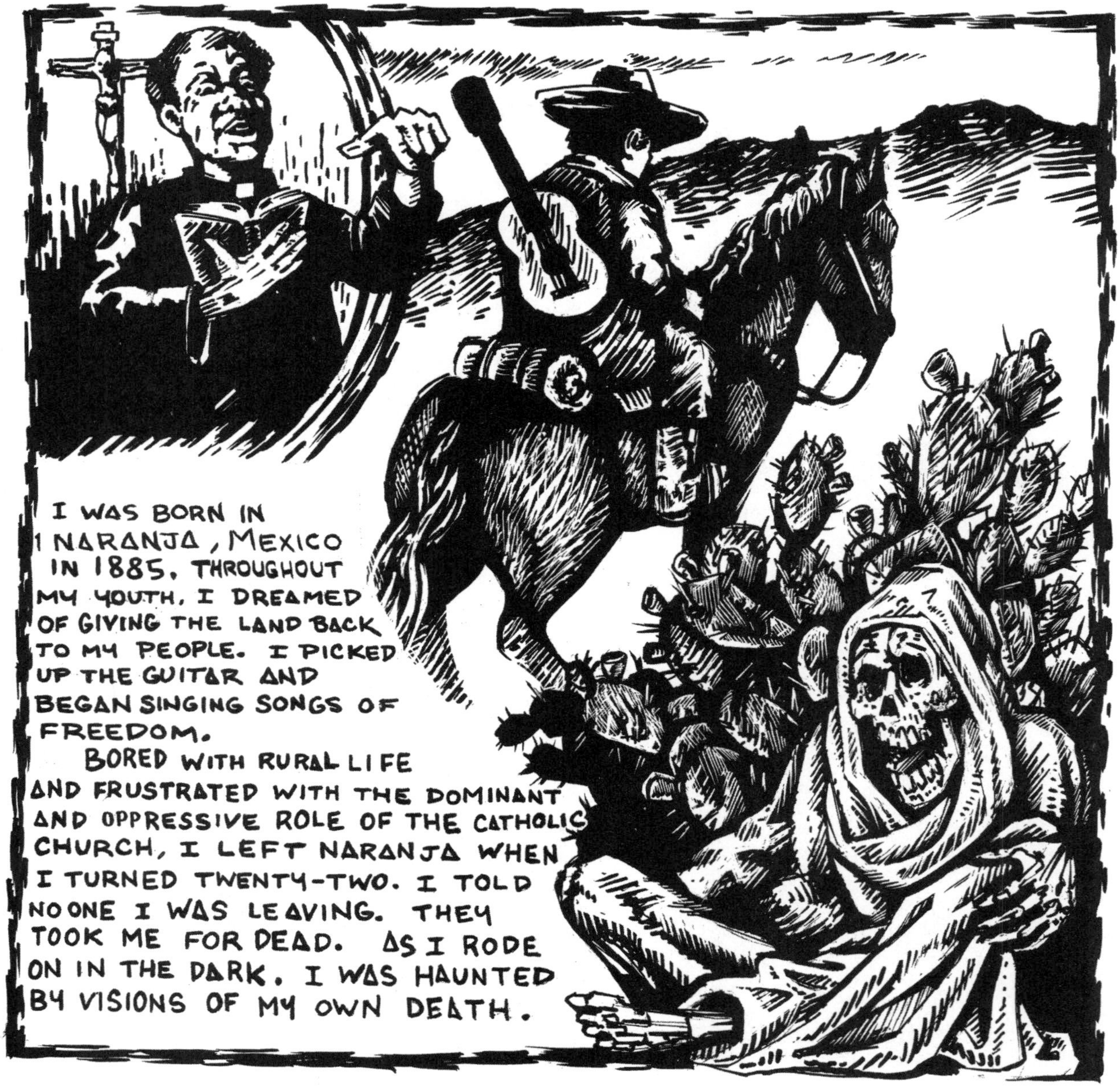
I WAS BORN IN NARANJA, MEXICO IN 1885. THROUGHOUT MY YOUTH, I DREAMED OF GIVING THE LAND BACK TO MY PEOPLE. I PICKED UP THE GUITAR AND BEGAN SINGING SONGS OF FREEDOM.
BORED WITH RURAL LIFE AND FRUSTRATED WITH THE DOMINANT AND OPPRESSIVE ROLE OF THE CATHOLIC CHURCH, I LEFT NARANJA WHEN I TURNED TWENTY-TWO. I TOLD NO ONE I WAS LEAVING. THEY TOOK ME FOR DEAD. AS I RODE ON IN THE DARK, I WAS HAUNTED BY VISIONS OF MY OWN DEATH.

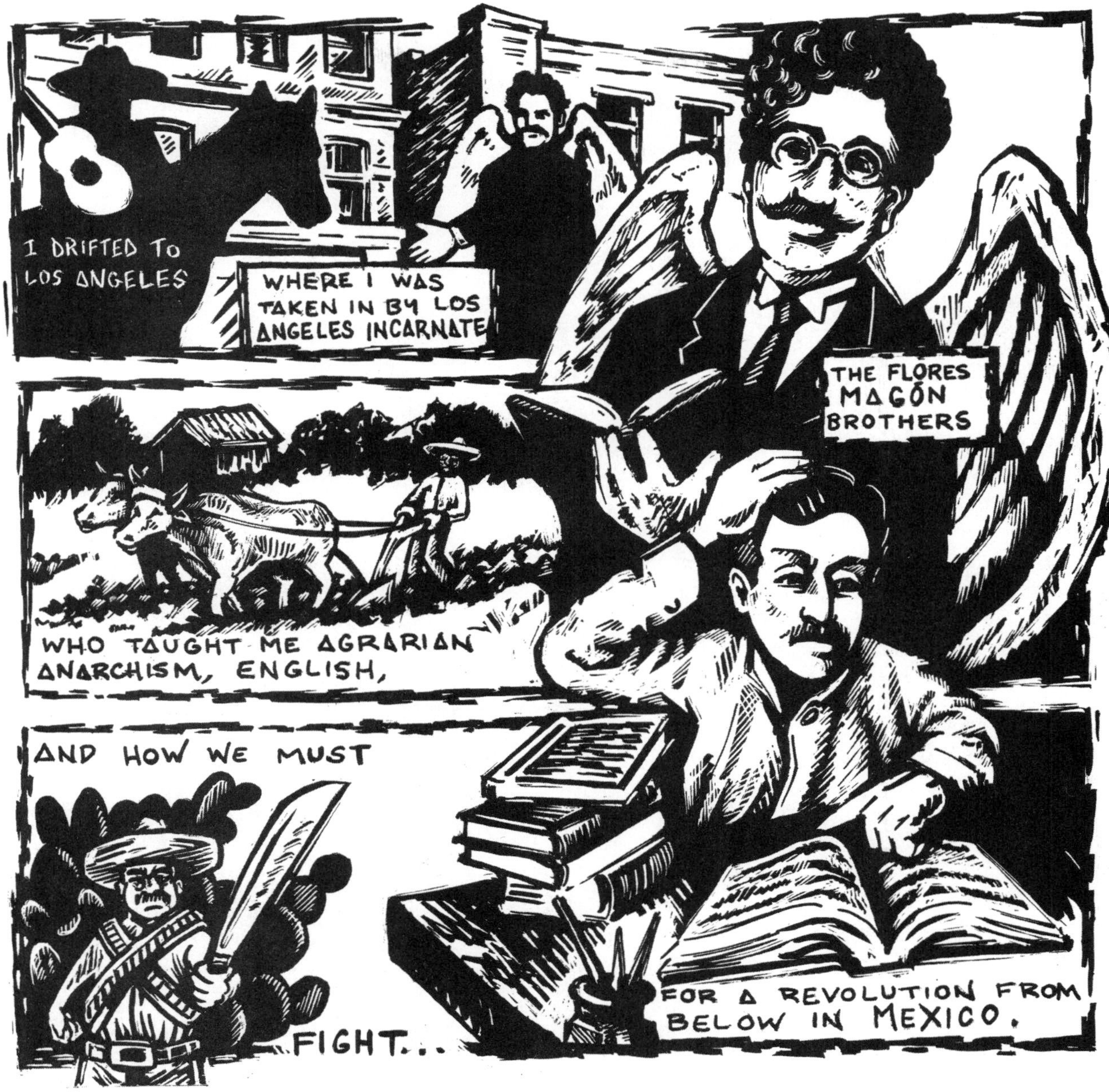
I DRIFTED TO LOS ANGELES
WHERE I WAS TAKEN IN BY LOS ANGELES INCARNATE
THE FLORES MAGÓN BROTHERS
WHO TAUGHT ME AGRARIAN ANARCHISM, ENGLISH,
AND HOW WE MUST
FIGHT...
FOR A REVOLUTION FROM BELOW IN MEXICO.

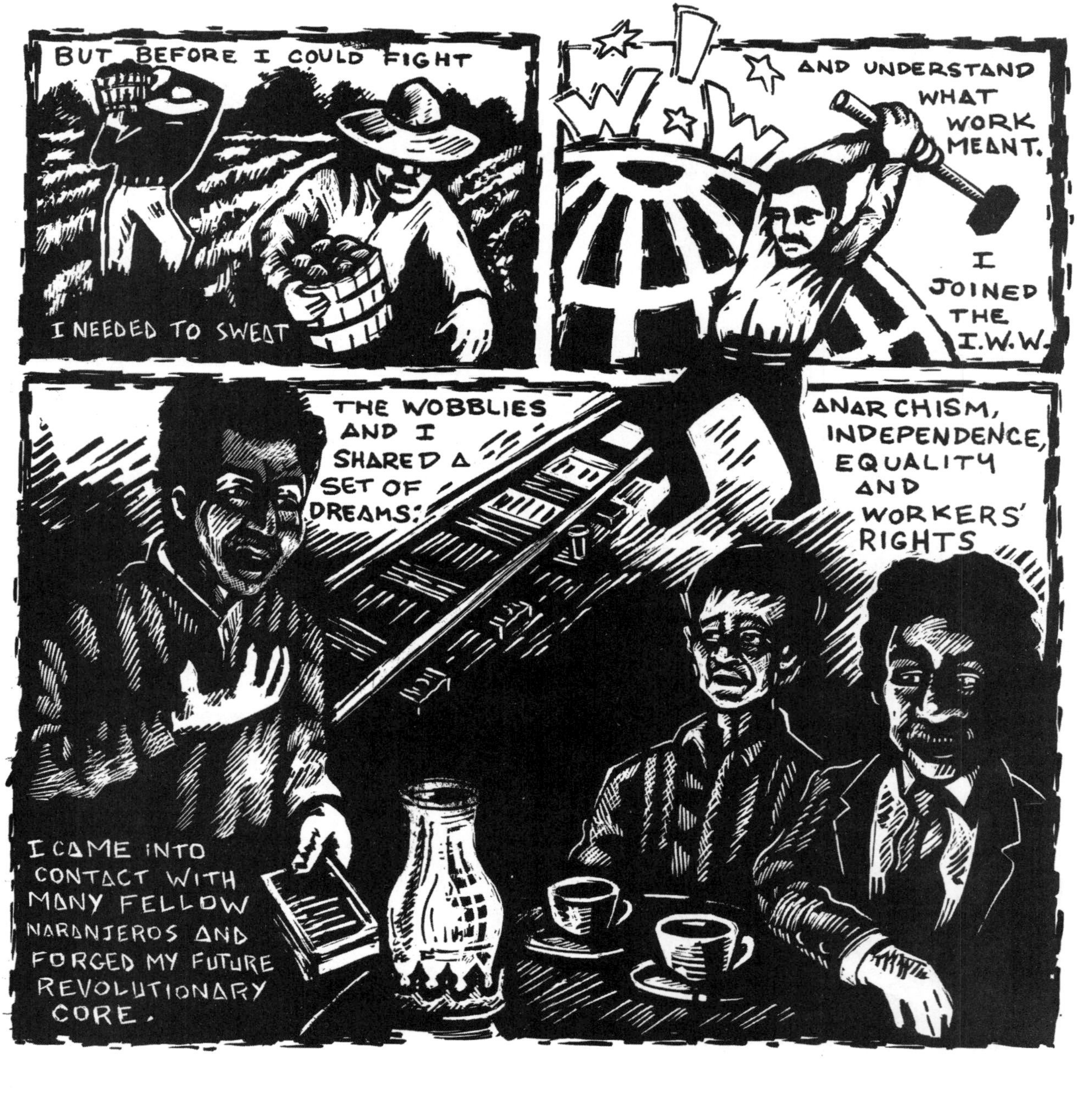
BUT BEFORE I COULD FIGHT
I NEEDED TO SWEAT
AND UNDERSTAND WHAT WORK MEANT.
I.W.W
I JOINED THE I.W.W.
THE WOBBLIES AND I SHARED A SET OF DREAMS:
ANARCHISM, INDEPENDENCE, EQUALITY AND WORKERS' RIGHTS
I CAME INTO CONTACT WITH MANY FELLOW NARANJEROS AND FORGED MY FUTURE REVOLUTIONARY CORE.

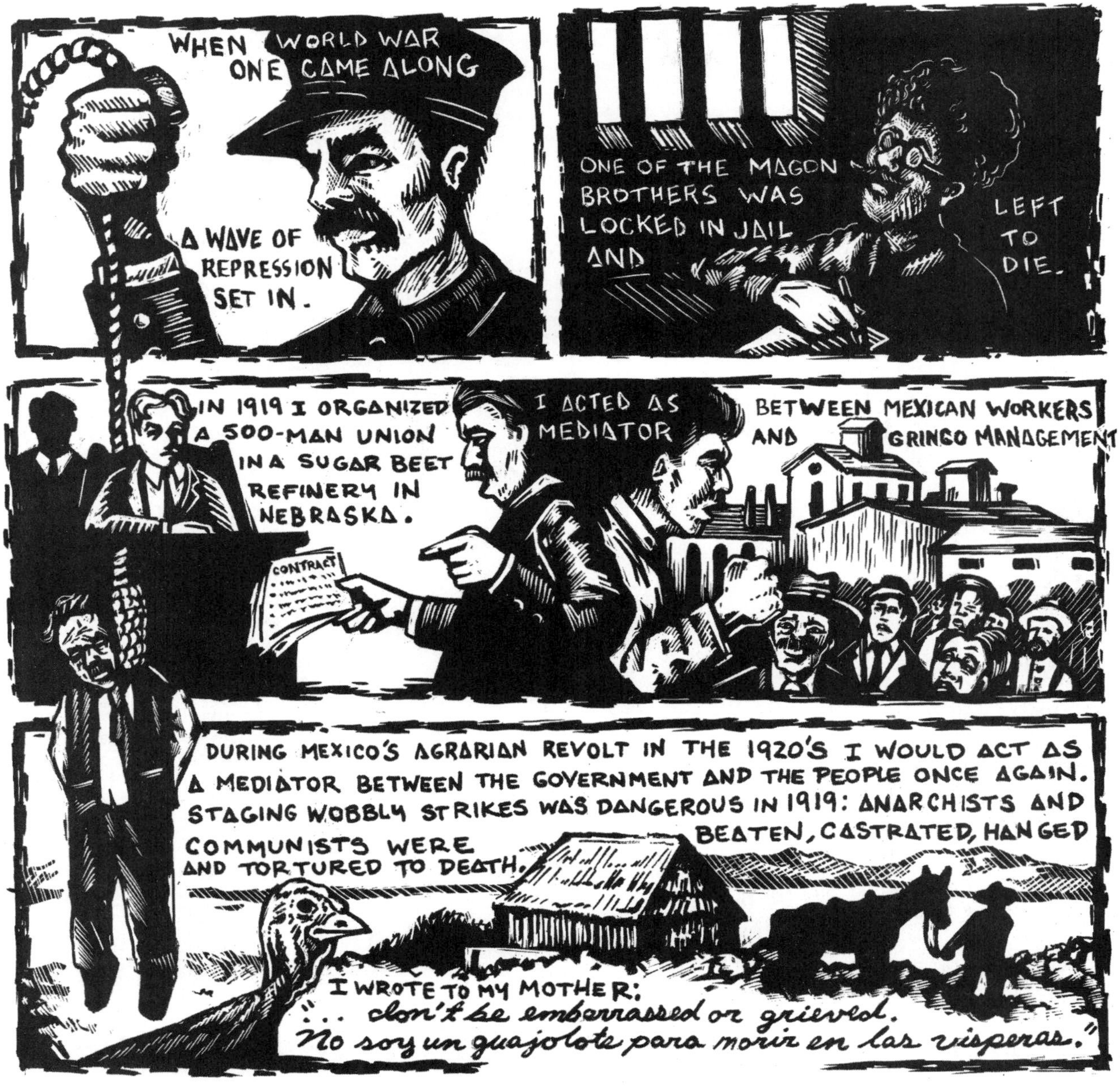
WHEN WORLD WAR ONE CAME ALONG
A WAVE OF REPRESSION SET IN.
ONE OF THE MAGON BROTHERS WAS LOCKED IN JAIL AND
LEFT TO DIE.
IN 1919 I ORGANIZED A 500-MAN UNION IN A SUGAR BEET REFINERY IN NEBRASKA.
CONTRACT
I ACTED AS MEDIATOR
BETWEEN MEXICAN WORKERS AND GRINGO MANAGEMENT
DURING MEXICO'S AGRARIAN REVOLT IN THE 1920'S I WOULD ACT AS A MEDIATOR BETWEEN THE GOVERNMENT AND THE PEOPLE ONCE AGAIN.
STAGING WOBBLY STRIKES WAS DANGEROUS IN 1919: ANARCHISTS AND COMMUNISTS WERE BEATEN, CASTRATED, HANGED AND TORTURED TO DEATH.
I WROTE TO MY MOTHER:
"... don't be embarrassed or grieved.
No soy un guajolote para morir en las visperas."

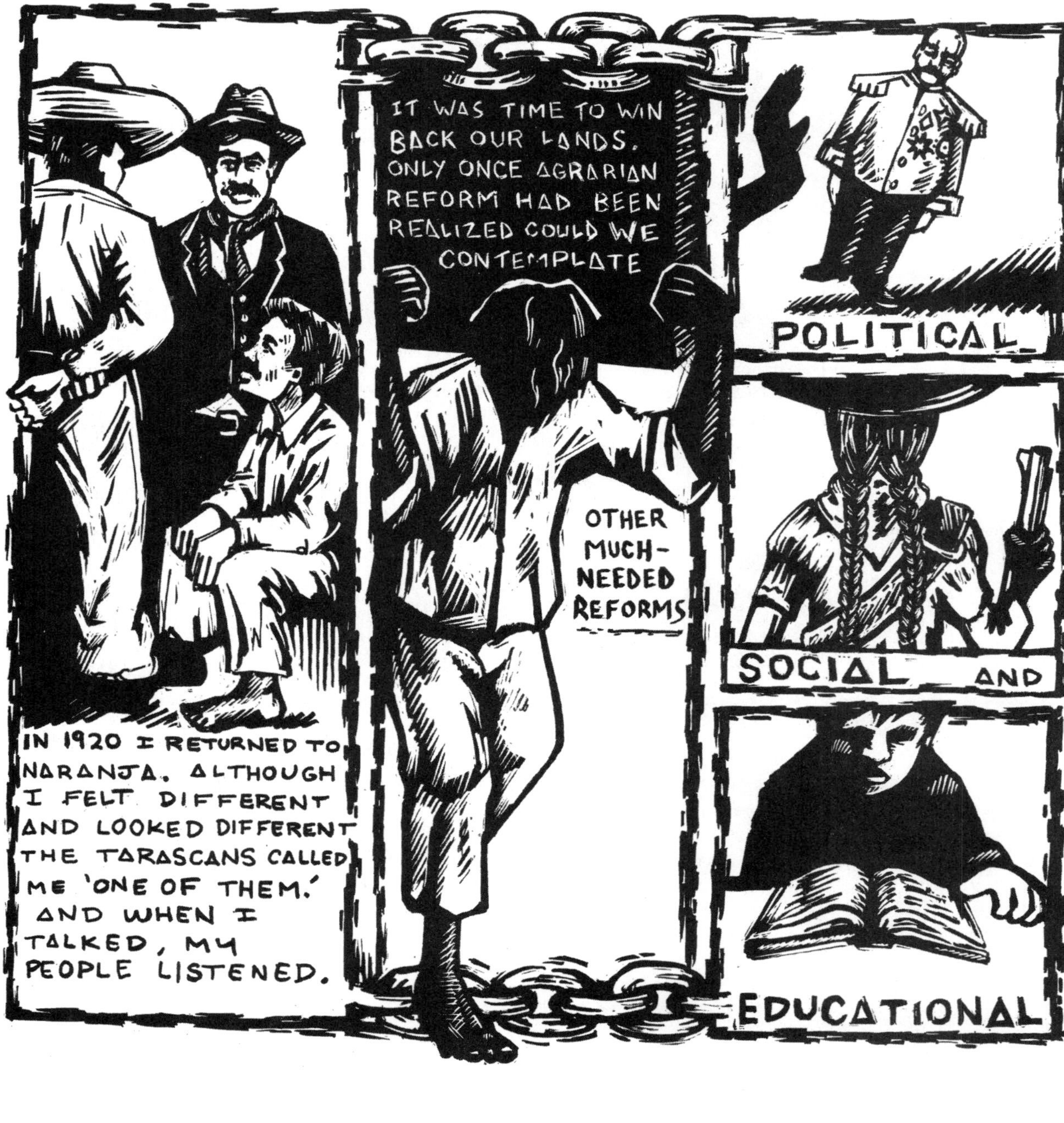
IN 1920 I RETURNED TO NARANJA. ALTHOUGH I FELT DIFFERENT AND LOOKED DIFFERENT THE TARASCANS CALLED ME 'ONE OF THEM.' AND WHEN I TALKED, MY PEOPLE LISTENED.
IT WAS TIME TO WIN BACK OUR LANDS. ONLY ONCE AGRARIAN REFORM HAD BEEN REALIZED COULD WE CONTEMPLATE
OTHER MUCH-NEEDED REFORMS
POLITICAL
SOCIAL AND
EDUCATIONAL

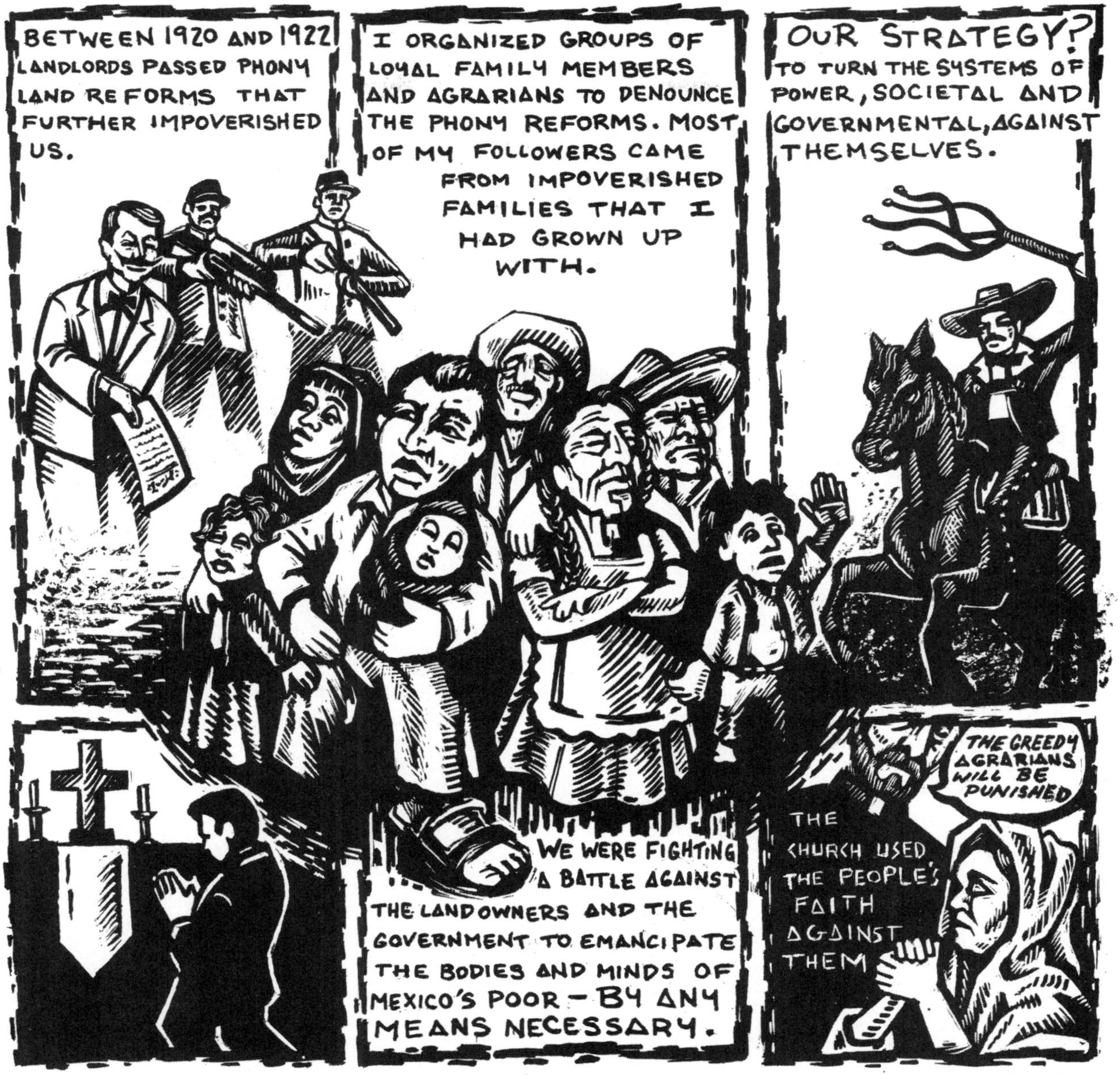
BETWEEN 1920 AND 1922 LANDLORDS PASSED PHONY LAND REFORMS THAT FURTHER IMPOVERISHED US.
I ORGANIZED GROUPS OF LOYAL FAMILY MEMBERS AND AGRARIANS TO DENOUNCE THE PHONY REFORMS. MOST OF MY FOLLOWERS CAME FROM IMPOVERISHED FAMILIES THAT I HAD GROWN UP WITH.
OUR STRATEGY?
TO TURN THE SYSTEMS OF POWER, SOCIETAL AND GOVERNMENTAL, AGAINST THEMSELVES.
WE WERE FIGHTING A BATTLE AGAINST THE LANDOWNERS AND THE GOVERNMENT TO EMANCIPATE THE BODIES AND MINDS OF MEXICO'S POOR – BY ANY MEANS NECESSARY.
THE GREEDY AGRARIANS WILL BE PUNISHED
THE CHURCH USED THE PEOPLE'S FAITH AGAINST THEM

IN 1920 I BECAME COMISSIONER OF THE LEAGUE OF AGRARIAN COMMUNITIES AND STRIVED TO ORGANIZE THE ENTIRE ZACAPU VALLEY REGION.

WE CONTINUED BUILDING STRENGTH LOCALLY. I HELPED THE WOMEN ORGANIZE, AND THE FEMININE LEAGUE WAS FORMED

THE WOBBLIES HAD TAUGHT ME THAT ORGANIZING MUST CUT ACROSS ALL BOUNDARIES.

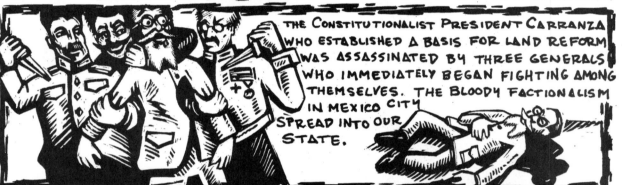

THE CONSTITUTIONALIST PRESIDENT CARRANZA WHO ESTABLISHED A BASIS FOR LAND REFORM WAS ASSASSINATED BY THREE GENERALS WHO IMMEDIATELY BEGAN FIGHTING AMONG THEMSELVES. THE BLOODY FACTIONALISM IN MEXICO CITY SPREAD INTO OUR STATE.

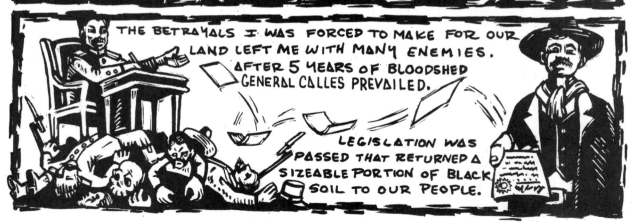

THE BETRAYALS I WAS FORCED TO MAKE FOR OUR LAND LEFT ME WITH MANY ENEMIES. AFTER 5 YEARS OF BLOODSHED GENERAL CALLES PREVAILED.

LEGISLATION WAS PASSED THAT RETURNED A SIZEABLE PORTION OF BLACK SOIL TO OUR PEOPLE.

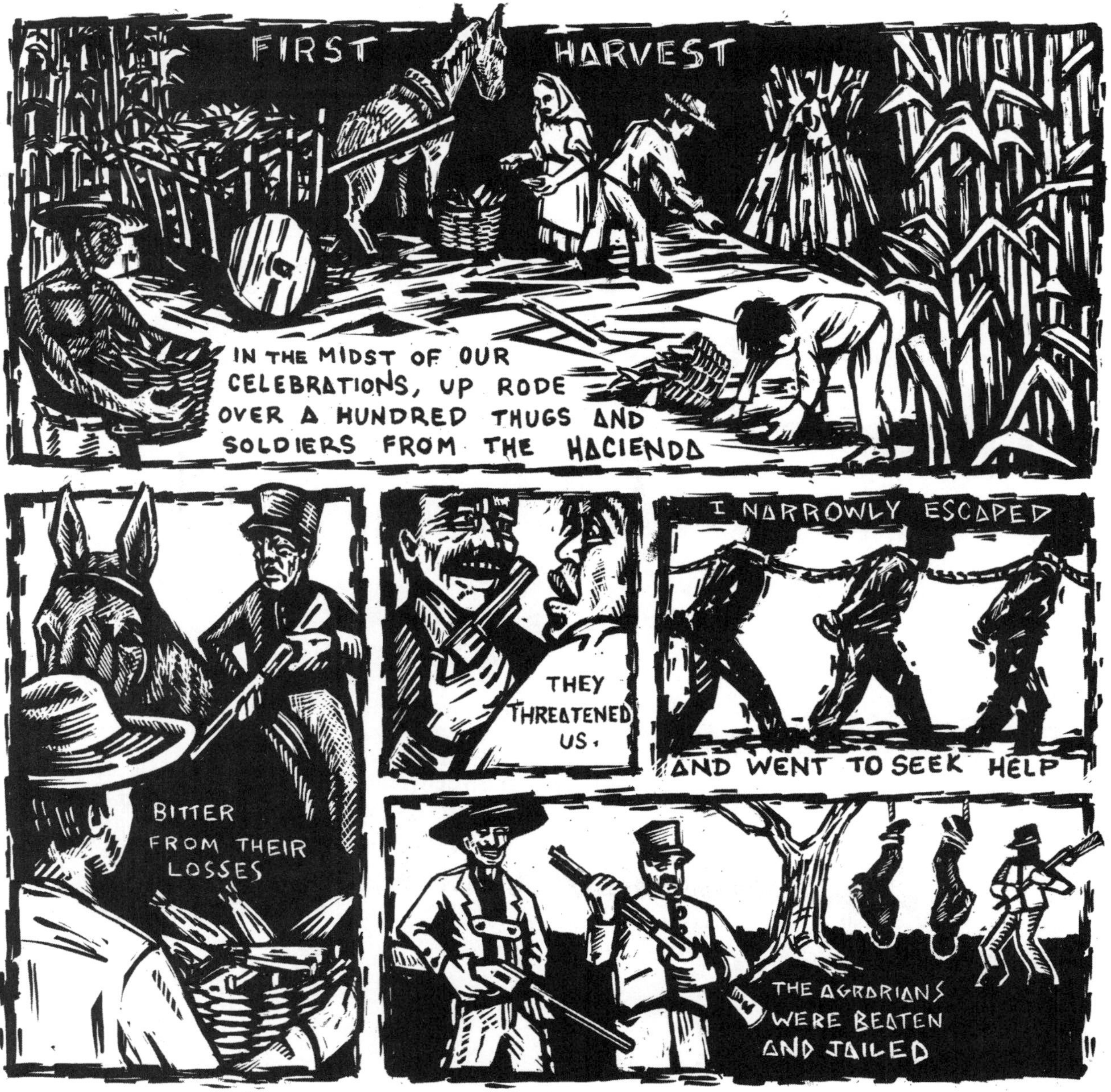
FIRST HARVEST
IN THE MIDST OF OUR CELEBRATIONS, UP RODE OVER A HUNDRED THUGS AND SOLDIERS FROM THE HACIENDA
BITTER FROM THEIR LOSSES
THEY THREATENED US.
I NARROWLY ESCAPED
AND WENT TO SEEK HELP
THE AGRARIANS WERE BEATEN AND JAILED

UNABLE TO TOLERATE THE HUMILIATION

THE WOMEN ATTACKED THE THUGS WHO WERE STEALING THE CORN AND FREED THE MEN.

THE WOMEN FOUGHT WITH STONES

THROUGH MY CLEVER USE OF STATE APPARATUS

I WAS ABLE TO GET AN ORDER TO HAVE THE STOLEN CORN RETURNED

36 WAGON LOADS WERE BROUGHT BACK FROM CANTABRIA

A YEAR'S SUPPLY OF CORN WAS GIVEN TO EACH FAMILY

IN NARANJA.

ON APRIL 26TH 1926

I WAS CAPTURED BY SOLDIERS DISGUISED AS PEASANTS.

THEY LED ME INTO THE MOUNTAINS.

MY BARE FEET BLED.

NIGHT FELL.

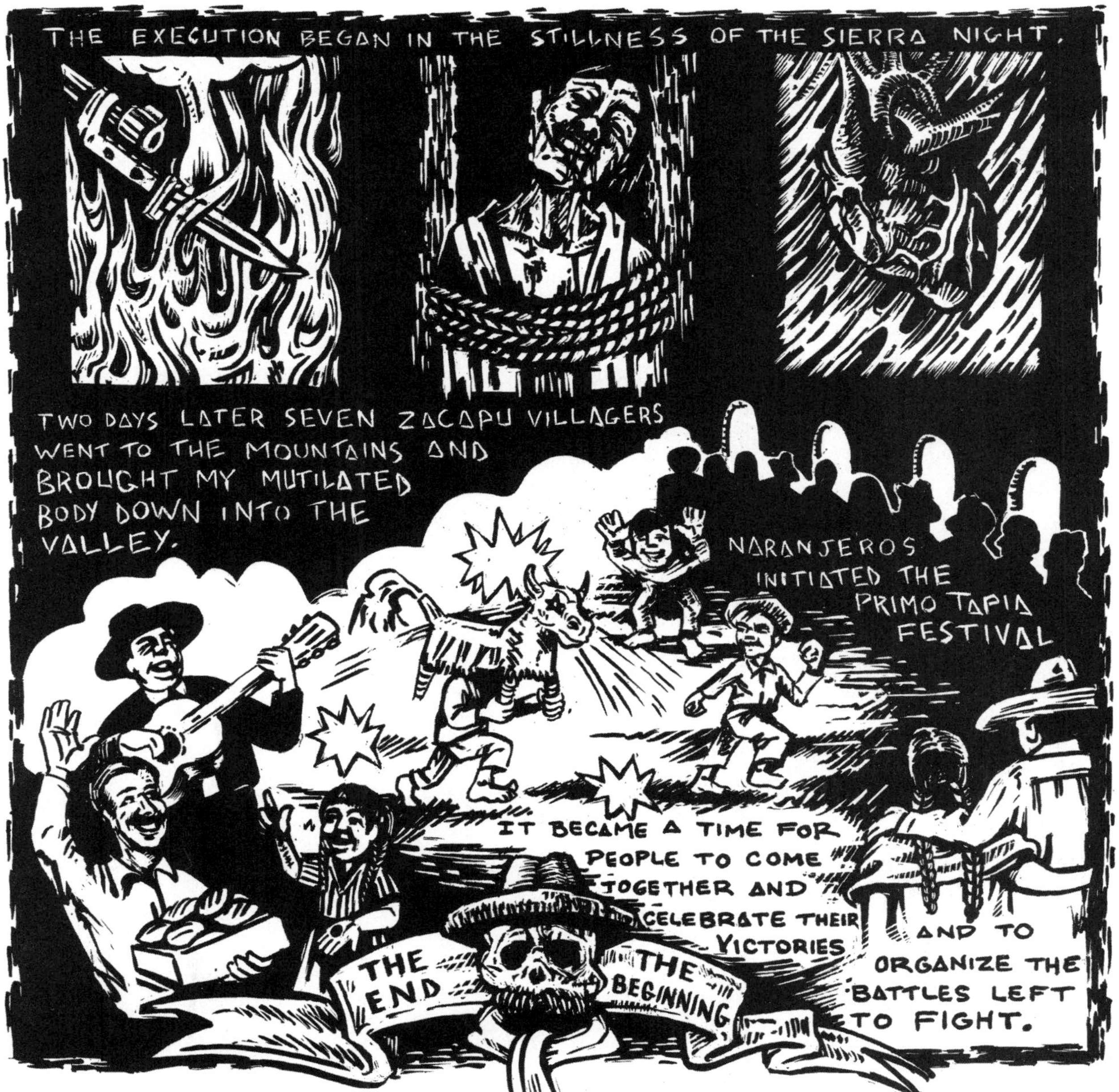
THE EXECUTION BEGAN IN THE STILLNESS OF THE SIERRA NIGHT.
TWO DAYS LATER SEVEN ZACAPU VILLAGERS WENT TO THE MOUNTAINS AND BROUGHT MY MUTILATED BODY DOWN INTO THE VALLEY.
NARANJEROS INITIATED THE PRIMO TAPIA FESTIVAL
IT BECAME A TIME FOR PEOPLE TO COME TOGETHER AND CELEBRATE THEIR VICTORIES
AND TO ORGANIZE THE BATTLES LEFT TO FIGHT.
THE END
THE BEGINNING

ESO "DEL ARTE POR EL ARTE MISMO" ES
UN ABSURDO Y SUS DEFENSORES HAN
CRISPADO SIEMPRE MIS NERVIOS.
SIENTO POR EL ARTE TAN REVERENTE
ADMIRACION Y AMOR QUE ME LASTIMA
VERLO PROSTITUIDO POR PERSONAS
QUE NO TENIENDO EL PODER DE HACER
SENTIR OTRAS LO QUE ELLAS SIENTEN
NI HACER LAS PENSAR LO QUE ELLAS
PIENSAN. OCULTAN SU IMPOTENCIA
BAJO EL MOTE DE "EL ARTE POR
EL ARTE MISMO"

Ricardo Flores-Magón

Movimiento
ARtistico
CHicano

PO BOX 2890   CHICAGO, ILLINOIS 60690

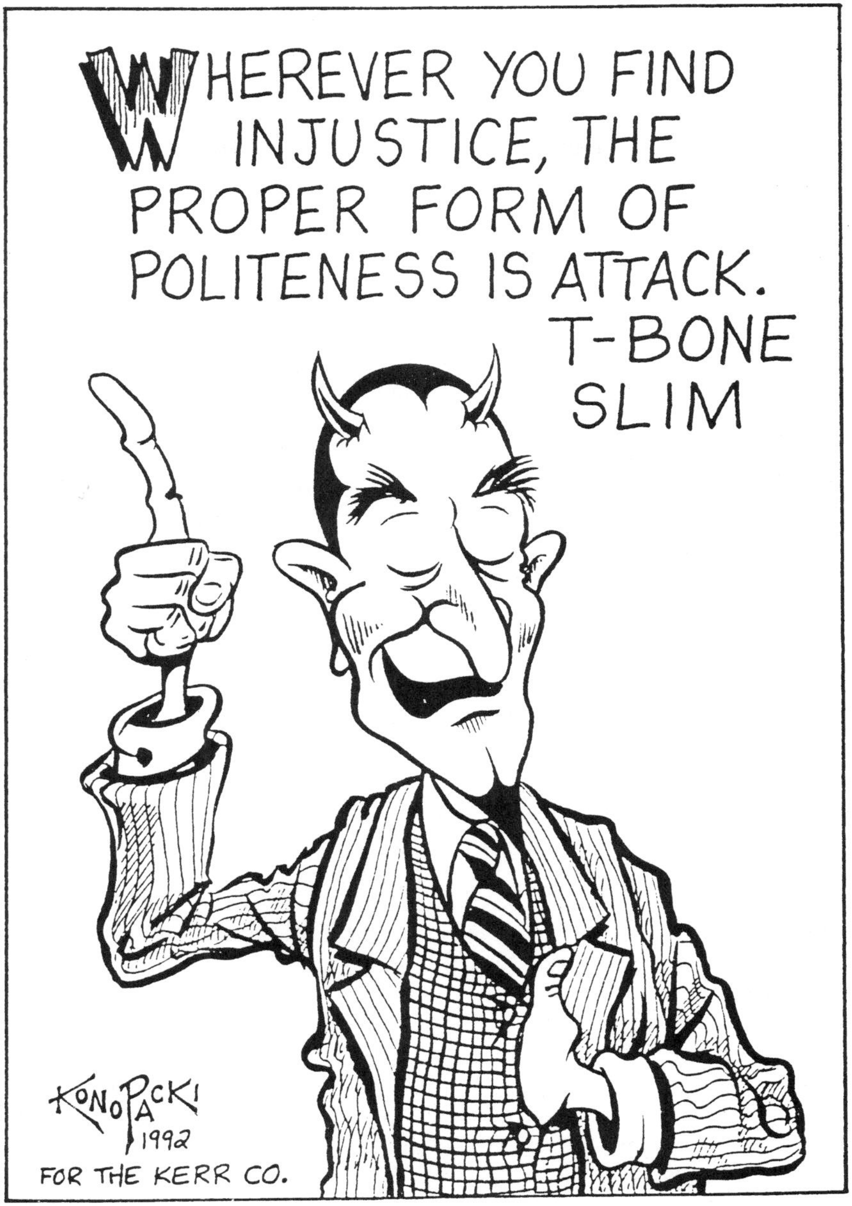
WHEREVER YOU FIND INJUSTICE, THE PROPER FORM OF POLITENESS IS ATTACK.
T-BONE SLIM
KONOPACKI 1992
FOR THE KERR CO.

TOM SCRIBNER: THE OLD WOBBLY OF SANTA CRUZ

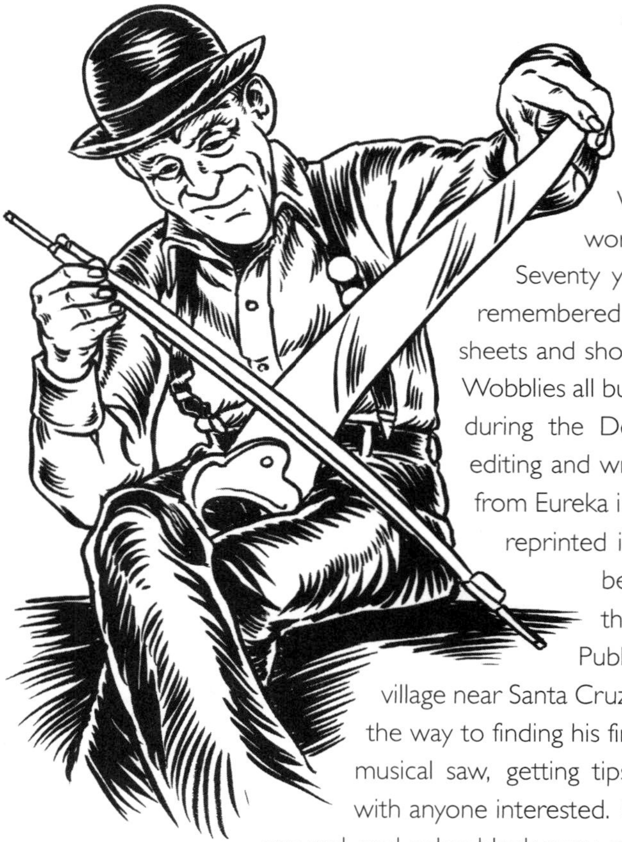

Tom Scribner was born in 1899 in Michigan's Upper Peninsula, the Copper Country, the grandson of a Civil War veteran. Selling magazines to loggers as a boy, he was asked to get them copies of socialist and Wobbly publications. In 1914, he joined the IWW, while working as a "swamper" in the woods for Weyerhauser. Seventy years later writing a never-published autobiography, he remembered his branch successfully demanding blankets, clean sheets and showers, then finally the eight-hour day. By the 1920s, the Wobblies all but gone, Tom hit the skidroad, continuing on to odd jobs during the Depression, settling (sometimes) in Eureka, California, editing and writing frequently for the Wobblyesque *Lumberjack News* from Eureka in the late 1950s and early 1960s, his articles sometimes reprinted in the anarchist *Vanguard*, of New York. For a while in between he had been a Communist, but eventually left the Party, dissatisfied. From 1949 he was on his own. Publishing *The Ripsaw News* from Davenport, an industrial village near Santa Cruz, California, devoted to producing concrete, he was on the way to finding his final home: on the main street in Santa Cruz, playing the musical saw, getting tips from tourists and locals, talking Wobbly philosophy with anyone interested. He lived in a downtown hotel in Santa Cruz from 1968 onward, and only a block away, and there he could be found most any day, until his death in 1982. A statue faithful to Tom remains, where he played and talked, in front of the town's leading independent bookstore. He can be seen as a talking head in the film, *Wobblies*.

THE COLLEGE OF COMPLEXES:

STORY © HARVEY · PEKAR ⊕ ART © JEROME · X350474

Slim Brundage was perhaps one of the most interesting bohemians to emerge in the twentieth century; though, considering his accomplishments among the least understood or appreciated.

YOU'RE KIND OF CUTE . . . . AND YOU LOOK LIKE YOU MIGHT BE INTELLIGENT TOO!

SO

MEET ME MON. ☐ TUES. ☐ WED. ☐ THUR. ☐ FRI. ☐ SAT. ☐ SUN. ☐

AT

COLLEGE OF COMPLEXES
862 N. State St. Chicago

"The Playground For People Who Think"

Meetings start at 9 p.m.

* ACTUAL INVITATION CARD

As founder & manager (he called himself the "Janitor") of Chicago's College of Complexes (1951-1961) Brundage owned a bar that was also one of the bastions of free speech in this nation. He was a great encourager of education (self & otherwise) and a facilitator of idea exchanging.

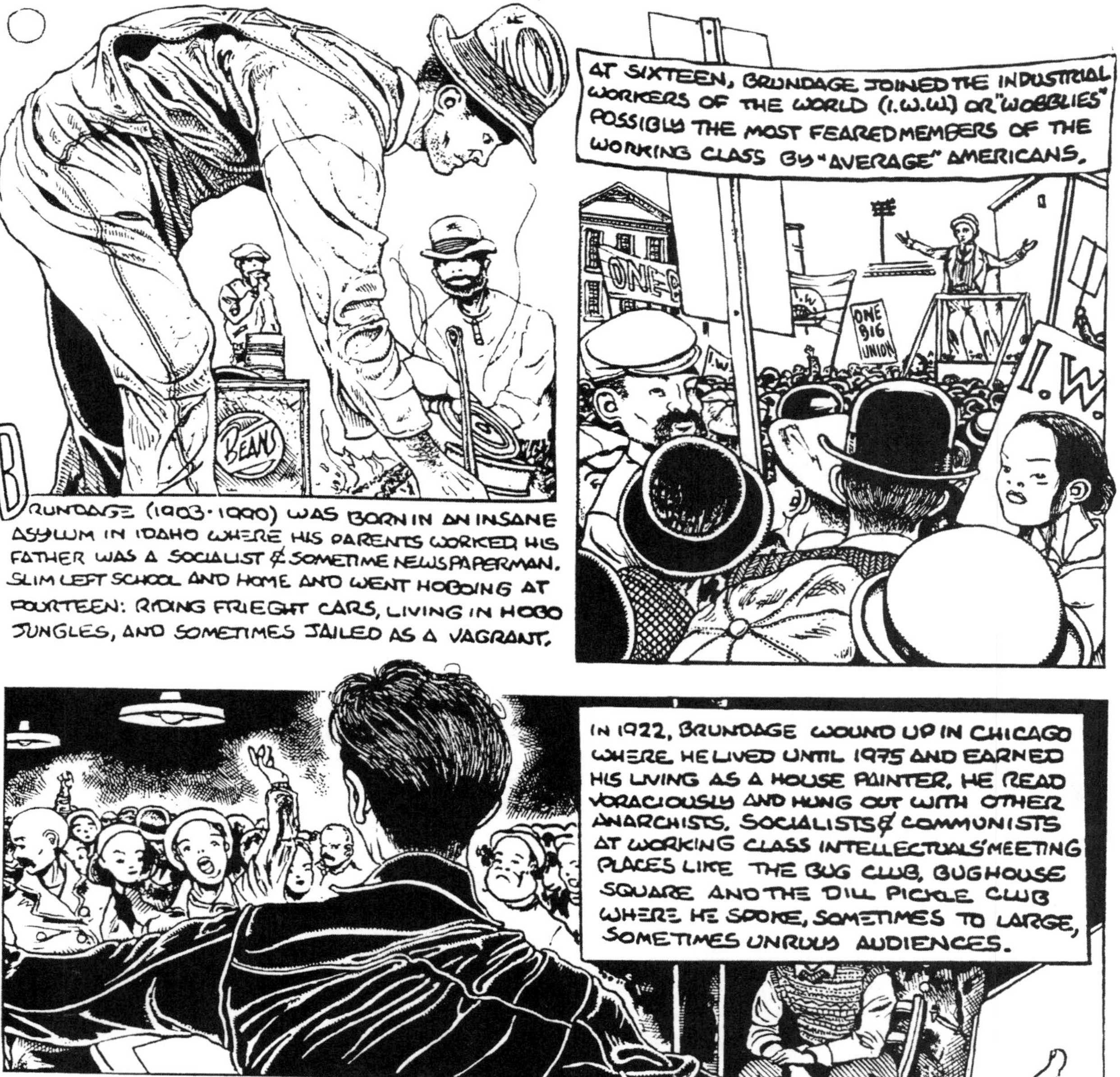
BEANS
BRUNDAGE (1903-1990) WAS BORN IN AN INSANE ASYLUM IN IDAHO WHERE HIS PARENTS WORKED. HIS FATHER WAS A SOCIALIST & SOMETIME NEWSPAPERMAN. SLIM LEFT SCHOOL AND HOME AND WENT HOBOING AT FOURTEEN: RIDING FRIEGHT CARS, LIVING IN HOBO JUNGLES, AND SOMETIMES JAILED AS A VAGRANT.
AT SIXTEEN, BRUNDAGE JOINED THE INDUSTRIAL WORKERS OF THE WORLD (I.W.W.) OR "WOBBLIES" POSSIBLY THE MOST FEARED MEMBERS OF THE WORKING CLASS BY "AVERAGE" AMERICANS.
ONE BIG UNION
I.W.
IN 1922, BRUNDAGE WOUND UP IN CHICAGO WHERE HE LIVED UNTIL 1975 AND EARNED HIS LIVING AS A HOUSE PAINTER. HE READ VORACIOUSLY AND HUNG OUT WITH OTHER ANARCHISTS, SOCIALISTS & COMMUNISTS AT WORKING CLASS INTELLECTUALS' MEETING PLACES LIKE THE BUG CLUB, BUGHOUSE SQUARE AND THE DILL PICKLE CLUB WHERE HE SPOKE, SOMETIMES TO LARGE, SOMETIMES UNRULY AUDIENCES.

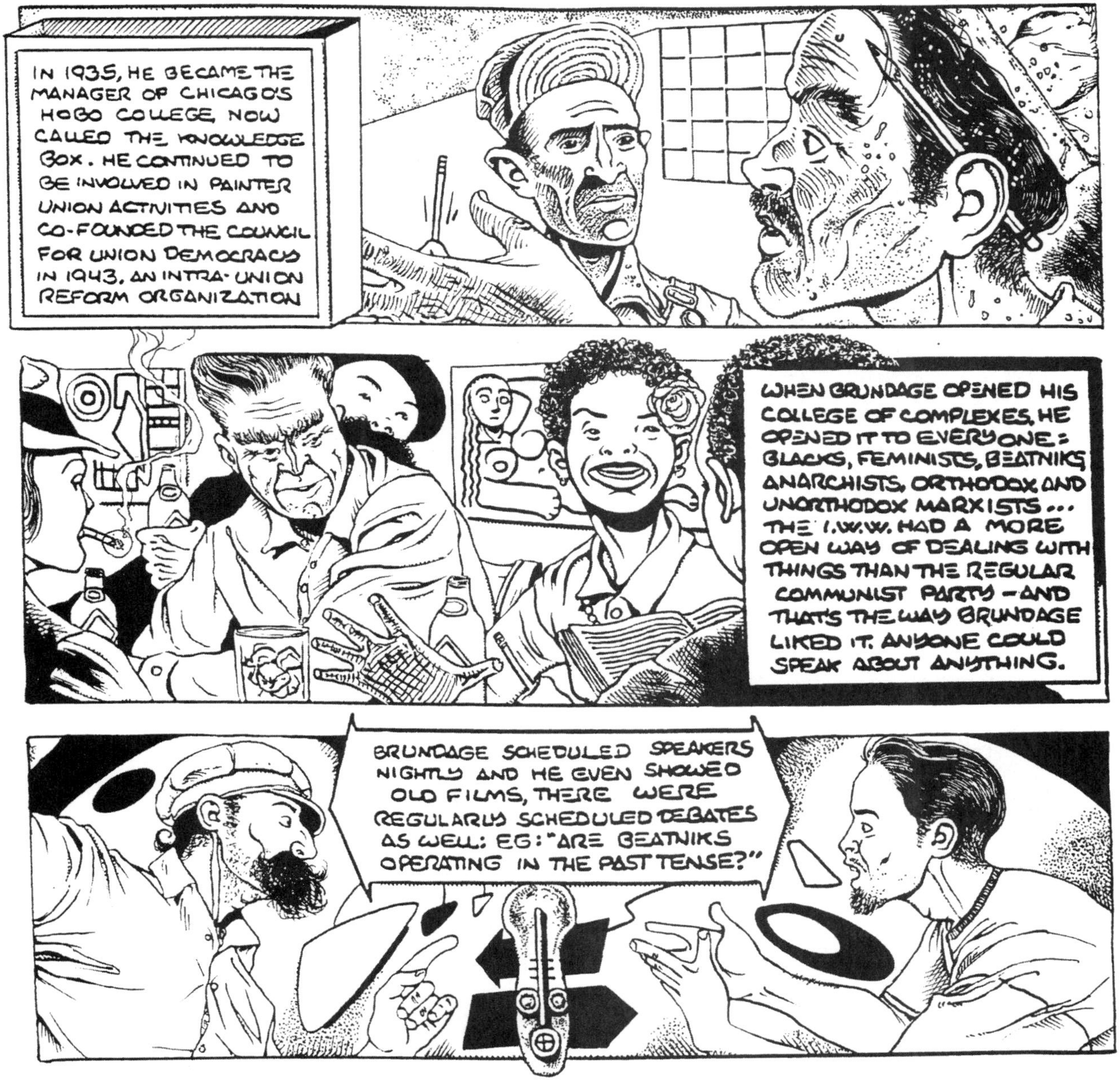
IN 1935, HE BECAME THE MANAGER OF CHICAGO'S HOBO COLLEGE, NOW CALLED THE KNOWLEDGE BOX. HE CONTINUED TO BE INVOLVED IN PAINTER UNION ACTIVITIES AND CO-FOUNDED THE COUNCIL FOR UNION DEMOCRACY IN 1943, AN INTRA-UNION REFORM ORGANIZATION
WHEN BRUNDAGE OPENED HIS COLLEGE OF COMPLEXES, HE OPENED IT TO EVERYONE: BLACKS, FEMINISTS, BEATNIKS ANARCHISTS, ORTHODOX AND UNORTHODOX MARXISTS... THE I.W.W. HAD A MORE OPEN WAY OF DEALING WITH THINGS THAN THE REGULAR COMMUNIST PARTY—AND THAT'S THE WAY BRUNDAGE LIKED IT. ANYONE COULD SPEAK ABOUT ANYTHING.
BRUNDAGE SCHEDULED SPEAKERS NIGHTLY AND HE EVEN SHOWED OLD FILMS, THERE WERE REGULARLY SCHEDULED DEBATES AS WELL: EG: "ARE BEATNIKS OPERATING IN THE PAST TENSE?"

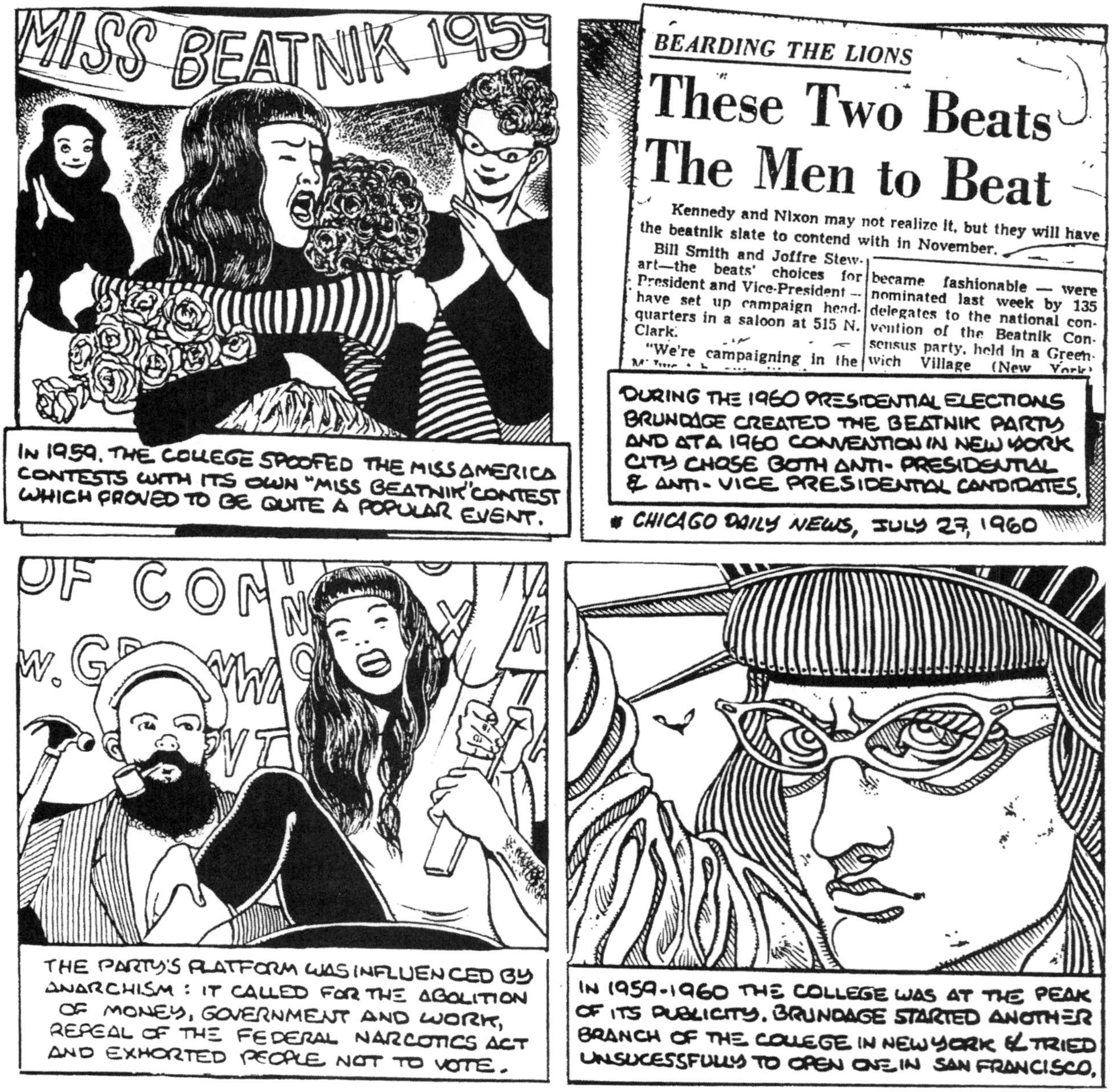
MISS BEATNIK 1959
IN 1959, THE COLLEGE SPOOFED THE MISS AMERICA CONTESTS WITH ITS OWN "MISS BEATNIK" CONTEST WHICH PROVED TO BE QUITE A POPULAR EVENT.
BEARDING THE LIONS
These Two Beats The Men to Beat
Kennedy and Nixon may not realize it, but they will have the beatnik slate to contend with in November.
Bill Smith and Joffre Stewart—the beats' choices for President and Vice-President—have set up campaign headquarters in a saloon at 515 N. Clark.
"We're campaigning in the
became fashionable — were nominated last week by 135 delegates to the national convention of the Beatnik Consensus party, held in a Greenwich Village (New York)
DURING THE 1960 PRESIDENTIAL ELECTIONS BRUNDAGE CREATED THE BEATNIK PARTY AND AT A 1960 CONVENTION IN NEW YORK CITY CHOSE BOTH ANTI-PRESIDENTIAL & ANTI-VICE PRESIDENTIAL CANDIDATES.
* CHICAGO DAILY NEWS, JULY 27, 1960
THE PARTY'S PLATFORM WAS INFLUENCED BY ANARCHISM: IT CALLED FOR THE ABOLITION OF MONEY, GOVERNMENT AND WORK, REPEAL OF THE FEDERAL NARCOTICS ACT AND EXHORTED PEOPLE NOT TO VOTE.
IN 1959-1960 THE COLLEGE WAS AT THE PEAK OF ITS PUBLICITY. BRUNDAGE STARTED ANOTHER BRANCH OF THE COLLEGE IN NEW YORK & TRIED UNSUCESSFULLY TO OPEN ONE IN SAN FRANCISCO.

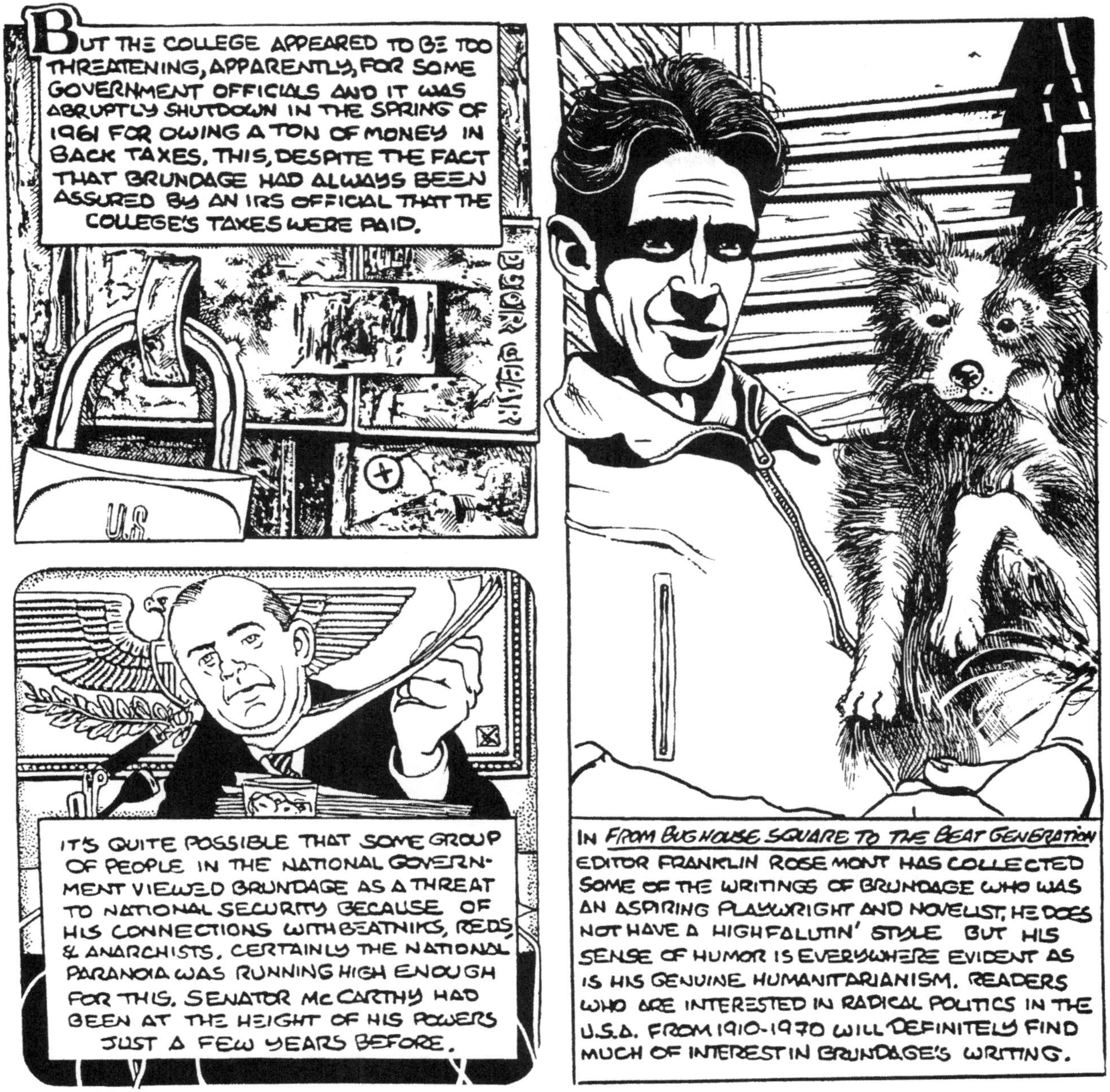
BUT THE COLLEGE APPEARED TO BE TOO THREATENING, APPARENTLY, FOR SOME GOVERNMENT OFFICIALS AND IT WAS ABRUPTLY SHUTDOWN IN THE SPRING OF 1961 FOR OWING A TON OF MONEY IN BACK TAXES. THIS, DESPITE THE FACT THAT BRUNDAGE HAD ALWAYS BEEN ASSURED BY AN IRS OFFICIAL THAT THE COLLEGE'S TAXES WERE PAID.
U.S
IT'S QUITE POSSIBLE THAT SOME GROUP OF PEOPLE IN THE NATIONAL GOVERNMENT VIEWED BRUNDAGE AS A THREAT TO NATIONAL SECURITY BECAUSE OF HIS CONNECTIONS WITH BEATNIKS, REDS, & ANARCHISTS. CERTAINLY THE NATIONAL PARANOIA WAS RUNNING HIGH ENOUGH FOR THIS. SENATOR McCARTHY HAD BEEN AT THE HEIGHT OF HIS POWERS JUST A FEW YEARS BEFORE.
IN FROM BUGHOUSE SQUARE TO THE BEAT GENERATION EDITOR FRANKLIN ROSEMONT HAS COLLECTED SOME OF THE WRITINGS OF BRUNDAGE WHO WAS AN ASPIRING PLAYWRIGHT AND NOVELIST. HE DOES NOT HAVE A HIGHFALUTIN' STYLE BUT HIS SENSE OF HUMOR IS EVERYWHERE EVIDENT AS IS HIS GENUINE HUMANITARIANISM. READERS WHO ARE INTERESTED IN RADICAL POLITICS IN THE U.S.A. FROM 1910-1970 WILL DEFINITELY FIND MUCH OF INTEREST IN BRUNDAGE'S WRITING.

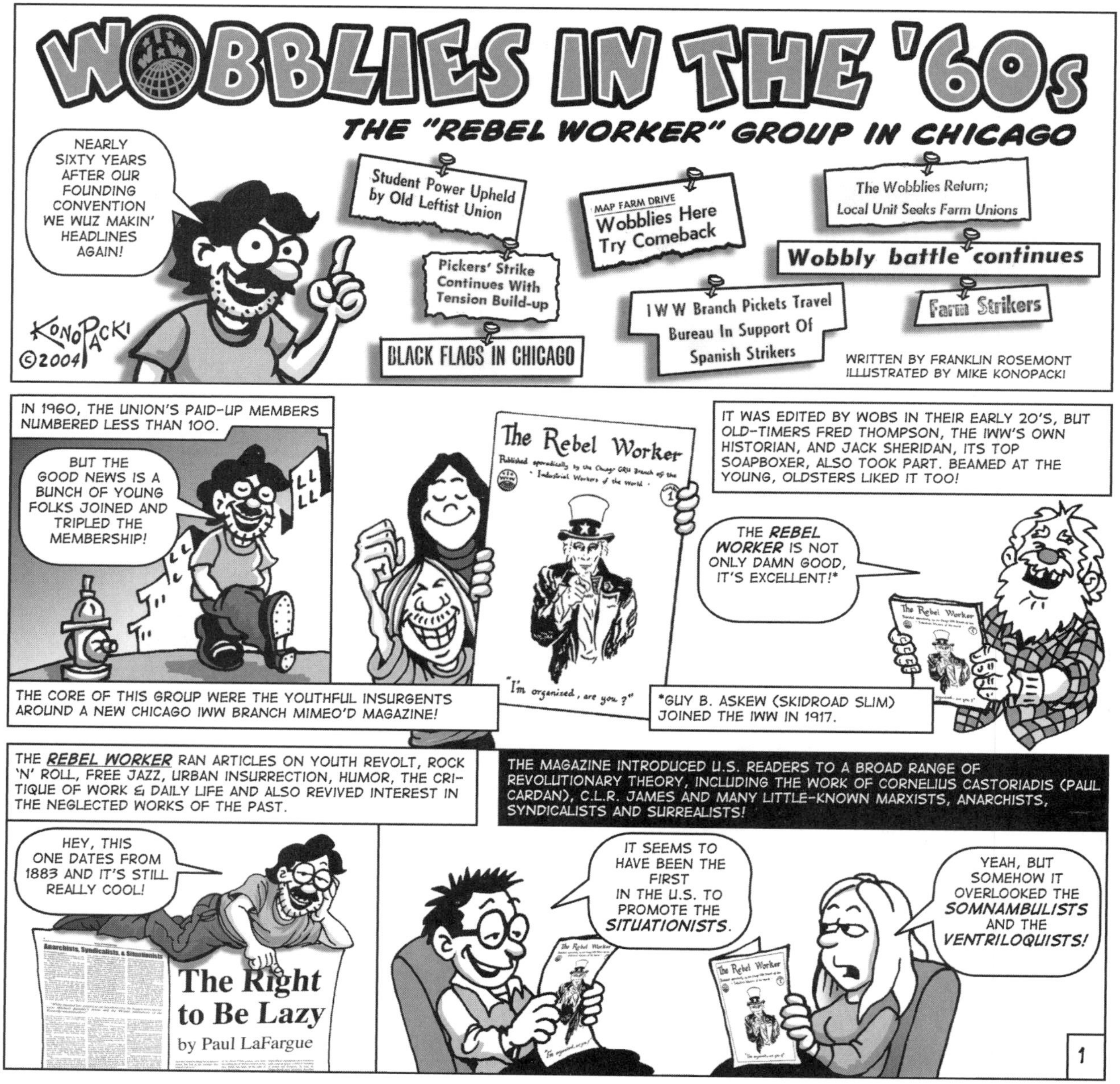
WOBBLIES IN THE '60s
THE "REBEL WORKER" GROUP IN CHICAGO
NEARLY SIXTY YEARS AFTER OUR FOUNDING CONVENTION WE WUZ MAKIN' HEADLINES AGAIN!
Student Power Upheld by Old Leftist Union
Pickers' Strike Continues With Tension Build-up
BLACK FLAGS IN CHICAGO
MAP FARM DRIVE
Wobblies Here Try Comeback
I W W Branch Pickets Travel Bureau In Support Of Spanish Strikers
The Wobblies Return; Local Unit Seeks Farm Unions
Wobbly battle continues
Farm Strikers
KONOPACKI ©2004
WRITTEN BY FRANKLIN ROSEMONT
ILLUSTRATED BY MIKE KONOPACKI
IN 1960, THE UNION'S PAID-UP MEMBERS NUMBERED LESS THAN 100.
BUT THE GOOD NEWS IS A BUNCH OF YOUNG FOLKS JOINED AND TRIPLED THE MEMBERSHIP!
THE CORE OF THIS GROUP WERE THE YOUTHFUL INSURGENTS AROUND A NEW CHICAGO IWW BRANCH MIMEO'D MAGAZINE!
The Rebel Worker
"I'm organized, are you?"
IT WAS EDITED BY WOBS IN THEIR EARLY 20'S, BUT OLD-TIMERS FRED THOMPSON, THE IWW'S OWN HISTORIAN, AND JACK SHERIDAN, ITS TOP SOAPBOXER, ALSO TOOK PART. BEAMED AT THE YOUNG, OLDSTERS LIKED IT TOO!
THE *REBEL WORKER* IS NOT ONLY DAMN GOOD, IT'S EXCELLENT!*
*GUY B. ASKEW (SKIDROAD SLIM) JOINED THE IWW IN 1917.
THE *REBEL WORKER* RAN ARTICLES ON YOUTH REVOLT, ROCK 'N' ROLL, FREE JAZZ, URBAN INSURRECTION, HUMOR, THE CRITIQUE OF WORK & DAILY LIFE AND ALSO REVIVED INTEREST IN THE NEGLECTED WORKS OF THE PAST.
HEY, THIS ONE DATES FROM 1883 AND IT'S STILL REALLY COOL!
Anarchists, Syndicalists, & Situationists
The Right to Be Lazy
by Paul LaFargue
THE MAGAZINE INTRODUCED U.S. READERS TO A BROAD RANGE OF REVOLUTIONARY THEORY, INCLUDING THE WORK OF CORNELIUS CASTORIADIS (PAUL CARDAN), C.L.R. JAMES AND MANY LITTLE-KNOWN MARXISTS, ANARCHISTS, SYNDICALISTS AND SURREALISTS!
IT SEEMS TO HAVE BEEN THE FIRST IN THE U.S. TO PROMOTE THE *SITUATIONISTS*.
YEAH, BUT SOMEHOW IT OVERLOOKED THE *SOMNAMBULISTS* AND THE *VENTRILOQUISTS!*
1

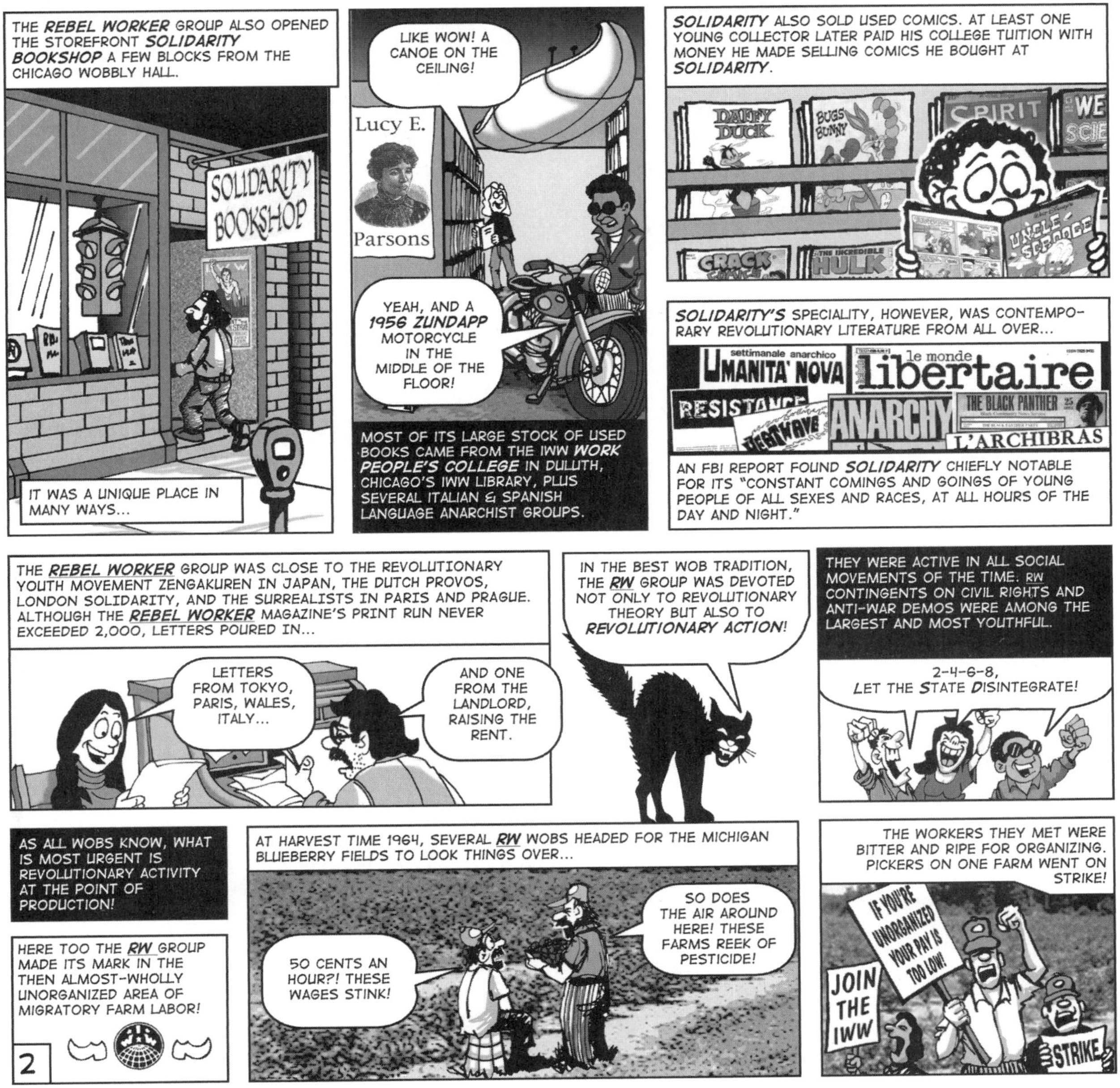
THE REBEL WORKER GROUP ALSO OPENED THE STOREFRONT SOLIDARITY BOOKSHOP A FEW BLOCKS FROM THE CHICAGO WOBBLY HALL.
SOLIDARITY BOOKSHOP
IT WAS A UNIQUE PLACE IN MANY WAYS...
LIKE WOW! A CANOE ON THE CEILING!
Lucy E. Parsons
YEAH, AND A 1956 ZUNDAPP MOTORCYCLE IN THE MIDDLE OF THE FLOOR!
MOST OF ITS LARGE STOCK OF USED BOOKS CAME FROM THE IWW WORK PEOPLE'S COLLEGE IN DULUTH, CHICAGO'S IWW LIBRARY, PLUS SEVERAL ITALIAN & SPANISH LANGUAGE ANARCHIST GROUPS.
SOLIDARITY ALSO SOLD USED COMICS. AT LEAST ONE YOUNG COLLECTOR LATER PAID HIS COLLEGE TUITION WITH MONEY HE MADE SELLING COMICS HE BOUGHT AT SOLIDARITY.
DAFFY DUCK
BUGS BUNNY
SPIRIT
CRACK COMICS
THE INCREDIBLE HULK
UNCLE SCROOGE
SOLIDARITY'S SPECIALITY, HOWEVER, WAS CONTEMPORARY REVOLUTIONARY LITERATURE FROM ALL OVER...
settimanale anarchico UMANITA' NOVA
le monde libertaire
RESISTANCE
ANARCHY
THE BLACK PANTHER
L'ARCHIBRAS
AN FBI REPORT FOUND SOLIDARITY CHIEFLY NOTABLE FOR ITS "CONSTANT COMINGS AND GOINGS OF YOUNG PEOPLE OF ALL SEXES AND RACES, AT ALL HOURS OF THE DAY AND NIGHT."
THE REBEL WORKER GROUP WAS CLOSE TO THE REVOLUTIONARY YOUTH MOVEMENT ZENGAKUREN IN JAPAN, THE DUTCH PROVOS, LONDON SOLIDARITY, AND THE SURREALISTS IN PARIS AND PRAGUE. ALTHOUGH THE REBEL WORKER MAGAZINE'S PRINT RUN NEVER EXCEEDED 2,000, LETTERS POURED IN...
LETTERS FROM TOKYO, PARIS, WALES, ITALY...
AND ONE FROM THE LANDLORD, RAISING THE RENT.
IN THE BEST WOB TRADITION, THE RW GROUP WAS DEVOTED NOT ONLY TO REVOLUTIONARY THEORY BUT ALSO TO REVOLUTIONARY ACTION!
THEY WERE ACTIVE IN ALL SOCIAL MOVEMENTS OF THE TIME. RW CONTINGENTS ON CIVIL RIGHTS AND ANTI-WAR DEMOS WERE AMONG THE LARGEST AND MOST YOUTHFUL.
2-4-6-8, LET THE STATE DISINTEGRATE!
AS ALL WOBS KNOW, WHAT IS MOST URGENT IS REVOLUTIONARY ACTIVITY AT THE POINT OF PRODUCTION!
HERE TOO THE RW GROUP MADE ITS MARK IN THE THEN ALMOST-WHOLLY UNORGANIZED AREA OF MIGRATORY FARM LABOR!
2
AT HARVEST TIME 1964, SEVERAL RW WOBS HEADED FOR THE MICHIGAN BLUEBERRY FIELDS TO LOOK THINGS OVER...
50 CENTS AN HOUR?! THESE WAGES STINK!
SO DOES THE AIR AROUND HERE! THESE FARMS REEK OF PESTICIDE!
THE WORKERS THEY MET WERE BITTER AND RIPE FOR ORGANIZING. PICKERS ON ONE FARM WENT ON STRIKE!
IF YOU'RE UNORGANIZED YOUR PAY IS TOO LOW!
JOIN THE IWW
STRIKE

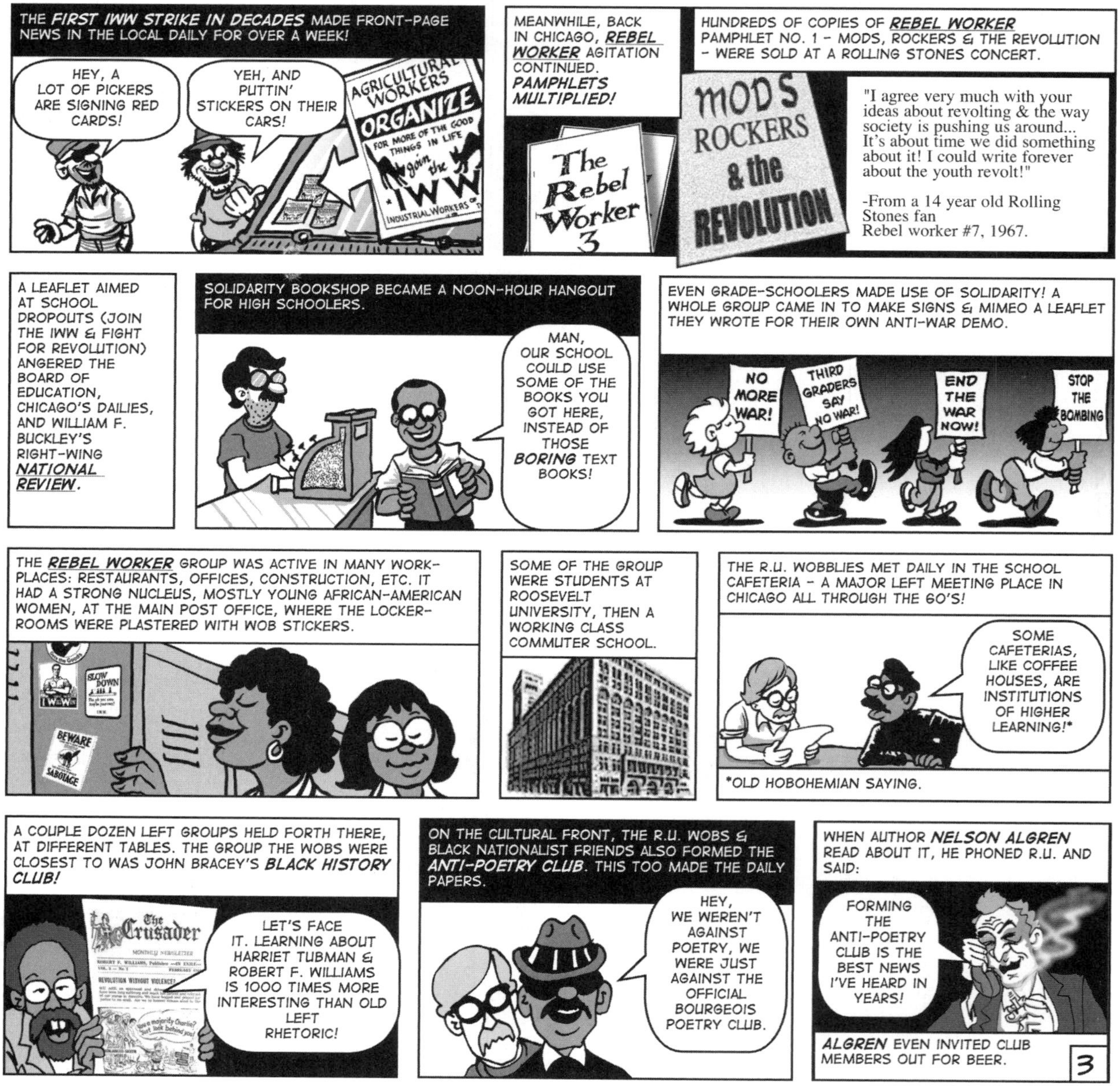
THE FIRST IWW STRIKE IN DECADES MADE FRONT-PAGE NEWS IN THE LOCAL DAILY FOR OVER A WEEK!
HEY, A LOT OF PICKERS ARE SIGNING RED CARDS!
YEH, AND PUTTIN' STICKERS ON THEIR CARS!
AGRICULTURAL WORKERS ORGANIZE FOR MORE OF THE GOOD THINGS IN LIFE join the IWW INDUSTRIAL WORKERS OF
MEANWHILE, BACK IN CHICAGO, REBEL WORKER AGITATION CONTINUED. PAMPHLETS MULTIPLIED!
The Rebel Worker 3
HUNDREDS OF COPIES OF REBEL WORKER PAMPHLET NO. 1 - MODS, ROCKERS & THE REVOLUTION - WERE SOLD AT A ROLLING STONES CONCERT.
MODS ROCKERS & the REVOLUTION
"I agree very much with your ideas about revolting & the way society is pushing us around... It's about time we did something about it! I could write forever about the youth revolt!"
-From a 14 year old Rolling Stones fan
Rebel worker #7, 1967.
A LEAFLET AIMED AT SCHOOL DROPOUTS (JOIN THE IWW & FIGHT FOR REVOLUTION) ANGERED THE BOARD OF EDUCATION, CHICAGO'S DAILIES, AND WILLIAM F. BUCKLEY'S RIGHT-WING NATIONAL REVIEW.
SOLIDARITY BOOKSHOP BECAME A NOON-HOUR HANGOUT FOR HIGH SCHOOLERS.
MAN, OUR SCHOOL COULD USE SOME OF THE BOOKS YOU GOT HERE, INSTEAD OF THOSE BORING TEXT BOOKS!
EVEN GRADE-SCHOOLERS MADE USE OF SOLIDARITY! A WHOLE GROUP CAME IN TO MAKE SIGNS & MIMEO A LEAFLET THEY WROTE FOR THEIR OWN ANTI-WAR DEMO.
NO MORE WAR!
THIRD GRADERS SAY NO WAR!
END THE WAR NOW!
STOP THE BOMBING
THE REBEL WORKER GROUP WAS ACTIVE IN MANY WORK-PLACES: RESTAURANTS, OFFICES, CONSTRUCTION, ETC. IT HAD A STRONG NUCLEUS, MOSTLY YOUNG AFRICAN-AMERICAN WOMEN, AT THE MAIN POST OFFICE, WHERE THE LOCKER-ROOMS WERE PLASTERED WITH WOB STICKERS.
SLOW DOWN
BEWARE SABOTAGE
SOME OF THE GROUP WERE STUDENTS AT ROOSEVELT UNIVERSITY, THEN A WORKING CLASS COMMUTER SCHOOL.
THE R.U. WOBBLIES MET DAILY IN THE SCHOOL CAFETERIA - A MAJOR LEFT MEETING PLACE IN CHICAGO ALL THROUGH THE 60'S!
SOME CAFETERIAS, LIKE COFFEE HOUSES, ARE INSTITUTIONS OF HIGHER LEARNING!*
*OLD HOBOHEMIAN SAYING.
A COUPLE DOZEN LEFT GROUPS HELD FORTH THERE, AT DIFFERENT TABLES. THE GROUP THE WOBS WERE CLOSEST TO WAS JOHN BRACEY'S BLACK HISTORY CLUB!
The Crusader
MONTHLY NEWSLETTER
ROBERT F. WILLIAMS, Publisher
REVOLUTION WITHOUT VIOLENCE?
LET'S FACE IT. LEARNING ABOUT HARRIET TUBMAN & ROBERT F. WILLIAMS IS 1000 TIMES MORE INTERESTING THAN OLD LEFT RHETORIC!
ON THE CULTURAL FRONT, THE R.U. WOBS & BLACK NATIONALIST FRIENDS ALSO FORMED THE ANTI-POETRY CLUB. THIS TOO MADE THE DAILY PAPERS.
HEY, WE WEREN'T AGAINST POETRY, WE WERE JUST AGAINST THE OFFICIAL BOURGEOIS POETRY CLUB.
WHEN AUTHOR NELSON ALGREN READ ABOUT IT, HE PHONED R.U. AND SAID:
FORMING THE ANTI-POETRY CLUB IS THE BEST NEWS I'VE HEARD IN YEARS!
ALGREN EVEN INVITED CLUB MEMBERS OUT FOR BEER.
3

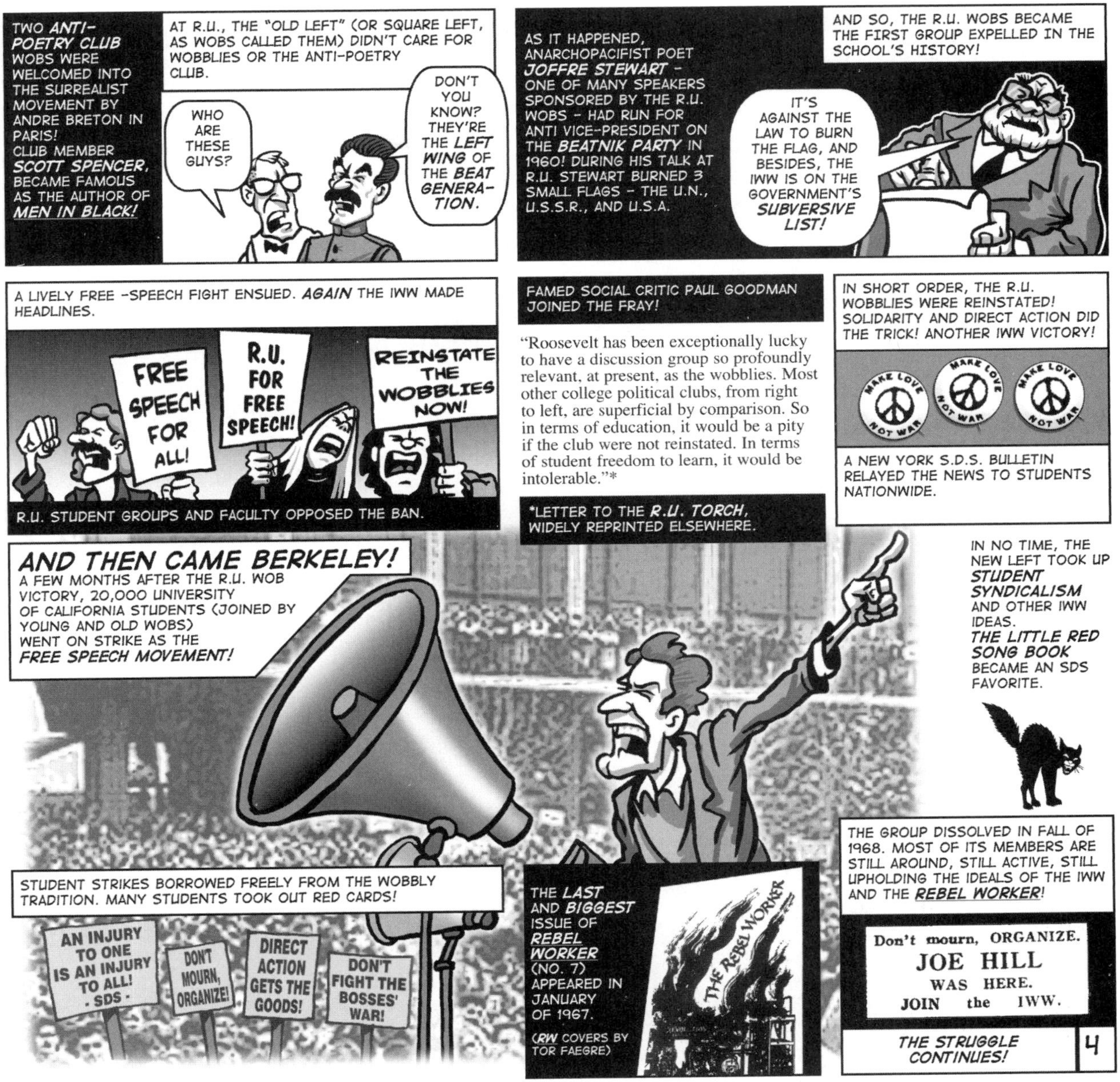
TWO ANTI-POETRY CLUB WOBS WERE WELCOMED INTO THE SURREALIST MOVEMENT BY ANDRE BRETON IN PARIS! CLUB MEMBER SCOTT SPENCER, BECAME FAMOUS AS THE AUTHOR OF MEN IN BLACK!
AT R.U., THE "OLD LEFT" (OR SQUARE LEFT, AS WOBS CALLED THEM) DIDN'T CARE FOR WOBBLIES OR THE ANTI-POETRY CLUB.
WHO ARE THESE GUYS?
DON'T YOU KNOW? THEY'RE THE LEFT WING OF THE BEAT GENERATION.
AS IT HAPPENED, ANARCHOPACIFIST POET JOFFRE STEWART – ONE OF MANY SPEAKERS SPONSORED BY THE R.U. WOBS – HAD RUN FOR ANTI VICE-PRESIDENT ON THE BEATNIK PARTY IN 1960! DURING HIS TALK AT R.U. STEWART BURNED 3 SMALL FLAGS – THE U.N., U.S.S.R., AND U.S.A.
AND SO, THE R.U. WOBS BECAME THE FIRST GROUP EXPELLED IN THE SCHOOL'S HISTORY!
IT'S AGAINST THE LAW TO BURN THE FLAG, AND BESIDES, THE IWW IS ON THE GOVERNMENT'S SUBVERSIVE LIST!
A LIVELY FREE -SPEECH FIGHT ENSUED. AGAIN THE IWW MADE HEADLINES.
FREE SPEECH FOR ALL!
R.U. FOR FREE SPEECH!
REINSTATE THE WOBBLIES NOW!
R.U. STUDENT GROUPS AND FACULTY OPPOSED THE BAN.
FAMED SOCIAL CRITIC PAUL GOODMAN JOINED THE FRAY!
"Roosevelt has been exceptionally lucky to have a discussion group so profoundly relevant, at present, as the wobblies. Most other college political clubs, from right to left, are superficial by comparison. So in terms of education, it would be a pity if the club were not reinstated. In terms of student freedom to learn, it would be intolerable."*
*LETTER TO THE R.U. TORCH, WIDELY REPRINTED ELSEWHERE.
IN SHORT ORDER, THE R.U. WOBBLIES WERE REINSTATED! SOLIDARITY AND DIRECT ACTION DID THE TRICK! ANOTHER IWW VICTORY!
MAKE LOVE NOT WAR
MAKE LOVE NOT WAR
MAKE LOVE NOT WAR
A NEW YORK S.D.S. BULLETIN RELAYED THE NEWS TO STUDENTS NATIONWIDE.
AND THEN CAME BERKELEY!
A FEW MONTHS AFTER THE R.U. WOB VICTORY, 20,000 UNIVERSITY OF CALIFORNIA STUDENTS (JOINED BY YOUNG AND OLD WOBS) WENT ON STRIKE AS THE FREE SPEECH MOVEMENT!
STUDENT STRIKES BORROWED FREELY FROM THE WOBBLY TRADITION. MANY STUDENTS TOOK OUT RED CARDS!
AN INJURY TO ONE IS AN INJURY TO ALL! - SDS -
DON'T MOURN, ORGANIZE!
DIRECT ACTION GETS THE GOODS!
DON'T FIGHT THE BOSSES' WAR!
THE LAST AND BIGGEST ISSUE OF REBEL WORKER (NO. 7) APPEARED IN JANUARY OF 1967.
(RW COVERS BY TOR FAEGRE)
THE REBEL WORKER
IN NO TIME, THE NEW LEFT TOOK UP STUDENT SYNDICALISM AND OTHER IWW IDEAS. THE LITTLE RED SONG BOOK BECAME AN SDS FAVORITE.
THE GROUP DISSOLVED IN FALL OF 1968. MOST OF ITS MEMBERS ARE STILL AROUND, STILL ACTIVE, STILL UPHOLDING THE IDEALS OF THE IWW AND THE REBEL WORKER!
Don't mourn, ORGANIZE.
JOE HILL
WAS HERE.
JOIN the IWW.
THE STRUGGLE CONTINUES!
4

SIX

THE IWW LIVES!

A remarkable sight appeared around 1966: IWW buttons on the lapels of the organizers in the fast-rising student radical movement, Students for a Democratic Society. Only a few years earlier, SDS had been the child of a campus social-democratic movement, the Student League for Industrial Democracy. In a famous conference of 1962 at Port Huron, Michigan, an SDS statement (drafted by Tom Hayden and others influenced, some said, by the ideas of Pan-African giant C.L.R. James as well as radical sociologist C. Wright Mills, among others) sounded less like Old Left Marxism and more like Wob doctrine. It urged "participatory democracy," not as proletarian as IWW ideas, to be sure, but as a movement from below rather than above, relying upon ordinary people rather than experts, however liberal or left-wing.

Over the next few years, IWW offices were confounded by thousands of inquiries, requests by unemployed youngsters to join (but without a branch or the prospect of organizing one), and renewed interest in the monthly tabloid, the *Industrial Worker*. Lamentably, the interest flagged with the crisis of the New Left and the takeover of SDS by one Maoist faction after another. A great opportunity had been lost as the revolutionary spirit of the time passed, and the remnants of the New Left and women's (also gay and lesbian) liberation movements, along with the Black (and Brown and Red and Yellow) Power movement, turned to reformism and mainly cultural pursuits.

But here and there fascinating local developments reminded observers that the IWW was very much alive. During the early 1960s, as recorded below, the Wobs took life on the Roosevelt College campus of Chicago, and among migrant workers northward. During the 1980s and early 1990s, Wobs could be found among youngsters, mainly, striving to save the mighty redwoods of California through an alliance with timber workers.

At the turn of the new century and after, Wob membership drifted up and down, scatterings of new locals (especially in counter-culture towns) were formed or disappeared, and a few, like the one in Portland, Oregon, seemed to set down firm roots. A successful employees' May 2004 vote and precarious victory (by IWW IU/660) at a Starbucks in mid-Manhattan—immediately appealed by the corporate giant—proved once again that Wobblies had a role where the mainstream labor movement had given up trying.

The Starbucks event, and IWW success among resentful, often part-time workers in low-paid sectors with few if any benefits, suggested the prospect that loomed ahead. The globalism that had been the very heart of the Wob understanding became increasingly real in daily life. Workers of many countries now had no choice. They were being forced into solidarity with each other for dignity and survival, even if the official labor leaders maintained an outdated and conservative approach to the rapidly changing world economy. Antiglobalization demonstrations from Seattle to Manhattan to Latin America, Europe, and Asia, often brought out Wobbly signs, for the best possible reasons. Perhaps, after a century, the organic basis for IWW-envisioned success had finally arrived. At any rate, given the accelerating attack of corporations upon the planet and all living creatures, it was getting close to now or never.

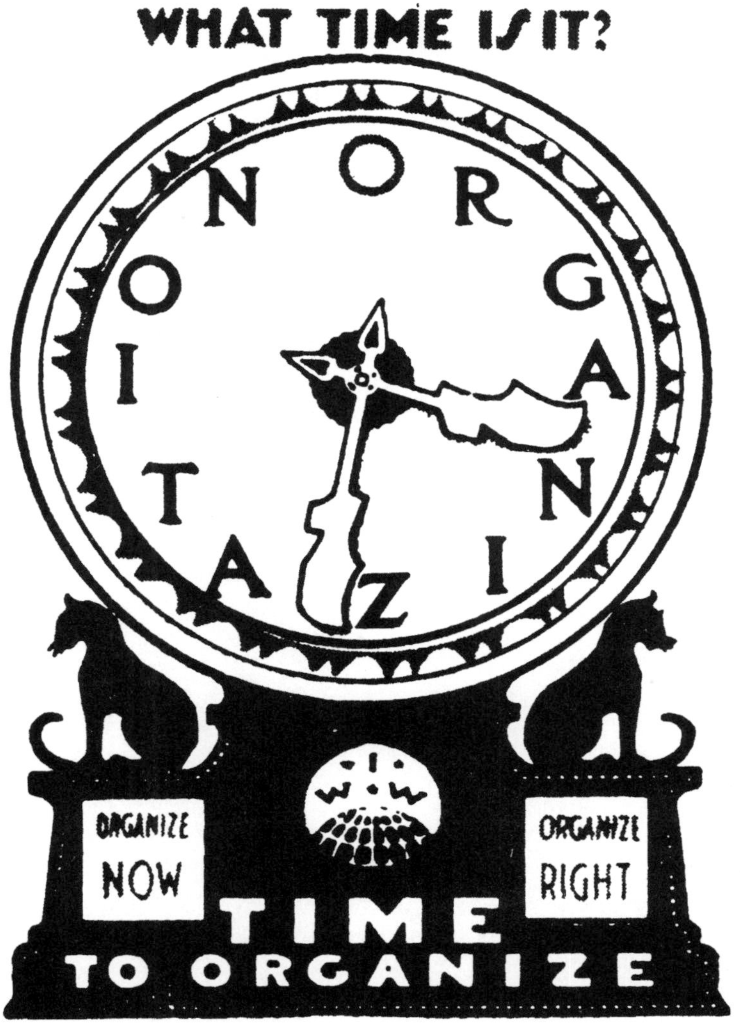
WHAT TIME IS IT?
ORGANIZATION
I.W.W.
ORGANIZE NOW
ORGANIZE RIGHT
TIME TO ORGANIZE

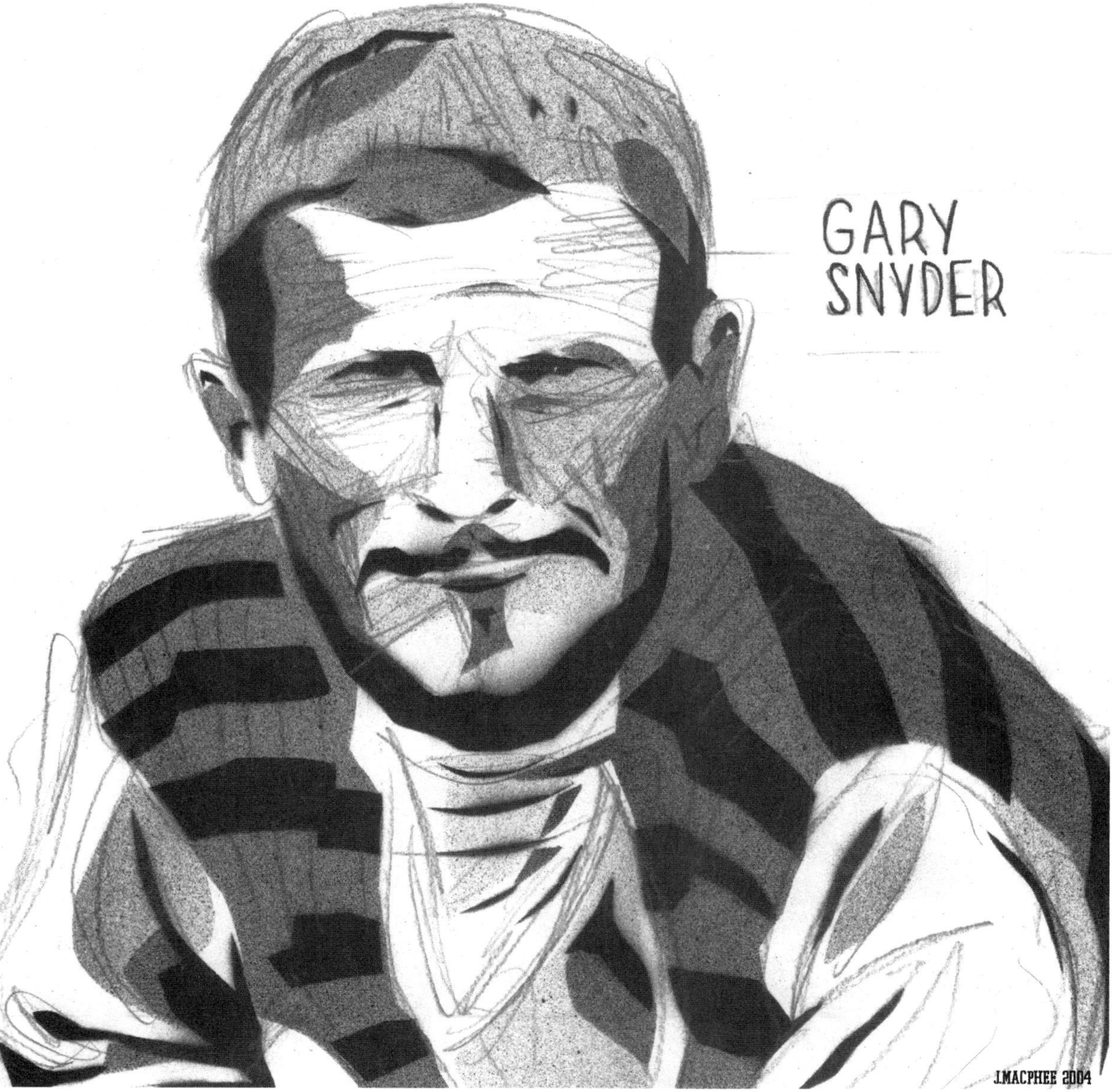
GARY
SNYDER
J.MACPHEE 2004

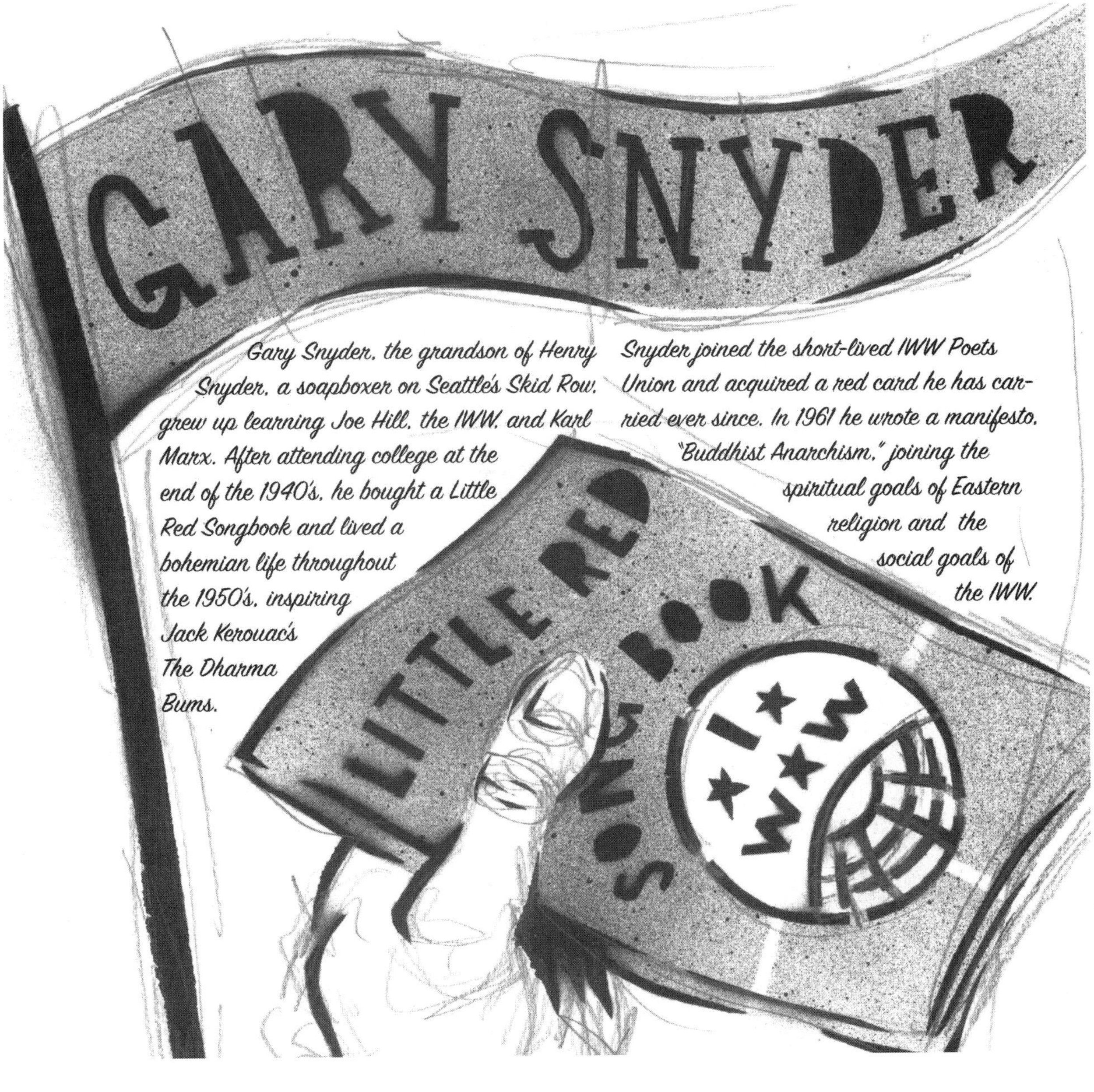
GARY SNYDER
LITTLE RED SONG BOOK
I★W★W

Gary Snyder, the grandson of Henry Snyder, a soapboxer on Seattle's Skid Row, grew up learning Joe Hill, the IWW, and Karl Marx. After attending college at the end of the 1940's, he bought a Little Red Songbook and lived a bohemian life throughout the 1950's, inspiring Jack Kerouac's The Dharma Bums.

Snyder joined the short-lived IWW Poets Union and acquired a red card he has carried ever since. In 1961 he wrote a manifesto, "Buddhist Anarchism," joining the spiritual goals of Eastern religion and the social goals of the IWW.

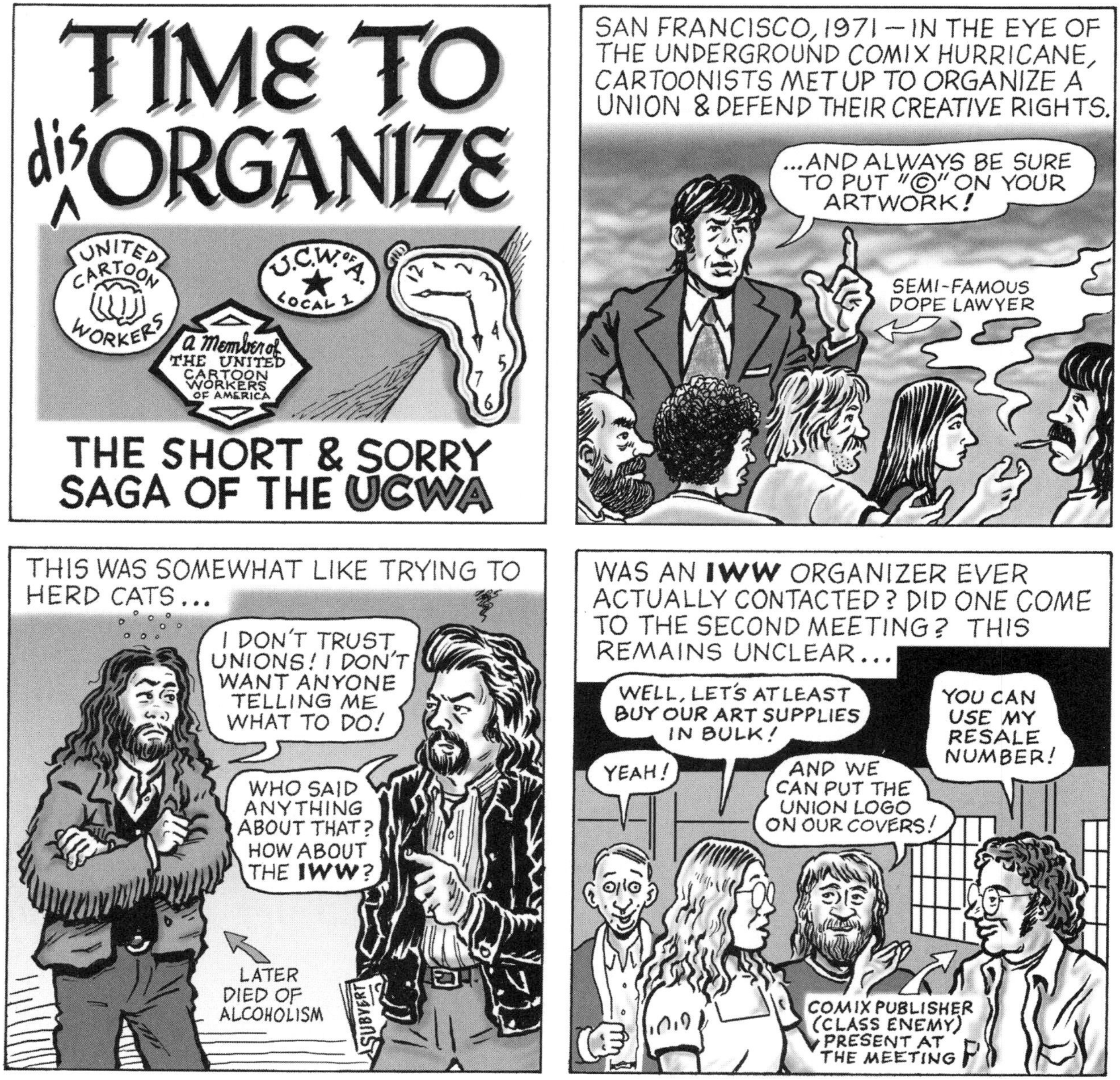
TIME TO disORGANIZE
UNITED CARTOON WORKERS
U.C.W. of A. LOCAL 1
a Member of THE UNITED CARTOON WORKERS OF AMERICA
THE SHORT & SORRY SAGA OF THE UCWA
SAN FRANCISCO, 1971 — IN THE EYE OF THE UNDERGROUND COMIX HURRICANE, CARTOONISTS MET UP TO ORGANIZE A UNION & DEFEND THEIR CREATIVE RIGHTS.
...AND ALWAYS BE SURE TO PUT "©" ON YOUR ARTWORK!
SEMI-FAMOUS DOPE LAWYER
THIS WAS SOMEWHAT LIKE TRYING TO HERD CATS...
I DON'T TRUST UNIONS! I DON'T WANT ANYONE TELLING ME WHAT TO DO!
WHO SAID ANYTHING ABOUT THAT? HOW ABOUT THE IWW?
LATER DIED OF ALCOHOLISM
SUBVERT
WAS AN IWW ORGANIZER EVER ACTUALLY CONTACTED? DID ONE COME TO THE SECOND MEETING? THIS REMAINS UNCLEAR...
YEAH!
WELL, LET'S AT LEAST BUY OUR ART SUPPLIES IN BULK!
AND WE CAN PUT THE UNION LOGO ON OUR COVERS!
YOU CAN USE MY RESALE NUMBER!
COMIX PUBLISHER (CLASS ENEMY) PRESENT AT THE MEETING

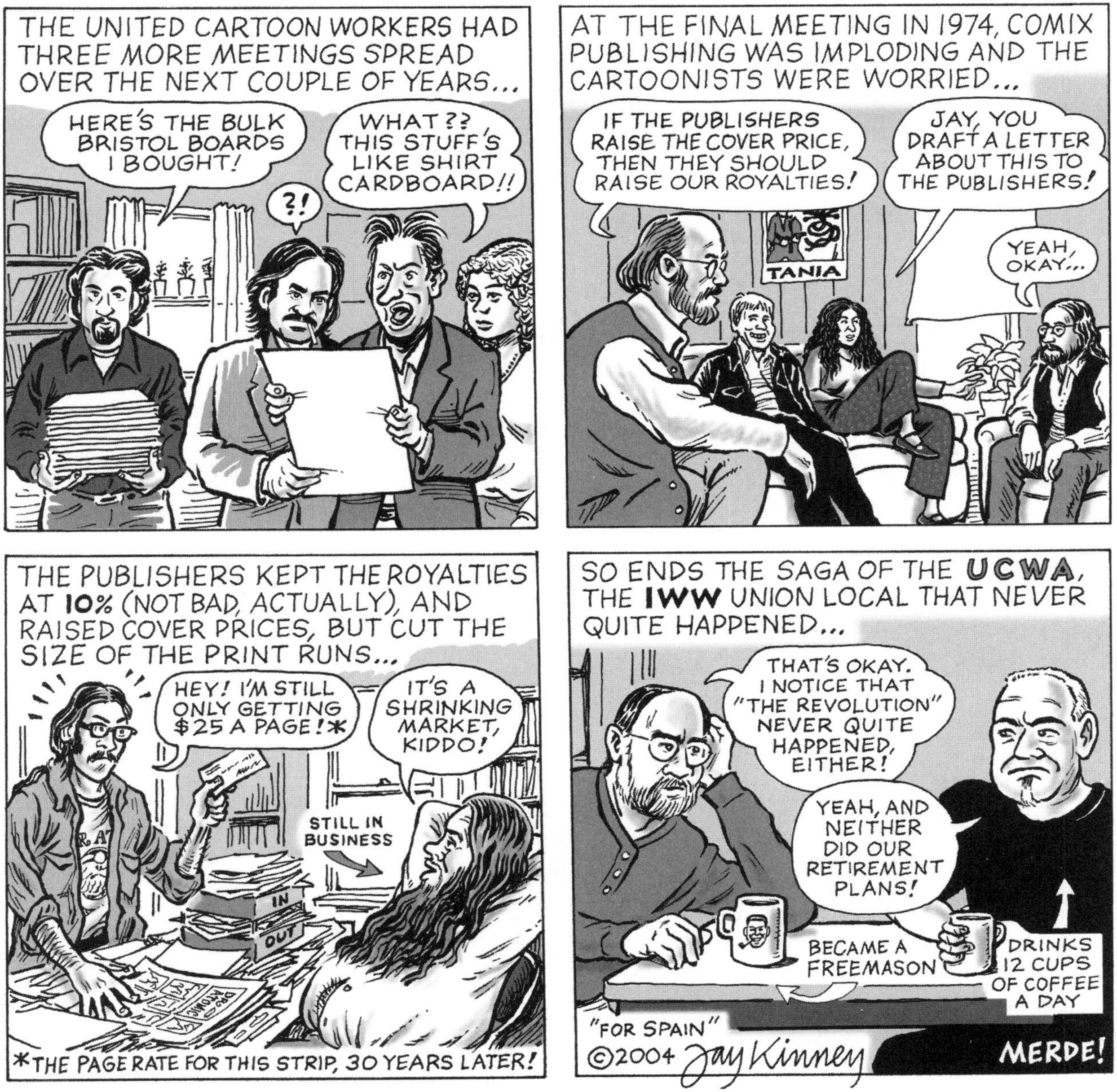
THE UNITED CARTOON WORKERS HAD THREE MORE MEETINGS SPREAD OVER THE NEXT COUPLE OF YEARS...
HERE'S THE BULK BRISTOL BOARDS I BOUGHT!
?!
WHAT?? THIS STUFF'S LIKE SHIRT CARDBOARD!!
AT THE FINAL MEETING IN 1974, COMIX PUBLISHING WAS IMPLODING AND THE CARTOONISTS WERE WORRIED...
IF THE PUBLISHERS RAISE THE COVER PRICE, THEN THEY SHOULD RAISE OUR ROYALTIES!
JAY, YOU DRAFT A LETTER ABOUT THIS TO THE PUBLISHERS!
TANIA
YEAH, OKAY...
THE PUBLISHERS KEPT THE ROYALTIES AT 10% (NOT BAD, ACTUALLY), AND RAISED COVER PRICES, BUT CUT THE SIZE OF THE PRINT RUNS...
HEY! I'M STILL ONLY GETTING $25 A PAGE!*
IT'S A SHRINKING MARKET, KIDDO!
STILL IN BUSINESS
IN
OUT
*THE PAGE RATE FOR THIS STRIP, 30 YEARS LATER!
SO ENDS THE SAGA OF THE UCWA, THE IWW UNION LOCAL THAT NEVER QUITE HAPPENED...
THAT'S OKAY. I NOTICE THAT "THE REVOLUTION" NEVER QUITE HAPPENED, EITHER!
YEAH, AND NEITHER DID OUR RETIREMENT PLANS!
BECAME A FREEMASON
DRINKS 12 CUPS OF COFFEE A DAY
"FOR SPAIN"
©2004 Jay Kinney
MERDE!

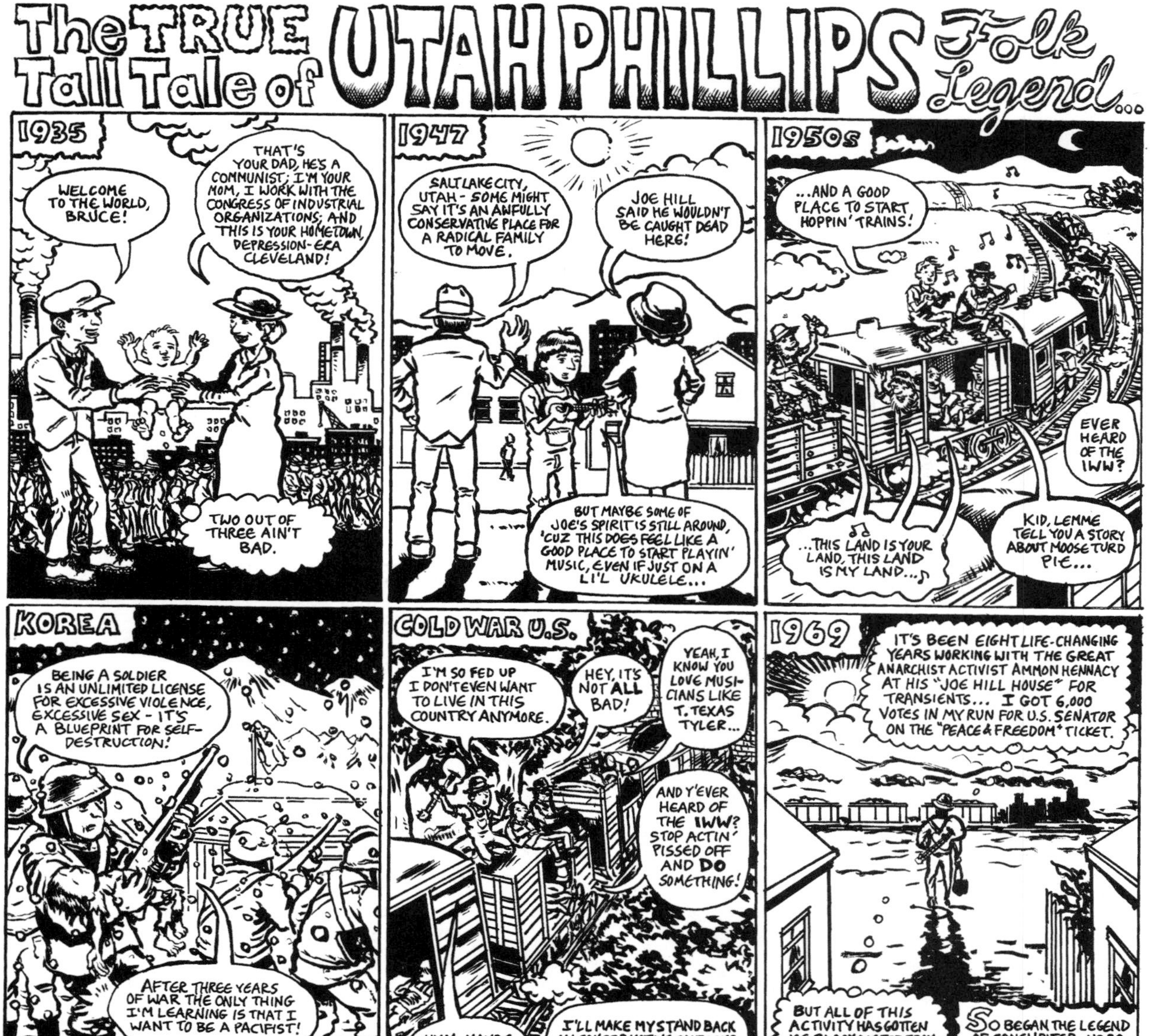
The TRUE Tall Tale of UTAH PHILLIPS Folk Legend...
1935
WELCOME TO THE WORLD, BRUCE!
THAT'S YOUR DAD, HE'S A COMMUNIST; I'M YOUR MOM, I WORK WITH THE CONGRESS OF INDUSTRIAL ORGANIZATIONS; AND THIS IS YOUR HOMETOWN, DEPRESSION-ERA CLEVELAND!
TWO OUT OF THREE AIN'T BAD.
1947
SALT LAKE CITY, UTAH - SOME MIGHT SAY IT'S AN AWFULLY CONSERVATIVE PLACE FOR A RADICAL FAMILY TO MOVE.
JOE HILL SAID HE WOULDN'T BE CAUGHT DEAD HERE!
BUT MAYBE SOME OF JOE'S SPIRIT IS STILL AROUND, 'CUZ THIS DOES FEEL LIKE A GOOD PLACE TO START PLAYIN' MUSIC, EVEN IF JUST ON A LI'L UKULELE...
1950s
...AND A GOOD PLACE TO START HOPPIN' TRAINS!
EVER HEARD OF THE IWW?
...THIS LAND IS YOUR LAND, THIS LAND IS MY LAND...
KID, LEMME TELL YOU A STORY ABOUT MOOSE TURD PIE...
KOREA
BEING A SOLDIER IS AN UNLIMITED LICENSE FOR EXCESSIVE VIOLENCE, EXCESSIVE SEX - IT'S A BLUEPRINT FOR SELF-DESTRUCTION!
AFTER THREE YEARS OF WAR THE ONLY THING I'M LEARNING IS THAT I WANT TO BE A PACIFIST!
COLD WAR U.S.
I'M SO FED UP I DON'T EVEN WANT TO LIVE IN THIS COUNTRY ANYMORE.
HEY, IT'S NOT ALL BAD!
YEAH, I KNOW YOU LOVE MUSICIANS LIKE T. TEXAS TYLER...
AND Y'EVER HEARD OF THE IWW? STOP ACTIN' PISSED OFF AND DO SOMETHING!
HMM, MAYBE I WILL...
I'LL MAKE MY STAND BACK IN CONSERVATIVE SALT LAKE... (AND THE NAME "U. UTAH" HAS A NICE RING TO IT...)
1969
IT'S BEEN EIGHT LIFE-CHANGING YEARS WORKING WITH THE GREAT ANARCHIST ACTIVIST AMMON HENNACY AT HIS "JOE HILL HOUSE" FOR TRANSIENTS... I GOT 6,000 VOTES IN MY RUN FOR U.S. SENATOR ON THE "PEACE & FREEDOM" TICKET.
BUT ALL OF THIS ACTIVITY HAS GOTTEN ME BLACKLISTED FROM MY JOB HERE IN UTAH... TIME TO TRAVEL ON.
SO BEGAN THE LEGEND OF SONGWRITER, HOBO, STORYTELLER, ACTIVIST UTAH PHILLIPS, "THE GOLDEN VOICE OF THE GREAT SOUTHWEST"

...AND 21st Century Wobbly

JEFFREY LEWIS '04

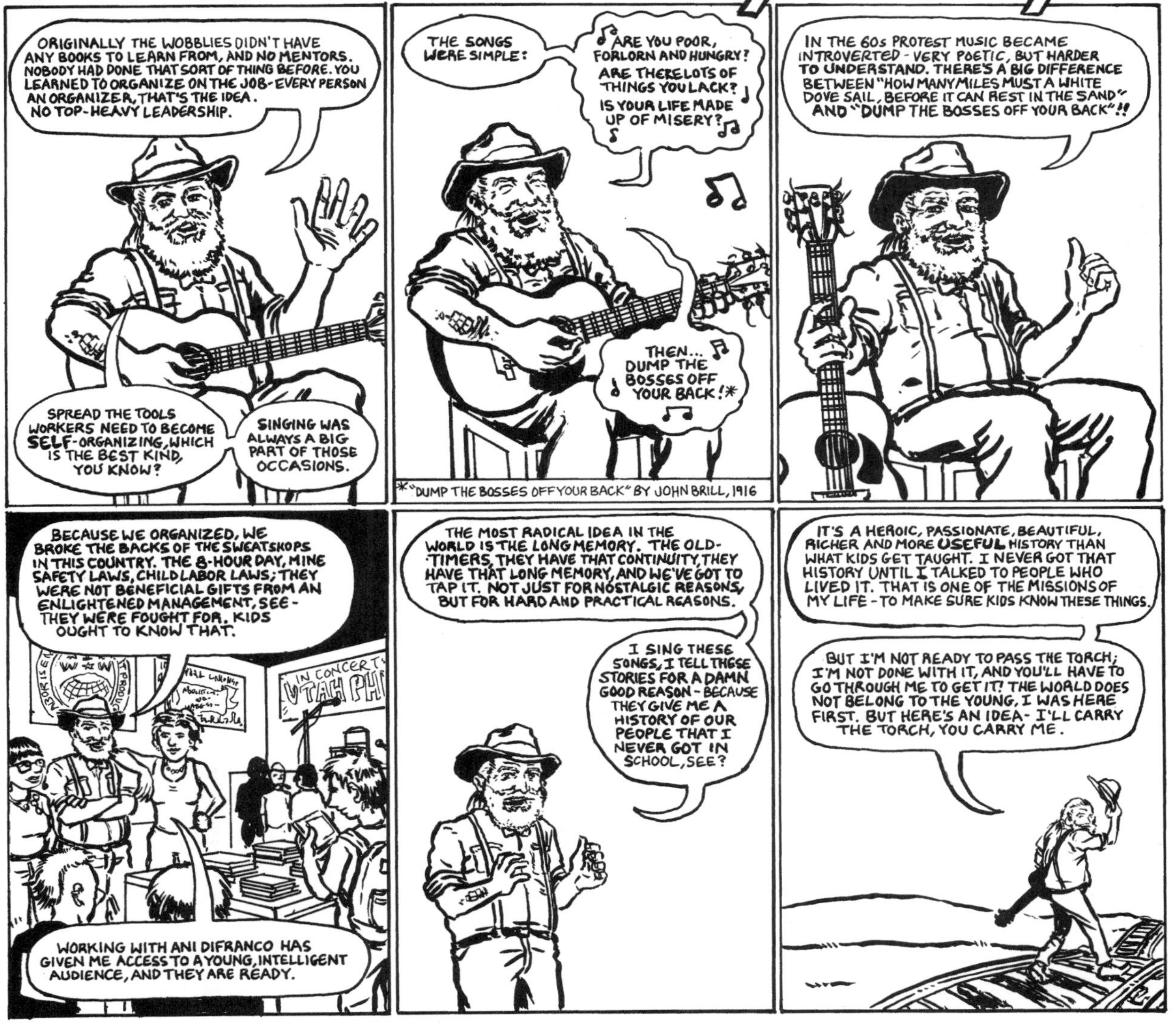

ORIGINALLY THE WOBBLIES DIDN'T HAVE ANY BOOKS TO LEARN FROM, AND NO MENTORS. NOBODY HAD DONE THAT SORT OF THING BEFORE. YOU LEARNED TO ORGANIZE ON THE JOB - EVERY PERSON AN ORGANIZER, THAT'S THE IDEA. NO TOP-HEAVY LEADERSHIP.
SPREAD THE TOOLS WORKERS NEED TO BECOME SELF-ORGANIZING, WHICH IS THE BEST KIND, YOU KNOW?
SINGING WAS ALWAYS A BIG PART OF THOSE OCCASIONS.
THE SONGS WERE SIMPLE:
ARE YOU POOR, FORLORN AND HUNGRY? ARE THERE LOTS OF THINGS YOU LACK? IS YOUR LIFE MADE UP OF MISERY?
THEN... DUMP THE BOSSES OFF YOUR BACK!*
* "DUMP THE BOSSES OFF YOUR BACK" BY JOHN BRILL, 1916
IN THE 60s PROTEST MUSIC BECAME INTROVERTED - VERY POETIC, BUT HARDER TO UNDERSTAND. THERE'S A BIG DIFFERENCE BETWEEN "HOW MANY MILES MUST A WHITE DOVE SAIL, BEFORE IT CAN REST IN THE SAND" AND "DUMP THE BOSSES OFF YOUR BACK"!!
BECAUSE WE ORGANIZED, WE BROKE THE BACKS OF THE SWEATSHOPS IN THIS COUNTRY. THE 8-HOUR DAY, MINE SAFETY LAWS, CHILD LABOR LAWS; THEY WERE NOT BENEFICIAL GIFTS FROM AN ENLIGHTENED MANAGEMENT, SEE - THEY WERE FOUGHT FOR. KIDS OUGHT TO KNOW THAT.
IN CONCERT
UTAH PHI
WORKING WITH ANI DIFRANCO HAS GIVEN ME ACCESS TO A YOUNG, INTELLIGENT AUDIENCE, AND THEY ARE READY.
THE MOST RADICAL IDEA IN THE WORLD IS THE LONG MEMORY. THE OLD-TIMERS, THEY HAVE THAT CONTINUITY, THEY HAVE THAT LONG MEMORY, AND WE'VE GOT TO TAP IT. NOT JUST FOR NOSTALGIC REASONS, BUT FOR HARD AND PRACTICAL REASONS.
I SING THESE SONGS, I TELL THESE STORIES FOR A DAMN GOOD REASON - BECAUSE THEY GIVE ME A HISTORY OF OUR PEOPLE THAT I NEVER GOT IN SCHOOL, SEE?
IT'S A HEROIC, PASSIONATE, BEAUTIFUL, RICHER AND MORE USEFUL HISTORY THAN WHAT KIDS GET TAUGHT. I NEVER GOT THAT HISTORY UNTIL I TALKED TO PEOPLE WHO LIVED IT. THAT IS ONE OF THE MISSIONS OF MY LIFE - TO MAKE SURE KIDS KNOW THESE THINGS.
BUT I'M NOT READY TO PASS THE TORCH; I'M NOT DONE WITH IT, AND YOU'LL HAVE TO GO THROUGH ME TO GET IT! THE WORLD DOES NOT BELONG TO THE YOUNG. I WAS HERE FIRST. BUT HERE'S AN IDEA - I'LL CARRY THE TORCH, YOU CARRY ME.

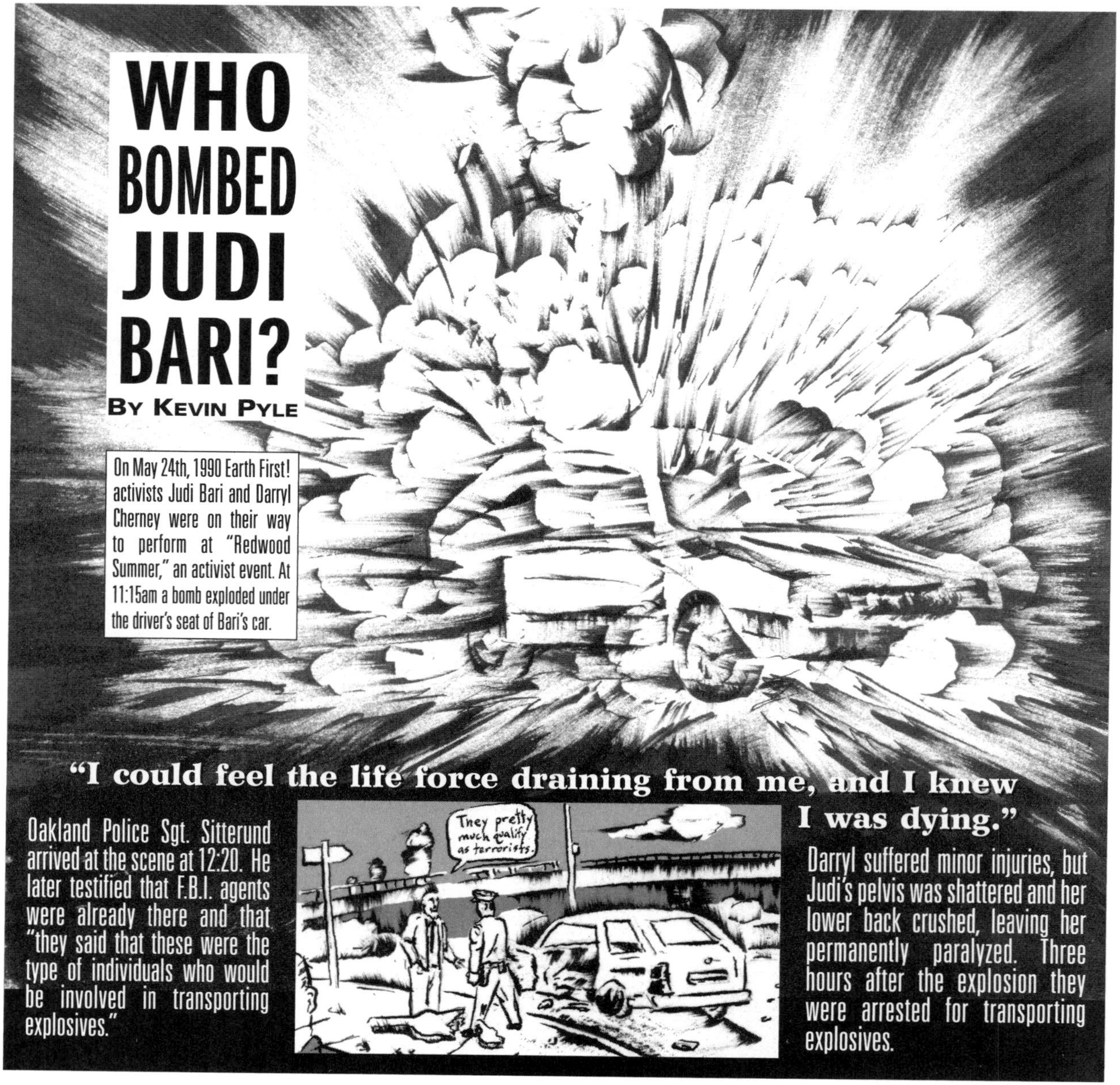
WHO BOMBED JUDI BARI?
BY KEVIN PYLE
On May 24th, 1990 Earth First! activists Judi Bari and Darryl Cherney were on their way to perform at "Redwood Summer," an activist event. At 11:15am a bomb exploded under the driver's seat of Bari's car.
"I could feel the life force draining from me, and I knew I was dying."
Oakland Police Sgt. Sitterund arrived at the scene at 12:20. He later testified that F.B.I. agents were already there and that "they said that these were the type of individuals who would be involved in transporting explosives."
They pretty much qualify as terrorists.
Darryl suffered minor injuries, but Judi's pelvis was shattered and her lower back crushed, leaving her permanently paralyzed. Three hours after the explosion they were arrested for transporting explosives.

Since 1988 Judi had been the contact person for Earth First! in Mendocino County, establishing herself as an effective and inspirational activist .

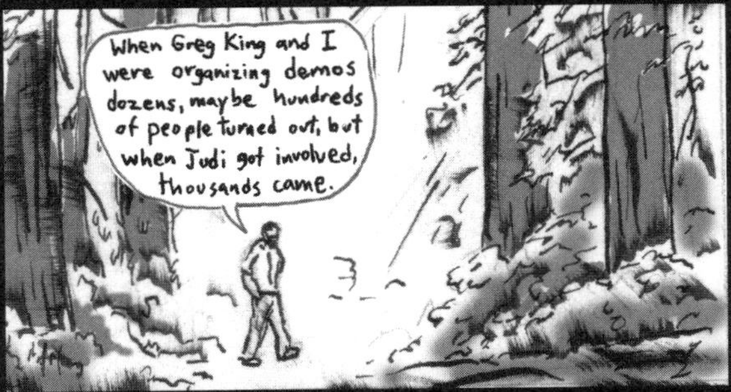
When Greg King and I were organizing demos dozens, maybe hundreds of people turned out, but when Judi got involved, thousands came.

She pushed for Earth First! to embrace non-violent direct action and to renounce the use of tree-spiking or any other tactic that could lead to injuries to timber and mill workers.

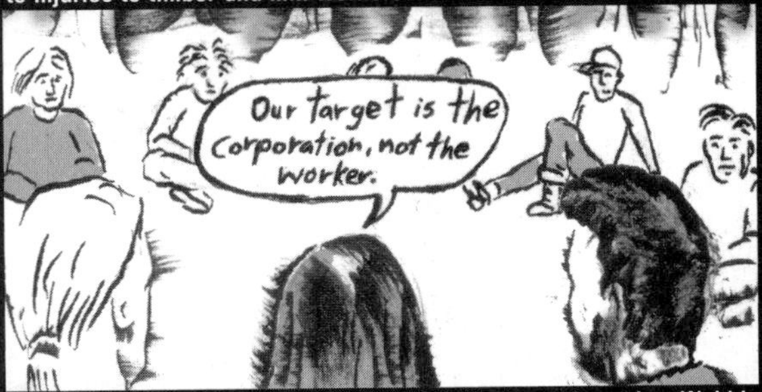
Our target is the corporation, not the worker.

In 1989 Judi joined an effort to support sawmill workers exposed to PCBs. She helped organize them into Local #1 of the IWW and win their case in U.S. Labor Court.

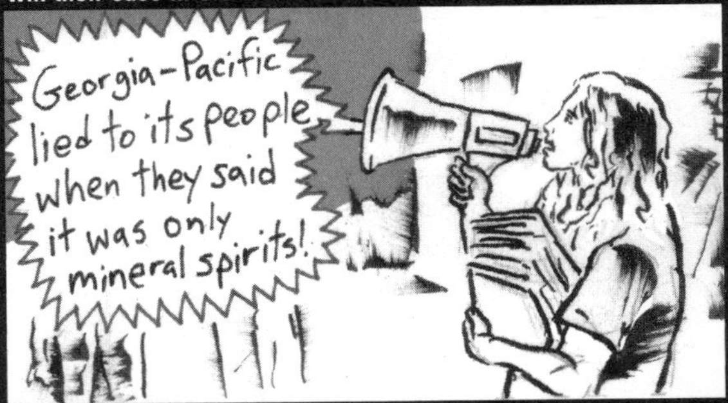
Georgia-Pacific lied to its people when they said it was only mineral spirits!

She wrote an article for the Industrial Worker advocating Wobbly organizing among timber workers and began speaking publicly about the link between unsustainable overcutting and worker layoffs.

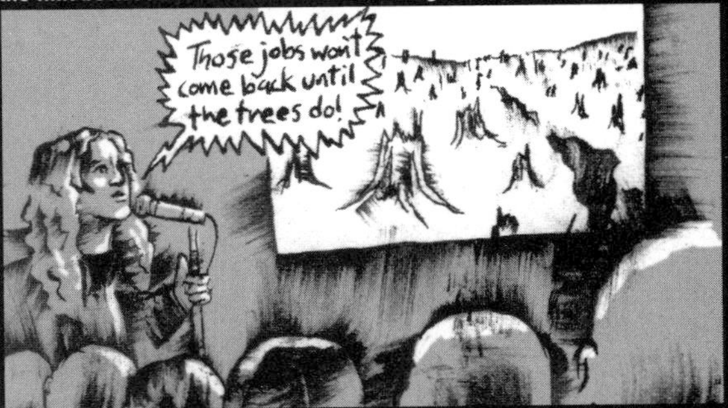
Those jobs won't come back until the trees do!

In August of 1989 Judi's car was rammed from behind by a logging truck she had helped blockade less than 24 hours earlier. No investigation followed.

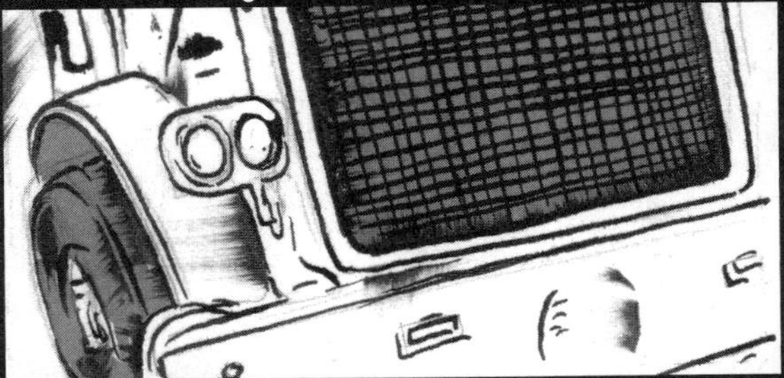

In the month prior to the bombing fake press releases falsely linking Earth First! to terrorism began surfacing in Mendecino. Judi received numerous death threats.

image from letter received by Judi

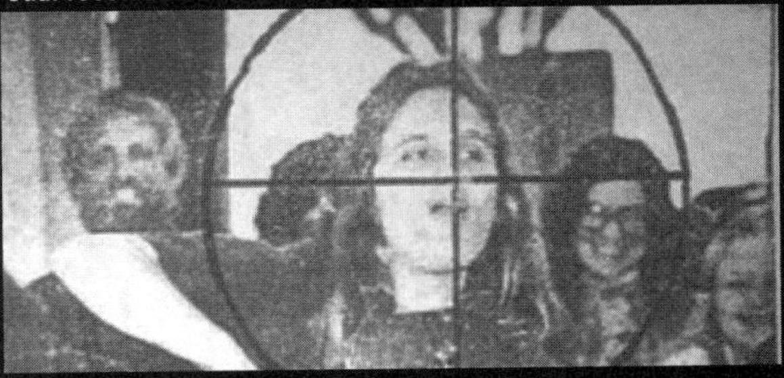

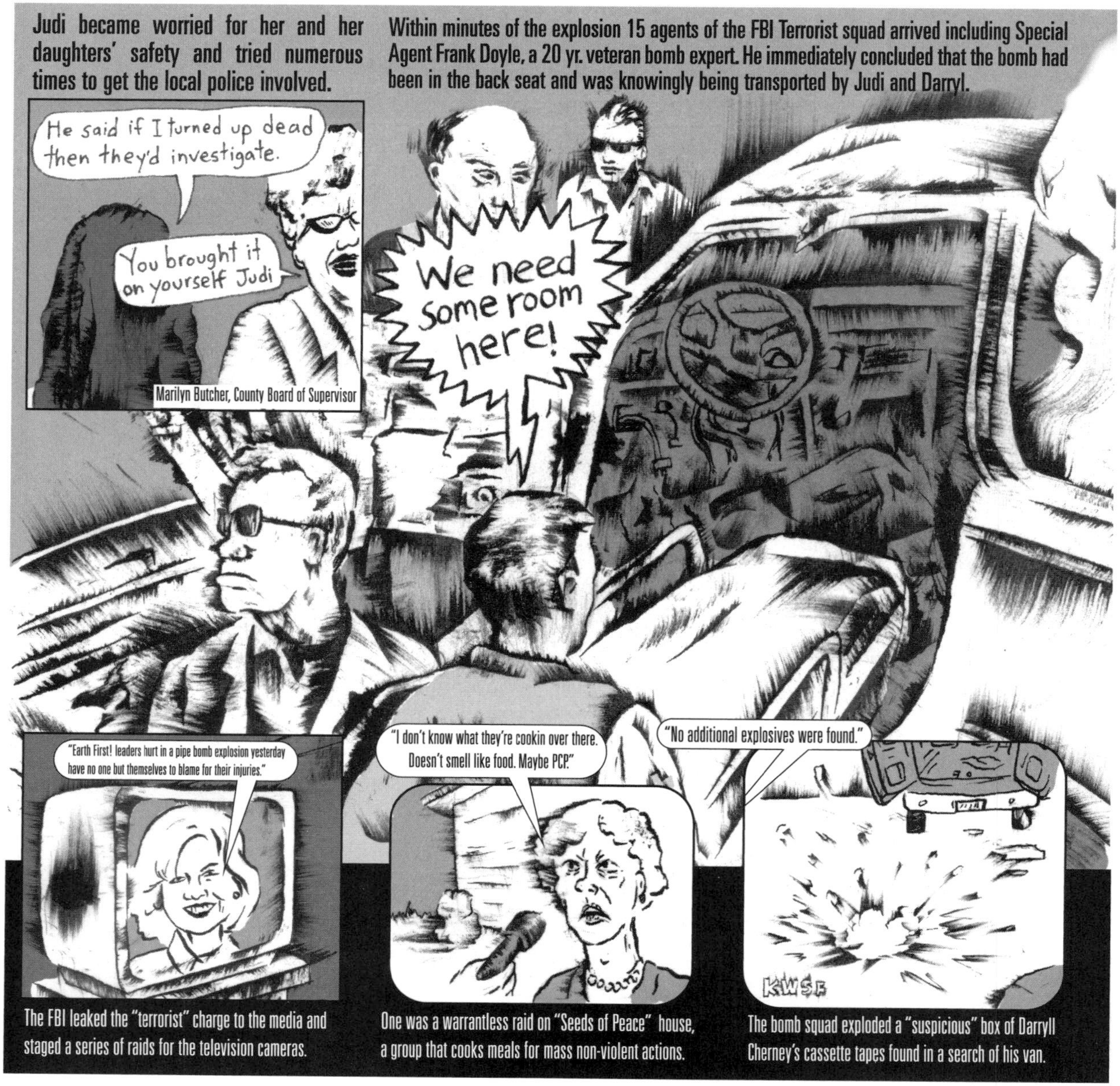

Judi became worried for her and her daughters' safety and tried numerous times to get the local police involved.
He said if I turned up dead then they'd investigate.
You brought it on yourself Judi
Marilyn Butcher, County Board of Supervisor
Within minutes of the explosion 15 agents of the FBI Terrorist squad arrived including Special Agent Frank Doyle, a 20 yr. veteran bomb expert. He immediately concluded that the bomb had been in the back seat and was knowingly being transported by Judi and Darryl.
We need some room here!
"Earth First! leaders hurt in a pipe bomb explosion yesterday have no one but themselves to blame for their injuries."
The FBI leaked the "terrorist" charge to the media and staged a series of raids for the television cameras.
"I don't know what they're cookin over there. Doesn't smell like food. Maybe PCP."
One was a warrantless raid on "Seeds of Peace" house, a group that cooks meals for mass non-violent actions.
"No additional explosives were found."
KWSF
The bomb squad exploded a "suspicious" box of Darryll Cherney's cassette tapes found in a search of his van.

The FBI attempted to link Judi and Darryl to a bomb exploded at the Cloverdale Sawmill two weeks before. The FBI crime lab in Washington was able to show that the two bombs were made with the same material but none of that matched the materials seized from Judi and Darryl's homes.

FBI Special Agent David Williams in Washington considered the bomb in Judi's car complex and well-crafted and concluded that it had clearly been placed under the front seat, not in the back as Agent Doyle had claimed.

SA Williams also said the recovered materials obviously indicated a booby trap device triggered by the motion of the car. This was noted and later crossed out on Judi's original arrest warrant.

pocketwatch
(second hand removed)
100 volt socket
drill holes
CAP
ball bearing
battery
looped wires
fill pipe w/gunpowder
wrap pipe w/nails & duck tape
PIPE
CAP
2"

In the eight weeks following the bombing the Oakland DA attempted to bring charges against Judi and Darryl three times. Each time they were turned away by the court for lack of evidence. After the third denial the charges were dropped.

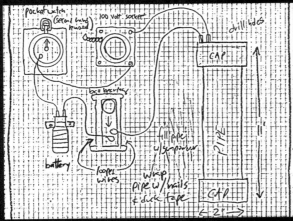

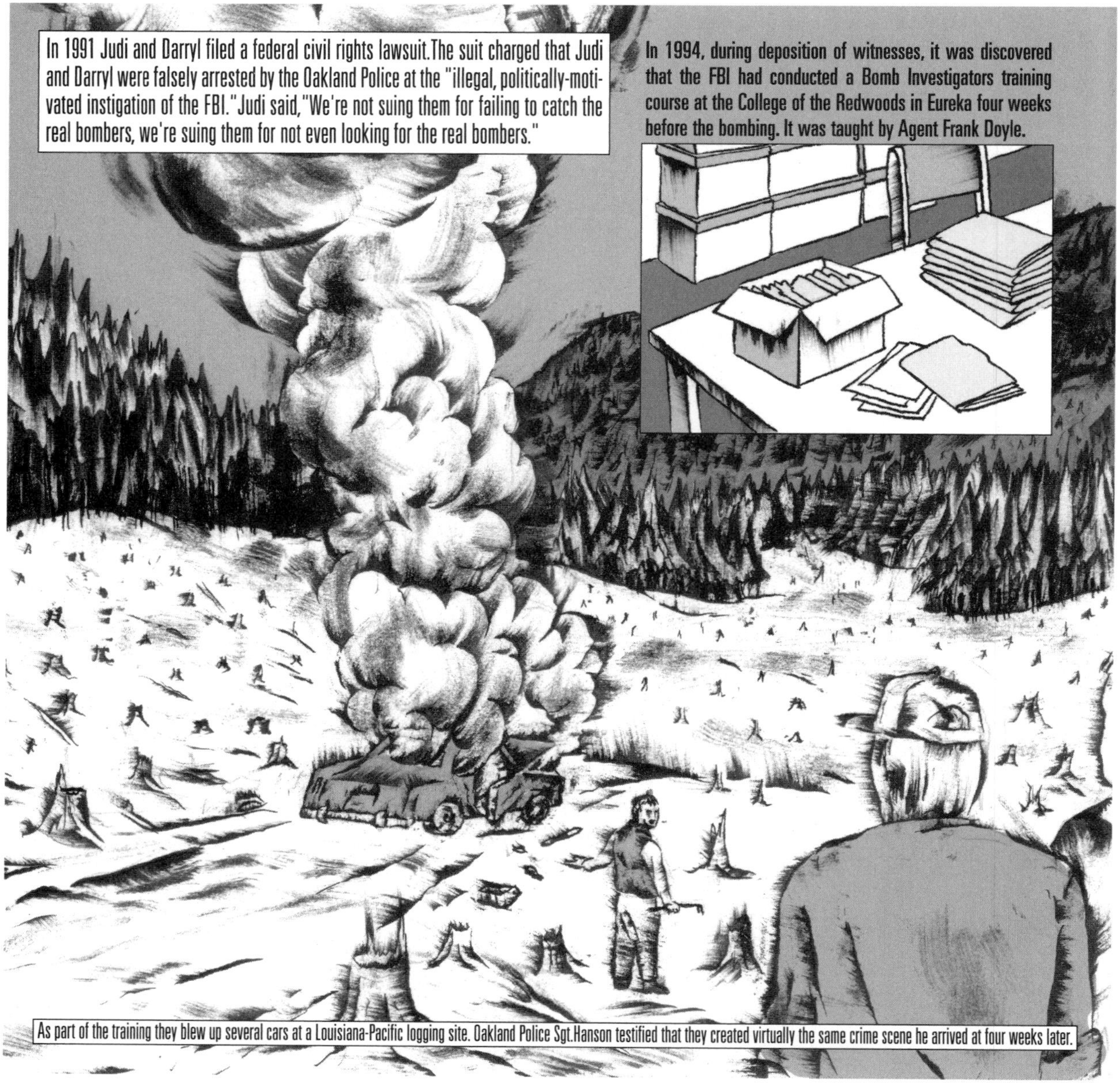
In 1991 Judi and Darryl filed a federal civil rights lawsuit.The suit charged that Judi and Darryl were falsely arrested by the Oakland Police at the "illegal, politically-motivated instigation of the FBI." Judi said,"We're not suing them for failing to catch the real bombers, we're suing them for not even looking for the real bombers."
In 1994, during deposition of witnesses, it was discovered that the FBI had conducted a Bomb Investigators training course at the College of the Redwoods in Eureka four weeks before the bombing. It was taught by Agent Frank Doyle.
As part of the training they blew up several cars at a Louisiana-Pacific logging site. Oakland Police Sgt.Hanson testified that they created virtually the same crime scene he arrived at four weeks later.

The course also focused on incendiary bombs like the one used in the Cloverdale Sawmill bombing, which occurred two weeks after the training. The FBI has claimed to have lost the roster of students attending the course.

The lawsuit also forced public release of the photos of Judi's car which clearly showed that the bomb exploded directly under the driver's seat. Richard Held, the FBI Special Agent in charge of the San Francisco office at the time of the bombing, resigned soon thereafter.

Hole left by bomb

Held had headed FBI operations to disrupt the Black Panther Party (BPP) and American Indian Movement (AIM) under the FBI code name COINTELPRO in the '60s and '70s. It was these operations that resulted in the imprisonment of BPP leader Geronimo Ji Jaga (Pratt) and AIM activist Leonard Peltier.

Though partially paralyzed and in constant pain, Judi continued to organize non-violent direct action against logging interests. "They bombed the wrong end of me."

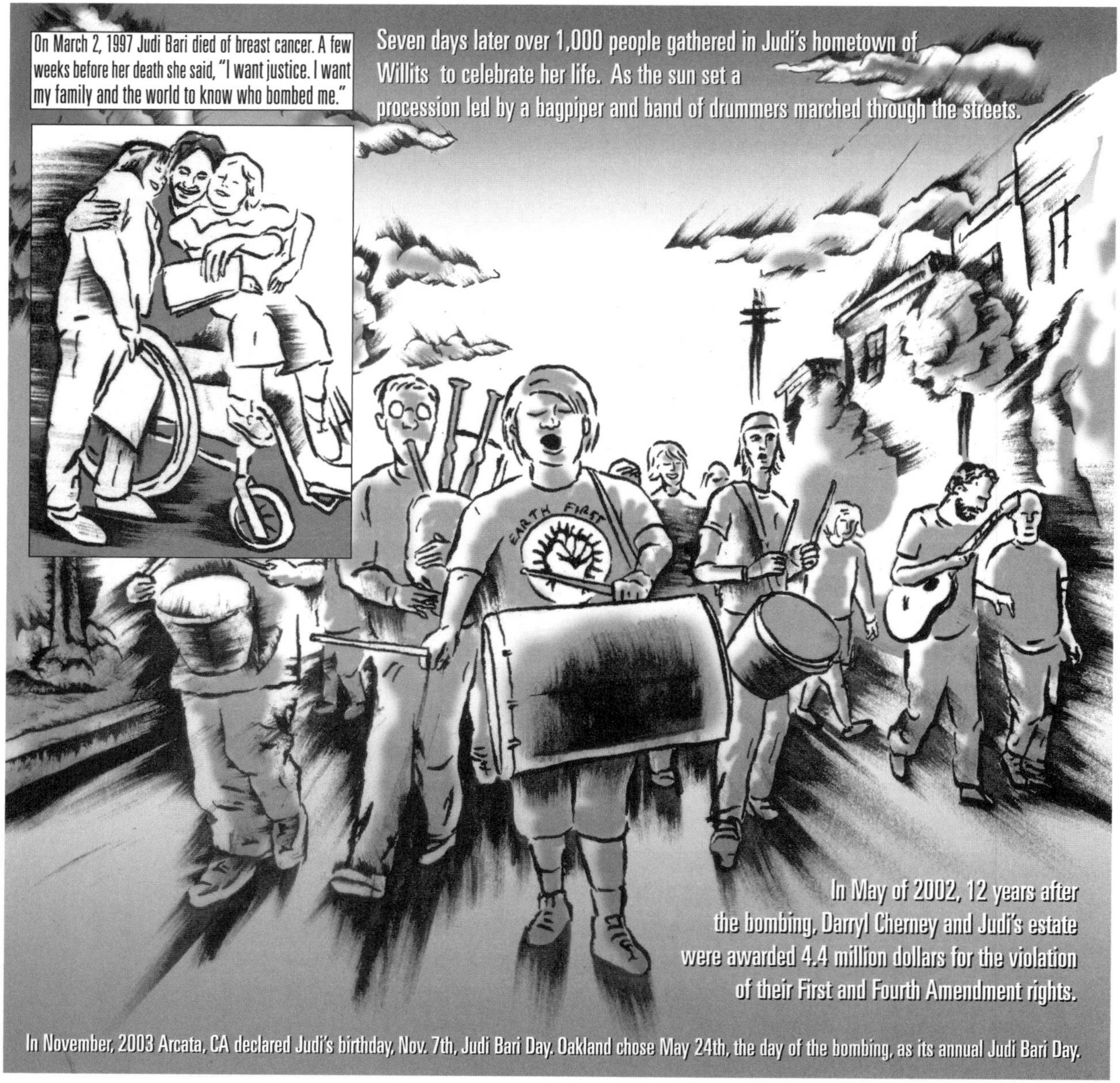
On March 2, 1997 Judi Bari died of breast cancer. A few weeks before her death she said, "I want justice. I want my family and the world to know who bombed me."
Seven days later over 1,000 people gathered in Judi's hometown of Willits to celebrate her life. As the sun set a procession led by a bagpiper and band of drummers marched through the streets.
EARTH FIRST
In May of 2002, 12 years after the bombing, Darryl Cherney and Judi's estate were awarded 4.4 million dollars for the violation of their First and Fourth Amendment rights.
In November, 2003 Arcata, CA declared Judi's birthday, Nov. 7th, Judi Bari Day. Oakland chose May 24th, the day of the bombing, as its annual Judi Bari Day.

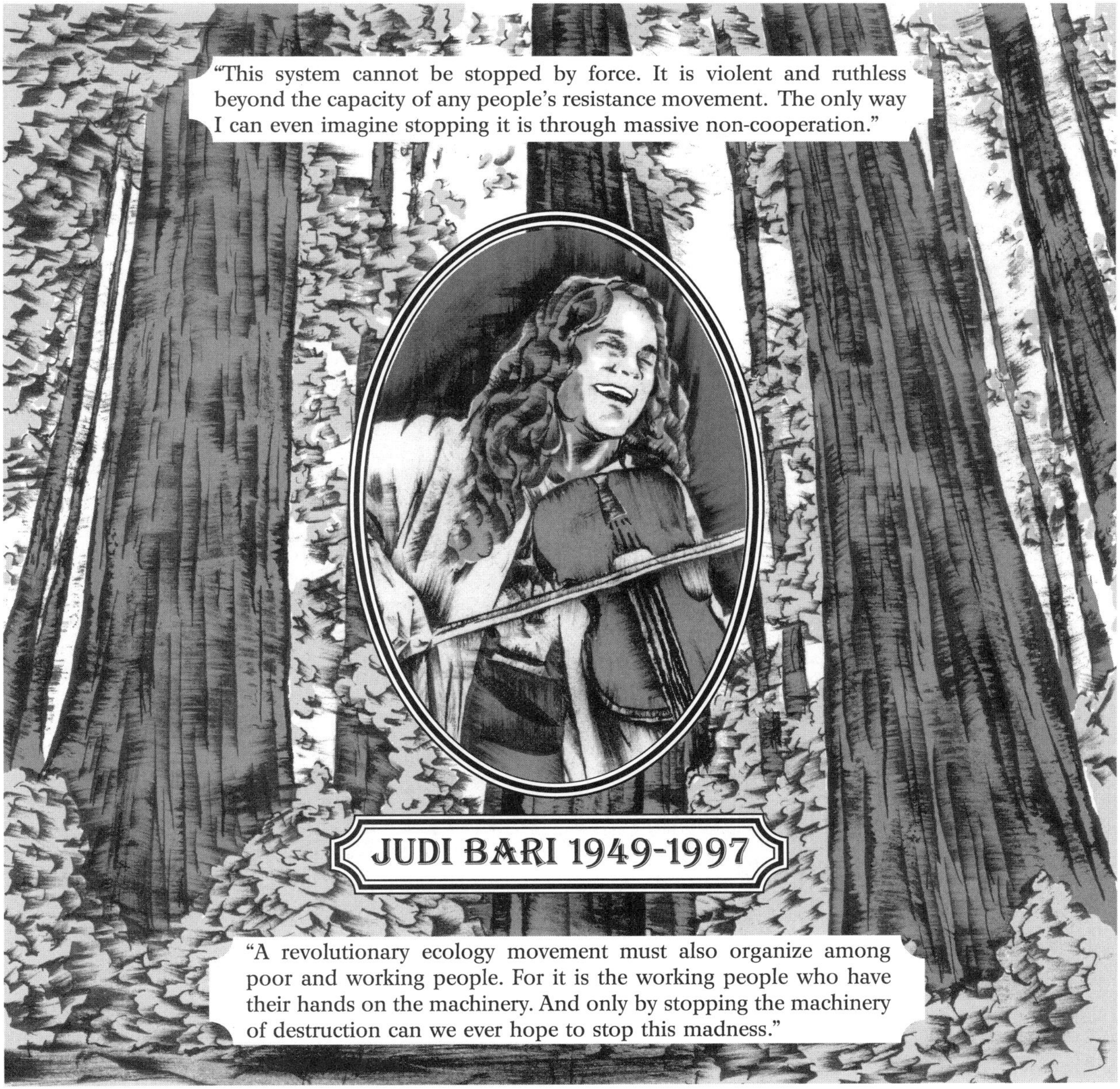
"This system cannot be stopped by force. It is violent and ruthless beyond the capacity of any people's resistance movement. The only way I can even imagine stopping it is through massive non-cooperation."
JUDI BARI 1949-1997
"A revolutionary ecology movement must also organize among poor and working people. For it is the working people who have their hands on the machinery. And only by stopping the machinery of destruction can we ever hope to stop this madness."

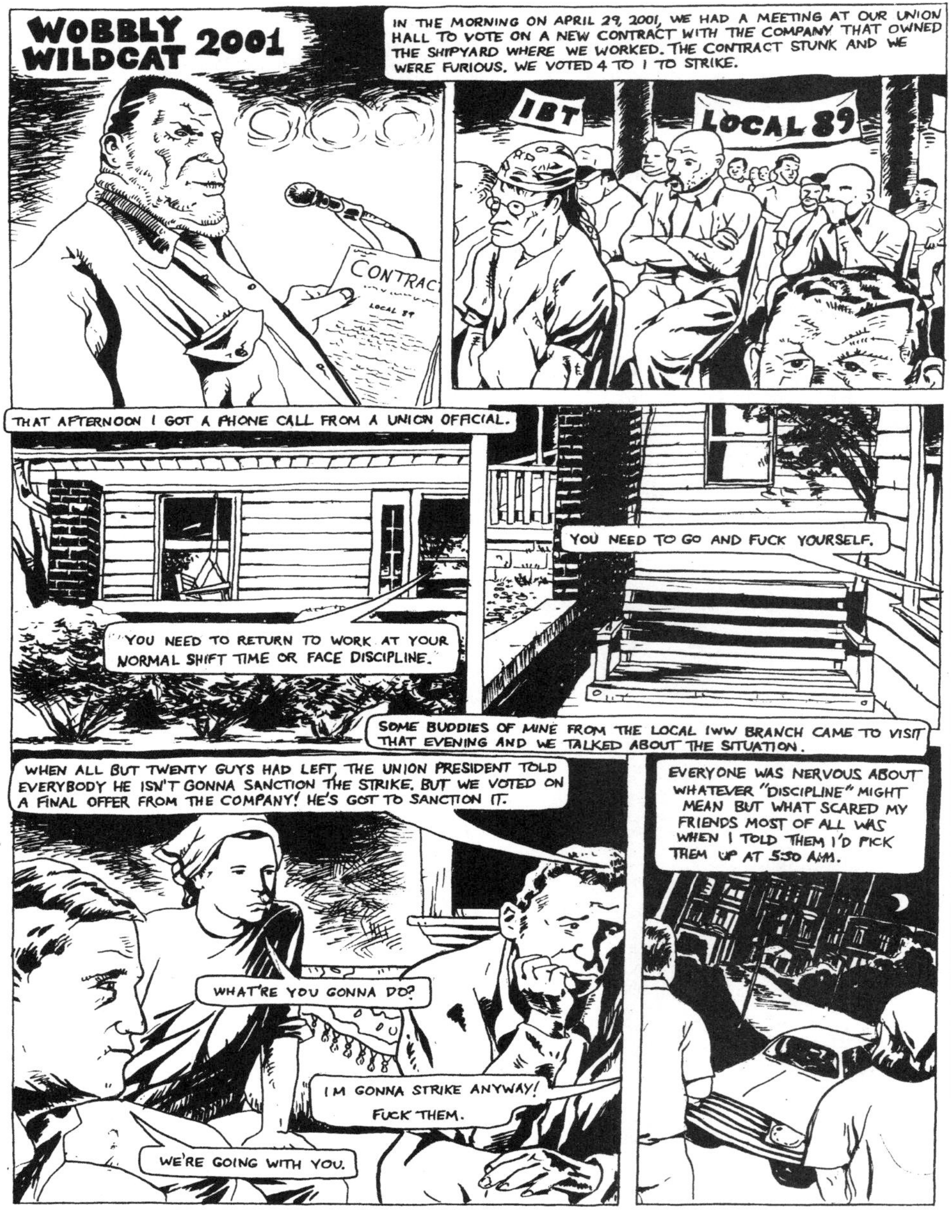
WOBBLY WILDCAT 2001
IN THE MORNING ON APRIL 29, 2001, WE HAD A MEETING AT OUR UNION HALL TO VOTE ON A NEW CONTRACT WITH THE COMPANY THAT OWNED THE SHIPYARD WHERE WE WORKED. THE CONTRACT STUNK AND WE WERE FURIOUS. WE VOTED 4 TO 1 TO STRIKE.
CONTRACT
LOCAL 89
IBT
LOCAL 89
WHEN ALL BUT TWENTY GUYS HAD LEFT, THE UNION PRESIDENT TOLD EVERYBODY HE ISN'T GONNA SANCTION THE STRIKE. BUT WE VOTED ON A FINAL OFFER FROM THE COMPANY! HE'S GOT TO SANCTION IT.
THAT AFTERNOON I GOT A PHONE CALL FROM A UNION OFFICIAL.
YOU NEED TO RETURN TO WORK AT YOUR NORMAL SHIFT TIME OR FACE DISCIPLINE.
YOU NEED TO GO AND FUCK YOURSELF.
SOME BUDDIES OF MINE FROM THE LOCAL IWW BRANCH CAME TO VISIT THAT EVENING AND WE TALKED ABOUT THE SITUATION.
WHAT'RE YOU GONNA DO?
I'M GONNA STRIKE ANYWAY! FUCK THEM.
WE'RE GOING WITH YOU.
EVERYONE WAS NERVOUS ABOUT WHATEVER "DISCIPLINE" MIGHT MEAN BUT WHAT SCARED MY FRIENDS MOST OF ALL WAS WHEN I TOLD THEM I'D PICK THEM UP AT 5:30 A.M.

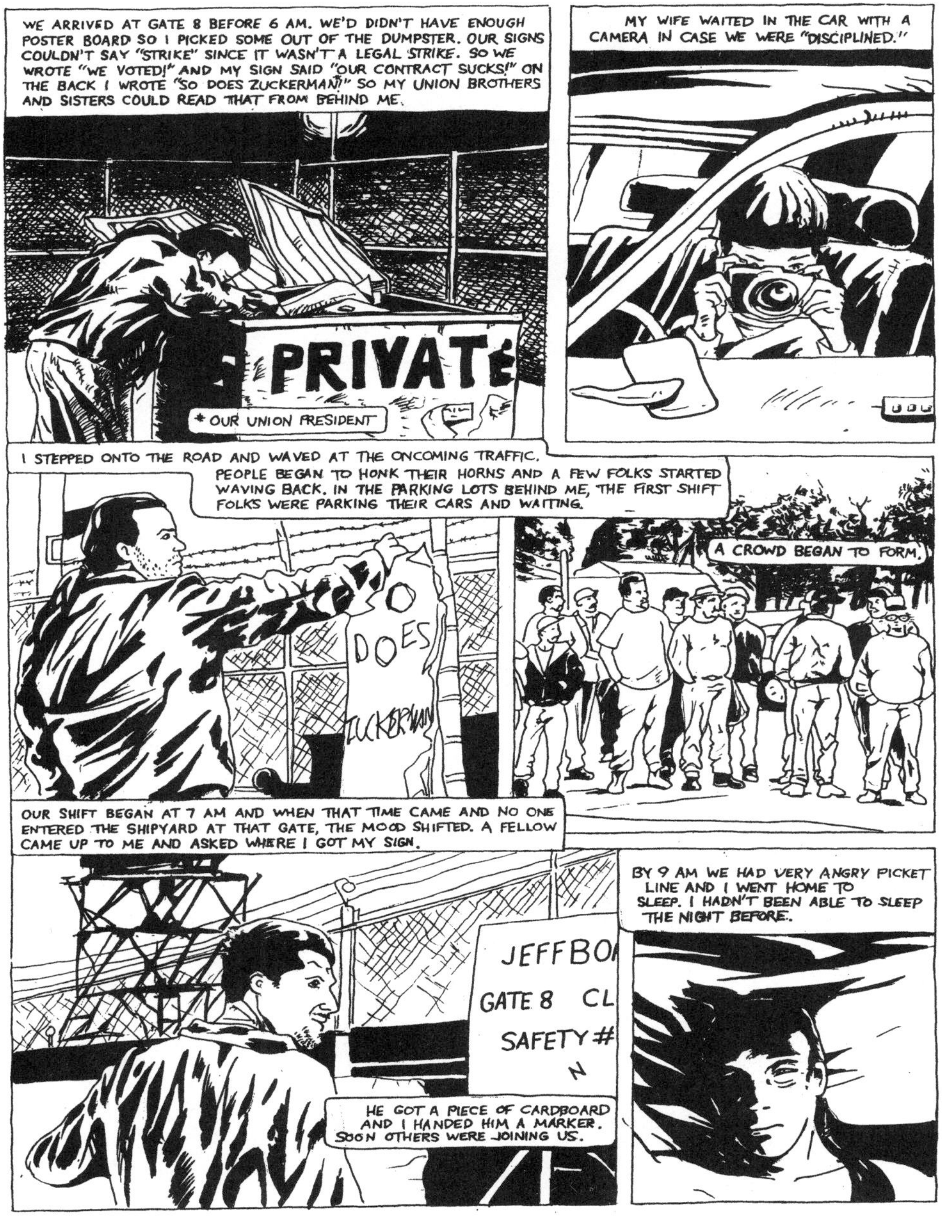
WE ARRIVED AT GATE 8 BEFORE 6 AM. WE'D DIDN'T HAVE ENOUGH POSTER BOARD SO I PICKED SOME OUT OF THE DUMPSTER. OUR SIGNS COULDN'T SAY "STRIKE" SINCE IT WASN'T A LEGAL STRIKE. SO WE WROTE "WE VOTED!" AND MY SIGN SAID "OUR CONTRACT SUCKS!" ON THE BACK I WROTE "SO DOES ZUCKERMAN!*" SO MY UNION BROTHERS AND SISTERS COULD READ THAT FROM BEHIND ME.
PRIVATE
* OUR UNION PRESIDENT
MY WIFE WAITED IN THE CAR WITH A CAMERA IN CASE WE WERE "DISCIPLINED."
I STEPPED ONTO THE ROAD AND WAVED AT THE ONCOMING TRAFFIC.
PEOPLE BEGAN TO HONK THEIR HORNS AND A FEW FOLKS STARTED WAVING BACK. IN THE PARKING LOTS BEHIND ME, THE FIRST SHIFT FOLKS WERE PARKING THEIR CARS AND WAITING.
SO DOES ZUCKERMAN
A CROWD BEGAN TO FORM.
OUR SHIFT BEGAN AT 7 AM AND WHEN THAT TIME CAME AND NO ONE ENTERED THE SHIPYARD AT THAT GATE, THE MOOD SHIFTED. A FELLOW CAME UP TO ME AND ASKED WHERE I GOT MY SIGN.
JEFFBO
GATE 8 CL
SAFETY #
N
HE GOT A PIECE OF CARDBOARD AND I HANDED HIM A MARKER. SOON OTHERS WERE JOINING US.
BY 9 AM WE HAD VERY ANGRY PICKET LINE AND I WENT HOME TO SLEEP. I HADN'T BEEN ABLE TO SLEEP THE NIGHT BEFORE.

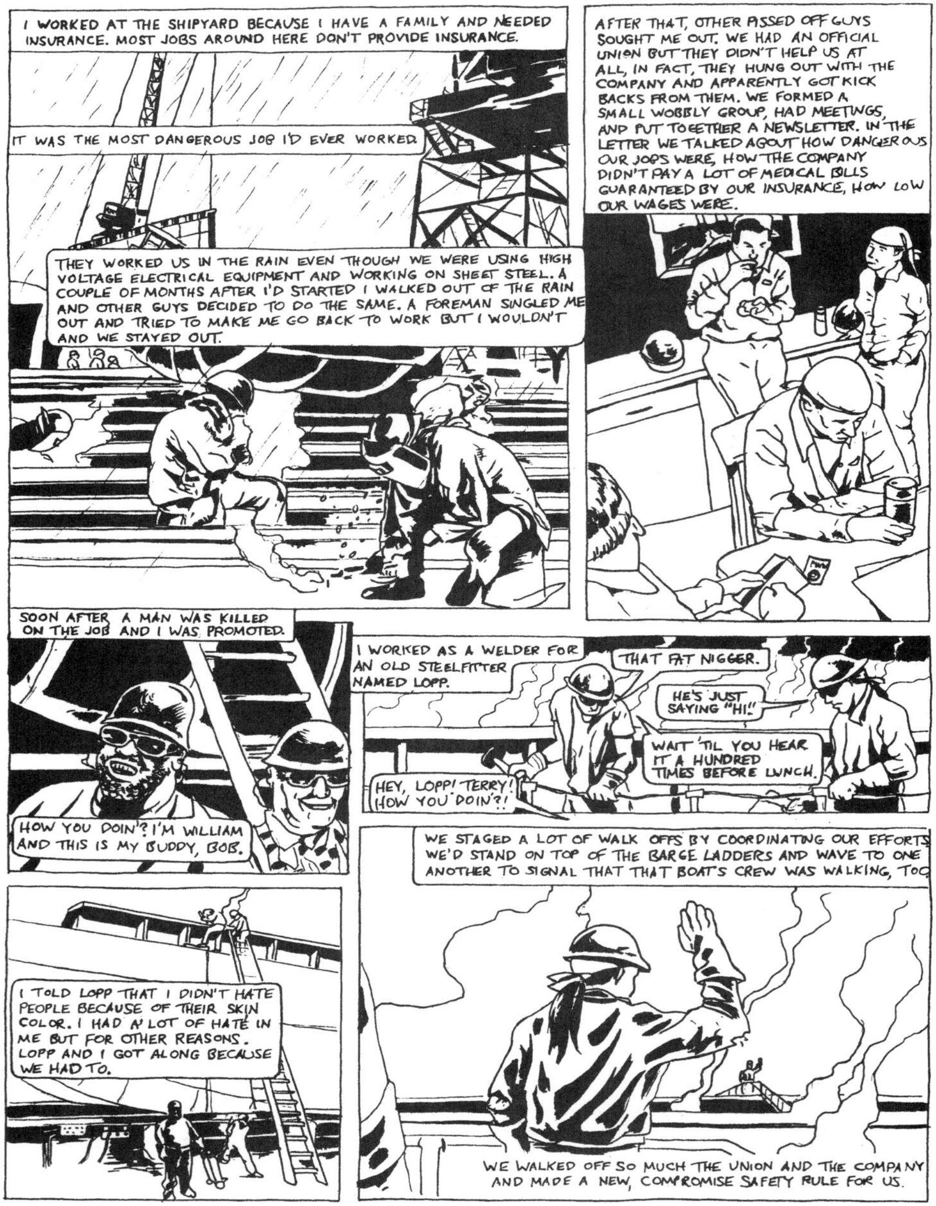
I WORKED AT THE SHIPYARD BECAUSE I HAVE A FAMILY AND NEEDED INSURANCE. MOST JOBS AROUND HERE DON'T PROVIDE INSURANCE.
IT WAS THE MOST DANGEROUS JOB I'D EVER WORKED.
THEY WORKED US IN THE RAIN EVEN THOUGH WE WERE USING HIGH VOLTAGE ELECTRICAL EQUIPMENT AND WORKING ON SHEET STEEL. A COUPLE OF MONTHS AFTER I'D STARTED I WALKED OUT OF THE RAIN AND OTHER GUYS DECIDED TO DO THE SAME. A FOREMAN SINGLED ME OUT AND TRIED TO MAKE ME GO BACK TO WORK BUT I WOULDN'T AND WE STAYED OUT.
AFTER THAT, OTHER PISSED OFF GUYS SOUGHT ME OUT. WE HAD AN OFFICIAL UNION BUT THEY DIDN'T HELP US AT ALL, IN FACT, THEY HUNG OUT WITH THE COMPANY AND APPARENTLY GOT KICK BACKS FROM THEM. WE FORMED A SMALL WOBBLY GROUP, HAD MEETINGS, AND PUT TOGETHER A NEWSLETTER. IN THE LETTER WE TALKED ABOUT HOW DANGEROUS OUR JOBS WERE, HOW THE COMPANY DIDN'T PAY A LOT OF MEDICAL BILLS GUARANTEED BY OUR INSURANCE, HOW LOW OUR WAGES WERE.
SOON AFTER A MAN WAS KILLED ON THE JOB AND I WAS PROMOTED.
HOW YOU DOIN'? I'M WILLIAM AND THIS IS MY BUDDY, BOB.
I WORKED AS A WELDER FOR AN OLD STEELFITTER NAMED LOPP.
THAT FAT NIGGER.
HE'S JUST SAYING "HI!"
WAIT 'TIL YOU HEAR IT A HUNDRED TIMES BEFORE LUNCH.
HEY, LOPP! TERRY! HOW YOU DOIN'?!
I TOLD LOPP THAT I DIDN'T HATE PEOPLE BECAUSE OF THEIR SKIN COLOR. I HAD A LOT OF HATE IN ME BUT FOR OTHER REASONS. LOPP AND I GOT ALONG BECAUSE WE HAD TO.
WE STAGED A LOT OF WALK OFFS BY COORDINATING OUR EFFORTS. WE'D STAND ON TOP OF THE BARGE LADDERS AND WAVE TO ONE ANOTHER TO SIGNAL THAT THAT BOAT'S CREW WAS WALKING, TO
WE WALKED OFF SO MUCH THE UNION AND THE COMPANY AND MADE A NEW, COMPROMISE SAFETY RULE FOR US.

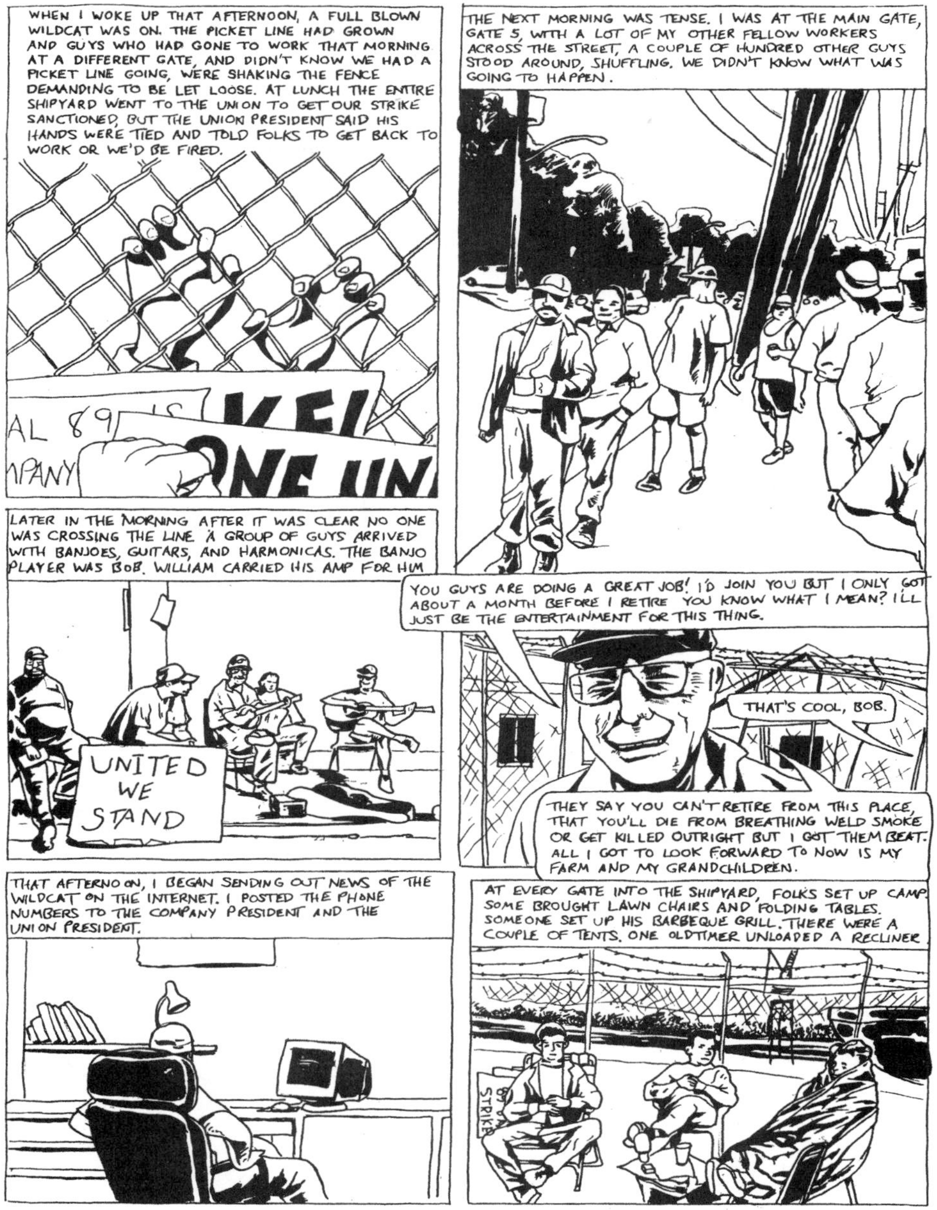
WHEN I WOKE UP THAT AFTERNOON, A FULL BLOWN WILDCAT WAS ON. THE PICKET LINE HAD GROWN AND GUYS WHO HAD GONE TO WORK THAT MORNING AT A DIFFERENT GATE, AND DIDN'T KNOW WE HAD A PICKET LINE GOING, WERE SHAKING THE FENCE DEMANDING TO BE LET LOOSE. AT LUNCH THE ENTIRE SHIPYARD WENT TO THE UNION TO GET OUR STRIKE SANCTIONED, BUT THE UNION PRESIDENT SAID HIS HANDS WERE TIED AND TOLD FOLKS TO GET BACK TO WORK OR WE'D BE FIRED.
THE NEXT MORNING WAS TENSE. I WAS AT THE MAIN GATE, GATE 5, WITH A LOT OF MY OTHER FELLOW WORKERS ACROSS THE STREET, A COUPLE OF HUNDRED OTHER GUYS STOOD AROUND, SHUFFLING. WE DIDN'T KNOW WHAT WAS GOING TO HAPPEN.
LATER IN THE MORNING AFTER IT WAS CLEAR NO ONE WAS CROSSING THE LINE A GROUP OF GUYS ARRIVED WITH BANJOES, GUITARS, AND HARMONICAS. THE BANJO PLAYER WAS BOB. WILLIAM CARRIED HIS AMP FOR HIM
UNITED WE STAND
YOU GUYS ARE DOING A GREAT JOB! I'D JOIN YOU BUT I ONLY GOT ABOUT A MONTH BEFORE I RETIRE YOU KNOW WHAT I MEAN? I'LL JUST BE THE ENTERTAINMENT FOR THIS THING.
THAT'S COOL, BOB.
THEY SAY YOU CAN'T RETIRE FROM THIS PLACE, THAT YOU'LL DIE FROM BREATHING WELD SMOKE OR GET KILLED OUTRIGHT BUT I GOT THEM BEAT. ALL I GOT TO LOOK FORWARD TO NOW IS MY FARM AND MY GRANDCHILDREN.
THAT AFTERNOON, I BEGAN SENDING OUT NEWS OF THE WILDCAT ON THE INTERNET. I POSTED THE PHONE NUMBERS TO THE COMPANY PRESIDENT AND THE UNION PRESIDENT.
AT EVERY GATE INTO THE SHIPYARD, FOLKS SET UP CAMP. SOME BROUGHT LAWN CHAIRS AND FOLDING TABLES. SOMEONE SET UP HIS BARBEQUE GRILL. THERE WERE A COUPLE OF TENTS. ONE OLDTIMER UNLOADED A RECLINER

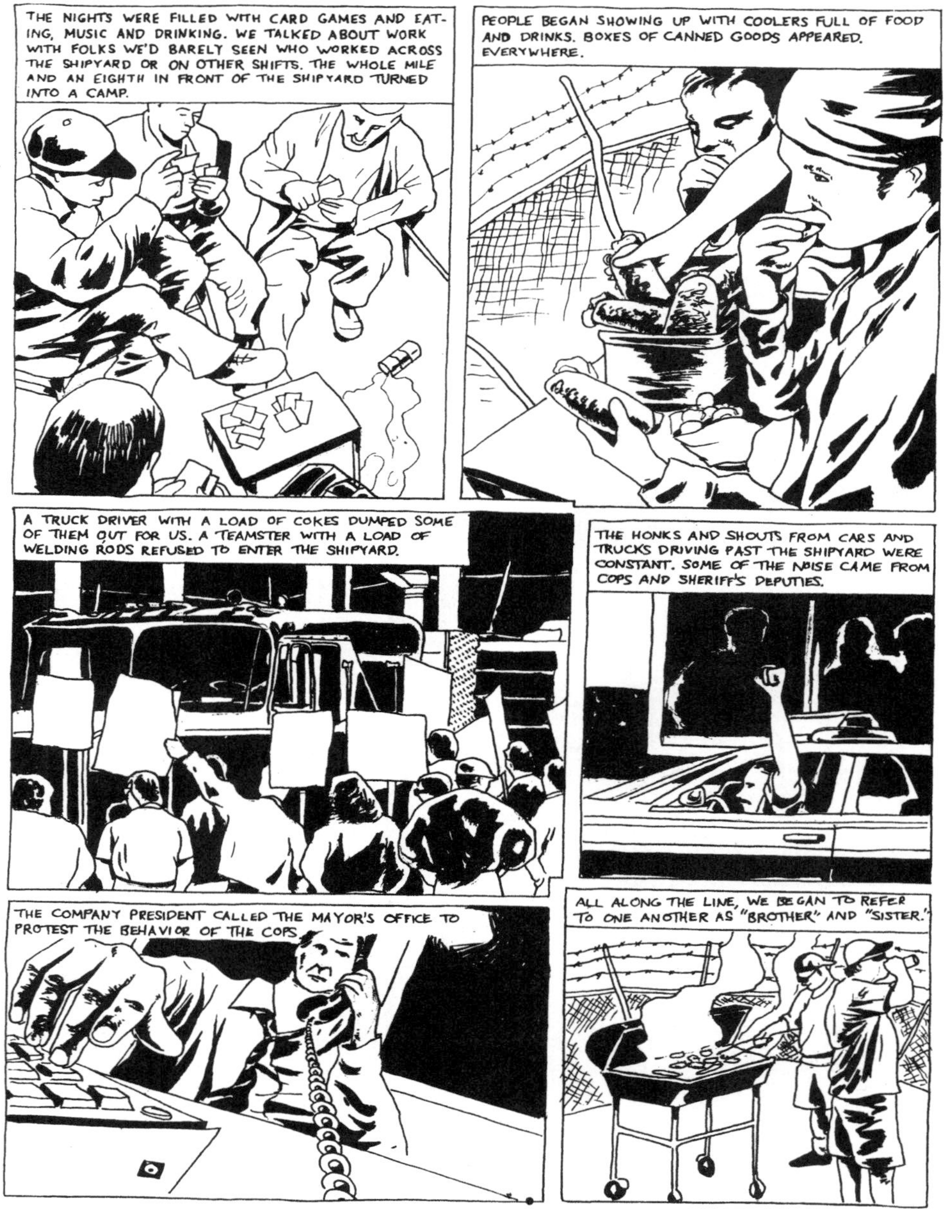
THE NIGHTS WERE FILLED WITH CARD GAMES AND EATING, MUSIC AND DRINKING. WE TALKED ABOUT WORK WITH FOLKS WE'D BARELY SEEN WHO WORKED ACROSS THE SHIPYARD OR ON OTHER SHIFTS. THE WHOLE MILE AND AN EIGHTH IN FRONT OF THE SHIPYARD TURNED INTO A CAMP.
PEOPLE BEGAN SHOWING UP WITH COOLERS FULL OF FOOD AND DRINKS. BOXES OF CANNED GOODS APPEARED. EVERYWHERE.
A TRUCK DRIVER WITH A LOAD OF COKES DUMPED SOME OF THEM OUT FOR US. A TEAMSTER WITH A LOAD OF WELDING RODS REFUSED TO ENTER THE SHIPYARD.
THE HONKS AND SHOUTS FROM CARS AND TRUCKS DRIVING PAST THE SHIPYARD WERE CONSTANT. SOME OF THE NOISE CAME FROM COPS AND SHERIFF'S DEPUTIES.
THE COMPANY PRESIDENT CALLED THE MAYOR'S OFFICE TO PROTEST THE BEHAVIOR OF THE COPS.
ALL ALONG THE LINE, WE BEGAN TO REFER TO ONE ANOTHER AS "BROTHER" AND "SISTER."

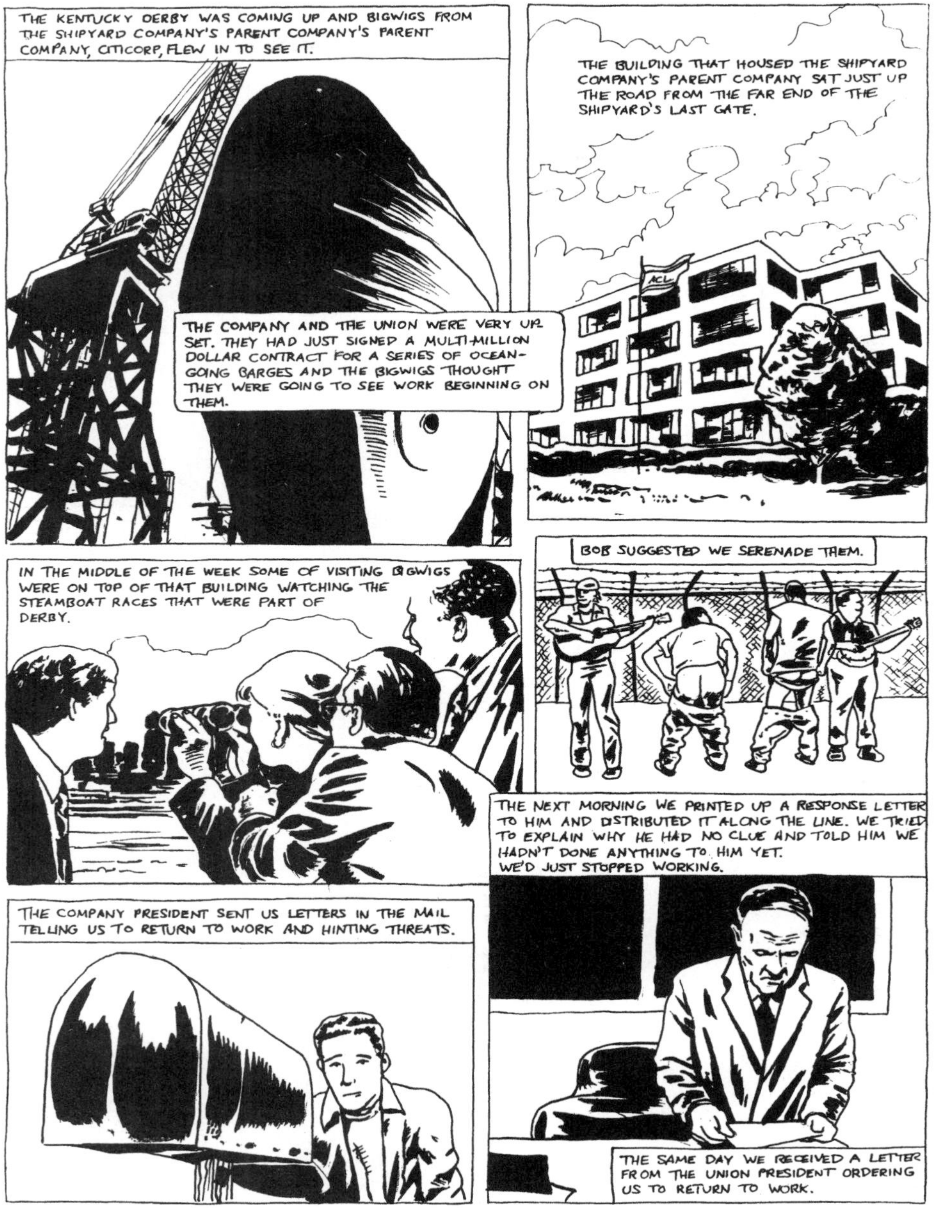
THE KENTUCKY DERBY WAS COMING UP AND BIGWIGS FROM THE SHIPYARD COMPANY'S PARENT COMPANY'S PARENT COMPANY, CITICORP, FLEW IN TO SEE IT.
THE COMPANY AND THE UNION WERE VERY UPSET. THEY HAD JUST SIGNED A MULTI-MILLION DOLLAR CONTRACT FOR A SERIES OF OCEAN-GOING BARGES AND THE BIGWIGS THOUGHT THEY WERE GOING TO SEE WORK BEGINNING ON THEM.
THE BUILDING THAT HOUSED THE SHIPYARD COMPANY'S PARENT COMPANY SAT JUST UP THE ROAD FROM THE FAR END OF THE SHIPYARD'S LAST GATE.
ACL
IN THE MIDDLE OF THE WEEK SOME OF VISITING BIGWIGS WERE ON TOP OF THAT BUILDING WATCHING THE STEAMBOAT RACES THAT WERE PART OF DERBY.
BOB SUGGESTED WE SERENADE THEM.
THE COMPANY PRESIDENT SENT US LETTERS IN THE MAIL TELLING US TO RETURN TO WORK AND HINTING THREATS.
THE NEXT MORNING WE PRINTED UP A RESPONSE LETTER TO HIM AND DISTRIBUTED IT ALONG THE LINE. WE TRIED TO EXPLAIN WHY HE HAD NO CLUE AND TOLD HIM WE HADN'T DONE ANYTHING TO HIM YET.
WE'D JUST STOPPED WORKING.
THE SAME DAY WE RECEIVED A LETTER FROM THE UNION PRESIDENT ORDERING US TO RETURN TO WORK.

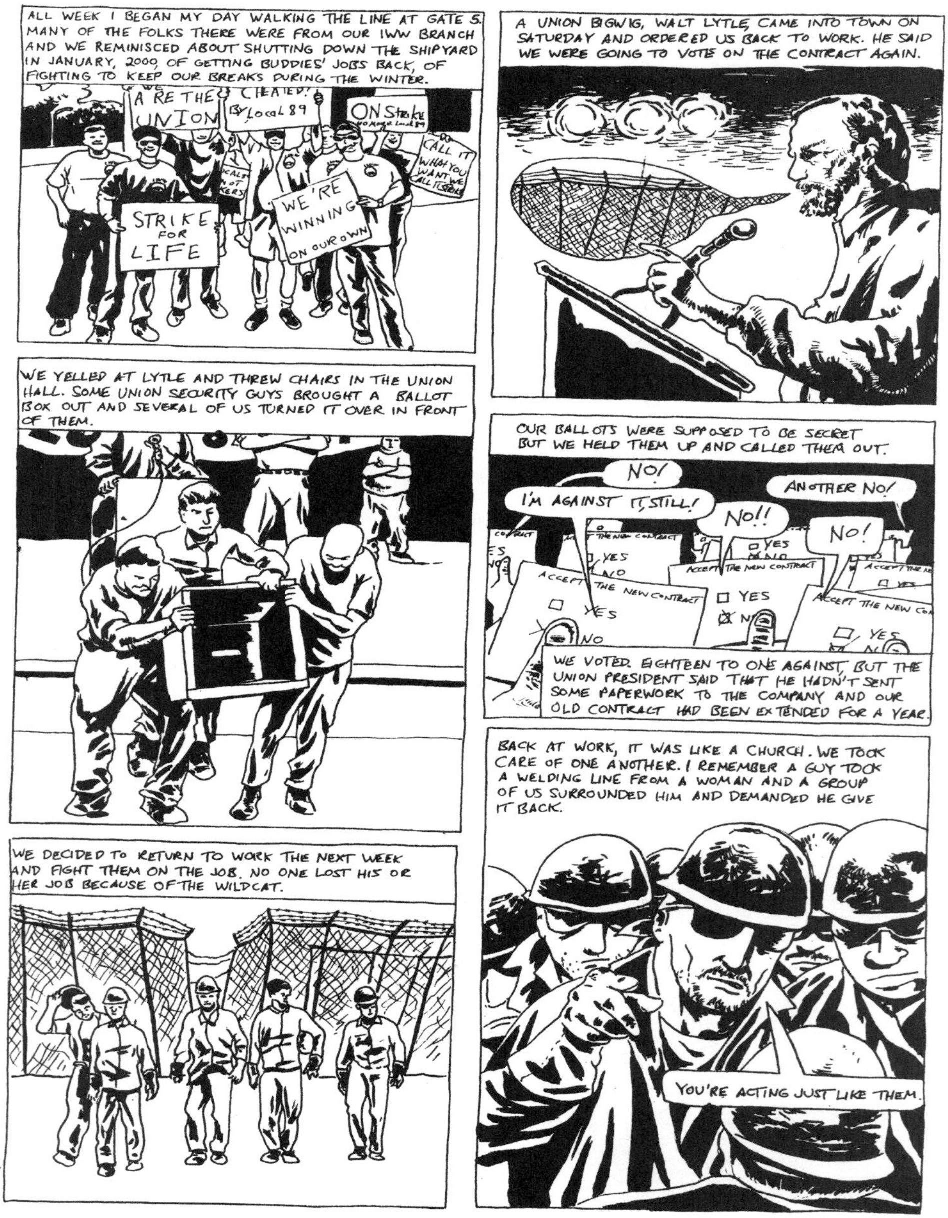
ALL WEEK I BEGAN MY DAY WALKING THE LINE AT GATE 5. MANY OF THE FOLKS THERE WERE FROM OUR IWW BRANCH AND WE REMINISCED ABOUT SHUTTING DOWN THE SHIPYARD IN JANUARY, 2000, OF GETTING BUDDIES' JOBS BACK, OF FIGHTING TO KEEP OUR BREAKS DURING THE WINTER.
ARE THE UNION
CHEATED! By Local 89
ON Strike
CALL IT WHAT YOU WANT WE CALL IT STRIKE
STRIKE FOR LIFE
WE'RE WINNING ON OUR OWN
A UNION BIGWIG, WALT LYTLE, CAME INTO TOWN ON SATURDAY AND ORDERED US BACK TO WORK. HE SAID WE WERE GOING TO VOTE ON THE CONTRACT AGAIN.
WE YELLED AT LYTLE AND THREW CHAIRS IN THE UNION HALL. SOME UNION SECURITY GUYS BROUGHT A BALLOT BOX OUT AND SEVERAL OF US TURNED IT OVER IN FRONT OF THEM.
OUR BALLOTS WERE SUPPOSED TO BE SECRET BUT WE HELD THEM UP AND CALLED THEM OUT.
NO!
I'M AGAINST IT, STILL!
ANOTHER NO!
NO!!
NO!
ACCEPT THE NEW CONTRACT
YES
NO
WE VOTED EIGHTEEN TO ONE AGAINST, BUT THE UNION PRESIDENT SAID THAT HE HADN'T SENT SOME PAPERWORK TO THE COMPANY AND OUR OLD CONTRACT HAD BEEN EXTENDED FOR A YEAR.
WE DECIDED TO RETURN TO WORK THE NEXT WEEK AND FIGHT THEM ON THE JOB. NO ONE LOST HIS OR HER JOB BECAUSE OF THE WILDCAT.
BACK AT WORK, IT WAS LIKE A CHURCH. WE TOOK CARE OF ONE ANOTHER. I REMEMBER A GUY TOOK A WELDING LINE FROM A WOMAN AND A GROUP OF US SURROUNDED HIM AND DEMANDED HE GIVE IT BACK.
YOU'RE ACTING JUST LIKE THEM.

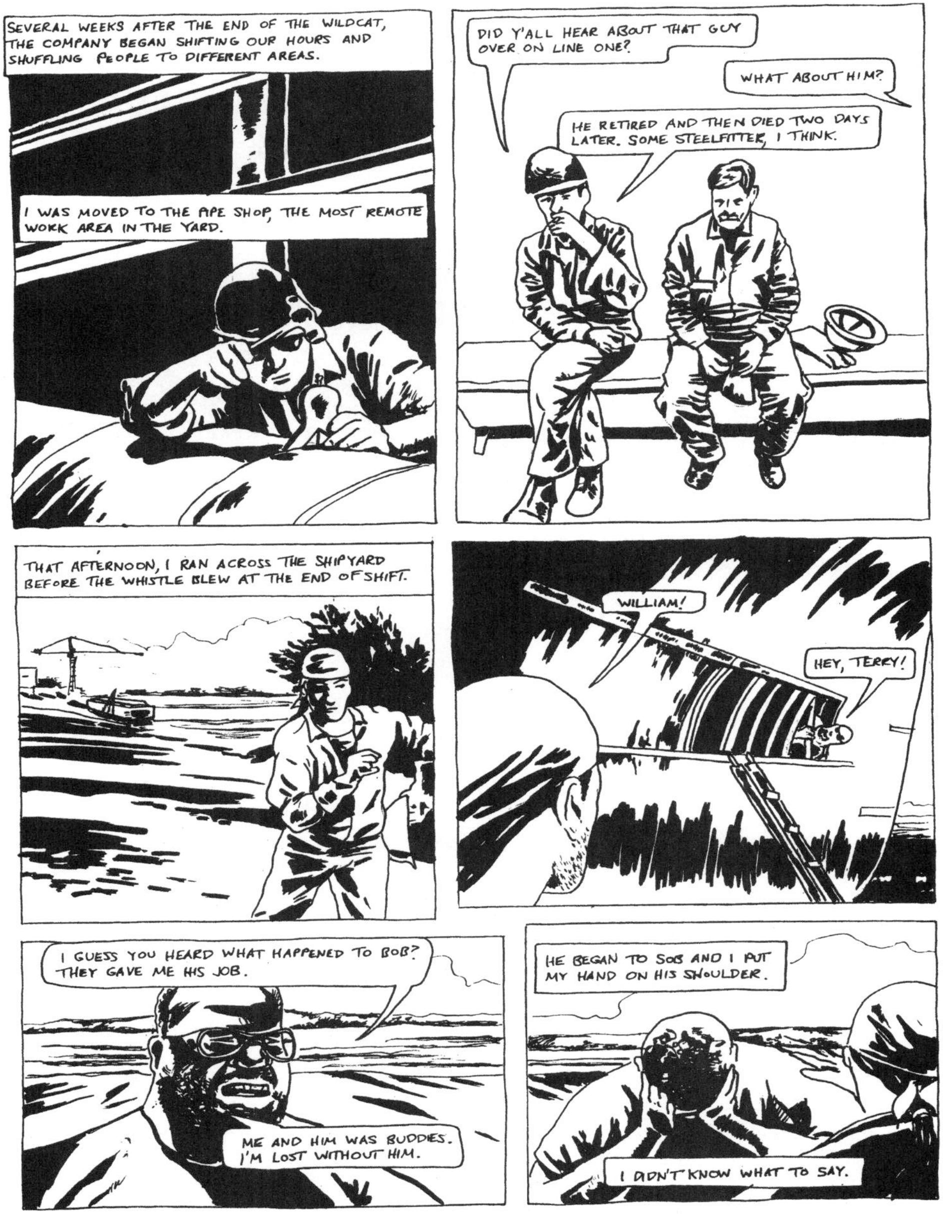
SEVERAL WEEKS AFTER THE END OF THE WILDCAT, THE COMPANY BEGAN SHIFTING OUR HOURS AND SHUFFLING PEOPLE TO DIFFERENT AREAS.
I WAS MOVED TO THE PIPE SHOP, THE MOST REMOTE WORK AREA IN THE YARD.
DID Y'ALL HEAR ABOUT THAT GUY OVER ON LINE ONE?
WHAT ABOUT HIM?
HE RETIRED AND THEN DIED TWO DAYS LATER. SOME STEELFITTER, I THINK.
THAT AFTERNOON, I RAN ACROSS THE SHIPYARD BEFORE THE WHISTLE BLEW AT THE END OF SHIFT.
WILLIAM!
HEY, TERRY!
I GUESS YOU HEARD WHAT HAPPENED TO BOB? THEY GAVE ME HIS JOB.
ME AND HIM WAS BUDDIES. I'M LOST WITHOUT HIM.
HE BEGAN TO SOB AND I PUT MY HAND ON HIS SHOULDER.
I DIDN'T KNOW WHAT TO SAY.

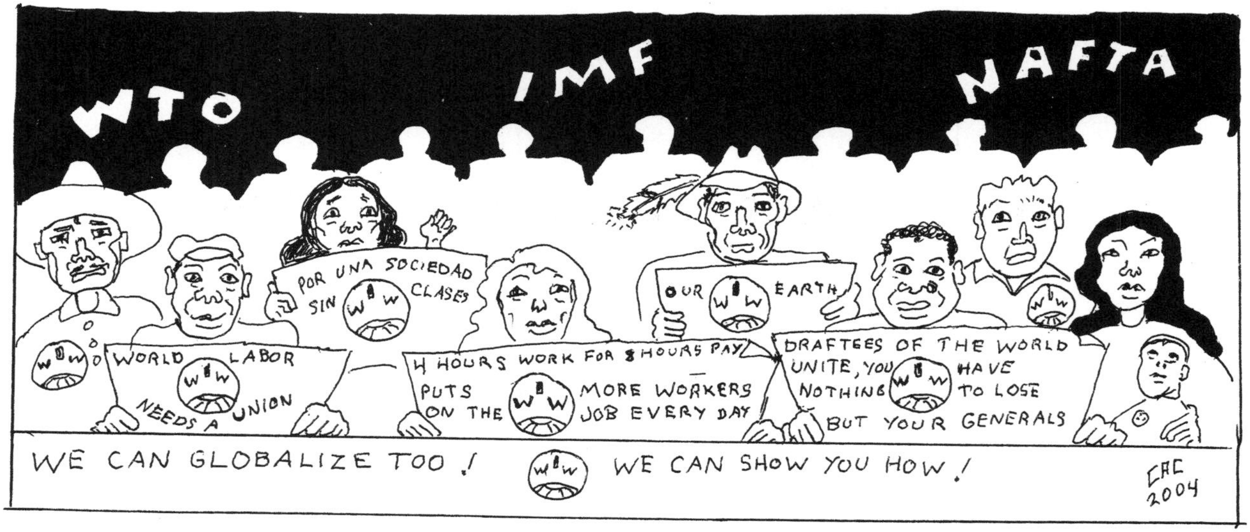
WTO
IMF
NAFTA
POR UNA SOCIEDAD SIN CLASES
OUR EARTH
WORLD LABOR NEEDS A UNION
4 HOURS WORK FOR 8 HOURS PAY
PUTS MORE WORKERS ON THE JOB EVERY DAY
DRAFTEES OF THE WORLD UNITE, YOU HAVE NOTHING TO LOSE BUT YOUR GENERALS
WE CAN GLOBALIZE TOO! WE CAN SHOW YOU HOW!
CAC 2004

"OUR D"

THE ART AND MUSIC OF THE IWW

The IWW, as Franklin Rosemont has pointed out, was no organization of trained artists; it had fewer of those than any other major radical movement during the twentieth century. Yet, it inspired dozens of talented artists, before 1920 some of the nation's most experimental and talented, and the IWW generated its own fabulous "school" of cartoonists.[1] Next to songs, cartoons probably brought more workers around than any other expression of Wob creativity. A few dozen self-taught artisans, including songster Joe Hill, drew with pen or stylus on paper, stencils, linoleum block or wood, almost always for an issue of a Wob publication ready to go to press (some of them also lettered signs for Wob halls). These rank-and-file artists appear to have received little or no pay for their work, choosing to go "on the bum" with their fellow Wobs, organize where possible, and take odd jobs to stay alive. Some of them signed their art only with the "red card number" on their Wobbly ID, or didn't sign cartoons at all. Only in later generations could artist-poet-agitator Carlos Cortez (sometime editor of the *Industrial Worker*) see his work exhibited in the Museum of Modern Art, or several of the card-holding members drawing for this book be called "professional artists."

The curious discrepancy between the degree of artistic accomplishment and the absence of formal training raises the largest questions about the influences upon this remarkable handful. The first place to look, certainly, is the contemporary newspaper cartoon and comic strip. Only in the later 1890s did the first real comic character appear: "The Yellow Kid," an ambiguously racial figure colored yellow (part of the "yellow press" introducing color in the one section appreciated most by the public: "the funny pages"), amid the chaos of "Hogan's Alley," an otherwise Irish slum scene of what would later be called juvenile delinquents-in-the-making. By the early years of the new century, comics took the dailies by storm, not only in English-language publications and not only in the US, but most completely here, because the wide readership and associated advertising base created careers for young men (and a very few women) with a sharp sense of what interested a semi-literate public.

There was often something radical about the mainstream comics, memorably in the oft-repeated scene of working-class kids throwing snowballs to knock off the top hat of the respectable "gent," typically a banker, lawyer, or businessman. Plenty of other types also challenged authority, in funny and visually striking ways. There was also plenty of racism and ethnocentrism, not to mention gendered strips making fun of women. But what was most radical was undoubtedly the *form* of comics. Like movies ("moving pictures"), then just emerging into real theaters, comics allowed artists to experiment with form, learning what the mostly working-class readership liked best. (By the 1920s, comics would also become successful movies: animated films, with a bright future ahead.) Amid lots of dreck, like the "he-she" jokes or fat ladies jumping into ponds splashing all the water out, there were wonderful, highly imaginative strips. History buffs like to remember "Little Nemo in Slumberland" by Windsor McKay, Rube Goldberg's fantastic inventions (that accomplished nothing), likewise the racetrack pair Mutt and Jeff (sometimes imitated directly by Wob cartoonists), among many others.

Easily the most famous of the Wob cartoon strips, and the only real continuing feature, was "Mr. Block," drawn by the elusive artist Ernest Riebe. Appearing first in the *Industrial Worker* of Spokane, Washington, in 1912, the blockhead Mr. Block reached publication as a booklet in 1913—arguably the first revolutionary comic book anywhere—and a later collection appeared in 1919, as *Crimes of the Bolsheviki*, a satirical take on the details of the capitalist propaganda (for instance, the charge that the Russians had "nationalized women") then being issued in response to the Russian Revolution. Mr. Block also became, of course, the source for one of the most famous of Wobbly songs, written by none other than Joe Hill.

Wob artists also took inspiration from the styles developed by editorial cartoonists, whether liberal, conservative or socialist, and from the artwork of the sympathetic *Masses* circle, whose artists' work was occasionally reprinted in IWW newspapers. Behind these influences could be seen, with a careful eye, the direction of radicals in the global art world, defecting from the salons of the rich to the working-class movements. Grappling with the contradictions of modern society, attacking capitalism relentlessly in every molecule of its poisonous being, these artists sought ways to look at the victims as potential saviors without making melodramatic or artificial claims. They also looked at themselves more carefully than their predecessors had: not only poverty (for those who did not draw or paint what the wealthy classes wanted) for self and family, but isolation in the studio, sardonic humor at the claims of capitalist society, and melancholy at the fate of the civilization depicted.

The revolt against the feigned prettiness and the religious orthodoxy of tradition arguably began with Hieronymus Bosch (1453–1516) and his unreserved attacks on clerics, money-men, soldiers, and the corrupting spirit of the emerging commercial society. But the manifestations were clearer in the late nineteenth century, as workers' movements and social critics (including novelists and poets, some radical and others just iconoclastic) gave shape to sentiment.

It was no simple thing. In Britain, for instance, William Morris' circle of socialists (with strong anarchist sympathies) had prompted a medieval-looking iconography by Walter Crane and others who saw socialism as the Golden Day ahead; beautiful, nearly naked bodies reaching out for paradise in nature freed from capitalist control. "Secession" impulses on the continent likewise blossomed, some of them influenced by Morris' Arts and Crafts movement (seeking to return artisanship to daily life), but most often simply seeking freedom for bohemian youngsters to draw and write what they saw as the new possibilities for human freedom. These were "modernists" who wanted to express the essence of the form, and so in experimenting they utilized the woodcut or linoleum cut, ideal for use in artistic prints (already a step away from the singular work created for the rich benefactor or collector), but also useful in more public statements, posters, and political leaflets. Like young avant-gardists every-where, these artists were deeply involved with each other, with love and eros as much as politics, and especially daring in their depictions of nudes and of "ugly" men and women, particularly those of the ruling classes. Among these artistic radicals could be counted famed figures such as Kathe Kollwitz, Edvard Munch, and Frans Masereel, who captured the pathos of the modern scene, among a host of others radicalized by the horrors of the First World War.

Closer to home, a small Dada rebellion may be said to have opened with the display of a urinal, signed "R. Mutt," by Frenchman (and future surrealist) Marcel Duchamp, at a Manhattan art show in 1917. Ephemeral magazines, illustrated by some of the same artists who drew for Emma Goldman's *Mother Earth*, blossomed and disappeared, reborn as the surrealist movement emerged in the Paris of the mid-1920s. Here we could place the origin, or at least precursors, of the alliance between surrealists and Wobblies around the *Rebel Worker* of the 1960s and the Charles H. Kerr publishing company, which has in recent decades become again what it was in the 1910s, an important publisher for IWW historical materials.[2]

What specific influences these two streams—commercial comic strips and rebellious contemporary art—had on the Wob cartoonists is impossible to quantify. Whether there really was an "invisible thread connecting Cubism and the IWW," as John Reed jocularly observed, is doubtful. And yet, the freedom to experiment, to move past existing forms, was the essence of the matter. We can say clearly that the Wob newspaper cartoon, whether didactic or satirical, flowed smoothly into the agitational poster or print (in miniature, postcard) and on into the "silent agitator," the small sticker that by the 1920s IWW members and sympathizers began placing in various odd spots from blank fences to bathroom stalls. In an important sense, this was the beginning of a new kind of public political art, the wall poster of future radical expression.

These streams continued to share something important with surrealism and Dadaism in the evocation of the dream of a better society (or just a more rebellious workforce) and the parody (in the sense seen most lavishly these days in Adbusters) of existing commercial or political salesmanship "turned around," revealing the truth behind the familiar lies.[3] Most of all, Wobbly cartoonists shared with the most advanced artists the vision of being free, not only personally, as artists, but as members of a freed homo sapiens. If the direction of modern art was in many ways a flight from content to form—and the rebellious intellectuals of the 1910s mocked by the compliant careerists of 1950s Cold War America who renounced anything but abstract expressionism and shamelessly promoted the glories of their sponsoring government agencies—then the recuperation of a really radical art would naturally return to the Wobbly spirit. The best of the 1960s–1980s "underground" comics (drawing on Mad Comics, also upon Walt Kelly and Jules Feiffer, among other rebellious artists of the 1950s); the best of the feminist art of the era to follow; the militantly anti-racist community mural movement; and the revival of the labor mural by Mike Alewitz—all these resonated, consciously or unconsciously, with memories of IWW visual agitation.[4] We look back upon the Wobbly cartoonists, then, as we do upon the Ash Can art of the *Masses* magazine: a century ahead of their time in their discoveries, but just ripe for our time—not to copy but to learn and grow from, amid the tasks of art and revolution ahead.[5]

Nothing made the Wobblies unique so much as their songs. *The Little Red Song Book* (sometimes called *The Wobbly Songbook*), in thirty-some editions since 1909, was far and away the best-selling radical publication in twentieth-century America, its endurance rivaled only by *My Life* by IWW supporter and modern dancer Isadora Duncan. As Wob music ethnographer Archie Green says, it grew directly out of song poems that readers of Wobbly newspapers would submit for publication and amateur musicians would put the words to music (often vaudeville tunes, gospel favorites or old radical songs: "The Battle Hymn of the Republic," written for Union victory and the abolition of slavery during the Civil War, thus became "Solidarity Forever," one of the all-time favorites). In 1909, the IWW branch in Spokane that published the newspaper *Solidarity* put out the first *Little Red Song Book* to raise consciousness and to raise money.

Some of the most famous songs are remembered for their dark humor. Wobblies just out of the mines or lumber camps, in small Western towns with only Salvation Army centers, bars, whorehouses, and Wobbly halls welcoming them, would stand next to the Salvation Army (they called it the "Starvation Army") singers and intone "Long-Haired Preachers" (sometimes called "Pie in the Sky") to the tune of the

Salvation Army favorite, "The Sweet Bye and Bye." Many of them were self-satirical, like T-Bone Slim's "The Popular Wobbly," or "I'm too Old to Be a Scab." Often they dwelt on the itinerant existence (like T-Bone Slim's "Mysteries of a Hobo's Life") and the beauty of the countryside, along with the dangers and poverty of the hobo camp and casual labor.

[1] Franklin Rosemont, "Industrial Workers of the World Cartoons," in *Encyclopedia of the American Left*, edited by Mari Jo Buhle, Paul Buhle, and Dan Georgakas, (New York: Oxford University Press, 1998 edition), pp. 359–61. Practically speaking, Rosemont has been the *only* scholar of Wobbly cartooning, and, with the mimeographed *Rebel Worker* of the 1960s, a participant in Wobbly graphics experiments.

[2] Surrealists have documented the affinity of spirit between the Wobs and assorted impulses within US culture. See for instance Franklin Rosemont, ed., *Surrealism and Its Popular Accomplices* (San Francisco: City Lights, 1983), a reprint of a special issue of *Cultural Correspondence*, published in its first years by Paul Buhle. Perhaps it is worth adding here that the second issue of *Radical America* (September–October, 1967) bore the famous "Labor Produces All" logo of the IWW on its cover, along with a lead article by IWW secretary-treasurer Fred Thompson: the signification of a spiritual affinity.

[3] Among those avowedly close to the Wobbly spirit was Larry Rivers (1923–2003), ceaselessly satirizing consumerist and pseudo-patriotic images.

[4] Among them, Alewitz encompassed Wobbly themes and signs most often. See Paul Buhle and Mike Alewitz, *Insurgent Images: the Agitprop Murals of Mike Alewitz* (New York: Monthly Review Press, 2002).

[5] Along with the work in this book, some of the most charming new Wobbly art can be found on the T-Shirts and bibs of Northland Products: "An Owe to One is an Owie to All," and "I'm a Little Wobbly," the first illustrated by a full-grown sabo-tabby, the second by a sabo-kitty.

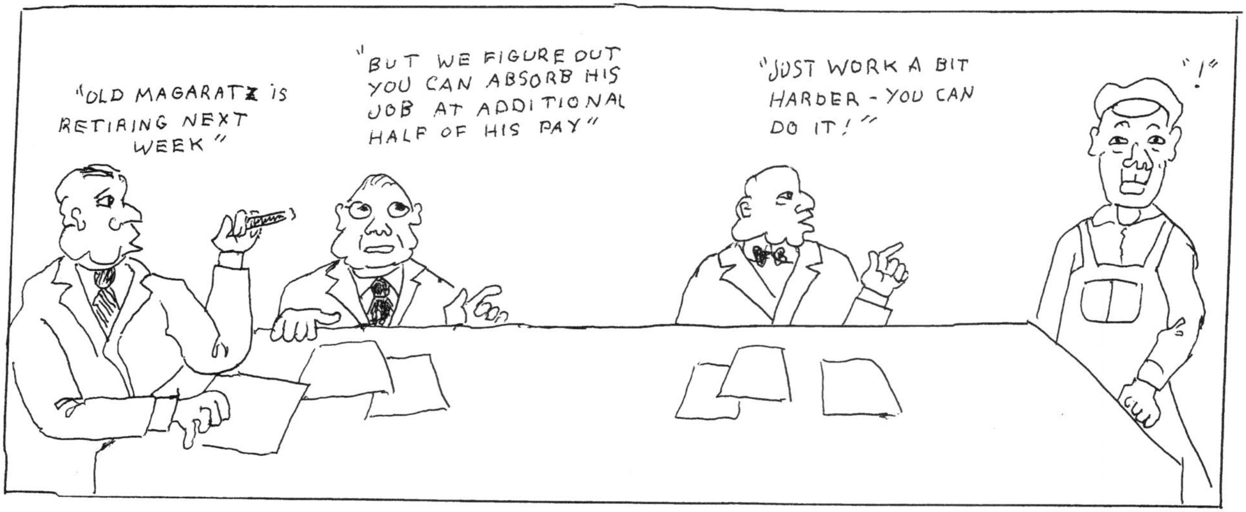
"OLD MAGARATZ IS RETIRING NEXT WEEK"
"BUT WE FIGURE OUT YOU CAN ABSORB HIS JOB AT ADDITIONAL HALF OF HIS PAY"
"JUST WORK A BIT HARDER - YOU CAN DO IT!"
"!"

"AD"

WOBBLY ORIGINALS

Joe Hill, *Industrial Worker*, April 4, 1913

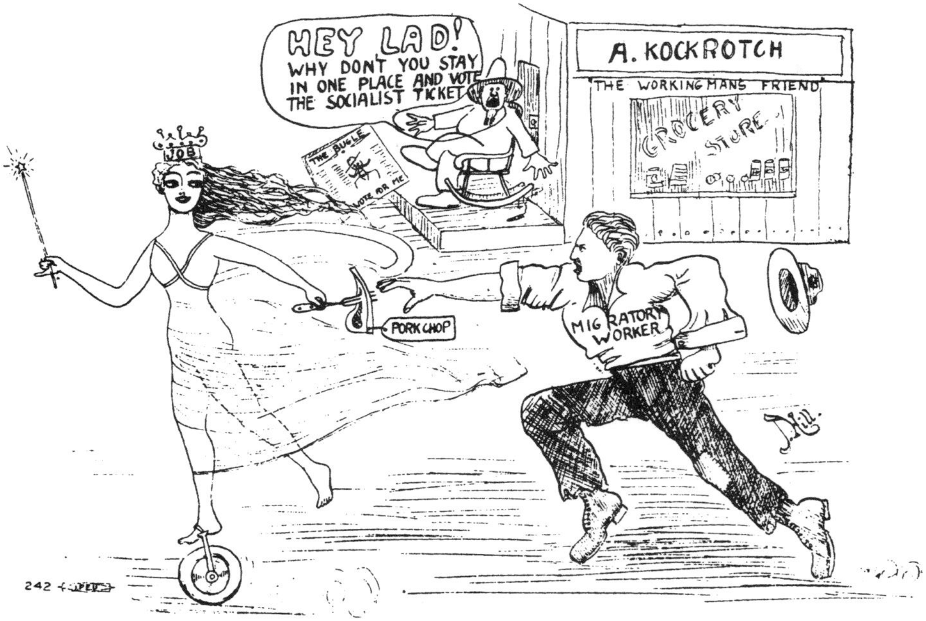
HEY LAD!
WHY DON'T YOU STAY IN ONE PLACE AND VOTE THE SOCIALIST TICKET
A. KOCKROTCH
"THE WORKINGMANS FRIEND"
GROCERY STORE
JOB
THE BUGLE
VOTE FOR ME
PORK CHOP
MIGRATORY WORKER
242

CONSTITUTIONAL GUARANTEE:--LIFE? LIBERTY? AND THE PURSUIT OF--A JOB!

Ralph Chaplin, *Solidarity*, June 16, 1917

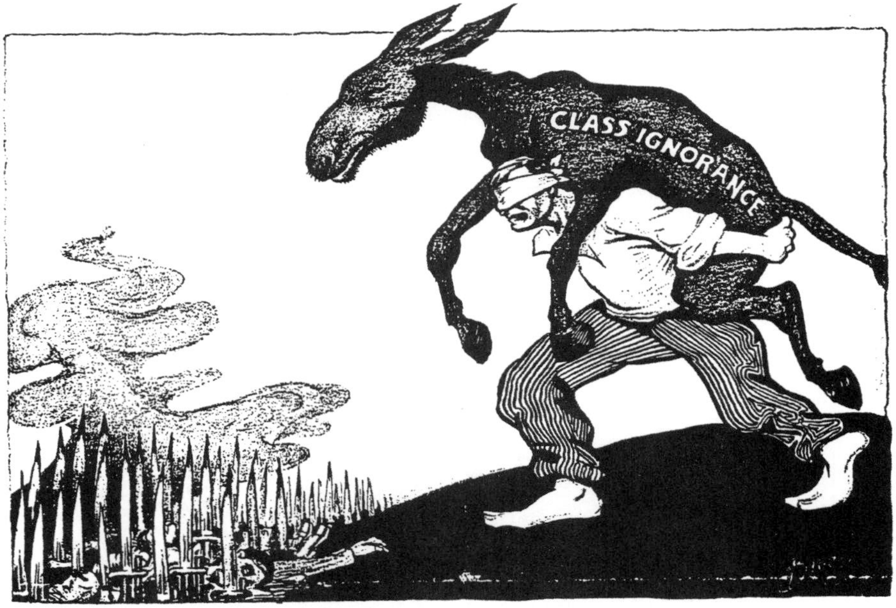
CLASS IGNORANCE

WILL HE CONTINUE, OR WILL HE BUCK?

BIG STRIKE IN BUTTE, MONTANA

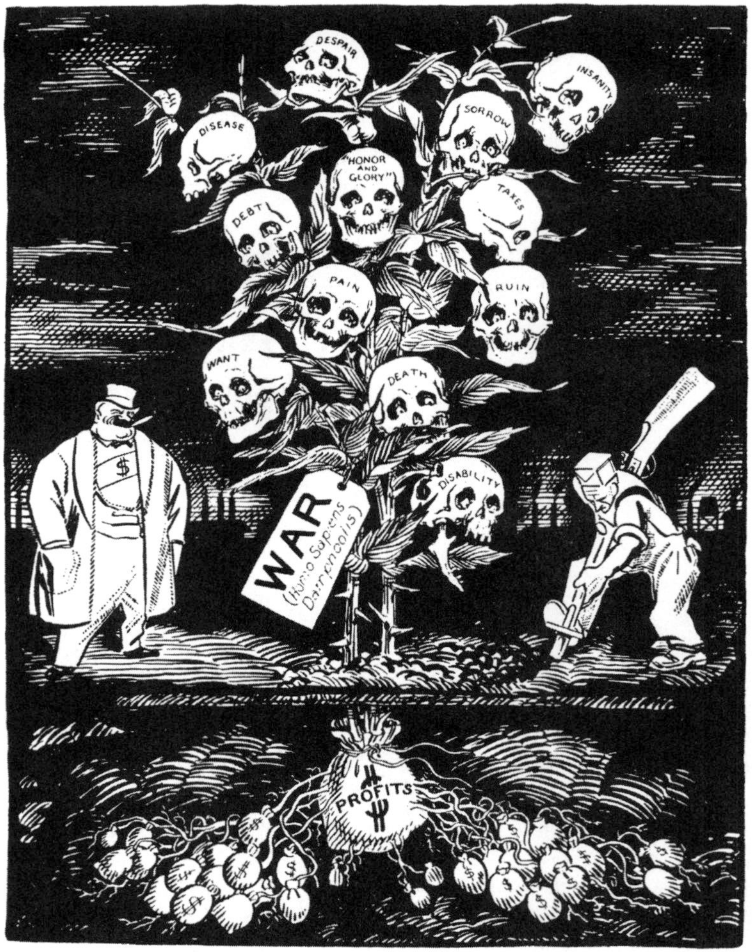
DESPAIR
INSANITY
DISEASE
SORROW
"HONOR AND GLORY"
DEBT
TAXES
PAIN
RUIN
WANT
DEATH
DISABILITY
WAR
(Homo Sapiens
PROFITS

BIG BUSINESS (to Labor, generously): "My good fellow, you'll be well paid for your patriotic action in 'tending this glorious plant; you shall have all the fruit above the ground—I'll take ONLY the roots!"

Industrial Worker, 1919

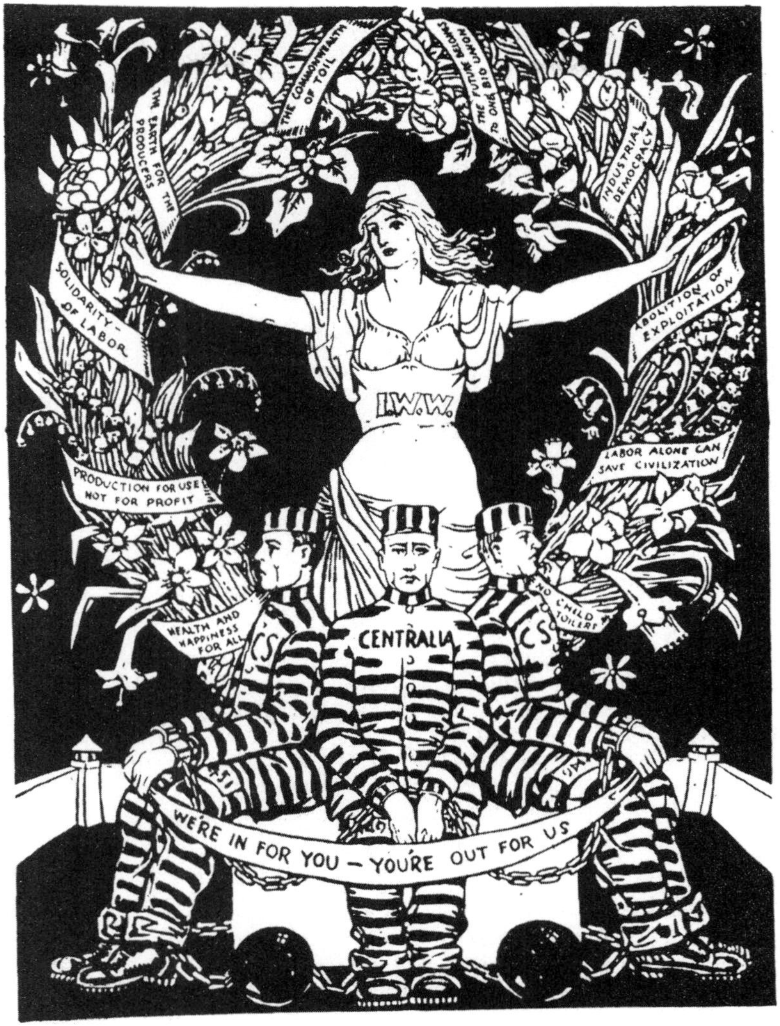
THE EARTH FOR THE PRODUCERS
THE COMMONWEALTH OF TOIL
THE FUTURE BELONGS TO ONE BIG UNION
INDUSTRIAL DEMOCRACY
SOLIDARITY OF LABOR
ABOLITION OF EXPLOITATION
I.W.W.
PRODUCTION FOR USE NOT FOR PROFIT
LABOR ALONE CAN SAVE CIVILIZATION
WEALTH AND HAPPINESS FOR ALL
NO CHILD TOILERS
CS
CENTRALIA
CS
WE'RE IN FOR YOU — YOU'RE OUT FOR US

Industrial Pioneer, August 1924

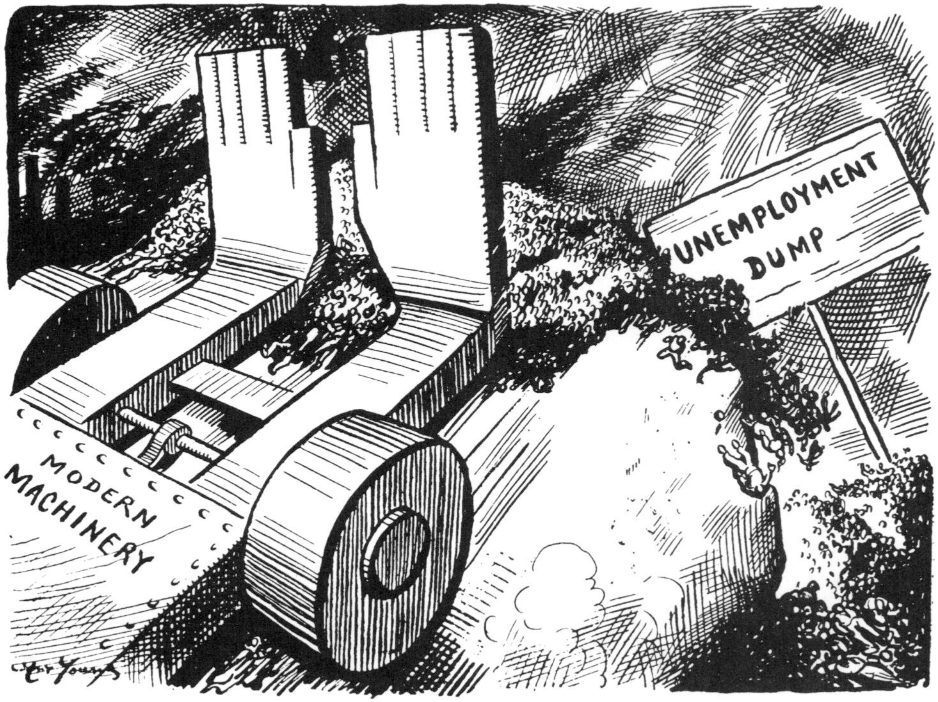
UNEMPLOYMENT DUMP
MODERN MACHINERY

Sabotage, Ralph Chaplin, *Solidarity*, April 7, 1917

SABOTAGE
EXPLOITATION
Bingo

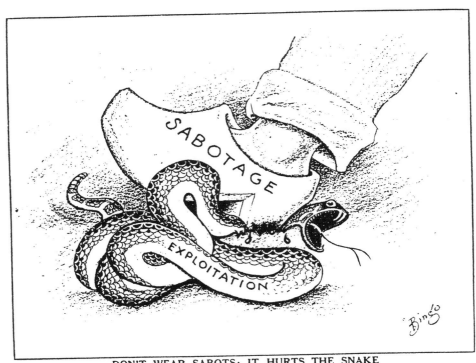

DON'T WEAR SABOTS; IT HURTS THE SNAKE

Thief!

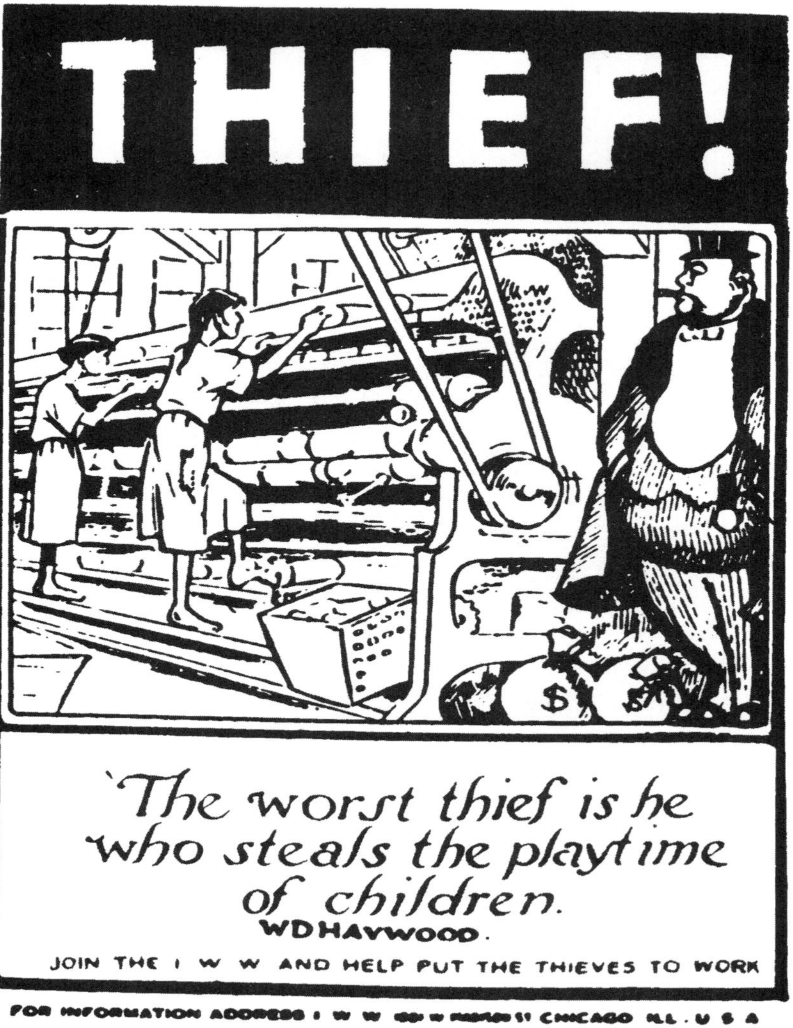
THIEF!
$
'The worst thief is he who steals the playtime of children.
W D HAYWOOD.
JOIN THE I W W AND HELP PUT THE THIEVES TO WORK
FOR INFORMATION ADDRESS I W W
CHICAGO ILL · U S A

Una Gran Union, From IWW foreign language pamphlet

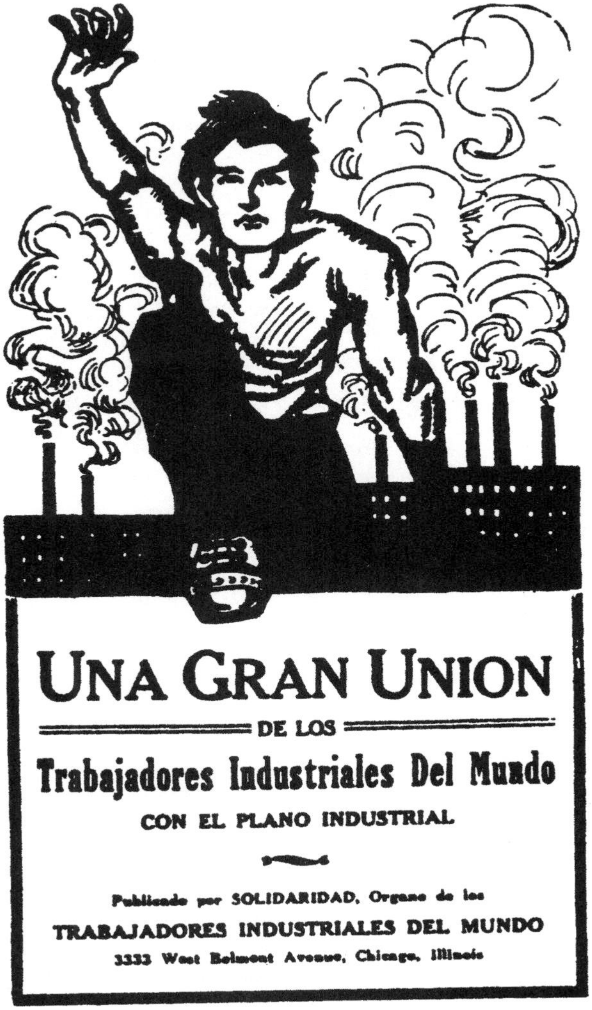
UNA GRAN UNION
DE LOS
Trabajadores Industriales Del Mundo
CON EL PLANO INDUSTRIAL
Publicado por SOLIDARIDAD, Organo de los
TRABAJADORES INDUSTRIALES DEL MUNDO
3333 West Belmont Avenue, Chicago, Illinois

Mr. Block, Ernst Riebe, *Industrial Worker*, August 21, 1913.

Mr. Block
He Goes Harvesting
HELP! HELP! HELP! HARVEST HANDS WANTED. FARMERS ARE UNABLE TO SECURE HELP AT $5.00 AND $6.00 A DAY. GO TO THE DAKOTAS AND MAKE A LITTLE FORTUNE. Eastern News Papers.
ALL THE PAPERS TELL THE SAME STORY. IT MUST BE SO.
I WILL HAVE TO TAKE THE SIDE DOOR PULLMAN WITH THE REST OF THE BOYS.
To South Dakota
THOSE HIGH WAGE STORIES ARE PUBLISHED TO SWAMP THE LABOR MARKET OF THE WEST IN ORDER TO REDUCE WAGES. JOIN THE I.W.W. AND HELP TO OVERTHROW THE SYSTEM OF EXPLOITATION.
I AM A PATRIOT AND I OBJECT TO ANARCHISM IN THIS BOX CAR.
MITCHEL, SOUTH DAKOTA
I AM LOOKING FOR A JOB HARVESTING
ALL THE JOBS ARE TAKEN AND THERE ARE 500 MEN LOOKING FOR WORK HERE. TAKE THE NEXT FREIGHT AND GET OUT.
Z-Z-Z-Z
DIDN'T I TELL YOU TO TAKE THE NEXT FREIGHT AND GET OUT OF TOWN?!
ALL THE BOX CARS WERE PACKED WITH HARVEST HANDS AND I COULD'NT GET IN.
WHY DIDN'T YOU RIDE THE BUMPERS?
1913.
242

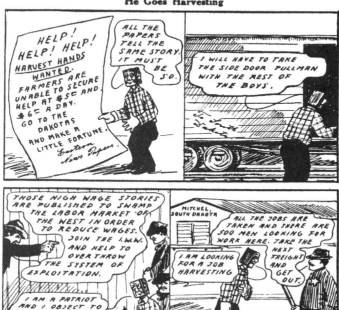

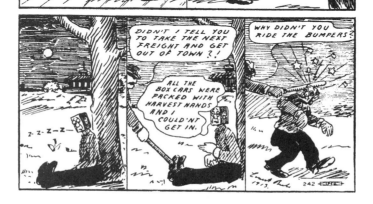

Wheel of Fortune, Father Thomas J. Hagerty, 1905

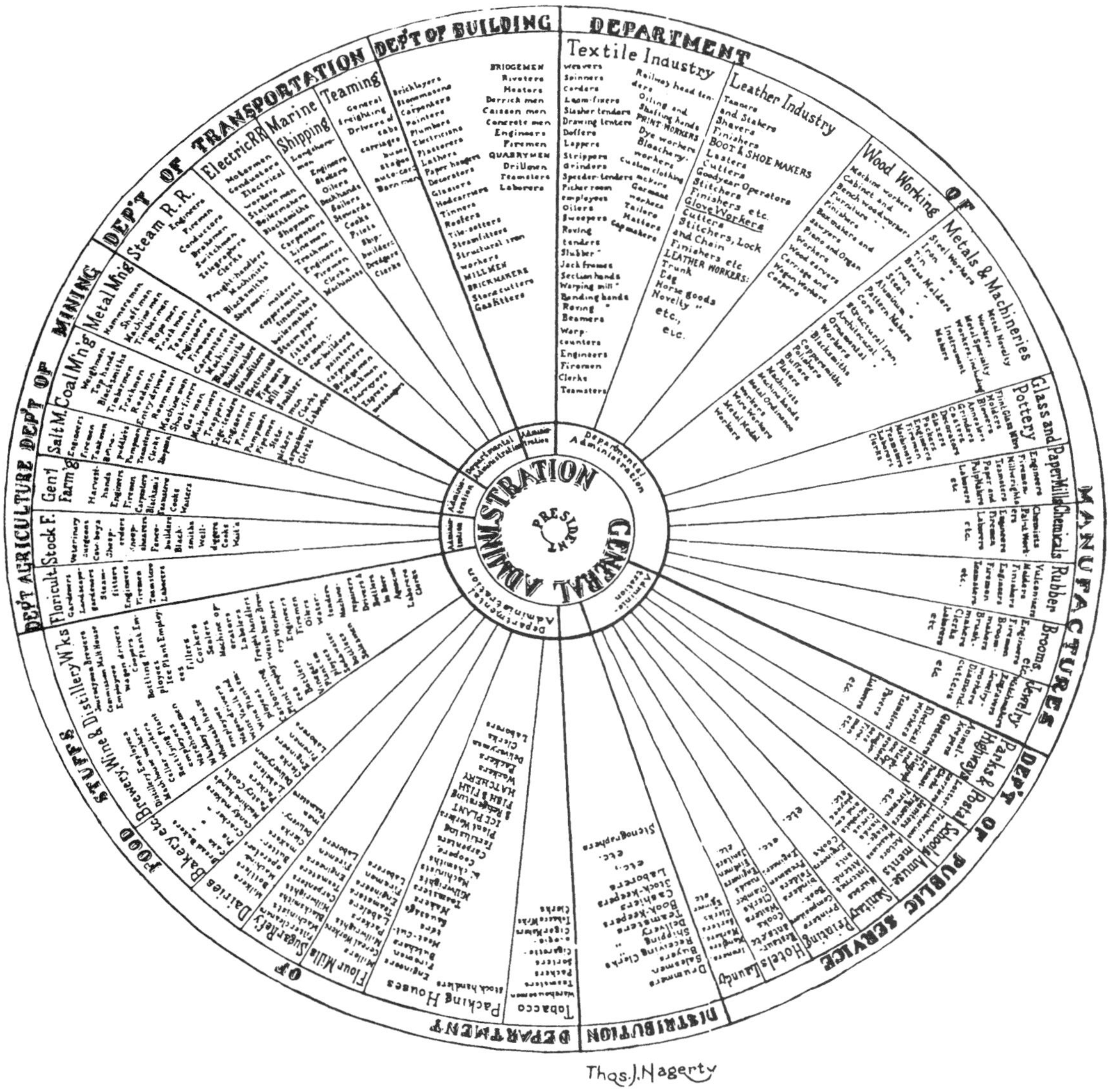
GENERAL ADMINISTRATION
PRESIDENT
Departmental Administration
DEPT OF BUILDING
DEPARTMENT OF MANUFACTURES
DEPT OF PUBLIC SERVICE
DISTRIBUTION DEPARTMENT
DEPARTMENT OF FOOD STUFFS
DEPT AGRICULTURE
DEPT OF MINING
DEPT OF TRANSPORTATION
Textile Industry
Leather Industry
Wood Working
Metals & Machineries
Glass and Pottery
PaperMills
Chemicals
Rubber
Brooms, etc.
Jewelry
Highway
Parks & Postal
Schools
Amusements
Sanitary
Printing
Building
Hotels
Laundry
Tobacco
Packing Houses
Flour Mills
Sugar Ref'y
Dairies
Bakery etc.
Brewery, Wine & Distillery W'ks
Floricult.
Stock F.
Gen'l Farm'g
Salt M.
Coal M'n'g
Metal M'n'g
Steam R.R.
Electric RR
Marine Shipping
Teaming
Thos. J. Hagerty

BIOGRAPHIES

Mike Alewitz is America's leading labor muralist, co-author of *Insurgent Images: the Agitprop Murals of Mike Alewitz*, and former chair of the Arts division of the Labor Party. He currently teaches mural-making at Central Connecticut State University.

Susan Simensky Bietila is a Wisconsin based artist/activist who grew up in Brooklyn, NY. She has continued to draw inspiration from the Wobblies since she first learned their history during the free-speech fight at Brooklyn College in 1965. Her first political artwork was published in the late 1960s in the *National Guardian* and in the second-wave feminist underground newspaper, the *RAT*. She is co-curator of "Drawing Resistance," a d.i.y. traveling art show, a group show of contemporary political art which has been touring North America since September 2001.

Her drawings, prints, and photographs have appeared recently in the New York storyboard magazine, *World War 3 Illustrated* and in other radical publications in the US and Canada.

Tauno Biltsted lives on the LES of Manhattan with his daughter, girlfriend and two cats. He and Mac McGill have fruitfully collaborated for ten years for *World War 3 Illustrated* and other publications. Tauno has been a squatter and community activist for all of his adult life and tries to bring an engaged sensibility to all of his work.

Clay Butler is the creator of the political comic strip "Sidewalk Bubblegum" and owner and director of www.claytowne.com Graphic and Web Design.

Christopher Cardinale earned a BFA with honors in 1996 from the University of New Mexico in Albuquerque. He then moved to Mexico City, where he immersed himself in the murals of the Mexican masters and worked with local political collectives. Cardinale has created large-scale murals, both individually and in collaboration with other artists, and had a number of one- and two-person shows in Mexico, New Mexico, Italy, Greece, and New York, where he has lived since 2001. In 2002, he was a resident at the Blue Mountain Center in the Adirondacks. Currently, he is co-editing the upcoming issue of *World War 3 Illustrated*, to which he has frequently contributed, with Seth Tobocman and Sabrina Jones. Cardinale's work has appeared in the *New York Times*, *Time* magazine and *New York Press*.

Giuliana Chamedes is a graduate of Brown and Cambridge universities and is studying for a PhD at Columbia in Law and History.

Sue Coe is an artist and activist, born in Tamworth, England in 1951. She studied at the Royal College of Art and has lived in the US since 1971. Sue's work has explored factory farming, meat-packing, apartheid, AIDS, and the horrors of war. Her many publications and prints are available on www.graphicwitness.org.

Carlos Cortez, born in 1923, is a longtime member, the son of a Mexican Wobbly father and German-American socialist mother. Cartoonist/poet Carlos Cortez (born 1923) is a longtime member of the IWW and has served as editor of the *Industrial Worker*. Well known for his linocut posters of IWWs Lucy Parsons, Joe Hill, Ben Fletcher, and others, he is also the author of three books of poems and editor of *Viva Posada! A Salute to the Great Printmaker of the Mexican Revolution* (2002). For many years he has been President of the Charles H. Kerr publishing co-op in Chicago.

Lisa DiPetto was born on Long Island and raised by a series of compassionate television sets, the losses of which she endured with rock-like stoicism. Sixties cartoons, advertising, and game shows were hardwired into her soul. Fortunately not too much of this reflects in her work. She is currently writing and illustrating several children's books. This is her first comic, but won't be her last.

Fly has been squatting in the Lower East Side of Manhattan since 1990, where she paints and draws comics and illustrations and sometimes paints murals. Her work has been published by: NY Press, *Juxtapoz*, *The Comics Journal*, *Village Voice*, *San Francisco Bay Guardian*, *Raygun*, *The Bradleys* (Fantagraphics), *World War 3 Illustrated*, *Punk*, *Maximumrocknroll*, and many more. Fly has self-published numerous comics and zines; a collection of these entitled *CHRON!IC!RIOTS!PA!SM!* was published in 1998 by Autonomedia. Her latest book *PEOPs*—a collection of almost 200 portraits of people and their stories—was released in July 2003 by Soft Skull/Shortwave.

Arthur Fonseca is an anarchist and activist who resides on the East side of the San Francisco Bay. He has been working since the mid '90s to preserve People's Park from the encroachments of the University of California at Berkeley's development schemes.

Roy Germon is an illustrator and painter living in Maine. A portfolio and contact info can be found at www.roygermon.com.

Ryan Inzana is an illustrator and cartoonist from Brooklyn, New York. His work can be seen in the *New York Times*, the *Wall Street Journal*, the *Nation*, the *Progressive*, and numerous other publications. Ryan's comic work can be found in the pages of *World War 3 Illustrated*, *New York Waste*, online in *Slate Magazine*, and in his latest graphic novel, *Johnny Jihad*. He is currently at work on an autobiographical graphic-novel series entitled *God-less America*.

Sabrina Jones is a native of Philadelphia, and has studied painting at the Pratt Institute and illustration at the School of Visual Arts. She created her first comics for *World War 3 Illustrated* and went on to edit many issues, as well as co-founding "Girltalk," an anthology of Women's autobiographical comics. Her comics and illustrations have appeared in the *New York Times*, *Bust*, *Citylimits*, *RealGirl*, *Legal Action Comics*, *Tikkun* and *InxArt*. She is included in the books, *The Great Women Cartoonists*, *From Girls to Grrrlz*, *Rare Books*, *WW3 Confrontational Comics*, *Angry Graphics*, and *Your House Is Mine*. Her work has traveled in the exhibit "She Draws Comics," from Vienna's Secession Gallery to San Francisco's Cartoon Art Museum. Sabrina also paints scenery for theater, film, and TV, as a member of United Scenic Artists Local 829. See more of her work at www.sabrinaland.com.

Tom Keough has been an artist all his life, trying to use his talents to do some good in this world. Tom says: "The *Industrial Worker* is my favorite newspaper. It has news you won't see in other papers." Tom's paintings and illustrations have been shown at the Museum of Modern Art, the United Nations offices, in union newsletters, and used by organizations such as the National Council of Churches and the War Resisters League.

Jay Kinney was a member of the first wave of underground cartoonists, with his first comic strip appearing in *Bijou Funnies* #1 in 1968. He co-founded the romance-comic parody, *Young Lust*, with Bill Griffith in 1970, created *Cover-up Lowdown* with Paul Mavrides in 1976, and founded *Anarchy Comics* in 1978. He was publisher and editor in chief of *Gnosis Magazine* (1985–99) and has co-authored (with Richard Smoley) *Hidden Wisdom: A Guide to the Western Inner Traditions* (1999) and edited *The Inner West: An Introduction to the Hidden Wisdom of the West* (2004). He resides in San Francisco with his wife, Dixie, and their two cats. His "Clinic of Cultural Collision" can be found at www.jaykinney.com.

Mike Konopacki is a labor cartoonist from Madison, Wisconsin. In 1983 he and Gary Huck, cartoonist for the United Electrical Radio and Machine Workers of America (UE), created Huck/Konopacki Labor Cartoons. Mike is author, along with Huck, of five collections of labor cartoons, their latest being "Two-headed Space Alien Shrinks Labor Movement." Along with writer Alec Dubro, Mike has produced labor comics for the APWU, CWA, Jobs With Justice, and Amnesty International USA. In 1995 Konopacki and Dubro created the thirty-two page full-color comic *The World Bank: A Tale of Power, Plunder, and Resistance*. It was translated into eleven languages worldwide. Huck and Konopacki's labor cartoons can be seen on the web at www.solidarity.com/hkcartoons.

Peter Kuper co-founded the political zine *World War 3 Illustrated* in 1979 and remains on its editorial board to this day. Peter Kuper's illustrations and comics appear regularly in *Time*, the *New York Times*, and *MAD*, where he illustrates SPY vs. SPY every month. His recent books include adaptations of Franz Kafka's "The Metamorphosis" and Upton Sinclair's "The Jungle," and *Sticks and Stones*, a wordless graphic novel about the rise and fall of empires. More of his work can be seen at www.peterkuper.com.

Barbara Laurence is Managing Editor of CAPITALISM/NATURE/SOCIALISM, and is Director of the non-profit Center for Political Ecology, in Santa Cruz, CA.

Jeffrey Lewis was born on roughly the same day that *Giant Size X-Men* #1 came out in November 1975. Raised by loving beatnik parents on New York's Lower East Side, and educated by the public school system, he is no longer in mint condition but has nevertheless accrued slightly in value. Currently he has a body that resides in Brooklyn when not on tour, a couple of albums of songs released on the Rough Trade label, and comics in various publications floating around the margins of western civilization. www.TheJeffreyLewisSite.com

Josh MacPhee is an artist based in Chicago, IL whose work often revolves around themes of radical politics and public space. He published his first book, *Stencil Pirates: A Global Survey of Street Stenciling*, in 2004 with Soft Skull Press. He also organizes the Celebrate People's History Poster Series and runs a small radical art distro at www.justseeds.org.

Mac McGill is a frequent contributor to *Tikkun* magazine and *World War 3 Illustrated*. His work has also been published by Seven Stories Press, Four Walls and Eight

Windows, the *Guardian Radical Newsweekly*, *The Shadow*, *Arthur* magazine and numerous other publications. Mac has exhibited his artwork and performed slideshow presentations of his work at: Babel Festival (Athens, Greece), Underground Festival (Milano, Italy), BD Amadora (Amadora, Portugal), Forte Presentino (Roma, Italy), Theater for the New City (New York City) and ABCnoRIO (New York City). He lives and works in the Lower East Side of New York City. He is a longtime squatter and activist and works at a homeless shelter for youth.

Dylan Miner is a doctoral candidate in the department of Art and Art History at the University of New Mexico. His academic writing focuses on the intersections between Chicana/o and Metis artistic production and anarchist praxis. He has published articles on Carlos Cortez Koyokuikatl, Diego Rivera, and the culture of Chicana/o anarchists in Michigan. His artwork has been shown in the United States, Canada and Mexico. He is a member of the Education Workers Industrial Union 620 and the Woodland Metis Tribe of Ontario.

Jerome Neukirch (a.k.a. Jerome x350474) is a persnickety perfectionist and a hopeless procrastinator. He has never turned in anything on time—including this bio. When not trying to draw, Jerome is an unimportant functionary in academia. He has been a Wob since 1999. He lives in Louisville, Kentucky with his two adoring cats who support his work and took a sustained interest in this project.

Harvey Pekar is the star persona of the film and autobiographical comic-book series *American Splendor*. He has been writing since 1957, with several collections of his works currently in print.

Kevin Pyle has done illustrations for the *New York Times*, the *New Yorker*, the *Progressive*, and the *Village Voice*, as well as numerous other publications. His docucomic, *Lab U.S.A.*—illuminated documents (Autonomedia)—received a silver medal from the Society of Illustrators. *Lab U.S.A.* is a history, in comic-book form, of medicine and science in the service of racist and political imperatives. He also produces installations and performances based on the text that have appeared at MassMOCA, the Brooklyn Museum of Art and numerous other art/performance venues. He is a longtime contributor/co-editor of *World War 3 Illustrated*, America's longest-running radical comic book.

Trina Robbins is founder of *It Ain't Me Babe*, the first of the Women's Liberation comics, and has written a number of books about women and comic art. She lives in San Francisco.

Spain Rodriguez was one of the founders of Underground Comix, most notably with his figure "Trashman of the Sixth International." His collection *MY TRUE STORY* is his true story, from the streets of Buffalo to San Francisco; many of his strips have offered intense historical views of revolutionary struggles.

Franklin Rosemont edited *The Rebel Worker* (1964–67). His latest book is a surrealist study, *An Open Entrance to the Shut Palace of Wrong Numbers* (2003). His books on the IWW include *Juice Is Stranger Than Friction: Selected Writings of T-Bone Slim* (1992) and *Joe Hill: The IWW and the Making of a Revolutionary Working-class Counterculture* (2003), both from Charles H. Kerr.

Sharon Rudahl was born in 1947 near Washington DC. She marched with Martin Luther King and graduated from Cooper Union in 1967. Sharon learned to draw comics during the Vietnam War and has been widely published in underground newspapers and magazines, as well as in Marvel Comics. Her art has been most recently exhibited in The Secession Art Gallery in Vienna. Sharon now lives in Hollywood with her husband, a professional chess player, and she has two sons. Her hobbies include civil disobedience and studying Mandarin.

Terry Tapp joined the IWW in 1998 after reading about them in a newspaper. He had been treated like hell at job after job, and the unions he talked to didn't seem to give a damn. He grew up in Kentucky among poor, working people who had a lot of talent and too many dreams for their lot. He has those dreams, too, and has managed to poke his head above constant work and frustration. Terry paints, draws, and writes comics and stories, and tattoo. His life is dedicated to his art and to giving the talent and dreams of other working people a chance to live. If there's an opportunity to raise hell, he takes it.

Nick Thorkelson years ago drew "The Earth Belongs to the People" and "The Underhanded History of the USA." Not so long ago he had a regular cartoon on local politics in the *Boston Globe*. His comics and cartoons have also appeared in *Itchy Planet*, *The Somerville Community News*, the *Progressive*, *Radical America*, *Dollars & Sense*, and *The Free Comix*, and publications of Greenpeace and Work Rights Press. His "Comic Strip of Neoliberalism" appears irregularly in *Dollars & Sense*, and can also be viewed online at www.nickthorkelson.com.

Seth Tobocman has been doing political comics since 1979 when he started the magazine *World War 3 Illustrated* with Peter Kuper. He has worked with a number of radical movements both as an artist and as an activist, including the movement to free South Africa, the Lower East Side Squatters Movement, as well as the

Anti-Globalization movement and the current antiwar movement. He has published three books of his comics: *You Don't Have to Fuck People Over to Survive* (1989), *War in the Neighborhood* (1999) and *Portraits of Israelis and Palestinians* (2003).

Susan Willmarth was born and raised in Albuquerque, NM and graduated from Parson's School of Design. She has worked for Push Pin Studios and *New York Magazine*. Sue has illustrated and designed books for Writer's and Reader's Publishers including "Black History for Beginners" and "McLuhan For Beginners". She currently illustrates for *World War 3 Illustrated* and keeps a day job at St. Marks Books in NYC.

Jordan Worley was born in Austin, Texas on August 8, 1973. He grew up in New York (Enwood, Yonkers, Brooklyn.) His work has been published in *World War 3 Illustrated*, and he has worked as co-editor on several issues of the magazine. Jordan has always drawn pictures to express himself and the world around him, and will continue to do so.

BIBLIOGRAPHY

Note: the following list is not intended to be exhaustive, but to include sources of a more general or recent scholarly nature used by the artists and others.

Adamic, Lewis. *The History of Class Violence in America*. Gloucester, Mass.: Harper & Brothers, 1934.

Ashbaugh, Carolyn. *Lucy Parsons, American Revolutionary*. Chicago: Charles H. Kerr, 1976.

Beck, Frank O. *Hobohemia: Emma Goldman, Lucy Parsons, Ben Reitman, and Other Agitators and Outsiders in 1920s/30s Chicago*. Chicago: Charles H. Kerr, 2000.

Bird, Stewart, Dan Georgakas, and Deborah Shaffer, eds. *Solidarity Forever: An Oral History of the I.W.W.* Chicago: Lake View Press, 1985, 2001.

Blaisdell, Lowell. *The Desert Revolution: Baja, California, 1911*. Madison: University of Wisconsin Press, 1962.

Brundage, Slim. *From Bughouse Square to the Beat Generation*. Chicago: Charles H. Kerr, 1997.

Buhle, Mari Jo, et al., eds. *Encyclopedia of the American Left*. New York: Oxford University Press, 2nd edition, 1998.

Buhle, Paul. *Taking Care of Business: Sam Gompers, George Meany, Lane Kirkland and the Tragedy of American Labor*. New York: Monthly Review Press, 1999.

Cahn, William. *Lawrence 1912, The Bread and Roses Strike*. Pilgrim Press, 1980.

Cameron, Ardis. *Radicals of the Worst Sort: Laboring Women in Lawrence, Massachusetts, 1860–1912*. Urbana: University of Illinois, 1993.

Camp, Helen. *Iron In Her Soul: Elizabeth Gurley Flynn and the American Left*. Pullman: Washington State Press, 1997.

Chaplin, Ralph, *Wobbly: The Rough and Tumble Story of an American Radical*. Chicago: University of Chicago Press, 1948.

Conlin, Joseph. *At the Point of Production: The Local History of the IWW*. Westport: Greenwood Press, 1981.

Cortez, Carlos. *"Wobbly": 80 Years of Rebel Art*. Chicago: Gato Negro Press, 1985.

Dubofsky, Melvyn. *We Shall Be All: A History of the Industrial Workers of the World*. Chicago: Quadrangle Books, 1969.

Foner, Philip S., ed. *Fellow Workers and Friends: IWW Free-Speech Fights as Told by the Participants*. Westport, CT: Greenwood Press, 1981.

Foner, Philip S. *History of the Labor Movement in the United States, IV: The Industrial Workers of the World, 1905–1917*. New York: International Publishers, 1965.

Forbath, William. *Law and the Shaping of the American Labor Movement*. Cambridge: Harvard University Press, 1991.

Founding Convention of the IWW: Proceedings. 2nd edition. New York: Merit Publishers, 1969.

Friedman, Robert L. *The Seattle General Strike*. Seattle: University of Washington, 1964.

Friedrich, Paul. *Agrarian Revolt in a Mexican Village*. Upper Saddle River, NJ: Prentice-Hall, 1970.

George, Harrison. *The IWW Trial*. 2nd Edition. New York: Arno Press, 1965.

Golin, Steve. *That Fragile Bridge: The Paterson Silk Strike—1913*. Philadelphia: Temple University Press, 1988.

Gomez-Quinones, Juan. Sembradores, *Ricardo Flores Magon y el Partido Liberal Mexicano: A Eulogy and a Critique*. Los Angeles: Chicano Studies, UCLA, 1973.

Green, Archie. *Wobblies, Pile Butts and Other Heroes: Laborlore Explorations*. Urbana: University of Illinois Press, 1993.

Green, James R. *Grassroots Socialism: Radical Movements in the Southwest, 1905–1943*. Baton Rouge: Louisiana State University Press, 1978.

Green, James R., William F. Hartford, and Tom Juravitch. *The Commonwealth of Toil*. Amherst: University of Massachusetts Press, 1996.

Green, Martin Burgess, *New York 1913: The Armory Show and the Paterson Strike Pageant*. New York: Scribner's, 1988.

Gutfield, Aaron. *Montana's Agony: Years of War and Hysteria, 1917–1921*. Gainesville: University of Florida Press, 1979.

Hall, Covington. *Labor Struggles in the Deep South and Other Writings*. Chicago: Charles H. Kerr, 1999.

Haywood, William. *Big Bill Haywood's Book*. New York: International Publishers, 1929.

Huberman, Leo. *The Labor Spy Racket*. New York: Modern Age Books, 1937.

Kornbluh, Joyce, ed. *Rebel Voices: An IWW Anthology*. 2nd edition. Chicago: Charles H. Kerr, 1998.

Leier, Mark. *Where the Fraser River Flows: The IWW in British Columbia*. Vancouver: New Star Books, 1990.

Luhan, Mabel Dodge, *Intimate Memories: The Autobiography of Mabel Dodge Luhan*, edited by Lois Palken Rudnick. Albuquerque: University of New Mexico Press, c1999.

Meltzer, Milton. *Bread and Roses: The Struggles of American Labor 1865–1915*. New York: New American Library, 1967.

McGuckin, Henry. *Memoirs of a Wobbly*. Chicago: Charles H. Kerr, 1987.

O'Connor, Harvey. *Revolution in Seattle*. New York: Monthly Review Press, 1964.

Preston, William, Jr. *Aliens and Dissenters: Federal Suppression of Radicals, 1903–1933.* 2nd Edition. Urbana: University of Ilinois Press, 1995.

Rabbin, David. *Free Speech in its Forgotten Years.* Cambridge, UK: Cambridge University Press, 1997.

Riebe, Ernest. *Mr. Block: Twenty-Four IWW Cartoons.* Chicago: Charles H. Kerr, 1984.

Roscoe, Will. *The Murder of Frank Little: "An Injury to One is an Injury to All,"* July 1, 1973 (unpublished).

Rosemont, Franklin. *Joe Hill: The IWW & the Making of a Revolutionary Working-class Counterculture.* Chicago: Charles H. Kerr, 2003.

Rosemont, Franklin, ed. *The Rise and Fall of the Dil Pickle: Jazz-Age Chicago's Wildest and Most Outrageously Creative Hobohemian Nightspot.* Chicago: Charles H. Kerr, 2004.

Rosemont, Franklin and Charles Radcliffe, eds. *Dancin' in the Streets: Anarchists, IWWs, Surrealists, Situationists and Provos in the 1960s, as recorded in the Pages of the* Rebel Worker *and* Heatwave. Chicago: Charles H. Kerr, 2005

Ruff, Allen. *"We Called Each Other Comrade": Charles H. Kerr, Radical Publishers.* Urbana: University of Illinois, 1997.

Salerno, Sal. *Red November, Black November: Culture and Community in the Industrial Workers of the World.* Albany: SUNY Press, 1989.

Seidman, Derek. "'They're as Bad as Wal-Mart': Starbucks Workers Get Organized," *Counterpunch* (on-line), August 26, 2004.

Sellers, Nigel Anthony. *Oil, Wheat and Wobblies: The Industrial Workers of the World in Oklahoma, 1905–1930*. Norman: University of Oklahoma, 1998.

Songs to Fan the Flames of Discontent. Chicago: IWW, 1923.

Thompson, Fred, and Patrick Murfin. *The IWW: Its First Seventy Years*. Chicago: IWW, 1976.

Tyler, Robert. *Rebels of the Woods: The IWW in the Pacific Northwest*. Eugene: University of Oregon Press, 1967.

Zinn, Howard. *A People's History of the United States*. New York: Harper and Row Publishers, 1980.

OTHER SOURCES:

An Injury to One. Directed by Travis Wilkerson. First Run/Icarus Films, 2003.

The Wobblies. Directed by Deborah Shaffer and Stewart Bird. First Run/Icarus Films, 1979.

Many periodicals were consulted. A small selection includes: the *Industrial Worker*, *Solidarity*, the *Labor Defender*, the *Butte Miner* and the *Butte Daily Post*.

Likewise, many websites now contain information on Wobblies. Some of those used most include:

Center for the Study of the Pacific Northwest, University of Washington, Special Collections: http://content.lib.washington.edu/index.html (Bisbee Deportation of 1917.)

Journal of the San Diego Historical Society: http://sandiegohistory.org/hissoc.html (Free-speech fights.)

http://lib.umich.edu/spec-coll/labadie/Labadie Collection (Many anarchist materials.)

http://lucy parsonsproject.org/index.html (Lucy Parsons.)

http://sunsite.berkeley.edu/Goldman/ (Emma Goldman Papers.)

www.wobblyshow.org

ARCHIVES:

The Emma Goldman Collection, University of California, Berkeley; Labadie Collection, University of Michigan, Ann Arbor; Tamiment Library, New York University.

For more information on

THE INDUSTRIAL WORKERS OF THE WORLD

IWW GENERAL HEADQUARTERS
Post Office Box 13476
Philadelphia, PA 19101
www.iww.org

THE LABADIE COLLECTION
University of Michigan, Special Collections Library
711 Harlan Hatcher Library
University of Michigan
Ann Arbor, Michigan 48109–1205
http://www.lib.umich.edu/spec-coll/labadie/

THE TAMIMENT LIBRARY
AND ROBERT F. WAGNER LABOR ARCHIVES
At New York University Bobst Library
70 Washington Square South
New York, NY 10012
http://www.nyu.edu/library/bobst/research/tam/

THE MONTANA HISTORICAL SOCIETY
P.O. Box 201201
225 North Roberts
Helena, MT 59620–1201
http://www.his.state.mt.us/default.asp

THE HOLT LABOR LIBRARY
50 Fell Street,
San Francisco, CA 94102
http://www.holtlaborlibrary.org/index.html